ENERGY TAX INCENTIVES AT A GLANCE

The chart below summarizes the key incentives that were added by the Energy Tax Incentives Act of 2005. These incentives are intended to improve energy production, transportation and efficiency. See the explanations in CCH's *Energy and Highway Tax Acts of 2005*: Law, Explanation and Analysis for a complete discussion of these changes.

INDIVIDUAL ENERGY INCENTIVES		
New credit for:	*In effect:*	*Maximum amount:*
• Energy efficient home improvements (Code Sec. 25C)	2006 and 2007	$500 lifetime
• Residential solar water heaters, photovoltaic and fuel cell property (Code Sec. 25D)	2006 and 2007	$2,000 heater, $2,000 photovoltaic, fuel cell (unlimited)
BUSINESS ENERGY INCENTIVES		
New credit for:	*In effect:*	*Maximum amount:*
• Construction of new energy efficient homes (Code Sec. 45L)	2006 and 2007	$2,000 per dwelling unit
• Manufacture of energy efficient appliances (Code Sec. 45M)	2006 and 2007	$75 million
New deduction for:	*In effect:*	*Amount:*
• Energy efficient commercial buildings (Code Sec. 179D)	2006 and 2007	$1.80 per sq. ft. less any prior year deduction
ALTERNATIVE FUEL VEHICLE CREDIT		
New credit for:	*In effect:*	*Maximum for car/light truck:*
• Hybrid vehicle (Code Sec. 30B)	2006-2010	$3,400
• Advanced lean-burn vehicle (Code Sec. 30B)	2006-2010	$3,400
• Alternative fuel vehicle (Code Sec. 30B)	2006-2010	$4,000
• Fuel cell vehicle (Code Sec. 30B)	2006-2014	$12,000
ENERGY PRODUCTION AND INVESTMENT INCENTIVES		
New credit for:	*In effect:*	*Amount:*
• New nuclear power facility producing electricity (Code Sec. 45J)	post-enactment thru 2020	1.8 cents per kilowatt hour for 8 year period
• Small agri-biodiesel producer (Code Sec. 40A(b)(5))	post-enactment thru 2008	10 cents per gallon, up to 15 million gallons per year
• Renewable diesel (Code Sec. 40A(f))	2006-2008	$1 per gallon
• Investment in alternative fuel refueling property (Code Sec. 30C)	2006-2009 (2006-2014 for hydrogen property)	$1,000 maximum credit ($30,000 for depreciable property)
• Fuel cell power plants (Code Sec. 48(a)(3)(A))	2006 and 2007	30% of basis
• Stationary microturbine power plants (Code Sec. 48(a)(3)(A))	2006 and 2007	10% of basis

© 2005 **CCH** INCORPORATED

CREDITS INCREASED, EXPANDED AND EXTENDED

- Solar energy credit **increased** from 10% to 30% of basis for 2006 and 2007 and **expanded** to cover hybrid solar lighting systems (Code Sec. 48)
- Renewable electricity production credit **expanded** to cover hydropower and Indian coal production (Code Sec. 45)
- Biodiesel income and excise tax credits **extended** thru 2008 (Code Secs. 40A(e), 6426(c) and 6427)
- Credit for fuel produced from nonconventional sources **expanded** to cover certain facilities producing coke and coke gas (Code Sec. 45K)
- Credit for small ethanol producer **expanded** to cover producers with alcohol production capacity up to 60 million gallons of alcohol, up from 30 million (Code Sec. 40(g))
- Research credit **expanded** to cover expenses paid to energy research consortia (Code Sec. 41)

DEPRECIATION AND EXPENSING

- Depreciation period for natural gas distribution lines **shortened** from 20 to 15 years, for property placed in service after April 11, 2005, and before 2011 (Code Sec. 168(e)(3)(E)(viii))
- Depreciation period for natural gas gathering line **established** as 7 years, for property placed in service after April 11, 2005 (Code Sec. 168(e)(3)(C)(iv))
- Depreciation period for assets used in transmission and distribution of electricity **shortened** from 20 to 15 years (Code Sec. 168(e)(3)(E)(vii))
- Cost of refinery investments that increase capacity **expensed** 50%, for property placed in service after the date of enactment and before 2012 (Code Sec. 179C)

AMORTIZATION

- Geological and geophysical exploration expenditures incurred in U.S. **amortized** over two years (Code Sec. 167(h))
- Cost of air pollution control facilities **amortized** over 84 months, for facilities placed in service after April 11, 2005 (Code Sec. 169(d)(5))

DEDUCTIONS

- Percentage depletion deduction for small refiners **extended** to refiners with refinery runs not exceeding 75,000 barrels (Code Sec. 613A(d)(4))
- Deduction for costs of compliance with EPA low sulfur diesel regulations may be passed through to cooperative owners (Code Sec. 179B(e))
- Deduction for contributions to qualified nuclear decommissioning fund available to regulated and unregulated taxpayers (Code Scc. 468A)

TAX-EXEMPT BONDS

- Safe harbor exception to tax-exempt bond arbitrage rules for certain prepaid gas contracts (Code Sec. 148(b)(4))

TAX RATE REDUCTIONS

- Tax rate on qualifying diesel-water fuel emulsions **reduced** from 24.3 cents to 19.7 cents per gallon (Code Sec. 4081(a)(2))

Energy Tax Incentives Act of 2005

As Signed by the President
on August 8, 2005

Safe, Accountable, Flexible, Efficient Transportation Equity Act of 2005

As Signed by the President
on August 10, 2005

Law, Explanation
and Analysis

CCH Editorial Staff Publication

CCH INCORPORATED
Chicago

A WoltersKluwer Company

This publication is designed to provide accurate and authoritative information in regard to the subject matter covered. It is sold with the understanding that the publisher is not engaged in rendering legal, accounting, or other professional service. If legal advice or other expert assistance is required, the services of a competent professional person should be sought.

ISBN 0-8080-1391-2

©2005, **CCH** INCORPORATED

4025 W. Peterson Ave.
Chicago, IL 60646-6085
1 800 248 3248
http://tax.cchgroup.com

No claim is made to original government works; however, within this Product or Publication, the following are subject to CCH's copyright: (1) the gathering, compilation, and arrangement of such government materials; (2) the magnetic translation and digital conversion of data, if applicable; (3) the historical, statutory and other notes and references; and (4) the commentary and other materials.

All Rights Reserved
Printed in the United States of America

Energy and Highway Tax Acts of 2005
A Little of This, A Little of That, But Something for Everyone

Prior to its August recess, Congress passed comprehensive legislation that had languished for months in conference awaiting agreement by House and Senate conferees. The Energy Policy Act of 2005 (Energy Act) (H.R. 6), as signed by President Bush on August 8, 2005, addresses energy policy while the SAFE Transportation Equity Act (Highway Act) (H.R. 3), as signed by President Bush on August 10, 2005, provides sweeping highway and mass transit incentives for the states. Buried within these Acts are numerous tax law changes impacting divergent taxpayer types and providing practitioners with planning opportunities to assist clients.

Energy Tax Incentives Act

Four years in the making with many fits and starts along the way, Congress, on July 29, 2005, finally passed major energy legislation that would shore up the nation's energy infrastructure and provide for future energy needs. The Energy Tax Incentives Act, Title XIII of H.R. 6, provides tax incentives of $14.5 billion over a 10-year period to boost conservation efforts, increase domestic energy production, and expand the use of alternative energy sources, such as solar, wind, ethanol, biomass, hydropower and clean coal technology. Beneficiaries of Congress's largesse range from oil, gas, and renewable energy companies to manufacturers of household appliances, as well as homeowners who make energy-efficient improvements to their principal residence. The cost of the tax incentives are offset by raising almost $3 billion from reinstating the Oil Spill Liability Trust Fund (Superfund) tax, extending the Leaking Underground Storage Tank (LUST) Tax Fund tax, and modifying the recapture rules for amortizable Code Sec. 197 intangibles.

Highway Act of 2005

The Highway Act, Title XI of H.R. 3, was also overwhelmingly passed by Congress on July 29, 2005, and extends authorization for trust fund expenditures through fiscal-year 2009 and for highway-related taxes through fiscal-year 2011. Such authorization was scheduled to expire in 2003, but was extended numerous times by Congress. The Highway Act also contains a multitude of provisions aimed at curbing fuel fraud, provides $15 billion of tax-exempt bond financing authority to finance highway projects and rail-truck transfer facilities, and modifies and simplifies various excise taxes, including highway, aquatic, aerial, alcohol, and sports excise taxes.

About This Work and CCH

In light of the almost simultaneous passage of the Energy and Highway Acts, CCH is providing practitioners with a single integrated law and explanation reference source, *Energy and Highway Tax Acts of 2005: Law, Explanation and Analysis*, encompassing both Acts. Along with the relevant Internal Revenue Code provisions, as amended by the Acts, and supporting committee reports, CCH editors, together with several leading tax practitioners and commentators, have put together a complete practical analysis of the new law. Tax professionals looking for the Conference Report, including the related bill text, can find it in a separate CCH publication.

Other books and tax services relating to the new legislation can be found at our website http://tax.cchgroup.com.

As always, CCH Tax and Accounting remains dedicated to responding to the needs of tax professionals in helping them quickly understand and work with these new laws as they take effect.

Mark A. Luscombe

Principal Analyst

CCH Tax and Accounting

August 2005

Outside Contributors

Katherine Breaks
Senior Manager
Washington National Tax, KPMG LLP
Washington, D.C.

William B. Gray
Excise Tax Manager
Sinclair Oil Corporation
Salt Lake City, Utah

Dr. Patrick Hennessee
Professor of Accounting
The University of Tulsa
Tulsa, Oklahoma

Vincent J. O'Brien
President
Vincent J. O'Brien, CPA, P.C.
Lynbrook, New York

CCH Tax and Accounting Publishing
EDITORIAL STAFF

Explanation and Analysis

Manish C. Bhatia, J.D.

Louis W. Baker, J.D., M.B.A.

David Becker, J.D.

Maureen Bornstein, J.D.,
Portfolio Managing Editor

Glenn L. Borst, J.D., LL.M.

Anne E. Bowker, J.D.

John O. Buchanan, J.D., LL.M.

Sarah Burch, M.S.T.

Mildred Carter, J.D.

Maurice M. Cashin, J.D.

Tom Cody, J.D., LL.M., M.B.A.

Eileen Corbett, J.D.

Heather Corbin, J.D.

Kurt Diefenbach, J.D.,
Managing Editor

Liliana Dimitrova, LL.B., LL.M.

Karen Elsner, C.P.A.

Alicia C. Ernst, J.D.

Shannon Jett Fischer, J.D.

Donna M. Flanagan, J.D.

John D. Flanagan, J.D., M.B.A.

Brant Goldwyn, J.D.

Irene Goodman, J.D.

Tony D. Graber, J.D., LL.M.

Bruno L. Graziano, J.D., M.S.A.

Joy A. Hail, J.D.

Carmela Harnett,
Managing Editor

Kay L. Harris, J.D.

Michael Henaghan, J.D., LL.M.

Karen Heslop, J.D.

Jane A. Hoffman, C.P.A.,
Portfolio Managing Editor

Dem A. Hopkins, J.D.

David Jaffe, J.D.

Angela C.K. Johnson, J.D.

George G. Jones, J.D., LL.M.,
Managing Editor

Geralyn A. Jover-Ledesma, LL.B.,
C.P.A.

Lynn S. Kopon, J.D.

Mary W. Krackenberger, J.D.

Thomas K. Lauletta, J.D.

John P. Logan, J.D.

Jennifer M. Lowe, J.D.

Laura M. Lowe, J.D.,
Managing Editor

Mark Luscombe, J.D., LL.M, C.P.A.,
Principal Analyst

Andrew J. Maschas, J.D.

Daniel J. McCarthy III, J.D.

Michael Menzhuber, J.D., LL.M.

Jela Miladinovich, J.D.

Sheri Wattles Miller, J.D.

Ellen Mitchell, EA

Robert A. Morse, J.D.

Tracy Gaspardo Mortenson, J.D.,
C.P.A., *Managing Editor*

John J. Mueller, J.D., LL.M.,
Managing Editor

Anita I. Nagelis, J.D.

Jean T. Nakamoto, J.D.

Jerome Nestor, J.D., C.P.A., M.B.A

Jennifer Nolan, C.P.A.

Larry Norris, M.S.,
Managing Editor

Karen A. Notaro, J.D., LL.M.,
Portfolio Managing Editor

Linda J. O'Brien, J.D., LL.M.,
Managing Editor

Marie O'Donnell, J.D., C.P.A.

John Old, J.D., LL.M.

Karin Old, J.D.

Lawrence A. Perlman, C.P.A., J.D.,
LL.M.

Deborah M. Petro, J.D., LL.M.

John W. Roth, J.D., LL.M.

Rosanne Schabinger, EA

Carolyn M. Schiess, J.D.

Michael G. Sem, J.D.

James Solheim, J.D., LL.M.

Raymond G. Suelzer, J.D., LL.M.

Kenneth L. Swanson, J.D., LL.M.

Deanna Tenofsky, J.D., LL.M.

Laura A. Tierney, J.D.

David Trice, J.D., CFP

James C. Walschlager, M.A.

Kelley Wolf, J.D.

George L. Yaksick, Jr., J.D.

Ken Zaleski, J.D.

Washington News Staff

Sarah Borchersen-Keto

Jeff Carlson, M.A.

Stephen K. Cooper

Paula L. Cruickshank

David A. Hansen, J.D.

Kathryn Hough

Catherine Hubbard, M.G.

Rosalyn Johns-Thomas

Joyce Mutcherson-Ridley

William Pegler

Electronic and Print Production

Elizabeth Albers,
Manager, Editorial Processes

Trent Allan

Maureen C. Beadle

Jeffrey R. Bosse

Douglas Bretschneider,
Managing Editor

Stella Brown

Angela D. Cashmore

Amelia Eslava

Connie Eyer

Amanda J. Felinski

Tara K. Fenske

Jane Fridman

Lien Giang

Mary Ellen Guth

Ann Hartmann

Kathleen M. Higgins

Denise Hirsch

Jennifer Holland

Kristine J. Jacobs

Jennifer L. Jones

Linda Kalteux

Faina Lerin

Rebecca Little

Irene B. Lopez

Chantal M. Mahler

Andrejs Makwitz

Fred Marshall

Tina Matos

Tim Mejudhon

Helen Miller

Lisa Moore, M.A.

Molly Munson

Elaine Ogawa,
Managing Editor

Melissa O'Keefe

Holly J. Porter

Diana Roozeboom

Jennifer K. Schencker

David Schuster

Diana H. Shkap

Monika Stefan

James F. Walschlager

Robert Williams

Laura M. Zenner,
Managing Editor

Christopher Zwirek

¶1 Features of This Publication

This publication is your complete guide to the Energy Tax Incentives Act of 2005, Title XIII of the larger Energy Policy Act of 2005, and the highway and mass transit tax provisions, Title XI of the Safe, Accountable, Flexible, Efficient Transportation Equity Act: A Legacy for Users (SAFETEA-LU) (often referred to within this work as the "SAFE Transportation Equity Act of 2005" or the "Highway Act"). The core portion of this publication contains the CCH Explanations and Analysis of these Acts. The CCH Explanations outline all of the law changes and what they mean for you and your clients. The explanations feature practical guidance, examples, planning opportunities and strategies, as well as pitfalls to be avoided as a result of the law changes. Insights supplied by expert tax practitioners are highlighted throughout our analysis.

The law text and committee reports are reproduced following the analysis. Any new or amended Internal Revenue Code sections appear here, with changes highlighted in *italics*. You will also see the law text for portions of the Acts that did not amend the tax code. The committee reports that provide the legislative history of each provision follows the law text.

The book also contains numerous other features designed to help you locate and understand the changes made by the Energy and Highway Acts. These features include highlight summaries of important provisions, cross references to related materials, detailed effective dates, and numerous finding tables and indexes. A more detailed description of these features appears below.

HIGHLIGHTS

Highlights are quick summaries of the major provisions of the Energy and Highway Acts. The Highlights are arranged by area of interest, such as residential and business property, motor vehicles, oil and gas, or fuel production and fuel excise taxes. At the end of each summary is a paragraph reference to the longer CCH Explanation on that topic, giving you an easy way to find the parts of the book that are of most interest to you. *Highlights start at ¶5.*

TAXPAYERS AFFECTED

The first chapter of the book, *Taxpayers Affected*, contains a detailed look at how the new laws affect specific categories of taxpayers. This chapter provides a quick reference for readers who want to know the immediate impact that the laws will have on their clients. Each section of this chapter highlights a different taxpayer type, noting the tax savings or costs that result from changes made by the Energy and Highway Acts. *Taxpayers Affected starts at ¶101.*

CCH EXPLANATIONS

CCH Explanations are designed to give you a complete, accessible understanding of the new law. Explanations are arranged by subject for ease of use. There are three main finding devices you can use to locate explanations on a given topic. These are:

- A detailed table of contents at the beginning of the publication listing all of the CCH Explanations of the new laws;
- A table of contents preceding each chapter; and
- An extensive topical index covering all subjects under the Energy and Highway Acts.

Each CCH Explanation contains special features to aid in your complete understanding of the new law. These include:

- A background or prior law discussion that puts the law changes into perspective;
- Practitioner commentary incorporated throughout the explanations, identifying planning opportunities and strategies, as well as pitfalls to avoid;
- Editorial aids, including examples, cautions, planning notes, elections, comments, compliance tips, key rates and figures, and state tax consequences, that highlight the impact of the new laws
- Charts and examples illustrating the ramifications of specific law changes;
- Captions at the end of each explanation identifying the Code sections added, amended or repealed, as well as the Act sections containing the changes;
- Cross references to the law and committee report paragraphs related to the explanation;
- A line highlighting the effective date of each law change, marked by an arrow symbol;
- References at the end of the discussion to related information in the Standard Federal Tax Reporter, Federal Tax Service, Federal Tax Guide and the Federal Excise Tax Reporter.

The CCH Explanations begin at ¶205.

AMENDED CODE PROVISIONS

Changes to the Internal Revenue Code made by the Energy and Highway Acts appear under the heading "Code Sections Added, Amended or Repealed." *Any changed or added law text is set out in italics.* Deleted Code text, or the Code provision prior to amendment, appears in the Amendment Notes following each reconstructed Code provision. An effective date for each Code change is also provided.

The amendment notes contain cross references to the corresponding Committee Reports and the CCH Explanations that discuss the new law. *The text of the Code begins at ¶5001.*

¶1

Sections of the Energy and Highway Acts that do not amend the Internal Revenue Code appear in full text following "Code Sections Added, Amended or Repealed." *The text of these provisions appears in Act Section order beginning at ¶7003.*

COMMITTEE REPORTS

The committee reports explain the intent of Congress in enacting legislation. Included in this publication for the Energy Act are portions of the House Committee Report accompanying H.R. 1541 (H.R. Rep. No. 109-45), and because no official reports were issued, the Joint Committee on Taxation explanations of the Senate bill (JCX-44-05 and JCX-46-05) and the Conference Agreement (JCX-60-05). Committee reports included in this publication for the Highway Act are the House Committee Report accompanying H.R. 996 (H.R. Rep. No. 109-13); the Senate Committee Report accompanying S. 1230 (S. Rep. No. 109-82); and the Conference Committee Report (H.R. Conf. Rep. No. 109-203). At the end of each section of Committee Report text, you will find references to the corresponding explanation and Code provisions. *Committee Reports appear in Act Section order beginning at ¶10,001.*

EFFECTIVE DATES

A table listing the major effective dates provides you with a reference bridge between Code Sections and Act Sections and indicates the retroactive or prospective nature of the laws explained. *This effective date table begins at ¶20,001.*

SPECIAL FINDING DEVICES

Other special tables and finding devices in this book include:

- A table cross-referencing Code Sections to the CCH Explanations (*see ¶25,001*);
- A table showing all Code Sections added, amended or repealed (*see ¶25,005*);
- A table showing provisions of other acts that were amended (*see ¶25,010*);
- A table of Act Sections not amending the Internal Revenue Code (*see ¶25,015*); and
- An Act Section amending Code Section table (*see ¶25,020*).
- A listing of the provisions dropped in conference (*see ¶27,001*).

¶2 Table of Contents

¶1	Features of This Publication	
¶5	Highlights	

EXPLANATION

¶101	Chapter 1	Taxpayers Affected
¶205	Chapter 2	Residential Property and Businesses
¶305	Chapter 3	Motor Vehicles
¶405	Chapter 4	Electricity
¶505	Chapter 5	Oil and Gas
¶605	Chapter 6	Coal
¶705	Chapter 7	Fuel Production and Fuel Excise Taxes
¶805	Chapter 8	Other Excise Taxes
¶905	Chapter 9	Highways and Railroads
¶1005	Chapter 10	Reports, Studies and Funding

LAW

¶5001	Code Sections Added, Amended or Repealed
¶7003	Act Sections Not Amending Code Sections

COMMITTEE REPORTS

¶10,001	Energy Tax Incentives Act of 2005
¶15,001	SAFE Transportation Equity Act of 2005

SPECIAL TABLES

Effective Dates Tables

¶20,001	Energy Tax Incentives Act of 2005
¶20,005	SAFE Transportation Equity Act of 2005

Other Tables

¶25,001	Code Section to Explanation Table
¶25,005	Code Sections Added, Amended or Repealed
¶25,010	Table of Amendments to Other Acts
¶25,015	Table of Act Sections Not Amending Internal Revenue Code Sections
¶25,020	Act Sections Amending Code Sections
¶27,001	Provisions Dropped in Conference

Page 563	Index

¶2

¶3 Detailed Table of Contents

CHAPTER 1. TAXPAYERS AFFECTED

Energy and Tax Incentives Act and SAFE Transportation Equity Act of 2005

¶101 Overview

Individuals

¶105 Overall effect on individuals
¶107 Effect on purchasers of environmentally friendly vehicles
¶109 Effect on homeowners
¶111 Effect on tax-exempt bond investors
¶113 Effect on patrons of cooperatives
¶115 Effect on sport fishermen

General Business

¶117 Overall effect on business
¶119 Effect on business expenditures for energy savings and research
¶121 Effect on business purchasers of environmentally friendly vehicles
¶123 Effect on home builders
¶125 Effect on commercial building owners
¶127 Effect on appliance manufacturers

Energy and Fuels

¶129 Overview of effect on energy

Oil

¶131 Effect on oil producers

Natural Gas

¶133 Effect on natural gas producers
¶135 Effect on natural gas utilities
¶137 Effect on natural gas distributors

Electricity and Nuclear Power

¶139 Effect on electricity producers
¶141 Effect on nuclear power industry
¶143 Effect on electricity transmission
¶145 Effect on electric utilities

Cooperatives

¶147 Effect on energy cooperatives

Coal and Coke
¶149   Effect on coal and coke producers

Fuels
¶151   Effect on gasoline producers
¶153   Effect on diesel and biodiesel producers
¶155   Effect on kerosene producers
¶157   Effect on liquefied petroleum gas producers
¶159   Effect on ethanol producers
¶161   Effect on special motor fuels producers
¶163   Effect on alcohol fuels producers
¶165   Effect on motor boat and small engine fuel producers
¶167   Effect on P Series fuels producers
¶169   Effect on liquid hydrocarbons from biomass
¶171   Effect on fuel blenders, pipeline operators, inventory position holders, and terminal and vessel operators
¶173   Effect on fuel importers
¶175   Effect on refiners

Energy Research
¶176   Effect on energy research

Other Affected Businesses
¶177   Overall effect on other businesses
¶178   Effect on trucking and limousine companies
¶179   Effect on alcoholic beverage producers
¶180   Effect on aviation
¶181   Effect on exporters
¶182   Effect on farmers
¶183   Effect on credit card issuers
¶184   Effect on custom gunsmiths
¶185   Effect on oil tanker operators
¶186   Effect on operators of deep draft vessels
¶187   Effect on recycling industry

Government Trust Funds
¶191   Effect on government trust funds

State Tax Energy Incentives
¶195   Energy conservation and production income tax credits

¶3

CHAPTER 2. RESIDENTIAL PROPERTY AND BUSINESSES

Residential Energy Incentives
¶205 Residential energy property credit
¶210 Credit for residential alternative energy expenditures

Business Energy Incentives
¶215 Energy-efficient commercial buildings property deduction
¶220 Homebuilder's credit for new energy-efficient homes
¶225 Manufacturer's credit for energy efficient appliances
¶230 Business solar investment tax credit
¶235 Expansion of research credit
¶240 Credit for business installation of qualified fuel cells and stationary microturbine power plants

Other Business Provisions
¶245 Recapture of Code Sec. 197 amortization

CHAPTER 3. MOTOR VEHICLES

¶305 Alternative motor vehicle credit
¶310 New qualified fuel cell motor vehicle credit
¶315 New advanced lean burn technology motor vehicle credit
¶320 New qualified hybrid motor vehicle credit
¶325 New qualified alternative fuel motor vehicle credit
¶330 Termination of deduction for clean-fuel vehicles
¶335 Limousines and the "gas guzzler" tax
¶340 Excise tax on heavy trucks and trailers sold at retail
¶345 Tire excise tax modification

CHAPTER 4. ELECTRICITY

Production Credit
¶405 Qualified energy resources
¶410 Qualified facilities used for production
¶415 Computation of renewable electricity production tax credit
¶420 Renewable electricity production credit for agricultural cooperatives

Transmission Property
¶425 Depreciation of electric transmission property

¶3

¶430 Five-year carryback for public utility NOLs to promote electrical transmission and pollution control investments
¶435 Sales of dispositions to implement FERC restructuring policy

Nuclear Power

¶440 Credit for production from advanced nuclear power facilities
¶445 Modification to special rules for nuclear decommissioning costs
¶450 Treatment of income of certain electric cooperatives

Energy Bonds

¶455 Tax credit bonds to subsidize non-profits' production of renewable energy electricity

CHAPTER 5. OIL AND GAS

¶505 Temporary election to expense qualified liquid fuel refineries
¶510 Determination of small refiner exception to oil depletion deduction
¶515 Depreciation of natural gas distribution lines
¶520 Depreciation of natural gas gathering pipelines
¶525 Geological and geophysical costs amortized over two years
¶530 Safe harbor from tax-exempt bond arbitrage rules for prepaid natural gas
¶535 Deduction for capital costs incurred in complying with EPA sulfur regulations
¶540 Oil Spill Liability Trust Fund financing rate

CHAPTER 6. COAL

¶605 Credit for investment in clean coal facilities
¶610 Credit for producing fuel from a nonconventional source extended to coke or coke gas facilities
¶615 Modification of credit for producing fuel from a nonconventional source
¶620 84-month amortization of air pollution control facilities

CHAPTER 7. FUEL PRODUCTION AND FUEL EXCISE TAXES

Diesel and Biodiesel

¶705 Extension of excise tax provisions and income tax credit for biodiesel
¶710 Small agri-biodiesel producer credit
¶715 Renewable diesel
¶720 Reduced excise tax rate on diesel-water fuel emulsion

¶3

Alternative Fuels

¶725 Excise tax credit for alternative fuels
¶730 Credit for installation of alternative fueling stations
¶735 Small ethanol producer credit extended to larger producers

Prevention of Fuel Fraud

¶740 Excise tax on kerosene used in aviation
¶745 Refunds of excise taxes on exempt sales of fuels by credit cards
¶750 Ultimate purchaser can claim refund for diesel fuel used on farms
¶755 Reregistration with change in ownership
¶760 Diesel fuel tax evasion report
¶765 Adulterated fuels penalty
¶770 Reconciliation of on-loaded cargo to entered cargo
¶775 Registration of deep-draft vessels
¶780 Motor fuel tax enforcement advisory committee

LUST Tax and Technical Corrections

¶785 Leaking Underground Storage Tank Trust Fund
¶787 Gasohol refund claims repealed
¶790 Reduced tax rate for aviation fuel used by registrants
¶795 Termination date for tax on aviation-grade kerosene
¶797 Small engine fuel taxes to fund coastal wetlands protection

Cross References

Extension of taxes and trust fund (see ¶905)
Oil Spill Liability Trust Fund financing rate (see ¶540)

CHAPTER 8. OTHER EXCISE TAXES

Air and Water Transportation

¶805 Modification of rural airport definition
¶810 Ticket tax exemption for seaplane transportation
¶815 Sightseeing flights exempt from taxes on air transportation
¶820 Fuel excise tax exemptions clarified for crop dusters
¶822 Fixed-wing aircraft engaged in forestry operations exempt from ticket taxes
¶825 Repeal of harbor maintenance tax on exports

Alcohol

¶830 Small alcohol excise taxpayers
¶835 Income tax credit for distilled spirits
¶840 Occupational taxes on producers and marketers of alcoholic beverages

Sporting Goods
¶845   Excise tax on fishing rods and poles
¶850   Custom gunsmiths

CHAPTER 9. HIGHWAYS AND RAILROADS
¶905   Extension of taxes and trust fund
¶910   Tax treatment of state ownership of railroad real estate investment trust
¶915   Tax-exempt bond financing for highway projects and rail-truck transfer facilities
¶920   National surface transportation infrastructure financing commission

CHAPTER 10. REPORTS, STUDIES AND FUNDING
REPORTS AND STUDIES
¶1005   National Academy of Sciences study and report
¶1010   Energy savings through recycling to be studied
¶1015   Study of highway fuels used by trucks for nontransportation purposes
¶1020   Study on the collection of excise tax on taxable tires

GOVERNMENT FUNDING
¶1025   Modification of adjustments and apportionments
¶1030   Elimination of Aquatic Resources Trust Fund and transformation of Sport Fish Restoration Account
¶1035   Transfers from the Leaking Underground Storage Tank Trust Fund

¶3

¶5 Highlights

RESIDENTIAL AND BUSINESS PROPERTY

¶205 **Energy-Efficient Home Improvement Credit.** Individuals can claim a tax credit for up to $500 of the cost of qualified energy efficiency home improvements. The maximum tax credit for windows is $200.

¶210 **Solar and Fuel Cell Equipment Installed on a Personal Residence.** Homeowners who install residential alternative energy equipment can qualify for a credit equal to 30 percent of the cost of eligible equipment, up to $2,000 for each category of solar equipment and up to $500 for each 0.5 kilowatt of capacity of fuel cell plants installed.

¶215 **Energy-Efficient Commercial Property Deduction.** A deduction of up to $1.80 per square foot is allowed for costs associated with energy efficient commercial building property.

¶220 **Homebuilder's Credit for Construction of New Energy-Efficient Home.** Eligible contractors who build new homes that meet energy-efficiency standards are eligible for a tax credit of up to $1,000 or $2,000 per dwelling unit, depending on the degree of energy efficiency.

¶225 **Manufacturer's Credit for Energy Efficient Appliances.** Manufacturers are eligible for a credit for the production of energy-efficient dishwashers, refrigerators and clothes washers.

¶230 **Business Solar Investment Tax Credit.** The business investment credit for solar energy property is increased from 10 percent to 30 percent.

¶235 **Energy Research Credit Expansion.** Expenditures to qualified energy research consortia are eligible for the 20 percent research and experimentation tax credit.

¶240 **Qualified Fuel Cell Power Plants Credits.** A 30 percent business tax credit is allowed for the purchase of qualified fuel cell power plants, and a 10 percent credit is allowed for the purchase of qualified stationary microturbine power plants.

¶245 **Code Sec. 197 Amortization.** Recapture of multiple Code Sec. 197 intangibles disposed of in a single transaction or series of transactions must be calculated as if all were a single asset.

MOTOR VEHICLES

¶305 **Alternative Motor Vehicle Credit.** A new series of tax credits is created to encourage the development, manufacture and use of alternative fuel vehicles.

¶310 **Qualified Fuel Cell Motor Vehicle Credit.** The qualified fuel cell motor vehicle credit ranges from $4,000 to $40,000 depending on the vehicle weight. The credit is enhanced for vehicles that achieve fuel-efficiency targets.

¶315 **Advanced Lean Burn Technology Motor Vehicle Credit.** The advanced lean burn technology motor vehicle credit ranges from $400 to $2,400, based on fuel economy, with an additional $250 to $1,000 lifetime conservation credit.

¶320 **Qualified Hybrid Motor Vehicle Credit.** The qualified hybrid motor vehicle credit ranges from $250 to $1,000 for lifetime fuel savings and from $400 to $2,400 for fuel economy.

¶325 **Qualified Alternative Fuel Motor Vehicle Credit.** The qualified alternative fuel motor vehicle credit ranges from $2,500 to $32,000, based on the vehicle weight.

¶330 **Termination of Code Sec. 179A.** The termination of clean-fuel deductions is accelerated so that the deductions do not apply to vehicles placed in service after December 31, 2005.

¶335 **Limousines and the "Gas Guzzler" Tax.** Limousines over 6,000 pounds are exempt from the "gas guzzler" tax.

¶340 **Heavy Trucks and Trailers.** Only tractors weighing over 19,500 pounds are subject to the federal excise tax on heavy trucks and trailers.

¶345 **Super Single Tires.** The definition of a "super single tire" does not include tires designed to steer the vehicle.

ELECTRICITY

¶405, ¶410, ¶415, ¶420 **Renewable Electricity Production Credit.** For purposes of the renewable electricity production credit, qualified energy resources are expanded for a limited time to include qualified hydropower production and Indian coal. Eligible agricultural cooperatives may elect to allocate any portion of their renewable electricity production credits to their patrons.

¶425 **Depreciation of Electric Transmission Property.** Certain electric transmission property is treated as MACRS 15-year property.

¶430 **Five-year NOL for Electric Transmission Equipment.** A public utility can elect a five-year carryback for a portion of its net operating losses based on its investment in qualified electric transmission and pollution control capital equipment.

¶435 **Tax Deferral for Gains on Electric Transmission Assets.** The rules allowing an eight-year deferral for recognizing qualified gain from a qualifying electric transmission transaction are extended to transactions occurring in 2007.

¶5

Highlights

¶440 **Advanced Nuclear Facility Business Tax Credit.** A new business tax credit is created for energy production from advanced nuclear power facilities.

¶445 **Nuclear Decommissioning Fund Contributions.** The limitation on deposits into the qualified nuclear decommissioning fund based on cost of service calculations is repealed. All taxpayers, including unregulated taxpayers, may deduct amounts contributed to a qualified fund.

¶450 **Treatment of Electric Cooperative Income.** The rules excluding certain types of income received or accrued by tax-exempt rural electric cooperatives for purposes of the 85-percent test are made permanent.

¶455 **Clean Renewable Energy Bonds.** Up to $800 million of tax credit bonds may be issued before December 31, 2007 to support renewable electricity production.

OIL AND GAS

¶505 **Expensing Liquid Fuel Refineries.** Taxpayers may make a temporary election to treat 50 percent of the cost of qualified refinery property as an expense that is not charged to capital account.

¶510 **Determination of Small Refiner Exception to Oil Depletion Deduction.** The 50,000 barrel-per-day limitation for small refiners is increased to an average daily run of 75,000 barrels.

¶515, ¶520 **Natural Gas Line Depreciation.** New natural gas gathering lines are treated as MACRS 7-year property regardless of whether they are owned by a producer or a nonproducer. New natural gas distribution lines are treated as MACRS 15-year property.

¶525 **Geological and Geophysical Costs.** Geological and geophysical expenses incurred in connection with domestic oil and gas exploration and development must be amortized ratably over 24 months.

¶530 **Safe Harbor for Natural Gas Prepayments.** A safe harbor exception to the tax-exempt bond arbitrage rules is created for qualified natural gas supply contracts purchased by state and local government utilities.

¶535 **Passthrough Sulfur Regulations Cost.** Deductions for costs incurred by a small business cooperative to comply with EPA low sulfur diesel regulations may be passed through to the members.

¶540 **Oil Spill Liability Trust Fund.** The five-cents-per-barrel Oil Spill Liability Trust Fund tax is reinstated.

¶5

COAL

¶605 **Clean Coal Investment Tax Credit.** Clean coal technology credits ranging from 15 to 20 percent of qualified costs are available for investments in clean coal facilities producing electricity.

¶610, ¶615 **Nonconventional Sources.** The tax credit for fuel produced by nonconventional sources is made part of the general business credit. A production credit is also available for qualified facilities that produce coke or coke gas.

¶620 **Amortization of Pollution Control Facilities.** Atmospheric pollution control facilities used in connection with coal-fired property may be amortized over 84 months, even if the property was not in operation before 1976.

FUEL PRODUCTION AND FUEL EXCISE TAXES

¶705, ¶710, ¶715 **Renewable Diesel and Biodiesel Fuel.** Income and excise tax credits for biodiesel fuel are extended through 2008 and a new credit is added for small agri-biodiesel producers. Renewable diesel is generally treated the same as biodiesel.

¶720 **Reduced Excise Tax Rate on Diesel-Water Fuel Emulsion.** A special tax rate of 19.7 cents per gallon is provided for diesel-water fuel emulsions to reflect their reduced Btu content.

¶725 **Alternative Fuels Excise Tax Credit.** The ethanol excise tax credit is expanded to include other alternative fuels that displace conventional petroleum products, and tax rates for these fuels are clarified.

¶730 **Alternative Fueling Stations.** A new credit is available for the installation of clean-fuel vehicle refueling property used in a trade or business or installed at the taxpayer's residence.

¶735 **Small Ethanol Producer.** The maximum size for a producer that can qualify for the small ethanol producer credit is doubled to include persons whose production capacity does not exceed 60 million gallons.

¶740, ¶790, ¶795 **Aviation-Grade Kerosene.** The rules governing excise taxes on kerosene used as aviation fuel are restructured. The reduced tax rate for fuel used in commercial aviation applies only if the user is registered with the IRS.

¶745 **Fuel Tax Refunds.** If a state or local government uses a credit card to purchase fuel, the credit card company is generally the only party entitled to seek a refund of any excise taxes paid on the purchase.

¶750 **Farm Use.** Excise tax refunds on exempt fuel used on farms will be paid only to ultimate purchasers, not ultimate vendors.

¶5

¶755 **Change in Ownership Reregistration.** Registered taxpayer blenders, importers, pipeline operators, position holders, refiners, terminal operators, and vessel operators must reregister in the event of change in ownership.

¶760 **Diesel Fuel Excise Tax Report.** The IRS must report to Congress on the availability of new technologies that can be employed to enhance collections of the excise tax on diesel fuel.

¶765 **Adulterated Fuels Penalty.** A $10,000 penalty may be imposed on anyone who knowingly sells diesel that does not comply with EPA sulfur-control regulations.

¶770 **Exported Taxable Fuels.** The Departments of Homeland Security and the Treasury must provide for the transmission to the IRS of information pertaining to imported taxable fuels.

¶775 **Deep-Draft Vessels.** Vessels, including large draft vessels, are required to register, but unregistered vessels can still make bulk entries of taxable fuels for use, consumption or warehousing in the U.S.

¶785, ¶1035 **Leaking Underground Storage Tank (LUST) Trust Fund.** The LUST Trust Fund financing rate is extended until October 1, 2011, and exemptions, refunds and credits are limited. A new provision has also been added to prevent monies from being spent for unauthorized purposes.

OTHER EXCISE TAXES

¶805, ¶810, ¶815, ¶820 **Air.** Crop dusters are exempt from fuel taxes while traveling to and from, and operating over a farm, and no longer need consent from the farm owner to apply for a refund. Helicopters used in timber operations and fixed-wing aircraft are exempt from ticket and flight segment taxes. The definition of "rural airport" is expanded. Sightseeing flights are exempt from the air transportation tax, and some transportation by seaplane is exempt from ticket taxes.

¶825, ¶1030 **Water.** The Aquatic Resources Trust Fund and the Boat Safety Account are eliminated, and the Sport Fish Restoration Account is redesignated as the Sport Fish Restoration and Boating Trust Fund. Exported cargo is exempt from the harbor maintenance tax.

¶830, ¶835, ¶840 **Alcohol.** Special occupational taxes on producers and marketers of alcoholic beverages are permanently repealed. A new income tax credit is available for business costs associated with having tax-paid distilled spirits in inventory. Small alcohol excise taxpayers can file excise taxes quarterly instead of semi-monthly.

¶845, ¶850 **Sporting Goods.** The 10–percent excise tax on fishing rods is capped at $10. Custom gunsmiths who manufacture fewer than 50 firearms per year are exempt from excise tax.

HIGHWAYS AND RAILROADS

¶905 **Trust Funds and Taxes.** Highway Trust Fund excise taxes that were scheduled to expire in 2005 are extended for six years.

¶910 **Railroad REITs.** A railroad real estate investment trust (REIT) that becomes 100 percent state-owned is not treated as a taxable C corporation, but is taxed as if its income from the performance of essential governmental functions accrued directly to the state.

¶915 **Tax-Exempt Financing.** $15 billion of tax-exempt bond authority is authorized to finance highway projects and rail-truck transfer facilities.

¶780, ¶920 **Temporary Commissions.** A temporary Motor Fuel Tax Enforcement Advisory Commission and a National Surface Transportation Infrastructure Financing Commission are established.

REPORTS, STUDIES & FUNDING

¶1005, ¶1010, ¶1015 **Treasury Studies.** The Treasury Department must study the use of highway motor fuel in trucks that is not used for the propulsion of the vehicle. The Treasury and Energy Departments must conduct a study to determine energy savings gained by recycling.

¶1020 **Tire Study.** The IRS must conduct a study of the excise tax on taxable tires.

¶1025 **Anti-deficit Provisions Modified.** The "Harry Byrd rule" will consider deficits in the Highway Trust Fund over a 48-month period, rather than a 24-month period.

¶5

Taxpayers Affected

ENERGY TAX INCENTIVES ACT AND SAFE TRANSPORTATION EQUITY ACT OF 2005

¶101 Overview

INDIVIDUALS

¶105 Overall effect on individuals
¶107 Effect on purchasers of environmentally friendly vehicles
¶109 Effect on homeowners
¶111 Effect on tax-exempt bond investors
¶113 Effect on patrons of cooperatives
¶115 Effect on sport fishermen

GENERAL BUSINESS

¶117 Overall effect on business
¶119 Effect on business expenditures for energy savings and research
¶121 Effect on business purchasers of environmentally friendly vehicles
¶123 Effect on home builders
¶125 Effect on commercial building owners
¶127 Effect on appliance manufacturers

ENERGY AND FUELS

¶129 Overview of effect on energy

OIL

¶131 Effect on oil producers

NATURAL GAS

¶133 Effect on natural gas producers
¶135 Effect on natural gas utilities
¶137 Effect on natural gas distributors

ELECTRICITY AND NUCLEAR POWER

¶139 Effect on electricity producers
¶141 Effect on nuclear power industry
¶143 Effect on electricity transmission
¶145 Effect on electric utilities

COOPERATIVES

¶147 Effect on energy cooperatives

COAL AND COKE

¶149 Effect on coal and coke producers

FUELS

¶151 Effect on gasoline producers
¶153 Effect on diesel and biodiesel producers
¶155 Effect on kerosene producers
¶157 Effect on liquefied petroleum gas producers
¶159 Effect on ethanol producers
¶161 Effect on special motor fuels producers
¶163 Effect on alcohol fuels producers
¶165 Effect on motor boat and small engine fuel producers
¶167 Effect on P Series fuels producers
¶169 Effect on liquid hydrocarbons from biomass
¶171 Effect on fuel blenders, pipeline operators, inventory position holders, and terminal and vessel operators
¶173 Effect on fuel importers
¶175 Effect on refiners

ENERGY RESEARCH

¶176 Effect on energy research

OTHER AFFECTED BUSINESSES

¶177 Overall effect on other businesses
¶178 Effect on trucking and limousine companies
¶179 Effect on alcoholic beverage producers
¶180 Effect on aviation
¶181 Effect on exporters

¶182 Effect on farmers
¶183 Effect on credit card issuers
¶184 Effect on custom gunsmiths
¶185 Effect on oil tanker operators
¶186 Effect on operators of deep draft vessels
¶187 Effect on recycling industry

GOVERNMENT TRUST FUNDS

¶191 Effect on government trust funds

STATE TAX ENERGY INCENTIVES

¶195 Energy conservation and production income tax credits

ENERGY TAX INCENTIVES ACT AND SAFE TRANSPORTATION EQUITY ACT OF 2005

¶101 Overview

The near simultaneous passage of the Energy Policy Act of 2005 (H.R. 6) and the SAFE Transportation Equity Act of 2005 (H.R. 3) tends to highlight the interrelationship of the two major areas of energy and transportation to the American economy. A major portion of energy usage goes to support transportation in its various forms and the taxation of energy resources serves as a major source of funding to build and maintain the transportation infrastructure.

It is expected that neither piece of legislation will have much, if any, immediate impact on the price consumers pay for gasoline. However, the tax title (Energy Tax Incentives Act, Title XIII of H.R. 6), does contain numerous benefits directed at traditional energy producers, such as the oil, coal, and electric power industries. In addition, the sometimes forgotten nuclear power industry also received attention from Congress. Finally, nontraditional sources of energy, including biodiesel and solar power, were also considered.

Although these legislative efforts were aimed primarily at the energy and transportation industries, that is not to say that individuals or general business should feel left out. In particular, car purchasers, homeowners, and commercial building owners will all have something to consider when doing their tax planning. In addition, the legislation contains the typical smattering of specialized provisions benefiting such diverse groups as small custom gunsmiths, sport fishermen, and certain segments of the alcoholic beverage industry.

INDIVIDUALS

¶105 Overall Effect on Individuals

Individual taxpayers were the recipients of two significant changes made by the Energy Tax Incentives Act of 2005 (Energy Act). First, prospective car and light truck purchasers will have new incentives to purchase a vehicle powered by other than a traditional gasoline engine (¶107). Due to certain restrictions contained in the statute, anyone contemplating such a purchase in the near future should study their options and consider the benefits of deciding sooner rather than later.

Another major class of beneficiaries of the Energy Act are homeowners. New incentives for energy-efficient changes to one's home, including the installation of certain solar or photovoltaic equipment should prove popular (¶109). In addition, a new credit is available for the installation of equipment to be used to refuel certain nontraditional vehicles (¶107).

¶107 Effect on Purchasers of Environmentally Friendly Vehicles

New credits on purchase or lease.—The Energy Tax Incentives Act of 2005 (Energy Act) did not neglect a growing segment of the American driving public consisting of purchasers of vehicles that are powered by other than a traditional gasoline engine. Such vehicles, which include pure electrics and hybrids, as well as those that run on natural gas, liquefied petroleum or natural gas, or 85-percent methanol have been growing in popularity as gasoline prices have risen. Hybrid cars, such as the Toyota Prius and Honda Insight, as well as more recent luxury entries like the Lexus RX 400h, have been garnering the bulk of the publicity. Particularly in the case of hybrids, price does not seem to have deterred sales, at least not to date. However, the typical hybrid model "stickers" for several thousand dollars more than its normally powered sibling. Over time, consumers may find it hard to justify such a price differential even when that initial price is offset by fuel savings over the life of the vehicle. For example, if the hybrid version of a vehicle averages 40 miles per gallon versus 25 for the gasoline version and, assuming gasoline averages $2.50 per gallon, a driver would have to travel over 80,000 miles to recover a $3,000 difference in price between the two vehicles. Of course, this is before the consideration of tax incentives that can drastically alter that equation.

The Energy Act effectively terminates the current law deduction for clean fuel vehicles (¶330) and replaces it with a series of credits for hybrids, lean-burn vehicles, fuel cell vehicles, and alternative fuel vehicles under the overall title of the "Alternative Motor Vehicle Credit" (¶305).

Hybrids and lean-burn vehicles.—Although prior law did provide tax incentives for the purchase of a hybrid or other nontraditional vehicle, the Energy Act sweetens the deal. Beginning January 1, 2006, purchasers *and lessors* of hybrids and so-called lean-burn vehicles are entitled to a two-part credit rather the deduction that had been in place before the new law (¶315 and ¶320). The two part credit consists of (1) a fuel economy credit and (2) conservation credit. The fuel economy credit is computed on the basis of a comparison with 2002 model year fuel economy for city driving. This portion of the credit ranges from $400 for a vehicle with fuel economy that is at least 125 percent better than the base amount and up to $2,400 for one that has fuel economy of at least 250 percent of the base amount. For example, a 2002 passenger car in the 3,500 pound class had a fuel economy rating of 22.6 miles per gallon. Accordingly, a hybrid vehicle that produces fuel economy of double that amount would be entitled to a $1,600 fuel economy credit under the new law. The conservation credit relates to the lifetime fuel savings of a vehicle and ranges from $250 for a savings of at least 1,200 gallons of gasoline to $1,000 for a savings of at least 3,000 gallons. A similar credit is available for commercial vehicles as well (¶121).

However, what Congress gives with one hand it often takes away with the other. The new credit for hybrid and lean-burn vehicles will be capped once a manufacturer sells 60,000 of such vehicles. Beginning with the second quarter after the 60,000th sale is recorded, purchasers would only be entitled to a reduced credit phasing down to no credit after the fifth quarter. Although the basic reason for such a cap may be the cost to the federal treasury, there has been some speculation that it was also included to give domestic auto manufacturers a needed break against some of their Japanese rivals that have been out front with this technology and are already selling enough such cars annually to easily exceed the cap limitations next year. The credit is set to expire generally December 31, 2010.

Alternative fuel vehicles.—Somewhat less sexy from a technological point of view than hybrids, alternative fuel vehicles are still an important segment of the current automotive market. Alternative fuels include natural gas, liquefied petroleum or natural gas, or 85-percent methanol. The Department of Energy lists over 20 models of 2005 cars and light trucks that are available as alternative fuel vehicles that are not hybrids. These include such mainstream models as the Ford Taurus, Dodge Ram pick up, and the Chevy Silverado. For alternative fuel cars and light trucks, the Energy Act provides a credit of up to $4,000 (¶325). A larger credit is available for trucks, buses, and vans (¶121). This credit also expires December 31, 2010.

Fuel cell vehicles.—Although fuel cell vehicles are extremely rare today, President Bush in his 2003 State of the Union address stated his interest in American industry developing viable hydrogen powered cars and trucks within the near future. The result is the President's Hydrogen Fuel Initiative, which, in conjunction with the FreedonCAR partnership with automakers, is intended to advance high-technology research needed to produce a practical, affordable hydrogen fuel cell that can significantly improve fuel economy over time. The drafters of the Energy Act did not forget to consider the potential future importance of fuel cell vehicles. Accordingly, a two-part credit is also provided for these vehicles with part one based on the vehicle's weight class and the second part based on fuel economy as compared to the 2002 model year figures (¶310). The base credit can run as high as $8,000 for cars, but tops at $4,000 in 2010 and later. The additional credit runs from $1,000 for vehicles having 150 percent better fuel economy than 2002 to $4,000 for those with 300 percent better fuel economy. The fuel cell credit would expire December 31, 2014. For a discussion of the fuel cell vehicle credit for heavy trucks, see ¶121.

¶107

Unfortunately, not all alternative vehicles received a boost from the Energy Act. A provision that would have extended the credit for electric vehicles was dropped in the Conference Agreement.

Residential clean-fuel refueling equipment.—If you own a vehicle that is powered by something other than gasoline, a serious practical problem may be how to refuel your vehicle. At the present time, it is not possible to simply drive down to the local service station and fill up your tank with 20 gallons of natural gas or to recharge your electric car. In answer to this point, beginning in 2006 for property placed in service in 2006, the Energy Act allows a new credit of up to $1,000 for the residential installation of alternative fuel vehicle refueling property (¶730). Such property would include storage tanks and dispensing units and charging stations for electric cars. Alternative fuels for purposes of this credit include mixtures that are at least 85-percent ethanol, natural gas, compressed natural gas, liquefied natural gas or petroleum gas or hydrogen, as well as biodiesel/diesel mixtures of at least 20-percent biodiesel A larger credit is available for commercial property (see ¶121). To claim this credit, qualifying property must have been put in service prior to 2010 or, in the case of hydrogen related property, 2015.

¶109 Effect on Homeowners

Energy-efficient improvements.—Although the main thrust of the Energy Tax Incentives Act of 2005 (Energy Act) is on energy producers and related industries, individuals, including homeowners, were not forgotten. Owners of existing homes will be entitled to a lifetime credit of up to $500 for energy-efficient improvements to their homes made in 2006 and 2007 (¶205). The credit is 10 percent of the cost of (1) energy-efficient improvements plus the cost of (2) residential energy property expenditures. Qualifying improvements must be expected to last for at least five years and include those for insulation, windows, skylights, and doors, although only $200 can be attributed to expenditures for windows. Metal roofs coated with heat-reducing pigments are also included.

The residential energy property expenditures included in the credit are broken down into three components each with their own separate limits:

- $50 for a main air circulating fan;
- $150 for a natural gas, propane or oil furnace or hot water boiler; and
- $300 for what is referred to as "energy efficient building property," which includes electric and geothermal pumps and central air conditioners.

The home for which the credit is being taken must be the taxpayer's principal residence. Although taxpayers are not required to certify their expenses for the credit, they will be required to reduce their basis in the qualifying property in the amount of the credit.

Solar or photovoltaic equipment.—Homeowners are also entitled to a 30-percent credit for the installation of solar hot water or photovoltaic (electricity generating solar) and fuel cell property (¶210). An annual credit limit of $2,000 per category is set for solar hot water and photovoltaic expenditures, and $500 for each half kilowatt of capacity of qualified fuel cell property. This credit is also available for property placed in service in 2006 and 2007. However, the credit cannot be taken for equipment used for heating swimming pools or hot tubs. Jointly occupied property, as well as condominiums and co-ops, are subject to proration rules.

¶111 Effect on Tax-Exempt Bond Investors

Clean energy renewable bonds.—With tax rates on capital gains and qualified dividends at historic lows, investors interested in tax-exempt bonds may be feeling somewhat neglected. However, the Energy Tax Incentives Act of 2005 (Energy Act) and the SAFE Transportation Equity Act of 2005 (Highway Act) do not disappoint in this regard. For example, the Energy Act adds new clean energy renewable bonds (CREBs) (¶455). These bonds can be issued by governmental bodies (including Indian tribal governments), the Tennessee Valley Authority, electric cooperatives, and others to finance renewable energy facilities. CREBs will not pay interest, but holders will be entitled to a tax credit for bonds issued in 2006 and 2007. A national limit of $800 million in such bonds is set.

New categories of exempt facilities bonds.—The Highway Act also provides motivation for tax-exempt bond investors. The Act adds a new category of exempt facility bonds for "qualified highway or surface freight transfer facilities" (¶915) A national limit of $15 billion is placed on the total face value of these bonds.

Bonds issued by state-owned REITs.—Another provision of the Highway Act provides that the income of certain state-owned corporations organized as real estate investment trusts (REITs) that also qualify as non-operating Class III railroads will be treated as accruing to the state. Accordingly, obligations issued by the corporation will not be treated as private activity bonds and, thus, interest paid on them will be tax exempt (¶910). In order to qualify under this provision, the state had to have become the owner of all of the corporation's voting stock after December 31, 2003, and before December 31, 2006.

¶113 Effect on Patrons of Cooperatives

Passthrough of electricity production credit.—The Energy Tax Incentives Act of 2005 allows eligible electric cooperatives to pass any portion of the new Code Sec. 45(e) credit through to their patrons (¶113 and ¶420). The credit may be apportioned based on the amount of business done by such patrons during the tax year. This credit applies to credits claimed by agricultural cooperatives in tax years ending after August 8, 2005.

Other pass-throughs.—Several additional provisions in the Energy Act clarify that particular credits may be passed through from cooperatives to their owners or patrons. These include the expensing election for qualified liquid fuel refinery property (¶505), the deduction permitted for costs of EPA Highway Diesel Fuel Sulphur Control Requirements incurred by a small refiner cooperative (¶535), the small agri-biodiesel producer credit (¶710), and the small ethanol producer credit (¶735).

¶115 Effect on Sport Fishermen

Excise tax on fishing poles and rods.—The SAFE Transportation Equity Act of 2005 places a cap on the excise tax imposed on the sale of fishing poles and rods. Effective for sales after September 30, 2005, the excise tax is limited to the lesser of 10 percent of the sale price or $10 (¶845).

GENERAL BUSINESS

¶117 Overall Effect on Business

Business generally fared well under provisions of both the Energy Tax Incentives Act of 2005 (Energy Act) and the SAFE Transportation Equity Act of 2005 (Highway Act). New incentives were added for the purchase and installation of fuel cell and microturbine power plants, as well as certain solar energy property (¶119). The research credit was also expanded to include certain expenditures on energy-related research. However, the benefits of the amortization of intangibles under Code Sec. 197, will be recaptured in some cases.

Business owners who purchase or lease vehicles may be able to take advantage of the revised credits available for the purchase/lease of hybrid and other types of alternative fuel vehicles that are also available to individuals (¶121). Home builders, including those producing manufactured homes, will be the recipients of new credits for energy-efficient homes (¶123). Commercial building owners could benefit from provisions that will reward them for energy-efficient expenditures on their properties (¶125). The hard-hit home appliance industry can receive new business credits for manufacturing clothes washers, refrigerators, and dishwashers (¶127).

¶119 Effect on Business Expenditures for Energy Savings and Research

Fuel cell and stationary microturbine power plants.—In another example of the potential importance of fuel cells to America's search for new energy resources, the Energy Tax Incentives Act of 2005 (Energy Act) allows a 30-percent business energy credit for the purchase of qualified fuel cell powerplants for businesses placed in service in 2006 and 2007 (¶240). Such a system integrates the fuel cell stack and associated components to convert fuel to electricity using electrochemical means with an electricity-only generating efficiency of more than 30 percent that generates at least one-half kilowatt of electricity. The credit for any fuel cell property is limited to $500 for each one-half kilowatt of capacity.

Although gas turbines have been around for decades, the field of microturbines is still considered emerging technology. Some commentators go so far as to claim that such technology will help propel the next great economic boom. In any event, Congress has decided to be in the forefront with this issue and offer businesses a 10-percent credit for the purchase of qualifying stationary microturbine power plants.

In order to qualify for the credit, the system must have an electricity-only generating efficiency of at least 26 percent based on International Standard Organization conditions and a capacity of less than 2,000 kilowatts. The credit is limited to the lesser of 10 percent of the qualifying property's basis or $200 for each kilowatt of capacity and is available for property placed in service in 2006 and 2007.

Telecommunications companies receive particularly good news with respect to the installation of fuel cell and microturbine power plants in that the Energy Act removes the Code Sec. 48 restriction that would otherwise have prevented them from claiming the new credit because of their status as public utilities.

Solar energy property.—A favorite of environmentalists, solar power also receives a boost from the Energy Act. The former 10-percent business energy credit for the cost of equipment that uses solar power to generate electricity for heating or cooling of a structure, to provide solar process heat or to produce, distribute, or use energy derived from a geothermal deposit, is increased to 30 percent (¶230). Besides the percentage change, the Energy Act indicates that equipment that uses fiber optic distributed sunlight to illuminate the inside of a structure qualifies as solar energy property. However, property used to heat a swimming pool is not eligible for the credit. The credit is available for property placed in service in 2006 and 2007.

Research credit expanded.—The Energy Act modifies the present-law Code Sec. 41 research credit for qualified energy research (¶235). Under the new law, a taxpayer may claim a credit of 20 percent of the expenditures on qualified energy research undertaken by an "energy research consortium." Qualified energy research expenditures are expenditures that would otherwise qualify for the existing research credit and include those related to the production, supply, and conservation of energy (including alternative energy sources). Research relating to hydrogen fuel cell vehicles would qualify for this credit if the research expenditures otherwise satisfy the current requirements of present-law as would qualifying research undertaken to improve the energy-efficiency of lighting.

An energy research consortium must be organized and operated primarily to conduct energy research and development in the public interest and to which at least five unrelated persons paid, or incurred amounts, to such organization within the calendar year. In addition, to be a qualified energy research consortium no single person can pay or incur more than 50 percent of the total amounts received by the research consortium during the calendar year. An energy research consortium cannot be a private foundation.

The amount of credit claimed is limited to expenditures within the tax year. However, in a change from the rules for the pre-existing research credit, the 20-percent energy research credit applies to all qualifying expenditures, not only those in excess of a base amount. The expanded research credit is available for amounts paid or incurred after August 8, 2005.

Recapture for amortization of intangibles.—The Energy Act places new restrictions on the use of Code Sec. 197, which allows businesses to amortize the cost of intangibles over a 15-year period (¶245). Specifically, the Energy Act requires that the benefits of amortization be recaptured if multiple intangibles are sold (or otherwise disposed of) in a single transaction or series of transactions, as if all of the Code Sec. 197 intangibles were a single asset. Thus, any gain on the sale (or other disposition) of the intangibles is recaptured as ordinary income to the extent of ordinary deprecia-

¶119

tion deductions previously claimed on any of these intangibles. However, the new rule does not apply if the adjusted basis of the intangible exceeds its fair market value.

¶121 Effect on Business Purchasers of Environmentally Friendly Vehicles

New credits for business purchasers and lessors.—As noted in the discussion of individual taxpayers (¶107), the Energy Tax Incentives Act of 2005 (Energy Act) effectively terminates the current law deduction for clean fuel vehicles (¶330) and replaces it with a series of credits for hybrids, lean-burn vehicles, fuel cell vehicles, and alternative fuel vehicles under the overall title of the "Alternative Motor Vehicle Credit" (¶305).

Hybrids and lean-burn vehicles.—Beginning January 1, 2006, the Energy Act provides purchasers *and lessors* of hybrids and so-called lean-burn vehicles with a two-part credit rather the deduction that had been in place before the new law (¶315 and ¶320). The two part credit consists of (1) a fuel economy credit and (2) conservation credit. The fuel economy credit is computed on the basis of a comparison with 2002 model year fuel economy for city driving. This portion of the credit ranges from $400 for a vehicle with fuel economy that is at least 125 percent better than the base amount and up to $2,400 for one that has fuel economy of at least 250 percent of the base amount. For example, a 2002 passenger car in the 3,500 pound class had a fuel economy rating of 22.6 miles per gallon. Accordingly, a hybrid vehicle that produces fuel economy of double that amount would be entitled to a $1,600 fuel economy credit under the new law. The conservation credit relates to the lifetime fuel savings of a vehicle and ranges from $250 for a savings of at least 1,200 gallons of gasoline to $1,000 for a savings of at least 3,000 gallons.

For many businesses, it is important to note that the credit is also available to lessors and is not only available for passenger cars, but also, potentially, for both light and heavy trucks. However, the credit for heavy trucks expires December 31, 2009, one year earlier than for hybrid cars, light trucks and other lean burn vehicles. In addition, the new credit for hybrid and lean-burn vehicles will be capped once a manufacturer sells 60,000 of such vehicles. Beginning with the second quarter after the 60,000th sale is recorded, purchasers would only be entitled to a reduced credit phasing down to no credit after the fifth quarter.

Fuel cell vehicles.—Although fuel cell vehicles are for the most part the subject of future technology, the Energy Act does provide incentives for their use by businesses (¶310). A two-part credit is also provided for these vehicles with part one based on the vehicle's weight class and the second part based on fuel economy as compared to the 2002 model year figures. The base credit can run as high as $40,000 for trucks over 26,000 pounds. The fuel cell vehicle credit expires December 31, 2014. For discussion of this credit with respect to cars and light trucks, see ¶107.

Alternative fuel vehicles.—A more mainstream choice than hybrids or fuel cell vehicles, particularly for business customers, are alternative fuel vehicles. Alternative fuels include natural gas, liquefied petroleum or natural gas, or 85-percent methanol. Vehicles available with this technology include such business favorites as the Dodge

Ram pick-up and the Chevy Silverado and Suburban. In fact, the Department of Energy lists over 20 models of 2005 cars and light trucks that are available as alternative fuel vehicles that are not hybrids. For alternative fuel cars and light trucks, the Energy Act provides a credit of up to $32,000 for trucks, buses, and vans over 26,000 pounds (¶325). A smaller credit is available for cars and light trucks (¶107). This credit expires December 31, 2010.

Commercial clean-fuel refueling equipment.—Beginning in 2006, the Energy Act allows a new credit of up to $30,000 for the commercial installation of alternative fuel vehicle refueling property (¶730). Such property would include storage tanks and dispensing units and charging stations for electric cars. Alternative fuels for purposes of this credit include mixtures that are at least 85-percent ethanol, natural gas, compressed natural gas, liquefied natural gas or petroleum gas or hydrogen, as well as biodiesel/diesel mixtures of at least 20-percent biodiesel A smaller credit is available for residential property (¶107). To claim this credit, qualifying property must have been put in service prior to 2010 or, in the case of hydrogen related property, 2015.

¶123 Effect on Home Builders

Energy-efficient homes.—Home builders are in for some good news as a result of passage of the Energy Tax Incentives Act of 2005 (Energy Act). For homes that are substantially completed after 2005 and purchased in 2006 and 2007, the Energy Act provides a credit of $2,000 if the home achieves a 50-percent improvement in energy efficiency versus a comparable dwelling constructed under the existing International Energy Conservation Code standards (¶220). The credit is referred to as the "New Energy Efficient Home Credit," which would seem to imply that it only applies to new construction. However, the statute indicates that the term construction includes "substantial reconstruction and rehabilitation." The credit is available only to the builder (or producer in the case of a manufactured home) who constructs the home, which must be used by the purchaser as a residence during the tax year. To be eligible for the credit, the home must also be in the United States.

Manufactured homes.—So as not to slight a growing part of the home construction industry, the energy-efficient home construction credit is also available for manufactured homes. In addition, a manufactured home can qualify for a lower $1,000 credit if the home meets a 30-percent efficiency standard.

¶125 Effect on Commercial Building Owners

Energy-efficient property expenditures.—The Energy Tax Incentives Act of 2005 (Energy Act) provides a new deduction for the cost of energy-efficient property expenditures for commercial buildings (¶215). The deduction is generally $1.80 per square foot for buildings that achieve a 50-percent energy savings with reference to Standard 90.1-2001 of the American Society of Heating, Refrigerating, and Air Conditioning Engineers and the Illuminating Engineering Society of North America. However, a reduced deduction for building subsystems of $0.60 per square foot is available for those building that fail the 50-percent test. The separate building systems are the same as those considered for purposes of the full deduction, i.e., (1) interior lighting, (2) heating, cooling, ventilation, and hot water, and (3) the "building envelope." The deduction is allowed for the year in which the qualifying property is placed in service and certification requirements must be met in order to qualify. The deduction is available for property placed in service in 2006 and 2007.

¶127 Effect on Appliance Manufacturers

Energy-efficient appliances.—With the recent news of a takeover bid for Maytag by a Chinese company, tax relief for appliance manufacturers could be considered timely. The Energy Tax Incentives Act of 2005 (Energy Act) adds new tax credits, as part of the general business credit, for the production of energy-efficient clothes washers, dishwashers, and refrigerators (¶225). The credit amounts vary and are only available for appliances produced in 2006 and 2007.

- *Clothes washers*—$100, if they meet the 2007 requirements of the Energy Star Program;
- *Refrigerators*—$75, if manufactured in 2006 and achieve 15-percent energy savings;
- *Refrigerators*—$125, if manufactured in 2006 or 2007 and achieve 20-percent energy savings;
- *Refrigerators*—$175, if manufactured in 2006 or 2007 and achieve 25-percent energy savings; and
- *Dishwashers*—The lesser of $100 or the energy savings amount, if they meet the 2007 requirements of the Energy Star Program.

In addition, an overall cap of $75 million per tax year is placed on the energy-efficient appliance credit, which is to be reduced for any credit taken in a prior year. No more than $20 million of the cap can be from the manufacture of refrigerators that meet the 15-percent energy savings.

ENERGY AND FUELS

¶129 Overview of Effect on Energy

Recent high energy prices and growing shortages of fossil fuels have generally made the energy industry one of the most profitable areas of the economy. Many of the tax provisions in this legislation are designed to help the industry eliminate bottlenecks in the system, reduce waste, and promote alternative sources of energy. In an effort to look at the entire energy industry, the Treasury is directed in this legislation to contract with the National Academy of Sciences to conduct a study evaluating the external costs and benefits associated with the production and consumption of energy (¶1005).

OIL

¶131 Effect on Oil Producers

Oil producers.—More oil producers are likely to meet the expanded definition of "independent producer" and qualify for special tax rules under the oil depletion deduction applicable to independent producers (¶510). The Oil Spill Liability Trust Fund tax has also been reinstated with a significantly larger funding goal (¶540). The credit for producing oil from shale and tar sands is made part of the general business credit, with the carryback and carryforward features of the general business credit (¶615). Geological and geophysical amounts incurred in connection with oil exploration in the U.S. may be amortized over two years (¶525).

NATURAL GAS

¶133 Effect on Natural Gas Producers

Natural gas producers.—With a growing shortage of domestic supplies of natural gas, the Energy Tax Incentives Act of 2005 looks at alternative sources of natural gas. A new investment credit is created for certain certified gasification projects designed to convert coal, petroleum reside, biomass, or other materials recovered for their energy or feedstock value into a synthesis gas (¶605). The credit for producing gas from geopressured brine, Devonian shale, coal seams, tight formations, or biomass has been made part of the general business credit, with the carryback and carryforward provisions associated with that credit (¶615). Geological and geophysical amounts incurred in connection with gas exploration in the U.S. may be amortized over two years (¶525).

¶135 Effect on Natural Gas Utilities

Tax-exempt bonds.—An exception is created to the general arbitrage restrictions on tax-exempt bonds permitting bonds to finance the prepayment of natural gas supply contracts of a government utility (¶530).

¶137 Effect on Natural Gas Distributors

Depreciation.—The Energy Tax Incentives Act of 2005 establishes shorter depreciation periods for natural gas gathering lines (¶520) and natural gas distribution lines (¶515).

ELECTRICITY AND NUCLEAR POWER

¶139 Effect on Electricity Producers

Electricity producers.—The Code Sec. 45 placed-in-service deadline for electric production projects from certain alternative sources is extended for qualifying wind facilities, closed-loop biomass facilities (including a facility co-firing the closed-loop biomass with coal, other biomass, or coal and other biomass), open-loop biomass facilities, geothermal facilities, small irrigation power facilities, landfill gas facilities, and trash combustion facilities (¶410 and ¶415). In addition, two new qualifying alternative resources have been added to Code Sec. 45: hydropower and Indian coal (¶405). A new category of tax credit bonds, called Clean Renewable Energy Bonds (CREBs), is created for financing Code Sec. 45 electricity production projects from alternative fuels (¶455). More pollution control facilities used in connection with coal-fired electric generation now qualify for favorable amortization, but the amortization period is 84 rather than 60 months (¶620).

¶141 Effect on Nuclear Power Industry

Nuclear power.—To help encourage a second generation of nuclear power plant construction, the Energy Tax Incentives Act of 2005 creates a new tax credit for producing electricity at a qualifying advanced nuclear power facility (¶440). Also the rules with respect to deductible contributions to nuclear decommissioning funds are relaxed by repealing the cost-of-service requirement to be eligible for a deduction and permitting contributions to funds for pre-1984 decommissioning costs (¶445). Even unregulated taxpayers can now qualify for deductions to a qualified nuclear decommissioning fund.

¶143 Effect on Electricity Transmission

Electricity transmission.—The recovery period for certain assets used in the transmission of electricity for sale and related land improvements is reduced to 15 years and the definition of qualifying Code Sec. 45 property is modified (¶425). The special rules under Code Sec. 451(i) for deferral of gain on the sale or other disposition of property used for providing electric transmission services are extended (¶435).

¶145 Effect on Electric Utilities

NOL carryback.—A five-year net operating loss carryback is provided for certain electric utility companies (¶430).

COOPERATIVES

¶147 Effect on Energy Cooperatives

Energy co-ops.—Several provisions in the Energy Tax Incentives Act of 2005 clarify that particular credits may be passed through from cooperatives to their owners or patrons. These include the Code Sec. 45 credit for production of electricity from alternative resources (¶420), the expensing election for qualified liquid fuel refinery property (¶505), the deduction permitted for costs of EPA Highway Diesel Fuel Sulphur Control Requirements incurred by a small refiner cooperative (¶535), the small agri-biodiesel producer credit (¶710), and the small ethanol producer credit (¶735). Mutual or cooperative electric companies are qualified borrowers for purposes of the new tax credit for Clean Renewable Energy Bonds (CREBs) (¶455). Certain sunset dates are removed for rural electric cooperatives with respect to excluding income received from open-access electric energy transmission or distribution services, any nuclear decommissioning transaction, and any asset exchange or conversion transaction under Code Sec. 501(c)(12); the rules that allow income from load loss transactions to be treated as member income; and the rule that permits taxable electric cooperatives to treat the receipt or accrual of income from load loss transactions as income from patrons (¶450).

COAL AND COKE

¶149 Effect on Coal and Coke Producers

Coal and coke.—A new investment credit applies to certified projects to generate power using integrated gasification combined cycle (IGCC) and other advanced coal-based electricity generation technologies (¶605). The Code Sec. 29 credit for producing liquid, gaseous, or solid synthetic fuels from coal (including lignite) is made part of the general business credit, with the carryback and carryforward features of the general business credit (¶615). The credit, redesignated Code Sec. 45K, is also expanded to apply to qualified facilities that produce coke and coke gas (¶610). Additional pollution control facilities used in connection with coal-fired electric generation qualify for favorable amortization, but the amortization period is 84 rather than 60 months (¶620).

The Code Sec. 45 credit for the production of electricity from renewal resources is expanded to add Indian coal as a new qualifying energy source (¶405). The existing credit with respect to closed-loop biomass facilities (including a facility co-firing the closed-loop biomass with coal, other biomass, or coal and other biomass) has also been extended (¶410 and ¶415). Diesel from coal is identified as an alternative fuel for purposes of the volumetric excise tax credit, and the calculations for the excise tax and credit are modified (¶725).

FUELS

¶151 Effect on Gasoline Producers

Gasoline.—The excise tax on gasoline and other fuels to fund the Leaking Underground Storage Tank (LUST) Trust Fund is extended and all fuel, including dyed fuel, is subject to the tax (¶785). Also, the reduction in the rate of excise tax on gasoline is postponed for six years (¶905). A temporary advisory commission is created to oversee motor fuel excise tax enforcement (¶780).

¶153 Effect on Diesel and Biodiesel Producers

Diesel and biodiesel.—A special excise tax rate is provided for diesel fuel blended with water into a diesel-water fuel emulsion (¶720). The income tax credit for biodiesel and qualified biodiesel mixtures as well as the excise tax credit for biodiesel mixtures are extended, together with the payment provisions related to the biodiesel fuel mixture credit (¶705). Similar incentives are created for renewable diesel (¶715). A new small agri-biodiesel producer credit is added to the biodiesel fuels credit (¶710). The excise tax on diesel and other fuels to fund the Leaking Underground Storage Tank (LUST) Trust Fund is extended and all fuel, including dyed fuel, is subject to the tax (¶785).

The reduction in the rate of excise tax on diesel fuel is postponed for six years (¶905). The Treasury is directed to undertake a study of the use of highway fuels in trucks for nonpropulsive purposes (¶1015). The IRS is also required to prepare a report on the availability of new technologies to enhance the collection of the excise taxes on diesel fuel (¶760). A new penalty is authorized for anyone who knowingly sells diesel that does not comply with EPA sulfur diesel regulations (¶765). Diesel from coal is identified as an alternative fuel for purposes of the volumetric excise tax credit (¶725).

¶155 Effect on Kerosene Producers

Kerosene.—The excise tax on kerosene and other fuels to fund the Leaking Underground Storage Tank (LUST) Trust Fund is extended and all fuel, including dyed fuel, is subject to the tax (¶785). Also, the reduction in the rate of excise tax on kerosene is postponed for six years (¶905). In addition, all removals of kerosene other than into the wing of an airplane will be taxed as diesel fuel (¶740). Technical corrections in the SAFE Transportation Equity Act of 2005 also clarify that IRS registration is required for the reduced aviation tax rate (¶790) and that the termination date for the tax on aviation-grade kerosene is the same as the termination date for aviation gasoline (¶795).

¶157 Effect on Liquefied Petroleum Gas Producers

LPG.—Liquified petroleum gas is identified as an alternative fuel for purposes of the volumetric excise tax credit (¶725).

¶159 Effect on Ethanol Producers

Ethanol.—The Code Sec. 40 small ethanol producer credit is modified to increase the limit on production capacity necessary to meet the definition of a small ethanol producer (¶735).

¶161 Effect on Special Motor Fuels Producers

Special motor fuels.—The excise tax on special motor fuels and other fuels to fund the Leaking Underground Storage Tank (LUST) Trust Fund is extended and all fuel, including dyed fuel, is subject to the tax (¶785). The reduction in the rate of excise tax on special motor fuels is postponed for six years (¶905). A temporary advisory commission is created to oversee motor fuel excise tax enforcement (¶780).

¶163 Effect on Alcohol Fuels Producers

Alcohol fuels.—The reduction in the rate of excise tax on alcohol fuels is postponed for six years (¶905). A technical correction is included in the SAFE Transportation Equity Act of 2005 conforming other Code provisions to the alcohol fuels changes in the American Jobs Creation Act of 2004 (P.L. 108-357) (¶787).

¶165 Effect on Motor Boat and Small Engine Fuel Producers

Small engine fuels.—The authority to transfer funds from the Highway Fund to the Sport Fish Restoration and Boating Trust Fund is extended for six years (¶905). A technical correction in the SAFE Transportation Equity Act of 2005 clarifies that amounts collected from small engine fuel taxes deposited into the Sport Fish Restoration and Boating Trust Fund may only be used to carry out the purposes of the Coastal Wetlands Planning, Protection and Restoration Act (¶797).

¶167 Effect on P Series Fuels Producers

P Series fuels.—P Series fuels are identified as an alternative fuel for purposes of the volumetric excise tax credit (¶725).

¶169 Effect on Liquid Hydrocarbons from Biomass

Liquid hydrocarbons.—Liquid hydrocarbons derived from biomass are identified as an alternative fuel for purposes of the volumetric excise tax credit (¶725).

¶171 Effect on Fuel Blenders, Pipeline Operators, Inventory Position Holders, and Terminal and Vessel Operators

Reregistration.—Persons required to register under Code Sec. 4101 are now required to reregister in the event of a change in ownership (¶755).

¶173 Effect on Fuel Importers

Fuel importers.—Importers required to register under Code Sec. 4101 are now required to reregister in the event of a change in ownership (¶755). The Departments of Homeland Security and Treasury are required to provide the IRS with information concerning taxable fuels destined for importation (¶770).

¶175 Effect on Refiners

Refiners.—In an effort to boost very tight U.S. refining capacity, a temporary expensing election is created for qualified refinery assets used in the refining of liquid fuels (¶505). More oil refiners are likely to meet the expanded definition of "independent producer" and qualify for special tax rules under the oil depletion deduction applicable to independent producers (¶510). Refiners required to register under Code Sec. 4101 are now required to reregister in the event of a change in ownership (¶755).

ENERGY RESEARCH

¶176 Effect on Energy Research

Research credit.—The research credit rules are relaxed for qualified energy research, permitting the credit for research undertaken by an energy research consortium, eliminating any base amount requirement, and permitting 100 percent of amounts paid to eligible small businesses, universities, and federal laboratories to qualify for the credit (¶235).

OTHER AFFECTED BUSINESSES

¶177 Overall Effect on Other Businesses

In addition to the major business provisions cited previously, there are a number of small targeted points contained in the Energy Tax Incentives Act of 2005 (Energy Act) and in the SAFE Transportation Equity Act of 2005 (Highway Act). Trucking and limousine businesses will benefit from new excise tax exemptions (¶178). Certain segments of the alcoholic beverage industry will see relief from occupational taxes and excise tax filing requirements, and some wholesalers and distillers may be entitled to a new tax credit (¶179). New rules contained in the Highway Act will also be felt by some in portions of the aviation industry, including crop sprayers, rural airport passengers, and the operators of sightseeing tours and seaplanes (¶180). Other businesses that should take note of changes made by the Highway Act or Energy Act include:

- Exporters (¶181);
- Farmers (¶182);
- Credit card issuers (¶183);
- Custom gunsmiths (¶184);
- Oil tanker operators (¶185);
- Operators of deep draft vessels (¶186); and
- Recyclers (¶187).

¶178 Effect on Trucking and Limousine Companies

New rules for super single tires.—"Super single tires" are subject to an excise tax of 4.725 cents per 10 pounds of excess rated load capacity over 3,500 pounds. The Energy Tax Incentives Act of 2005 (Energy Act) clarifies that the definition of a super single tire is a single tire greater than 13 inches in cross section width designed to replace two tires in a dual fitment (¶345). In other words, super single tires are not considered steering tires. Steering tires do not qualify for the special reduced tax rate. Because the effective date of this provision relates back to the related provision in the American Jobs Creation Act of 2004 (P.L. 108-357), it is effective for sales in calendar years beginning after January 1, 2005.

Truck tractors exempt from excise tax.—The SAFE Transportation Equity Act of 2005 (Highway Act) excludes tractors with a gross vehicle weight of 19,500 pounds or less from the 12-percent excise tax ordinarily imposed on the first retail sale of truck chassis and bodies, truck trailers and semitrailer chassis and bodies, and tractors used primarily for highway transportation in conjunction with a trailer or semitrailer (¶340). However, in order to qualify for the exemption, the gross vehicle weight of the tractor, when combined with a trailer or semitrailer, cannot exceed 33,000 pounds. The exclusion is available for sales after September 30, 2005.

¶178

No "gas guzzler" tax for limos.—The so called gas guzzler tax is imposed on vehicles that fail to achieve an average fuel economy of at least 22.5 miles per gallon, but the tax is generally only imposed on vehicles that have an unloaded gross vehicle weight of 6,000 pounds or less. The tax can range from $1,000 to $7,700 for vehicles that average less than 12.5 miles per gallon. Although emergency vehicles and nonpassenger automobiles are exempt from the tax, limousines are not, regardless of their weight. Beginning October 1, 2005, the Highway Act redresses this apparent inequity by exempting limousines having an unloaded gross vehicle weight in excess of 6,000 pounds from the gas guzzler tax (¶335).

Related reports and studies.—In addition to the provision on tires described above, the Energy Act mandates that, no later than July 1, 2007, the IRS is to report to Congress concerning the amount of tax collected during the one-year period beginning January 1, 2006, for each class of taxable tire (e.g. biasply, super single, or other) and the number of tires in each such class on which tax is imposed (¶1020). The Highway Act includes a different mandate that directs the Treasury to prepare a study of highway fuels used by trucks for nontransportation purposes (¶1015).

¶179 Effect on Alcoholic Beverage Producers

Occupational taxes.—Special occupational taxes are currently imposed on the producers and marketers of alcoholic beverages. However, effective July 1, 2008, the SAFE Transportation Equity Act of 2005 (Highway Act) repeals the special occupation taxes (¶840). Certain registration, recordkeeping, and inspection rules that are required for wholesale and retail alcohol dealers will be retained, as will the criminal penalties for failure to comply.

Excise tax filing for small producers.—Beginning in 2006, small domestic producers and importers of distilled spirits, wine, and beer are provided with eased excise tax requirements under a provision of the Highway Act (¶830). If they qualify, the producer/importer will be allowed to pay (and presumably file) excise taxes within 14 days after the end of each calendar quarter, rather than semi-monthly, beginning in 2006. In order to qualify as "small," the producer/importer's tax liability for the previous year must have been $50,000 or less and they must have at least a reasonable expectation that this will be the case in the current year as well. However, transactions made under deferred payment bonds do not qualify for quarterly filing and payment.

Wholesalers and distillers.—Effective for tax years beginning after September 30, 2005, the Highway Act provides a new income tax credit for the cost of carrying tax-paid domestic distilled spirits in wholesale inventories (¶835). The credit is computed based on the average tax-financing cost per case of distilled spirits for the most recent calendar year using the corporate overpayment interest rates for an assumed holding period of 60 days at an assumed excise tax rate of $25.68 per case. A limited credit is available for distillers and importers who are not eligible wholesalers.

¶180 Effect on Aviation

Treatment of aviation grade kerosene.—Aviation grade kerosene that is removed from a refinery or terminal directly into an aircraft for purposes of commercial aviation will be taxed at a reduced rate of 4.3 cents per gallon, assuming the person using the fuel is properly registered (¶155 and ¶740). Kerosene removed from a refinery or terminal directly into an aircraft that is used in noncommercial aviation will still be taxed at 21.8 cents per gallon, but is scheduled to drop to 4.3 cents after September 30, 2007. New rules also clarify that an exemption involving refueling trucks at a terminal in an airport is only applicable if the terminal is located at a secured area of the airport. Technical corrections in the SAFE Transportation Equity Act of 2005 also clarify that IRS registration is required for the reduced aviation tax rate (¶790) and that the termination date for the tax on aviation-grade kerosene is the same as the termination date for aviation gasoline (¶795).

Crop sprayers and foresters.—Aerial applicators will no longer have to obtain written consent from the farm owner or operator to claim an exemption from excise taxes imposed on aviation gasoline under a provision of the Highway Act that is effective for fuel used after September 30, 2005 (¶820). In addition, the exemption from such taxes for helicopters used in timber operations will include fixed-wing aircraft if the aircraft is not using a federally funded airport and airway services.

Rural airport passengers.—Customers at rural airports will benefit from the Highway Act's expanded definition of the term "rural airport," thus qualifying for an exemption from the excise tax on flight segments (¶805). Effective October 1, 2005, the new definition of a rural airport includes those that (1) are not connected by paved roads to another airport and (2) had less than 100,000 commercial passengers departing on flight segments of at least 100 miles during the second preceding calendar year.

Seaplane operators and passengers.—The Highway Act clarifies that, effective after September 30, 2005, the air passenger and air cargo taxes do not apply to transportation on a seaplane if the flight segment takes off from and lands on water (¶810). However, an additional condition requires that the takeoff and landing sites must not have received and must not be receiving financial assistance from the Airport and Airway Trust Fund. The benefits of this tax break may be offset by the classification of seaplanes as noncommercial aviation, thus subjecting fuel for such planes to the higher noncommercial tax rate.

Sightseeing tour operators and passengers.—Sightseeing tours also receive a benefit from the Highway Act. Effective for transportation beginning after September 30, 2005, the exception to the air passenger tax for small aircraft operated on nonestablished lines will include those in which sightseeing is the sole purpose of the flight (¶815).

¶181 Effect on Exporters

Harbor maintenance tax.—In conforming the Internal Revenue Code to the Supreme Court's decision in *United States Shoe Corp.*, SCt, 98-1 USTC ¶70,091, 523 U.S. 360, 118 S.

Ct. 1290, the SAFE Transportation Equity Act of 2005 (Highway Act) repeals the harbor maintenance tax on exports (¶825). The repeal is effective before, on, and after August 10, 2005.

¶182 Effect on Farmers

Direct refund for nontaxable use.—A provision of the SAFE Transportation Equity Act of 2005 (Highway Act) eliminates the rule requiring that only the ultimate vendor of diesel fuel or kerosene used for farming purposes could apply for a refund of excise taxes paid on the fuel (¶750). Accordingly, after September 30, 2005, refunds can be paid to the ultimate purchaser (farmer) under the rules that otherwise apply to nontaxable uses of diesel fuel or kerosene.

¶183 Effect on Credit Card Issuers

Government purchases of fuel by credit card.—The SAFE Transportation Equity Act of 2005 (Highway Act) replaces the oil company credit card rule as it applied to sales of gasoline to an entity that is exempt from excise taxes, such as a state or local government (¶745). Under the new rule, effective for sales after December 31, 2005, only credit card issuers who are "registered" will be entitled to a credit or refund of excise taxes on credit card sales of any taxable fuel to a state or local government or sales of gasoline to a nonprofit educational organization for its exclusive use. Registered card issuers must also show that they have not collected the tax from the purchaser or have obtained the written consent of the purchaser to allow the credit or refund and that they have agreed to pay the tax to the ultimate vendor or have obtained written consent from the vendor allowing the credit or refund. Credit card issuers who are not registered or cannot meet the other cited requirements are required to collect the necessary taxes from the ultimate purchaser of the fuel, and only an exempt purchaser is entitled to claim a credit or refund from the IRS. Penalties apply to unregistered credit card issuers who fail to collect the proper amount of tax.

¶184 Effect on Custom Gunsmiths

Low production exemption.—Although guns would not seem to be a topic for a bill that is primarily concerned with highways and transportation infrastructure, the SAFE Transportation Equity Act of 2005 (Highway Act) does make a beneficial change for some small gun manufacturers (¶850). Specifically, the Highway Act provides an exemption from the firearms excise tax for pistols, revolvers, and other firearms manufactured, produced, or imported by someone who manufactures, produces, or imports less than 50 such pieces in a calendar year. A controlled group is treated as a single person for purposes of the 50-item limit. The provision is effective for articles sold after September 30, 2005.

¶185 Effect on Oil Tanker Operators

New reconciliation requirement.—In an effort to stem the tide of fuel tax fraud, the SAFE Transportation Equity Act of 2005 (Highway Act) requires that within one year after August 10, 2005, the Secretary of Homeland Security, after consultation with the Secretary of the Treasury, is to establish an electronic data interchange system through which the U.S. Customs and Border Protection shall transmit to the IRS information pertaining to cargoes of any taxable fuel that the U.S. Customs and Border Protection has obtained electronically (¶770). In addition, within the same time frame, all filers of required cargo information for these taxable fuels will have to provide such information to the U.S. Customs and Border Protection through the electronic data interchange system.

¶186 Effect on Operators of Deep Draft Vessels

Registration requirement.—Another anti-fraud provision in the SAFE Transportation Equity Act of 2005 (Highway Act) requires the registration of deep draft vessels (i.e., ships used primarily on the high seas that have a draft height of more than 12 feet) with the Secretary of the Treasury (¶775). However, the registration requirement does not apply if the operator uses the vessel exclusively for the entry of taxable fuel nor does it apply for purposes of the bulk transfer exemption.

¶187 Effect on Recycling Industry

Study.—Although Congress considered certain tax incentives for recycling, it decided as an initial step to have the Treasury undertake a study to determine the energy savings gained by various types of recycling (¶1010).

GOVERNMENT TRUST FUNDS

¶191 Effect on Government Trust Funds

Government trust funds.—The SAFE Transportation Equity Act of 2005 (Highway Act) includes several provisions affecting the administration of government trust funds. One of the primary purposes of the Highway Act is to extend authority to make expenditures from the Highway Trust Fund and Mass Transit Account (¶905). The Treasury must now look out four years rather than two years to determine the extent that unfunded highway authorizations exceed projected net Highway Trust Fund tax receipts (¶1025). The Sport Fish Restoration Account has become the Sport Fish Restoration and Boating Trust Fund, the Aquatic Resources Trust Fund has been eliminated, and the remaining funds in the Boat Safety Account will be depleted to carry out the purposes of the Dingell-Johnson Sport Fish Restoration Act (¶1030). Finally, a new measure seeks to ensure that transfers are only made from the Leaking Underground Storage Tank (LUST) Trust Fund for purposes authorized by statute (¶1035).

STATE TAX ENERGY INCENTIVES

¶195 Energy Conservation and Production Income Tax Credits

Taxpayers taking advantage of the federal tax incentives offered by the Energy Tax Incentives Act of 2005 may be able to benefit as well from a number of state energy conservation and production income tax credits. Many of these state credits are similar to the energy incentives enacted by the Energy Act. A state-by-state description of these incentives follows. Each description notes whether the credit is a personal income tax credit and/or a corporate income tax credit.

Arkansas

- Recycling equipment corporate and personal income tax credit in the amount of 30 percent of the cost, including installation, of equipment purchased exclusively for use in the business of reducing, reusing, or recycling solid waste material for commercial purposes. (Sec. 26-51-506, A.C.A.)

Arizona

- Solar energy device personal income tax credit equal to 25 percent, up to $1,000, of solar energy device installed in the taxpayer's Arizona residence. (Sec. 43-1083, A.R.S.)
- Home builders corporate or personal income tax credit for each solar hot water plumbing stub out and each outlet for recharging an electric vehicle that is installed in a newly constructed Arizona residence. The amount of the credit is limited to a maximum of $75 for each installation for each separate house or dwelling unit. (Sec. 43-1090, A.R.S.; Sec. 43-1090(B), A.R.S.; Sec. 43-1176, A.R.S.)
- Corporate income tax credit for the cost of installing a slow-fill vehicle refueling apparatus, including storage tanks, on a taxpayer's property for personal, noncommercial use or for the cost of installing any infrastructure necessary for the operation of a vehicle refueling apparatus. The amount of the credit is the cost of purchasing a vehicle refueling apparatus or the cost of the installation of the infrastructure. (Sec. 43-1174.01, A.R.S.)
- Corporate income tax credit for building or operating fuel stations that pump alternative fuels equal to 100 percent of the costs of building or operating fuel stations for alternative fuels vehicles, up to a maximum of $400,000 for stations open to the general public and for stations pumping renewable fuels. For all other stations, the credit is limited to 50 percent of the costs, up to a maximum of $200,000. (Sec. 43-1174.02, A.R.S.)

California

- Solar or wind energy system corporate or personal income tax credit equal to the lesser of either 7.5 percent of the net cost paid or incurred by a taxpayer for the purchase and installation of a solar or wind energy system in California; or $4.50 per rated watt of generating capacity of that system. (Sec. 23684, Rev. & Tax Code)

Connecticut

- Alternative fuel corporate income tax credit for amounts expended or incurred on alternative fuel (natural gas or electricity used as motor vehicle fuel) vehicles, equipment, and related filling or recharging stations. The amount of the credit is either 10 percent or 50 percent of the expenditure, depending on the type of expenditure. (Sec. 12-217i, G.S.)

Colorado

- Alternative fuel vehicles and refueling facilities corporate and personal income tax credit for a motor vehicle that uses or is converted to use an alternative fuel, has its power source replaced with a power source that uses an alternative fuel or is a hybrid vehicle. The credit is a percentage applied against the cost amount as determined by the certification level of the vehicle under the Colorado Clean Fuel Fleet Program. (Sec. 39-22-516(2.5), C.R.S.)
- Plastic recycling personal income tax credit for investment in new plastic recycling technology in the state that is equal to 20 percent of the taxpayer's net expenditures to third parties, up to the maximum of $10,000 in net expenditures. The tax credit is applicable only to income related to expenditures for rent, wages, supplies, consumable tools, equipment, test inventory, and utilities in connection with the plastic recycling technology. The maximum tax credit is $2,000 a year. (Sec. 39-22-114.5, C.R.S.)

Georgia

- Low-emission or zero-emission vehicles corporate and personal income tax credit equal to the lesser of 10 percent of the cost of the vehicle or $2,500 for any new low-emission vehicle, and the lesser of 20 percent of the cost of the vehicle or $5,000 for any new zero emission vehicle. The credit for conversion of a conventionally fueled vehicle to a low or zero-emission vehicle equals 10 percent of the cost of conversion, subject to a cap of $2,500 for each converted vehicle. The amount of the credit for an electric vehicle charger is the lesser of 10 percent of the cost of the charger or $2,500. (Sec. 48-7-40.16, Code)
- Federal qualified transportation fringe benefit corporate and personal income tax credit for employers that provide federal qualified transportation fringe benefits to their employees. The credit is $25 per employee receiving the benefit per year. (Sec. 48-7-29.3, Code)

Hawaii

- Solar thermal energy system, or photovoltaic energy system, corporate or personal income tax credit equal to 35 percent of the actual cost or $1,750, whichever is less, for single family residential property; 35 percent of the actual cost or $350 per unit, whichever is less, for multifamily residential property; and 35 percent of the actual cost or $250,000, whichever is less, for commercial property. (Haw Rev Stat Sec. 235-12.5)
- Wind-powered energy systems corporate or personal income tax credit equal to 20 percent of the actual cost or $1,500, whichever is less, for single family residential property; 20 percent of the actual cost or $200 per unit, whichever is less, for multifamily residential property; and 20 percent of the actual cost or $250,000, whichever is less, for commercial property. (Haw Rev Stat Sec. 235-12.5)

Kansas

- Alternative-fueled motor vehicle or alternative fuel fueling station corporate income tax credit for owners and operators of a fleet of 10 or more motor vehicles. The average fuel consumption for the fleet must be at least 2,000 gallons per year. The credit is equal to 40 percent of the incremental cost or conversion cost for each vehicle, up to a maximum of $2,400 per vehicle. For each qualified alternative-fueling station, the credit is an amount equal to 40 percent of the total amount expended for each fueling station, but not to exceed $160,000 for each station. Alternatively, a taxpayer may claim a credit of 5 percent of the cost of an alternative fuel system, or $750, whichever is less. This credit is only available to the first individual to take title to the motor vehicle, other than for resale, and the taxpayer must present proof of purchase. The vehicle must be capable of operating on a blend of 85 percent ethanol and 15 percent gasoline. (Sec. 79-32,201, K.S.A.)

Kentucky

- Recycling equipment corporate and personal income tax credit for the purchase of recycling or composting equipment to be used exclusively in Kentucky for recycling or composting postconsumer waste or for any taxpayer that has a major recycling project containing recycling or composting equipment to be used exclusively in Kentucky for recycling or composting postconsumer waste. The credit is equal to 50 percent of the cost of the installed equipment. The credit for purchased equipment is limited to 10 percent of the total credit allowable and 25 percent of the tax liability for the tax year. The credit for a major recycling project is limited to the lesser of 50 percent of the excess of the total of each tax liability over the tax liability of the taxpayer for the most recent tax year ending prior to January 1, 2005; or $2,500,000. (Sec. 141.390(2)(a), KRS)

- Biodiesel fuel production and blending corporate and personal income tax credit for producers or blenders that use agricultural crops, agricultural residues, or waste products to manufacture biodiesel fuel in Kentucky. The amount of the credit is $1 per gallon of biodiesel fuel, unless the total amount of approved credits for all producers and blenders exceeds the annual credit cap of $1,500,000. (Ch. 168 (H.B. 272), Part III, Sec. 137, Laws 2005)

- Coal incentive corporate and personal income tax credit for owners or operators of a coal-fired electric generation plant. The amount of the credit is $2 for each incentive ton of coal that is subject to Kentucky coal severance tax and is purchased and used to generate electric power (Sec. 141.0405, KRS). There is a similar credit for clean coal facilities; the taxpayer may take one or the other, but not both. (Ch. 168 (H.B. 272), Part III, Sec. 142, Laws 2005)

Louisiana

- Alternative motor vehicle fuel conversion corporate and personal income tax credit in an amount equal to 20 percent of the cost of the qualified clean-burning motor vehicle fuel property. If the taxpayer does not determine the amount of the vehicle cost that is attributable to the qualified property, the credit amount is the lesser of 20 percent of 10 percent of the cost of the vehicle or $1,500. (Sec. 47:287.757, R.S.)

¶195

- Recycling equipment corporate and personal income tax credit equal to 20 percent of the cost of new recycling manufacturing or process equipment and/or qualified service contracts to be used or performed exclusively within Louisiana. (Sec. 47:6005, R.S.)

Maryland

- Green base building corporate or personal income tax credit for building owners equal to 6 percent of costs for construction of the portion of a building not intended for occupancy by an owner or tenant meeting energy efficiency and environmental standards established by the Maryland Energy Administration or for rehabilitation of a building to be a green base building. (Sec. 10-722, Tax General Art.)
- Green tenant space corporate or personal income tax credit for building owners or tenants equal to 6 percent of allowable costs for tenant improvements paid or incurred in constructing or completing tenant space that meets energy efficiency and environmental standards established by the Maryland Energy Administration or for rehabilitating tenant space to be green tenant space. (Sec. 10-722, Tax General Art.)
- Green whole building corporate or personal income tax credit for building owners or tenants equal to 8 percent of allowable costs for construction of a building in which the base building qualifies as a green base building and all tenant space qualifies as green tenant space or for rehabilitation of a building to be a green whole building. (Sec. 10-722, Tax General Art.)
- Building-integrated photovoltaic module corporate and personal income tax credit equal to (1) 20 percent of the incremental cost paid or incurred for building-integrated photovoltaic modules, and (2) 25 percent of the cost of nonbuilding-integrated photovoltaic modules, including the cost of the foundation or platform and labor costs. (Sec. 10-722, Tax General Art.)
- Fuel cell corporate or personal income tax credit for building owners and tenants equal to 30 percent of the capitalized costs associated with the installation of a fuel cell that is a qualifying alternate energy source and is installed to serve a green whole building, green base building, or green tenant space. (Sec. 10-722, Tax General Art.)
- Wind turbine corporate or personal income tax credit for building owners and tenants equal to 25 percent of the capitalized costs paid or incurred for the installation of a wind turbine that is a qualifying alternate energy source and is installed to serve a green whole building, green base building, or green tenant space, including the cost of the foundation or platform and labor costs. (Sec. 10-722, Tax General Art.)

Massachusetts

- Solar and wind energy personal income tax credit for owners and tenants of residential property located in Massachusetts who occupy the dwelling as their principal residence equal to the lesser of $1,000 or 15 percent of the net expenditure made for property that transmits or uses solar or wind energy, or another form of renewable energy, for purposes of heating or cooling the dwelling or providing hot water or electricity for use within the dwelling. (Sec. 6(d), Ch. 62, G.L.; 830 CMR 62.6.1)

Montana

- Nonfossil energy system personal income tax credit for Montana residents who complete installation of an energy system using a recognized nonfossil form of energy generation in the principal dwelling equal to the cost of the system, including installation costs, less grants received, not to exceed $500. (MCA 15-32-201)
- Recycling corporate and personal income tax credit for investments in depreciable property used primarily to collect or process reclaimable material or to manufacture a product from reclaimed material. The credit is 25 percent of the cost of the property on the first $250,000 invested, 15 percent of the cost of the property on the next $250,000 invested, and 5 percent of the cost of the property on the next $500,000 invested, not to exceed $1 million. (MCA 15-32-602; MCA 15-32-603)
- Alternative fuel corporate and personal income tax credit for the equipment and labor costs assumed in converting a motor vehicle licensed in Montana to operate on alternative fuel. The credit is allowed in an amount equal to 50 percent of the equipment and labor costs incurred, but may not exceed $500 for conversion of a motor vehicle with a gross weight of 10,000 pounds or less, or $1,000 for conversion of a motor vehicle with a gross vehicle weight over 10,000 pounds. (MCA 15-30-164)
- Low emission wood or biomass combustion device personal income tax credit for Montana resident taxpayers for installation of an energy system using a low emission wood or biomass combustion device in their principal dwelling. The tax credit is for an amount equal to the cost of the system, including installation costs, less grants received, not to exceed $500. (MCA 15-32-201)
- A personal income tax credit for energy-conserving expenditures for Montana resident taxpayers. The credit is 25 percent of the taxpayer's capital investment, not to exceed $500, in the physical attributes of a building or installation of a water, heating, or cooling system in the building so long as either type of investment is for energy conservation purposes. (MCA 15-30-125)

New Mexico

- Renewable electric energy production corporate income tax credit for taxpayers that hold title to an energy generator that generates electrical energy using only solar light or heat, wind, or biomass. The amount of the credit equals $.01 per kilowatt-hour of the first four hundred thousand megawatt-hours of electricity produced, provided that the total amount of tax credits claimed by all taxpayers for a single qualified energy generator in a taxable year does not exceed $.01 per kilowatt-hour of the first four hundred thousand megawatt-hours of electricity produced by the qualified energy generator. (Section 7-2A-19 NMSA 1978)

New York

- Solar energy personal income tax credit for New York residents who install solar electric generating equipment in their primary New York residence equal to 25 percent of equipment costs, up to $3,750. (Sec. 606(g-1), Tax Law)
- Fuel cell electric generating equipment personal income tax credit equal to 20 percent of qualified fuel cell electric generating equipment expenditures, up to $1,500. (Sec. 606(g-2), Tax Law)

¶195

- Green base building corporate and personal income tax credit for building owners equal to 1 percent of allowable costs for either the construction of a green base building or for the rehabilitation of a base building into a green base building (1.2 percent, if the building is located in an economic development area), up to $150 per square foot. (Sec. 19(a)(3), Tax Law)
- Green whole building corporate and personal income tax credit for building owners and tenants equal to 1.4 percent of allowable costs for either the construction of a green building or the rehabilitation of a building into a green building (1.6 percent, if the building is located in an economic development area), up to $150 per square foot for the base building and $75 per square foot for tenant space. (Sec. 19(a)(2), Tax Law)
- Green tenant space corporate and personal income tax credit for building owners and tenants equal to 1 percent of costs for tenant improvements by owner or tenant in constructing or completing green tenant space, or in rehabilitating space into green tenant space (1.2 percent, if the building is located in an economic development area), up to $75 per square foot. (Sec. 19(a)(4), Tax Law)
- Green building fuel cell corporate or personal income tax credit for building owners and tenants equal to 6 percent of capitalized costs of fuel cell installed to serve a green building, green base building or green tenant space, including the cost of the foundation or platform and labor costs, up to $1,000 per kilowatt. (Sec. 19(a)(5), Tax Law)
- Green building photovoltaic module corporate or personal income tax credit equal to 20 percent of the incremental costs of a green building-integrated module or 5 percent of the cost of a nonintegrated module, up to $3 per watt. (Sec. 19(a)(6), Tax Law)
- Green building refrigerant corporate or personal income tax credit equal to 2 percent of the cost of new air conditioning equipment (including chillers and absorption chillers, water or air cooled unitary equipment, water-cooled heat pumps, packaged terminal heat pumps, air conditioners, and other similar air conditioning equipment) that uses an EPA-approved, non-ozone depleting refrigerant and is installed to serve a green building, green base building or green tenant space. (Sec. 19(a)(7), Tax Law)

North Carolina

- Wind energy equipment corporate income tax credit equal to 35 percent of the cost of equipment required to capture and convert wind energy into electricity or mechanical power and related devices for converting, conditioning, and storing the electricity, up to $250,000 for each nonresidential installation or $10,000 for each residential installation. (Sec. 105-129.16A, G.S.)
- Solar energy equipment corporate income tax credit equal to 35 percent of cost of equipment that uses solar radiation as a substitute for traditional energy for water heating, active space heating and cooling, passive heating, daylighting, generating electricity, distillation, desalination, detoxification, or the production of industrial or commercial process heat, including related devices necessary for collecting, storing, exchanging, conditioning, or converting solar energy to other useful forms of energy, up to $250,000 for each nonresidential installation, or for residential installations, $1,400 per dwelling unit for equipment for domestic heating, and

¶195

$3,500 per dwelling unit for equipment for active space heating, combined active space and domestic hot water systems, and passive space heating. (Sec. 105-129.16A, G.S.)
- Recycling equipment corporate income tax credit for purchases or leases of machinery and equipment for a recycling facility in North Carolina equal to 50 percent of the amount payable by the owner of a facility defined as a "major" recycling facility during the tax year to purchase or lease the machinery and equipment. Machinery and equipment purchases for a facility defined as a "large" recycling facilities are entitled to a credit equal to 20 percent of the amount payable by the owner during the tax year. (Sec. 105-129.26, G.S.; Sec. 105-129.27, G.S.)

Oklahoma

- Energy-efficient residential construction corporate and personal income tax credit for eligible expenditures incurred by contractors who construct energy-efficient residential property of 2,000 square feet or less, effective November 1, 2005. The amount of the credit is $2,000 for an eligible energy-efficient residential property that is constructed and certified as between 20 percent and 39 percent above the International Energy Conservation Code 2003 and any supplement, and $4,000 for an eligible property certified as 40 percent or more above the International Energy Conservation Code 2003 and any supplement. The term "eligible expenditure" includes an energy-efficient heating or cooling system; insulation material or a system primarily designed to reduce heat gain or loss; exterior windows, including skylights; exterior doors; and a metal roof that is coated to reduce heat gain. (68 O.S. Sec. 2357.46)
- Clean burning motor vehicle fuel property corporate and personal income tax credit in an amount equal to 50 percent of the cost of the qualified clean-burning motor vehicle fuel property. In cases where a motor vehicle is bought by a taxpayer with qualified clean-burning motor vehicle fuel property installed by the vehicle's manufacturer and the taxpayer is unable or elects not to determine the exact basis attributable to the property, the taxpayer may claim a credit in an amount equal to the lesser of 10 percent of the cost of the motor vehicle or $1,500. (68 O.S. Sec. 2357.22)
- Ethanol production facility corporate and personal income tax credit equal to 20 cents per gallon of ethanol produced for five years beginning with the first month for which an ethanol production facility is eligible to receive the credit and ending before December 31, 2010. The credit is limited to 25 million gallons of ethanol produced annually or 125 million gallons over five years. (68 O.S. Sec. 2357.66)
- Electricity generated by Oklahoma zero-emissions facilities corporate and personal income tax credit equal to $0.0050 for each kilowatt-hour of electricity generated after 2003 but before 2007, and $0.0025 for each kilowatt-hour of electricity generated after 2006 but before 2012. (68 O.S. Sec. 2357.32A)

Oregon

- Alternative energy device personal income tax credit equal to, (1) for devices used for space heating, cooling, electrical energy, or domestic water heating, the first year energy yield in kilowatt hours per year x 60 cents per dwelling unit, up to $1,500, (2) for devices used for swimming pool, spa, or hot tub heating, the lesser of 50 percent of the cost of the device or the first year energy yield in kilowatt hours per year x 15 cents, up to $1,500, or (3) for energy-efficient appliances, 40 cents per kilowatt hour saved, or the equivalent for other fuel saved, up to $1,000. (Sec. 316.116, ORS)

- Alternative fuel station corporate income tax credit for the costs incurred in constructing or installing in a dwelling a fueling station for alternative fuel vehicles. The credit is 25 percent of the cost of the fueling station but cannot exceed $750. S corporation shareholders may use their distributive share of the credit against their personal income tax liability. (Sec. 317.115, ORS)
- Plastics recycling corporate and personal income tax credit for certified investments made to collect, transport, process or manufacture a reclaimed plastic product. The maximum credit allowed in any one tax year is the lesser of the taxpayer's tax liability or 10 percent of the certified cost of the taxpayer's investment. (Sec. 315.324, ORS)

Rhode Island

- Alternative fuel personal and corporate income tax credits are allowed for: (1) 50 percent of the capital, labor, and equipment costs incurred directly for the construction of or improvements to any filling station that provides alternative fuel or recharging of electric vehicles; and (2) 50 percent of the incremental costs incurred for the purchase of alternative fuel motor vehicles or for the cost of converting vehicles into alternative fuel vehicles. (RI Gen Laws Sec. 44-39.2-2)
- Residential renewable energy corporate and personal income tax credit for the cost of installing photovoltaic, solar hot water or space heating, wind energy, or geothermal systems in a Rhode Island residence. The amount of the credit varies depending on the type of system installed. (RI Gen Laws Sec. 44-57-5)

South Carolina

- Recycling investment corporate income tax credit for taxpayers that construct or operate a qualified recycling facility equal to 30 percent of a taxpayer's investment in recycling property during the tax year. (Sec. 12-6-3460, S.C. Code)

Utah

- Energy system corporate and personal income tax credit for the cost of an active solar, passive solar, wind, or hydroenergy system used to supply energy to any residence or business or as a commercial business, or a biomass system used to supply energy to a business or as a commercial business, equal to, for residential energy systems, 25 percent of the cost of the system, including installation costs, up to $2,000 per residential unit, and for businesses, 10 percent of the cost of the system installed, including installation costs, up to $50,000 per commercial unit. (Sec. 59-7-614(2)(a), Utah Code Ann., Sec. 59-7-614(2)(b), Utah Code Ann., and Sec. 59-10-134, Utah Code Ann.)
- Clean fuel vehicle corporate and personal income tax credit for motor vehicles that use cleaner-burning fuel such as propane, natural gas, or electricity. The credit amount is either 50 percent of the incremental cost of an OEM vehicle minus the amount of any clean fuel grant received, up to $3,000 per vehicle, or 50 percent of the cost of equipment for conversion minus the amount of any clean fuel grant received, up to $2,500 per vehicle. (Sec. 59-7-605, Utah Code Ann., Sec. 59-10-127, Utah Code Ann.)

¶195

Virginia

- Recycling machinery and equipment corporate income tax credit for 10 percent of the purchase price paid during the taxable year for recycling machinery and equipment used exclusively in or on the premises of manufacturing facilities or plant units, within Virginia, that manufacture, process, compound, or produce items of tangible personal property from recyclable materials for sale. (Sec. 58.1-439.7, Code)
- Clean fuel vehicles corporate and personal income tax credit equal to 10 percent of the deduction allowed for placing clean fuel vehicles and clean fuel vehicle refueling property in service under IRC Sec. 179A for purchases of clean fuel vehicles principally garaged in Virginia or certain refueling property placed in service in Virginia. (Sec. 58.1-438.1, Code)

West Virginia

- Alternative-fuel motor vehicles corporate and personal income tax credit for a new, retrofitted, or converted motor vehicle that operates solely on one alternative fuel, operates on one or more such fuels singly or in combination, or operates on an alternative fuel but is also capable of operating on gasoline or diesel fuel. Alternative fuels include compressed or liquefied natural gas, liquefied petroleum gas, methanol, ethanol, certain fuel mixtures containing 85 percent or more methanol, ethanol, or other alcohols, coal-derived liquid fuels and electricity (including electricity from solar energy). The maximum total credit allowed is: $3,750 for vehicles weighing not more than 10,000 pounds; $9,250 for vehicles weighing over 10,000 pounds and up to 26,000 pounds; and $50,000 for a truck or van of more than 26,000 pounds or a bus capable of seating at least 20 adults. However, taxpayers who claim the credit for an alternative-fuel vehicle that operates exclusively on electricity may claim an additional credit of 10 percent of the credit otherwise allowed, provided the total amount does not exceed the actual cost of conversion or the incremental difference in purchase price. (W.Va. Code Sec. 11-6D-1, W. Va. Code Sec. 11-6D-2, W.Va. Code Sec. 11-6D-3, W. Va. Code Sec. 11-6D-5, W. Va. Code Sec. 11-6D-6)

¶195

Residential Property and Businesses

RESIDENTIAL ENERGY INCENTIVES

¶205   Residential energy property credit
¶210   Credit for residential alternative energy expenditures

BUSINESS ENERGY INCENTIVES

¶215   Energy-efficient commercial buildings property deduction
¶220   Homebuilder's credit for new energy-efficient homes
¶225   Manufacturer's credit for energy efficient appliances
¶230   Business solar investment tax credit
¶235   Expansion of research credit
¶240   Credit for business installation of qualified fuel cells and stationary microturbine power plants

OTHER BUSINESS PROVISIONS

¶245   Recapture of Code Sec. 197 amortization

RESIDENTIAL ENERGY INCENTIVES

¶205 Residential Energy Property Credit

BACKGROUND

Residential utility company customers may exclude from income subsidies provided, directly or indirectly, by public utilities for the purchase or installation of an energy conservation measure (Code Sec. 136(a)). The exclusion is limited to subsidies received for any installation or modification designed to reduce electricity or natural gas consumption or to improve the management of energy demand with respect to a dwelling unit (Code Sec. 136(c)). There are no other federal income tax benefits available to taxpayers for energy conservation modifications made to their homes.

Since residential heating and cooling requirements represent a significant share of national energy consumption, improving the energy efficiency of dwelling unit

BACKGROUND

envelopes could have a direct impact on reducing energy demand nationwide. According to the U.S. Department of Energy, *the building envelope includes everything that separates the interior of a building from the outdoor environment, including the windows, walls, foundation, basement, slab, ceiling, roof, and insulation.* Conserving electricity and natural gas could also reduce the nation's reliance on foreign suppliers and reduce pollution.

NEW LAW EXPLAINED

Residential energy property credit.—A tax credit of up to $500 is available to individuals for nonbusiness energy property, such as residential exterior doors and windows, insulation, heat pumps, furnaces, central air conditioners and water heaters (Code Sec. 25C, as added by the Energy Tax Incentives Act of 2005). The credit is equal to (1) the *residential energy property expenditures* plus (2) 10 percent of the cost of *qualified energy efficiency improvements* installed during the year at the taxpayer's principal residence in the United States. The residential energy property credit is limited to a maximum of $500 for all tax years and no more than $200 of the credit can be based on expenditures for windows (Code Sec. 25C(b), as added by the Energy Act). The residential energy property credit applies to qualified energy efficiency improvements and qualified energy property placed in service in 2006 and 2007 (Code Sec. 25C(g), as added by the Energy Act).

Eligible improvements include:

- insulation materials;
- exterior windows, including skylights;
- exterior doors;
- metal roofs with special pigmented coatings;
- electric heat pump water heaters;
- electric and geothermal heat pumps;
- central air conditioners;
- natural gas, propane, or oil water heaters or furnaces;
- hot water boilers; and
- advanced main air circulating fans.

> **Practical Analysis:** George Jones of CCH Tax and Accounting, Washington, D.C., notes that there are some circumstances technically allowed under the new Code provisions (and not contradicted by any official Committee Report) that may not be readily apparent:
>
> - Skylights and windows installed in a new location, not only replacement skylights and windows, appear to qualify for the credit.

NEW LAW EXPLAINED

> - Set-back thermostats and ceiling fans, although they help reduce energy consumption, are not included in Code Sec. 25C(c)'s definition of qualified energy efficiency improvements.
> - Insulated garage door replacements qualify as exterior doors and, if sufficiently insulated, are a qualified energy efficiency improvement.
> - Do-it-yourself installations are permitted, but documentation becomes more critical.
> - The cost of certain maintenance items, such as outdoor caulking and replacement of weather-stripping appear to qualify as a qualified energy efficiency improvement if done according to IECC code and likely to last at least five years.

Credit limits. The residential energy property credit is a $500 lifetime credit. The credit is equal to 10 percent of the cost of qualified energy efficiency improvements (windows, doors, insulation) *plus* the cost of qualified energy property (heat pumps, water heaters, furnaces, central air units) up to the $500 lifetime maximum, subject to the following specific credit amount limits:

(1) $200 for window components,

(2) $50 for an advanced main air circulating fan

(3) $150 for any qualified natural gas, propane, or oil furnace or hot water boiler, and

(4) $300 for any item of energy-efficient building property (see chart under *Energy-efficient building property*) (Code Sec. 25C(b), as added by the Energy Act).

Qualified energy efficiency improvements. A qualified energy efficiency improvement is defined as an energy efficient building envelope component that meets the criteria set forth in the 2000 International Energy Conservation Code (IECC), as in effect on August 8, 2005, or a metal roof that meets the Energy Star Program requirements. The building envelope component must be installed on or in connection with the taxpayer's principal residence within the United States, originally placed into service by the taxpayer, and the component must be reasonably expected to remain in use for at least five years (Code Sec. 25C(c)(1), as added by the Energy Act).

Comment: It is not clear whether labor costs associated with the installation of building envelope components can be included in computing the credit. There is no statutory reference to labor costs in connection with qualified energy efficiency improvements. Labor costs are specifically included in the cost of qualified energy property, by statute. Therefore, it is probable that the credit for building envelope components must be based on the cost of the components, exclusive of any associated labor costs.

Building envelope components are specifically defined as:

(1) any insulation material or system specifically designed to reduce the heat loss or gain of a dwelling unit when installed in or on the dwelling unit;

(2) exterior windows (including skylights);

¶205

NEW LAW EXPLAINED

(3) exterior doors; and

(4) any metal roof but only if it has appropriate pigmented coatings specifically and primarily designed to reduce the heat gain of the dwelling unit (Code Sec. 25C(c)(2), as added by the Energy Act).

The 2000 IECC prescribes R-values for insulation at various locations in the building and U-factors for window and door glass, as well as the percentage of gross exterior wall area for these components depending on the type of building and the climate zone. In addition, the 2000 IECC provides specifications for heating and cooling systems, including duct systems and related insulation, temperature and humidity controls, and water heating systems. The Energy Star program requirements control in the case of metal roofs coated with heat-reduction pigment.

Comment: Not all insulation materials designed to regulate heat gain or loss are qualified energy efficiency improvements. For example, lined or insulated draperies are not insulation materials. Only the building envelope components discussed in the 2000 IECC appear to be qualified energy efficiency improvements for purposes of this credit.

Planning Note: Use of a reputable contractor for any energy-efficient home improvement is highly advisable to ensure familiarity with the 2000 IECC criteria. Taxpayers should be sure that the contract specifies that the building envelope components involved comply with the 2000 IECC criteria.

Residential energy property expenditures. Costs incurred for qualified energy property installed on or in connection with the taxpayer's principal residence within the United States, and originally placed in service by the taxpayer, are residential energy property expenditures. Labor costs associated with the onsite preparation, assembly or original installation of qualified energy property are included in residential energy property expenditures (Code Sec. 25C(d)(1), as added by the Energy Act).

Qualified energy property includes:

(1) energy-efficient building property,

(2) a qualified natural gas, propane or oil furnace or hot water boiler, or

(3) an advanced main air circulating fan.

This property must meet any performance and quality standards prescribed by IRS regulations in effect at the time the property is acquired, erected, or constructed. Measurements of the energy efficiency ratio (EER) for central air conditioners and electric heat pumps must be based on published data that is tested by manufacturers at 95 degrees Fahrenheit, and may be based on the data of the Air Conditioning and Refrigeration Institute. For purposes of the EER for geothermal heat pumps, testing must take place under the conditions of ARI/ISO Standard 13256-1 for Water Source Heat Pumps, or ARI 870 for Direct Expansion GeoExchange Heat Pumps, and include evidence that water heating was provided through a desuperheater or integrated water heating system connected to the storage water heater tank (Code Sec. 25C(d)(2), as added by the Energy Act).

Energy-efficient building property. The chart below lists the types of building property that qualify for the residential energy property credit and includes the minimum energy standards that must be satisfied (Code Sec. 25C(d)(3), as added by the Energy Act).

¶205

NEW LAW EXPLAINED

Energy-Efficient Building Property Minimum Standards

	Energy Factor	HSPF [1]	SEER [2]	EER [3]	COP [4]	CEE [5]
Electric heat pump water heater	2.0					
Electric heat pump		9	15	13		
Geothermal heat pump:						
Closed loop				14.1	3.3	
Open loop				16.2	3.6	
Direct expansion				15	3.5	
Central air conditioner						Highest efficiency tier
Natural gas, propane or oil water heater	.80					

[1] Heating seasonal performance factor
[2] Seasonal energy efficiency ratio
[3] Energy efficiency ratio
[4] Heating coefficient of performance
[5] Consortium for Energy Efficiency as in effect January 1, 2006

Qualified natural gas, propane, or oil furnace or hot water boiler. A natural gas, propane, or oil furnace or hot water boiler that achieves an annual fuel utilization efficiency rate of at least 95 qualifies for the residential energy property credit (Code Sec. 25C(d)(4), as added by the Energy Act).

Advanced main air circulating fan. A fan that is used in a natural gas, propane, or oil furnace qualifies for the credit if it has an annual electricity use of no more than two percent of the total annual energy use of the furnace (Code Sec. 25C(d)(5), as added by the Energy Act).

Eligible dwelling units. For purposes of building envelope components, the term *dwelling unit* includes a manufactured home that conforms to Federal Manufactured Home Construction and Safety Standards (Code Sec. 25C(c)(3), as added by the Energy Act). Building envelope component and qualified energy property improvements to condominiums and cooperative housing structures also qualify for the credit, as does an improvement covering two or more dwelling units. A tenant-stockholder in a cooperative housing corporation or a condominium owner who is a member of a condominium management association is treated as having paid or incurred a proportionate share of the cost of any qualified energy efficiency improvements paid or incurred by the corporation or association (Code Secs. 25C(e)(1), 25D(e)(5), and 25D(e)(6), as added by the Energy Act).

¶205

NEW LAW EXPLAINED

> **Example (1):** The Great Oaks Condominium Association governs a twelve-unit condominium structure containing four three-bedroom corner units, six two-bedroom units and two one-bedroom units constituting 14,800 square feet. The association constitution and by laws provide for computation of the monthly assessment on the basis of square foot of ownership. Myles Davis owns and occupies an 800-square-foot one-bedroom unit. The association replaces the two outside doors and the overhead garage door with qualified energy efficient models in May of 2006 at a cost of $9,000. Since Myles owns 5.4 (800 ÷ 14,800) percent of the condominium residential space, his allocated share of the expenditures is $486 ($9,000 × .054). Myles is entitled to a credit of $48.60 ($486 × .10) in 2006.

The residential energy property credit may be split between joint owners (two or more) of a dwelling unit owned and used as a principal residence, but the total of all allowable credits cannot exceed the $500 maximum limitation. The percentage of the credit claimed by each co-owner is the same as the percentage of the total energy improvement costs borne by that co-owner (Code Secs. 25C(e)(1) and 25D(e)(4), as added by the Energy Act).

> **Example (2):** The facts are the same as in Example (1). Three brothers, Dan, Mike and Pat, own and occupy a 1500-square-foot three-bedroom unit. Dan owns 50 percent of the unit, Mike owns 30 percent and Pat owns 20 percent. They share the cost of the monthly assessment based on their percentage of ownership. Together the brothers own 10.13 (1500 ÷ 14,800) percent of the condominium residential space; therefore, together their allocated costs for the doors are $912 ($9,000 × .1013). Dan's allocated cost is $456 ($912 × .50); therefore, his credit is $45.60 ($456 × .10). Mike's allocated cost is $274 ($912 × .30) and his credit is $27.40 ($274 × .10 percent). Pat's credit is $18.20 ($182 × .10) based on an allocated cost of $182 ($912 × .20).

Comment: Vacation homes and rental dwelling units do not qualify for the credit.

With respect to improvements on two or more dwelling units, the home improvement energy credit is computed separately, with separate maximum limits, on each unit (Code Sec. 25C(e)(2), as added by the Energy Act).

Credit limitations. The following limitations apply to the residential energy property credit:

(1) *Credit period.* The home improvement energy credit only applies to property placed in service in 2006 and 2007.

NEW LAW EXPLAINED

(2) *Property with mixed business and nonbusiness use.* If less than 80 percent of otherwise eligible property is for nonbusiness use, then only the percentage of the costs properly allocated to nonbusiness uses can be taken into account in calculating the credit (Code Secs. 25C(e)(1) and 25D(e)(7), as added by the Energy Act).

(3) *Property purchased with subsidized energy financing is not eligible for the credit.* Any expenditures made with funds obtained from subsidized energy financing are ineligible for the credit (Code Secs. 25C(e)(1) and 25D(d)(9), as added by the Energy Act). Subsidized energy loans are defined under Code Sec. 48(a)(4)(C) and include any financing provided under a federal, state, or local program with the principal purpose of providing subsidized financing for projects designed to conserve or produce energy.

(4) *Amount of credit.* The home improvement energy credit is a $500 lifetime credit. If a home improvement energy credit is claimed by the taxpayer in a prior tax year, the amount of the credit otherwise allowable to that taxpayer for the current tax year cannot exceed $500 reduced by the sum of the credit allowed in the prior year (Code Sec. 25C(b)(1), as added by the Energy Act). A taxpayer who moves to a new principal residence presumably cannot start over with a new $500 credit limit. The credit is based on 10 percent of the cost of building envelope components plus the total cost, including labor, of qualifying energy property up to the $500 maximum. No more than $200 of the $500 maximum credit can be applied to expenditures for window components. The credit amount is also limited to:

(a) $50 for an advanced main air circulating fan,

(b) $150 for any qualified natural gas propane, or oil furnace or hot water boiler, and

(c) $300 for any item of energy-efficient building property (see chart) (Code Sec. 25C(b)(2) and (3), as added by the Energy Act).

When expenditure is considered made. An expenditure is considered made when the original installation of the equipment is complete. Property that is installed as part of an overall construction project is treated as made when the original use of the constructed or reconstructed structure by the taxpayer begins (Code Secs. 25C(e)(1) and 25D(e)(8), as added by the Energy Act).

Planning Note: Tax year 2005 installations do not qualify for the home improvement energy credit, so taxpayers might want to postpone any planned 2005 installations until early 2006. Since this credit is only applicable for installations completed in tax years 2006 and 2007, care should be exercised to ensure that installations begun in 2007 are completed in 2007.

Practical Analysis: George Jones of CCH Tax and Accounting, Washington, D.C., observes that installations presently underway or planned for the Fall can qualify for the credit if not "placed in service" until 2006. "Placed in service" has

66 Energy and Highway Tax Acts of 2005

NEW LAW EXPLAINED

> always been a definition subject to some conflicting interpretations and, no doubt, the new residential energy property will add participants to the debate. Proposed Reg. §1.168-2(l)(2) defines "placed in service" to mean "the time that property is first placed by the taxpayer in a condition or state of readiness and availability for a specifically assigned function . . . ." This definition implies that actual use is not necessary and that property substantially ready may be considered placed in service at that time. While replacement windows are either in or out in one year, the installation of a new fuel-efficient furnace or similar equipment may provide some flexibility in shifting "placed in service" into 2006 to qualify for the credit. The voluntarily hold-back on installation in any case must be of a key component.

Tax liability limitation. The residential energy property credit is a nonrefundable personal credit (Act Sec. 1333(a) of the Energy Act). The credit may be offset against the excess of the regular tax over the alternative minimum tax liability.

Comment: The nonrefundable energy credit has no carryforward provision.

Basis. The taxpayer's basis in the property, including the cost of the qualified energy efficiency improvements, must be reduced by the amount of the home improvement energy credit (Code Secs. 25C(f) and 1016(a)(34), as added by the Energy Act).

Planning Note: When considering energy efficient home improvements, state and local energy incentives should also be explored. What may appear to be a 10-percent-off replacement window and door sale in 2006 and 2007 may actually turn out to be a 20-percent or more sale if there are state and/or county tax benefits in addition to the federal residential energy property credit. However, any expenditures made with funds obtained from subsidized energy financing are ineligible for the credit (Code Secs. 25C(e)(1) and 25D(d)(9), as added by the Energy Act).

State Tax Consequences: Many states provide energy incentives through personal and corporate income tax credits. See ¶195 for a state-by-state summary of available credits.

▶ **Effective date.** The provision applies to property placed in service after December 31, 2005 (Act Sec. 1333(c) of the Energy Tax Incentives Act of 2005). The credit terminates and is not available with respect to property placed in service after December 31, 2007 (Code Sec. 25C(g), as added by the Energy Act).

Law source: Law at ¶5015 and ¶5240. Committee Report at ¶10,210.

— Act Sec. 1333(a) of the Energy Tax Incentives Act of 2005, adding Code Sec. 25C;

— Act Sec. 1333(b), amending Code Sec. 1016(a) and adding Code Sec. 1016(a)(34);

— Act Sec. 1333(c), providing the effective date.

Reporter references: For further information, consult the following CCH reporters.

— Standard Federal Tax Reporter, 2005FED ¶29,412.042

— Federal Tax Service, FTS §A:19.20

¶205

¶210 Credit for Residential Alternative Energy Expenditures

BACKGROUND

Homeowners have not been able to claim a federal credit for residential alternative energy expenditures since 1985. Businesses that purchase solar energy or geothermal equipment are eligible for the energy investment component of the general business credit equal to 10% of the amount invested (Code Sec. 48).

From 1977 through 1985, the federal tax code allowed a residential energy credit for renewable energy source equipment or conservation expenditures (former Code Sec. 23, prior to repeal by P.L. 101-508; this was Code Sec. 44C prior to being renumbered in 1986). The renewable energy source portion of the credit was 40% of eligible expenditures up to $10,000, for a maximum credit of $4,000 (former Code Sec. 23(a)(2)).

States and regional utilities offer a variety of rebates, tax credits, and buy-down programs to encourage homeowners to install alternative energy equipment. Federal tax provisions reinforce some of these programs. Payments received from a utility buy-down program for the purchase or installation of energy conservation equipment are excludable from federal taxable income (Code Sec. 136). Tax-free reimbursements may cover the costs of installing or modifying equipment intended to reduce electricity and natural gas consumption or to improve the management of household energy demands, but any reimbursement that is excluded from income under this provision cannot be taken into account in calculating any deduction or credit under the tax code (Code Sec. 136).

The United States has many reasons for trying to reduce reliance on traditional electricity sources, and this has been true throughout the decades that have gone by without a federal residential alternative energy tax credit. Encouraging homeowner investments in alternative energy can help reduce pollution, lessen dependence on foreign oil, and prevent strain on the nation's electricity grids and natural gas pipelines. On-site generation of electricity and solar heated water can also lead to household savings.

NEW LAW EXPLAINED

Credit for solar and fuel cell equipment installed on a personal residence.—A tax credit is available to help individual taxpayers pay for residential alternative energy equipment (Code Sec. 25D, as added by the Energy Tax Incentives Act of 2005). The residential alternative energy credit is 30 percent of the cost of eligible solar water heaters, solar electricity equipment (photovoltaics) and fuel cell plants. The maximum credit is $2,000 per tax year for *each* category of solar equipment, and $500 for each half kilowatt of capacity of fuel cell plants installed per tax year. Cooperative and condominium dwellers can claim the credit by splitting the cost of installing equipment with other unit owners. Eligible equipment must be placed in service after December 31, 2005, and before 2008 (Code Sec. 25D(g), as added by the Energy Act).

NEW LAW EXPLAINED

> **Comment:** Numerous state and local programs provide significant financial incentives to homeowners wishing to install renewable energy equipment. Available incentives include state tax credits, rebates, grants, utility buy-down programs, and special financing. The total available from these programs may add up to significantly more than the federal tax credit. State sponsored programs are tracked by the Database of State Incentives for Renewable Energy (DSIRE) at www.dsireusa.org. Any subsidy that is excludable from federal taxable income cannot be taken into account in calculating the credit (Code Sec. 136(b)). Expenditures made from subsidized energy financing provided by federal, state or local incentive programs do not qualify for the federal credit (Code Sec. 25D(e)(9), as added by the Energy Act).
>
> **Comment:** A person would need to spend $6,667 on solar panels or other eligible property to qualify for a $2,000 credit ($6,667 × .30 = $2,000). A typical installation for solar panels might cost $7,000-$10,000 per kilowatt, depending on the location of the residence.
>
> **Planning Note:** Regulations that were issued under the residential energy credit that expired at the end of 1985 contained details about some issues that may again be relevant under this credit and the new credit for residential energy property (Code Sec. 25C, as added by the Energy Act; see ¶205). Those with access to the Federal Tax Archives can consult the 1986 Standard Federal Tax Reporter, ¶461 *et seq.*, for regulations and rulings issued under former Code Sec. 44C.

Tax liability limitation. The residential alternative energy credit is a nonrefundable personal credit. It can be used to offset the excess of the individual's regular tax liability over any AMT liability, but cannot be used to get a refund if the tax liability drops below zero (Code Sec. 25D(c), as added by the Energy Act).

> **Comment:** The tax liability limitation rule of Code Sec. 26(a), as effective in 2006, applies to the residential alternative energy credit. Currently Code Sec. 26(a) provides for the offset of nonrefundable credits against regular tax *and* AMT liabilities, however, this provision is scheduled to expire for tax years beginning after December 31, 2005. Therefore, when the residential alternative energy credit becomes effective in 2006, it can only be offset against the excess of the individual's regular tax liability over any AMT liability.

Carryforward of credit. Unused credits may be carried forward and added to a residential alternative energy credit for the succeeding tax year (Code Sec. 25D(c), as added by the Energy Act).

> **Comment:** Since the residential alternative energy credit is only in effect for property placed in service during tax years 2006 and 2007, the carryforward provision is limited to unused credits from 2006 that are carried forward and applied in tax year 2007.

Eligible categories of alternative energy property. The residential alternative energy credit covers expenditures for three specific categories of property:

- solar water heating property;
- photovoltaic property (to generate electricity from sunlight); and
- qualified fuel cell property (Code Sec. 25D(a), as added by the Energy Act).

NEW LAW EXPLAINED

Solar panels that are used for water heating and photovoltaic systems are eligible for the credit even if they constitute a structural component of the building on which they are installed (Code Sec. 25D(e)(2), as added by the Energy Act). The credit does not apply to expenditures that are properly allocable to a swimming pool, hot tub, or other medium that has a function other than energy storage (Code Sec. 25D(e)(3), as added by the Energy Act).

Solar water heating property. This category includes any property that uses solar energy to heat water for use in a dwelling unit (Code Sec. 25D(d)(1), as added by the Energy Act). Eligible solar water heaters must be certified for performance by the nonprofit Solar Rating and Certification Corporation (SRCC) (www.solar-rating.org) or by a comparable entity endorsed by the government of the state in which the heater is installed (Code Sec. 25D(b)(2)). A water heating system certified by SRCC will be labeled as "OG 300 Certified." The summary of water heater systems ratings posted at www.solar-rating.org lists names and addresses of participating suppliers. Home-made, uncertified solar water heaters are not eligible for the credit. The water heating system must be installed in a U.S. dwelling used as a residence by the taxpayer, and at least half of the energy used by the solar water heating system must come from the sun (Code Sec. 25D(d)(1), as added by the Energy Act).

Comment: There is no requirement that a water heater achieve a particular efficiency rating to qualify for the credit.

Photovoltaic property. Photovoltaic means "electricity from light." The most likely application in a residential setting is the use of modular solar panels as a supplemental or even exclusive source of electricity. These are known as photovoltaics, PV panels, or PVs. The tax definition of photovoltaic property expenditures eligible for the residential alternative energy credit is very broad and includes any expenditure for property that uses solar energy to generate electricity for use in a dwelling unit located in the United States and used as a residence by the taxpayer (Code Sec. 25D(d)(2), as added by the Energy Act).

Comment: Any expenditures for photovoltaics qualify for the credit (subject to the credit limits) regardless of how many kilowatt hours are generated by the system or what percentage of the consumer's electric power use is supplied by the system.

Photovoltaics are modular silicon cells laminated with plastic or glass that are mounted on the roof of a house or nearby hillside to absorb sunlight. Each module might represent from 50 to 300 watts of power, installed in an interlocking way to produce a total system of 2000-2500 watts or more. A 2.5 kW system could produce 10 kW of electricity per day, representing 300 kW or 60% of a typical 500 kW monthly electric bill. Output varies by location and with weather conditions.

Example (1): Steve installs a 2.5 kW PV system on the roof of his colonial house in Lansing, NY, at a cost of $9,000 per kW or $22,500 for his entire system before incentives. He pays cash for his system. The New York State Energy Research and Development Authority (NYSERDA) offers a buy-down of $4 per watt, or $10,000 for Steve's system. He also is entitled to a New York tax credit of $3,125 for his expenditure. For purposes of the federal residential alternative energy

¶210

NEW LAW EXPLAINED

credit, his $22,500 expenditure is reduced by the $10,000 utility buy-down, to $12,500. His 30% federal credit is $2,000 ($12,500 × .30 = $3,750, but limited to $2,000 maximum). Overall, the federal and state incentives total $15,125 and bring the net cost of his system down to $7,375. (NY income taxes on the buy-down amount might add to this cost.)

Example (2): In Example (1), above, assume that Steve finances his out-of-pocket costs for his PV system with an Energy Smart Loan (a state loan available in New York) at 4% below market rate. In this case Steve does not qualify for any credit because all of his project is financed with subsidized financing.

Example (3): Mary Ann installs a PV system identical to Steve's in Example (1) on her house in Chicago, IL. Mary Ann's 2.5 kW system has a pre-incentive cost of $22,500. Mary Ann applies for and receives an Illinois Renewable Energy Resources Program grant of 60% of her costs or $13,500. Mary Ann also qualifies for a Chicago utility program, Spire Solar Chicago, which provides her with a rebate of $1,000 per kW or $2,500. Mary Ann's unsubsidized expenditures equal $6,500, so her federal credit is $1,950 ($6,500 out of pocket cost × .30). When this credit is added to her other incentives, Mary Ann's net cost is $4,550.

Comment: The credit for residential photovoltaics does not contain any specific certification or output requirements. However, consumers should check requirements for any available state and local incentive programs before committing to a product.

Qualified fuel cell property. A fuel cell is a battery-like device that generates electricity from the chemical energy of hydrogen and oxygen. Fuel cells are electrochemical, generating electricity without the inefficiency or pollution of combustion. Fuel cell by-products are water vapor and heat (which can also be captured to heat buildings). Hydrogen used in fuel cells may come from an additional step that converts natural gas to hydrogen. Fuel cells are most widely used in alternative fuel vehicles and are famous for their use on NASA space shuttles.

Fuel cell property is eligible for the residential alternative energy credit if it is a fuel cell power plant that generates at least .5 kilowatt of electricity using an electrochemical process and has an electricity-only generation efficiency of greater than 30 percent (Code Secs. 25D(d)(3) and 48(c)(1), as added by the Energy Act). A fuel cell power plant is defined as an integrated system, comprised of a fuel stack assembly and associated balance of plant components, which converts a fuel into electricity using electrochemical means (Code Sec. 48(c)(3), as added by the Energy Act). A fuel cell

NEW LAW EXPLAINED

power plant must be installed on or in connection with the taxpayer's U.S. *principal* residence (Code Sec. 25D(d)(3), as added by the Energy Act).

Residential use of stationary fuel cell power systems is rare in the United States and systems may be difficult to locate. Manufacturers or potential manufacturers include H Power, IdaTech, Ballard, Siemens, Plug Power, and Avista Labs. Information about these manufacturers can be found at www.usfcc.com. Portable fuel cell generators are available for home use; however, these mobile generators do not appear to be eligible for the credit because they are not "installed" on or in connection with the home, and the "integrated system" requirement may require the fuel cell to be connected to an electric grid. Examples of portable fuel cell generators include AirGen, which runs for 10-12 hours on a separately purchased hydrogen canister, and the Voller Energy Portapack.

> **Example (4):** Joe Nash owns a vacation home near Boulder, Colorado which is frequently subject to power brownouts. Joe purchases a new $6,000 portable AirGen fuel cell generator, fueled by separately purchased hydrogen fuel cylinders, to serve as his emergency home office power backup. The generator does not qualify for the credit because it is not being used with regard to Joe's *principal* residence. The generator might also be disqualified for several other reasons. The generator is mobile, rather than installed, and it might not be considered an integrated system. At 1 kW output, the generator does meet the minimum output requirements for the credit, but it may not meet the greater than 30 percent electricity-only generation efficiency.

The available credit for qualified fuel cell property expenditures is 30 percent of the cost of the equipment, up to a maximum of $500 for each .5 kilowatt of capacity purchased by the homeowner per year (Code Sec. 25D(a)(3) and (b)(1)(C), as added by the Energy Act). There is no overall credit limit for this category. A typical home installation to power a 2,000 square foot home might be 7 kW, leading to a maximum credit of $7,000.

> **Comment:** An amendment to the energy credit under Code Sec. 48(a) allows a similar credit for fuel cells installed at a business property (Code Sec. 48(c), as added by the Energy Act). See ¶ 240.

Labor costs. The costs of labor to prepare the site and assemble and install the qualified property are includable in total qualified property expenses for purposes of computing the credit. Piping or wiring costs to connect qualified property to the dwelling are also includable in qualified expenditures (Code Sec. 25D(e)(1), as added by the Energy Act).

General requirements for claiming the credit. Equipment eligible for the residential alternative energy credit must be installed on or in connection with an individual taxpayer's U.S. residence (Code Sec. 25D(d), as added by the Energy Act). Other requirements are outlined below:

¶210

NEW LAW EXPLAINED

(1) *The property must be installed on or in connection with a dwelling unit located in the United States and used as a residence by the taxpayer.* The alternative energy credit is limited to residential equipment installed in the United States. For purposes of solar water heating and photovoltaic property, the language of the statute says that the site of the installation must be "used as a residence by the taxpayer," not *the* residence of the taxpayer, meaning that second and vacation home installations are eligible.

(2) *Principal residence requirement for fuel cell property.* Expenditures for fuel cell property qualify for the credit only if the property is installed on or in connection with a dwelling unit located in the United States that is used as a *principal* residence by the taxpayer. Vacation or second homes do not qualify for the credit as to fuel cell property.

(3) *Solar water heaters must be certified* for performance by the Solar Rating and Certification Corporation or a comparable organization in the state where the property is located.

(4) *Half of the energy used by solar water heating systems must come from the sun.*

Credit limitations. The following restrictions apply to the residential alternative energy credit:

(1) *Credit period.* The residential alternative energy credit applies to property placed in service only in 2006 and 2007.

(2) *The credit is not available as a subsidy for swimming pools and hot tubs.* Expenses related to hot tubs or swimming pools, such as heating water or running electrical pumps, do not qualify for the credit (Code Sec. 25D(e)(3), as added by the Energy Act).

(3) *Property purchased with subsidized energy financing is not eligible for the credit.* Any expenditures made with funds obtained from subsidized energy financing are ineligible for the credit (Code Sec. 25D(d)(9), as added by the Energy Act). Subsidized energy loans are defined under Code Sec. 48(a)(4)(C) and include any financing provided under a federal, state, or local program with the principal purpose of providing subsidized financing for projects designed to conserve or produce energy.

(4) *Property with mixed business and nonbusiness use.* If less than 80 percent of otherwise eligible property is for nonbusiness use, then only the percentage of the costs properly allocated to nonbusiness uses can be taken into account in calculating the credit (Code Sec. 25D(e)(7), as added by the Energy Act).

(5) *Tax liability limitation.* The residential alternative energy credit is a nonrefundable personal credit. It can be used to offset the excess of the individual's regular tax liability over any AMT liability, but cannot be used to get a refund if the tax liability drops below zero. Unused credits may be carried forward and added to any residential alternative energy credit for the succeeding tax year (Code Sec. 25D(c), as added by the Energy Act).

(6) *Amount of credit.* The allowable credit is 30 percent of expenditures for qualifying solar water heating property and photovoltaic property. The maximum credit

NEW LAW EXPLAINED

for each of these types of property is $2,000 per tax year. A taxpayer could claim $4,000 in credits in one year: $2,000 each for water heating and photovoltaics (not counting any credits for fuel cell property). The fuel cell component of the credit is 30 percent of any expenditures for qualified fuel cell power plants. The credit for any fuel cell may not exceed $1,000 for each kilowatt of capacity ($500 for each .5 kW) per tax year. The credit for fuel cell property is not subject to any cumulative limits (Code Sec. 25D(a), as added by the Energy Act).

Caution Note: Costs for which a nontaxable reimbursement was received under a utility buy-down program cannot be included in any credit calculation (Code Sec. 136(b)). This limit may place further restrictions on the allowable amount of the credit for many taxpayers.

When expenditure is considered made. An expenditure is considered made when the original installation of the equipment is complete. Property that is installed as part of an overall construction project is treated as made when the original use of the constructed or reconstructed structure by the taxpayer begins (Code Sec. 25D(e)(8), as added by the Energy Act).

Planning Note: Since the residential alternative energy credit applies to qualified property placed in service after December 31, 2005, completion of equipment installations that are currently scheduled should be put off until January 1, 2006, or after. Qualifying property should be placed in service before January 1, 2008.

Residence occupied by two or more taxpayers. Energy-efficient equipment may be installed on a home occupied by individuals who file separate tax returns. In this case the tax credit is split among all of the co-owners, and the total credit claimed by the combined owners may not exceed $2,000 per tax year for solar water heating property or photovoltaic property and $500 for each .5 kW of capacity for qualified fuel cell property per tax year. The percentage of the credit claimed by each co-owner is the same as the percentage of the total installation costs borne by that co-owner (Code Sec. 25D(e)(4), as added by the Energy Act).

Example (5): JoAnn and Blanche together own a duplex Victorian row house in San Francisco. Blanche is highly compensated and strongly wishes to preserve the environment, and she contributes $4,500 (after rebates) toward the installation of photovoltaic panels for their house. JoAnn contributes $1,500, or 25% of the out-of-pocket cost. Their available credit of $1,800 ($6,000 × .30) is split, with $450 (25%) going to JoAnn and $1,350 (75%) going to Blanche.

Condominiums and cooperatives splitting energy-efficient property expenditures. A shareholder in a cooperative apartment building may claim a proportionate share of any expenditures made by the corporation on property eligible for the credit. The cooperative stockholder's allocable share of the expenditures is the same as his or her proportionate share of the cooperative's total outstanding stock (including any stock held by the corporation) (Code Sec. 25D(e)(5), as added by the Energy Act). A condominium owner may similarly claim a proportionate share of any expenditures made by the management association, in proportion to the unit owner's share in the

¶210

NEW LAW EXPLAINED

association (Code Sec. 25D(e)(6), as added by the Energy Act). Under regulations applicable to former Code Sec. 44C, which is quite similar to the new credit rules, in the case of a special assessment to cover purchases of energy conservation property the unit owner's allocation would be based on the assessment amount (former Reg. § 1.44C-3(i)).

Basis reductions. The taxpayer's basis in the dwelling is reduced by the amount of any credit claimed (Code Secs. 1016(a)(35) and 25D(f), as added by the Energy Act).

> **Comment:** Conforming amendments to the carryforward provisions of the adoption credit (Code Sec. 23(c)), the credit for interest paid on mortgage credit certificates (Code Sec. 25(e)(1)(C)), and the first-time homebuyer's credit (Code Sec. 1400C(d)) were apparently inadvertently made to the respective Code provisions in effect through 2005. However, the residential alternative energy credit is only effective for property placed in service in 2006 and 2007.
>
> **State Tax Consequences:** Many states provide energy incentives through personal and corporate income tax credits. See ¶195 for a state-by-state summary of available credits.

▶ **Effective date.** The provision applies to property placed in service after December 31, 2005, in tax year ending after that date(Act Sec. 1335(c) of the Energy Tax Incentives Act of 2005). The credit terminates and is not available for property placed in service after December 31, 2007 (Code Sec. 25D(g), as added by the Energy Act).

Law source: Law at ¶5005, ¶5010, ¶5020, ¶5240 and ¶5260. Committee Report at ¶10,230.

— Act Sec. 1335(a) of the Energy Tax Incentives Act of 2005, adding Code Sec. 25D;
— Act Sec. 1335(b), amending Code Sec. 23(c), Code Sec. 25(e)(1)(C), Code Sec. 1400C(d) and adding Code Sec. 1016(a)(35);
— Act Sec. 1335(c), providing the effective date.

Reporter references: For further information, consult the following CCH reporters.
— Standard Federal Tax Reporter, 2005FED ¶29,412.042
— Federal Tax Service, FTS § A:19.20

BUSINESS ENERGY INCENTIVES

¶215 Energy-Efficient Commercial Buildings Property Deduction

BACKGROUND

A large percentage of domestic energy consumption can be attributed to commercial buildings. Such buildings are estimated to use approximately one-fourth of all the electrical energy consumed in the United States. Currently, no significant federal tax incentive exists to encourage the use of energy-efficient property in the construction of these commercial structures.

BACKGROUND

According to commentators, approximately 9 out of 10 commercial buildings were built over 15 years ago, and only a small percentage of those buildings have been updated to meet current energy usage standards. No significant federal tax incentive exists to encourage energy-efficient renovation of older commercial structures.

NEW LAW EXPLAINED

Deduction for energy-efficient commercial building property.—Taxpayers may claim a deduction for costs associated with energy-efficient commercial building property placed in service after December 31, 2005, and before January 1, 2008 (Code Sec. 179D(a), as added by the Energy Tax Incentives Act of 2005). The maximum amount that can be deducted is $1.80 per square foot of the building in question, less the total amount of deductions taken under this provision, with respect to the building, in any prior tax years. The basis of any property generating a deduction must be reduced by the amount deducted (Code Sec. 179D(b) and (e), as added by the Energy Act).

> **Comment:** According to the Joint Committee on Taxation, Description and Technical Explanation of the Energy Tax Incentives Act of 2005 (JCX-60-05), if an individual credit for residential energy property under new Code Sec. 25C, as added by the Energy Act (¶205), or residential alternative energy property under new Code Sec. 25D, as added by the Energy Act (¶210), is allowed, with respect to property for which a deduction under this provision may be claimed, it is to be assumed that, in determining the annual energy and power costs of the building, the building contains the property for which the credit has been allowed, and any such costs cannot be taken into account for purposes of this provision.

> **Comment:** Although this deduction has value to owners of commercial lease property (see Comment below under *Partial allowance of deduction*), it is believed to be primarily targeted toward real estate businesses.

Public property. The IRS is required to issue regulations that allow a transfer of the deduction for energy-efficient commercial building property with respect to public property (Code Sec. 179D(d)(4), as added by the Energy Act). The regulations are to permit an allocation of any deduction associated with energy-efficient property installed in public buildings to the "person primarily responsible for designing the property." The deduction, therefore, will go to the party responsible for creating the energy-efficient environment, rather than to the public entity owner who is not a taxpayer. By expanding the incentive to include designers as well as owners, the intent is to encourage energy-efficient design and innovation in municipal buildings, such as public schools.

Energy-efficient commercial building property. In order to qualify costs as pertaining to "energy-efficient commercial building property," several criteria must be met. First, the costs must be associated with depreciable (or amortizable in lieu of depreciable) property that is installed in a domestic building that is within the scope of Standard 90.1-2001 (see *Comment* below for a discussion of this Standard). Second, the property in question must be installed as part of:

¶215

NEW LAW EXPLAINED

(1) the interior lighting system,

(2) the heating, cooling, ventilation and hot water systems, or

(3) the building envelope (Code Sec. 179D(c)(1)(C), as added by the Energy Act).

> **Comment:** Code Sec. 179D does not define "building envelope" for the purposes of qualifying property as energy-efficient commercial building property eligible for the deduction. The term is defined, however, in new Code Sec. 25C(c)(2) as part of the definitions relating to the credit for residential energy-efficient property (Code Sec. 25C(c)(2), as added by the Energy Act; see ¶205). While Code Sec. 25C applies to residential and not commercial buildings, it would seem likely that a similar definition would apply for purposes of Code Sec. 179D. The U.S. Department of Energy defines a building envelope to include "everything that separates the interior of a building from the outdoor environment, including the windows, walls, foundation, basement slab, ceiling, roof system and insulation."

Third, the property must be installed pursuant to a plan intended to reduce the total annual energy and power costs of the building (with respect to interior lighting, heating, cooling, ventilation and hot water supply systems) by 50 percent or more in comparison to a reference building that meets the minimum requirements of Standard 90.1-2001. Such a plan must be certified by the IRS (see *Certification*, below) (Code Sec. 179D(c)(1)(D), as added by the Energy Act). The IRS is directed to consult with the Secretary of Energy and issue regulations describing detailed methods of calculating and verifying energy and power costs for this purpose using qualified computer software based on the provisions of the 2005 California Nonresidential Alternative Calculation Method Approval Manual (Code Sec. 179D(d)(2) and (3), as added by the Energy Act; see *Regulations*, below).

> **Caution Note:** While attempting to summarily describe the legislation, some commentators have stated that the deduction is available when property is installed pursuant to a plan to reduce total energy costs of a building by 50 percent. This is somewhat misleading. The actual legislative text states that costs must be reduced "by 50 percent or more *in comparison to a reference building which meets the minimum requirements of Standard 90.1-2001*" (emphasis added). While it is not clear from the Internal Revenue Code or Committee Reports exactly what this comparison entails, industry commentators are inferring that the energy consumption of the building in question must equal 50 percent or less of the amount of energy used by a comparable building that meets the requirements of Standard 90.1-2001. This seems like a logical conclusion considering the fact that newly constructed buildings have no historic consumption level to reduce.

> **Comment:** It is also worthwhile to note that the 50-percent reduction refers to a reduction in energy and power *cost* to the taxpayer, rather than a reduction in actual units of energy consumed. As a result, a reduction in peak electricity usage will be more beneficial for a taxpayer trying to meet the 50-percent reduction goal than a reduction of energy used in non-peak hours, because energy used at peak times is significantly more expensive.

¶215

NEW LAW EXPLAINED

Caution Note: In order to qualify for the full deduction, the overall cost reduction plan must target all the systems specifically identified in Code Sec. 179D(c)(1)(D), namely the interior lighting, heating, cooling, ventilation *and* hot water supply systems. The targeted reduction applies to the overall energy savings, not the savings of any particular system.

Comment: Standard 90.1-2001 is a publication of the American Society of Heating, Refrigerating, and Air Conditioning Engineers (ASHRAE) and the Illuminating Engineering Society of North America (IESNA) (Code Sec. 179D(c)(2), as added by the Energy Act). The Standard provides minimum requirements for the design of energy efficient buildings other than low-rise residential buildings. It has general industry acceptance and has been incorporated in the International Energy Conservation Code (IECC) for 2003. Its language is often adopted into new building codes, and it also addresses modifications to existing buildings. A copy of the Standard and of the Tables referenced in Code Sec. 179D(f) can be accessed at www.ashrae.com.

Comment: The 2005 California Nonresidential Alternative Calculation Method Approval Manual is published by the California Energy Commission. It contains requirements for designing a calculation computer program for use with California energy standards. A copy of the Manual can be accessed at http://www.energy.ca.gov/title24/2005standards/nonresidential_acm/index.html.

According to the Joint Committee on Taxation, Description and Technical Explanation of the Energy Tax Incentives Act of 2005 (JCX-60-05), the methods for calculating energy and power costs must be fuel-neutral. In other words, the energy-efficiency measures must not discriminate between fuel sources. A building will be eligible for the deduction, therefore, regardless of whether it uses a gas or oil furnace or boiler, an electric heat pump or another fuel source. It is also the intention of the Joint Committee that the calculation methods provide suitable calculated energy savings for design methods and technologies not otherwise credited in either Standard 90.1-2001 or in the 2005 California Nonresidential Alternative Calculation Method Approval Manual, including:

(1) natural ventilation;

(2) evaporative cooling;

(3) automatic lighting controls, such as occupancy sensors, photocells and time clocks;

(4) daylighting;

(5) designs utilizing semi-conditioned spaces that maintain adequate comfort conditions without air conditioning or heating;

(6) improved fan system efficiency, including reductions in static pressure;

(7) advanced unloading mechanisms for mechanical cooling, such as multiple or variable speed compressors;

(8) on-site generation of electricity, including combined heat and power systems, fuel cells and renewable energy generation, such as solar energy; and

¶215

NEW LAW EXPLAINED

(9) wiring with lower energy losses than wiring that satisfies Standard 90.1-2001 requirements for building power distribution systems.

Certification. The definition of energy-efficient commercial building property requires that the taxpayer obtain certification of a plan to reduce the overall energy and power costs in connection with the installation of the property (Code Sec. 179D(c)(1)(D), as added by the Energy Act). While the IRS is charged with designing and governing this certification process, Congress has mandated a few procedural guidelines. First, certification must include inspection and testing by individuals recognized by an IRS-approved organization. These inspections and tests must be designed to ensure compliance with the energy saving plans and targets. Second, the procedures used in such testing must be comparable to the requirements in the Mortgage Industry National Accreditation Procedures for Home Energy Rating Systems (taking into account the differences between commercial and residential buildings) (Code Sec. 179D(d)(6), as added by the Energy Act).

Partial allowance of deduction. A reduced deduction may be available with respect to a building even if the relevant energy-efficient property is not installed as part of a certified plan to reduce overall energy and power costs (Code Sec. 179D(d)(1), as added by the Energy Act). The IRS is directed to issue regulations containing specific energy efficiency targets, and methods of calculating such targets, for each of the separate systems listed in Code Sec. 179D(c)(1)(C), namely, interior lighting, heating, cooling, ventilation and hot water (Code Sec. 179D(d)(1)(B), as added by the Energy Act). A taxpayer who replaces any of these systems in an existing building and meets the designated target will be eligible for a partial deduction (Code Sec. 179D(d)(1)(A), as added by the Energy Act). Interim targets for lighting systems have already been issued and are incorporated as part of Code Sec. 179D (see *Interim rules for lighting systems,* below).

The partial deduction is available for the costs of the energy-efficient system installed up to $0.60 per square foot of the building. These system-specific improvements are also subject to the IRS-designed certification process discussed above (Code Sec. 179D(d)(1)(A), as added by the Energy Act). Each certification will include an explanation to the building owner regarding the energy-efficiency features of the building and the projected annual energy costs (Code Sec. 179D(d)(5), as added by the Energy Act).

> **Comment:** This partial deduction will be especially relevant to owners of commercial lease properties. Historically, such owners have avoided improving outdated systems because of the significant capital investment required and because their utility costs are simply passed on to tenants. It is hoped that the availability of this partial deduction will cause them to reconsider investing in energy-efficient systems.

Interim rules for lighting systems. As mentioned above, the IRS is directed to issue regulations setting forth energy-efficiency targets for each of the specific systems described in Code Sec. 179D(c)(1)(C). Prior to the release of these regulations, interim guidelines for lighting systems are provided by Code Sec. 179D(f).

To qualify for the $0.60-per-square-foot deduction for system-specific energy-efficient property (see *Partial allowance of deduction* above), a lighting system must reduce

¶215

NEW LAW EXPLAINED

lighting power density (LPD) by 40 percent of the minimum requirements contained in Table 9.3.1.1 or Table 9.3.1.2 of Standard 90.1-2001 (not including additional interior lighting power allowances). If the reduction in LPD is 25 percent of the minimum requirements, a $0.25-per-square-foot deduction is allowed. If the reduction is below 25 percent of the minimum requirements (50 percent in the case of warehouses), the target has not been met and no deduction is allowed (Code Sec. 179D(f), as added by the Energy Act).

If the reduction of LPD is between 25 percent and 40 percent of the minimum requirements, only a certain percentage of the deduction will be allowed (Code Sec. 179D(f)(2)(A), as added by the Energy Act). The deduction will be reduced by a percentage equal to the sum of 50 and the amount that bears the same ratio to 50 as the excess of the reduction over 25 percentage points bears to 15 (Code Sec. 179D(f)(2)(B), as added by the Energy Act).

> **Example (1):** Assume Jones Corporation operates a 4,000-square-foot family restaurant. In an effort to save energy, Jones installs a new lighting system that reduces its LPD by 3,200 watts. Assume also that the minimum requirement contained in Table 9.3.1.1 for family restaurants is 1.6 watts/square foot or 6,400 watts for the Jones restaurant (4,000 × 1.6). Because Jones has reduced its lighting power usage by 3,200 watts, which is 50% of the minimum requirement (3,200 / 6,400), it is eligible for the entire amount of the partial deduction of $0.50 per square foot, or $2,000.

> **Example (2):** If, however, Jones Corporation reduces its LPD by only 30% of the minimum requirements, or 1,920 watts (6,400 watts × 30%), the amount of the deduction will be prorated. Jones Corporation will only be able to deduct $1,334, or 66.67% of the otherwise allowable deduction ($2,000 × 66.67%). This percentage is equal to 50 plus 16.67. The 16.67 percentage points is the amount which bears the same ratio to 50 as 5 (30% minus 25%) bears to 15. In other words, 16.67/50 is equal to 5/15. Therefore, 16.67 is added to 50 to find the applicable percentage of the otherwise allowable deduction.

This interim guidance does not apply, however, to certain lighting systems. Systems whose controls and circuitry do not fully comply with Standard 90.1-2001 are not covered by these rules, nor do the rules apply to systems that do not include bi-level switching in all occupancies (except hotel and motel guest rooms, store rooms, restrooms and public lobbies). Lastly, systems failing to meet the minimum requirements for calculated lighting levels contained in the Illuminating Engineering Society of North America (IESNA) Lighting Handbook, Performance and Application, Ninth Edition, 2000, are not governed by this interim guidance (Code Sec. 179D(f)(2)(C), as added by the Energy Act).

> **Comment:** It is interesting to note that interim guidelines were provided for lighting systems, but not for heating, cooling, ventilation or hot water systems. A

¶215

NEW LAW EXPLAINED

possible explanation for this is that Congress understood that lighting costs account for almost 50 percent of older commercial building energy usage and that lighting is relatively easy to upgrade. Simple solutions, such as dimming and room occupancy sensors, can reduce energy usage drastically. Also, an appropriate and fair gauge of lighting efficiency was readily available. Another factor might have been the lobbying tenacity of the National Electrical Manufacturers Association, which strongly supported and proposed language for the interim guidelines.

Regulations. As mentioned above, the IRS is charged with issuing regulations that will govern the certification process. These regulations must include the proper methods of calculating and verifying various energy and power costs using qualified computer software, based on the provisions of the 2005 California Nonresidential Alternative Calculation Method Approval Manual (Code Sec. 179D(d)(2) and (3), as added by the Energy Act). In addition, Code Sec. 179D(g) directs the IRS to issue any regulations necessary to account for new technologies regarding energy efficiency and renewable energy for the purpose of determining energy efficiency and savings. The IRS must also issue regulations that will mandate a recapture of the deduction if any certified energy savings plan is not fully implemented (Code Sec. 179D(g), as added by the Energy Act).

Comment: The deduction for energy-efficient commercial building property garnered Congressional and public support largely because it was performance, rather than cost, based. In other words, the availability of the deduction is dependent on quantitative reductions in energy usage, rather than on the amount of money paid for energy-efficient products. Tying the deduction to strongly enforced performance goals was seen as a method of fostering competition between, and innovation by, suppliers of different technologies. Price or cost-based incentives, on the other hand, are generally viewed more skeptically as artificially inflating prices and inviting corruptive practices.

Performance-based incentives, however, are harder to administer. This puts an onus on the IRS to promulgate regulations that incorporate strong, efficient and enforceable measures of energy efficiency. This is no small task.

Comment: The fact that this deduction is not effective retroactively creates somewhat of an inequity for taxpayers who sought to achieve energy efficiency prior to the passage of the Energy Act. The full deduction is available only for property placed in service after December 31, 2005, that is installed pursuant to a certified plan of overall cost reduction targeting multiple systems. A taxpayer who builds new construction using energy-efficient systems or installs the systems during a total renovation of an existing structure after December 31, 2005, therefore, will be entitled to a full deduction. In addition, a taxpayer who improves an existing building by installing energy-efficient systems on a piecemeal basis after August 8, 2005, may be eligible for a partial deduction. However, taxpayers who built completely energy-efficient buildings or updated existing systems prior to January 1, 2006, receive no deduction. Although such taxpayers will have benefitted from other tax incentives such as bonus depreciation, they were unable to claim an immediate deduction for such costs.

¶215

NEW LAW EXPLAINED

State Tax Consequences: Many states provide energy incentives through personal and corporate income tax credits. See ¶195 for a state-by-state summary of available credits.

▶ **Effective date.** The provision applies to property placed in service after December 31, 2005 (Act Sec. 1331(d) of the Energy Tax Incentives Act of 2005). Code Sec. 179D, however, contains a termination clause rendering the deduction unavailable with respect to property placed in service after December 31, 2007 (Code Sec. 179D(h), as added by the Energy Act).

Law source: Law at ¶5195, ¶5205, ¶5210, ¶5240, ¶5245 and ¶5250. Committee Report at ¶10,190.

— Act Sec. 1331(a) of the Energy Tax Incentives Act of 2005, adding Code Sec. 179D;
— Act Sec. 1331(b), adding Code Sec. 1016(a)(32), amending Code Sec. 1245(a) and Code Sec. 1250(b)(3), adding Code Sec. 263(a)(1)(K) and amending Code Sec. 312(k)(3)(B), as amended by Energy Act Sec. 1323(b)(3);
— Act Sec. 1331(d), providing the effective date.

Reporter references: For further information, consult the following CCH reporters.

— Standard Federal Tax Reporter, 2005FED ¶29,412.023 and ¶30,909.025
— Federal Tax Service, FTS § G:24.20

¶220 Homebuilder's Credit for New Energy-Efficient Homes

BACKGROUND

The general business tax credit (Code Sec. 38) is a combination of several separate credits for specific types of business activities. Unused general business credits can generally be carried back one year, and carried forward for 20 years. The general business credit includes a rehabilitation credit for expenses incurred in renovating old buildings (Code Sec. 47), and a business energy credit for certain solar or geothermal energy property (Code Sec. 48).

The residential sector accounts for 20 percent of the energy consumed in the United States. Energy used in the average American home costs over $1,400 per year, produces about 11 tons of carbon dioxide, and accounts for about 20 percent of all American greenhouse gas emissions. In fact, the average American home produces twice as much greenhouse gas pollution as the average car. The government estimates that roughly 44 percent of home energy use is devoted to space heating and cooling, 33 percent is used for lights and appliances, 14 percent is used for water heating, and 9 percent is used for refrigeration.

Substantial energy savings could be achieved if energy-efficient features were incorporated into the approximately 1.5 million new homes that are built each year. The Alliance to Save Energy estimates that if all states adopted modern building energy codes, the average homeowner would save 12 percent in energy bills. The Alliance

BACKGROUND

further estimates that less than two percent of American homes are built to a high level of energy efficiency that could be achieved with existing, readily available technology.

Energy efficiency is determined based on the *building envelope*, which is everything about the house that serves to shield the living space from the outdoors. It includes the wall and roof assemblies, insulation, air/vapor retarders, windows, and weather-stripping and caulking. The current standard for energy-efficient construction is the International Energy Conservation Code (IECC), which is a climate-adjusted model code developed by the private sector to employ existing off-the-shelf technology to produce a reasonably energy-efficient home. The IECC provides standards for sealing joints, penetrations and other openings in the envelope to prevent air leakage; air/vapor retarders that inhibit the flow of air and water vapor into and out of a home; insulation and other materials; ducts and piping; temperature controls; swimming pools; and water heaters.

One of the principal federal programs to improve home energy efficiency is the Energy Star program, a public-private partnership operated by the Environmental Protection Agency. More than 7,000 organizations have joined this voluntary labeling program designed to identify and promote energy-efficient products and deliver technical information and tools that consumers can use to choose energy-efficient solutions and best management practices. Any single-family or multi-family residence that is three stories or less in height can qualify as an Energy Star home. An Energy Star home must be independently verified to be at least 30 percent more energy-efficient than homes built to the 1993 national Model Energy Code, or 15 percent more efficient than the applicable state energy code, whichever is more rigorous. Energy Star homes can qualify for special mortgages that allow the home buyer to qualify for a larger loan, reduce closing costs, and offset the cost of energy-efficient features.

NEW LAW EXPLAINED

Homebuilder's credit for new energy-efficient homes.—An eligible contractor may claim a tax credit of $1,000 or $2,000 for a qualified new energy-efficient home that a person acquires from the contractor during 2006 and 2007 for use as a residence during the tax year (Code Sec. 45L(a) and Code Sec. 45L(g), as added by the Energy Tax Incentives Act of 2005).

> **Comment:** Some experts believe that consumer-oriented credits are ineffective tools to improve home energy efficiency, and that a credit targeted at builders will increase the stock of energy-efficient housing and make energy-efficient homes more affordable.

Eligible contractor. An eligible contractor is a person who constructs a new energy-efficient home, or a manufacturer that produces a qualified new energy-efficient manufactured home (Code Sec. 45L(b)(1), as added by the Energy Act). To be a *qualified new energy-efficient home*:

¶220

NEW LAW EXPLAINED

- the home must be located in the United States,
- its construction must be substantially completed after the date that the statute creating this credit is enacted, and
- it must meet the energy saving requirements discussed below.

The term "construction" includes substantial reconstruction and rehabilitation, and the term "acquire" includes purchases (Code Sec. 45L(b)(3) and (b)(4), as added by the Energy Act).

> **Comment:** The Conference Committee apparently intended to make the credit applicable to homes that are substantially completed after 2005, but the statutory language provides that the home must be substantially completed after the date the statute is enacted (Joint Committee on Taxation, Description and Technical Explanation of the Energy Tax Incentives Act of 2005 (JCX-60-05)).

A *$2,000 credit* is available if the home meets the following energy-savings requirements:

(1) the home must be certified to have a level of annual heating and cooling energy consumption at least 50 percent below the annual heating and cooling energy consumption of a comparable dwelling unit, *and*

(2) the home must be certified to have building envelope component improvements that account for at least one-fifth of that 50 percent improvement in heating and cooling energy consumption (Code Sec. 45L(a)(2)(A) and (c)(1), as added by the Energy Act).

A *manufactured home* can also qualify for the $2,000 credit if it meets these same tests and conforms to the Federal Manufactured Home Construction and Safety Standards set forth at Title 24 CFR § 3280 (Code Sec. 45L(c)(2), as added by the Energy Act). A manufactured home that does not meet these tests can nevertheless qualify for a *$1,000 credit* if it conforms to the Federal Manufactured Home Construction and Safety Standards, and:

- it is certified to have a level of annual heating and cooling energy consumption at least 30 percent below the annual heating and cooling energy consumption of a comparable dwelling unit, and to have building envelope component improvements that account for at least one-third of that 30-percent improvement; *or*
- it meets the requirements established by the Environmental Protection Agency under the Energy Star Labeled Homes Program (Code Sec. 45L(a)(2)(B) and (c)(3), as added by the Energy Act).

A *comparable dwelling unit* is one that is constructed in accordance with the standards of chapter 4 of the 2003 International Energy Conservation Code (including supplements) in effect on the date the credit is enacted, with heating and cooling equipment efficiencies that correspond to the minimum allowed under regulations established by the Department of Energy under the National Appliance Energy Conservation Act of 1987 in effect at the time construction was completed (Code Sec. 45L(c)(1)(A), as added by the Energy Act).

Certification. The certification of a qualified new energy-efficient home must be made in accordance with guidance that will be provided by the Treasury Department after

¶220

NEW LAW EXPLAINED

consultation with the Energy Department. The guidance will specify procedures and methods for calculating energy and cost savings. The certification must be in writing, and must specify in a readily verifiable fashion the energy-efficient building envelope components and heating or cooling equipment installed in the home, and their respective rated energy efficiency performance (Code Sec. 45L(d), as added by the Energy Act).

The homebuilder's credit is a part of the general business credit (Code Sec. 38(b)(23), as added by the Energy Act). Expenditures taken into account under the rehabilitation (Code Sec. 47) and energy (Code Sec. 48) components of the investment tax credit are not taken into account under this new credit (Code Sec. 45L(f), as added by the Energy Act). If the credit is allowed in connection with an expenditure that would normally increase basis in the property, any such basis increase must be reduced by the amount of the credit (Code Secs. 45L(e) and 1016(a)(33), as added by the Energy Act). Like most other components of the business credit, unused portions of the homebuilder's credit can be carried over to other tax years (Code Sec. 196(c)(13), as added by the Energy Act).

> **State Tax Consequences:** Many states provide energy incentives through personal and corporate income tax credits. See ¶195 for a state-by-state summary of available credits.

▶ **Effective date.** The provision applies to qualified new energy-efficient homes acquired after December 31, 2005, in tax years ending after that date (Act Sec. 1332(f) of the Energy Tax Incentives Act of 2005). The provision does not apply to any qualified new energy-efficient home acquired after December 31, 2007 (Code Sec. 45L(g), as added by the Energy Act).

Law source: Law at ¶5040, ¶5085, ¶5200 and ¶5240. Committee Report at ¶10,200.

— Act Sec. 1332(a) of the Energy Tax Incentives Act of 2005, adding Code Sec. 45L;
— Act Sec. 1332(b), amending Code Sec. 38(b) and adding Code Sec. 38(b)(23);
— Act Sec. 1332(c), amending Code Sec. 1016(a) and adding Code Sec. 1016(a)(33);
— Act Sec. 1332(d), amending Code Sec. 196(c) and adding Code Sec. 196(c)(13);
— Act Sec. 1332(f), providing the effective date.

Reporter references: For further information, consult the following CCH reporters.

— Standard Federal Tax Reporter, 2005FED ¶4251.021 and ¶29,412.023
— Federal Tax Service, FTS § G:24.20

¶225 Manufacturer's Credit for Energy Efficient Appliances

BACKGROUND

The general business credit (under Code Sec. 38) is a limited nonrefundable credit against income tax that is claimed after all other nonrefundable credits (except the Code Sec. 53 credit for prior year alternative minimum tax). The general business credit for a tax year is the sum of: (1) the business credit carryforwards to such year;

BACKGROUND

(2) the amount of the current year business credits; and (3) the business credit carrybacks for such year (Code Sec. 38(a)).

The current year business credit consists of the investment tax credit, the credit for alcohol used as a fuel, the biodiesel fuel credit, the research credit, the low-income housing credit, the enhanced oil recovery credit, the disabled access credit, the renewable electricity production credit, the Indian employment credit, the employer Social Security credit, the orphan drug credit, the new markets credit, the new retirement plan setup credit, the railroad track maintenance credit, the low sulfur diesel fuel production credit, the marginal well production credit, and the employer-provided child care credit. This list of specific credits frequently changes from year to year as individual credits are added or expire.

For credits arising in tax years beginning after 1997, any unused general business credit generally may be carried back one year and carried forward 20 years (Code Sec. 39).

NEW LAW EXPLAINED

New credit for manufacturing energy efficient appliances.—The Energy Tax Incentives Act of 2005 adds a new credit for the manufacture of energy-efficient appliances, including only dishwashers, clothes washers and refrigerators. The credit is a part of the general business credit and will be used to determine a taxpayer's current year business credit (Code Sec. 38(b)(24), as added by the Energy Act).

The total amount of credit available for a tax year is equal to the sum of the credit amount separately calculated for each type of qualified energy-efficient appliance produced by the taxpayer during the calendar year ending with or within that tax year. The credit amount for each type of qualified appliance is determined by multiplying the eligible production for that type of appliance by the type's applicable amount (Code Sec. 45M(a)(2), as added by the Energy Act). There are three types of qualified energy efficient appliances for purposes of this new credit.

Dishwashers. In order for a manufactured dishwasher to meet the required standard for application of this credit, the dishwasher must be manufactured during calendar year 2006 or 2007 and meet the requirements of the Energy Star program as in effect for dishwashers in 2007 (Code Sec. 45M(b)(1)(A), as added by the Energy Act). The applicable amount for qualified dishwashers is the energy savings amount, which is equal to the lesser of $100 or the product of $3 and 100 multiplied by the energy savings percentage. The energy savings percentage is the ratio of: (1) the energy factor (EF) established by the Department of Energy for compliance with the Federal energy conservation standards (the Energy Star program) for dishwashers in 2007, minus the EF required by the Energy Star program for dishwashers in 2005; to (2) the EF required by the Energy Star program for dishwashers in 2007 (Code Sec. 45M(b)(2), as added by the Energy Act).

> **Comment:** For this purpose, a "dishwasher" means a residential dishwasher that is subject to the Department of Energy conservation standards (Code Sec. 45(f)(2), as added by the Energy Act).

¶225

NEW LAW EXPLAINED

Clothes washer. In order for a manufactured clothes washer to meet the required standard for application of the new energy efficient appliance credit, the clothes washer must be manufactured during calendar year 2006 or 2007 and meet the requirements of the Energy Star program as in effect for clothes washers in 2007 (Code Sec. 45M(b)(1)(B), as added by the Energy Act). The clothes washer must be a residential clothes washer, and this includes residential style coin operated washers (Code Sec. 45M(f)(3), as added by the Energy Act). The applicable amount for qualified clothes washers in determining the credit is $100 (Code Sec. 45M(b)(1)(B), as added by the Energy Act).

Refrigerator. In order for a manufactured refrigerator to meet the required standard for application of the energy efficient appliance credit, the refrigerator must have an interior volume of at least 16.5 cubic feet and be equipped with automatic defrost for the refrigerator and freezer compartments (Code Sec. 45M(f)(4), as added by the Energy Act). For purposes of calculating the energy efficient appliance credit, refrigerators may fall into one of three types, each with a different applicable amount.

If a refrigerator is manufactured during calendar year 2006 and consumes at least 15 percent—but not more than 20 percent—less kilowatt hours per year than the conservation standards for refrigerators promulgated by the Department of Energy that took effect on July 1, 2001, then the applicable amount for purposes of calculating the credit is $75 (Code Sec. 45M(b)(1)(C), as added by the Energy Act). If a refrigerator is manufactured during calendar years 2006 or 2007 and consumes at least 20 percent—but not more than 25 percent—less kilowatt hours per year than the 2001 energy conservation standards, then the applicable amount is $125. If a refrigerator is manufactured during calendar year 2006 or 2007 and consumes at least 25 percent less kilowatt hours per year than the 2001 energy conservation standards, then the applicable amount is $175.

Eligible production. The eligible production amount for a particular type of energy efficient appliance is determined by subtracting the average number of qualified appliances described above that the taxpayer produced during the preceding three-calendar-year period from the number of appliances of the same type that the taxpayer produced during the applicable calendar year. For this purpose, only qualified appliances produced in the United States apply (Code Sec. 45M(c)(1), as added by the Energy Act).

A special rule applies to calculating eligible production for refrigerators. For this type of appliance, eligible production is determined by subtracting 110 percent of the average number of qualified refrigerators that the taxpayer produced during the preceding three-calendar-year period from the number of qualified refrigerators that the taxpayer produced during the applicable calendar year. Again, only qualified refrigerators produced in the United States apply (Code Sec. 45M(c)(2), as added by the Energy Act).

Limitations. The maximum amount of the new credit allowable to a taxpayer is capped at $75 million per tax year for all qualifying appliances manufactured during that year (Code Sec. 45M(e)(1), as added by the Energy Act). In each subsequent year the cap is reduced by the amount (if any) of the credit used in any prior tax year. Of that $75 million (or reduced) cap, no more than $20 million of credit amount in a

¶225

NEW LAW EXPLAINED

single tax year may result from the manufacture of refrigerators to which the $75 applicable amount applies (i.e., refrigerators which are at least 15 percent but no more than 20 percent below 2001 energy conservation standards) (Code Sec. 45M(e)(2), as added by the Energy Act).

In addition to the $75 million cap on the credit allowed, the overall credit amount claimed for a particular tax year may not exceed two percent of the taxpayer's average annual gross receipts for the preceding three tax years (Code Sec. 45M(e)(3), as added by the Energy Act). For this purpose, the aggregation rules under Code Sec. 448(c)(2) and (3) for determining a taxpayer's eligibility to use the cash method of accounting apply in determining the taxpayer's gross receipts. For example, all persons will be treated as a single employer under the controlled group rules. Gross receipts will be adjusted for taxpayers that were not in existence for the full three-year period or that had tax years of less than 12 months. Gross receipts will be decreased by returns and allowances for the taxpayer's predecessors within the three-year base period.

In addition, all persons treated as a single employer under the controlled group rules of Code Sec. 52 are treated as a single manufacturer for purposes of the credit. The fact that a foreign corporation may be a member of a consolidated group that produces energy-efficient appliances will not preclude claiming the credit on the consolidated return, and the consolidated group will be considered as a single manufacturer for this purpose (Code Sec. 45M(g), as added by the Energy Act).

▶ **Effective date.** The amendments made by this section shall apply to appliances produced after December 31, 2005 (Act Sec. 1334(d) of the Energy Tax Incentives Act of 2005).

Law source: Law at ¶5040 and ¶5090. Committee Report at ¶10,220.

— Act Sec. 1334(a) of the Energy Tax Incentives Act of 2005, adding Code Sec. 45M;

— Act Sec. 1334(b), amending Code Sec. 38(b)(22) and Code Sec. 38(b)(23), and adding Code Sec. 38(b)(24);

— Act Sec. 1334(d), providing the effective date.

Reporter references: For further information, consult the following CCH reporters.

— Standard Federal Tax Reporter, 2005FED ¶4251.021

— Federal Tax Service, FTS § G:24.20

¶230 Business Solar Investment Tax Credit

BACKGROUND

A nonrefundable, business credit of 10 percent is allowed for the cost of the following types of energy property placed in service during the year: (1) solar equipment that uses solar energy to generate electricity, to heat or cool or provide hot water for use in a structure, or to provide solar process heat, or (2) geothermal equipment used to produce, distribute, or use energy derived from a geothermal deposit. Solar energy property includes equipment such as collectors, storage tanks, rockbeds, thermostats

88 Energy and Highway Tax Acts of 2005

BACKGROUND

and heat exchangers. However, property that uses fuel or energy derived indirectly from solar energy, such as ocean thermal energy, fossil fuel or wood, is not considered solar energy property.

The business energy tax credits are components of the general business credit. These credits when combined with all other components of the general business credit, generally may not exceed for a tax year the excess of the taxpayer's net income tax over the greater of (1) 25 percent of so much of the net regular tax liability as exceeds $25,000 or (2) the tentative minimum tax. An unused general business credit generally may be carried back one year and carried forward 20 years.

NEW LAW EXPLAINED

Business solar investment tax credit percentage increased.—The business investment credit for solar energy property is increased from 10 percent to 30 percent (Code Sec. 48(a)(2)(A), as amended by the Energy Tax Incentives Act of 2005).

> **Comment:** The credit for solar energy property, hybrid solar lighting systems and qualified fuel cell property is 30 percent. For any other energy property, the credit percentage is only 10 percent.

The increased credit applies to (1) equipment which uses solar energy to generate electricity, to heat or cool (or provide hot water for use in) a structure, or to provide solar process heat, and (2) equipment which uses solar energy to illuminate the inside of a structure using fiber-optic distributed sunlight, effective for periods ending before January 1, 2008. Property used to generate solar energy for purposes of heating swimming pools is not eligible solar energy property.

> **Compliance Tip:** Business energy credits are allowable in the year that the qualified property is first placed in service and are claimed on Form 3468, Investment Tax Credit.

> **State Tax Consequences:** Many states provide energy incentives through personal and corporate income tax credits. See ¶195 for a state-by-state summary of available credits.

▶ **Effective date.** The provision applies to periods after December 31, 2005, in tax years ending after such date, under rules similar to the rules of Code Sec. 48(m) (as in effect on the day before the date of the enactment of the Revenue Reconciliation Act of 1990, November 4, 1990).

Law source: Law at ¶5100. Committee Report at ¶10,250.

— Act Sec. 1337(a) of the Energy Tax Incentives Act of 2005, amending Code Sec. 48(a)(2)(A);
— Act Sec. 1337(b), amending Code Sec. 48(a)(3)(A);
— Act Sec. 1337(c), amending Code Sec. 48(a)(3)(A)(i);
— Act Sec. 1337(d), providing the effective date.

Reporter references: For further information, consult the following CCH reporters.
— Standard Federal Tax Reporter, 2005FED ¶4671.021
— Federal Tax Service, FTS § G:24.20

¶230

¶235 Expansion of Research Credit

BACKGROUND

In general, Code Sec. 41 provides for a research tax credit equal to the sum of 20 percent of the amount by which a taxpayer's qualified research expenses for a tax year exceed a base amount for that year, plus 20 percent of the basic research payments made for the tax year (commonly referred to as the university basic research payments). The amount of basic research payments equals the excess of 100 percent of corporate cash payments paid for basic research conducted by universities and certain nonprofit scientific research organizations over the sum of the greater of two minimum basic research floors plus an amount reflecting any decrease in nonresearch giving to universities by the corporation as compared to such giving during a fixed base period, as adjusted for inflation. The research credit is scheduled to expire on December 31, 2005 and will generally not apply to amounts paid or incurred after that date.

Alternative incremental credit. For tax years beginning after June 30, 1996, taxpayers may elect an alternative three-tiered credit regime that applies reduced credit rates and fixed-base percentages (Code Sec. 41(c)(4)). The election applies to the tax year to which it relates and all subsequent tax years unless revoked with the consent of the IRS. Using the alternative regime, a taxpayer's research credit is equal to the sum of the three tiers:

(1) Tier 1 Credit: 2.65 percent of current year qualified research expenses in excess of a base amount computed by using a fixed-base percentage of one percent (the base amount equals one percent of the taxpayer's average gross receipts for the four preceding years), but not in excess of a base amount computed using a fixed-base percentage of 1.5 percent;

(2) Tier 2 Credit: 3.2 percent of current year qualified research expenses in excess of a base amount computed by using a fixed-base percentage of 1.5 percent, but not in excess of a base amount computed using a fixed-base percentage of two percent; and

(3) Tier 3 Credit: 3.75 percent of current year qualified research expenses in excess of a base amount computed by using a fixed-base percentage of two percent.

Eligible expenses. Qualified research expenses that are eligible for the research tax credit consist of:

(1) wages for employees involved in the research activity;

(2) cost of supplies used in research;

(3) time-sharing costs for computer use in the conduct of research; and

(4) 65 percent of the costs of contracting with another party to conduct research on the taxpayer's behalf (contract research expenses) (Code Sec 41(b)).

In the case of amounts paid to a qualified research consortium, 75 percent (rather than 65 percent as in (4) above) of amounts paid for qualified research is treated as qualified research expenses eligible for the research credit. A qualified research consortium is any organization which:

BACKGROUND

(1) is a tax-exempt organization described in Code Sec. 501(c)(3) or Code Sec. 501(c)(6)
(2) is organized and operated primarily to conduct scientific research;
(3) conducts qualified research on behalf of the taxpayer and one or more persons not related to the taxpayer; and
(4) is not a private foundation.

To be eligible for the credit, the research must satisfy the requirements of Code Sec. 174 for the deduction of research expenses. Furthermore, the research must be undertaken for the purpose of discovering information that is technological in nature and the application of which is intended to be useful in the development of a new or improved business component of the taxpayer. In addition, substantially all of the research activities must constitute elements of a process of experimentation related to a new or improved function, performance, or reliability or quality of a business component.

NEW LAW EXPLAINED

Energy research credit.—The Energy Tax Incentives Act of 2005 modifies the research tax credit as it applies to qualified energy research. The new provision provides that a taxpayer may claim a credit equal to 20 percent of amounts paid or incurred by the taxpayer during the tax year to an energy research consortium (Code Sec. 41(a)(3) as added by the Energy Act). The 20 percent credit applies to all expenditures for research by an energy research consortium, not only those in excess of a base amount. An energy research consortium is an organization:

(1) which is a tax-exempt organization described in Code Sec. 501(c)(3) and is organized and operated primarily to conduct energy research or is organized and operated primarily to conduct energy research in the public interest (within the meaning of Code Sec. 501(c)(3));
(2) which is not a private foundation;
(3) to which at least five unrelated persons paid or incurred amounts to such organization during the calendar year for energy research; and
(4) to which no single person paid or incurred during the calendar year more than 50 percent of the total amounts received by such organization for energy research during such calendar year (Code Sec. 41(f)(6) as added by the Energy Act).

All persons treated as a single employer under Code Sec. 52(a) or Code Sec. 52(b) are treated as related persons for purposes of (3) above, and as a single person for purposes of (4) above (Code Sec. 41(f)(6)(B), as added by the Energy Act).

Repeal of limitation on contract research expenses paid to eligible small businesses, universities and federal laboratories. The Energy Act also provides that 100 percent of the amounts paid or incurred by the taxpayer to an eligible small business, a university or a Federal laboratory for qualified research which is energy research constitutes contract research expenses. This increased percentage for energy research replaces the

NEW LAW EXPLAINED

65 percent level for amounts paid for qualified research allowed under present law (Code Sec. 41(b)(3)(D) as added by the Energy Act).

An eligible small business is a small business in which the taxpayer does not own a 50 percent or greater interest in the business, and the business has employed, on average, 500 or fewer employees during either of the two preceding calendar years. If the small business is a corporation, the 50 percent ownership test (above) is determined with reference to the taxpayer's ownership of the business' outstanding corporate stock (determined by vote, or by value). If the small business is not a corporation, the taxpayer's ownership in the business is determined with reference to the taxpayer's percentage of ownership in the capital and profits interests of the small business. With respect to startups, controlled groups and predecessors, rules similar to those of Code Sec. 220(c)(4)(B) and (D) apply in determining eligible small business status. The term "Federal laboratory" is defined in section 4(6) of the Stevenson-Wydler Technology Innovation Act of 1980 (15 U.S.C. 3703(6)).

Expenditures for qualified energy research are those that would otherwise qualify for the research credit under present law. Such expenditures relate to the production, supply and conservation of energy, including otherwise qualifying research expenditures related to alternative energy sources or the use of alternative energy sources (Joint Committee on Taxation, Description and Technical Explanation of the Energy Tax Incentives Act of 2005 (JCX-60-05)).

> **Example:** Research relating to hydrogen fuel cell vehicles is qualified energy research, if the research expenditures would otherwise satisfy the criteria of Code Sec. 41. Similarly, otherwise qualifying research aimed at improving the energy efficiency of lighting would qualify for the energy research credit (Joint Committee on Taxation, Description and Technical Explanation of the Energy Tax Incentives Act of 2005 (JCX-60-05)).

Comment: The credit for increasing research activities under Code Sec. 41 is due to expire after December 31, 2005 (Code Sec. 41(h)(1)(B)). The Energy Act does not include a provision extending the termination date.

▶ **Effective date.** The provision is effective for amounts paid or incurred after August 8, 2005, in tax years ending after such date (Act Sec. 1351(c) of the Energy Act).

Law source: Law at ¶5055. Committee Report at ¶10,320.
— Act Sec. 1351(a)(1) of the Energy Tax Incentives Act of 2005, amending Code Sec. 41(a);
— Act Sec. 1351(a)(2), amending Code Sec. 41(f);
— Act Sec. 1351(a)(3), amending Code Sec. 41(b)(3)(C);
— Act Sec. 1351(b), amending Code Sec. 41(b)(3);
— Act Sec. 1351(c), providing the effective date.

Reporter references: For further information, consult the following CCH reporters.
— Standard Federal Tax Reporter, 2005FED ¶4362.035 and ¶4362.038
— Federal Tax Service, FTS § G:24.80
— Federal Tax Guide, 2005FTG ¶2450

¶235

¶240 Credit for Business Installation of Qualified Fuel Cells and Stationary Microturbine Power Plants

BACKGROUND

A nonrefundable 10-percent business energy credit is allowed for the cost of energy property placed in service during the tax year (Code Sec. 48(a)(2)). Energy property includes solar energy equipment and geothermal energy equipment. Solar energy equipment is that which uses solar energy to generate electricity to heat or cool or provide hot water for use in a structure or to provide solar process heat (Code Sec. 48(a)(3)(A)(i)). Geothermal equipment is that which is used to produce, distribute, or use energy derived from a geothermal deposit (Code Sec. 48(a)(3)(A)(ii)). To qualify for the energy credit, the property must be either constructed, erected, or reconstructed by the taxpayer, or acquired by the taxpayer if the original use of the property commences with the taxpayer. In addition, the property must qualify for depreciation or amortization. The property must also meet performance and quality standards (if any) that have been prescribed by the IRS (after consultation with the Department of Energy) and which are in effect when the property is acquired. Public utility property does not qualify as energy property.

The business energy tax credits are components of the general business credit (Code Sec. 38(b)(1)). The business energy tax credits, when combined with all other components of the general business credit, generally may not exceed for any tax year the excess of the taxpayer's net income tax over the greater of (1) 25 percent of the net regular tax liability above $25,000 or (2) the tentative minimum tax. For credits arising in tax years beginning after December 31, 1997, an unused general business credit generally can be carried back one year and carried forward 20 years.

NEW LAW EXPLAINED

Credit for qualified fuel cell property and stationary microturbine power plants.—Energy property now includes qualified fuel cell property and stationary microturbine property for purposes of the business energy credit (Code Sec. 48(a)(3)(A), as amended by the Energy Tax Incentives Act of 2005). The credit is 30 percent of the basis of qualified fuel cell property placed in service during the tax year. The energy credit for any qualified fuel cell property shall not exceed an amount equal to $500 for each 0.5 kilowatt of capacity of such property. The credit is not available for qualified fuel cell property and stationary microturbine power plants for any period after December 31, 2007. See ¶210 for a discussion of the credit for qualified residential fuel cell property expenditures.

The credit for stationary microturbine power plants is 10 percent of the basis of such property placed in service during the tax year. The energy credit for stationary microturbine power plants shall not exceed an amount equal to $200 for each kilowatt of capacity of such property.

NEW LAW EXPLAINED

Compliance Tip: Business energy credits are allowable in the year that the qualified property is first placed in service and are claimed on Form 3468, Investment Tax Credit.

Qualified fuel cell property. Qualified fuel cell property is defined as a fuel cell power plant that generates at least 0.5 kilowatt of electricity using an electrochemical process and has an electricity-only generation efficiency greater than 30 percent. A fuel cell power plant is defined as an integrated system comprised of a fuel cell stack assembly and associated balance of plant components which converts a fuel into electricity using electrochemical means (Code Sec. 48(c)(1), as added by the Energy Act).

Stationary microturbine power plant. A stationary microturbine power plant is an integrated system comprised of a gas turbine engine, a combustor, a recuperator or regenerator, a generator or alternator and associated balance of plant components that converts a fuel into electricity and thermal energy. It also includes all secondary components located between the existing infrastructure for fuel delivery and the existing infrastructure for power distribution, including equipment and controls for meeting relevant power standards, such as voltage, frequency and power factors (Code Sec. 48(c)(2), as added by the Energy Act).

Telecommunication companies. The new credits apply to qualified fuel cell property and to qualified microturbine property used predominately in the trade or business of furnishing or selling telephone services, domestic telegraph services or other telegraph services (other than international telegraph services).

Comment: For telecommunication companies, the new law removes the restriction under Code Sec. 48(a)(3)(D) that would otherwise prevent them from claiming the new credits due to their status as public utilities.

State Tax Consequences: Many states provide energy incentives through personal and corporate income tax credits. See ¶195 for a state-by-state summary of available credits.

▶ **Effective date.** The provision applies to periods after December 31, 2005, in tax years ending after such date, under rules similar to the rules of Code Sec. 48(m) as in effect on the day before the date of enactment of the Revenue Reconciliation Act of 1990, November 4, 1990 (P.L. 101-508) (Act Sec. 1336(e) of the Energy Tax Incentives Act of 2005).

Law source: Law at ¶5100. Committee Report at ¶10,240.

— Act Sec. 1336(a) of the Energy Tax Incentives Act of 2005, amending Code Sec. 48(a)(3)(A);

— Act Sec. 1336(b), adding Code Sec. 48(c);

— Act Sec. 1336(c), amending Code Sec. 48(a)(2)(A);

— Act Sec. 1336(d), amending Code Sec. 48(a)(1);

— Act Sec. 1336(e), providing the effective date.

Reporter references: For further information, consult the following CCH reporters.

— Standard Federal Tax Reporter, 2005FED ¶4671.026

— Federal Tax Service, FTS § G:24.20

¶240

OTHER BUSINESS PROVISIONS

¶245 Recapture of Code Sec. 197 Amortization

BACKGROUND

With certain exceptions, amortizable Code Sec. 197 intangibles generally are purchased intangibles held by a taxpayer in the conduct of a business. The following are Code Sec. 197 intangibles: (1) goodwill, going concern value, and covenants not to compete entered into in connection with the acquisition of a trade or business; (2) workforce in place; (3) information base; (4) a patent, copyright, formula, design, or similar item; (5) any customer-based intangible; (6) any supplier-based intangible; (7) any license, permit, or other right granted by a governmental unit or agency; and (8) any franchise, trademark, or trade name (Code Sec. 197(d)).

The cost of amortizable Code Sec. 197 intangibles are recoverable using the straight-line method of amortization over a uniform life of fifteen years.

Under Code Sec. 1245, gain on the sale of depreciable property must be recaptured as ordinary income to the extent of depreciation deductions previously claimed. The recapture amount is computed separately for each item of property. Code Sec. 197 intangibles are treated as property of a character subject to the allowance for depreciation and, therefore, are subject to these recapture rules.

NEW LAW EXPLAINED

Recapture of Code Sec. 197 amortization modified.—If multiple Code Sec. 197 intangibles are sold, or otherwise disposed of, in a single transaction or series of transactions, the seller must calculate recapture as if all of the Code Sec. 197 intangibles were a single asset (Code Sec. 1245(b)(9)(A), as added by the Energy Tax Incentives Act of 2005). Thus, any gain on the sale or other disposition of the intangibles is recaptured as ordinary income to the extent of ordinary depreciation deductions previously claimed on any of the Code Sec. 197 intangibles.

> **Example:** In year 1, Don Trupp acquires two Code Sec. 197 intangible assets for a total of $45,000. Asset A is assigned a cost basis of $15,000 and asset B is assigned a cost basis of $30,000. Don is entitled to a total of $3,000 amortization per year ($45,000 divided by 15 years).
>
> In year 6, the basis of asset A is $10,000 and asset B is $20,000. Don sells the assets for an aggregate sale price of $45,000, resulting in gain of $15,000. The character of this gain depends on the recapture amount, which depends in turn on the relative sales prices of the individual assets. With respect to asset A, Don has claimed $5,000 of amortization, and therefore has $5,000 of recapture potential. With respect to asset B, he has claimed $10,000 of amortization, and therefore has $10,000 of recapture potential.

NEW LAW EXPLAINED

> Under the Energy Act modifications, Don calculates recapture as if assets A and B were a single asset. For purposes of the calculation, the proceeds are $45,000 and the gain is $15,000. Because a total of $15,000 of amortization has been claimed with respect to assets A and B, the full $15,000 gain is recaptured as ordinary income.

Comment: Under prior law, the allocation of the sales proceeds between the assets would be determinative of the recapture amount. In the above example, if the sale proceeds were allocated $15,000 to asset A and $30,000 to asset B, the gain on assets A and B would be $5,000 and $10,000, respectively. These amounts match the recapture potential for each asset, so under the prior rules the full amount of the gain would have been recaptured as ordinary income.

However, if the sale proceeds instead were allocated $25,000 to asset A and $20,000 to asset B, the full $15,000 gain would have been recognized with respect to asset A, and only $5,000 (full recapture potential with respect to A) would have been recaptured as ordinary income. The remaining $10,000 of gain attributable to A would have been treated as capital gain. No gain (and thus no recapture) would have been recognized with respect to asset B, and only $5,000 of the $15,000 recapture potential would have been recognized.

The new modified rules make the allocation of sales proceeds unnecessary for purposes of determining the amortization recapture amount.

Caution Note: The new rule requiring that when multiple Code Sec. 197 intangibles are sold in a single transaction or series of transactions, the seller must calculate recapture as if all of the Code Sec. 197 intangibles were a single asset, **does not apply** to any amortizable Code Sec. 197 intangible with respect to which the adjusted basis exceeds the fair market value (Code Sec. 1245(b)(9)(B), as added by the Energy Act).

▶ **Effective date.** The provision applies to dispositions of property after August 8, 2005 (Act Sec. 1363(b) of the Energy Tax Incentives Act of 2005).

Law source: Law at ¶5245. Committee Report at ¶10,370.
— Act Sec. 1363(a) of the Energy Tax Incentives Act of 2005, adding Code Sec. 1245(b)(9);
— Act Sec. 1363(b), providing the effective date.

Reporter references: For further information, consult the following CCH reporters.
— Standard Federal Tax Reporter, 2005FED ¶12,455.021
— Federal Tax Service, FTS § G:22.40

¶245

Motor Vehicles

¶305   Alternative motor vehicle credit
¶310   New qualified fuel cell motor vehicle credit
¶315   New advanced lean burn technology motor vehicle credit
¶320   New qualified hybrid motor vehicle credit
¶325   New qualified alternative fuel motor vehicle credit
¶330   Termination of deduction for clean-fuel vehicles
¶335   Limousines and the "gas guzzler" tax
¶340   Excise tax on heavy trucks and trailers sold at retail
¶345   Tire excise tax modification

¶305 Alternative Motor Vehicle Credit

BACKGROUND

The only tax incentive designed to encourage development of alternative fuels is the deduction for certain costs of clean-fuel vehicles and related property (Code Sec. 179A). A qualified clean-fuel vehicle is one that consumes clean-burning fuels, including hybrid-electric vehicles but not qualified electric vehicles (Code Sec. 30). Clean-burning fuels include natural gas, liquefied natural gas, liquefied petroleum gas, hydrogen, electricity, and any other fuel at least 85 percent of which is methanol, ethanol, any other alcohol or ether (Code Sec. 179A(e)(1)). The maximum amount of the deduction is:

- $50,000 for a truck or van with a gross vehicle weight over 26,000 pounds or a bus with a seating capacity of at least 20 adults,
- $5,000 in the case of a truck or van with a gross vehicle weight between 10,000 and 26,000 pounds, and
- $2,000 in the case of any other motor vehicle (Code Sec. 179A(b)(1)).

The amount of the costs related to clean-fuel properties that may be used to claim the deduction is reduced by 75 percent in 2006 and terminated for tax years after December 31, 2006.

BACKGROUND

This deduction, however, is limited and does not apply to many vehicles which employ new energy-efficient technology. Congress believes that a stronger incentive is necessary to encourage use, innovation and technological development of energy-efficient motor vehicles.

NEW LAW EXPLAINED

Overview.—The Energy Tax Incentives Act of 2005 creates a series of new tax credits to encourage the development, manufacture and use of alternative fuel motor vehicles (Code Sec. 30B, as added by the Energy Act). The credits are collectively claimed under the title of the "Alternative Motor Vehicle Credit." This credit is equal to the sum of the four separate credit components:

(1) the new qualified fuel cell motor vehicle credit (Code Sec. 30B(b), as added by the Energy Act) (¶310),

(2) the new advanced lean burn technology motor vehicle credit (Code Sec. 30B(c), as added by the Energy Act) (¶315),

(3) the new qualified hybrid motor vehicle credit (Code Sec. 30B(d), as added by the Energy Act) (¶320), and

(4) the new qualified alternative fuel motor vehicle credit (Code Sec. 30B(e), as added by the Energy Act) (¶325).

Common elements of the Alternative Motor Vehicle Credit. Each separate credit component is unique but there are certain elements common to all four credits which are outlined below.

Qualifying vehicles. The overall definition of a qualifying vehicle is specific for each credit, but there are three common elements in each definition. The common elements are:

(1) the original use of the vehicle commences with the taxpayer,

(2) the vehicle is acquired for use or lease by the taxpayer and not for resale, and

(3) the vehicle is made by a manufacturer.

Coordination with other credits. Taxpayers with qualified motor vehicles that are used in a trade or business and subject to depreciation will claim the alternative motor vehicle credit as a part of and subject to the rules of the general business credit. Thus, any unused credit in a tax year will be eligible to be carried back three years and forward 20 years. However, under Code Sec. 39, no credit amount may be carried back to the year before the year the credit first became available (Code Secs. 30B(g)(1) and 38(b)(25), as added by the Energy Act).

If the credit is to be claimed by an individual as a personal credit, the credit amount is limited to the excess of the regular tax less the sum of the taxpayer's credits under Subpart A (the dependent care credit, the elderly and permanent disabled credit, the child tax credit, the home mortgage credit, the educational credits, the retirement contribution savings credit), and Code Secs. 27 and 30 (the foreign tax credit and the electric vehicle credit) over the tentative minimum tax (Code Sec. 30B(g)(2), as added by the Energy Act).

¶305

NEW LAW EXPLAINED

Tax-exempt entities. Generally, the buyer of a qualified vehicle would claim the credit. However, the seller (but not the lessor) of a qualified vehicle to a tax-exempt entity, a governmental unit or a foreign entity (for use as described in Code Sec. 50(b)(3) or (4)) may claim the credit, providing the seller gives written notice of intent to claim the credit and the credit's amount to the buyer (Code Sec. 30B(h)(6), as added by the Energy Act).

Other definitions and special rules. The following terms and rules apply to all four of the separate credit components of the alternative motor vehicle credit.

Motor vehicle. The term "motor vehicle" means any vehicle that is manufactured primarily for use on public streets, roads and highways, and which has at least four wheels (see Code Sec. 30(c)(2)) (Code Sec. 30B(h)(1), as added by the Energy Act).

Other vehicle descriptive terms. The terms "automobile," "passenger automobile," "medium duty passenger automobile," "light truck," and "manufacturer" are defined by reference to regulations prescribed by the Administrator of the Environmental Protection Agency under Title II of the Clean Air Act (42 U.S.C. §7521 and following) (Code Sec. 30B(h)(3), as added by the Energy Act).

> **Comment:** The Clean Air Act and accompanying regulations may be found at www.epa.gov.

City fuel economy. City fuel economy for any vehicle shall be measured under rules similar to those found in Code Sec. 4064(c) (Code Sec. 30B(h)(2), as added by the Energy Act).

Basis reduction. The basis of any vehicle is reduced by the amount of alternative motor vehicle credit allowed (Code Secs. 30B(h)(4) and 1016(a)(36), as added by the Energy Act).

Denial of double benefits. The alternative motor vehicle credit also reduces the amount of any other deduction or credit allowable for a particular vehicle in the tax year (Code Sec. 30B(h)(5), as added by the Energy Act).

Recapture. The IRS is required to issue regulations providing for the recapture of any alternative motor vehicle credit amounts if the qualified vehicle should cease to be eligible property (Code Sec. 30B(h)(8), as added by the Energy Act).

> **Comment:** The language of this subsection makes clear that any recapture of credit amounts is to include amounts claimed under a lease whose term is for less than the economic life of the vehicle. However, the term "economic life" is not defined.

Exceptions for foreign use of property and overlapping Code Sec. 179 deductions. No credit amount will be allowed for any qualified vehicle that is not used within the United States (see Code Sec. 50(b)). In addition, no credit amount will be allowed for any portion of the cost of the vehicle that is used to claim a Code Sec. 179 deduction (Code Sec. 30B(h)(7), as added by the Energy Act).

Election. The claiming of the alternative motor vehicle credit is at the election of the taxpayer (Code Sec. 30B(h)(9), as added by the Energy Act).

Motor vehicle safety and air quality standards. A qualified vehicle under the alternative motor vehicle credit must comply with motor vehicle safety standards of 49 U.S.C.

¶305

NEW LAW EXPLAINED

§§ 30,101 through 30,169. In addition, it also must comply with the applicable provisions of the Clean Air Act for the make and model year of the vehicle. A vehicle must comply with the state air quality laws for those states that have adopted such provisions under a waiver under § 209(b) of the Clean Air Act (Code Sec. 30B(h)(10), as added by the Energy Act).

> **Comment:** Individuals who want to claim an alternative motor vehicle credit must ensure that the vehicle meets any more stringent air quality standards adopted by their state.

Regulations. The IRS is authorized to promulgate regulations as necessary to carry out the provisions of Code Sec. 30B. The regulations identifying eligible vehicles will be issued in coordination with the Secretary of Transportation and the Administrator of the Environmental Protection Agency (Code Sec. 30B(i), as added by the Energy Act).

> **State Tax Consequences:** Many states provide energy incentives through personal and corporate income tax credits. See ¶ 195 for a state-by-state summary of available credits.

▶ **Effective date.** This provision is effective for qualifying property placed in service after December 31, 2005, in tax years ending after that date (Act Sec. 1341(c) of the Energy Tax Incentives Act of 2005).

Law source: Law at ¶ 5030, ¶ 5040, ¶ 5130, ¶ 5240 and ¶ 5440. Committee Report at ¶ 10,260.

— Act Sec. 1341(a) of the Energy Tax Incentives Act of 2005, adding Code Sec. 30B;
— Act Sec. 1341(b), amending Code Secs. 38(b), 55(c)(2), 1016(a), and 6501(m);
— Act Sec. 1341(c), providing the effective date.

Reporter references: For further information, consult the following CCH reporters.
— Standard Federal Tax Reporter, 2005FED ¶ 4251.021 and ¶ 29,412.023
— Federal Tax Service, FTS § A:19.20

¶ 310 New Qualified Fuel Cell Motor Vehicle Credit

New qualified fuel cell motor vehicle credit.—The first component of the alternative motor vehicle credit is the new qualified fuel cell motor vehicle credit (Code Sec. 30B(b), as added by the Energy Tax Incentives Act of 2005).

Qualifying fuel cell motor vehicles. To be eligible as a qualifying fuel cell motor vehicle, the motor vehicle must meet several criteria including the three requirements common to all the credit components of the alternative motor vehicle credit (see ¶ 305, *Qualifying vehicles*). These requirements are:

(1) the original use of the vehicle must commence with the taxpayer (Code Sec. 30B(b)(3)(C), as added by the Energy Act),

(2) the vehicle must be acquired for the use or lease of the taxpayer and not for resale (Code Sec. 30B(b)(3)(D), as added by the Energy Act), and

(3) the vehicle must be made by a manufacturer (Code Sec. 30B(b)(3)(E), as added by the Energy Act).

In the case of passenger automobiles or light trucks, two additional criteria must be met. The vehicle must be certified as meeting or exceeding the Bin 5, Tier II emission standard established in the regulations under the Clean Air Act for that make and model year vehicle (Code Sec. 30B(b)(3)(B), as added by the Energy Act). For states, such as California, that have passed equivalent qualifying emission standards, the vehicle is required to also be certified for those standards for that particular make and model year (Code Sec. 30B(h)(10)(A), as added by the Energy Act).

In addition, the vehicle must be propelled by power derived from one or more cells which convert chemical energy directly into electricity by combining oxygen with hydrogen fuel (Code Sec. 30B(b)(3)(A), as added by the Energy Act).

Credit amount. The amount of credit attributable to the placing in service of a qualified fuel cell motor vehicle during the tax year is determined using the following table (Code Sec. 30B(b)(1), as added by the Energy Act):

In the case of a vehicle which has a gross vehicle weight rating of—	The new qualified fuel cell motor vehicle credit is—
Not more than 8,500 lbs	$8,000
(if placed in service after December 31, 2009	$4,000)
More than 8,500 lbs but not more than 14,000 lbs	$10,000
More than 14,000 lbs but not more than 26,000 lbs	$20,000
More than 26,000 lbs	$40,000

Qualified fuel cell vehicles that meet the definition of either a "passenger automobile" or "light truck" (see ¶ 305) and meet certain standards for increased fuel efficiency will be able to increase their credit amount based on the increase in fuel efficiency over the 2002 city fuel economy standards (Code Sec. 30B(b)(2)(A), as added by the Energy Act). The additional amount is determined using the following table:

In the case of a vehicle which achieves a fuel economy (expressed as a percentage of the 2002 model year city fuel economy) of—	The additional credit amount is—
At least 150 percent but less than 175 percent	$1,000
At least 175 percent but less than 200 percent	$1,500
At least 200 percent but less than 225 percent	$2,000
At least 225 percent but less than 250 percent	$2,500
At least 250 percent but less than 275 percent	$3,000
At least 275 percent but less than 300 percent	$3,500
At least 300 percent	$4,000

The 2002 model year city fuel economy for such vehicles is determined using the following tables (Code Sec. 30B(b)(2)(B), as added by the Energy Act):

Passenger Automobiles

If vehicle inertia weight class is:	The 2002 model year city fuel economy is:
1,500 or 1,750 lbs	45.2 mpg
2,000 lbs	39.6 mpg
2,250 lbs	35.2 mpg
2,500 lbs	31.7 mpg
2,750 lbs	28.8 mpg

¶310

If vehicle inertia weight class is:	The 2002 model year city fuel economy is:
3,000 lbs	26.4 mpg
3,500 lbs	22.6 mpg
4,000 lbs	19.8 mpg
4,500 lbs	17.6 mpg
5,000 lbs	15.9 mpg
5,500 lbs	14.4 mpg
6,000 lbs	13.2 mpg
6,500 lbs	12.2 mpg
7,000 to 8,500 lbs	11.3 mpg

Light Trucks

If vehicle inertia weight class is:	The 2002 model year city fuel economy is:
1,500 or 1,750 lbs	39.4 mpg
2,000 lbs	35.2 mpg
2,250 lbs	31.8 mpg
2,500 lbs	29.0 mpg
2,750 lbs	26.8 mpg
3,000 lbs	24.9 mpg
3,500 lbs	21.8 mpg
4,000 lbs	19.4 mpg
4,500 lbs	17.6 mpg
5,000 lbs	16.1 mpg
5,500 lbs	14.8 mpg
6,000 lbs	13.7 mpg
6,500 lbs	12.8 mpg
7,000 to 8,500 lbs	12.1 mpg

The term "vehicle inertia weight class" is given the same meaning as in the regulations under Title II of the Clean Air Act (42 U.S.C. §7521 and following) (Code Sec. 30B(b)(2)(C), as added by the Energy Act).

Other requirements. The new qualified fuel cell motor vehicle credit is also subject to the credit amount limitations and the other definitions and special rules discussed at ¶ 305.

Termination. The new qualified fuel cell motor vehicle credit cannot be claimed for any vehicle purchased after December 31, 2014 (Code Sec. 30B(j)(1), as added by the Energy Act).

▶ **Effective date.** This provision is effective for vehicles placed in service after December 31, 2005, in tax years ending after such date (Act Sec. 1341(c) of the Energy Tax Incentives Act of 2005). The provision terminates and will not apply to any vehicle purchased after December 31, 2014 (Code Sec. 30B(j)(1), as added by the Energy Act).

Law source: Law at ¶ 5030. Committee Report at ¶ 10,260.

— Act Sec. 1341(a) of the Energy Tax Incentives Act of 2005, adding Code Sec. 30B;

— Act Sec. 1341(b), amending Code Secs. 38(b), 55(c)(2), 1016(a), and 6501(m);

— Act Sec. 1341(c), providing the effective date.

Reporter references: For further information, consult the following CCH reporters.
— Standard Federal Tax Reporter, 2005FED ¶4251.021 and ¶29,412.023
— Federal Tax Service, FTS § A:19.20

¶315 New Advanced Lean Burn Technology Motor Vehicle Credit

New advanced lean burn technology motor vehicle credit.—The second component of the alternative motor vehicle credit is the new advanced lean burn technology motor vehicle credit (Code Sec. 30B(c), as added by the Energy Tax Incentives Act of 2005).

New advanced lean burn technology motor vehicles. To be eligible as a qualified new advanced lean burn technology motor vehicle, the motor vehicle must meet several criteria including the three requirements common to all the credit components of the alternative motor vehicle credit (see ¶ 305, *Qualifying vehicles*). These requirements are:

(1) the original use of the vehicle must commence with the taxpayer (Code Sec. 30B(c)(3)(B), as added by the Energy Act),

(2) the vehicle must be acquired for the use or lease of the taxpayer and not for resale (Code Sec. 30B(c)(3)(C), as added by the Energy Act), and

(3) the vehicle must be made by a manufacturer (Code Sec. 30B(c)(3)(D), as added by the Energy Act).

An eligible vehicle must be a passenger automobile or light truck with an internal combustion engine which:

- is designed to operate primarily using more air than is necessary for complete combustion of the fuel,
- incorporates direct injection, and
- achieves at least 125 percent of the 2002 model year city fuel economy (see ¶ 310) (Code Sec. 30B(c)(3)(A), as added by the Energy Act).

Vehicles from model year 2004 and later must also receive a certificate that the vehicle meets or exceeds the Bin 5, Tier II emission standard established under the Clean Air Act for that make and model year, if the gross vehicle weight rating is 6,000 pounds or less. Vehicles with a gross vehicle weight rating of more than 6,000 pounds but not more than 8,500 pounds must be certified to meet or exceed the Bin 8, Tier II emission standard established under the Clean Air Act (Code Sec. 30B(c)(3)(A)(iv), as added by the Energy Act).

Credit amount. The credit amount attributable to the placing in service of a new qualified advanced lean burn technology motor vehicle during the tax year is determined by using the following table (Code Sec. 30B(c)(2)(A), as added by the Energy Act):

¶315

In the case of a vehicle which achieves a fuel economy (expressed as a percentage of the 2002 model year city fuel economy) of—	The credit amount is—
At least 125 percent but less than 150 percent	$400
At least 150 percent but less than 175 percent	$800
At least 175 percent but less than 200 percent	$1,200
At least 200 percent but less than 225 percent	$1,600
At least 225 percent but less than 250 percent	$2,000
At least 250 percent	$2,400

Conservation credit. The credit amount for new advanced lean burn technology motor vehicles may be increased by a conservation credit (Code Sec. 30B(c)(2)(B), as added by the Energy Act). The increased amount for the conservation credit will be determined using the following table:

In the case of a vehicle which achieves a lifetime fuel savings (expressed in gallons of gasoline) of—	The conservation credit amount is—
At least 1,200 but less than 1,800	$250
At least 1,800 but less than 2,400	$500
At least 2,400 but less than 3,000	$750
At least 3,000	$1,000

The "lifetime fuel savings" for a vehicle is equal to the excess (if any) of

- 120,000 divided by the 2002 model year city fuel economy for the vehicle inertia weight class (see ¶ 310), over
- 120,000 divided by the city fuel economy for the vehicle (Code Sec. 30B(c)(4), as added by the Energy Act).

Additional requirements. The new advanced lean burn technology motor vehicle credit is also subject to the credit amount limitations and the other definitions and special rules discussed at ¶ 305 plus the following additional limitations.

Quantity limitation. The amount of credit for the new advanced lean burn technology motor vehicle credit and the new qualified hybrid motor vehicle credit (¶ 320) is limited by the sum total of the number of units sold by the manufacturer. The credit amounts will be phased out when a manufacturer of these vehicles certifies that it has sold a combined total of 60,000 of these vehicles for use in the United States after December 31, 2005. For these purposes, controlled groups of corporations are considered to be a single entity and related foreign corporations are included in the single entity (Code Sec. 30B(f)(4), as added by the Energy Act).

For vehicles purchased in the calendar quarter that includes the date of the sale of the 60,000th unit, and the next calendar quarter, taxpayers will be allowed to continue to claim the full allowable credit amount. The credit amount will be limited to 50 percent of the allowable credit amount for vehicles purchased in the next two calendar quarters and to 25 percent of the allowable credit amount for vehicles purchased in the next two calendar quarters. The credit will be disallowed for all calendar quarters thereafter (Code Sec. 30B(f)(1), (2) and (3), as added by the Energy Act).

> **Example:** A manufacturer announces in February of 2007 that it has sold a combined sum of qualified hybrid and advanced lean burn technology motor

> vehicles totaling 60,000 units. Taxpayers may continue to claim the full amount of either of these credits for vehicles that are purchased from the manufacturer before July 1, 2007. Taxpayers that make purchases of qualified vehicles on or after July 1, 2007, but before January 1, 2008, are entitled to claim 50 percent of the otherwise allowable credit amount. Taxpayers that make purchases of qualified vehicles on or after January 1, 2008, but before July 1, 2008, are entitled to claim 25 percent of the otherwise allowable credit. For vehicles purchased on or after July 1, 2008, no credit amount will be allowed (Joint Committee on Taxation, Description and Technical Explanation of the Energy Tax Incentives Act of 2005 (JCX-60-05)).

Termination. The new advanced lean burn technology motor vehicle credit cannot be claimed for any vehicle purchased after December 31, 2010 (Code Sec. 30B(j)(2), as added by the Energy Act).

▶ **Effective date.** The provision is effective for vehicles placed in service after December 31, 2005, in tax years ending after such date (Act Sec. 1341(c) of the Energy Tax Incentives Act of 2005). The provision terminates and will not apply to any vehicle purchased after December 31, 2010 (Code Sec. 30B(j)(2), as added by the Energy Act).

Law source: Law at ¶5030. Committee Report at ¶10,260.

— Act Sec. 1341(a) of the Energy Tax Incentives Act of 2005, adding Code Sec. 30B;
— Act Sec. 1341(b), amending Code Secs. 38(b), 55(c)(2), 1016(a), and 6501(m);
— Act Sec. 1341(c), providing the effective date.

Reporter references: For further information, consult the following CCH reporters.

— Standard Federal Tax Reporter, 2005FED ¶4251.021 and ¶29,412.023
— Federal Tax Service, FTS § A:19.20

¶320 New Qualified Hybrid Motor Vehicle Credit

New qualified hybrid motor vehicle credit.—The third component of the alternative motor vehicle credit is the new qualified hybrid motor vehicle credit (Code Sec. 30B(d), as added by the Energy Tax Incentives Act of 2005).

Qualifying hybrid motor vehicles. In order to be eligible as a qualified hybrid motor vehicle, the motor vehicle must meet several criteria including the three requirements common to all the credit components of the alternative motor vehicle credit (see ¶ 305, *Qualifying vehicles*). These requirements are:

(1) the original use of the vehicle must commence with the taxpayer (Code Sec. 30B(d)(3)(A)(v), as added by the Energy Act),

(2) the vehicle must be acquired for the use or lease of the taxpayer and not for resale (Code Sec. 30B(d)(3)(A)(vi), as added by the Energy Act), and

(3) the vehicle must be made by a manufacturer (Code Sec. 30B(d)(3)(A)(vii), as added by the Energy Act).

The vehicle must draw propulsion energy from onboard sources of stored energy that are both an internal combustion or heat engine using consumable fuel, and a rechargeable energy storage system. Passenger automobiles or light trucks must receive a certificate of conformity under the Clean Air Act, and meet or exceed the equivalent qualifying California low emission vehicle standard under §243(e)(2) of the Clean Air Act for that make and model year. In addition, if the vehicle has a gross weight rating of 6,000 pounds or less, it must meet or exceed the Bin 5, Tier II emission standard established in the regulations under the Clean Air Act for that make and model year. Vehicles with a gross weight rating of more than 6,000 pounds but not more than 8,500 pounds must meet or exceed the Bin 8, Tier II emission standard. Finally, the vehicle must have a maximum available power of at least:

- 4 percent, in the case of a passenger automobile or light truck with a gross vehicle weight rating of not more than 8,500 pounds,
- 10 percent, in the case of a vehicle which has a gross vehicle weight rating of more than 8,500 pounds but not more than 14,000 pounds, or
- 15 percent, in the case of a vehicle which has a gross vehicle weight rating in excess of 14,000 pounds (Code Sec. 30B(d)(3)(A)(i), (ii), and (iii), as added by the Energy Act).

Vehicles from model years 2004 through 2007, other than passenger automobiles or light trucks with a gross weight rating of not more than 8,500 pounds with an internal combustion or heat engine, must receive a certificate of conformity under the Clean Air Act as meeting the emission standard established in the regulations for either a diesel heavy duty engine or an ottocycle heavy duty engine (Code Sec. 30B(d)(3)(A)(iv), as added by the Energy Act).

The term qualified hybrid motor vehicle shall **not** include any vehicle which is not a passenger automobile or light truck if the vehicle has a gross vehicle weight rating of less than 8,500 pounds (Code Sec. 30B(d)(3)(A), as added by the Energy Act).

> **Comment:** This, apparently, is an attempt by Congress to exclude buyers of sports utility vehicles (SUVs) from claiming the qualified motor vehicle credit.

The term "consumable fuel" is defined to mean any solid, liquid, or gaseous matter which releases energy when consumed by an auxiliary power unit (Code Sec. 30B(d)(3)(B), as added by the Energy Act). "Maximum available power" is defined to mean:

- in the case of passenger automobiles or light trucks which have a gross vehicle weight rating of not more than 8,500 pounds, the maximum power available from the rechargeable energy storage system, during a standard 10-second pulse power or equivalent test, divided by such maximum power and the Society of Automotive Engineers (SAE) net power of the heat engine, or
- in the case of all other vehicles, the maximum power available from the rechargeable energy storage system during the standard 10 second pulse power or equivalent test, divided by the vehicle's total traction power. "Total traction power" means the sum of the peak power from the rechargeable energy storage system and the heat engine peak power of the vehicle. If, however, the sole means by which the vehicle can be driven is by the rechargeable energy storage system, then the "total traction power" is the peak power of such storage system (Code Sec. 30B(d)(3)(C), as added by the Energy Act).

Credit amount. The credit amount attributable to the placing in service of a qualified hybrid motor vehicle during the tax year, in the case of passenger automobiles or light trucks with a gross vehicle weight rating of not more than 8,500 pounds, is determined by referring to credit amounts determined under Code Sec. 30B(c)(2)(A), the advanced lean burn technology motor vehicle credit (see ¶315), as represented by the following table (Code Sec. 30B(d)(2)(A)(i), as added by the Energy Act):

In the case of a vehicle which achieves a fuel economy (expressed as a percentage of the 2002 model year city fuel economy) of—	The credit amount is—
At least 125 percent but less than 150 percent	$400
At least 150 percent but less than 175 percent	$800
At least 175 percent but less than 200 percent	$1,200
At least 200 percent but less than 225 percent	$1,600
At least 225 percent but less than 250 percent	$2,000
At least 250 percent	$2,400

This credit amount may be increased by a conservation credit (Code Sec. 30B(d)(2)(A)(ii), as added by the Energy Act), the amount of which is determined by referring to the conservation credit amounts under Code Sec. 30B(c)(2)(B), the advanced lean burn technology motor vehicle credit (see ¶315), as represented by the following table:

In the case of a vehicle which achieves a lifetime fuel savings (expressed in gallons of gasoline) of—	The conservation credit amount is—
At least 1,200 but less than 1,800	$250
At least 1,800 but less than 2,400	$500
At least 2,400 but less than 3,000	$750
At least 3,000	$1,000

If the qualified hybrid motor vehicle is not a passenger automobile or light truck with a gross vehicle weight rating under 8,500 pounds, the credit amount is equal to an applicable percentage times the qualified incremental hybrid cost of the vehicle as certified by the manufacturer in accordance with guidance to be issued by the IRS (Code Sec. 30B(d)(2)(B), as added by the Energy Act). Such guidance shall specify the procedures and methods for calculating the fuel economy savings and the incremental hybrid costs (Code Sec. 30B(d)(2)(B)(v), as added by the Energy Act).

The applicable percentages are as follows:

- 20 percent, if the vehicle achieves an increase in city fuel economy relative to a comparable vehicle of at least 30 percent but less than 40 percent,
- 30 percent, if the vehicle achieves an increase in city fuel economy relative to a comparable vehicle of at least 40 percent but less than 50 percent, and
- 40 percent, if the vehicle achieves an increase in city fuel economy relative to a comparable vehicle of at least 50 percent (Code Sec. 30B(d)(2)(B)(ii), as added by the Energy Act).

The qualified incremental hybrid cost is equal to the amount of the excess of the manufacturer's suggested retail price (MSRP) for the hybrid vehicle over the MSRP of a comparable vehicle. The incremental hybrid cost cannot exceed:

- $7,500, if the hybrid vehicle has a gross vehicle weight rating of not more than 14,000 pounds,

¶320

- $15,000, if the hybrid vehicle has a gross vehicle weight rating of more than 14,000 pounds but not more than 26,000 pounds, or
- $30,000, if the hybrid vehicle has a gross vehicle weight rating of more than 26,000 pounds (Code Sec. 30B(d)(2)(B)(iii), as added by the Energy Act).

A "comparable vehicle" is any vehicle that is powered solely by a gasoline or diesel internal combustion engine and that is comparable in weight, size and use to the hybrid vehicle in question (Code Sec. 30B(d)(2)(B)(iv), as added by the Energy Act).

Additional requirements. The new qualified hybrid motor vehicle credit is also subject to the credit amount limitations and the other definitions and special rules discussed at ¶305, plus the following additional requirements.

Quantity limitation. The amount of credit for the new qualified hybrid motor vehicle credit and the new advanced lean burn technology motor vehicle credit (¶315) is limited by the combined sum total of the number of units sold by the manufacturer. The credit amounts will be phased out when a manufacturer of these vehicles certifies that it has sold a combined total of 60,000 of these vehicles after December 31, 2005, for use in the United States. For these purposes, controlled groups of corporations are considered to be a single entity and related foreign corporations are included in the single entity (Code Sec. 30B(f)(4), as added by the Energy Act).

For vehicles purchased in the calendar quarter that includes the date of the sale of the 60,000th unit and the next calendar quarter, taxpayers will be allowed to continue to claim the full allowable credit amount. The credit amount will be limited to 50 percent of the allowable credit for vehicles purchased in the next two calendar quarters and 25 percent of the allowable credit amount for vehicles purchased in the next two calendar quarters. The credit will be disallowed thereafter (Code Sec. 30B(f)(1), (2), (3), as added by the Energy Act).

> **Example:** A manufacturer announces in February of 2007 that it has sold a combined sum of qualified hybrid and advanced lean burn technology motor vehicles totaling 60,000 units. Taxpayers may continue to claim the full amount of either of these credits for vehicles purchased from the manufacturer before July 1, 2007. Taxpayers that make purchases of qualified vehicles on or after July 1, 2007, but before January 1, 2008, are entitled to claim 50 percent of the otherwise allowable credit amount. Taxpayers that make purchases of qualified vehicles on or after January 1, 2008, but before July 1, 2008, are entitled to claim 25 percent of the otherwise allowable credit. For vehicles purchased on or after July 1, 2008, no credit amount will be allowed (Joint Committee on Taxation, Description and Technical Explanation of the Energy Tax Incentives Act of 2005 (JCX-60-05)).

Comment: The quantity limitation disfavors automobile manufacturers that already have an established market for their qualified hybrid motor vehicles, some of which could reach the 60,000 unit mark early in the credit's first year. However, the limitation may work to encourage those manufacturers that have not yet developed automobiles using hybrid or advanced lean burn technologies to bring these products to market faster.

Termination. The new qualified hybrid motor vehicle credit for passenger automobiles and light trucks of not more than 8,500 pounds is set to terminate for vehicles purchased after December 31, 2010 (Code Sec. 30B(j)(2), as added by the Energy Act).

The new qualified hybrid motor vehicle credit for any other vehicle that does not qualify as a passenger automobile or light truck of not more than 8,500 pounds is set to terminate for vehicles purchased after December 31, 2009 (Code Sec. 30B(j)(3), as added by the Energy Act).

▶ **Effective date.** The provision is effective for vehicles placed in service after December 31, 2005, in tax years ending after such date (Act Sec. 1341(c) of the Energy Tax Incentives Act of 2005).

Law source: Law at ¶5030. Committee Report at ¶10,260.

— Act Sec. 1341(a) of the Energy Tax Incentives Act of 2005, adding Code Sec. 30B;

— Act Sec. 1341(b), amending Code Secs. 38(b), 55(c)(?), 1016(a), and 6501(m);

— Act Sec. 1341(c), providing the effective date.

Reporter references: For further information, consult the following CCH reporters.

— Standard Federal Tax Reporter, 2005FED ¶4251.021 and ¶29,412.023

— Federal Tax Service, FTS § A:19.20

¶325 New Qualified Alternative Fuel Motor Vehicle Credit

New qualified alternative fuel motor vehicle credit.—The fourth and final component of the alternative motor vehicle credit is the new qualified alternative fuel motor vehicle credit (Code Sec. 30B(e), as added by the Energy Tax Incentives Act of 2005).

Qualifying alternative fuel motor vehicles. To be eligible as a qualified alternative motor vehicle, the motor vehicle must meet several criteria including the three requirements common to all the credit components of the alternative motor vehicle credit (see ¶ 305, *Qualifying vehicles*). These requirements are:

(1) the original use of the vehicle must commence with the taxpayer (Code Sec. 30B(e)(4)(A)(ii), as added by the Energy Act),

(2) the vehicle must be acquired for the use or lease of the taxpayer and not for resale (Code Sec. 30B(e)(4)(A)(iii), as added by the Energy Act), and

(3) the vehicle must be made by a manufacturer (Code Sec. 30B(e)(4)(A)(iv), as added by the Energy Act).

The only other requirement is that the vehicle is only capable of operating using an alternative fuel (Code Sec. 30B(e)(4)(A)(i), as added by the Energy Act).

"Alternative fuels" are compressed natural gas, liquefied natural gas, liquefied petroleum gas, hydrogen, and any liquid at least 85 percent of the volume of which consists of methanol (Code Sec. 30B(e)(4)(B), as added by the Energy Act).

> **Comment:** This definition of alternative fuels does not include ethanol or other alcohols as does the definition of clean-fuel (see Code Sec. 179A(e)(1)).

Credit amount. The amount of credit attributable to the placing in service of a qualified alternative fuel motor vehicle is equal to the applicable percentage times the incremental cost of the vehicle (Code Sec. 30B(e)(1), as added by the Energy Act). The applicable percentage is:

- 50 percent, plus
- 30 percent, if the vehicle
  — has received a certificate of conformity under the Clean Air Act and meets or exceeds the most stringent standard available for certification under the Clean Air Act for that make and model year vehicle (other than a zero emission standard), or
  — has received an order certifying the vehicle as meeting the same requirements as vehicle which may be sold or leased in California and meets or exceeds the most stringent standard available for certification under the state laws of California for that make or model year vehicle (other than a zero emission standard).

  For a qualified alternative fuel motor vehicle with a gross vehicle weight rating of more than 14,000 pounds, the most stringent standard available shall be such standard available for certification on August 8, 2005 (Code Sec. 30B(e)(2), as added by the Energy Act).

"Incremental cost" for any new qualified alternative fuel motor vehicle is equal to the excess of the manufacturer's suggested retail price (MSRP) for the vehicle over the MSRP for a gasoline or diesel fuel motor vehicle of the same model, to the extent that amount does not exceed:

- $5,000, if the vehicle has a gross vehicle weight rating of not more than 8,500 pounds,
- $10,000, if the vehicle has a gross vehicle weight rating of more than 8,500 pounds but not more than 14,000 pounds,
- $25,000, if the vehicle has a gross vehicle weight rating of more than 14,000 pounds but not more than 26,000 pounds, and
- $40,000, if the vehicle has a gross vehicle weight rating of more than 26,000 pounds (Code Sec. 30B(e)(3), as added by the Energy Act).

Mixed-fuel vehicles credit. The new qualified alternative fuels motor vehicle credit may be claimed in a reduced amount for vehicles that use a mixture of alternative fuel and petroleum-based fuels (Code Sec. 30B(e)(5), as added by the Energy Act).

Qualifying mixed-fuel vehicle. A qualifying mixed-fuel vehicle is:

- a vehicle whose gross vehicle weight rating is more than 14,000 pounds,
- a vehicle that is certified by the manufacturer as being able to perform efficiently in normal operation on a combination of an alternative fuel and a petroleum-based fuel
- a vehicle that either:
  — has received a certificate of conformity under the Clean Air Act, or

— has received an order certifying the vehicle as meeting the same requirements as vehicles which may be sold or leased in California and meets or exceeds the low emission vehicle standard for that make and model year vehicle, and

- a vehicle that meets the three requirements common to all the credit components of the alternative motor vehicle credit (see ¶305, *Qualifying vehicles*). These requirements are:

    (1) the original use of the vehicle must commence with the taxpayer

    (2) the vehicle must be acquired for the use or lease of the taxpayer and not for resale, and

    (3) the vehicle must be made by a manufacturer (Code Sec. 30B(e)(5)(B), as added by the Energy Act).

Credit amount. The credit amount for mixed-fuel vehicles is expressed as a percentage of the new qualified alternative fuel motor vehicle credit. If a mixed fuel vehicle uses a 75/25-percent mixture (at least 75-percent alternative fuel and at most 25-percent petroleum based fuel), it is eligible for 70 percent of the credit. If it uses a 90/10-percent mixture (at least 90-percent alternative fuel and at most 10-percent petroleum-based fuel), it is eligible for 90 percent of the qualified alternative fuels motor vehicle credit (Code Sec. 30B(e)(5)(A), as added by the Energy Act).

Other requirements. The new qualified alternative fuel motor vehicle credit is also subject to the credit amount limitations and the other definitions and special rules discussed at ¶305.

Termination. The new qualified alternative fuel motor vehicle credit is set to terminate for vehicles purchased after December 31, 2010 (Code Sec. 30B(j)(4), as added by the Energy Act).

▶ **Effective date.** The provision is effective for vehicles placed in service after December 31, 2005, in tax years ending after such date (Act Sec. 1341(c) of the Energy Tax Incentives Act of 2005).

Law source: Law at ¶5030. Committee Report at ¶10,260.

— Act Sec. 1341(a) of the Energy Tax Incentives Act of 2005, adding Code Sec. 30B;

— Act Sec. 1341(b), amending Code Secs. 38(b), 55(c)(2), 1016(a), and 6501(m);

— Act Sec. 1341(c), providing the effective date.

Reporter references: For further information, consult the following CCH reporters.

— Standard Federal Tax Reporter, 2005FED ¶4251.021 and ¶29,412.023

— Federal Tax Service, FTS § A:19.20

¶330 Termination of Deduction for Clean-Fuel Vehicles

BACKGROUND

Taxpayers are allowed a deduction for the cost of any qualified clean-fuel vehicle property placed in service during the tax year (Code Sec. 179A). A qualified clean-fuel vehicle is any motor vehicle that may be propelled by a clean-burning fuel, such as natural gas, liquefied natural gas, liquefied petroleum gas, hydrogen, electricity, or

BACKGROUND

any other fuel at least 85 percent of which is methanol, ethanol, or any other alcohol or ether. An electric vehicle that qualifies for the 10-percent credit for qualified electric vehicles under Code Sec. 30 will not be treated as a qualified clean-fuel vehicle for this purpose. The deduction may only be claimed for qualified clean-fuel property that is acquired for original use by the taxpayer and not acquired for resale.

> **Comment:** Gasoline-hybrid vehicles may qualify for the deduction, even if they are not used for business purposes.

The maximum amount of deduction allowed for any vehicle is limited to $50,000 for a truck or van with a gross vehicle weight of more than 26,000 pounds or a bus with a seating capacity of 20 or more adults (Code Sec. 179A(b)). The deduction is limited to $5,000 for a truck or van with gross vehicle weight of more than 10,000 pounds, but not more than 26,000 pounds. The deduction is limited to $2,000 for all other qualified vehicles.

The maximum amount of the deduction was scheduled to be phased out. Prior to the Working Families Tax Relief Act of 2004 (P.L. 108-311), the maximum amount of deduction that could have been claimed was reduced by 25 percent for property placed in service in 2004, 50 percent for property placed in service in 2005, and 75 percent for property placed in service in 2006. No deduction was available for vehicles placed in service after 2006 (Code Sec. 179A(f)). The Working Families Tax Act eliminated the phaseout for 2004 and 2005.

NEW LAW EXPLAINED

Early termination of clean-fuel deduction.—The phaseout of the deduction for qualified clean-fuel vehicles has been accelerated one year. No deduction is available to taxpayers for vehicles placed in service after December 31, 2005 (Code Sec. 179A(f), as amended by the Energy Tax Incentives Act of 2005).

> **Planning Note:** The deduction is being eliminated due to the addition of a new credit for alternative motor vehicles (see ¶305, ¶310, ¶315, ¶320 and ¶325).

Practical Analysis: Vincent O'Brien, President of Vincent J. O'Brien, CPA, PC, Lynbrook, New York, observes that, in the past, it was easy for practitioners to overlook the tax incentives related to hybrid automobiles (generally a vehicle that uses both gas and electric motors), since the use of such vehicles was not widespread.

However, hybrids are becoming more popular. Practitioners need to be aware of the special tax incentives available for such vehicles, and they should ask clients about whether they have purchased a hybrid vehicle.

The clean-fuel vehicle deduction, which was available in 2004 and earlier years, remains available for 2005. For individuals, the deduction is taken above the line on page 1 of Form 1040 and is limited to $2,000. Federal income tax savings will vary from $500 (for individuals with a marginal federal income tax rate of 25

¶330

Explanation   113

NEW LAW EXPLAINED

> percent) to $700 (for a marginal rate of 35 percent). (For simplicity, this ignores the effects of the reduction of adjusted gross income on other deductions.)
>
> The deduction is available only for vehicles that are certified by the IRS (such as the Ford Escape Hybrid—model year 2005, or the Toyota Prius—model years 2001 through 2005). Eligible taxpayers claim the deduction on Form 1040 by writing "Clean-Fuel" next to the subtotal line of the adjusted gross income section of the form, which is line 35 on the 2004 version. The clean-fuel deduction is a one-time deduction that must be taken in the year the vehicle is originally put into use. It is available only to the original owner of the vehicle.
>
> The clean-fuel vehicle deduction was scheduled to decrease to $500 in 2006 and was scheduled to expire after 2006. The new law accelerates the expiration, so that it will now expire after 2005, but it will be replaced with the new alternative technology vehicle credit.
>
> The new credit will vary, based on the specific fuel economy of the vehicle purchased. The minimum credit should be $650, while the maximum credit should be $3,400. Therefore, comparing the tax savings available under the clean-fuel vehicle deduction in 2005 to the savings afforded by the new credit in 2006 and later years, individuals should receive at least as much tax benefit and possibly a substantially higher benefit, if they purchase a vehicle that has a very high fuel economy rating.

▶ **Effective date.** No specific effective date is provided by the Act. The provision is, therefore, considered effective on August 8, 2005.

Law source: Law at ¶5180. Committee Report at ¶10,260.

— Act Sec. 1348 of the Energy Tax Incentives Act of 2005, amending Code Sec. 179A(f).

Reporter references: For further information, consult the following CCH reporters.

— Standard Federal Tax Reporter, 2005FED ¶12,133.025
— Federal Tax Service, FTS § A:10.54
— Federal Tax Guide, 2005FTG ¶9065

¶335 Limousines and the "Gas Guzzler" Tax

BACKGROUND

A "gas guzzler" tax is imposed on the sale by the manufacturer or importer of any automobile that does not meet statutory standards for fuel economy. The tax begins at $1,000 for automobile models that do not meet a 22.5-miles-per-gallon standard and increases to $7,700 for models with a fuel economy rating of less than 12.5 miles per gallon (Code Sec. 4064(a)). For purposes of the tax, an "automobile" is any four-wheeled vehicle propelled by fuel, which is manufactured primarily for use on public streets, roads, and highways, and rated at 6,000 pounds unloaded gross vehicle weight or less. A limousine is considered an "automobile" subject to the tax, regardless of its weight (Code Sec. 4064(b)(1)(A)).

¶335

NEW LAW EXPLAINED

Gas guzzler tax repealed for limousines.—The gas guzzler tax, as it applies to limousines rated at greater than 6,000 pounds unloaded gross vehicle weight, is repealed. The gas guzzler tax's definition of "automobile" no longer includes a limousine (Code Sec. 4064(b)(1)(A), as amended by the SAFE Transportation Equity Act of 2005).

▶ **Effective date.** The amendment takes effect on October 1, 2005 (Act Sec. 11111(b) of the SAFE Transportation Equity Act of 2005).

Law source: Law at ¶5275. Committee Report at ¶15,020.

— Act Sec. 11111(a) of the SAFE Transportation Equity Act of 2005, amending Code Sec. 4064(b)(1)(A);

— Act. Sec. 11111(b), providing the effective date.

Reporter references: For further information, consult the following CCH reporters.

— Federal Tax Service, FTS § E:2.171[10]

— Federal Tax Guide, 2005FTG ¶21,130

— Excise Tax Reporter, ETR ¶7615.01 and ¶7615.03

¶340 Excise Tax on Heavy Trucks and Trailers Sold At Retail

BACKGROUND

A 12-percent tax is imposed on the sale price of the first retail sale of (1) truck bodies and chassis suitable for use with a vehicle having a gross weight of over 33,000 pounds; (2) truck trailer and semitrailer bodies and chassis suitable for use with a vehicle having a gross vehicle weight of over 26,000 pounds; and (3) tractors of the kind chiefly used for highway transportation with a trailer or semitrailer (Code Sec. 4051(a)). In general, tractors and truck chassis completed as tractors are subject to the excise tax regardless of their gross vehicle weight (Temporary Reg. § 145.4051-1(a)(2)).

Temporary IRS regulations provide that "tractor" means a highway vehicle which is primarily designed to tow a vehicle such as a trailer or semitrailer, but which does not carry cargo on the same chassis as the engine. The regulations presume that a vehicle equipped with air brakes and/or towing package is primarily designed as a tractor (Temporary Reg. § 145.4051-1(e)(1)(i)).

In *Freightliner of Grand Rapids, Inc.*, (DC Mich., 2005-1 USTC ¶70,234), a truck dealer was held liable for the retail tax on heavy trucks and trailers on a set of chassis cabs that were converted into custom RV tow vehicles. They were characterized as tractors because they were designed primarily to tow trailers rather than to transport a load on the same chassis as the engine. Under the holding of this case, these types of vehicles are subject to tax regardless of their gross vehicle weight.

NEW LAW EXPLAINED

Exclusion for Tractors Weighing 19,500 Pounds or Less.—If each of two weight restrictions is met, the SAFE Transportation Equity Act of 2005 provides an exemption from the excise tax for highway tractors used in combination with a trailer or semitrailer. To qualify for this exemption, the tractor must have a gross vehicle weight of 19,500 pounds or less, *and*, when combined with a trailer or semitrailer, must have a combined weight of 33,000 pounds or less.

> **Caution Note:** The Conference Committee Report for the Highway Act (H.R. Conf. Rep. No. 109-203) warns that no inference is intended from this provision regarding the proper classification of vehicles as tractors or trucks.

▶ **Effective date.** The exclusion is effective for sales after September 30, 2005.

Law source: Law at ¶5270. Committee Report at ¶15,030.

— Act Sec. 11112(a) of the SAFE Transportation Equity Act of 2005, amending Code Sec. 4051(a);

— Act Sec. 11112(b), providing the effective date.

Reporter references: For further information, consult the following CCH reporters.

— Federal Tax Guide, 2005FTG ¶21,110

— Excise Tax Reporter, ETR ¶6325.01 and ¶6325.04

¶345 Tire Excise Tax Modification

BACKGROUND

The American Jobs Creation Act of 2004 (P.L. 108-357) replaced the excise tax on tires based on tire weight with tax rates based on the load capacity of a tire, and also added definitions of "taxable tires," "biasply tires" and "super single tires." The tax is imposed on taxable tires sold by a manufacturer, producer, or importer at the rate of 9.45 cents (4.725 cents for biasply or super single tires) for every 10 pounds of tire load capacity in excess of 3,500 pounds (Code Sec. 4071(a)). A taxable tire means any tire of the type used on highway vehicles if wholly or partly made of rubber and marked for highway use pursuant to federal regulations (Code Sec. 4072(a)). A biasply tire is a pneumatic tire on which the ply cords that extend to the beads are laid at alternate angles substantially less than 90 degrees to the centerline of the tread (Code Sec. 4072(d)). A super single tire is a single tire greater than 13 inches in cross section width designed to replace two tires in a dual fitment (Code Sec. 4072(e)).

> **Comment:** The administration of the excise tax on tires was simplified when the tax was based on the load capacity of a tire instead of the tire weight. Sample batches of tires no longer need to be weighed by both the tire manufacturers and the IRS for purposes of determining the applicable tax rates. Instead, the tax will be based on the tire load capacity stamped on the side of highway tires as required by the Department of Transportation.

NEW LAW EXPLAINED

Definition of super single tire amended.—The Energy Tax Incentives Act of 2005 clarifies that super single tires, as defined under Code Sec. 4072(e), do not include any tire designed for steering. Steering axles are not equipped with dual fitment and are, therefore, any tire attached to a steering axle cannot be "designed to replace two tires in a dual fitment." Steering tires are "taxable tires" if they are used on highway vehicles, are wholly or partly made of rubber and marked for highway use pursuant to federal regulations (Code Sec. 4072(a)). However, since steering tires cannot be classified as super single tires or biasply tires, they do not qualify for the special rate (4.725 cents); instead, the general rate of 9.45 cents for every 10 pounds of tire load capacity in excess of 3,500 pounds shall apply.

▶ **Effective date.** The amendment applies to sales in calendar years beginning on or after January 1, 2005 (Act Sec. 1364(b) of the Energy Tax Incentives Act of 2005; Act Sec. 869(e)[(f)] of the American Jobs Creation Act of 2004 (P.L. 108-357)).

Law source: Law at ¶5285. Committee Report at ¶10,380.

— Act Sec. 1364(a) of the Energy Tax Incentives Act of 2005, amending Code Sec. 4072(e);

— Act Sec. 1364(b), providing the effective date.

Reporter references: For further information, consult the following CCH reporters.

— Federal Tax Guide, 2005FTG ¶21,135

Electricity

PRODUCTION CREDIT

¶405 Qualified energy resources
¶410 Qualified facilities used for production
¶415 Computation of renewable electricity production tax credit
¶420 Renewable electricity production credit for agricultural cooperatives

TRANSMISSION PROPERTY

¶425 Depreciation of electric transmission property
¶430 Five-year carryback for public utility NOLs to promote electrical transmission and pollution control investments
¶435 Sales of dispositions to implement FERC restructuring policy

NUCLEAR POWER

¶440 Credit for production from advanced nuclear power facilities
¶445 Modification to special rules for nuclear decommissioning costs
¶450 Treatment of certain income of electric cooperatives

ENERGY BONDS

¶455 Tax credit bonds to subsidize non-profits' production of renewable energy electricity

PRODUCTION CREDIT

¶405 Qualified Energy Resources

BACKGROUND

A nonrefundable tax credit is available for the domestic production of electricity from certain "qualified energy resources" (QERs) (Code Sec. 45(a)). The eight types of QERs are wind, closed-loop biomass, open-loop biomass, geothermal energy, solar

BACKGROUND

energy, small irrigation power, municipal solid waste, and refined coal. The Tax Code provides the following definitions for six QERs:

(1) *Closed-loop biomass.* The term "closed-loop biomass" means any organic material from a plant which is planted exclusively for purposes of being used at a qualified facility to produce electricity.

(2) *Open-loop biomass.* The term "open-loop biomass" means any agricultural livestock (cow, swine, poultry, and sheep) manure and litter including wood shavings, straw, rice hulls, and other bedding material for the disposition of manure. It also means any solid, nonhazardous, cellulosic (woody portion of a plant) waste material derived from: (a) certain forest-related resources (e.g., mill and harvesting residues, precommercial thinnings, slash, and brush); (b) certain solid wood waste materials (e.g., waste pallets, crates, dunnage, manufacturing and construction wood wastes), and landscape or right-of-way tree trimmings; or (c) agriculture sources, including orchard tree crops, vineyard, grain, legumes, sugar, and other crop by-products or residues that are segregated from other waste materials.

(3) *Geothermal energy.* The term "geothermal energy" means energy derived from a geothermal deposit (a geothermal reservoir consisting of natural heat that is stored in rocks or in an aqueous liquid or vapor).

(4) *Small irrigation power.* The term "small irrigation power" means power generated without any dam or impoundment of water through an irrigation system canal or ditch. The nameplate or installed capacity rating cannot be less than 150 kilowatts, but must be less than five megawatts.

(5) *Municipal solid waste.* The term "municipal solid waste" includes any garbage, refuse, sludge from a waste treatment plant, water supply treatment plant, or air pollution control facility. Also included are other discarded material, including solid, liquid, semisolid, or contained gaseous material resulting from industrial, commercial, mining, and agricultural operations, and from community activities (Section 2(27) of the Solid Waste Disposal Act (42 U.S.C. 6903)). The term does *not* include solid or dissolved material in domestic sewage, or solid or dissolved materials in irrigation return flows or industrial discharges that are subject to special permits, or certain materials defined by the Atomic Energy Act of 1954.

(6) *Refined coal.* The term "refined coal" means a fuel that is: (a) a liquid, gaseous, or solid synthetic fuel produced from coal, including lignite, or high carbon fly ash (e.g., fuel used as feedstock); (b) sold by the taxpayer with the reasonable expectation that it will be used to produce steam; (c) certified by the taxpayer as resulting in a "qualified emission reduction" when the fuel is used to produce steam; and (d) produced in a manner that results in at least a 50-percent increase in the market value of the refined coal, when compared to the value of the feedstock coal (not including any increase that results from the addition of any materials during the production process).

The electricity from the QER must be produced at a qualified facility. See ¶410 for information concerning qualified facilities.

¶405

BACKGROUND

For 2005, the renewable electricity production credit is 1.9 cents multiplied by the kilowatt hours of electricity sold by the taxpayer during the tax year and produced from qualified energy resources at a qualified facility. However, the credit rate is reduced by one-half to 0.95 cents per kilowatt hour for electricity produced by certain qualified facilities. Specific rules apply for the computation of the credit for refined coal. See ¶415 for information concerning the computation of the renewable electricity production credit. Only sales of electricity that is produced in the United States or a U.S. possession are taken into account. When a facility has more than one owner, production must be allocated in proportion to the respective ownership interest in gross sales from the facility.

NEW LAW EXPLAINED

Expansion in types of "qualified energy resources."— Under the new legislation, the types of "qualified energy resources" (QERs) producing electricity that are eligible for the renewable electricity production credit have been expanded from eight to ten resources by the addition of "qualified hydropower production" and "Indian coal" (Code Sec. 45(c)(1), as amended by the Energy Tax Incentives Act of 2005).

Qualified hydropower production. The term "qualified hydropower production" means the incremental hydropower production from a hydroelectric or nonhydroelectric dam that is attributable to efficiency improvements or additions of capacity placed in service after August 8, 2005 (Code Sec. 45(c)(8), as added by the Energy Act). The incremental production is determined by using the same water flow information used to establish the facility's historic average annual hydropower production baseline certified by the Federal Energy Regulatory Commission. Operational changes not related to efficiency improvements or additions of capacity are disregarded.

"Hydroelectric dam" means a hydroelectric dam that was placed in service on or before August 8, 2005. "Nonhyrdoelectric dam" means a facility that on August 8, 2005, did not produce hydroelectric power, but turbines and other electricity generating equipment are added after August 8, 2005, but before January 1, 2008, provided there is no enlargement of the structure, construction or enlargement of the bypass channel, or impoundment or withholding of any additional water from the natural stream channel (Code Sec. 45(c)(8)(C)(iii) and 45(d)(9)(A) and (B), as added by the Energy Act).

Indian coal. The term "Indian coal" means coal produced from coal reserves that were owned by an Indian tribe or by the United States for the benefit of an Indian tribe on June 14, 2005 (Code Sec. 45(c)(9), as added by the Energy Act). "Indian tribe" is defined as any Indian tribe, band, nation, or other organized group or community which is recognized as eligible for the special programs and services provided by the United States to Indians because of their status as Indians (Code Sec. 7871(c)(3)(E)(ii)).

Comment: The Senate version of the Energy Act contained two additional QERs, fuel cell energy and wave, current, tidal and ocean thermal energy, that were removed from the final version of the Energy Act at conference (Joint Committee

NEW LAW EXPLAINED

on Taxation, Description and Technical Explanation of the Energy Tax Incentives Act of 2005 (JCX-60-05)).

Clarification of certain open-loop biomass. In addition to any solid, nonhazardous, cellulosic waste material being included as open-loop biomass, any nonhazardous lignin waste material is added to the material segregated and derived from forest-related and agricultural resources (Code Sec. 45(c)(3)(A)(ii), as amended by the Energy Act).

State Tax Consequences: Many states provide energy incentives through personal and corporate income tax credits. See ¶195 for a state-by-state summary of available credits.

▶ **Effective date.** These provisions are effective on August 8, 2005 (Act Sec. 1301(g)(1) of the Energy Tax Incentives Act of 2005). The clarification regarding the definition of open-loop biomass is effective for electricity produced and sold after October 22, 2004, in tax years ending after that date (Act Sec. 1301(g)(2) of the Energy Act; Act Sec. 710 of the American Jobs Creation Act of 2005 (P.L. 108-357)).

Law source: Law at ¶5065 and ¶7005. Committee Report at ¶10,010.

— Act Sec. 1301(c) of the Energy Tax Incentives Act of 2005, amending Code Sec. 45(c) by adding new Code Sec. 45(c)(1)(H) and Code Sec. 45(c)(8);

— Act Sec. 1301(d), adding new Code Sec. 45(c)(9);

— Act Sec. 1301(f), amending Code Sec. 45(c)(3)(A)(ii);

— Act Sec. 1301(g), providing the effective date.

Reporter references: For further information, consult the following CCH reporters.

— Standard Federal Tax Reporter, 2005FED ¶4415.01

— Federal Tax Service, FTS § G:24.240

— Federal Tax Guide, 2005FTG ¶2575

¶410 Qualified Facilities Used for Production

BACKGROUND

In order to be eligible for the renewable electricity production credit, the electricity must be produced from a qualified energy resource (QER) and it must be produced at a "qualified facility" (QF). The eight types of QFs are:

(1) wind energy facilities placed in service after 1993 and before January 1, 2006;

(2) closed-loop biomass (organic material planted exclusively to produce electricity) facilities placed in service after 1992 and before January 1, 2006, or facilities placed in service and modified before January 1, 2006, to use closed-loop biomass to co-fire with coal, with other biomass, or with coal and other biomass;

(3) open-loop biomass (agricultural livestock waste nutrients) facilities placed in service after October 22, 2004 and before January 1, 2006, other open-loop biomass (certain wood waste or waste from forest-related or agricultural re-

BACKGROUND

sources) facilities placed in service before January 1, 2006, and certain poultry waste facilities placed in service before January 1, 2004;

(4) geothermal (natural heat stored in rocks, aqueous liquid or vapor) or solar facilities placed in service after October 22, 2004, and before January 1, 2006;

(5) small irrigation power (generation of electricity without a dam or impoundment of water through an irrigation system canal or ditch) facilities placed in service after October 22, 2004, and before January 1, 2006;

(6) landfill gas (methane gas derived from the biodegradation of municipal solid waste) facilities placed in service after October 22, 2004, and before January 1, 2006;

(7) trash combustion (burning of municipal solid waste) facilities placed in service after October 22, 2004, and before January 1, 2006; and

(8) refined coal (liquid, gaseous, or solid synthetic fuel produced from coal, including lignite, or high carbon fly ash) production facilities placed in service after October 22, 2004, and before January 1, 2009.

Electricity produced at wind energy, closed-loop biomass and refined coal QFs is only eligible for the tax credit during the 10-year period beginning on the date the facility was originally placed in service (Code Sec. 45(a)(2)(A)(ii)). However, for a modified closed-loop biomass QF, the 10-year period will begin no earlier than October 22, 2004 (Code Sec. 45(d)(2)(B)(i)). The remaining QFs will only be eligible for the tax credit during the five-year period beginning on the date the facility was originally placed in service (Code Sec. 45(b)(4)(B)(i)). The QF must be owned by the taxpayer and the electricity must be sold to an unrelated person during the tax year in order for the taxpayer to be eligible for the tax credit (Code Sec. 45(a)(2)(B)).

NEW LAW EXPLAINED

New types of qualified facilities.—The new law expands the types of qualified facilities (QFs) that may be used to produce electricity from qualified energy resources (QERs) to include "qualified hydropower production facilities" and "Indian coal production facilities" (Code Sec. 45(d), as amended by the Energy Tax Incentives Act of 2005). This expansion is a necessary corollary to the expansion of the types of resources that qualify as QERs (see ¶405). The new law also expands the placed-in-service dates for all QFs and provides clarification of trash combustion facilities.

Qualified hydropower facilities. When a facility placed in service on or before August 8, 2005, produces incremental hydropower production (hydroelectric dam) attributable to efficiency improvements or additions to capacity, a qualified facility is defined to mean any facility owned by the taxpayer to which efficiency improvements or additions to capacity are placed in service after August 8, 2005, and before January 1, 2008 (Code Sec. 45(d)(9), as added by the Energy Act). When a facility was placed in service before August 8, 2005, but did not produce hydroelectric power (nonhydroelectric dam), a qualified facility is defined to mean any facility to which turbines and other electricity generating equipment is added after August 8, 2005, and before January 1, 2008.

¶410

NEW LAW EXPLAINED

Indian coal production facilities. When a facility produces Indian coal, a qualified facility is defined to mean any facility owned by a taxpayer, and that is originally placed in service before January 1, 2009 (Code Sec. 45(d)(10), as added by the Energy Act).

Expansion of placed in service dates for qualified facilities. The new law expands the period for which certain QFs are placed in service as follows:

(1) wind energy facilities placed in service after 1993 and before January 1, 2008;

(2) closed-loop biomass facilities placed in service after 1992 and before January 1, 2008, or facilities placed in service and modified before January 1, 2008, to use closed-loop biomass to co-fire with coal, with other biomass, or with both;

(3) open-loop biomass facilities using agricultural livestock waste nutrients placed in service after October 22, 2004, and before January 1, 2008, and other open-loop biomass facilities using certain wood waste or waste from forest-related or agricultural resources placed in service before January 1, 2008;

(4) geothermal facilities placed in service after October 22, 2004, and before January 1, 2008;

(5) small irrigation power facilities placed in service after October 22, 2004, and before January 1, 2008;

(6) landfill gas facilities placed in service after October 22, 2004, and before January 1, 2008; and

(7) trash combustion facilities placed in service after October 22, 2004, and before January 1, 2008 (Code Sec. 45(d), as amended by the Energy Tax Incentives Act of 2005).

Caution: Certain poultry waste facilities, as defined by Code Sec. 45(c)(3)(C) as of October 22, 2004, were subject to a grandfather provision under the American Jobs Creation Act of 2004 (P.L. 108-357). Those facilities were not subject to changes made by the 2004 Jobs Act provided the facilities were placed in service before January 1, 2004. Under the new law, facilities that were placed in service before January 1, 2005, continue to receive grandfathered status. Grandfathered poultry waste facilities are not subject to the tax credit reduction for electricity produced at open-loop biomass facilities (Act Sec. 710(g)(4) of the 2004 Jobs Act, as amended by the Energy Act).

Planning Note: The placed in service dates for solar facilities (after October 22, 2004, and before January 1, 2006) and refined coal facilities (after October 22, 2004, and before January 1, 2009) remain untouched by the new law.

Clarification of trash combustion facilities. Trash combustion facilities include existing facilities that add new units placed in service on or before October 22, 2004, that increase electricity production at the facility. The electricity produced at the new unit qualifies for the renewable electricity production tax credit to the extent that the amount of electricity produced at the facility is increased at the entire facility due to the new unit (Code Sec. 45(d)(7), as amended by the Energy Act).

Comment: The Joint Committee on Taxation, Description and Technical Explanation of the Energy Tax Incentives Act of 2005 (JCX-60-05) provides further

NEW LAW EXPLAINED

information regarding the new unit. Generally, the new unit includes new burners, boilers and turbines. The new unit and other existing units at the facility may share certain common equipment, such as trash handling equipment.

Clarification of coordination of credits. Facilities that receive a credit under Code Sec. 29 for production of electricity from gas derived from the biodegradation of municipal solid waste or refined coal are not qualified facilities for purposes of the renewable electricity production credit (Code Sec. 45(e)(9), as amended by the Energy Act).

▶ **Effective date.** These provisions are effective on August 8, 2005 (Act Sec. 1301(g)(1) of the Energy Tax Incentives Act of 2005). The provisions regarding the definition of trash combustion facilities and coordination of credits apply to electricity produced and sold after October 22, 2004, in tax years ending after that date (Act Sec. 1301(g)(2) of the Energy Act; Act Sec. 710 of the American Jobs Creation Act of 2005 (P.L. 108-357)).

Law source: Law at ¶5065. Committee Report at ¶10,010.

— Act Sec. 1301(a), (c), (d) and (e), amending Code Sec. 45(d);

— Act Sec. 1301(f), amending Code Sec. 45(e)(9) and (e)(8)(C), and Act Sec. 710(g) of the American Jobs Creation Act of 2004;

— Act Sec. 1301(g), providing the effective date.

Reporter references: For further information, consult the following CCH reporters.

— Standard Federal Tax Reporter, 2005FED ¶4415.01

— Federal Tax Service, FTS § G:24.240

— Federal Tax Guide, 2005FTG ¶2575

¶415 Computation of Renewable Electricity Production Tax Credit

BACKGROUND

For 2005, the renewable electricity production tax credit is 1.9 cents (as adjusted for inflation) per kilowatt hour of electricity produced from a qualified energy resource at a wind energy, closed-loop biomass, geothermal energy, or solar energy qualified facility. The renewable electricity production credit is reduced by one-half to 0.95 cents per kilowatt hour for electricity produced from a qualified resource at an open-loop biomass, small irrigation power, landfill gas, or trash combustion facility.

The credit may be claimed during the 10-year period beginning on the date a wind energy, closed-loop biomass, or refined coal facility is placed in service (but no earlier than October 22, 2004, for modified closed-loop biomass facilities) (Code Sec. 45(a)). It may be claimed during the five-year period beginning on the date an open-loop biomass, geothermal energy, solar energy, small irrigation power, landfill gas, and trash combustion facility is placed in service (Code Sec. 45(b)(4)(B)(i)). Under a special rule, a five-year credit period that begins on October 22, 2004, applies to open-loop biomass facilities that use material other than agricultural livestock waste

BACKGROUND

nutrients that were placed in service before October 22, 2004 (Code Sec. 45(b)(4)(B)(ii)). In order to qualify for the credit, the electricity produced must be sold during the tax year by the taxpayer to an unrelated person. The credit is subject to phaseout as the market price of electricity exceeds certain threshold levels (as adjusted for inflation) (Code Sec. 45(b)(1)).

The renewable electricity production credit is reduced by: (1) government grants; (2) tax-exempt bonds; (3) direct or indirect subsidized financing through government programs; or (4) any other credit allowable with respect to the property (e.g., the business energy investment credit). The reduction cannot, however, exceed 50 percent of the otherwise allowable credit (Code Sec. 45(b)(3)).

Special rules apply to modified closed-loop biomass and refined coal production facilities when determining the allowable renewable electricity production credit for electricity produced from these facilities. For modified closed-loop biomass facilities, the allowable credit is computed by multiplying the credit (under Code Sec. 45(a)) by a ratio of the thermal content of the closed-loop biomass used at the modified facility to the thermal content of all fuels used at the modified facility (Code Sec. 45(d)(2)(B)(ii)), but is not reduced by grants, tax-exempt bonds, subsidized financing, or other credits (Code Sec. 45(b)(3)). For refined coal production facilities, the renewable electricity production credit for 2005 is computed at a rate of $5.481 per ton of qualified refined coal that is produced at the facility and sold to an unrelated person during the 10-year period that begins on the date the facility was originally placed in service.

NEW LAW EXPLAINED

Eligibility period for claiming the credit expanded.—The new law provides a time period for which electricity produced by new qualified energy resources (¶405) at a qualified facility (¶410) will be eligible for the renewable electricity production tax credit. It also increases the credit period for electricity produced at certain qualified facilities.

Computation of credit for electricity produced by qualified hydropower production. A qualified hydropower production at a qualified hydropower production facility producing incremental hydropower production will only be eligible for the tax credit during the 10-year period beginning on the date the efficiency improvements or additions to capacity are placed into service (Code Sec. 45(d)(9)(C), as added by the Energy Tax Incentives Act of 2005).

The renewable electricity production tax credit for electricity produced from qualified hydropower production at a qualified hydropower production facility is computed at one-half the credit rate for electricity produced from a qualified energy resource at a wind energy, closed-loop biomass, geothermal energy, or solar energy qualified facility (Code Sec. 45(b)(4)(A), as amended by the Energy Act). For 2005, the credit rate for wind energy, closed-loop biomass, geothermal energy, and solar energy is 1.9 cents (as adjusted for inflation) per kilowatt hour of electricity produced. Thus, the renewable electricity production credit rate for electricity produced by qualified hydropower production is 0.95 cents per kilowatt hour.

¶415

NEW LAW EXPLAINED

Computation of credit for electricity produced by Indian fuel. The electricity produced by Indian coal production at a qualified Indian coal production facility will only be eligible for the tax credit during a seven-year period beginning January 1, 2006 (Code Sec. 45(e)(10)(A), as added by the Energy Act).

For 2006 through 2009, the credit is $1.50 per ton of Indian coal produced at a qualified Indian coal production facility during a seven-year period beginning January 1, 2006 (Code Sec. 45(e)(10)(A) and (B), as added by the Energy Act). For 2010 and after, the credit is $2.00 per ton of Indian coal produced. The credit rates, beginning in 2006, are to be adjusted for inflation. The tax credit for Indian coal is treated as a specified credit for purposes of the general business credit under Code Sec. 38(c)(4)(A) for a period of four years beginning on the later of January 1, 2006 and the date the facility is placed in service (Code Sec. 45(e)(10)(D), as added by the Energy Act).

Increased credit period for electricity produced at certain qualified facilities. The new law increases the credit period for which a renewable electricity production tax credit is allowable for electricity produced at certain qualified facilities from five years to 10 years. Electricity produced at the following qualified facilities that are placed in service after August 8, 2005, are eligible for the tax credit for electricity produced during the 10-year period beginning on that date (Code Sec. 45(b)(4)(B), as amended by the Energy Act):

(1) open-loop biomass facilities,

(2) geothermal energy facilities,

(3) solar energy facilities,

(4) small irrigation power facilities,

(5) landfill gas facilities, and

(6) trash combustion facilities.

> **Caution:** The five-year credit period continues to apply to open-loop biomass, geothermal energy, solar energy, small irrigation power, landfill gas, and trash combustion facilities that were placed in service on or between January 1, 2005, and August 8, 2005.

Clarification of credit period for certain open-loop biomass facilities. The special rule of a five-year credit period beginning on October 22, 2004, that applies to certain open-loop biomass facilities using material other than agricultural livestock waste materials and which were placed in service before October 22, 2004, is now a 10-year period that begins on January 1, 2005, and applies to such facilities that were placed in service before January 1, 2005 (Code Sec. 45(b)(4)(B)(ii), as amended by the Energy Act).

▶ **Effective date.** These provisions are effective on August 8, 2005 (Act Sec. 1301(g)(1) of the Energy Tax Incentives Act of 2005). The clarification regarding the credit period for certain open-loop biomass facilities is effective for electricity produced and sold after October 22, 2004, in tax years ending after such date (Act Sec. 1301(g)(2) of the Energy Act; Act Sec. 710 of the American Jobs Creation Act of 2004 (P.L. 108-357)).

NEW LAW EXPLAINED

Law source: Law at ¶5065. Committee Report at ¶10,010.

— Act Sec. 1301(b) of the Energy Tax Incentives Act of 2005, amending Code Sec. 45(b)(4)(B);

— Act Sec. 1301(c), amending Code Sec. 45(b)(4)(A) and adding Code Sec. 45(d)(9);

— Act Sec. 1301(d), adding Code Sec. 45(e)(10);

— Act Sec. 1301(f), amending Code Sec. 45(b)(4)(B), striking Code Sec. 45(e)(6), and amending Code Sec. 168(e)(3)(B)(vi)(I);

— Act Sec. 1301(g), providing the effective date.

Reporter references: For further information, consult the following CCH reporters.

— Standard Federal Tax Reporter, 2005FED ¶4415.01

— Federal Tax Service, FTS § G:24.240

— Federal Tax Guide, 2005FTG ¶2575

¶420 Renewable Electricity Production Credit for Agricultural Cooperatives

BACKGROUND

Farmers' cooperatives, that is, cooperatives of farmers, fruit growers, and persons engaged in similar pursuits, may qualify for tax-exempt status (Code Sec. 521). In order to qualify, the cooperative must be organized and operated for the purpose of marketing the products of members and returning the net proceeds to the members or purchasing supplies and equipment for the use of members at cost plus expenses (Code Sec. 1382). Qualifying farmers' cooperatives are subject to special rules of taxation such as the allowance of certain deductions from gross income and other deductions permitted to corporations (Code Secs. 1381-1388). Corporations to which these special rules do not apply include organizations exempt from taxation (other than as a cooperative), mutual savings banks, cooperative banks, domestic building and loan associations, insurance companies, or any corporation that furnishes electric energy or telephone service to persons in rural areas.

A farmers' cooperative is allowed a deduction for dividends paid to its members (or patrons) during the year. Generally, patronage dividends may be deducted only to the extent of net income derived from transactions with the cooperative's patrons. To qualify for the deduction, the patronage dividends must be based on the quantity or value of the business that is done with or for the patrons. In addition, the amount paid must be determined by reference to the cooperative's net earnings from the business that the cooperative has done with or for its patrons (Code Sec. 1388(a)). The payment period for patronage dividends begins on the first day of the cooperative's tax year and ends on October 15th of the following year (Code Sec. 1382(d)).

Renewable electricity production credit. A nonrefundable tax credit is available for the domestic production of electricity from qualified energy resources, such as open-loop biomass (Code Sec. 45(c)). Open-loop biomass derives electricity from: (1) agricultural livestock (cow, swine, poultry, and sheep) waste nutrients; or (2) certain wood waste

BACKGROUND

or waste from forest-related or agricultural resources (Code Sec. 45(c)(1)(C)). The electricity produced by qualified energy resources must be produced at a qualified facility (Code Sec. 45(d)).

The credit is permitted only for the sale of electricity produced in the United States or a U.S. possession (Code Sec. 45(e)). When a facility has more than one owner, production must be allocated in proportion to the respective ownership interests in gross sales from the facility. However, there is no provision providing for cooperatives to pass any portion of the credit to its patrons.

For 2005, the renewable electricity production credit is 1.9 cents multiplied by the kilowatt hours of electricity sold by the taxpayer during the tax year. However, the tax credit rate of 1.9 cents per kilowatt hour is reduced by one-half to 0.95 cents per kilowatt hour for electricity produced by certain qualified facilities, such as open-loop biomass facilities.

NEW LAW EXPLAINED

Election to allocate renewable electricity production credit to patrons of agricultural cooperatives.—Eligible agricultural cooperatives that receive a renewable electricity production credit for the sale of electricity produced by a qualified energy resource at a qualified facility may elect to allocate any portion of that credit to its patrons (Code Sec. 45(e)(11), as added by the Energy Incentives Act of 2005). An eligible cooperative is one that is more than 50 percent owned by agricultural producers or entities owned by agricultural producers (Code Sec. 45(e)(11)(D), as added by the Energy Act). The allocation must be based on the amount of business the patrons have done with the cooperative during the tax year.

Form of election. The election must be made on a timely filed return for the tax year the credit is claimed. Once made, the election is irrevocable (Code Sec. 45(e)(11)(A)(ii), as added by the Energy Act). In addition, the election will only take effect if the eligible cooperative designates the apportionment in a written notice mailed to its patrons during the payment period for patronage dividends pursuant to Code Sec. 1382(d).

Treatment of the allocation to the cooperative and its patrons. The eligible cooperative may only claim the portion of the credit that is not otherwise allocated to its patrons (Code Sec. 45(e)(11)(B)(i), as added by the Energy Act). A patron receiving a credit allocation must include the amount in the tax year ending on or after the last day of the cooperative's patronage dividend payment period or, if earlier, on or after the date that the patron receives notice of the allocation (Code Sec. 45(e)(11)(B)(ii), as added by the Energy Act).

If the amount of the credit calculated under Code Sec. 45(a) is less than the amount of the credit shown on the cooperative's return, the cooperative's tax liability is increased by the excess of the reduction in the credit over the amount not apportioned to the patrons (Code Sec. 45(e)(11)(C), as added by the Energy Act). Any increase imposed, however, is not treated as tax imposed for purposes of determining the amount of any other tax credit.

¶420

NEW LAW EXPLAINED

> **Example:** Agripower, Inc. produces electricity at its qualified open-loop biomass facility. For 2006, Agripower claims a renewable electricity production credit, of $3,000, $2,300 of which it allocates to its patrons and $700 of which is retains. However, Agripower should have claimed a credit of $1,000 as determined under Code Sec. 45(a). Thus, under Code Sec. 45(e)(11)(C), the cooperative's tax liability is increased by $1,300 ($2,000 - $700).

Caution Note: The IRS could disallow the remaining $700 credit claimed by the cooperative, thus recovering the entire reduction of $2,000 ($1,300 increase plus $700 disallowed).

Alternative minimum tax. Any increase in tax attributable to the election is not included in computation of regular tax for purposes of the alternative minimum tax (Code Sec. 55(c)(1), as amended by the Energy Act).

▶ **Effective date.** These provisions are effective on August 8, 2005 (Act Sec. 1302(c) of the Energy Act).

Law source: Law at ¶5065 and ¶5130. Committee Report at ¶10,010.

— Act Sec. 1302(a) of the Energy Tax Incentives Act of 2005, adding Code Sec. 45(e)(11);

— Act Sec. 1302(b), amending Code Sec. 55(c)(1);

— Act Sec. 1302(c), providing the effective date.

Reporter references: For further information, consult the following CCH reporters.

— Standard Federal Tax Reporter, 2005FED ¶4415.01, ¶5101.04 and ¶32,328.021

— Federal Tax Service, FTS § G:24.240

— Federal Tax Guide, 2005FTG ¶2575

TRANSMISSION PROPERTY

¶425 Depreciation of Electric Transmission Property

BACKGROUND

Under the Modified Accelerated Cost Recovery System (MACRS), assets used in the transmission and distribution of electricity for sale and related land improvements are assigned a 20-year recovery period (Asset Class 49.14 of Rev. Proc. 87-56). A 30-year recovery period applies for purposes of the MACRS alternative depreciation system (ADS). Initial clearing and grading land improvements specified in Rev. Rul. 72-403 are specifically excluded from Asset Class 49.14. However, such improvements, if placed in service after October 22, 2004, and used in connection with any electric utility transmission and distribution plant are considered MACRS 20-year property with a 25-year ADS period (Code Sec. 168(e)(3)(F) and (g)(3)(B), as amended by the 2004 American Jobs Creation Act (P.L. 108-357)). Previously, such improve-

BACKGROUND

ments were classified as MACRS 7-year property on the basis of their status as Code Sec. 1245(a)(3) real property for which no class life is provided.

NEW LAW EXPLAINED

Electric transmission property treated as MACRS 15-year property.—The new law treats certain electric transmission property originally placed in service after April 11, 2005, as MACRS 15-year property (Code Sec. 168(e)(3)(E)(vii), as added by the Energy Tax Incentives Act of 2005). A 30-year recovery period is assigned for purposes of the MACRS alternative depreciation system (ADS) (Code Sec. 168(g)(3)(B), as amended by the Energy Act). Thus, the regular recovery period for qualifying property is reduced from 20 years to 15 years and the ADS recovery period is unchanged.

The provision applies to any section 1245 property (as defined in Code Sec. 1245(a)(3)) used in the transmission at 69 or more kilovolts of electricity for sale, the original use of which commences with the taxpayer after April 11, 2005 (Code Sec. 168(e)(3)(E)(vii), as added by the Energy Act).

> **Comment:** Code Sec. 1245(a)(3) includes tangible depreciable personal property (other than a building or its structural components) used as an integral part of producing or furnishing electrical energy (i.e., Code Sec. 1245 real property) (Code Sec. 1245(a)(3)(B)(i)). Thus, the provision can apply to depreciable land improvements (other than buildings and structural components) used as an integral part in the transmission at 69 or more kilovolts of electricity for sale. Presumably, however, this provision does not have the effect of reducing the depreciation period of initial grading and clearing land improvements from the 20-year period generally prescribed by Code Sec. 168(e)(3)(F) to 15 years even if such improvements are integral in the transmission of electricity.

> **Comment:** Since alternative minimum tax (AMT) adjustments were previously eliminated for MACRS 15- and 20-year property placed in service after 1998, no AMT adjustment is required on electrical transmission assets which are depreciable over 15 years under the new law (Code Sec. 56(a)(1), as amended by the Taxpayer Relief Act of 1997 (P.L. 105-34)).

The original use of the electrical transmission assets must begin with the taxpayer after April 11, 2005. This means that used property, such as property acquired as part of the purchase of a business, will not qualify (Code Sec. 168(e)(3)(E)(vii), as added by the Energy Act).

> **Comment:** The Energy Tax Policy Bill of 2003, which was reported out of Conference but not enacted into law, contained a similar provision (Bill Section 1323). The Conference Report for that provision included a discussion on original use which is not contained in the Joint Committee on Taxation, Description and Technical Explanation of the Energy Tax Incentives Act of 2005 (JCX-60-05) but which presumably remains equally relevant. Specifically, the 2003 Conference Report indicated that in determining whether the original use requirement is satisfied, the factors used to determine whether property qualified as "new section 38 property" for purposes of the investment tax credit apply. Thus, Reg.

¶425

NEW LAW EXPLAINED

§1.48-2(b) and related investment credit cases and rulings apply in determining whether the original use requirement is satisfied.

According to the 2003 Conference Report, additional capital expenditures incurred to recondition or rebuild acquired or owned property will also satisfy the original use requirement. However, the cost of reconditioned or rebuilt property acquired by a taxpayer does not satisfy the requirement. The following example is based on an example that appears in the 2003 Conference Committee Report.

Example: A taxpayer pays $200,000 for previously used transmission lines. The taxpayer then makes a $50,000 expenditure on the property that must be capitalized. The $50,000 expenditure satisfies the original use requirement and the 15-year recovery period applies whether the expenditure is added to the cost of the original purchase or is treated as a separate asset.

The bonus depreciation regulation under MACRS dealing with original use may also provide some useful insight on the original use requirement. See Temporary Reg. § 1.168(k)-1T(b)(3).

Comment: See ¶430 for a discussion of a new law provision that allows utilities to elect a five-year net operating loss carryback period if an investment is made in certain electric transmission or pollution control equipment.

▶ **Effective date.** The provision applies to property placed in service after April 11, 2005. However, the provision does not apply to any property with respect to which the taxpayer or a related party has entered into a binding contract for the construction thereof on or before April 11, 2005, or, in the case of self-constructed property, has started construction on or before such date (Act Sec. 1308(c) of the Energy Tax Incentives Act of 2005).

Law source: Law at ¶5165. Committee Report at ¶10,070.

— Act Sec. 1308(a) of the Energy Tax Incentives Act of 2005, adding Code Sec. 168(e)(3)(E)(vii);
— Act Sec. 1308(b), amending Code Sec. 168(g)(3)(B);
— Act Sec. 1308(c), providing the effective date.

Reporter references: For further information, consult the following CCH reporters.

— Standard Federal Tax Reporter, 2005FED ¶11,279.023
— Federal Tax Service, FTS § G:16.83[5]
— Federal Tax Guide, 2005FTG ¶9110

¶430 Five-Year Carryback for Public Utility NOLs to Promote Electrical Transmission and Pollution Control Investments

BACKGROUND

A taxpayer has a net operating loss (NOL) if certain deductions exceed gross income in a particular tax year (Code Sec. 172(c)). The taxpayer may be able to carry back or

BACKGROUND

carry over this amount to the extent the loss was incurred in a trade or business, from a casualty loss, or from a loss on the sale of depreciable property or real estate used in a trade or business (Code Sec. 172(b)). The carried over NOL will reduce the taxpayer's tax for the carryover year. The general rule is that an NOL can be carried back to the two tax years immediately preceding the NOL loss year and then carried forward for up to 20 tax years (Code Sec. 172(b)(1)(a)). A taxpayer may waive the carryback period and simply carry forward the NOL (Code Sec. 172(b)(3)).

There are exceptions to the two-year carryback rule. For example, a three-year carryback period is available for taxpayers with NOLs arising from certain casualty and theft losses, and for small business taxpayers and farmers with respect to NOLs attributable to presidentially declared disasters (Code Sec. 172(b)(1)(F)). A five-year period is available for farming losses (whether caused by a disaster or not) (Code Sec. 172(b)(1)(G)). A five-year period is available for NOLs arising in tax years ending in 2001 or 2002 (Code Sec. 172(b)(1)(H)).

NOLs are first applied to the earliest tax year to which the loss may be carried (Code Sec. 172(b)). Certain "specified liability losses" (for example, losses attributable to product liability, environmental remediation, or decommissioning of a nuclear powerplant) are entitled to a 10-year carryback, but are treated separately for ordering purposes. They are used in a carryover year only to the extent the remainder of the carried over NOL has already been used up (Code Sec. 172(f)(5)).

NEW LAW EXPLAINED

Five-year carryback available for 2003, 2004, and 2005 loss years.—The new law allows electric utilities to elect a five-year NOL carryback period for NOLs generated in tax years ending in 2003, 2004, and 2005 in an amount based on the taxpayer's preelection investment in certain electric transmission or pollution control equipment (Code Sec. 172(b)(1), as amended by the Energy Tax Incentives Act of 2005).

A taxpayer can elect the five-year carryback period in any tax year ending after December 31, 2005, and before January 1, 2009. If the five-year period is elected, the carried back NOL amount is limited to 20 percent of the sum of electric transmission property capital expenditures and pollution control facility capital expenditures for the tax year preceding the tax year in which the election is made (Code Sec. 172(b)(1)(I)(i), as added by the Energy Act).

> **Example:** The Public Service Co. spends $10,000,000 in qualifying investments in its 2005 tax year. In the 2006 tax year, Public Service can elect to use the five-year carryback period for up to $2,000,000 of NOLs from loss years ending 2003, 2004, or 2005.

Qualifying investments. An electrical transmission property capital expenditure is any expenditure, chargeable to a capital account, made by the taxpayer which is attributable to electric transmission property used by the taxpayer in the transmission at 69 or more kilovolts of electricity for sale. A pollution control facility capital expenditure is

¶430

NEW LAW EXPLAINED

any expenditure, chargeable to capital account, made by an electric utility company (as defined in the Public Utilities Holding Company Act) which is attributable to a facility which will qualify as a certified pollution control facility under Code Sec. 169(d)(1) (disregarding the requirement that facility be new or in operation before January 1, 1976) (Code Sec. 172(b)(1)(I)(vi), as added by the Energy Act).

> **Comment:** Expenditures that are currently deductible are not counted as qualifying expenditures.

Any expenditures that may be refunded or the purpose of which may be changed at the taxpayer's option so as to cause it to cease to be a qualified expenditure, is not a qualified expenditure (Code Sec. 172(b)(1)(I)(vi), as added by the Energy Act).

> **Comment:** To qualify for the five-year carryback, it is only necessary that the taxpayer make the expenditure, not that it place the equipment or facility in service. However, the taxpayer must be permanently committed to completing the investment in order to qualify for the extended carryback (Joint Committee on Taxation, Description and Technical Explanation of the Energy Tax Incentives Act of 2005 (JCX-60-05)).

Example: Taxpayer makes a cash deposit with respect to a contract to purchase electric transmission property. The contract contains an option under which the taxpayer may change its mind and apply the deposit to other kinds of equipment. The deposit is not a qualifying investment.

Limits on election. The ability to elect the five-year carryback period is limited. First, no more than one election can be made with respect to any NOL in a tax year. Second, an election cannot be made for more than one tax year beginning in the same calendar year. Accordingly, the taxpayer can make only one election in any election year and once an election has been made with respect to a loss year, no subsequent election is available with respect to that loss year. (Code Sec. 172(b)(1)(I)(ii), as added by the Energy Act).

Example: The Public Service Co. has two short tax years beginning in calendar year 2006. Public Service may make an election in only one of those two short tax years that begins in calendar year 2006.

Separately treated for ordering rules. For purposes of applying the ordering rules under Code Sec. 172(b), NOLs for which the taxpayer has elected a five-year carryback period are treated the same way specified liability losses are treated (Code Sec. 172(f)(5)). Accordingly, they are treated as separate NOLs, to be used in a carryover year only after the remaining NOLs are used up (Code Sec. 172(b)(1)(I)(iii), as added by the Energy Act).

Statutes of limitations extended. A taxpayer can apply under Code Sec. 6411(a) for a tentative carryback refund of the tax for a tax year to which an NOL is carried back. Generally, the refund application (e.g., Form 1139, Corporate Application for Tenta-

NEW LAW EXPLAINED

tive Refund) must be filed within 12 months of the close of the tax year in which the NOL arose (i.e., the NOL loss year). However, for purposes of NOLs for which the five-year carryback period is elected under this new provision, the Energy Act extends this date by an additional 24 months (Code Sec. 172(b)(1)(I)(iv), as added by the Energy Act). The Energy Act also extends the statute of limitations for claiming a refund attributable to an NOL carryback (Code Sec. 6511(d)(2)(A)), by treating the limitations period expiration date as three years from the due date of the return for the election tax year rather than as three years from the due date of the return for the NOL loss year. The Energy Act provides a similar rule for calculating interest on overpayments (Code Sec. 6611(f)(1)), and the assessment of deficiencies (Code Sec. 6501(h)), both of which are also determined under the new law with reference to the election year rather than the loss year (Code Sec. 172(b)(1)(I)(v), as added by the Energy Act).

> **Election:** Congress left it to the IRS to determine how a taxpayer should make the election. The filing of a refund claim should suffice to make the election provided that the taxpayer attaches a statement specifying the election year, the loss year, and the amount of qualifying investment in electric transmission property and pollution control facilities in the preceding tax year (Joint Committee on Taxation, Description and Technical Explanation of the Energy Tax Incentives Act of 2005 (JCX-60-05)).

Practical Analysis: Katherine Breaks, Senior Manager, Washington National Tax, KPMG LLP,[*] notes that the Energy Tax Incentives Act of 2005 provides an election for certain electric utility companies to extend the carryback period to five years for a portion of net operating losses (NOLs) arising in 2003, 2004 and 2005 ("loss years"). The election may be made during any tax year ending after December 31, 2005, and before January 1, 2009 ("election years"). The portion of the loss year NOL to which the election may apply is limited to 20 percent of the amount of the taxpayer's qualifying investment in the tax year prior to the year in which the election is made (the "qualifying investment limitation"). The Energy Act extends the statute of limitations to permit eligible taxpayers to file refund claims for net operating losses arising in the 2003, 2004 and 2005 tax years. Taxpayers have a significant amount of time—more than four years after making a qualifying investment—to decide whether to take advantage of this special carryback provision.

▶ **Effective dates.** No specific effective date is provided by the Energy Act. The provision is, therefore, considered effective on August 8, 2005.

---

[*] The views and opinions expressed herein are those of the author and do not necessarily represent the views and opinions of KPMG LLP in the United States. The information in this article is general in nature and based on authorities that are subject to change. Applicability to specific situations is to be determined through consultation with your tax adviser.

¶430

NEW LAW EXPLAINED

Law source: Law at ¶5175. Committee Report at ¶10,100.
— Act Sec. 1311 of the Energy Tax Incentives Act of 2005, adding Code Sec. 172(b)(1)(I).

Reporter references: For further information, consult the following CCH reporters.
— Standard Federal Tax Reporter, 2005FED ¶12,014.023
— Federal Tax Service, FTS § G:14.82
— Federal Tax Guide, 2005FTG ¶10,830

¶435 Sales or Dispositions to Implement FERC Restructuring Policy

BACKGROUND

A taxpayer can elect to recognize qualified gain from a qualifying electric transmission transaction over an eight-year period (Code Sec. 451(i)). The qualified gain is immediately recognized beginning in the tax year of the transaction to the extent the amount realized from the transaction exceeds:

(1) the cost of exempt utility property that is purchased by the taxpayer during the four-year period beginning on the date of the transaction, reduced by

(2) any portion of the cost previously taken into account under these gain deferral rules (Code Sec. 451(i)(1)(A)).

The cost of exempt utility property taken into account under this formula cannot be reduced below zero. Any remaining qualified gain would be recognized ratably over eight years (Code Sec. 451(i)(1)(B)).

For this purpose, qualified gain is:

(1) any ordinary income derived from a qualifying electric transmission transaction that would be required to be recognized under Code Secs. 1245 or 1250, and

(2) any income from a transaction in excess of that amount which is required to be included in gross income for the tax year (Code Sec. 451(i)(2)).

Qualifying electric transmission transaction. A qualifying electric transmission transaction is any sale or other disposition to an independent transmission company of: (1) property used in the trade or business of providing electric transmission services; or (2) an ownership interest in a corporation or partnership whose principal trade or business consists of providing such services. The sale or disposition must be made before January 1, 2007 (Code Sec. 451(i)(3)). An independent transmission company is:

(1) an independent transmission provider approved by the Federal Energy Regulatory Commission (FERC);

(2) a person:

  (a) who the FERC determines is not a "market participant," and

  (b) whose transmission facilities to which the deferral election applies are under the operational control of a FERC-approved independent transmission provider within a specified time frame; or

BACKGROUND

(3) in the case of facilities subject to the jurisdiction of the Public Utility Commission of Texas, a person approved by that commission as consistent with Texas state law regarding an independent transmission organization, or a political subdivision or affiliate whose transmission facilities are controlled by that person (Code Sec. 451(i)(4)).

In the case of item (2) above, the transmission facilities must be under the control of the independent transmission provider before the close of the period specified in the FERC authorization of the transaction (Code Sec. 451(i)(4)(B)(ii)). In any event, control must be exercised by January 1, 2007 (Code Sec. 451(i)(4)(B)(ii); Conference Committee Report, H.R. Conf. Rep. No. 108-375).

NEW LAW EXPLAINED

Tax deferral extended for gains on electric transmission assets.—Deferral treatment of sales or other dispositions to independent transmission companies has been extended one year to transactions occurring before January 1, 2008 (Code Sec. 451(i)(3), as amended by the Energy Tax Incentives Act of 2005).

▶ **Effective date.** The provision applies to transactions occurring after August 8, 2005 (Act Sec. 1305(c) of the Energy Tax Incentives Act of 2005).

Law source: Law at ¶5215. Committee Report at ¶10,040.

— Act Sec. 1305(a) of the Energy Tax Incentives Act of 2005, amending Code Sec. 451(i)(3);

— Act Sec. 1305(b), amending Code Sec. 451(i)(4)(B)(ii);

— Act Sec. 1305(c), providing the effective date.

Reporter references: For further information, consult the following CCH reporters.

— Standard Federal Tax Reporter, 2005FED ¶21,030.06

NUCLEAR POWER

¶440 Credit for Production from Advanced Nuclear Power Facilities

BACKGROUND

Code Sec. 45 provides that for purposes of the general business credit under Code Sec. 38, a renewable electricity production credit is allowed for electricity that is produced by a taxpayer from qualified energy resources at a qualified facility and sold to an unrelated person during the tax year. The base amount of the credit is 1.5 cents per kilowatt-hour (indexed for inflation) of electricity produced; for 2005, the credit is 1.9 cents per kilowatt-hour. While qualified facilities include wind energy facilities, solar energy facilities, "closed-loop" biomass facilities, open-loop biomass facilities (including livestock waste nutrients), geothermal energy facilities, small

BACKGROUND

irrigation power facilities, landfill gas facilities, and trash combustion facilities, a credit is not provided for electricity produced at advanced nuclear power facilities.

NEW LAW EXPLAINED

Advanced nuclear facility business tax credit.—A new business tax credit is created for energy production from advanced nuclear power facilities (Code Secs. 38(b) and 45J, as added by the Energy Tax Incentives Act of 2005). The credit is equal to 1.8 cents times the number of kilowatt hours of electricity that are: (1) produced by the taxpayer at an advanced nuclear power facility during the eight-year period beginning on the date the facility was originally placed in service; and (2) sold by the taxpayer to an unrelated person during the tax year.

A qualifying advanced nuclear power facility is any advanced nuclear facility that is owned by the taxpayer, uses nuclear energy to produce electricity, and is placed in service after August 8, 2005, and before January 1, 2021 (Code Sec. 45J(d)(1), as added by the Energy Act). An advanced nuclear facility is any nuclear facility the reactor design for which is approved after December 31, 1993, by the Nuclear Regulatory Commission and such design or a substantially similar design of comparable capacity was not approved on or before such date (Code Sec. 45J(d)(2), as added by the Energy Act).

> **Comment:** The date restrictions provide an incentive to quickly bring more nuclear powerplants into service in order to receive this tax credit before January 1, 2021.

The amount of the business tax credit that is allowed per tax year, per facility, is limited to the ratio of the national megawatt capacity limitation of the facility to the total megawatt nameplate capacity of the facility under a national limitation (Code Sec. 45J(b)(1), as added by the Energy Act). The national megawatt capacity limitation will be 6,000 megawatts and the Secretary of Treasury shall allocate the national megawatt capacity limitation in such manner as necessary (Code Sec. 45J(b)(2) and (3), as added by the Energy Act). However, no later than six months after August 8, 2005, regulations are to be issued that provide a certification process under which the Secretary of Treasury, in consultation with the Secretary of Energy, will approve and allocate the national megawatt capacity limitation (Code Sec. 45J(b)(4), as added by the Energy Act). The amount of the credit allowable for any tax year shall not exceed an amount that bears the same ratio to $125,000,000 as the national megawatt capacity limitation allocated to the facility bears to 1,000 (Code Sec. 45J(c)(1), as added by the Energy Act).

> **Example:** A taxpayer operates a 1,350 megawatt rated nameplate capacity system and has received an allocation from the Secretary for 1,350 megawatts of capacity eligible for the credit. The taxpayer's annual limitation on credits that may be claimed is equal to 1.35 times $125 million, or $168.75 million. If the taxpayer operates a facility with a nameplate rated capacity of 1,350 megawatts, but has received an allocation from the Secretary for 750 megawatts of credit

NEW LAW EXPLAINED

> eligible capacity, then the two limitations apply. The taxpayer may claim a credit equal to 1.35 cents per kilowatt hour of electricity produced, subject to an annual credit limitation of $93.75 million in credits (three-quarters of $125 million) (Joint Committee on Taxation, Description and Technical Explanation of the Energy Tax Incentives Act of 2005 (JCX-60-05)).

Rules similar to those in Code Sec. 45(b)(1) for the renewable electricity credit will apply for a phaseout of the credit (Code Sec. 45J(c)(2) and (e), as added by the Energy Act). The Joint Committee on Taxation's report clarifies that the credit allowable to the taxpayer will be reduced by reason of grants, tax-exempt bonds, subsidized energy financing, and other credits. However, this reduction cannot exceed 50 percent of the otherwise allowable credit (Joint Committee on Taxation, Description and Technical Explanation of the Energy Tax Incentives Act of 2005 (JCX-60-05)).

▶ **Effective date.** The credit for production from advanced nuclear power facilities applies to production in tax years beginning after August 8, 2005 (Act Sec. 1306(d) of the Energy Tax Incentives Act of 2005).

Law source: Law at ¶5040 and ¶5075. Committee Report at ¶10,050.

— Act Sec. 1306(a) of the Energy Tax Incentives Act of 2005, adding Code Sec. 45J;
— Act Sec. 1306(b), amending Code Sec. 38(b)(19)–(21), as amended by the SAFE Transportation Equity Act of 2005;
— Act Sec. 1306(c);
— Act Sec. 1306(d), providing the effective date.

Reporter references: For further information, consult the following CCH reporters.

— Standard Federal Tax Reporter, 2005FED ¶4251.021
— Federal Tax Service, FTS § G:24.240
— Federal Tax Guide, 2005FTG ¶2575

¶445 Modification to Special Rules for Nuclear Decommissioning Costs

BACKGROUND

Currently, utilities that own or operate a nuclear powerplant are required by federal and state laws to decommission the plant at the end of its useful life. An accrual-basis utility can determine with reasonable accuracy the costs that it must incur to decommission a nuclear powerplant. Those costs, however, may not be deducted until economic performance occurs (Code Sec. 468A(a) and (c)(2)).

In lieu of waiting for economic performance to occur, a utility may elect to currently deduct contributions it makes to a Nuclear Decommissioning Reserve Fund established to help pay the decommissioning costs of a nuclear powerplant (Code Sec. 468A(a) and (e)). Contributions to a qualified fund are limited to the lesser of:

BACKGROUND

(1) the amount of nuclear decommission costs allocable to the fund which is included in the taxpayer's cost of service for ratemaking purposes for the tax year; or

(2) the "ruling amount" applicable to that tax year (Code Sec. 468A(b)).

The "ruling amount" is a schedule obtained from the IRS upon request that specifies the annual payments that must be made into the fund to cover the amount of decommission costs allocable to the fund over its existence (e.g., post-decommissioning costs) (Code Sec. 468A(d)). For this purpose, decommissioning costs are considered to accrue ratably over a nuclear powerplant's estimated useful life. Thus, if the present value of the total decommissioning costs of a nuclear powerplant is $100, but the fund was not in existence during 25 percent of the powerplant's estimated useful life, then the total amount of decommissioning costs allocable to the fund is limited to $75.

Amounts withdrawn from a qualified fund to pay for decommissioning costs must be included in the taxpayer's income (Code Sec. 468A(c)(1)). The taxpayer may then deduct the nuclear decommissioning costs as economic performance occurs (Code Sec. 468A(c)(2)).

NEW LAW EXPLAINED

Nuclear decommissioning cost rules modified.—The special rules for deducting nuclear decommissioning costs have been modified. Effective for tax years beginning after December 31, 2005, contributions by a taxpayer to a Nuclear Decommissioning Reserve Fund for any tax year are limited to the "ruling amount" applicable for the tax year (Code Sec. 468A(b), as amended by the Energy Tax Incentives Act of 2005). The limitation regarding cost of service requirements has been repealed. Thus, all taxpayers, including unregulated taxpayers, are allowed a deduction for amounts contributed to a qualified decommissioning fund (Joint Committee on Taxation, Description and Technical Explanation of the Energy Tax Incentives Act of 2005 (JCX-60-05)).

> **Practical Analysis:** Mark Luscombe, Principal Analyst, CCH Tax and Accounting, observes that the statement that all taxpayers, even unregulated taxpayers, are allowed a deduction for amounts contributed to a qualified decommissioning fund may have some unintended consequences. The precise purpose of the language is not clear. Perhaps it is intended merely to permit patrons of cooperatives making contributions to nuclear decommissioning funds to get the passthrough on the deduction, a theme that seems to run through many provisions in the Energy Act.
>
> Some state utility regulators, however, have permitted decommissioning charges to be passed through to utility customers and appear on monthly utility bills. Is it possible that every individual and business that pays a decommissioning charge on their monthly utility bill is entitled to an annual deduction for

¶445

NEW LAW EXPLAINED

> contributions to a nuclear decommissioning fund? There is no indication in the legislation that this provision was intended to create a deduction for utility customers. Still, the Joint Committee on Taxation language would seem to open up that possibility.

Exception to ruling amount. A utility will be permitted to contribute more than the "ruling amount" in only one limited circumstance. Specifically, a taxpayer that is maintaining a qualified fund is permitted to make contributions of amounts necessary to fund the total nuclear decommissioning costs of the powerplant over its estimated useful life (Code Sec. 468A(f)(1), as added by the Energy Act). In other words, the taxpayer may contribute up to the present value of the total decommissioning costs for the nuclear powerplant that were previously excluded (generally, pre-1984 decommissioning costs). For example, if the present value of the total decommissioning costs of a nuclear powerplant is $100, under the rules prior to the Energy Act, the fund was only permitted to accumulate $75 of decommissioning costs if the fund was not in existence during 25 percent of the powerplant's useful life. Under the Energy Act, the taxpayer may now transfer the remaining $25 to the qualified fund (Joint Committee on Taxation, Description and Technical Explanation of the Energy Tax Incentives Act of 2005 (JCX-60-05)).

It is anticipated that the amount that is allowed to be transferred will be determined based on the estimate of total decommissioning costs used for purposes of determining the taxpayer's most recent ruling amount (Joint Committee on Taxation, Description and Technical Explanation of the Energy Tax Incentives Act of 2005 (JCX-60-05)). No gain or loss is recognized on this contribution and, if appreciated property is transferred, the amount of the deduction is limited to the adjusted basis of the transferred property (Code Sec. 468A(f)(2)(D), as added by the Energy Act). The exception to the "ruling amount" limitation will not apply unless the taxpayer requests a new schedule of "ruling amounts" from the IRS in connection with the transfer (Code Sec. 468A(f)(3), as added by the Energy Act). The taxpayer's basis in any fund will not be increased by reason of any transfer permitted under these rules (Code Sec. 468A(f)(4), as added by the Energy Act).

> **Planning Note:** Effective for tax years beginning after December 31, 2005, a taxpayer will be required to request a new schedule of "ruling amounts" upon each renewal of the operating license for the nuclear powerplant (Code Sec. 468A(d)(1), as amended by the Energy Act).

Deductions for amounts transferred into the qualified fund under this provision are allowed ratably over the remaining estimated useful life of the nuclear powerplant beginning with the tax year in which the transfer is made (Code Sec. 468A(f)(2)(A), as added by the Energy Act). A deduction is denied for any transfer of an amount for which the taxpayer or a predecessor was previously allowed a deduction or for which a corresponding amount was not included in the gross income of the taxpayer or a predecessor (Code Sec. 468A(f)(2)(B), as added by the Energy Act). A ratable portion of each transfer is treated as being from previously deducted or excluded amounts to the extent of the transfer. If the qualified fund itself is later transferred, the transferor can claim any deduction for tax years ending after the date the fund is

¶445

NEW LAW EXPLAINED

transferred for the tax year which includes such date (Code Sec. 468A(f)(2)(C), as added by the Energy Act).

▶ **Effective date.** The provision applies to tax years beginning after December 31, 2005 (Act Sec. 1310(f) of the Energy Tax Incentives Act of 2005).

Law source: Law at ¶5220. Committee Report at ¶10,090.

— Act Sec. 1310(a) of the Energy Tax Incentives Act of 2005, amending Code Sec. 468A(b);
— Act Sec. 1310(b)(1), redesignating Code Sec. 468A(f) and (g) as (g) and (h), and adding new Code Sec. 468A(f);
— Act Sec. 1310(b)(2), amending Code Sec. 468A(d)(2)(A);
— Act Sec. 1310(c), amending Code Sec. 468A(d)(1);
— Act Sec. 1310(d), amending Code Sec. 468A(e)(3);
— Act Sec. 1310(e)(1)-(3), amending Code Sec. 468A(e)(2)
— Act Sec. 1310(f), providing the effective date.

¶450 Treatment of Certain Income of Electric Cooperatives

BACKGROUND

Local benevolent life insurance associations, mutual ditch or irrigation companies, mutual or cooperative telephone companies and like organizations (not defined in the Internal Revenue Code or regulations, but including mutual or cooperative electric companies) are exempt from tax under Code Sec. 501(c)(12)(A) if at least 85 percent of the income of the organization consist of amounts collected from members for the sole purpose of meeting losses and expenses.

The 85-percent test is applied annually so that an electric cooperative could be taxable one year and tax-exempt the next year. Code Sec. 501(c)(12) and the regulations do not define income. However, Rev. Rul. 74-362, 1974-2 CB 170, states that the term means "gross income" for purposes of the 85-percent member-income test. Income received or accrued by a rural electric cooperative is excluded for purposes of the 85-percent test for exemption under Code Sec. 501(c)(12) if the income is from:

(1) the provision or sale of electric energy transmission services or ancillary services on a nondiscriminatory open access basis under an open access transmission tariff approved or accepted by the Federal Energy Regulatory Commission (FERC) or under an independent transmission provider agreement approved or accepted by FERC;

(2) the provision or sale of electric energy distribution services or ancillary services, as long as the services are provided on a nondiscriminatory open access basis to distribute electric energy not owned by the cooperative:

(a) to end-users who are served by distribution facilities not owned by the cooperative or any of its members, or

BACKGROUND

   (b) generated by a generation facility that is not owned or leased by the cooperative or any of its members and that is directly connected to distribution facilities owned by the cooperative or any of its members;

(3) a nuclear decommissioning transaction; or

(4) an asset exchange or conversion transaction (Code Sec. 501(c)(12)(C)).

Receipt or accrual of income from load loss transactions, by mutual or cooperative electric companies, is treated as income from patrons who are members of the cooperative. A load loss transaction is any wholesale or retail sale of electric energy to the extent that the aggregate amount of the sales during a seven-year period beginning with the start-up year does not exceed the limit placed on such sales. That limit is the sum for all seven years of the amount by which sales to members in each year are less than the amount of sales to members in a base year. The base year is the year before the start-up year or, at the company's election, the second or third year before the start-up year. Load loss transactions do not include sales to cooperative members (Code Sec. 501(c)(12)(H)).

The exclusions from income for open access transactions, nuclear decommissioning transactions, asset exchange, and conversion transactions are scheduled to expire after December 31, 2006. The special rule for income received or accrued by a tax-exempt rural electric cooperative or a taxable electric cooperative from a load loss transaction is scheduled to expire after December 31, 2006.

NEW LAW EXPLAINED

Cooperative income from certain transactions sunset date eliminated.—The sunset date has been eliminated for the rules excluding income received or accrued by tax-exempt rural electric cooperatives from open access electric energy transmission or distribution services, any nuclear decommissioning transaction, and any asset exchange or conversion transaction for purposes of the 85-percent test under Code Sec. 501(c)(12) (Code Sec. 501(c)(12)(C), as amended by the Energy Tax Incentives Act of 2005). The sunset date has also been eliminated for the rules that:

(1) allow income from load loss transactions to be treated as member income in determining whether a rural electric cooperative satisfies the 85-percent test; and

(2) permit taxable electric cooperatives to treat the receipt or accrual of income from load loss transactions as income from patrons who are members of the cooperative (Code Sec. 501(c)(12)(H), as amended by the Energy Act).

▶ **Effective date.** The provision is effective for tax years beginning on August 8, 2005 (Act Sec. 1304(c) of the Energy Tax Incentives Act of 2005).

Law source: Law at ¶5225. Committee Report at ¶10,030.

— Act Sec. 1304(a) of the Energy Tax Incentives Act of 2005, amending Code Sec. 501(c)(12)(C);

— Act Sec. 1304(b), amending Code Sec. 501(c)(12)(H);

— Act Sec. 1304(c), providing the effective date.

¶450

NEW LAW EXPLAINED

Reporter references: For further information, consult the following CCH reporters.
— Standard Federal Tax Reporter, 2005FED ¶22,634.01
— Federal Tax Guide, 2005FTG ¶16,025

ENERGY BONDS

¶455 Tax Credit Bonds to Subsidize Non-Profits' Production of Renewable Energy Electricity

BACKGROUND

Increasing awareness of the political and environmental dangers of dependence on nonrenewable energy sources has led to efforts to encourage the development of clean, renewable energy sources. State regulators are increasingly adopting renewable portfolio standards, which require all electricity suppliers to provide a certain amount of electricity generated from renewable sources. However, according to the American Public Power Association, "renewable resources (exclusive of hydropower) account for less than two percent of the nation's overall generating portfolio."

A federal income tax credit is allowed under Code Sec. 45 for the production from qualified facilities of electricity that is sold by the taxpayer to an unrelated person. Qualified facilities are those which generate power from certain specified fuels, including wind energy, geothermal energy, solar energy, biomass, landfill gas and trash combustion. The credit is generally available with respect to energy produced at a particular facility for the 10-year period commencing with the date the facility is placed in service. The amount of the credit is phased out if the market price of electricity exceeds certain threshold levels.

While the tax credit for production of electricity from renewable sources provides a subsidy to private energy companies, about 25 percent of Americans are served by public power companies or rural electric cooperatives which are unable to take advantage of the credit because they are not subject to income tax. The federal government subsidizes state and local government activities by excluding from gross income the interest on state and local bonds that meet certain requirements. This reduces the amount of interest that borrowers must pay. A more recently developed method of providing a subsidy to state and local governments and other tax-exempt entities is to authorize them to issue tax credit bonds. A tax credit bond essentially provides the issuer with an interest-free loan. The bond holders receive a federal income tax credit at the credit rate, instead of interest payments, and the issuer only has to repay the principal. The bond holders must include the credit amount in income, then claim the credit against tax on their return.

> **Example:** Lee holds a $1,000 tax-credit bond with a credit rate of five percent throughout 2007. Lee must report $50 in income on his tax return even though

BACKGROUND

> he does not actually receive the $50. After calculating his tax liability, Lee would be entitled to claim a credit of $50. If his marginal tax rate was 30 percent, the tax liability on the $50 of income would be $15. After taking into account the tax credit of $50, Lee would net $35. That is exactly the same amount that he would net after taxes if he had received the $50 in cash income on a conventional $1,000 bond paying five percent interest.

The only tax credit bonds that have been authorized are Qualified Zone Academy Bonds (QZABs) under Code Sec. 1397E, added by the Taxpayer Relief Act of 1997 (P.L. 105-34). QZABs are issued by state or local governments, with the proceeds generally restricted to use for the renovation or improvement of schools in certain geographic areas.

NEW LAW EXPLAINED

Tax credit bonds for tax exempt producers of renewable energy electricity.—The Energy Tax Incentives Act of 2005 authorizes the issuance of up to $800 million of tax credit bonds, to be known as clean renewable energy bonds (CREBs), during 2006 and 2007 to finance capital expenditures by tax-exempt electricity producers to increase their capacity to produce electricity from clean renewable sources (Code Sec. 54, as added by the Energy Tax Incentives Act of 2005). The bonds may be issued by governmental bodies, cooperative electricity companies, or cooperative lenders owned by cooperative electricity companies. These bonds provide a federal subsidy to allow nonprofit electricity providers, including cooperatives and government-owned utilities, to compete more evenly with for-profit companies that can take advantage of the existing tax credit under Code Sec. 45. The $800 million national limit is to be allocated among qualified projects at the discretion of the IRS, except that not more than $500 million can be allocated to governmental projects (Code Sec. 54(f), as added by the Energy Act).

Calculating the credit. A taxpayer holding a CREB on one or more credit allowance dates during a tax year is allowed a credit equivalent to the interest that the bond would otherwise pay (Code Sec. 54(a), as added by the Energy Act). Credit allowance dates are March 15, June 15, September 15, December 15, and the last day the bond is outstanding. The credit with respect to each credit allowance date is generally equal to 25 percent of the annual credit for the bond, though a pro rata reduction applies for the quarters in which the bond is issued, redeemed or matures. The annual credit is equal to the face amount of the bond multiplied by a credit rate determined by the IRS. The credit rate is the rate that the IRS estimates will allow the issuance of bonds with a specified maturity without discount and without interest cost to the issuer (Code Sec. 54(b), as added by the Energy Act).

The amount of the credit allowed to the taxpayer must be included in gross income and treated as interest income (Code Sec. 54(g), as added by the Energy Act). For purposes of the requirement to pay estimated taxes, the holder of a bond is treated as having made an estimated tax payment in the amount of the credit on the credit allowance date (Code Sec. 54(l)(5), as added by the Energy Act).

¶455

NEW LAW EXPLAINED

> **Caution Note:** Although items of income generally increase the basis of a partner or S corporation shareholder in their interest, that basis is not increased by the amount of the credit included in income (Code Sec. 54(l)(3)(B), as added by the Energy Act).

The credit is not refundable (Code Sec. 54(c), as added by the Energy Act). In the case of a person who receives a passthrough of the credit from a partnership, trust, S corporation or other entity, the credit cannot exceed the tax attributable to the portion of the person's income attributable to the passthrough entity (Code Sec. 54(l)(3)(A), as added by the Energy Act). The rules for this limitation are to be similar to the rules under Code Sec. 41(g) that limit the passthrough of the research credit. The IRS is to prescribe procedures to allocate the credit among the shareholders of a regulated investment company holding CREBs (Code Sec. 54(l)(4), as added by the Energy Act).

> **Comment:** As enacted, the credit is available with respect to bonds issued after December 31, 2005, and before January 1, 2008. The credit under Code Sec. 45 for electricity produced from renewable sources is scheduled to expire at the same time (Code Sec. 45(d), as amended by the Energy Act). Presumably in the future these two provisions will be extended or allowed to expire simultaneously.

Clean renewable energy bonds (CREBs). A bond is a CREB if it meets the following requirements:

(1) it is issued by a qualified issuer (i.e., a cooperative electric company, a clean renewable energy lender, or a governmental body) that has received an allocation of the national limitation (Code Secs. 54(d)(1)(A) and 54(j)(4), as added by the Energy Act);

(2) 95 percent or more of the proceeds of the bond issue are to be used for capital expenditures to be incurred by a qualified borrower (i.e., a mutual or cooperative electric company or a governmental body) for one or more qualified projects (Code Secs. 54(d)(1)(B) and 54(j)(5), as added by the Energy Act);

(3) the maturity of the bond does not exceed the statutory maximum term (Code Sec. 54(e), as added by the Energy Act);

(4) the issue provides for an equal amount of principal to be repaid during each calendar year that the issue is outstanding (Code Sec. 54(l)(6), as added by the Energy Act);

(5) the bond is in registered form and the issuer designates it to be a CREB (Code Sec. 54(d)(1)(C), as added by the Energy Act); and

(6) the issue meets additional expenditure requirements (Code Sec. 54(d)(1)(D), as added by the Energy Act).

95 percent use requirement. At least 95 percent of the proceeds of a CREB issue must be used for capital expenditures for one or more qualified projects. A qualified project is any qualified facility (generally as defined for purposes of the credit as electricity produced from renewable sources) owned by a qualified borrower (Code Sec. 54(d)(2)(A), as added by the Energy Act). Qualified facilities include facilities producing electricity using:

¶455

NEW LAW EXPLAINED

- wind,
- closed-loop biomass,
- open-loop biomass,
- geothermal or solar energy,
- small irrigation power,
- landfill gas,
- trash combustion, or
- qualified hydropower.

Facilities producing refined coal are also qualified facilities (Code Sec. 45(d), as amended by the Energy Act). Qualified borrowers are mutual and cooperative electric companies and governmental bodies, including state and local governments and Indian tribal bodies (Code Sec. 54(j)(5), as added by the Energy Act).

CREB proceeds generally must be used to pay costs incurred after the issuance of the bond. Thus, CREB proceeds cannot be used to refinance a project that was originally financed before the passage of the Energy Act (Code Sec. 54(d)(2)(B), as added by the Energy Act). However, CREB proceeds can be used to reimburse a borrower for amounts paid after the passage of the Energy Act, but before the issuance of the bond, if:

(1) before making the original expenditure, the borrower declared its intent to reimburse the expenditure with CREB proceeds;

(2) not later than 60 days after the expenditure, the issuer adopts an official intent to reimburse the expenditure with CREB proceeds; and

(3) not later than 18 months after the expenditure, the reimbursement is made (Code Sec. 54(d)(2)(C), as added by the Energy Act).

Proceeds are not treated as used for a qualified project to the extent the borrower or issuer takes any action within its control that results in the proceeds not being used for a qualified project (Code Sec. 54(d)(2)(D), as added by the Energy Act). The IRS is to prescribe regulations describing methods for remedying changes in the use of proceeds within 120 days of August 8, 2005 (Act Sec. 1303(d) of the Energy Act).

Maximum maturity requirement. CREBs are subject to a maximum maturity limitation to be determined and published by the IRS on a monthly basis. The maximum term will be the term estimated by the IRS to result in the present value of the obligation to repay the principal on the bond being equal to 50 percent of the bond's face value. The discount rate to be used in calculating the present value for a month is the average annual interest rate of tax-exempt obligations having a term of ten years or more that are issued during the preceding month. If the term as so determined is not a multiple of a whole year, the maximum term will be the next higher whole year (Code Sec. 54(e), as added by the Energy Act).

Comment: The maximum maturity for qualified zone academy bonds (QZABs) is determined using the same discount rate (Code Sec. 1397E(d)(3)). However, regulations state that the discount rate for QZAB purposes will be equal to 110 percent of the long-term adjusted AFR, compounded semi-annually, for the

NEW LAW EXPLAINED

month in which the bond is issued (Reg. § 1.1397E-1(d)). During the first seven months of 2005, the maximum maturity for QZABs has been 15 or 16 years.

Expenditure requirements. In order for a bond to be a CREB, the issuer must reasonably have the following expectations regarding the spending of the bond proceeds as of the date of issuance:

(1) at least 95 percent of the proceeds of the issue will be spent on qualified projects within the five-year period beginning on the date of issuance of the bond;

(2) a binding commitment with a third party to spend at least 10 percent of the proceeds of the issue will be entered into within the six-month period beginning on the issue date, or, if the proceeds of the issue are to be reloaned to multiple qualified borrowers, within the six-month period beginning on the date of the first loan to a qualified borrower; and

(3) the projects involved will be completed, and the proceeds of the issue will be spent, with due diligence (Code Sec. 54(h)(1), as added by the Energy Act).

The IRS can extend the five-year period if the issuer requests an extension before the period has ended and establishes that the failure to satisfy the spending requirement is due to reasonable cause and the related projects will continue to proceed with due diligence (Code Sec. 54(h)(2), as added by the Energy Act). If 95 percent of the proceeds of an issue are not spent by the close of the five-year period or any extended period approved by the IRS, the issuer is required to redeem all of the nonqualified bonds within 90 days of the end of the period. The amount of bonds required to be redeemed is determined as it is for the redemption of exempt facility bonds under Code Sec. 142 (Code Sec. 54(h)(3), as added by the Energy Act).

Comment: By the terms of the Energy Act, the issuer must reasonably expect at the time of issuance to spend 95 percent of the issue proceeds, within five years, on qualified projects. In contrast, the requirement to redeem nonqualified bonds applies if 95 percent of the proceeds of the issuance are not spent within five years, without reference to whether the proceeds are spent on qualified projects. The "spent on qualified projects" restriction applies to both expected and actual spending (Joint Committee on Taxation, Description and Technical Explanation of the Energy Tax Incentives Act of 2005 (JCX-60-05)). A technical correction to reflect that intention may be forthcoming.

Certain tax-exempt bond rules apply. Although CREBs are not tax-exempt bonds, they are subject to certain of the rules developed for tax-exempt bonds. Thus, a bond is not a CREB unless the issuer meets the arbitrage requirements of Code Sec. 148 with respect to the issue (Code Sec. 54(i), as added by the Energy Act). Generally those requirements are satisfied if the proceeds of the issue are not reasonably expected to be used to acquire higher yielding investments, with limited exceptions for temporary periods. Also, issuers of CREBs must file information reports with the IRS similar to those required of tax-exempt bond issuers under Code Sec. 149(e) (Code Sec. 54(l)(7), as added by the Energy Act). That provision requires issuers to file a statement identifying the issuer and listing the details of the issue not later than the 15th day of the second month after the end of the calendar quarter in which the bond is issued.

¶455

NEW LAW EXPLAINED

Definitions. A "cooperative electric company" means a mutual or cooperative electric company described in Code Secs. 501(c)(12) or 1381(a)(2)(C), or a not-for-profit electric utility that has received a loan or loan guarantee under the Rural Electrification Act (Code Sec. 54(j)(1), as added by the Energy Act).

A "clean renewable energy lender" means a lender that is a cooperative owned by, or having outstanding loans to, 100 or more cooperative electric companies and in existence on February 1, 2002. A clean renewable energy lender includes any affiliated entity controlled by the lender (Code Sec. 54(j)(2), as added by the Energy Act).

A "governmental body" means any state, territory, U.S. possession, Indian tribal government or the District of Columbia, and any political subdivision of any of these (Code Sec. 54(j)(3), as added by the Energy Act).

Information reporting. The "interest" on CREBs must be reported on Form 1099-INT as though it were actually paid on the credit allowance date. The IRS is authorized to prescribe any necessary or appropriate regulations implementing the reporting requirement, including regulations requiring more frequent or more detailed reporting (Code Sec. 6049(d)(8), as added by the Energy Act).

> **Compliance Tip:** Although interest payments to corporations, securities dealers, real estate investment trusts, registered investment companies, common trust funds, and charitable remainder trusts are generally not required to be reported, CREB "interest" accrued by those entities must be reported (Code Sec. 6049(d)(8)(B), as added by the Energy Act).

▶ **Effective date.** These provisions apply to bonds issued after December 31, 2005 (Act Sec. 1303(e) of the Energy Tax Incentives Act of 2005). These provisions do not apply to any bond issued after December 31, 2007 (Code Sec. 54(m), as added by the Energy Act).

Law source: Law at ¶5125, ¶5255, ¶5385, and ¶7010. Committee Report at ¶10,020.

— Act Sec. 1303(a) of the Energy Tax Incentives Act of 2005, adding new Code Sec. 54;
— Act Sec. 1303(b), adding new Code Sec. 6049(d)(8);
— Act Sec. 1303(c), amending Code Secs. 1397E(c)(2), 1397E(h), and 6401(b)(1);
— Act Sec. 1303(d);
— Act Sec. 1303(e), providing the effective date.

Oil and Gas

¶505 Temporary election to expense qualified liquid fuel refineries
¶510 Determination of small refiner exception to oil depletion deduction
¶515 Depreciation of natural gas distribution lines
¶520 Depreciation of natural gas gathering pipelines
¶525 Geological and geophysical costs amortized over two years
¶530 Safe harbor from tax-exempt bond arbitrage rules for prepaid natural gas
¶535 Deduction for capital costs incurred in complying with EPA sulfur regulations
¶540 Oil Spill Liability Trust Fund financing rate

¶505 Temporary Election to Expense Qualified Liquid Fuel Refineries

BACKGROUND

Under the present law, petroleum refining assets are depreciated for regular tax purposes over a 10-year recovery period using the double declining balance method under the Modified Accelerated Cost Recovery System (MACRS) of Code Sec. 168. Petroleum refining assets are assets used for distillation, fractionation, and catalytic cracking of crude petroleum into gasoline and its other components (Rev. Proc. 87-56, 1987-2 CB 674). Small business refiners are generally allowed to expense 75 percent of qualified capital costs incurred in complying with Environmental Protection Agency sulfur regulations (Code Sec. 179B).

Taxation of cooperatives and their patrons. Cooperatives are generally taxed as corporations except that they are allowed to deduct patronage dividends to the extent of the income derived from transactions with their patrons (Code Sec. 1382). Patronage dividend distributions are taxable to the patrons when paid in the form of money, a qualified written notice of allocation or other property (Code Sec. 1385(a)). Thus,

BACKGROUND

cooperatives are treated as conduits with respect to patronage source income derived from business transacted with cooperative owners.

NEW LAW EXPLAINED

Election to expense qualified liquid fuel refineries.—The Energy Tax Incentives Act of 2005 allows taxpayers to make a temporary election to expense 50 percent of the cost of a qualified refinery property (Code Sec. 179C(a), as added by the Energy Act). The expensing deduction is allowed for the tax year in which the qualified refinery property is placed in service. An election for a particular tax year is made on the taxpayer's return for that year, as provided by regulations. Once made, the election may be revoked only with the consent of the IRS (Code Sec. 179C(b), as added by the Energy Act).

> **Comment:** The remaining 50 percent of the taxpayer's qualifying expenditures are recovered under Code Sec. 168 and Code Sec. 179B, if applicable.
>
> **Comment:** The expensing deduction allowed by this provision is intended to encourage the construction of new refineries and the expansion of existing refineries to enhance the nation's refinery capacity. This result is much needed in light of increased gasoline consumption and climbing gasoline prices. In addition, the tax incentive for upgrading refinery equipment will promote investment in newer technologies resulting in more reliable and efficient refineries.

Qualified refinery property. Qualified refinery property eligible for expensing includes any portion of a qualified refinery:

(1) the original use of which commences with the taxpayer;

(2) which is placed in service by the taxpayer after August 8, 2005, and before January 1, 2012;

(3) which meets certain production capacity requirements (in the case of an expansion of an existing refinery);

(4) which meets all applicable environmental laws in effect on the date such portion was placed in service;

(5) no written binding contract for the construction of which was in effect on or before June 14, 2005; and

(6) the construction of which is subject to a written binding construction contract entered into before January 1, 2008, which is placed in service before January 1, 2008, or, in the case of self-constructed property, the construction of which began after June 14, 2005 and before January 1, 2008 (Code Sec. 179C(c)(1), as added by the Energy Act).

A "qualified refinery" means any refinery located in the United States that is designed to serve the primary purpose of processing liquid fuel from crude oil or qualified fuels (Code Sec. 179C(d), as added by the Energy Act). Qualified fuels include oil produced from shale and tar sands; gas produced from geopressured brine, Devonian shale, coal seams, or a tight formation or biomass; and synthetic fuels produced from coal.

NEW LAW EXPLAINED

> **Comment:** The definition of qualified fuels for purposes of the new provision is the same as the definition provided under former Code Sec. 29(c), prior to being redesignated as Code Sec. 45K(c) by the Energy Act. However, the domestic production limitation under former Code Sec. 29(d), prior to being redesignated as Code Sec. 45K(d) by the Energy Act, is not applicable to the definition of a refinery under the new provision. Thus, an otherwise qualifying refinery will be eligible for the expensing election even though the primary purpose of the refinery is the processing of oil produced from shale or tar sands outside the United States. A facility that processes coal via gas into liquid fuel will also qualify as a refinery under the new provision (Joint Committee on Taxation, Description and Technical Explanation of the Energy Tax Incentives Act of 2005 (JCX-60-05)).

An exception to the original use requirement in (1) above is provided if the property is originally placed in service by a person after August 8, 2005, and, within three months, it is sold and leased back by the same person (Code Sec. 179C(c)(2), as added by the Energy Act). In such cases, the property is treated as originally placed in service not earlier than the date on which the property is used under the leaseback.

The production capacity requirement in (3) above is met if the portion of the existing qualified refinery enables the existing refinery: (a) to increase its total volume output, as measured by the total volume of finished products other than asphalt or lube oil, by five percent or more on an average daily basis, or (b) to process qualified fuels at a rate which is equal to or greater than 25 percent of the total output of such refinery on an average daily basis (Code Sec. 179C(e), as added by the Energy Act).

> **Comment:** For this purpose, the output of a refinery is measured on the basis of barrels per calendar day, which is the amount of fuels that a facility can process under usual operating conditions, expressed in terms of capacity during a 24-hour period and reduced to account for down time and other limitations (Joint Committee on Taxation, Description and Technical Explanation of the Energy Tax Incentives Act of 2005 (JCX-60-05)).

In determining whether the environmental law compliance requirement in (4) above is met, a waiver under the Clean Air Act will not be taken into account (Code Sec. 179C(c)(3), as added by the Energy Act).

> **Comment:** The environmental law compliance requirement applies only with respect to the refinery or any portion of it that is placed in service after August 8, 2005. Therefore, any portion of the refinery placed in service prior to the effective date that does not meet the applicable environmental laws will not prevent the taxpayer from making an expensing election with respect to an otherwise qualified refinery property.

Ineligible refinery property. The expensing election is not available with respect to a refinery property that is primarily used as a topping plant, asphalt plant, lube oil facility, crude or product terminal, or blending facility (Code Sec. 179C(f), as added by the Energy Act). Nor is it available with respect to a refinery property built solely to comply with consent decrees or projects mandated by the federal, state or local governments.

¶505

NEW LAW EXPLAINED

Reporting. The expensing deduction for qualified refinery property will be allowed for any tax year only if the taxpayer files a report with the IRS providing information about its refinery operations (Code Sec. 179C(h), as added by the Energy Act).

▶ **Effective date.** The amendments made by this section shall apply to properties placed in service after August 8, 2005 (Act Sec. 1323(c) of the Energy Tax Incentives Act of 2005).

Law source: Law at ¶5190, ¶5205, ¶5210, and ¶5245. Committee Report at ¶10,120.

— Act Sec. 1323(a) of the Energy Tax Incentives Act of 2005, adding Code Sec. 179C;

— Act Sec. 1323(b), amending Code Secs. 263(a)(1), 312(k)(3)(B), and 1245(a);

— Act Sec. 1323(c), providing the effective date.

Reporter references: For further information, consult the following CCH reporters.

— Standard Federal Tax Reporter, 2005FED ¶13,709.01

— Federal Tax Service, FTS § L:6.80

¶510 Determination of Small Refiner Exception to Oil Depletion Deduction

BACKGROUND

Oil and gas producers are generally allowed to claim depletion deductions determined under the cost depletion method (Code Sec. 613A(a)). Independent producers and royalty owners are, however, exempt from this rule and can use percentage depletion instead of deducting the costs of their producing wells based on the actual production from the wells. The percentage depletion in such cases is limited to a certain percentage of the average daily production of domestic oil and natural gas, subject to a maximum depletable quantity (Code Sec. 613A(c)).

The percentage depletion allowed to independent producers and royalty owners does not apply to taxpayers who are considered to be "retailers" or "refiners." A refiner is any taxpayer who directly or through a related person engages in the refining of crude oil, but only if the refinery runs of the taxpayer and such related persons exceeds 50,000 barrels on any given day during the tax year (Code Sec. 613A(d)(4)). Thus, an independent producer whose refining operations exceed the 50,000 barrel-per-day refinery limitation will lose its status as such and may not use the percentage depletion.

For purposes of the refinery limitation, a refinery run equals the volume of inputs of crude oil (excluding any product derived from oil) into the refining stream (Reg. § 1.613A-7(s)). In addition, a taxpayer is considered to be "related" to a refiner if a five-percent or more ownership interest in either the taxpayer or the refiner is held by the other person, or if a third party has such an ownership interest in both parties (Code Sec. 613A(d)(3)).

¶510

NEW LAW EXPLAINED

Refinery limitation on independent producers increased.—The 50,000 barrel-per-day refinery limitation for purposes of the independent producer exemption has been increased to 75,000 barrels (Code Sec. 613A(d)(4), as amended by the Energy Tax Incentives Act of 2005). The new limitation is determined based on the average, instead of the actual, daily refinery runs for the tax year. The average daily refinery run for the tax year is calculated by dividing the aggregate refinery runs for the tax year by the total number of days in the tax year.

▶ **Effective date.** The amendment made by this section applies to tax years ending after August 8, 2005 (Act Sec. 1328(b) of the Energy Tax Incentives Act of 2005).

Law source: Law at ¶5230. Committee Report at ¶10,170.

— Act Sec. 1328(a) of the Energy Tax Incentives Act of 2005, amending Code Sec. 613A(d)(4);
— Act Sec. 1328(b), providing the effective date.

Reporter references: For further information, consult the following CCH reporters.

— Standard Federal Tax Reporter, 2005FED ¶23,988.04
— Federal Tax Service, FTS § L:4.100
— Federal Tax Guide, 2005FTG ¶9645

¶515 Depreciation of Natural Gas Distribution Lines

BACKGROUND

Natural gas distribution lines installed by gas utilities are currently considered 20-year property under the Modified Accelerated Cost Recovery System (MACRS) (Rev. Proc. 87-56, 1987-2 CB 674, Asset Class 49.21 (Gas Utility Distribution Facilities)). A 35-year recovery period applies for purposes of the MACRS alternative depreciation system (ADS).

NEW LAW EXPLAINED

Natural gas distribution lines treated as MACRS 15-year property.—The new law provides that a natural gas distribution line placed in service after April 11, 2005, and before January 1, 2011, is depreciable as MACRS 15-year property (Code Sec. 168(e)(3)(E)(viii), as added by the Energy Tax Incentives Act of 2005). For MACRS alternative depreciation system (ADS) purposes, a 35-year recovery period is assigned (Code Sec. 168(g)(3)(B), as amended by the Energy Act). Thus, the regular MACRS depreciation period is temporarily decreased from 20 years to 15 years but the ADS period remains unchanged. The term "natural gas distribution line" is not specifically defined.

> **Comment:** Presumably, the definition is the same as applies to Asset Class 49.21 (Gas Utility Distribution Facilities) in Rev. Proc. 87-56, 1987-2 CB 674. However, while Asset Class 49.21 refers to natural gas distribution lines installed by gas

NEW LAW EXPLAINED

utilities, there is no limitation in the new law that the line be installed by a "gas utility."

Caution Note: The *original use* of the distribution line must commence with the taxpayer after April 11, 2005 (Code Sec. 168(e)(3)(E)(viii), as added by the Energy Act). Accordingly, used distribution lines purchased from an existing business or received as an asset in connection with the taxable acquisition of an existing business do not qualify for the 15-year recovery period. See ¶425 for additional commentary regarding the "original use" requirement. A distribution line also does not qualify for the 15-year recovery period if the taxpayer or a related party entered into a binding contract for its construction on or before April 11, 2005, or, in the case of self-constructed property, started construction on or before April 11, 2005 (Act Sec. 1325(c) of the Energy Act). The provision does not appear to define the term "related party."

Comment: There is no alternative minimum tax depreciation adjustment on natural gas distribution lines depreciable under this provision as 15-year property or which do not qualify and must be depreciated as 20-year property. This is because the AMT adjustment for MACRS 15- and 20-year property was previously eliminated for property placed in service after 1998 (Code Sec. 56(a)(1), as amended by the Taxpayer Relief Act of 1997 (P.L. 105-34)).

Comment: Another provision in the new law treats natural gas *gathering* lines as MACRS 7-year property, effective for property placed in service after April 11, 2005, if the original use begins with the taxpayer and no binding contract was in effect. See ¶520.

▶ **Effective date.** The provision applies to property placed in service after April 11, 2005, provided that the taxpayer or a related party has not entered into a binding contract for the construction thereof, on or before April 11, 2005, or, in the case of self-constructed property, has not started construction on or before such date (Act Sec. 1325(c) of the Energy Tax Incentives Act of 2005).

Law source: Law at ¶5165. Committee Report at ¶10,140.

— Act Sec. 1325(a) of the Energy Tax Incentives Act of 2005, adding Code Sec. 168(e)(3)(E)(viii);

— Act Sec. 1325(b), amending Code Sec. 168(g)(3)(B);

— Act Sec. 1325(c), providing the effective date.

Reporter references: For further information, consult the following CCH reporters.

— Standard Federal Tax Reporter, 2005FED ¶11,279.023

— Federal Tax Service, FTS § G:16:83[5]

— Federal Tax Guide, 2005FTG ¶9110

¶520 Depreciation of Natural Gas Gathering Pipelines

BACKGROUND

There is currently a conflict among the courts on the proper recovery period under the Modified Accelerated Cost Recovery System (MACRS) for natural gas gathering lines that are owned by nonproducers of natural gas. The two possible classifications are:

(1) Asset Class 13.2 of Rev. Proc. 87-56, 1987-2 CB 674, which provides a 7-year recovery period for "assets used by petroleum and natural gas producers for drilling of wells and production of petroleum and natural gas, including gathering pipelines..." and

(2) Asset Class 46.0 of Rev. Proc. 87-56, 1987-2 CB 674, which provides a 15-year recovery period for "assets used in the private, commercial, and contract carrying of petroleum, gas, and other products by means of pipes and conveyors..."

The IRS maintains that natural gas gathering pipelines owned by a nonproducer are described in Asset Class 46.0 and have a 15-year recovery period. This view has been followed by the Tax Court (*Duke Energy Natural Gas Corporation*, 109 TC 416, CCH Dec. 52,395and *Clajon Gas Co., L.P.*, 119 TC 197, CCH Dec. 54,919). The Courts of Appeal for the Sixth, Eighth, and Tenth Circuits, however, have held that natural gas gathering lines owned by nonproducers are described in Asset Class 13.2 and have a 7-year recovery period (*Saginaw Bay Pipeline Co.*, CA-6, 2003-2 USTC ¶50,592, *rev'g* DC Mich., 2001-2 USTC ¶50,642; *Clajon Gas Co. L.P.*, CA-8, 2004-1 USTC ¶50,123, *rev'g* 119 TC 197, CCH Dec. 54,919; *Duke Energy Natural Gas Corporation*, CA-10, 99-1 USTC ¶50,449 (*nonacq.*, 1992-2 CB xvi.), *rev'g* 109 TC 416, CCH Dec. 52,395). The IRS agrees that natural gas gathering lines owned by producers of natural gas are 7-year property (Asset Class 13.2).

NEW LAW EXPLAINED

Natural gas gathering lines treated as MACRS 7-year property.—The new law treats certain natural gas gathering lines placed in service after April 11, 2005, as MACRS 7-year property regardless of whether owned by a producer or a nonproducer (Code Sec. 168(e)(3)(C)(iv) and 168(i)(17), as added by the Energy Tax Incentives Act of 2005). A 14-year recovery period is assigned for purposes of the MACRS alternative depreciation system (ADS) (Code Sec. 168(g)(3)(B), as amended by the Energy Act).

> **Caution Note:** The provision only applies if the *original use* of the property commences with the taxpayer after April 11, 2005. In other words, the pipeline must be new. See ¶425 for additional commentary on the "original use" requirement. In addition, the provision does not apply if the taxpayer or a related party entered into a binding contract for the construction of the pipeline on or before April 11, 2005 (or, in the case of self-constructed property, began construction on or before that date) (Act Sec. 1326(e)(2) of the Energy Act).

NEW LAW EXPLAINED

Planning Note: Case law will continue to apply to gas gathering lines that do not qualify for the 7-year recovery period under this provision. These include lines placed in service before the effective date and used lines purchased after the effective date. The Joint Committee on Taxation, Description and Technical Explanation of the Energy Tax Incentives Act of 2005 (JCX-60-05), indicates that no inference regarding the proper depreciation period for gathering lines that are not subject to this provision should be drawn from the enactment of the provision.

Comment: In a separate provision, the new law treats natural gas *distribution* lines placed in service after April 11, 2005, as 15-year MACRS property with a 35-year ADS period. Under current law, these pipelines are treated as 20-year property with a 35-year ADS recovery period. See ¶515.

A natural gas gathering line is defined as:

(1) the pipe, equipment, and appurtenances determined to be a gathering line by the Federal Energy Regulatory Commission, and
(2) the pipe, equipment, and appurtenances used to deliver natural gas from the wellhead or a commonpoint to the point at which the gas first reaches either:

   (a) a gas processing plant,
   (b) an interconnection with a transmission pipeline for which a certificate as an interstate transmission pipeline has been issued by the Federal Energy Regulatory Commission,
   (c) an interconnection with an intrastate transmission pipeline, or
   (d) a direct interconnection with a local distribution company, a gas storage facility, or an industrial consumer (Code Sec. 168(i)(17), as added by the Energy Act).

Practical Analysis: Dr. Patrick Hennessee, Professor of Accounting at The University of Tulsa, notes that by legislatively defining natural gas gathering lines and classifying them as seven-year MACRS property, the Energy Tax Incentives Act of 2005 (Energy Act) resolves an almost decade-long controversy and uncertainty as to the cost recovery period (seven years versus 15 years) for gas gathering lines placed in service after April 11, 2005. The Energy Act only applies to original use property for which the taxpayer (or related party) had a binding acquisition contract on or before April 11, 2005. Thus, it remains to be seen whether the IRS will continue its unsuccessful litigation of gathering lines existing prior to this date. The Tenth Circuit, the Sixth Circuit and the Eighth Circuit of the Federal Courts of Appeal have already ruled that natural gas gathering lines qualified as seven-year MACRS property (*Duke Energy Natural Gas Corp.*, CA-10, 99-1 USTC ¶50,449, 172 F3d 1255, *rev'g*, 109 TC 416, Dec. 52,395 (1997); *Saginaw Bay Pipeline Co.*, CA-6, 2003-2 USTC ¶50,592, 338 F3d 600, *rev'g*, DC Mich., 2001-2 USTC ¶50,642, 124 FSupp2d 465; *Clajon Gas Co.*,

¶520

NEW LAW EXPLAINED

L.P., CA-8, 2004-1 USTC ¶50,123, 354 F3d 786, *rev'g,* 119 TC 197, Dec. 54,919 (2002)).

Alternative minimum tax. No depreciation adjustment is required for alternative minimum tax purposes for depreciation claimed on a natural gas gathering line that is treated as 7-year property under this provision (Code Sec. 56(a)(1)(B), as amended by the Energy Act).

Comment: The term "related party" is not defined by the new law.

▶ **Effective date.** The provision applies to property placed in service after April 11, 2005. However, the provision does not apply to property with respect to which the taxpayer or a related party has entered into a binding contract for the construction thereof on or before April 11, 2005, or, in the case of self-constructed property, has started construction on or before that date (Act Sec. 1326(e) of the Energy Tax Incentives Act of 2005).

Law source: Law at ¶5135 and ¶5165. Committee Report at ¶10,150.

— Act Sec. 1326(a) of the Energy Tax Incentives Act of 2005, redesignating Code Sec. 168(e)(3)(C)(iv) as (e)(3)(C)(v) and adding new Code Sec. 168(e)(3)(C)(iv);

— Act Sec. 1326(b), adding new Code Sec. 168(i)(17);

— Act Sec. 1326(c), amending Code Sec. 168(g)(3)(B);

— Act Sec. 1326(d), amending Code Sec. 56(a)(1);

— Act Sec. 1326(e), providing the effective date.

Reporter references: For further information, consult the following CCH reporters.

— Standard Federal Tax Reporter, 2005FED ¶5210.0215 and ¶11,279.023

— Federal Tax Service, FTS § G:6:83[3]

— Federal Tax Guide, 2005 FTG ¶9110

¶525 Geological and Geophysical Costs Amortized Over Two Years

BACKGROUND

Geological and geophysical expenditures are costs incurred for the purpose of obtaining and accumulating data that will serve as the basis for the acquisition and retention of mineral properties by taxpayers exploring for minerals, including gas and oil. Courts have found these expenses are capital in nature, and allocable to the property acquired or retained. IRS guidance provides rules on how to allocate such expenses incurred in a project area to particular areas of interest, if any are found (Rev. Rul. 77-188 (1977-1 CB 76), as amplified by Rev. Rul. 83-105 (1983-2 CB 51)). If no area of interest is found, the costs can be taken as a loss in the year the project area is abandoned.

NEW LAW EXPLAINED

Two-year amortization applies for all U.S. oil and gas geological and geophysical expenses.—The new law simplifies the treatment of geological and geophysical expenses. Such expenses paid or incurred in connection with oil and gas exploration or development in the United States must be amortized ratably over a 24-month period beginning on the mid-point of the tax-year that the expenses were paid or incurred (Code Sec. 167(h)(1) and (h)(2), as added by the Energy Tax Incentives Act of 2005). This is the exclusive method for claiming these expenses (Code Secs. 167(h)(3), as added by the Energy Act). Thus, in the case of property abandoned or retired during the 24-month amortization period, any remaining basis may not be recovered in the year of abandonment (Code Sec. 167(h)(4), as added by the Energy Act).

> **Comment:** Most taxpayers will benefit from the faster write-off. However, whatever advantage a taxpayer might have attained by capitalizing these costs is no longer available.

Treatment of offshore wells. Only payments made with respect to oil and gas wells located in the United States as defined in Code Sec. 638 qualify for 24-month amortization (Code Sec. 167(h)(1), as added by the Energy Act). For purposes of this provision, the United States includes the seabed and subsoil of those submarine areas which are adjacent to the territorial waters of the United States and over which the United States has exclusive exploration and exploitation rights under international law.

> **Comment:** This provision does not change the rules for the capitalization and amortization of geological and geophysical expenses with respect to minerals other than oil and gas.

Practical Analysis: Katherine Breaks, Senior Manager, Washington National Tax, KPMG LLP, observes that the Energy Tax Incentives Act of 2005 allows geological and geophysical expenditures incurred in connection with oil and gas exploration in the United States to be amortized over two years. Under prior law, geological and geophysical costs could not be recovered until production began or until the property was abandoned. The Energy Act provides certainty regarding the recovery of these expenditures and offers taxpayers guidance in managing their costs for these types of projects.

Deduction not capitalized under UNICAP rules. Amounts amortized under this provision are not subject to capitalization under the uniform capitalization (UNICAP) rules (Code Sec. 263A(c)(3), as amended by the Energy Act).

▶ **Effective date.** This provision applies to amounts paid or incurred in tax years beginning after August 8, 2005 (Act Sec. 1329(c) of the Energy Tax Incentives Act of 2005).

Law source: Law at ¶5160, ¶5205 and ¶5207. Committee Report at ¶10,180.

— Act Sec. 1329(a) of the Energy Tax Incentives Act of 2005, redesignating Code Sec. 167(h) as (i), and adding new Code Sec. 167(h);

¶525

NEW LAW EXPLAINED

— Act Sec. 1329(b), amending Code Sec. 263A(c)(3);

— Act Sec. 1329(c), providing the effective date.

Reporter references: For further information, consult the following CCH reporters.

— Standard Federal Tax Reporter, 2005FED ¶13,709.021

— Federal Tax Service, FTS § L:6.80

¶530 Safe Harbor from Tax-Exempt Bond Arbitrage Rules for Prepaid Natural Gas

BACKGROUND

Although state and local governments are allowed to issue tax-exempt bonds to finance various activities, certain arbitrage limitations are imposed by Code Sec. 148 in order to restrict entities from profiting on the investment of proceeds from such bonds. Arbitrage bonds are defined as bonds, the proceeds of which can reasonably be expected to be used to purchase higher yielding investment property or to replace funds used to acquire such investments. Thus, arbitrage earned from taxable securities, annuities, and other investment-type property is restricted if the yield on the property is materially higher than that on the bonds (Code Sec. 148(b)). Unless an exception applies, interest on an arbitrage bond is not excludable from income (Code Sec. 103(b)(2)).

> **Comment:** Private activity bonds that are not "qualified bonds" within the meaning of Code Sec. 141 are also covered by this provision (Code Sec. 103(b)(1)). Private activity bonds include those used to acquire "nongovernmental output property" as defined in Code Sec. 141(d)(2).

Under the applicable regulations (Reg. § 1.148-1(e)(2)), prepayments for property or services generally are considered to result in the acquisition of investment-type property if the principal purpose of the prepayment is to receive an investment return from the time the prepayment is made until the time the payment would otherwise have been made. However, there are exceptions to this general rule. For example, Reg. § 1.148-1(e)(1)(iii) generally exempts "qualified prepayments" for natural gas from the definition of investment-type property. In order to be considered a qualified prepayment, the payment must be made by a utility owned by a governmental entity (i.e., a municipal utility) and at least 90 percent of the prepaid natural gas financed by the bond issue must be put to a qualifying use. Qualifying use includes, among other things: (1) natural gas that is used by retail gas customers of the issuing municipal utility who are located in the municipal utility's natural gas service area and (2) natural gas used to produce electricity that will be furnished to retail electric customers of the municipal utility located in its electric service area.

NEW LAW EXPLAINED

Safe harbor for natural gas prepayments.—A safe harbor from the arbitrage rules is provided for qualifying prepaid natural gas supply contracts purchased by certain state and local government utilities (Code Sec. 148(b)(4), as added by the Energy Tax Incentives Act of 2005). Accordingly, qualified prepayments under such contracts are not considered to result in the acquisition of investment-type property.

Contract requirements. In order to meet the requirements of a qualified natural gas supply contract, the amount of gas permitted to be acquired under the contract by the utility during any year cannot exceed the sum of: (1) the annual average amount of natural gas purchased (other than for resale) during the testing period by customers of the utility located within its service area, plus (2) the amount of natural gas used to transport the prepaid natural gas to the utility during the year (Code Sec. 148(b)(4)(B), as added by the Energy Act). In computing the annual average in (1), natural gas that is used to generate electricity can be taken into account *only* if the electricity is generated by a government-owned utility and *only* to the extent that electricity is sold (other than for resale) to customers of the utility located within its service area (Code Sec. 148(b)(4)(C), as added by the Energy Act).

The new rules do allow for an adjustment to reflect the acquisition of new customers after the testing period ends, but before the bond issuance takes place. However, an overall limit states that the average under (1) above cannot exceed the annual amount of natural gas reasonably expected to be purchased for a reason other than resale by persons located within the utility's service area and who are its customers as of the date of the bond issue (Code Sec. 148(b)(4)(D), as added by the Energy Act). Governmental entities have the opportunity to request a ruling to argue for a higher average based on growth in population or consumption (Code Sec. 148(b)(4)(E), as added by the Energy Act).

An "applicable share" of natural gas on hand when the bond issuance takes place must be subtracted from the amount of natural gas otherwise permitted to be acquired. That reduction must include natural gas which the utility has the right to acquire during the period. The term "applicable share" means that the amount of natural gas must be allocated ratably over the period to which the prepayment applies (Code Sec. 148(b)(4)(F), as added by the Energy Act).

Intentional acts not permitted. Intentional acts on the part of a governmental entity to artificially inflate the volume of natural gas acquired by prepayment to exceed the sum of the amount of gas needed for purposes other than resale by its customers who are located within its service area, plus that amount of gas used to transport such natural gas to the utility, will result in loss of safe-harbor treatment (Code Sec. 148(b)(4)(G), as added by the Energy Act).

Definitions. For purposes of the safe-harbor rule, the term "testing period," used in the computation of the annual average amount of natural gas purchased, is the most recent five calendar years ending prior to the date of the bond issue (Code Sec. 148(b)(4)(H), as added by the Energy Act). In addition, in the case of a government-owned utility, the utility's "service area" is defined as any area through which the utility provided natural gas transmission or distribution services or electric distribution services (Code Sec. 148(b)(4)(I), as added by the Energy Act). Also, the term

NEW LAW EXPLAINED

includes an area within a county contiguous to the area just described, if retail customers of the utility are not served by another natural gas or electric service utility. Finally, a utility's service area includes any area recognized as such by state or federal law.

Exemption from private activity bond rules. A conforming amendment provides an exception to the private activity bond rules for qualified electric and natural gas supply contracts covered by the safe-harbor rule. Such contracts will not be considered nongovernmental output property for purposes of the private activity rules (Code Sec. 141(d)(7), as added by the Energy Act). In addition, the private loan financing test is not applicable to a qualified natural gas supply contract (Code Sec. 141(c)(2), as amended by the Energy Act).

> **Caution Note:** In a note contained in the Description and Technical Explanation of the Conference Agreement of H.R. 6, Title XIII (JCX-60-05), but not otherwise reflected in the law, the conferees recognize the existence of so-called state law joint action agencies that serve as purchasing agents for member municipal gas utilities. The conferees indicate that they intend for these buying arrangements to be subject to the same limitations as if an individual utility were purchasing gas directly. Thus, in the case of these buying arrangements, the requirements of the safe-harbor rule are to be tested at the individual municipal utility level based on the amount of gas that would be allocated to a member utility during any year covered by the contract.
>
> **Comment:** In light of the current lower capital gains tax rates and the equally advantageous treatment of qualifying dividends, municipal bond issuers find themselves faced with competition for the investor's dollar at a time when many governments are in troubled, if not dire, economic straits. Addition of this new safe-harbor rule should prove welcome news to state and local governments and assist them in protecting against increases in the cost of natural gas.

▶ **Effective date.** The safe harbor from the arbitrage rules for prepaid natural gas is applicable to obligations issued after August 8, 2005 (Act Sec. 1327(d) of the Energy Tax Incentives Act of 2005).

Law source: Law at ¶5140 and ¶5155. Committee Report at ¶10,160.

— Act Sec. 1327(a) of the Energy Tax Incentives Act of 2005, adding Code Sec. 148(b)(4);

— Act Sec. 1327(b), amending Code Sec. 141(c)(2);

— Act Sec. 1327(c), adding Code Sec. 141(d)(7);

— Act Sec. 1327(d), providing the effective date.

Reporter references: For further information, consult the following CCH reporters.

— Standard Federal Tax Reporter, 2005FED ¶7707.032 and ¶7889.023

— Federal Tax Service, FTS § E:17.220

— Federal Tax Guide, 2005FTG ¶4811

¶535 Deduction for Capital Costs Incurred in Complying with EPA Sulfur Regulations

BACKGROUND

The Environmental Protection Agency (EPA) has issued rules to limit the amount of sulfur in gasoline and highway diesel fuel (i.e., the Highway Diesel Fuel Sulfur Control Requirements of the EPA). These regulations require refiners to start producing diesel fuel with a sulfur content of no more than 15 parts per million (ppm) beginning June 1, 2006. At the terminal level, highway diesel fuel sold as low sulfur fuel must meet the sulfur standard as of July 15, 2006. Many refiners will need to invest in expensive hydro-treater technology for desulfurization, while fuel transporters and retailers most likely will need to purchase segregated tanks. The EPA has allowed small refiners to stagger compliance with these regulations, yet small refiners still face substantially increased costs when the grace period ends.

Taxpayers are generally allowed annual depreciation deductions for property used in a trade or business, which would include investments in refinery property. These allowances take into account the exhaustion, wear and tear of the underlying asset (Code Sec. 167(a)). However, under limited circumstances, a taxpayer may elect to expense immediately the cost of certain depreciable business assets (Code Sec. 179).

Code Sec. 179B(a), as added by the 2004 American Jobs Creation Act (P.L. 108-357), allows a small business refiner to make an election to deduct 75 percent of qualified capital costs paid or incurred during the tax year to comply with EPA sulfur regulations during the period beginning on January 1, 2003 through December 31, 2009. These costs include expenditures for the construction of new process operation units or the dismantling and reconstruction of existing process units that are to be used in the production of diesel fuel with a sulfur content of no more than 15 ppm, associated adjacent or offsite equipment (including tankage, catalyst, and power supply), engineering, construction period interest, and sitework.

Small business refiner defined. For this purpose, a small business refiner is a taxpayer who (1) is in the business of refining crude oil; (2) employs no more than 1,500 employees in the refinery operations of the business on any day during the tax year; and (3) had average daily domestic refinery run or average retained production for all facilities for the one-year period that ended on December 31, 2002, that did not exceed 205,000 barrels. The deduction is reduced *pro rata* for taxpayers with capacity in excess of 155,000 barrels per day.

Small refiner cooperative. Where a small business refiner is owned by a cooperative, Code Sec. 40(g)(6)(A)(i) allows a cooperative to elect to pass any production credits to patrons of the organization. Such amounts are included in the patron's gross income as patronage dividends under Code Secs. 1385(a) and 1388(a). The patron, and not the cooperative, claims the benefit of the credit to the extent the patron includes patronage dividends derived from such credit in the patron's income for the tax year. Cooperatives are not presently allowed to pass through to their patrons, the deduction permitted for the costs paid or incurred for the purpose of complying with the EPA rules.

BACKGROUND

Taxation of cooperatives and their patrons. A cooperative is an association, generally organized in corporate form, through which producers or consumers of various commodities, referred to as patrons, increase their market power by combining to sell or purchase the commodities collectively. Cooperatives, both exempt and nonexempt, are generally taxed as corporations, but they are allowed to take special deductions from gross income (Code Secs. 1381 and 1382). For example, cooperatives may deduct distributions to their patrons of cash dividends derived from sources directly related to the cooperative's marketing, purchasing, or service activities. These dividends are referred to as patronage dividends.

Exempt farmers' cooperatives are given the added advantage of being able to deduct dividends on capital stock and amounts paid or allocated from income not derived from patronage (Code Sec. 521). To qualify as an exempt farmers' cooperative, an entity must be organized on a cooperative basis and be engaged in prescribed activities. It must also comply with restrictions on its capital stock, it must not maintain excess reserves (a reserve required by State law or a reasonable reserve for any necessary purpose is permissible), and it must comply with restrictions on transacting business with nonmembers.

NEW LAW EXPLAINED

Small business refiner cooperatives can elect to pass through deduction to their patrons.—The Energy Tax Incentives Act of 2005 allows a small business refiner cooperative to elect to allocate all or a portion of the deduction permitted for costs paid or incurred for the purpose of complying with the EPA sulfur regulations *pro rata* among any other cooperatives that directly hold an ownership interest in the refiner (Code Sec. 179B(e)(1), as added by the Energy Act). Accordingly, to the extent the deduction is passed through to its patrons, the cooperative is denied deductions it would otherwise be entitled to relating to such costs.

> **Election:** Pass through treatment for cooperative patrons must be elected on a timely filed return of the organization for the relevant tax year (Code Sec. 179B(e)(2), as added by the Energy Act). Once made, the election is irrevocable for that tax year. The Energy Act does not contain any guidance as to the form the election should take.

Written notice. Any cooperative making such an election must provide cooperative owners written notice of the allocated amount by the due date for the tax return on which the election is made (Code Sec. 179B(e)(3), as added by the Energy Act).

▶ **Effective date.** This amendment applies to expenses paid or incurred after December 31, 2002, in tax years ending after that date (Act Sec. 1324(b) of the Energy Tax Incentives Act of 2005).

Law source: Law at ¶5185. Committee Report at ¶10,130.

— Act Sec. 1324(a) of the Energy Tax Incentives Act of 2005, adding Code Sec. 179B(e);

— Act Sec. 1324(b), providing the effective date.

NEW LAW EXPLAINED

Reporter references: For further information, consult the following CCH reporters.
— Standard Federal Tax Reporter, 2005FED ¶ 12,136.01
— Federal Tax Service, FTS § L:6.20

¶540 Oil Spill Liability Trust Fund Financing Rate

BACKGROUND

The Oil Spill Liability Trust Fund ("Oil Spill Fund") was established primarily to pay for certain removal costs and related costs associated with oil spills (Omnibus Budget Reconciliation Act of 1986, P.L. 99-509). The Oil Spill Fund was financed in part by a five-cent-per-barrel tax ("oil spill tax") on domestic crude oil received at a United States refinery, on imported petroleum products that entered into the United States for consumption, use, or warehousing and on domestic crude oil used in or exported from the United States not yet subjected to the tax before its use or exportation (Code Sec. 4611(a) and (b)). The oil spill tax was imposed on the operator of a United States refinery receiving the domestic crude oil, on the person importing the petroleum products and the person using or exporting the crude oil (Code Sec. 4611(d)).

> **Comment:** There used to be a tax of 14.7 cents per barrel on crude oil. This tax had two components: (1) 9.7 cents per barrel, which funded the Hazardous Substance Superfund Trust Fund, and (2) 5 cents per barrel, which funded the Oil Liability Trust Fund. Often these two taxes were lumped together and called "Superfund" taxes.

The oil spill tax was suspended effective July 1, 1994, because the Treasury Department estimated that the Oil Spill Fund would have an unobligated balance of over $1 billion at the end of the second calendar quarter of 1993 (IRS Announcement 93-90, I.R.B. 1993-23). The tax was, however, reapplied effective July 1, 1994, until December 31, 1994, when it expired by operation of law (IRS Announcement 97-74, I.R.B. 1994-22).

NEW LAW EXPLAINED

Reinstatement of the oil spill tax.—The Oil Spill Liability Trust Fund financing rate ("oil spill tax") of five cents per barrel is reinstated on April 1, 2006, until the Oil Spill Fund reaches an unobligated balance of $2.7 billion (Code Sec. 4611(f), as amended by the Energy Tax Incentives Act of 2005). Thereafter, the oil spill tax will be reinstated 30 days after the last day of any calendar quarter for which the IRS estimates that, as of the close of that quarter, the unobligated balance of the Oil Spill Fund is less than $2 billion. The oil spill tax will cease to apply after December 31, 2014, regardless of the Oil Spill Fund balance.

> **Compliance Tip:** Taxpayers liable for the oil spill tax pay and report the tax on Form 6627, Environmental Taxes and attach to Form 720, Quarterly Federal Excise Tax Return.

NEW LAW EXPLAINED

> **Practical Analysis:** William B. Gray (Bill), Excise Tax Manager, Sinclair Oil Corporation, observes that payors of this tax may want to consider passing it on to customers as a line-item tax on the invoice. There's nothing to prevent this. To accurately pass the tax on, you'd probably base the calculation on the proportion of gas and diesel that is produced from a barrel of crude oil.
>
> Most companies will want to consider what the competition will do. Will your competitors accept this as an additional cost and perhaps increase the price of the finished product as necessary, or will your competitors add a line item tax on their invoice? Most companies have not passed it on as a separate line item in the past.

▶ **Effective date.** No specific effective date is provided by the Act. The provision is, therefore, considered effective on August 8, 2005.

Law source: Law at ¶5365. Committee Report at ¶10,350.

— Act Sec. 1361 of the Energy Tax Incentives Act of 2005, amending Code Sec. 4611(f).

Reporter references: For further information, consult the following CCH reporters.

— Federal Tax Service, FTS §G:24.260
— Federal Tax Guide, 2005FTG ¶21,750
— Excise Tax Reporter, ETR ¶31,675.04

¶540

Coal 6

¶605 Credit for investment in clean coal facilities

¶610 Credit for producing fuel from a nonconventional source extended to coke or coke gas facilities

¶615 Modification of credit for producing fuel from a nonconventional source

¶620 84-month amortization of air pollution control facilities

¶605 Credit for Investment in Clean Coal Facilities

BACKGROUND

The general business credit under Code Sec. 38 is a limited nonrefundable credit against income tax that is claimed after all other nonrefundable credits. One of the components of the general business credit is the investment credit of Code Sec. 46, which consists, in part, of the business energy credit.

The business energy credit is a nonrefundable, 10-percent investment tax credit that is allowed for the cost of new property that is equipment (1) that uses solar energy to generate electricity to heat or cool a structure, or to provide solar heat process, or (2) that is used to produce, distribute, or use energy derived from a geothermal deposit, but only in the case of electricity generated by geothermal power, up to the electric transmission stage. The credit equals 10 percent of the basis of qualified energy property placed in service during the tax year (Code Sec. 48).

No energy credit is currently provided for electricity generating units that use coal as a fuel or for the gasification of coal or other materials. "Clean coal technologies," a controversial subject on Capitol Hill, allow coal to be burned more efficiently, with reduced emissions of sulphur and nitrogen oxides compared to older coal-burning systems. Proponents of the technology tout it as a reliable source of domestic energy with great potential. Opponents argue that the technology is harmful to the environment.

NEW LAW EXPLAINED

New tax credits for investment in clean coal facilities.—Two new credits for investment in clean coal facilities are added to the investment credit provisions of Code Sec. 46 (Code Sec. 46(3) and Code Sec. 46(4), as added by the Energy Tax Incentives Act of 2005). The first credit is the "Qualifying Advanced Coal Project Credit" (Code Sec. 48A, as added by the Energy Act). The second credit is the "Qualifying Gasification Project Credit" (Code Sec. 48B, as added by the Energy Act). Each credit is available only to taxpayers who have applied for and received certification that their project satisfies the relevant requirements. The IRS and the Energy Department will jointly establish programs to evaluate applications for such certifications.

> **Comment:** The adoption of "clean coal" investment credits not only reflects congressional recognition of the abundance of coal as a fuel source, but also demonstrates political sensitivity to the environmental impact of burning coal for the production of electricity. The credits are designed to encourage the burning of coal in a more efficient and environmentally friendly manner.

Qualifying advanced coal project credit. The IRS, in consultation with the Secretary of Energy, is required to establish a qualifying advanced coal project program to support the deployment of advanced coal-based generation technologies within 180 days of the passage of the Energy Act (Code Sec. 48A(d)(1), as added by the Energy Act). Under the program, taxpayers seeking subsidies for their advanced coal projects will file applications for certification. Up to $1,300,000,000 in credits will be allocated to taxpayers whose applications for certification are approved. The IRS is authorized to allocate a maximum of $800,000,000 in credits for integrated gasification combined cycle (IGCC) projects, and a maximum of $500,000,000 in credits for projects using other advanced coal-based generation technologies (Code Sec. 48A(d)(3), as added by the Energy Act).

Amount of qualifying advanced coal project credit. The amount of the qualifying advanced coal project credit for a tax year is (1) 20 percent of the qualified investment for the tax year for IGCC projects certified by the IRS, and (2) 15 percent of the qualified investment for the tax year for projects using other technologies (Code Sec. 48A(a)(1), as added by the Energy Act).

Qualified investment. The qualified investment for any tax year is the basis of eligible property placed in service by the taxpayer during the tax year that is part of the qualifying advanced coal project. Eligible property is limited to property for which depreciation or amortization is available and (1) the construction, reconstruction, or erection of which is completed by the taxpayer, or (2) which is acquired by the taxpayer, if the original use of the property commences with the taxpayer (Code Sec. 48A(b)(1), as added by the Energy Act). The basis of property, for purposes of calculating the qualified investment, is reduced to the extent the property was financed by tax-exempt private activity bonds or subsidized energy financing (Code Sec. 48A(b)(2), as added by the Energy Act). In addition, certain qualified progress expenditure rules, similar to the rules for the former investment tax credit under Code Sec. 46(c)(4) and Code Sec. 46(d) are applicable (Code Sec. 48A(b)(3), as added

¶605

NEW LAW EXPLAINED

by the Energy Act). These rules allow the credit to be taken for certain progress payments even before the property has been placed in service.

Eligible property. In the case of a qualifying advanced coal project using an IGCC, any property which is a part of the project and necessary for the gasification of coal, including any coal handling and gas separation equipment, is eligible property (Code Sec. 48A(c)(3), as added by the Energy Act). Investments in equipment that could operate by drawing fuel directly from a natural gas pipeline do not qualify for the credit (Joint Committee on Taxation, Description and Technical Explanation of the Energy Tax Incentives Act of 2005 (JCX-60-05)). In the case of any other qualifying advanced coal project, any property which is part of the project is eligible property (Code Sec. 48A(c)(3), as added by the Energy Act).

Qualifying advanced coal project program. Under the qualifying advanced coal project program, taxpayers seeking to claim the credit must submit an application for certification which shows that the planned project will satisfy the requirements of the program. Once an application is accepted, the applicant must make additional specified progress on the project. If specified steps are completed within two years, the IRS will certify the project. A certified project must be placed in service within five years after the certification.

As noted above, the IRS is required by law to establish the program within 180 days after the passage of the Energy Act. Taxpayers will be able to apply for an allocation of credits under the qualifying advanced coal project program during the three-year period beginning on the date the program is established (Code Sec. 48A(d)(2)(A), as added by the Energy Act). The IRS will determine what information is required in order to make a decision to accept or reject an application for certification. The application will be not be disclosed to the public to the extent that it contains privileged or confidential trade secrets or commercial or financial information (Code Sec. 48A(d)(2)(B), as added by the Energy Act). The IRS is required to accept or reject each application within 60 days following its submission (Code Sec. 48A(d)(2)(C), as added by the Energy Act). Each accepted applicant for certification has two years from the date of acceptance by the IRS to provide the IRS with evidence that the second stage criteria for certification have been met (Code Sec. 48A(d)(2)(D), as added by the Energy Act). A certified applicant will have five years from the date of issuance of certification to place the project in service. Failure to do so within the five year time frame will result in the certificate no longer being valid (Code Sec. 48A(d)(2)(E), as added by the Energy Act).

Initial requirements. A project is a qualifying advanced coal project that may obtain certification if the IRS determines that:

(1) the project uses an advanced coal-based generation technology to power a new electric generation unit or to refit or repower an existing electric generation unit (including an existing natural gas-fired combined cycle unit);

(2) the fuel input for the project, when completed, will be at least 75-percent coal;

(3) the electric generation unit or units at the project site will have a total nameplate generating capacity of at least 400 megawatts;

NEW LAW EXPLAINED

(4) a majority of the output of the project is reasonably expected to be acquired or utilized;

(5) the applicant/taxpayer provides evidence of ownership or control of a site of sufficient size to allow the proposed project to be constructed and to operate on a long term basis; and

(6) the project will be located in the United States (Code Sec. 48A(e)(1), as added by the Energy Act).

The IRS must issue a determination as to whether the applicant meets these initial requirements within 60 days after the filing of an application. If the application is accepted, the applicant has two years to provide evidence that the additional criteria for certification have been met.

Additional criteria for certification. A project for which an application has been accepted will be eligible for certification when:

(1) the applicant has received all federal and state environmental authorizations or reviews necessary to begin construction of the project; and

(2) the applicant, except in the case of a retrofit or repower of an existing electric generation unit, has purchased or entered into a binding contract for the purchase of the main steam turbine or turbines for the project. However, a contract for the purchase of the main steam turbine or turbines may be contingent upon receipt of certification (Code Sec. 48A(e)(2), as added by the Energy Act).

Priority for IGCC projects. In selecting which advanced coal projects to certify, the IRS is required to:

(1) certify capacity in relatively equal amounts to projects using bituminous coal as a primary feedstock, projects using subbituminous coal as primary feedstock, and projects using lignite as a primary feedstock, and

(2) give high priority to projects which include greenhouse gas capture capability, increased by-product utilization, and other benefits, as determined by the IRS (Code Sec. 48A(e)(3), as added by the Energy Act).

Greenhouse gas capture capability. Greenhouse gas capture capability means an IGCC technology facility that is able to add components that can capture, separate on a long-term basis, isolate, remove, and sequester greenhouse gases which result from generating electricity (Code Sec. 48A(c)(5), as added by the Energy Act).

IRS review and redistribution of credits. Not later than six years after the passage of the Energy Act, the IRS must review the credits that have been allocated at that point (Code Sec. 48A(d)(4)(A), as added by the Energy Act). If at that time there are available credits under either the IGCC limit or the non-IGCC limit, the IRS may reallocate the available credits if it determines that there is an insufficient quantity of qualifying applications for certification pending at the time of review or any previously granted certification has been revoked because the project has been delayed as a result of third party opposition or litigation (Code Sec. 48A(d)(4)(B), as added by the Energy Act). If credits are available for reallocation, the IRS is authorized to

NEW LAW EXPLAINED

conduct an additional program for applications for certification (Code Sec. 48A(d)(4)(C), as added by the Energy Act).

Definitions. "Advanced coal-based generation technology" and other terms used in advanced coal-based generation technology are described below.

(1) *Advanced coal-based generation technology.* An electric generation unit uses advanced coal-based generation technology if the unit uses integrated gasification combined cycle (IGCC) technology or has a design net heat rate of 8530 Btu/kWH (40-percent efficiency).

An exception exists to the 40-percent efficiency requirement for existing units. Any electric generation unit in existence on the date the law was enacted that uses advanced coal-based generation technology is required to achieve a minimum efficiency of 35 percent and an overall thermal design efficiency improvement, compared to the efficiency of the unit as operated, of not less than:

(A) seven percentage points for coal of more than 9,000 Btu;

(B) six percentage points for coal of 7,000 to 9,000 Btu; or

(C) four percentage points for coal of less than 7,000 Btu (Code Sec. 48A(f)(3) as added by the Energy Act).

The unit must also be designed to meet the following performance requirements:

Performance characteristic:	Design level for project:
SO_2 (percent removal)	99 percent
NO_x (emissions)	0.07 lbs/MMBTU
PM* (emissions)	0.015 lbs/MMBTU
Hg (percent removal)	90 percent

(Code Sec. 48A(c)(2) and Code Sec. 48A(f)(1), as added by the Energy Act).

The design net heat rate with respect to an electric generation unit must:

(A) be measured in Btu per kilowatt hour (higher heating value);

(B) be based on the design annual heat input to the unit and the rated net electrical power, fuels, and chemicals output of the unit (determined without regard to the cogeneration of steam by the unit);

(C) be adjusted for the heat content of the design coal to be used by the unit

(a) if the heat content is less than 13,500 Btu per pound, but greater than 7,000 Btu per pound, according to the following formula: design net heat rate = unit net heat rate x [1 – [(13,500-design coal heat content, Btu per pound/1,000)* 0.013]], and

(b) if the heat content is less than or equal to 7,000 Btu per pound, according to the following formula: design net heat rate = unit net heat rate x [1 – [(13,500-design coal heat content, Btu per pound/1,000)* 0.018]]; and

(D) be corrected for the site reference conditions of:

(a) elevation above sea level of 500 feet;

(b) air pressure of 14.4 pounds per square inch absolute;

NEW LAW EXPLAINED

  (c) temperature, dry bulb of 63/o/F;

  (d) temperature, wet bulb of 54/o/F; and

  (e) relative humidity of 55 percent (Code Sec. 48A(f)(2), as added by the Energy Act).

(2) *Electric generation unit.* Electric generation unit means any facility with at least 50 percent of its total annual net output being electrical power, including an otherwise eligible facility that is used in an industrial application (Code Sec. 48A(c)(6), as added by the Energy Act).

(3) *Integrated gasification combined cycle (IGCC).* Integrated gasification combined cycle means an electric generation unit that provides electricity by converting coal to synthesis gas which is used to fuel a combined-cycle plant which produces electricity from both a combustion turbine (including a combustion turbine/fuel cell hybrid) and a steam turbine (Code Sec. 48A(c)(7), as added by the Energy Act).

Applicability. No use of technology (or level of emission reduction solely by reason of the use of technology) or emission reduction by the demonstration of any technology or performance level, by or at one or more facilities with respect to which the Code Sec. 48A credit is allowed, will be considered to indicate that the technology or performance level is:

(1) adequately demonstrated for purposes of the Clean Air Act (42 U.S.C. §7411);

(2) achievable for purposes of the Clean Air Act (42 U.S.C. §7479); or

(3) achievable in practice for purposes of the Clean Air Act (42 U.S.C. §7501) (Code Sec. 48A(g), as added by the Energy Act).

Qualifying gasification project credit. The IRS, in consultation with the Secretary of Energy, is required to establish a qualifying gasification project program to certify qualified investments eligible for the qualifying gasification project credit within 180 days of the passage of the Energy Act. Under the program, taxpayers seeking subsidies for their gasification projects will file applications for certification. Up to $350,000,000 in credits will be allocated to taxpayers whose applications for certification are approved (Code Sec. 48B(d)(1), as added by the Energy Act).

  Comment: Coal gasification is an alternative to coal combustion. Instead of burning coal directly, a coal gasifier reacts coal with steam and controlled amounts of air or oxygen under high temperatures and pressure. This process breaks apart the chemical bonds in the coal's molecular structure, causing chemical reactions to form a gaseous mixture. This mixture is called synthesis gas or syngas. It is primarily made up of carbon monoxide and hydrogen, which is then combusted in a gas turbine to generate electricity.

Amount of qualifying gasification project credit. In general, the qualifying gasification project credit for any tax year is equal to 20 percent of the qualified investment for the tax year (Code Sec. 48B(a), as added by the Energy Act).

NEW LAW EXPLAINED

Qualified investment. The qualified investment for any tax year is the basis of eligible property placed in service by the taxpayer during the tax year that is part of the qualifying gasification project. Eligible property is limited to property for which depreciation or amortization is available and (1) the construction, reconstruction, or erection which is completed by the taxpayer, or (2) which is acquired by the taxpayer, if the original use of the property commences with the taxpayer (Code Sec. 48B(b)(1), as added by the Energy Act). The basis of property, for purposes of calculating the qualified investment, is reduced to the extent the property was financed by tax-exempt private activity bonds or subsidized energy financing (Code Sec. 48B(b)(2), as added by the Energy Act). In addition, certain qualified progress expenditure rules, similar to the rules for the former investment tax credit under Code Sec. 46(c)(4) and Code Sec. 46(d) are applicable (Code Sec. 48B(b)(3), as added by the Energy Act). These rules allow the credit to be taken for certain progress payments even before the property has been placed in service.

Eligible property. Eligible property is property that is part of a qualifying gasification project and is necessary for the gasification technology of the project (Code Sec. 48B(c)(3), as added by the Energy Act).

Qualifying gasification project program. Under the qualifying gasification project program, taxpayers seeking to use the credit must apply for a certification (Code Sec. 48B(d)(1), as added by the Energy Act). A certificate of eligibility may be issued only during the 10-fiscal year period beginning on October 1, 2005 (Code Sec. 48B(d)(2), as added by the Energy Act).

> **Comment:** New Code Sec. 48B(d)(1) states that "the total amounts of credit that may be allocated under the [qualifying gasification project] program shall not exceed $350,000,000 under rules similar to the rules of section 48A(d)(4)." It is not clear what this means. The rules of Code Sec. 48A(d)(4) allow the IRS to *reallocate* the qualifying advanced coal project credits between the IGCC and non-IGCC categories if there is an excess of demand for one category and a shortfall in the other. It may be that the provision was intended to refer to Code Sec. 48A(d)(2), which provides procedures for the certification process. There are no such procedures provided in Code Sec. 48B.

Qualifying gasification project. A qualifying gasification project is a project that (1) employs gasification technology, (2) will be carried out by an eligible entity, and (3) any portion of the qualified investment of which is certified under the qualifying gasification program as eligible for a credit under Code Sec. 48B. The qualified investment in a particular project cannot exceed $650,000,000 (Code Sec. 48B(c)(1), as added by the Energy Act). Since the credit is equal to 20 percent of the qualified investment, the maximum credit for any single project is $130,000,000.

The IRS is not allowed to make a competitive certification award for qualified investment for the credit unless the recipient has documented to the satisfaction of the IRS that:

(1) the award recipient is financially viable without the receipt of additional federal funding associated with the proposed project;

¶605

NEW LAW EXPLAINED

(2) the recipient will provide sufficient information to the IRS so the IRS is assured that the qualified investment is spent efficiently and effectively;

(3) a market exists for the products of the proposed project as evidenced by contracts or written statements of intent from potential customers;

(4) the fuels identified with respect to the gasification technology for the project will comprise at least 90 percent of the fuels required by the project for the production of chemical feedstocks, liquid transportation fuels, or coproduction of electricity;

(5) the award recipient's project team is competent in the construction and operation of the gasification technology proposed, with preference given to recipients with experience that demonstrates successful and reliable operations of the technology on domestic fuels so identified; and

(6) the award recipient has met other criteria established and published by the IRS (Code Sec. 48B(d)(3), as added by the Energy Act).

Comment: In 1984, the Clean Coal Technology Program (CCTP) began as a public-private partnership between the Department of Energy (DOE) and energy companies to develop less polluting coal plants. Since 1985, the DOE has appropriated $2.75 billion for clean coal projects. In evaluating the CCTP, the Government Accounting Office (GAO) described the program as having had "its ups and downs." Although the GAO cited numerous examples of successes in the program, it found that from a "management perspective" many projects had experienced delays, cost overruns, bankruptcies, and performance problems. The GAO also expressed concerns about some of the projects the DOE had selected. In 2000, the GAO examined 13 CCTP projects and found that eight had serious delays or financial problems (six were behind their original schedules by two to seven years) and two projects were bankrupt and would not be completed. The seemingly stringent requirements to participate in the Qualifying Gasification Project Program is likely an attempt to prevent the type of problems that the GAO highlighted in its review of the CCTP.

Definitions. "Gasification technology" and other terms used in gasification technology are defined below.

(1) *Gasification technology.* Gasification technology is any process that converts a solid or liquid product from coal, petroleum residue, biomass, or other materials that are recovered for their energy or feedstock value into a synthesis gas composed primarily of carbon monoxide and hydrogen for direct use or subsequent chemical or physical conversion (Code Sec. 48B(c)(2), as added by the Energy Act).

(2) *Biomass.* In general, the term biomass means any:

  (A) agricultural or plant waste;

  (B) byproduct of wood or paper mill operations, including lignin in spent pulping liquors; and

  (C) other products of forestry maintenance.

¶605

NEW LAW EXPLAINED

Biomass does not include commonly recycled paper (Code Sec. 48B(c)(4), as added by the Energy Act).

(3) *Carbon capture capability.* Carbon capture capability is a gasification plant design that is determined by the IRS to reflect reasonable consideration for, and be capable of, accommodating the equipment likely to be necessary to capture carbon dioxide from the gaseous stream, for later use or sequestration, which would otherwise be emitted in the flue gas from a project that uses nonrenewable fuel (Code Sec. 48B(c)(5), as added by the Energy Act).

(4) *Eligible entity.* An eligible entity is any person whose application for certification is principally intended for use in a domestic project that employs domestic gasification applications related to chemicals, fertilizers, glass, steel, petroleum residues, forest products, and agriculture, including feedlots and dairy operations (Code Sec. 48B(c)(7), as added by the Energy Act).

(5) *Petroleum residue.* Petroleum residue is the carbonized product of high-boiling hydrocarbon fractions obtained in petroleum processing (Code Sec. 48B(c)(8), as added by the Energy Act).

Denial of double benefit. A credit will not be allowed under Code Sec. 48B for any qualified investment that receives a credit under Code Sec. 48A (Code Sec. 48B(e), as added by the Energy Act).

State Tax Consequences: Many states provide energy incentives through personal and corporate income tax credits. See ¶195 for a state-by-state summary of available credits.

▶ **Effective date.** The provisions apply to periods after August 8, 2005, under rules similar to the rules of Code Sec. 48(m) (as in effect on the day before the enactment of the Revenue Reconciliation Act of 1990, November 4, 1990) (P.L. 101-508) (Act Sec. 1307(d) of the Energy Tax Incentives Act of 2005).

Under those rules the credit is available with respect to eligible property constructed, reconstructed or erected by the taxpayer after August 8, 2005, to the extent the basis is attributable to the taxpayer's efforts after that date. With respect to property acquired by the taxpayer after August 8, 2005, the entire basis of the eligible property can be taken into account. If qualified progress expenditures are taken into account, only the portion of basis attributable to progress expenditures made after August 8, 2005, are taken into account.

Law source: Law at ¶5095, ¶5105, ¶5110 and ¶5115. Committee Report at ¶10,060.

— Act Sec. 1307(a) of the Energy Tax Incentives Act of 2005, adding Code Sec. 46(3) and (4);

— Act Sec. 1307(b), adding new Code Secs. 48A and 48B;

— Act Sec. 1307(c), amending Code Sec. 49(a)(1)(C);

— Act Sec. 1307(d), providing the effective date.

Reporter references: For further information, consult the following CCH reporters.

— Standard Federal Tax Reporter, 2005FED ¶4580.01

— Federal Tax Service, FTS § G:24.20

¶605

¶ 610 Credit for Producing Fuel from a Nonconventional Source Extended to Coke or Coke Gas Facilities

BACKGROUND

Code Sec. 29 provides a nonrefundable credit for the production and sale of energy from alternative sources. This provision was originally enacted as part of the Crude Oil Windfall Profit Tax Act of 1980 (P.L. 96-223). There were two primary reasons for the enactment. First, the credit was intended to reduce U.S. dependence on imported energy. Second, the credit was intended to enhance the long-term competitiveness of alternative fuel sources.

The credit is generally equal to $3.00 (adjusted for inflation) multiplied by the number of barrel-of-oil equivalents of qualified fuels produced and sold during the tax year. The credit for 2004 was $6.56 per barrel-of-oil equivalent, which is approximately $1.16 per thousand cubic feet of natural gas. A barrel-of-oil equivalent is an amount of fuel which has the energy equivalent of 42 U.S. gallons. The energy equivalence is based on the Btu content of the fuels.

Certain fuels (oil, gas and synthetic fuels) may qualify for the credit. Oil may qualify if it is from shale or tar sands. Gas may qualify if it is from geopressured brine, Devonian Shale, coal seams, and tight formations ("tight sands") or biomass. Liquid, gaseous, or solid synthetic fuels produced from coal (including lignite) may also qualify.

To be eligible for the credit, the production of a qualified fuel must occur within the United States or a possession of the United States. In general, only production that is sold to an unrelated person qualifies for the credit.

The production that qualifies for the credit is subject to specific time constraints. Wells must be drilled within a certain time frame; facilities must be placed in service within specific dates; fuel produced must be sold prior to termination dates.

Qualified fuels generally must be produced from wells drilled after December 31, 1979, and before January 1, 1993, or produced in a facility placed in service after December 31, 1979, and before January 1, 1993. An exception extends the January 1, 1993, expiration date for facilities producing gas from biomass and synthetic fuel from coal if the facility producing the fuel is placed in service before July 1, 1998, pursuant to a binding contract entered into before January 1, 1997. The qualifying alternative fuel produced must generally be sold after December 31, 1979, and before January 1, 2003 (in the case of nonconventional sources subject to the January 1, 1993, expiration date) or January 1, 2008 (in the case of biomass gas and synthetic fuel facilities eligible for the extension period), to qualify for the credit.

The Code Sec. 29 credit, including the provision dealing with the production of coke or coke gas, has expired, except for certain biomass gas and synthetic fuels sold before January 1, 2008, and produced at facilities placed in service after December 31, 1992, and before July 1, 1998.

¶610

NEW LAW EXPLAINED

Extension and modification of credit for producing fuel from a nonconventional source.—The Code Sec. 29 credit for producing fuel from a nonconventional source has been redesignated as Code Sec. 45K (Code Sec. 45K, as redesignated by Act. Sec. 1322 of the Energy Tax Incentives Act of 2005, see ¶615) and extended to facilities producing coke or coke gas (Code Sec. 45K(h), as added by the Energy Act).

The credit can be claimed for coke or coke gas (1) produced in facilities that were placed in service before January 1, 1993, or after June 30, 1998, and before January 1, 2010, and (2) sold during the period beginning on the later of January 1, 2006, or the date that the facility is placed in service and ending on the date that is four years after the date such period began (Code Sec. 45K(h)(1), as added by the Energy Act).

Special rules. Special rules are provided for determining the amount of the credit allowed solely as a result of the new coke and coke gas provision contained in Code Sec. 45K(h)(1). The amount of qualified fuels sold during a tax year for which a credit can be claimed cannot exceed an average barrel-of-oil equivalent of 4,000 barrels per day with respect to any facility. Days prior to the date the facility is placed in service are not taken into account in determining the average (Code Sec. 45K(h)(2)(A), as added by the Energy Act).

> **Caution Note:** The average daily 4,000 barrel-of-oil equivalent limit with respect to any coke or coke gas producing facility is a new limitation that does not apply to other nonconventional fuel sources eligible for the credit. Although the new provision does not provide a definition of "facility," the Joint Committee on Taxation, Description and Technical Explanation of the Energy Tax Incentives Act of 2005 (JCX-60-05) states that the "conferees understand that a single facility for the production of coke or coke gas is generally composed of multiple coke ovens or similar structures."

For fuels sold after 2005, in determining the amount of the credit related to facilities producing coke and coke gas as provided in Code Sec. 45K(h), the $3.00 credit amount is adjusted for inflation using 2004 as the base year instead of 1979 (Code Sec. 45K(h)(2)(B), as added by the Energy Act). The credit allowed as a result of Code Sec. 45K(h) does not apply to any facility producing qualified fuels that received a credit under Code Sec. 45K for the tax year or any preceding tax year as a result of the provisions under Code Sec. 45K(g). (Code Sec. 45K(h)(2)(C), as added by the Energy Act).

> **Comment:** Although not provided for in the new law, the conference report contained language encouraging the IRS to consider issuing private letter rulings and other taxpayer-specific guidance regarding the Code Sec. 45K credit on an expedited basis to taxpayers who had pending ruling requests at the time the IRS imposed a moratorium on Code Sec. 45K guidance (formerly Code Sec. 29 guidance) (Joint Committee on Taxation, Description and Technical Explanation of the Energy Tax Incentives Act of 2005 (JCX-60-05)).

▶ **Effective date.** This provision applies to fuel produced and sold after December 31, 2005, in tax years ending after that date (Act Sec. 1321(b) of the Energy Tax Incentives Act of 2005).

NEW LAW EXPLAINED

Law source: Law at ¶5080. Committee Report at ¶10,110.

— Act Sec. 1321(a) of the Energy Tax Incentives Act of 2005, adding Code Sec. 29(h) (redesignated as Code Sec. 45K(h), by Act Sec. 1322);

— Act Sec. 1321(b), providing the effective date.

Reporter references: For further information, consult the following CCH reporters.

— Standard Federal Tax Reporter, 2005FED ¶4051.01

— Federal Tax Service, FTS § G:24.20

— Federal Tax Guide, 2005FTG ¶2350

¶615 Modification of Credit for Producing Fuel from a Nonconventional Source

BACKGROUND

Code Sec. 29 provides a nonrefundable credit for the production and sale of energy from alternative sources. This provision was originally enacted as part of the Crude Oil Windfall Profit Tax Act of 1980 (P.L. 96-223). There were two primary reasons for the enactment. First, the credit was intended to reduce U.S. dependence on imported energy. Second, the credit was intended to enhance the long-term competitiveness of alternative fuel sources.

The credit is generally equal to $3.00 (adjusted for inflation) multiplied by the number of barrel-of-oil equivalents of qualified fuels produced and sold during the tax year. The credit for 2004 was $6.56 per barrel-of-oil equivalent, which is approximately $1.16 per thousand cubic feet of natural gas. A barrel-of-oil equivalent is an amount of fuel which has the energy equivalent of 42 U.S. gallons. The energy equivalence is based on the Btu content of the fuels.

Certain fuels (oil, gas and synthetic fuels) may qualify for the credit. Oil may qualify if it is from shale or tar sands. Gas may qualify if it is from geopressured brine, Devonian Shale, coal seams, and tight formations ("tight sands") or biomass. Liquid, gaseous, or solid synthetic fuels produced from coal (including lignite) may also qualify.

To be eligible for the credit, the production of a qualified fuel must occur within the United States or a possession of the United States. In general, only production that is sold to an unrelated person qualifies for the credit. The regulations under Code Sec. 52(b) apply in determining whether a seller and purchaser are related. Accordingly, a sale within certain parent-subsidiary or controlled groups may not qualify as a sale to an unrelated person.

BACKGROUND

The production that qualifies for the credit is subject to specific time constraints. Wells must be drilled within a certain time frame; facilities must be placed in service within specific dates; and fuel produced must be sold prior to termination dates.

Qualified fuels generally must be produced from wells drilled after December 31, 1979, and before January 1, 1993, or produced in a facility placed in service after December 31, 1979, and before January 1, 1993. An exception extends the January 1, 1993, expiration date for facilities producing gas from biomass and synthetic fuel from coal if the facility producing the fuel is placed in service before July 1, 1998, pursuant to a binding contract entered into before January 1, 1997. The qualifying alternative fuel produced must generally be sold after December 31, 1979, and before January 1, 2003 (in the case of nonconventional sources subject to the January 1, 1993, expiration date) or January 1, 2008 (in the case of biomass gas and synthetic fuel facilities eligible for the extension period), to qualify for the credit.

The Code Sec. 29 credit has expired, except for certain biomass and synthetic fuels sold before January 1, 2008, and produced at facilities placed in service after December 31, 1992, and before July 1, 1998.

NEW LAW EXPLAINED

Modification of credit for producing fuel from a nonconventional source.—The Code Sec. 29 credit for producing fuel from a nonconventional source has been redesignated as Code Sec. 45K by the Energy Tax Incentives Act of 2005. The credit for producing fuel from a nonconventional source is now included in the computation of the general business credit (Code Sec. 38(b)(22), as added by the Energy Act; Code Sec. 45K(a), as redesignated and amended by the Energy Act). Any unused credit can now be carried forward or back as provided in Code Sec. 39. Subject to some limitations, unused business credits can be carried back one year and carried forward 20 years (Code Sec. 39).

The determination of whether any gas is produced from geopressured brine, Devonian shale, coal seams, or a tight formation is required to be made by the IRS in accordance with section 503 of the Natural Gas Policy Act of 1978 (as in effect before the repeal of the section) (Code Sec. 45K(c)(2), as amended by the Energy Act).

> **Comment:** In an earlier version of this bill (the Energy Tax Policy Act of 2003), a provision would have required the IRS to consult with the Federal Energy Regulatory Commission to determine whether fuels qualified for the nonconventional fuel source credit. It was believed that such a provision would have reduced the number of disputes and litigation under Code Sec. 45K, and imposed some uniformity. This provision was dropped from the new law. There have been many disputes and court cases litigating whether fuels qualified for the credit. Courts have been asked to decide such issues as the proper definition of "tar sands" and whether the Natural Gas Policy Act of 1978 required that a well category determination be made as a prerequisite for obtaining a credit for gas produced from tight sands or coal seams.

¶615

NEW LAW EXPLAINED

> **Practical Analysis:** Katherine Breaks, Senior Manager, Washington National Tax, KPMG LLP, observes that the Energy Tax Incentives Act of 2005 makes the credit for producing fuel from a non-conventional source part of the general business credit. Under prior law, unused Code Sec. 29 credits could not be carried forward or carried back to other tax years. If the taxpayer was unable to claim the Code Sec. 29 credit solely because it would reduce tax liability below the taxpayer's tentative minimum tax (TMT), the unused Code Sec. 29 credit increased the taxpayer's minimum tax credit. The minimum tax credit could be recovered in subsequent years if regular tax liability exceeded tentative minimum tax. By making the credit a general business credit, any unused credit can be carried back one year and carried forward 20 years.

▶ **Effective date.** Except as provided below, this provision applies to credits determined under the Internal Revenue Code of 1986 for tax years ending after December 31, 2005 (Act Sec. 1322(c)(1) of the Energy Tax Incentives Act of 2005). The provision pertaining to determinations under the Natural Gas Policy Act of 1978 takes effect on the date of the enactment of the Energy Tax Incentives Act of 2005 (Act Sec. 1322(c)(2) of the Energy Act).

Law source: Law at ¶5025, ¶5040, ¶5060, ¶5065, ¶5070, ¶5080, ¶5120, ¶5130, ¶5230 and ¶5235. Committee Report at ¶10,110.

— Act Sec. 1322(a)(1) of the Energy Tax Incentives Act of 2005, redesignating Code Sec. 29, as amended by this Act, as Code Sec. 45K;

— Act. Sec. 1322(a)(2), amending Code Sec. 38(b) and adding Code Sec. 38(b)(22);

— Act Sec. 1322(a)(3), amending Code Secs. 30(b)(3)(A), 43(b)(2), 45(e)(9), 45I(b)(2)(C)(i), 45I(c)(2)(A), 45I(d)(3), 45K(a), 45K(b), 53(d)(1)(B)(iii), 55(c)(3), 613A(c)(6)(C), 772(a), and 772(d)(5);

— Act Sec. 1322(b)(1), amending Code Sec. 29(c)(2)(A), striking Code Sec. 29(e), and redesignating Code Sec. 29(f), (g) and (h) as (e), (f) and (g), respectively, prior to redesignation as Code Sec. 45K(c)(2)(A), (e), (f) and (g);

— Act Sec. 1322(c), providing the effective date.

Reporter references: For further information, consult the following CCH reporters.

— Standard Federal Tax Reporter, 2005FED ¶4051.01 and ¶4251.021

— Federal Tax Service, FTS § G:24.220

— Federal Tax Guide, 2005FTG ¶2350

¶620 84-Month Amortization of Air Pollution Control Facilities

BACKGROUND

Taxpayers may elect to amortize a certified pollution control facility used in connection with a plant or other property that was in operation before January 1, 1976, over

BACKGROUND

a 60-month period (Code Sec. 169). In general, a certified pollution control facility is defined as a new identifiable treatment facility used in connection with a plant or other property in operation before January 1, 1976, to abate or control water or atmospheric pollution (Code Sec. 169(d)(1)). The original use of an acquired facility must begin with the taxpayer (Code Sec. 169(d)(4)). Corporate taxpayers must reduce the amount of basis eligible for the 60-month amortization period by 20 percent (Code Sec. 291(a)(5)). If a certified pollution control facility has a useful life in excess of 15 years, only the basis allocable to the first 15 years of the facility's useful life may be amortized (Code Sec. 169(f)(2)). For example, if the facility has a $100,000 basis and a 20-year useful life, $75,000 is amortizable over 60 months ($100,000 ×15/20). The $25,000 excess basis is depreciated using the Modified Accelerated Cost Recovery System (MACRS) (Code Sec. 169(g)).

NEW LAW EXPLAINED

Expansion of amortization deduction for atmospheric pollution control facilities.— Effective for air pollution control facilities placed in service after April 11, 2005, the new law eliminates the requirement that the facility must be used in connection with a plant that was in operation before January 1, 1976, if the plant is an electric generation plant or other property that is primarily coal-fired. However, the amortization period for a certified air pollution control facility qualifying by reason of this change is increased from 60 months to 84 months (Code Sec. 169(d)(5), as added by the Energy Tax Incentives Act of 2005).

> **Comment:** The amortization period for atmospheric pollution control facilities placed in service after April 11, 2005 and used in connection with a plant in operation before January 1, 1976 continues to be 60 months. Such facilities are not affected by this provision. Similarly, water pollution control facilities are not affected by the provision.

The provision only applies if construction, reconstruction, or erection of the facility is completed by the taxpayer after April 11, 2005, or the facility is acquired after April 11, 2005 (and the original use of the facility commences with the taxpayer after that date) (Code Sec. 169(d)(4)(B), as amended by the Energy Act).

> **Comment:** If an air pollution control facility is constructed, reconstructed, or erected by a taxpayer and qualifies for 84-month amortization by reason of the new law, only the portion of the basis attributable to construction, reconstruction, or erection by the taxpayer which is completed after April 11, 2005, qualifies for 84-month amortization. If the taxpayer acquires the facility, the original use of the property must begin with the taxpayer (Code Sec. 169(d)(4)(B), as added by the Energy Act).

> **Comment:** The new law contains no "binding contract" rule. Thus, a facility placed in service after April 11, 2005, may qualify for amortization even if it was acquired or constructed under a pre-April 12, 2005 binding contract.

> **Comment:** The new law also makes a technical correction to Code Sec. 169(d)(3) by changing a reference to the "Secretary of Health, Education, and Welfare" to the "Secretary of Health and Human Services."

¶620

NEW LAW EXPLAINED

Comment: The new law does not alter the rule requiring a corporate taxpayer to reduce its amortizable basis by 20 percent (Code Sec. 291(a)(5)) or the rule requiring a basis reduction for facilities with a useful life in excess of 15 years (Code Sec. 169(f)(2)).

▶ **Effective date.** The provision applies to air pollution control facilities placed in service after April 11, 2005 (Act Sec. 1309(e) of the Energy Tax Incentives Act of 2005).

Law source: Law at ¶5170. Committee Report at ¶10,080.

— Act Sec. 1309(a) of the Energy Tax Incentives Act of 2005, adding new Code Sec. 169(d)(5);
— Act Sec. 1309(b), amending Code Sec. 169(d)(4)(B);
— Act Sec. 1309(c), amending the heading for Code Sec. 169(d);
— Act Sec. 1309(d), amending Code Sec. 169(d)(3);
— Act Sec. 1309(e), providing the effective date.

Reporter references: For further information, consult the following CCH reporters.

— Standard Federal Tax Reporter, 2005FED ¶11,517.01
— Federal Tax Service, FTS §G:22.60
— Federal Tax Guide, 2005FTG ¶9550

¶620

Fuel Production and Fuel Excise Taxes

DIESEL AND BIODIESEL

¶705   Extension of excise tax provisions and income tax credit for biodiesel
¶710   Small agri-biodiesel producer credit
¶715   Renewable diesel
¶720   Reduced excise tax rate on diesel-water fuel emulsion

ALTERNATIVE FUELS

¶725   Excise tax credit for alternative fuels
¶730   Credit for installation of alternative fueling stations
¶735   Small ethanol producer credit extended to larger producers

PREVENTION OF FUEL FRAUD

¶740   Excise tax on kerosene used in aviation
¶745   Refunds of excise taxes on exempt sales of fuels by credit cards
¶750   Ultimate purchaser can claim refund for diesel fuel used on farms
¶755   Reregistration with change in ownership
¶760   Diesel fuel tax evasion report
¶765   Adulterated fuels penalty
¶770   Reconciliation of on-loaded cargo to entered cargo
¶775   Registration of deep-draft vessels
¶780   Motor fuel tax enforcement advisory committee

LUST TAX AND TECHNICAL CORRECTIONS

¶785   Leaking Underground Storage Tank Trust Fund
¶787   Gasohol refund claims repealed
¶790   Reduced tax rate for aviation fuel used by registrants
¶795   Termination date for tax on aviation-grade kerosene
¶797   Small engine fuel taxes to fund coastal wetlands protection

CROSS REFERENCES

Extension of taxes and trust fund (*see ¶905*)

Oil Spill Liability Trust Fund financing rate (*see ¶540*)

DIESEL AND BIODIESEL

¶705 Extension of Excise Tax Provisions and Income Tax Credit for Biodiesel

BACKGROUND

Tax provisions and incentives for alternative fuel sources, such as biodiesel, were included in the American Jobs Creation Act of 2004 (P.L. 108-357). With regard to biodiesel, the 2004 Jobs Act added a biodiesel fuels income tax credit under Code Sec. 40A as part of the general business credit under Code Sec. 38. The 2004 Jobs Act also added certain excise tax provisions applicable to biodiesel (Code Secs. 6426 and 6427(e)). The reduced rates of excise tax for most alcohol blended fuels were eliminated and, in their place, the 2004 Jobs Act provided a credit for alcohol fuel and biodiesel mixtures that is claimed against the excise tax imposed by Code Sec. 4081 on certain removals, entries and sales of taxable fuels (Code Sec. 6426). These income and excise tax credits are coordinated so that any benefit is received just once.

Both the biodiesel fuels income tax credit and the biodiesel mixture excise tax credit apply to fuel produced, sold or used after December 31, 2004. Similarly, under current law the biodiesel fuels income tax credit and the biodiesel mixture excise tax credit will not apply to any sale, use or removal for any period after December 31, 2006 (Code Secs. 40A(e) and 6426(c)(6), respectively). Additionally, the excise tax payment provision under Code Sec. 6427(e) will not apply with respect to any biodiesel mixture (as defined in Code Sec. 6426(c)(3)) sold or used after December 31, 2006 (Code Sec. 6427).

NEW LAW EXPLAINED

Extension through 2008.—The biodiesel fuels income tax credit under Code Sec. 40A, the biodiesel mixture excise tax credit under Code Sec. 6426, and the related payment provision under Code Sec. 6427(e) are extended through December 31, 2008 (Code Sec. 40A(g), as amended and redesignated by the Energy Tax Incentives Act of 2005; Code Secs. 6426(c)(6); and 6427(e)(3)(B), as amended by the Energy Act).

> **Comment:** The text of the Energy Act actually refers to Code Sec. 6427(e)(4)(B) with respect to the extension of the payment provision. This appears to be a typographical error in need of a technical correction.

As to the new time limit, the biodiesel mixture credit under Code Sec. 6426(c) will not apply to any sale, use or removal for any period after December 31, 2008. Additionally, the payment provision under Code Sec. 6427(e) will not apply with respect to any biodiesel mixture (as defined in Code Sec. 6426(c)(3)) sold or used after Decem-

NEW LAW EXPLAINED

ber 31, 2008. Likewise, the biodiesel fuels income tax credit under Code Sec. 40A(a) will not apply to any sale or use after December 31, 2008.

> **Planning Note:** The Energy Act also provides new tax treatment for renewable diesel that is similar to the tax treatment for biodiesel. See ¶715 for a discussion of the credits relating to renewable diesel.
>
> **State Tax Consequences:** Many states provide energy incentives through personal and corporate income tax credits. See ¶195 for a state-by-state summary of available credits.

▶ **Effective date.** The provisions are effective on August 8, 2005 (Act Sec. 1344(b) of the Energy Tax Incentives Act of 2005).

Law source: Law at ¶5050, ¶5425 and ¶5430. Committee Report at ¶10,290.

— Act Sec. 1344(a) of the Energy Tax Incentives Act of 2005, amending redesignated Code Sec. 40A(g), and amending Code Secs. 6426(c)(6) and 6427(e)(3)(B);

— Act Sec. 1344(b), providing the effective date.

Reporter references: For further information, consult the following CCH reporters.

— Standard Federal Tax Reporter, 2005FED ¶4320.01

— Federal Tax Service, FTS § G:24.60

— Excise Tax Reporter, ETR ¶2325.01, ¶49,250.01 and ¶49,685.095

¶710 Small Agri-Biodiesel Producer Credit

BACKGROUND

As part of an effort to lessen America's dependence on foreign oil, Congress has enacted tax incentives designed to encourage the production and use of renewable and alternative energy sources. One incentive is a nonrefundable income tax credit for certain biodiesel fuels under Code Sec. 40A. The biodiesel fuels credit is actually the sum of two credits—the "biodiesel mixture credit" (Code Sec. 40A(b)(1)) and the "biodiesel credit" (Code Sec. 40A(b)(2)). The biodiesel fuels credit is treated as a general business credit (Code Sec. 38). The amount of the biodiesel fuels credit is included in gross income under Code Sec. 87. The biodiesel fuels credit is also coordinated with the excise tax credit allowed under Code Secs. 6426 and 6427(e).

> **Comment:** The biodiesel fuels credit was added to the Code as part of the American Jobs Creation Act of 2004 (P.L. 108-357). The credit applies to fuel produced, and sold or used, after December 31, 2004, in tax years ending after that date.

The biodiesel mixture credit is 50 cents for each gallon of biodiesel used by the taxpayer in the production of a qualified biodiesel mixture (Code Sec. 40A(b)(1)(A)). A qualified biodiesel mixture is a mixture of biodiesel and diesel fuel determined without regard to any use of kerosene, that is sold by the producer to any person for use as fuel, or used as a fuel by the taxpayer producing the mixture. In order to qualify for the credit, the sale or use must be in a trade or business of the taxpayer,

BACKGROUND

and the biodiesel must be taken into account for the tax year in which the sale or use occurs. Casual off-farm production of a biodiesel mixture is not eligible for the credit.

> **Comment:** See Notice 2005-62, I.R.B. 2005-35, for the definition of a "biodiesel mixture" for purposes of the excise tax credit under Code Sec. 6426(c)(3).

The biodiesel credit is 50 cents for each gallon of biodiesel that is *not* in a mixture with diesel fuel and during the tax year is either (1) used by the taxpayer as a fuel in a trade or business, or (2) sold by the taxpayer at retail to a person and placed in the fuel tank of the retail purchaser's vehicle (Code Sec. 40A(b)(2)(A)). However, no user credit is allowed for any biodiesel that was sold in a retail sale.

Special rule for agri-biodiesel. For any biodiesel that is agri-biodiesel, the biodiesel mixture credit and the biodiesel credit is increased to $1 dollar per gallon (up from 50 cents per gallon) (Code Sec. 40A(b)(3)).

Certification required. In order to claim the biodiesel fuels credit, the taxpayer must obtain a certification from the producer or importer of the biodiesel identifying the product and the percentage of biodiesel and agri-biodiesel in the product (Code Sec. 40A(b)(4)).

> **Comment:** The IRS has issued guidance relating to the biodiesel fuels credit (Notice 2005-4, I.R.B. 2005-2, 289, modified by Notice 2005-62, I.R.B. 2005-35). Notice 2005-4 states that the credit is claimed on Form 8864, Biodiesel Fuels Credit. Notice 2005-4 also provides a model certificate that can be used to support a claim for the credit. Notice 2005-62 revises this model certificate to clarify that the taxpayer can obtain the certificate either directly from the producer of the biodiesel or indirectly from a "biodiesel reseller" (see section 2(h)(3) of Notice 2005-4, as revised by Notice 2005-62). Notice 2005-62 also provides that the taxpayer generally must submit a copy of the certificate with its claim for a biodiesel fuels credit.

Definitions. The terms "biodiesel" and "agri-biodiesel" are specifically defined in Code Sec. 40A(d). Biodiesel is defined as the "monoalkyl esters of long chain fatty acids derived from plant or animal matter" that meet; (1) the registration requirements for fuels and fuel additives established by the EPA under Section 211 of the Clean Air Act; and (2) the requirements of the American Society of Testing and Materials D6751. Agri-biodiesel means biodiesel derived solely from virgin oils, including esters derived from virgin vegetable oils from corn, soybeans, sunflower seeds, cottonseeds, canola, crambe, rapeseeds, safflowers, flaxseeds, rice bran, and mustard seeds, and from animal fats.

> **Comment:** With respect to the definition of agri-biodiesel, Notice 2005-62 clarifies that the list above is not exclusive. Therefore, biodiesel derived solely from virgin oils may include esters derived from palm oil and fish oil.

Tax imposed in certain cases. If a biodiesel fuels credit was claimed with respect to biodiesel used in the production of a biodiesel mixture and any person subsequently separates the biodiesel from the mixture, or without separation uses the biodiesel mixture other than as a fuel, a tax is imposed on that person in an amount necessary to recover the credit. A similar rule applies if a biodiesel credit was claimed with

BACKGROUND

respect to the retail sale of biodiesel and any person mixes that biodiesel or uses it other than as a fuel (Code Sec. 40A(d)(3)).

Termination of credit. Under current law, the biodiesel fuels credit does not apply to any sale or use after December 31, 2006.

NEW LAW EXPLAINED

Income tax credit for small agri-biodiesel producer.—The biodiesel fuels credit now includes a third component, the small agri-biodiesel producer credit (Code Sec. 40A(a), as amended by the Energy Tax Incentives Act of 2005). The small agri-biodiesel producer credit of any eligible small agri-biodiesel producer is 10 cents for each gallon of qualified agri-biodiesel production (up to 15 million gallons per tax year) (Code Secs. 40A(b)(5)(A) and 40A(b)(5)(C), as added by the Energy Act).

> **Comment:** The small agri-biodiesel producer credit mirrors the small ethanol producer credit (Code Sec. 40(a)(3)). The small ethanol producer credit is 10 cents for each gallon of qualified ethanol fuel production, up to 15 million gallons per tax year (Code Sec. 40(b)(4)).

Qualified agri-biodiesel production defined. The term "qualified agri-biodiesel production" means any agri-biodiesel that is produced by an eligible small agri-biodiesel producer, and which during the tax year is sold by that producer to another person:

(1) for use by the other person in the production of a qualified biodiesel mixture in that person's trade or business (other than casual off-farm production),

(2) for use by that other person as a fuel in a trade or business, or

(3) who sells the agri-biodiesel at retail to another person and places the agri-biodiesel in the fuel tank of that other person.

The term "qualified agri-biodiesel production" also means any agri-biodiesel that is produced by an eligible small agri-biodiesel producer, and which during the tax year is used or sold by the producer for any of the purposes described in (1)–(3) above (Code Sec. 40A(b)(5)(B), as added by the Energy Act).

> **Comment:** The text of Code Sec. 40A(b)(5)(B) refers to any agri-biodiesel "(determined without regard to the last sentence of subsection (d)(2))." This appears to be a drafting error, as (1) Code Sec. 40A(d)(2), which defines "agri-biodiesel," has only one sentence, and (2) the quoted parenthetical language, if applied literally, would effectively negate the small agri-biodiesel producer credit.

Production limitation. The qualified agri-biodiesel production of any producer for any tax year cannot exceed 15 million gallons (Code Sec. 40A(b)(5)(C), as added by the Energy Act).

Eligible small agri-biodiesel producer defined. The term "eligible small agri-biodiesel producer" means a person who, at all times during the tax year, has a productive capacity for agri-biodiesel that does not exceed 60 million gallons (Code Sec. 40A(e)(1), as amended by the Energy Act).

Special rules for small agri-biodiesel producer credit. For purposes of the 15 million gallon limitation and the 60 million gallon limitation described above, all members of the

¶710

NEW LAW EXPLAINED

same controlled group of corporations (within the meaning of Code Sec. 267(f)) and all persons under common control (within the meaning of Code Sec. 52(b) but determined by treating an interest of more than 50 percent as a controlling interest) are treated as one person (Code Sec. 40A(e)(2), as amended by the Energy Act). In addition, for a partnership, trust, S corporation, or other passthrough entity, the 15 and 60 million gallon limitations are applied at the entity level and at the partner or similar level (Code Sec. 40A(e)(3), as amended by the Energy Act). For a facility in which more than one person has an interest, the productive capacity is allocated among such persons "in such manner as the Secretary may prescribe" (Code Sec. 40A(e)(4), as amended by the Energy Act).

IRS authorized to issue regulations. The IRS is authorized to prescribe regulations that are necessary:

(1) to prevent the small agri-biodiesel producer credit from directly or indirectly benefitting any person with a productive capacity of more than 60 million gallons of agri-biodiesel during the tax year; or

(2) to prevent any person from directly or indirectly benefitting with respect to more than 15 million gallons during the tax year (Code Sec. 40A(e)(5), as amended by the Energy Act).

Allocation of credit to patrons of cooperative. A cooperative organization (as described in Code Sec. 1381(a), such as a tax-exempt farmers' cooperative) may elect to allocate any portion of the small agri-biodiesel producer credit for the tax year pro rata among the patrons of the organization on the basis of the quantity or value of business done with or for such patrons for the tax year (Code Sec. 40A(e)(6)(A)(i), as amended by the Energy Act).

Election: The cooperative organization must make the apportionment election on a timely filed return for the applicable tax year. Once made, the election is irrevocable for that tax year. The election is not effective unless the organization designates the apportionment in a written notice that is mailed to its patrons during the payment period described in Code Sec. 1382(d) (Code Sec. 40A(e)(6)(A)(ii), as amended by the Energy Act).

The amount of the credit not apportioned to patrons is included in the cooperative organization's credit for the tax year of the organization. The amount of the credit apportioned is included in the patron's credit for the first tax year of each patron ending on or after the last day of the payment period (as defined in Code Sec. 1382(d)) for the tax year of the organization or, if earlier, for the tax year of each patron ending on or after the date on which the patron receives notice of the apportionment (Code Sec. 40A(e)(6)(B), as amended by the Energy Act).

Special rules applicable to cooperative. If the amount of the cooperative organization's credit for a tax year is less than the amount of the credit shown on its tax return for that year, an amount equal to the excess of the reduction in the credit over the amount not apportioned to patrons for the tax year is treated as an increase in federal income tax imposed on the organization. The excess is not treated as an increase in taxes for purposes of determining the amount of any Federal income tax credit or for

NEW LAW EXPLAINED

purposes of the alternative minimum tax (Code Sec. 40A(e)(6)(B)(iii), as amended by the Energy Act).

Tax imposed if fuel not used for required purposes. If a small agri-biodiesel producer credit was determined under Code Sec. 40A(a)(3) (as amended by the Energy Act), and any person does not use the fuel for a purpose specified in Code Sec. 40A(b)(5)(B) (as amended by the Energy Act) (see "Qualified agri-biodiesel production defined," above), a tax is imposed on that person. The tax is equal to 10 cents a gallon for each gallon of such agri-biodiesel (Code Sec. 40A(d)(3)(C), as amended by the Energy Act).

> **Comment:** This provision parallels the recovery tax provisions applicable to the biodiesel mixture credit and the biodiesel credit (Code Sec. 40A(d)(3) and 40A(d)(3)(B)).

Termination of credit. The biodiesel fuels credit, which includes the small agri-biodiesel producer credit, does not apply to any sale or use after December 31, 2008 (Code Sec. 40A(g), as amended by the Energy Act). Thus, the Energy Act has extended the biodiesel fuels credit for an additional two years.

> **State Tax Consequences:** Many states provide energy incentives through personal and corporate income tax credits. See ¶ 195 for a state-by-state summary of available credits.

▶ **Effective date.** The small agri-biodiesel producer credit provisions apply to tax years ending after August 8, 2005 (Act Sec. 1345(e) of the Energy Tax Incentives Act of 2005).

Law source: Law at ¶ 5050. Committee Report at ¶ 10,300.

— Act Sec. 1345(a) of the Energy Tax Incentives Act of 2005, amending Code Sec. 40A(a);
— Act Sec. 1345(b), amending Code Sec. 40A(b);
— Act Sec. 1345(c), redesignating Code Sec. 40A(e) as (f) and adding new Code Sec. 40A(e);
— Act Sec. 1345(d), amending Code Sec. 40A(b), redesignating Code Sec. 40A(d)(3)(C) as (D), and adding new Code Sec. 40A(d)(3)(C);
— Act Sec. 1345(e), providing the effective date.

Reporter references: For further information, consult the following CCH reporters.
— Standard Federal Tax Reporter, 2005FED ¶ 4320.01
— Federal Tax Service, FTS § G:24.60
— Excise Tax Reporter, ETR ¶ 2325.03

¶715 Renewable Diesel

BACKGROUND

Renewable and alternative energy sources, such as biodiesel, have gained prominence in the news recently, particularly in light of America's interest in freeing itself from dependence on foreign oil. Special tax treatment for biodiesel was included in the American Jobs Creation Act of 2004 (P.L. 108-357). Pursuant to the 2004 Jobs Act, a biodiesel fuels income tax credit, consisting of the sum of a "biodiesel mixture

BACKGROUND

credit" and a "biodiesel credit," is available under Code Sec. 40A. Each of the two credits is calculated at a rate of 50 cents per gallon ($1 per gallon for agri-biodiesel). Additionally, with regard to excise taxes, the 2004 Jobs Act eliminated the reduced rates of tax for most alcohol-blended fuels and provided a credit for alcohol fuel and biodiesel mixtures that may be claimed against the excise tax imposed by Code Sec. 4081 on certain removals, entries and sales of taxable fuels. With respect to biodiesel, the biodiesel mixture excise tax credit is determined by multiplying the number of gallons of biodiesel used by the taxpayer to produce any biodiesel mixture for sale or use in the taxpayer's trade or business by 50 cents ($1 in the case of agri-biodiesel) (Code Sec. 6426(c)). To claim the biodiesel mixture excise tax credit, the taxpayer must obtain an appropriate certificate that identifies the product and the percentages of biodiesel and agri-biodiesel in the product (Code Sec. 6426(c)(4)). (A similar certificate is required to claim the biodiesel fuels income tax credit (Code Sec. 40A(b)(4)). The excise tax credit is coordinated with the income tax credit for biodiesel so that the same biodiesel cannot be claimed for both income and excise tax purposes (Code Sec. 40A(c)).

> **Comment:** The IRS has issued Notice 2005-4, I.R.B. 2005-2, 289, which provides a model certificate used to comply with the certification requirement. The model certificate in Notice 2005-4 was subsequently modified by Notice 2005-62.

If any person produces a biodiesel mixture described in Code Sec. 6426 in his or her trade or business, the IRS is to pay that person an amount equal to the biodiesel mixture credit (Code Sec. 6427(e)). However, no amount is payable for any mixture with respect to which an amount is allowed as a credit under Code Sec. 6426 (Code Sec. 6427(e)(2)). To the extent that the biodiesel fuel mixture credit exceeds a taxpayer's Code Sec. 4081 liability, an income tax credit or a payment under Code Sec. 6427(e) is available to the producer of the mixture (Notice 2005-4).

Additionally, pursuant to the 2004 Jobs Act, persons claiming benefits under the income and excise tax provisions discussed above must file quarterly information returns with the IRS (Code Sec. 4104). The 2004 Jobs Act also extended the registration requirements of Code Sec. 4101 to producers and importers of biodiesel and alcohol (Code Sec. 4101).

NEW LAW EXPLAINED

Renewable diesel treated as biodiesel.—The Internal Revenue Code treatment of renewable diesel is now the same as that of biodiesel, except that: (1) the biodiesel mixture income tax credit and the biodiesel income tax credit are determined using a rate of $1 per gallon (rather than 50 cents) with respect to renewable diesel; and (2) the agri-biodiesel credit and the small agri-biodiesel producer credit under Code Sec. 40A(b)(5), as added by the Energy Tax Incentives Act of 2005, do not apply to renewable diesel (Code Sec. 40A(f), as added by the Energy Act). Thus, an income tax credit, excise tax credit and payment system is provided for renewable diesel that is similar to that provided for biodiesel under the 2004 Jobs Act.

> **Comment:** The treatment of renewable diesel in the same manner as biodiesel for excise tax credit and payment purposes is accomplished via Code Sec. 6426(c)(5),

NEW LAW EXPLAINED

which provides that any term used in Code Sec. 6426(c) that is also used in Code Sec. 40A (such as "biodiesel") has the meaning given to it by Code Sec. 40A.

Caution Note: The new tax treatment of renewable diesel applies to fuel sold or used after December 31, 2005 (Act Sec. 1346(c) of the Energy Act). However, it will not apply to any sale or use after December 31, 2008 (Code Sec. 40A(g), as amended and redesignated by the Energy Act).

Definition of renewable diesel. Renewable diesel is defined as diesel fuel derived from biomass using a thermal depolymerization process (Code Sec. 40A(f)(3), as added by the Energy Act). Biomass, which is defined according to the provisions under Code Sec. 45K(c)(3) (formerly Code Sec. 29(c)(3)) governing the credit for producing fuel from a nonconventional source) is any organic material other than (1) oil and natural gas (or any product thereof) or (2) coal, including lignite (or any product thereof) (Code Sec. 40A(f)(3), as added by the Energy Act). According to the Joint Committee on Taxation, thermal depolymerization is a process in which complex organic materials, such as turkey offal, are reduced into light crude oil. In the process, pressure and heat are used to decompose long chain polymers of hydrogen, oxygen, and carbon into short-chain petroleum hydrocarbons with a maximum length of around 18 carbons (Joint Committee on Taxation, Description and Technical Explanation of the Energy Tax Incentives Act of 2005 (JCX-60-05)).

Renewable diesel must also meet the registration requirements for fuels and fuel additives established by the Environmental Protection Agency under section 211 of the Clean Air Act (42 U.S.C. 7545) and the requirements of the American Society of Testing and Materials D975 or D396 (Code Sec. 40A(f)(3), as added by the Energy Act).

Certification, registration and information reporting. As with biodiesel, in order to claim an income tax credit, an excise tax credit, or payment for renewable diesel, the taxpayer must obtain appropriate certification (Code Sec. 40A(f)(1), as added by the Energy Act, Code Sec. 40A(b)(4) and Code Sec. 6426(c)(4)). Additionally, persons claiming benefits under the new income and excise tax provisions for renewable diesel must file quarterly information returns with the IRS (Code Sec. 4104). Furthermore, the registration requirements of Code Sec. 4101 also apply to producers and importers of renewable diesel.

Tax imposed on later separation or failure to use as fuel. Similar to the credits for biodiesel, a tax is imposed if renewable diesel for which a credit has been claimed is used other than as a fuel or separated from a mixture (Code Sec. 40A(f)(1), as added by the Energy Act, Code Sec. 40A(d)(3) and Code Sec. 6426(d)).

Income tax provisions. Taxpayers may now claim an income tax credit for renewable diesel that is calculated in the same manner as the biodiesel fuels income tax credit (Code Sec. 40A(f), as added by the Energy Act). However, the biodiesel fuels income tax credit for renewable diesel (the "renewable diesel fuels credit") is calculated at a rate of $1 per gallon, rather than 50 cents (Code Sec. 40(f)(2)(A)). Like the biodiesel fuels income tax credit, the renewable diesel fuels credit is treated as a general business credit under Code Sec. 38 and is one of the qualified business credits listed in Code Sec. 196(c) that qualify for a deduction if it remains unused at the end of the applicable carryforward period. Passthrough rules similar to those found in Code

NEW LAW EXPLAINED

Sec. 52(d) will also apply to apportion the renewable diesel fuels credit between an estate or trust and its beneficiaries (Code Sec. 40A(d)(4)). Additionally, the amount of the renewable diesel fuels credit is includible in gross income under Code Sec. 87.

The renewable diesel fuels credit is the sum of two credits—the "biodiesel mixture credit" with respect to renewable diesel (the "renewable diesel mixture credit") and the "biodiesel credit" with respect to renewable diesel (the "renewable diesel credit").

> **Comment:** The rate used to calculate the biodiesel mixture credit and the biodiesel credit remains at 50 cents per gallon ($1 for agri-biodiesel) where renewable diesel is not involved.

The first credit, the renewable diesel mixture credit, is $1 for each gallon of renewable diesel used by the taxpayer in the production of a "qualified biodiesel mixture" ("qualified renewable diesel mixture") (Code Sec. 40A(f)(1), as added by the Energy Act, and Code Sec. 40A(b)(1)(A)). A qualified renewable diesel mixture is a mixture of renewable diesel and diesel fuel (as defined in Code Sec. 4083(a)(3)), determined without regard to any use of kerosene, that is sold by the taxpayer producing the mixture to any person for use as a fuel or is used as a fuel by the taxpayer producing the mixture. In order to qualify for the credit, the sale or use must be in a trade or business of the taxpayer, and must be for the tax year in which the sale or use occurs (Code Sec. 40A(b)(1)(C)). Casual off-farm production is not eligible for the credit (Code Sec. 40A(b)(1)(D)).

The second credit, the renewable diesel credit, is $1 for each gallon of renewable diesel that is not in a mixture with diesel fuel and during the tax year is either (1) used by the taxpayer as a fuel in a trade or business, or (2) sold by the taxpayer at retail to a person and placed in the fuel tank of the retail purchaser's vehicle (Code Sec. 40A(b)(2)(A)). However, no user credit is allowed for any renewable diesel that was sold in a retail sale (Code Sec. 40A(b)(2)(B)).

The renewable diesel fuels income tax credit is coordinated with the excise tax credit so that the amount of the credit otherwise determined under Code Sec. 40A is reduced to account for any benefit provided under the excise tax credit provision (Code Sec. 40A(f)(1), as added by the Energy Act, and Code Sec. 40A(c)).

Excise tax provisions. Renewable diesel is now treated in the same manner as biodiesel for purposes of the biodiesel mixture credit under Code Sec. 6426 (Code Sec. 40A(f), as added by the Energy Act). Renewable diesel is also treated like biodiesel under the payment provisions of Code Sec. 6427(e). Thus, to the extent that the biodiesel mixture credit for renewable diesel (the "renewable diesel mixture credit") exceeds a taxpayer's Code Sec. 4081 liability, an income tax credit or a payment under Code Sec. 6427(e) is available to the producer of the mixture (Code Sec. 40A(f)(1), as added by the Energy Act, and Code Sec. 6427(e); see also Notice 2005-4, I.R.B. 2005-2, 289).

The renewable diesel mixture credit is calculated by multiplying the number of gallons of renewable diesel used by the taxpayer to produce any "biodiesel mixture" ("renewable diesel mixture") for sale or use in the taxpayer's trade or business by the applicable amount (Code Sec. 6426(c)). The "applicable amount" is 50 cents, except for agri-biodiesel (Code Sec. 6426(c)(2)). Unlike the income tax credit under Code Sec. 40A, the Energy Act does not contain specific language that raises the rate to $1 per gallon for renewable diesel in computing the excise tax credit.

¶715

NEW LAW EXPLAINED

Comment: In providing a rate of $1 per gallon in calculating the income tax credit under Code Sec. 40A, the new law specifically refers to the income tax credit provisions in Code Sec. 40A(b)(1)(A) and Code Sec. 40A(b)(2)(A), which provide the per-gallon rate. On the other hand, the Joint Committee on Taxation, in describing the income tax credit, excise tax credit, and payment system for renewable diesel, states that "[t]he amount of the credit for renewable diesel is $1.00 per gallon," without distinguishing between the income tax credit and the excise tax credit (Joint Committee on Taxation, Description and Technical Explanation of the Energy Tax Incentives Act of 2005 (JCX-60-05)).

A renewable diesel mixture is any mixture of renewable diesel and diesel fuel (as defined in Code Sec. 4083(a)(3)), determined without regard to any use of kerosene, that is sold by the producer to any person for use as a fuel or is used as a fuel by the producer (Code Sec. 6426(c)(3)).

▶ **Effective date.** The new tax treatment of renewable diesel applies with respect to fuel sold or used after December 31, 2005. (Act. Sec. 1346(c) of the Energy Tax Incentives Act of 2005).

Law source: Law at ¶5050. Committee Report at ¶10,290.

— Act Sec. 1346(a) of the Energy Tax Incentives Act of 2005, redesignating Code Sec. 40A(f) as (g) and adding new Code Sec. 40A(f);

— Act Sec. 1346(b), amending the heading for Code Sec. 40A and the item in the table of contents relating to Code Sec. 40A;

— Act Sec. 1346(c), providing the effective date.

Reporter references: For further information, consult the following CCH reporters.

— Standard Federal Tax Reporter, 2005FED ¶4320.01

— Federal Tax Service, FTS § G:24.60

— Excise Tax Reporter, ETR ¶2325.01

¶720 Reduced Excise Tax Rate on Diesel-Water Fuel Emulsion

BACKGROUND

Diesel fuel is subject to an excise tax of 24.3 cents per gallon, which is used to finance the Highway Trust Fund (Code Sec. 4081(a)(2)(A)(iii)). Gasoline and most special motor fuels are subject to an 18.3-cents-per-gallon excise tax (Code Secs. 4041(a)(2)(B)(i) and 4081(a)(2)(A)(i)). Special motor fuels are subject to reduced tax rates based on the energy equivalence of these fuels to gasoline (Code Sec. 4041(a)(2)(B), (a)(3) and (m)(1)(A)). Special motor fuels include propane, liquefied natural gas, methanol derived from petroleum or natural gas, and compressed natural gas. Diesel fuel blended into a diesel-water emulsion fuel has no special tax rate, despite having fewer Btus than unmixed diesel fuel.

NEW LAW EXPLAINED

Special excise tax rate for diesel fuel blended with water.—A special excise tax rate of 19.7 cents per gallon has been set for diesel-water fuel emulsions (Code Sec. 4081(a)(2)(D), as added by the Energy Tax Incentives Act of 2005). This rate reflects the reduced Btu content per gallon caused by the water. The emulsion fuels eligible for the special rate must consist of not more than 86 percent diesel fuel (and other minor chemical additives) and at least 14 percent water. A U.S. manufacturer must register the emulsion additive with the Environmental Protection Agency, pursuant to Section 211 of the Clean Air Act (as in effect on March 31, 2003) (Code Sec. 4081(a)(2)(D), as added by the Energy Act).

Any person claiming the special rate of tax for the removal, sale, or use of the diesel-water fuel emulsion must be registered with the IRS under Code Sec. 4101 (Code Sec. 4081(a)(2)(D), as added by the Energy Act). Claims for refund based on the incentive rate may be filed quarterly if the person can claim at least $750 (Code Sec. 6427(i)(2)). If at least $750 cannot be claimed at the end of quarter, the amount can be carried over to the next quarter and soon. If the person cannot claim at least $750 at the end of the tax year, however, the credit must be claimed on the person's income tax return.

If diesel fuel on which the regular tax rate was imposed is used by any person in producing a diesel-water fuel emulsion that is sold or used in the person's trade or business, the IRS will refund, without interest, an amount equal to the excess of the regular tax rate (24.3 cents per gallon) over the incentive tax rate (19.7 cents per gallon) (Code Sec. 6427(m), as added by the Energy Act).

The Energy Act also provides that any person who separates the diesel fuel from a diesel-water fuel emulsion that was taxed under the incentive tax rate provided by Code Sec. 4081(a)(2)(D) (as added by the Energy Act) is treated as a refiner of the taxable fuel. This includes a diesel-water fuel emulsion with respect to which a credit or payment was previously allowed under Code Sec. 6427. Such person is liable for the difference between the amount of tax due on the latest removal of the separated fuel and the amount of tax imposed and not credited or refunded on any prior removal or entry of the fuel (Code Sec. 4081(c), as added by the Energy Act).

▶ **Effective date.** This provision takes effect on January 1, 2006 (Act Sec. 1343(c) of the Energy Tax Incentives Act of 2005).

Law source: Law at ¶5290 and ¶5430. Committee Report at ¶10,280.

— Act Sec. 1343(a) of the Energy Tax Incentives Act of 2005, adding new Code Sec. 4081(a)(2)(D);

— Act Sec. 1343(b)(1), redesignating Code Sec. 6427(m)–(p) as Code Sec. 6427(n)–(q) and adding new Code Sec. 6427(m);

— Act Sec. 1343(b)(2), adding new Code Sec. 4081(c);

— Act Sec. 1343(b)(3), amending Code Sec. 6427(i);

— Act Sec. 1343(c), providing the effective date.

Reporter references: For further information, consult the following CCH reporters.

— Excise Tax Reporter, ETR ¶8915.015 and ¶49,685.03

¶720

ALTERNATIVE FUELS

¶725 Excise Tax Credit for Alternative Fuels

BACKGROUND

An excise tax is imposed on the removal of any taxable fuel from a refinery or terminal, the entry of any taxable fuel into the United States, or the sale of any taxable fuel (Code Sec. 4081). Taxable fuels include gasoline, kerosene, and diesel fuel. The tax is equal to 18.3 cents per gallon for gasoline and 24.3 cents per gallon for kerosene and diesel fuel. Fuels are also subject to a 0.1 cent LUST tax. A back-up tax is imposed on the retail sale or use of these fuels if they were not taxed under Code Sec. 4081 or if the tax was credited or refunded (Code Sec. 4041). The retail back-up tax also applies to special motor fuels. Any liquid other than gas oil, fuel oil, gasoline, kerosene and diesel fuel is a special motor fuel. Special motor fuels include liquefied petroleum gas, liquefied natural gas, benzol, benzene, and naptha. Most special motor fuels are taxed at 18.3 cents per gallon, though some are taxed at different rates determined on an energy equivalent basis.

Prior to the American Jobs Creation Act of 2004 (P.L. 108-357), there were reduced tax rates for gasohol and for gasoline that was to be blended with alcohol to make gasohol. The 2004 Act eliminated the reduced rates and substituted a tax credit for fuels used to produce an eligible mixture.

NEW LAW EXPLAINED

Excise tax credit for alternative fuels.—The SAFE Transportation Equity Act of 2005 replaces the category of "special motor fuels" with "alternative fuels," provides a list of the fuels that are "alternative fuels," and makes changes in the treatment of those fuels similar to the changes made by the American Jobs Creation Act of 2004 in the treatment of alcohol-blended fuels. The Highway Act reduces the variety of tax rates on alternative fuels, adds alternative fuel and alternative fuel mixture credits to the existing credits for alcohol fuel and biodiesel mixtures in Code Sec. 6426, and allows for payments in lieu of the credits. The credit and payment provisions for alternative fuels and alternative fuel mixtures generally expire and do not apply to any sale or use after September 30, 2009 (September 30, 2014, in the case of a sale or use of liquefied hydrogen or an alternative fuel mixture involving liquefied hydrogen) (Code Secs. 6426(d)(4), (e)(3), 6427(e)(5)(C) and (5)(D), as added by the Highway Act).

Tax rates. The default tax rate on the sale or use of what are now known as alternative fuels as fuel in a motor vehicle or motorboat remains 18.3 cents per gallon. For liquefied natural gas, any liquid fuel (other than ethanol or methanol) derived from coal (including peat), and liquid hydrocarbons derived from biomass, the tax rate is 24.3 cents per gallon (Code Sec. 4041(a)(2)(B)(ii), as amended by the Highway Act). For compressed natural gas, the former tax rate of 48.54 cents per thousand cubic feet

NEW LAW EXPLAINED

(MCF) is replaced by a rate of 18.3 cents per energy equivalent of a gallon of gasoline (Code Sec. 4041(a)(3), as amended by the Highway Act).

Alternative fuel credit. The alternative fuel tax credit is a credit against the excise tax imposed on the retail sale or use of alternative fuels under Code Sec. 4041 (Code Sec. 6426(a)(2), as amended by the Highway Act). The alternative fuel credit is 50 cents per gallon of alternative fuel (or gasoline gallon equivalents of a nonliquid alternative fuel) sold by the taxpayer for use as fuel in a motor vehicle or motorboat, or so used by the taxpayer (Code Sec. 6426(d)(1), as amended by the Highway Act). The gasoline gallon equivalent for a nonliquid fuel is the amount of the fuel having a Btu content of 124,800 (higher heating value) (Code Sec. 6426(d)(3), as added by the Highway Act). Alternative fuels include:

- liquefied petroleum gas
- compressed or liquefied natural gas
- liquefied hydrogen
- any liquid fuel derived from coal (including peat) through the Fischer-Tropsch process
- liquid hydrocarbons derived from biomass and
- P Series fuels, as defined by the Secretary of Energy.

The term biomass means any organic material other than oil and natural gas (or any product thereof), and coal (including lignite) or any product thereof (Code Sec. 29(c)(3)). P-Series fuels are blends of natural gas liquids, ethanol, and a biomass-derived co-solvent. Alternative fuels, for purposes of the credit, do not include ethanol, methanol, or biodiesel (Code Sec. 6426(d)(2), as amended by the Highway Act).

Alternative fuel mixture credit. The alternative fuel mixture tax credit is a credit against the excise tax on certain removals, entries and sales imposed under Code Sec. 4081 (Code Sec. 6426(a)(1), as amended by the Highway Act). The alternative fuel mixture credit is 50 cents per gallon of alternative fuel used by the taxpayer in producing any alternative fuel mixture for sale or use in a trade or business of the taxpayer (Code Sec. 6426(e)(1), as added by the Highway Act).

An alternative fuel mixture is a mixture of alternative fuel and taxable fuel (i.e., gasoline, diesel fuel or kerosene) which is sold by the taxpayer producing it to any person for use as fuel, or is used as a fuel by the producer (Code Sec. 6426(e)(2), as added by the Highway Act).

> **Compliance Tip:** Taxpayers must register with the IRS in order to claim the credit or obtain repayments of the alternative fuel or alternative fuel mixture excise taxes (Code Secs. 6426(a) and 6427(e)(4), as amended and added by the Highway Act). The application for registration is IRS Form 637.

Payments in lieu of credit. Taxpayers who are subject to the excise tax on either the sale or use of alternative fuels or the production of alternative fuel mixtures can apply for

¶725

NEW LAW EXPLAINED

a payment in the amount of the credit in lieu of claiming the credit (Code Sec. 6427(e)(1), (e)(2), as amended by the Highway Act).

▶ **Effective date.** The provisions generally apply to any sale or use for any period after September 30, 2006 (Act Sec. 11113(d) of the SAFE Transportation Equity Act of 2005).

Law source: Law at ¶5265, ¶5305, ¶5425 and ¶5430. Committee Report at ¶15,040.

— Act Sec. 11113(a) of the SAFE Transportation Equity Act of 2005, amending Code Sec. 4041(a)(2) and (a)(3);

— Act Sec. 11113(b), amending Code Secs. 6426 and 6427(e);

— Act Sec. 11113(c), amending Code Sec. 4041(a)(1);

— Act Sec. 11113(d), providing the effective date.

Reporter references: For further information, consult the following CCH reporters.

— Federal Tax Service, FTS § G:24.340

— Federal Tax Guide, 2005FTG ¶2350

— Excise Tax Reporter, ETR ¶5700.03, ¶5700.034, ¶49,250.01 and ¶49,685.095

¶730 Credit for Installation of Alternative Fueling Stations

BACKGROUND

Currently, property used to refuel clean-fuel vehicles qualifies for a deduction under Code Sec. 179A in the year in which the property is placed in service. Clean-fuel vehicle refueling property includes property to store or dispense clean-fuel-burning fuel, but only if the fuel storage or dispensing is at the point where the fuel is delivered into a fuel tank of a motor vehicle. Clean-fuel refueling property also includes property for recharging electric vehicles, but only if the property is located where the electric vehicle is recharged. A taxpayer may expense and deduct up to $100,000 of the value of clean-fuel vehicle property placed in service with respect to each location of the taxpayer having such property.

Clean-burning fuels dispensed at the property must be any of the following: natural gas; liquefied natural gas; liquefied petroleum gas; hydrogen; electricity and any other fuel that is at least 85 percent methanol, ethanol, or any other alcohol or ether.

The Code Sec. 179A deduction available for clean-burning vehicle refueling property is scheduled to expire with respect to costs incurred after December 31, 2005 (the Energy Tax Incentives Act of 2005 sunsets this deduction a year earlier than originally scheduled, see ¶310).

NEW LAW EXPLAINED

Credit replaces deduction for installation of clean-fuel vehicle refueling property.—A new credit for the installation of alternative fuel (clean-fuel) vehicle property used in a trade or business, or installed at the taxpayer's residence, applies to property placed in service after December 31, 2005 (Code Sec. 30C, as added by the Energy Tax Incentive Act of 2005). A taxpayer may elect not to claim a credit under this new provision (Code Sec. 30C(e)(4), as added by the Energy Act). However, the tax basis of any property for which the credit is claimed will be reduced by the portion of the property's cost that is taken into account in computing the credit (Code Sec. 30C(e)(1), as added by the Energy Act). This credit replaces the Code Sec. 179A deduction for clean-fuel vehicle refueling property, which is unavailable for property placed in service after December 31, 2005 (see ¶310).

Amount of credit allowed. A taxpayer will be allowed a tax credit of up to 30 percent of the cost of "qualified alternative fuel vehicle refueling property," that is placed in service during the tax year (Code Sec. 30C(a), as added by the Energy Act). In addition to the 30-percent limit, there is a yearly cap on the dollar amount of the credit. For commercial (retail) taxpayers (that is, taxpayers for whom the property would be subject to a depreciation deduction), the maximum yearly credit is $30,000. However, taxpayers who install qualified vehicle refueling property at their principal residence will be limited to a $1,000 yearly credit (Code Sec. 30C(b), as added by the Energy Act). The Joint Committee on Taxation, Description and Technical Explanation of the Energy Tax Incentives Act of 2005 (JCX-60-05) indicates that a taxpayer may carry forward unused credits for 20 years.

Qualified alternative fuel vehicle refueling property defined. Except for a new definition of alternative fuels, the definition of qualified alternative fuel vehicle refueling property for purposes of the new credit closely follows the definition of qualified clean-fuel vehicle refueling property under Code Sec. 179A(d). Thus, to qualify for the credit, the property (which cannot include a building or its structural components) must:

- be of a character that would be subject to the depreciation deduction;
- be property originally used by the taxpayer;
- be at the site at which the vehicle is refueled (if the property is for the storage or dispensing of alternative fuels into the fuel tank of a vehicle propelled by the fuel); or
- be located at the point where the vehicles are recharged (if the property is for recharging electrically-propelled vehicles) (Code Sec. 30C(c)(1), as added by the Energy Act).

The above rules also apply to refueling property installed at a residence, except that the property does not have to be of a type that qualifies for the depreciation deduction (Code Sec. 30C(c)(2), as added by the Energy Act).

Definition of alternative fuels. In order to qualify for the credit, the fuels to be stored or dispensed must:

¶730

NEW LAW EXPLAINED

- at least 85 percent in volume consist of one or more of the following: ethanol, natural gas, compressed natural gas, liquefied natural gas, liquefied petroleum gas, or hydrogen (Code Sec. 30C(c)(1)(A), as added by the Energy Act); or

- be any mixture of biodiesel and diesel fuel (determined without regard to any use of kerosene) containing at least 20 percent of biodiesel (Code Sec. 30C(c)(1)(B), as added by the Energy Act).

   Comment: Except for the addition of biodiesel fuel, this list of qualified alternative fuels closely follows the clean-burning fuels listed under Code Sec. 179A(e)(1).

Application with other credits. The business portion of the credit for alternative fuel vehicle refueling property (that is, the portion relating to property of a character subject to depreciation) is treated as a portion of the general business credit under Code Sec. 38 (Code Sec. 30C(d)(1), as added by the Energy Act). The remaining portion of the credit (that is, the credit related to residential or nonbusiness property) is allowable to the extent of the excess of the regular tax (reduced by the nonrefundable credits of subpart A, the foreign tax credit (Code Sec. 27), the electric vehicle credit (Code Sec. 30), and the new credit for alternate motor vehicles (Code Sec. 30B)) over the alternative minimum tax for the tax year (Code Sec. 30C(d)(2), as added by the Energy Act).

Property used by a tax-exempt entity. If certain requirements are met, the person who sells qualified alternative fuel vehicle refueling property to a tax-exempt entity (or to a governmental unit or foreign persons or entities) will be treated as the taxpayer who places the property into service (Code Sec. 30C(e)(2), as added by the Energy Act). In order for this to happen, the qualifying property must not be subject to lease, and the seller must clearly disclose in a written document the amount of qualified alternative fuel vehicle refueling credit that is allowable with respect to the property sold.

Property used outside of United States. No alternative fuel vehicle refueling property credit will be allowed for property that is used predominately outside the United States (Code Sec. 30C(e)(3), as added by the Energy Act).

Interaction with Code Sec. 179. No alternative fuel vehicle refueling property credit will be allowed with respect to the portion of the cost of any property taken into account under Code Sec. 179 (i.e., election to expense certain depreciable business assets) (Code Sec. 30C(e)(3)).

Recapture rules. Rules similar to the recapture rules of Code Sec. 179A(e)(4) are to apply to the newly-enacted credit for alternative fuel vehicle refueling property (Code Sec. 30C(e)(5), as added by the Energy Act). Thus, the IRS is directed to issue regulations providing for the recapture of the benefits of any credit previously allowed with respect to a property that ceases to be eligible for the credit.

Termination of the credit. Generally, no credit for qualified alternative fuel vehicle refueling property will be available for property placed in service after December 31, 2009. However, for qualified refueling property relating to hydrogen, the credit will

¶730

NEW LAW EXPLAINED

not apply to property placed in service after December 31, 2014 (Code Sec. 30C(g), as added by the Energy Act).

State Tax Consequences: Many states provide energy incentives through personal and corporate income tax credits. See ¶195 for a state-by-state summary of available credits.

▶ **Effective date.** The provision applies to property placed in service after December 31, 2005, in tax years ending after such date (Act Sec. 1342(c) of the Energy Act of 2005).

Law source: Law at ¶5035, ¶5040, ¶5130, ¶5240, and ¶5440. Committee Report at ¶10,270.

— Act Sec. 1342(a) of the Energy Tax Incentives Act of 2005, adding new Code Sec. 30C;

— Act Sec. 1342(b), amending Code Secs. 38(b), 55(c)(2), 1016(a) and 6501(m);

— Act Sec. 1342(c), providing the effective date.

Reporter references: For further information, consult the following CCH reporters.

— Standard Federal Tax Reporter, 2005FED ¶12,133.01

— Federal Tax Service, FTS § G:6.300

— Federal Tax Guide, 2005FTG ¶9065

¶735 Small Ethanol Producer Credit Extended to Larger Producers

BACKGROUND

A number of tax benefits are available for ethanol and methanol produced from renewable sources that are used as a motor fuel or that are blended with other fuels for that use. One benefit is an income tax credit for small ethanol producers (Code Sec. 40(b)(4)(A)). A small ethanol producer is a person whose ethanol production capacity does not exceed 30 million gallons per year (Code Sec. 40(g)(1)). The credit is 10 cents per gallon of ethanol produced during the tax year for up to a maximum of 15 million gallons (Code Sec. 40(b)(4)(C). The small ethanol producer credit and the other credits that make up the alcohol fuels tax credit are includible in income (Code Sec. 87), and like tax credits generally, are subject to limitations and cannot be used to offset alternative minimum tax liability. Under coordination rules with the federal excise tax exemptions for gasohol, the alcohol fuels credit is subject to reduction to account for any tax benefit the taxpayer received with respect to the same alcohol under the excise tax provisions (Code Sec. 40(c)).

Cooperatives are generally treated as pass-through entities to the extent they distribute their profits to their patrons in the form of patronage dividends (Code Secs. 1381, 1382, 1385). Under changes made by the American Jobs Creation Act of 2004 (P.L. 108-357), the small ethanol producer credit is now among the credits that cooperatives are allowed to pass-through to their patrons if the cooperative so elects (Code Sec. 40(g)). The cooperative must apportion the credit pro rata among patrons

BACKGROUND

on the basis of the quantity or value of business done with or for such patrons in the tax year.

NEW LAW EXPLAINED

The definition of "small ethanol producer" is expanded to include larger producers.—The Energy Tax Incentives Act of 2005 expands the definition of an eligible small ethanol producer to include persons whose production capacity does not exceed 60 million gallons (Code Sec. 40(g), as amended by the Energy Act). This provision doubles the maximum size of producers that can qualify for the credit.

Cooperatives that elect to passthrough credit must notify patrons of apportionment. The Energy Act requires cooperatives to notify their patrons in writing of the apportionment of the credit. The notice must be mailed to the patron within the payment period described in Code Sec. 1382(d) (Code Sec. 40(g)(6)(A)(ii), as amended by the Energy Act). That period for any tax year begins with the first day of the tax year and ends with the 15th day of the ninth month following the close of the tax year.

> **Comment:** Apportioned amounts are included in the patron's gross income as patronage dividends (Code Secs. 1385(a) and 1388(a)). The patron, rather than the cooperative, claims the benefit of the credit to the extent the patron includes patronage dividends derived from the credit in the patron's income for the tax year (Code Sec. 40(g)(6)(B)).
>
> **Election:** Pass-through treatment for cooperative patrons must be elected on a timely filed return for the relevant tax year. Once made, the election is irrevocable for that tax year (Code Sec. 40(g)(6)(A)(ii)). Form 6478, Credit for Alcohol Used as Fuel, is used to claim the credit.
>
> **State Tax Consequences:** Many states provide energy incentives through personal and corporate income tax credits. See ¶195 for a state-by-state summary of available credits.

▶ **Effective date.** The amendments are effective for tax years ending after August 8, 2005 (Act Sec. 1347(c) of the Energy Tax Incentives Act of 2005).

Law source: Law at ¶5045. Committee Report at ¶10,310.

— Act Sec. 1347(a) of the Energy Tax Incentives Act of 2005, amending Code Sec. 40(g);

— Act Sec. 1347(b), amending Code Sec. 40(g)(6);

— Act Sec. 1347(c), providing the effective date.

Reporter references: For further information, consult the following CCH reporters.

— Standard Federal Tax Reporter, 2005FED ¶4304.01 and ¶4304.05

— Federal Tax Service, FTS §G:24.60

— Federal Tax Guide, 2005FTG ¶2400

— Excise Tax Reporter, ETR ¶2215.06

¶735

PREVENTION OF FUEL FRAUD

¶740 Excise Tax on Kerosene Used in Aviation

BACKGROUND

Diesel fuel and kerosene are generally subject to an excise tax of 24.3 cents per gallon (Code Sec. 4081(a)(2)(A)(iii)). However, *aviation-grade kerosene* is taxed at 21.8 cents per gallon (Code Sec. 4081(a)(2)(A)(iv)), and aviation-grade kerosene used in *commercial aviation* is taxed at 4.3 cents per gallon (Code Sec. 4081(a)(2)(C)). An additional tax of 0.1 cent per gallon is imposed and goes into the Leaking Underground Storage Tank (LUST) Trust Fund (Code Sec. 4081(d)(3)), for a total tax rate of 24.4 cents, 21.9 cents, or 4.4 cents per gallon, respectively (Code Sec. 4081(a)(2)(B)).

> **Comment:** The 24.3-cent tax on kerosene was scheduled to drop to 4.3 cents after September 30, 2005, but that decrease has been postponed until after September 30, 2011 (see ¶905). In addition, the 0.1-cent LUST tax was scheduled to expire after September 30, 2005, but it has been extended through September 30, 2011 (see ¶785).

The 4.4-cent excise tax is imposed on aviation-grade kerosene used in commercial aviation when the fuel is removed from a refinery or terminal directly into the fuel tank of the aircraft (Code Sec. 4081(a)(2)(C)). A *refueler truck, tanker or tank wagon* qualifies as part of a terminal if:

- the terminal is located within a secured area of an airport,
- the aviation-grade kerosene loaded into the truck, tanker or wagon is for delivery only into aircraft at the airport where the terminal is located,
- the terminal does not load aviation-grade fuel into any vehicle registered for highway use, and
- the truck, tanker or wagon has storage tanks, hose, and coupling equipment designed and used for fueling aircraft, it is not registered for highway use, and it is operated by the terminal operator or by a person that provides the terminal operator with a daily accounting of each delivery from the truck, tanker or wagon (Code Sec. 4081(a)(3)(A) and (B)).

Aviation-grade kerosene that is not taxed under these rules is taxed at the 21.8-cent rate (21.9 cents with the LUST tax) when it is sold to or used by an owner, lessor or operator of an aircraft. However, this *backup tax* does not apply if the fuel was previously taxed upon delivery from a terminal directly into an aircraft, and the tax was not credited or refunded (Code Sec. 4041(c)).

Aviation-grade kerosene is presumed taxable upon its sale or use unless it is used for an exempt purpose. If the fuel is exempt from excise tax on its sale or use, it is also exempt from the excise tax imposed on fuel delivered from a refinery or terminal directly into an aircraft (Code Sec. 4082(e)). The *exempt uses* for aviation fuel (Code Sec. 4041(f), (g), (h) and (l)) include:

BACKGROUND

- use other than as aircraft fuel,
- use on a farm for farming purposes,
- export,
- use in foreign trade,
- use in certain helicopters and fixed-wing aircraft,
- exclusive use of a nonprofit educational organization,
- exclusive use of a state,
- use in an aircraft owned by an aircraft museum, and
- use in military aircraft.

Credit or refund. If excise taxes are paid on aviation-grade kerosene that is used for exempt purposes or resold, the taxes are credited or refunded (Code Sec. 6427(l)(4)). For this purpose, nontaxable uses include use of the kerosene in commercial aviation (Code Sec. 6247(l)(2)(B)(ii)). The *credit or refund* is generally made to the purchaser, but it can be made to an *ultimate vendor* if these requirements are met (Code Secs. 6416(a) and 6427(l)(4)(B)):

(1) the purchaser waives the right to the refund and assigns it to the vendor,

(2) the vendor is registered with the IRS under Code Sec. 4101, and

(3) the vendor satisfies one of these tests:

    (a) the vendor did not include the tax in the price of the fuel,

    (b) the vendor repaid the tax to the purchaser, or

    (c) the vendor obtained the purchaser's written consent for the credit or refund to be made to the vendor, and filed that consent with the IRS.

The amount credited or refunded is generally equal to the taxes paid. However, for aviation-grade kerosene that was used in commercial aviation, the amount credited or refunded does not include amounts attributable to the LUST tax (0.1 cent) or the tax on aviation-grade fuel used in commercial aviation (4.3 cents); thus, the first 4.4 cents per gallon of the tax is not refunded (Code Sec. 6427(l)).

The excise taxes on aviation-grade kerosene that are imposed at the 21.8 and 4.3 cent-per-gallon rates are credited to the Airport and Airway Trust Fund. Refunds and credits of these taxes are paid from the Airport and Airway Trust Fund into the general fund of the U.S. Treasury (Code Sec. 9502(b) and (d)). Taxes that are imposed at the 24.3 cent-per-gallon rate are credited to the Highway Trust Fund (Code Sec. 9503(b)(1)(D)).

NEW LAW EXPLAINED

Excise tax restructured for kerosene used in aviation.—A variety of law changes are intended to improve the collection of excise taxes on aviation fuel. *Aviation-grade kerosene* is eliminated as a category of fuel with its own tax rate, and all kerosene is ostensibly taxed at the highest rate of 24.3 cents per gallon (Code Sec. 4081(a)(2)(A), as amended by the SAFE Transportation Equity Act of 2005). However, special tax rates apply to kerosene that is used in aviation.

¶740

NEW LAW EXPLAINED

Kerosene that is removed from a refinery or terminal directly into the fuel tank of an aircraft for use in *commercial aviation* can still qualify for the 4.3 cents-per-gallon tax rate (4.4 cents with the LUST tax). However, the person who uses the fuel must be registered for commercial use under Code Sec. 4101 (Code Sec. 4081(a)(2)(C)(i), as amended by the Highway Act) (See also ¶790). As under present law, the fuel is treated as used when it is removed from the fuel tank, and the person who uses the fuel is liable for paying the tax (Code Sec. 4081(a)(4), as amended by the Highway Act).

When kerosene is removed from a refinery or terminal directly into the fuel tank of an aircraft and used in *noncommercial aviation*, the tax rate remains 21.8 cents per gallon (21.9 cents with the LUST tax) (Code Sec. 4081(a)(2)(C)(ii), as amended by the Highway Act). This rate, and the 19.3-cent rate for aviation gasoline, are scheduled to revert to 4.3 cents after September 30, 2007 (Code Sec. 4081(d)(2)(A), as amended by the Highway Act).

> **Comment:** A technical correction to the existing statute also provides for this reversion of the tax rates (see ¶795).

For purposes of the 21.8-cent tax rate, a *refueler truck, tanker or tank wagon* can be treated as part of a terminal if the terminal is located in an airport, even if it is not located in a secured area. However, the terminal must be located in a secured area in order for the 4.3-cent tax rate to apply. For both tax rates, the other present-law requirements for treating trucks, tankers and wagons as a terminal continue to apply. That is, the terminal cannot load kerosene into any vehicle registered for highway use. Truck, tanker or wagon must deliver fuel only to airplanes at the airport where the terminal is located, it must be designed and used for fueling aircraft, it cannot be registered for highway use, and it must be operated by the terminal operator or someone who provides the terminal operator with a daily accounting of deliveries (Code Sec. 4081(a)(3)(D), as amended by the Highway Act).

> **Comment:** The Conference Committee Report for the Highway Act states that the list of airports with a terminal in a secured area should include Los Angeles International Airport (Terminal T-95-CA-4812) and Federal Express Corporation Memphis Airport (Terminal T-62-TN-2220) (Conference Committee Report (H.R. Conf. Rep. No. 109-203)).

The *backup tax* on any previously untaxed liquid for use as a fuel (other than aviation gasoline) continues to apply when the fuel is sold to or used by an aircraft owner, lessee or operator. The tax rates are the same: that is, 4.3 cents per gallon for fuel used in commercial aviation, and 21.8 cents per gallon for fuel used for noncommercial aviation. These backup taxes are not imposed if the fuel was taxed upon its removal from a terminal, entry into the U.S., or sale, as long as that tax was not credited or refunded (Code Sec. 4041(c), as amended by the Highway Act). If kerosene is *exempt* from this backup tax for any reason other than having been previously taxed (that is, if it is used for an exempt purpose), no tax is imposed when the kerosene is delivered from a refinery or terminal directly into an aircraft. For this purpose, a refueler truck, tanker or tank wagon is treated as part of a terminal only if the terminal is located in a secured area of an airport (Code Sec. 4082(e), as amended by the Highway Act).

¶740

NEW LAW EXPLAINED

Credit or refund. New rules govern the refund or credit of taxes on kerosene used in noncommercial aviation. If the fuel was taxed at the full 24.3-cent-per-gallon rate and was used for a non-exempt purpose, the refund or credit amounts to 2.5 cents per gallon because amounts attributable to the LUST tax (0.1 cent) and the tax on kerosene used in noncommercial aviation (21.8 cents) are not refundable (Code Sec. 6427(l)(5), as added by the Highway Act). An exempt use is any use that is exempt from the tax imposed by Code Sec. 4041(c) for a reason other than having been previously taxed. Commercial use is no longer identified as a nontaxable use (Code Sec. 6247(l)(2), as amended by the Highway Act). The refund is payable *only* to the ultimate vendor of the fuel. As under present law, the ultimate vendor must be registered with the IRS under Code Sec. 4101, and must have omitted the tax from the price of the fuel, repaid the tax to the purchaser, or provided the IRS with the purchaser's written consent to the vendor receiving the refund (Code Sec. 6427(l)(5)(B)), as added by the Highway Act).

> **Caution Note:** The amended statute actually states that the refund attributable to *any* kerosene shall be paid only to the ultimate vendor, but this language appears in a subsection that addresses kerosene used in noncommercial aviation. The Conference Committee Report for the Highway Act confirms that this ultimate vendor rule is limited to refunds arising from kerosene used in non-commercial aviation (Conference Committee Report (H.R. Conf. Rep. No. 109-203)).

Each month, the Treasury Secretary must transfer amounts from the Highway Trust Fund into the Airport and Airway Trust Fund that are equal to the estimated amount of refunds and credits for taxes on kerosene used in aviation. The transferred amounts are equivalent to 21.8 cents per gallon for refund and credit claims made with respect to kerosene used for noncommercial aviation, and 4.3 cents per gallon for refund and credit claims made with respect to kerosene used for commercial aviation. These transfer rules apply to taxes received on or after October 1, 2005, and before October 1, 2011 (Code Sec. 9503(a)(7), as added by the Highway Act). Refunded taxes on kerosene used for exempt purposes in commercial and noncommercial aviation are no longer included in amounts transferred from the Airport and Airway Trust Fund into the general fund of the U.S. Treasury (Code Sec. 9502(d), as amended by the Highway Act).

▶ **Effective date.** These amendments apply to fuels or liquids removed, entered or sold after September 30, 2005 (Act Sec. 11161(e), of the SAFE Transportation Equity Act of 2005).

Law source: Law at ¶5265, ¶5290, ¶5295, ¶5430, ¶5480 and ¶5485. Committee Report at ¶15,260.

— Act Sec. 11161(a) of the SAFE Transportation Equity Act of 2005, amending Code Secs. 4081(a), and 4082(b), (d) and (e);

— Act Sec. 11161(b), amending Code Secs. 4041(a)(1)(B) and (c), 4082(d)(2)(B) and 6427(i)(4)(A) and (l);

— Act Sec. 11161(c), amending Code Sec. 9502(a) and (b)(1), striking Code Sec. 9503(b)(3), and adding new Code Sec. 9503(c)(7);

— Act Sec. 11161(d), amending Code Sec. 9502(d)(2) and (3);

— Act Sec. 11161(e), providing the effective date.

¶740

NEW LAW EXPLAINED

Reporter references: For further information, consult the following CCH reporters.

— Excise Tax Reporter, ETR ¶8915.015, ¶8919.01, ¶9215.047, ¶49,685.065 and ¶49,685.13

¶745 Refunds of Excise Taxes on Exempt Sales of Fuels by Credit Cards

BACKGROUND

Certain uses of gasoline are exempt from tax, including uses by a nonprofit educational organization or a state or local government. Because fuel is taxed early in the chain of distribution, the tax has already been imposed by the time the exempt entity purchases the fuel. As a result, a claim for refund or credit arises. A question then emerges as to who in the chain of the fuel's distribution is entitled to claim the refund.

Prior to the enactment of the American Jobs Creation Act of 2004 (P.L. 108-357), the general rule was that a wholesale distributor who sold gasoline directly to the ultimate purchaser was treated as the only person who paid the excise tax and could therefore claim a refund (Code Sec. 6416(a)(4), prior to amendment by P.L. 108-357). If, however, an exempt entity—a state or local government or nonprofit educational organization—purchased gasoline using an oil company credit card, and the oil company reimbursed the seller based on a price that included the tax, the seller was not deemed to have made a direct sale to the exempt entity. In that case, the person that actually *paid* the tax (in most cases the oil company) was treated as the only person eligible to make a refund claim (Notice 89-29, 1989-1 CB 669).

The 2004 Jobs Act, however, changed the rule for refunds by expressly providing that the *ultimate vendor* of gasoline is the proper party to request a refund from the IRS, so long as the ultimate vendor is registered with the IRS. This change conformed the payment of refunds on gasoline sales with the procedures established for diesel fuel and kerosene sales, where the ultimate vendor made the claim for refund.

In light of the 2004 Jobs Act law changes regarding ultimate vendor claims, a question arose as to whether the oil company credit card rule was still applicable. Notice 2005-4, I.R.B. 2005-2, 289, extended the existing credit card rule through February 28, 2005, but it questioned whether the rule—which essentially takes the refund away from the ultimate vendor—continued to apply.

A letter dated February 25, 2005, sent by Senate Finance Committee Chairman Charles E. Grassley and ranking member Max Baucus, and signed by House Ways and Means Committee Chairman William M. Thomas, said that their intent with the 2004 Jobs Act changes was to retain the existing treatment with respect to sales on an oil company credit card. As a result, the IRS issued Notice 2005-24, I.R.B. 2005-12, 757, in which it extended the credit card rule until Congress had the opportunity to address the issue.

NEW LAW EXPLAINED

New rules for purchases facilitated by oil company credit cards.—New rules apply to purchases of gasoline, diesel fuel and kerosene using a credit card by a state or local government for its exclusive use. If a purchase of taxable fuel is made by a credit card issued to a state or local government, the credit card issuer that extends the credit to the state or local government is the only person entitled to apply for the credit or refund of the tax *if* the credit card issuer:

(1) is registered with the IRS,

(2) has not collected the tax from the purchaser of the fuel or has obtained written consent from the purchaser to seek the refund or credit, and

(3) has either repaid or agreed to repay the amount of tax to the ultimate vendor, has obtained the written consent of the ultimate vendor to the allowance of the credit or refund, or has otherwise made arrangements that directly or indirectly reimburse the ultimate vendor for the tax.

If these three conditions are not met, the credit card issuer must collect the tax from the ultimate purchaser of the fuel (e.g., the local government entity), which can then seek the credit or refund (Code Secs. 6416(a)(4)(B) and 6427(l)(6)(D), as added by the SAFE Transportation Equity Act of 2005).

> **Comment:** According to the Conference Committee Report for the Highway Act (H.R. Conf. Rep. No. 109-203), an indirect arrangement may consist of a contractual undertaking by the oil company and the credit card issuer that the oil company will pay the amount of tax to the ultimate vendor, and a corresponding contractual undertaking by the oil company and the ultimate vendor that this is the agreement. In this case, the oil company would be entitled to claim the credit or refund of tax.

The new rules also apply to gasoline purchased by a nonprofit educational organization for its exclusive use.

Practical Analysis: William B. Gray (Bill), Excise Tax Manager, Sinclair Oil Corporation, observes that this provision simplifies the differences in refunds between gasoline and diesel and focuses the refund claims on a single clearly defined party—the person extending the credit (usually the credit card company). This will get the oil companies and other intermediate vendors out of the refund business and will shift the burden to credit card companies—the first time that anyone other than a taxpayer or fuel seller is entitled to claim credit for nontaxable sales. If the credit card companies choose not to administer the exemption, the refund right, and burden, falls to the ultimate purchaser.

Registration. Credit card issuers who want to claim a credit or refund of tax on fuels sold to state or local governments or gasoline sold to nonprofit educational organizations must be registered with the IRS (Code Sec. 4101(a)(4), as added by the Highway Act). An unregistered credit card issuer that does not collect the tax from the ultimate

¶745

NEW LAW EXPLAINED

purchaser of the fuel is liable for the penalties for failing to register under Code Secs. 6719, 7232 and 7272.

Under Code Sec. 4101(a), the IRS has the authority to preclude persons that are registered credit card issuers under the new rules from issuing nonregistered credit cards. According to the Conference Committee Report for the Highway Act (H.R. Conf. Rep. No. 109-203), Congress anticipates that credit card issuers will use a separate registered entity for the issuance of credit cards subject to these rules. Congress intends that the IRS will review the registration of a credit card issuer who has engaged in multiple or flagrant violations of the new rules.

Timing of claims. The present law rules relating to the timing of claims for registered ultimate vendors are extended to registered credit card issuers (Code Sec. 6416(a)(4)(C), as redesignated and amended by the Highway Act). Thus, refund claims may be filed for any period of at least one week for which $200 or more is payable, and the claim must be filed on or before the last day of the first quarter following the earliest quarter included in the claim (Code Sec. 6427(i)(4)). The IRS must pay interest on refunds that remain unpaid after 45 days. Electronic claims for refund will be paid with interest if the claim is not paid within 20 days of the date it is filed. Note, however, that the rule for electronic claims only applies if the credit card issuer certifies to the IRS that all of the credit card issuer's ultimate purchasers are state or local governments or nonprofit educational organizations for the most recent quarter of the tax year (Code Sec. 6416(a)(4)(C), as amended by the Highway Act).

▶ **Effective date.** The new rules apply to sales after December 31, 2005 (Act Sec. 11163(e) of the SAFE Transportation Equity Act of 2005).

Law source: Law at ¶5305, ¶5395, ¶5410, ¶5430 and ¶5445. Committee Report at ¶15,280.

— Act Sec. 11163(a) of the SAFE Transportation Equity Act of 2005, adding new Code Sec. 4101(a)(4);

— Act Sec. 11163(b), amending Code Secs. 6416(a)(4) and (b)(2);

— Act Sec. 11163(c), amending Code Sec. 6427(I)(6);

— Act Sec. 11163(d), amending Code Secs. 6206 and 6675;

— Act Sec. 11163(e), providing the effective date.

Reporter references: For further information, consult the following CCH reporters.

— Excise Tax Reporter, ETR ¶10,945.02, ¶48,215.02 and ¶49,685.12

¶750 Ultimate Purchaser Can Claim Refund for Diesel Fuel Used on Farms

BACKGROUND

A credit or refund may be claimed for diesel fuel and kerosene taxes paid on undyed fuel used for certain nontaxable uses. Use on a farm for farming purposes is one exempt use (Code Sec. 6427(c)).

BACKGROUND

Generally, the ultimate purchaser of the fuels is the proper party to claim income tax credits or payments for taxed diesel fuel and kerosene put to nontaxable uses. However, the registered ultimate *vendor* is the proper party to make claims relating to diesel fuel and kerosene sold for use on a farm for farming purposes. A registered ultimate vendor is a person who sells undyed diesel fuel or undyed kerosene to any of the following:

(1) the owner, tenant, or operator of a farm for use by that person on a farm for farming purposes, or

(2) a person other than the owner, tenant, or operator of a farm for use by that person on a farm in connection with cultivating, raising, or harvesting.

In addition, this vendor must be registered by the IRS.

If a registered ultimate vendor has a claim of at least $200 ($100 for kerosene), the vendor may seek weekly refunds from the IRS (Code Sec. 6427(i)(4)(A)).

NEW LAW EXPLAINED

Claims by ultimate vendors repealed.—Ultimate vendor refund claims resulting from diesel fuel and kerosene used on a farm for farming purposes are repealed for sales after September 30, 2005 (Code Sec. 6427(l)(6)(A), as amended by the SAFE Transportation Equity Act of 2005). Thus, for diesel fuel or kerosene used on a farm for farming purposes, refund claims will be paid or credited to the ultimate purchaser rather than the ultimate vendor (Code Sec. 6427(l)(1)).

As a result, the "ultimate purchaser rules" will apply to farm-related refund claims of diesel fuel and kerosene. Specifically, a refund will be allowed to the ultimate purchaser of the fuel used on the farm if the tax was imposed on the diesel fuel or kerosene to which the claim relates, the claimant produced or bought the fuel and did not resell it, and the claim is properly filed (Reg. §48.6427-8(b)).

An ultimate purchaser of diesel fuel or kerosene used on a farm for farming purposes may make a claim for refund for any quarter of a tax year so long as the ultimate purchaser can claim at least $750 (Code Sec. 6427(i)(2)). If the purchaser cannot claim $750 by the end of the quarter, he or she can carry it over to the next quarter, and so on, until the $750 amount is reached. If, however, the ultimate purchaser cannot claim $750 by the end of the tax year, the purchaser must claim a credit (instead of seeking a refund) on his or her income tax return.

> **Practical Analysis:** William B. Gray (Bill), Excise Tax Manager, Sinclair Oil Corporation, observes that the ultimate vendor is relieved of responsibility in administering the refund. The burden of proof shifts to the farmer where many think the abuses have occurred. This will be costly to farmers, both in administering the refund process and waiting for the refund to be granted.

¶750

NEW LAW EXPLAINED

▶ **Effective date.** The new rules for diesel fuel and kerosene used on a farm apply to sales after September 30, 2005 (Act Sec. 11162(c) of the SAFE Transportation Equity Act of 2005).

Law source: Law at ¶5430. Committee Report at ¶15,270.

— Act Sec. 11162(a) and (b) of the SAFE Transportation Equity Act of 2005, amending Code Sec. 6427(l)(6);

— Act Sec. 11162(c), providing the effective date.

Reporter references: For further information, consult the following CCH reporters.

— Federal Tax Service, FTS § G:24.341
— Federal Tax Guide, 2005FTG ¶2375
— Excise Tax Reporter, ETR ¶49,685.05 and ¶49,685.12

¶755 Reregistration With Change in Ownership

BACKGROUND

Under Code Sec. 4101, blenders, enterers, pipeline operators, position holders, refiners, terminal operators, and vessel operators, all of whom are taxed on special fuels under Code Sec. 4041(a)(1) and on aviation and motor fuels under Code Sec. 4081, are required to register with the IRS. The American Jobs Creation Act of 2004 (P.L. 108-357) created a penalty under Code Sec. 6719 and imposes a $10,000 assessable penalty for an initial failure to register. That amount is increased by $1,000 per day as long as the failure continues. There is, however, a reasonable cause exception to this penalty. Additionally, the 2004 Jobs Act also created a nonassessable penalty of $10,000 for failure to register under Code Sec. 7272.

In addition to the civil penalties, failure to register also carries a criminal penalty of not more than $10,000 or imprisonment of not more than five years, or both, together with the costs of prosecution. Prior to the amendment of Code Sec. 7232 by the 2004 Jobs Act, the penalty was $5,000 or imprisonment of not more than five years, or both, together with the costs of prosecution

Treasury Regulation § 48.4101-1(h)(1)(v) requires that a change in the information the registrant submitted in connection with its application for registration, such as a change in ownership, requires notification of the Secretary within 10 days of the change. Moreover, the Secretary has the discretion to revoke the registration of a noncompliant registrant.

NEW LAW EXPLAINED

Reregistration requirements with a change in ownership.—Reregistration with a change in ownership is now required of persons taxed on special fuels under Code Sec. 4041(a)(1) and aviation and motor fuels under Code Sec. 4081 (Code Sec. 4101(a) as amended by the SAFE Transportation Equity Act of 2005). A change in ownership

NEW LAW EXPLAINED

is defined as more than 50 percent of the ownership interest in, or assets of, a registrant being held by persons other than persons (or person related thereto) who held more than 50 percent of such interests or assets before the transaction (or series of related transactions). The new law does not apply to corporations whose stock is regulary traded on an established securities market. The penalties for failure to reregister are the same as the current civil penalties in Code Secs. 6719 and 7272. The criminal penalties for failure to reregister are also the same as the current penalties under Code Sec. 7232.

▶ **Effective date.** This provision applies to actions, or failures to act after August 10, 2005 (Act Sec. 11164(c) of the SAFE Transportation Equity Act of 2005).

Law source: Law at ¶5305, ¶5450, ¶5465 and ¶5470. Committee Report at ¶15,290.

— Act Sec. 11164(a) of the SAFE Transportation Equity Act of 2005, amending Code Sec. 4101(a);

— Act Sec. 11164(b), amending Code Secs. 6719, 7232 and 7272;

— Act Sec. 11164(c), providing the effective date.

Reporter references: For further information, consult the following CCH reporters.

— Excise Tax Reporter, ETR ¶10,945.02, ¶51,860.01, ¶54,375.01 and ¶55,275.01

¶760 Diesel Fuel Tax Evasion Report

BACKGROUND

An excise tax is a selective sales tax levied on a specific commodity or service, or a charge to pursue a certain trade or occupation. The following fuels are subject to excise taxes: gasoline including aviation gasoline and gasoline blendstocks; diesel fuel; kerosene; aviation-grade kerosene; special motor fuels (including LPG); compressed natural gas; and fuels used in commercial transportation on inland waterways.

An excise tax is imposed upon: (1) the removal of any taxable fuel from a refinery or terminal, (2) the entry of any taxable fuel into the United States, or (3) the sale of any taxable fuel to any person who is not registered with the IRS to receive untaxed fuel, unless there was a prior taxable removal or entry (Code Sec. 4081(a)(1)). The tax does not apply to any removal or entry of taxable fuel transferred in bulk by pipeline or vessel to a terminal or refinery if the person removing or entering the taxable fuel, the operator of the pipeline or vessel and the operator of the terminal or refinery, are registered with the IRS (Code Sec. 4081(a)(1)(B)).

Diesel fuel and kerosene that is to be used for a nontaxable purpose will not be taxed upon removal from the terminal if it is dyed to indicate its nontaxable purpose. The IRS has the authority to prescribe marking requirements for diesel fuel and kerosene destined for a nontaxable use, but has not prescribed any marking requirements to date.

NEW LAW EXPLAINED

Diesel Fuel Tax Evasion Report.—The IRS Commissioner is required to provide a report concerning diesel fuel tax evasion to the Senate Finance Committee, Senate Committee on Environment and Public Works, the House Ways and Means Committee and the House Transportation and Infrastructure Committee. The report must be submitted no later than 360 days after August 10, 2005, the date of enactment of the SAFE Transportation Equity Act of 2005. Specifically, the IRS Commissioner must report on:

(1) the availability of new technologies, including forensic or chemical molecular markers, that can be employed to enhance collections of the excise tax on diesel fuel and the plans of the IRS to employ these technologies;

(2) the design of a test to place forensic or chemical molecular markers in any excluded liquid, as defined in Reg. § 48.4081-1(b);

(3) the design of a test, in consultation with the Department of Defense, to place forensic or chemical molecular markers in all nonstrategic bulk level deliveries of diesel fuel to the military; and

(4) the design of a test to place forensic or chemical molecular markers in all diesel fuel bound for export utilizing the Gulf of Mexico.

▶ **Effective date.** No specific effective date is provided by the Act. The provision is, therefore, considered effective on August 10, 2005.

Law source: Law at ¶7080. Committee Report at ¶15,190.

— Act Sec. 11145 of the SAFE Transportation Equity Act of 2005.

¶765 Adulterated Fuels Penalty

BACKGROUND

Excise taxes are imposed on all diesel fuels, gasoline and kerosene. Diesel fuel includes any liquid, other than gasoline, that without further processing or blending is suitable for use in a diesel-powered highway vehicle or diesel-powered train. Beginning in 2005, transmix and diesel fuel blendstocks identified by the IRS are taxed as if they were diesel fuel, regardless of whether the mixture contains gasoline (Code Sec. 4083(a)(3)). Some persons who transfer, sell or hold out for sale diesel fuel mixtures or additives, and some retailers claim that certain diesel fuel mixtures or additives are not suitable for use in a diesel-powered highway vehicle or diesel-powered train because they are not approved as additives or mixtures by the Environmental Protection Agency (EPA).

In 2001, the EPA finalized regulations, the Highway Diesel Fuel Sulfur Control Requirements, that set new emissions standards for diesel-powered highway vehicles and established new diesel fuel quality standards. Beginning in 2006, refiners must begin producing highway diesel fuel that meets a maximum sulfur standard of 15 parts per million.

NEW LAW EXPLAINED

Penalty imposed for failing to meet EPA standards for diesel fuel additives.—A new $10,000 penalty may be imposed against any person (other than a retailer) who knowingly transfers for resale, sells for resale or holds out for resale for use in a diesel-powered highway vehicle or train any liquid that does not meet applicable EPA regulations. The penalty may be assessed for each transfer, sale or holding out for resale, in addition to any tax on the liquid, if applicable (Code Sec. 6720A(a), as added by the SAFE Transportation Equity Act). Likewise, a $10,000 penalty may be imposed on a retailer for knowingly holding out for sale any such liquid. The penalty may be assessed for each holding out for sale, in addition to any tax on the liquid, if applicable (Code Sec. 6720A(b), as added by the Highway Act). "Applicable EPA regulations," for purposes of the penalty, refers to the Highway Diesel Fuel Sulfur Control Requirements (Code Sec. 6720A(a), as added by the Highway Act). The amount of the penalty collected is appropriated to the Highway Trust Fund (Code Sec. 9503(b)(5), as amended by the Highway Act).

▶ **Effective date.** This provision applies to any transfer, sale, or holding out for sale or resale occurring after August 10, 2005 (Act Sec. 11167(d) of the SAFE Transportation Equity Act).

Law source: Law at ¶5455 and ¶5485. Committee Report at ¶15,320.

— Act Sec. 11167(a) of the SAFE Transportation Equity Act, adding new Code Sec. 6720A;
— Act Sec. 11167(b), amending Code Sec. 9503(b);
— Act Sec. 11167(d), providing the effective date.

¶770 Reconciliation of On-loaded Cargo to Entered Cargo

BACKGROUND

Section 343 of the Trade Act of 2002 (P.L. 107-210) directed the government to set out regulations providing for the transmission to the Customs Service, through an electronic data interchange system, of information pertaining to cargo to be brought into the United States or to be sent from the United States, prior to the arrival or departure of the cargo.

Receiving advance electronic cargo information from all modes of transportation allows Customs and Border Patrol to identify and intercede high-risk cargo before the cargo enters the commerce of the United States (or departs and cannot be recovered). By identifying high-risk cargo at an early stage, the movement of low-risk imports and exports will be facilitated, according to the Treasury Advisory Committee on Commercial Operations (Executive Summary: *Advance Electronic Cargo Information*).

Certain carriers of bulk cargo are exempt from the requirements. An exemption applies to cargo that is composed of free-flowing articles, such as oil, coal and ore. Thus, taxable fuels are not covered by the Cargo Declaration requirement (Customs

BACKGROUND

Form 1302, *Inward Cargo Declaration*) or an electronic alternative, which Customs must receive from a carrier.

NEW LAW EXPLAINED

Electronic transmission of data system to be established.—The Secretary of Homeland Security and the Secretary of the Treasury are required to establish an electronic data interchange system so that the U.S. Customs and Border Protection (USCBP) can transmit information to the IRS relating to cargo that consists of Code Sec. 4083 taxable fuels (Act Sec. 11165(a) of the SAFE Transportation Equity Act of 2005). All filers of required cargo information for taxable fuels, under regulations adopted under the Trade Act of 2002, must provide the information to the USCBP through the electronic system. The electronic system is required to be established within one year of this provision's enactment, August 10, 2005.

▶ **Effective date.** The provision is effective on August 10, 2005 (Act Sec. 11165(b) of the SAFE Transportation Equity Act of 2005).

Law source: Law at ¶7095. Committee Report at ¶15,300.

— Act Sec. 11165(a) of the SAFE Transportation Equity Act of 2005, amending section 343(a) of the Trade Act of 2002 (P.L. 107-210);

— Act Sec. 11165(b), providing the effective date.

¶775 Registration of Deep-Draft Vessels

BACKGROUND

Code Sec. 4101 requires that all persons taxed on special fuels under Code Sec. 4041 and motor and aviation fuels under Code Sec. 4081 register with the Secretary of the Treasury. Generally, both taxes are considered to be manufacturers taxes, with taxes paid at retail only where the tax was not previously paid. The rate of the taxes varies depending on the year and classification of the fuels. The persons taxed under these provisions include blenders, enterers, pipeline operators, position holders, refiners, terminal operators and vessel operators. Under Reg. § 48.4101-1(b)(8), a vessel operator is any person who operates a vessel within the bulk transfer/terminal system. However, the regulation excludes from the definition any deep-draft ocean-going vessel. Code Sec. 4042(c)(1) defines a deep-draft ocean-going vessel as any vessel designed for use on the high seas with a draft of 12 or more feet.

Under Code Sec. 4081, gasoline, diesel fuel and kerosene are taxed upon removal from any refinery or terminal; upon entry into the United States for consumption, use or warehousing; or upon the sale of the fuel to any party not registered under Code Sec. 4101, unless the fuel was previously taxed due to the occurrence of any of the above events. However, the tax does not apply to a bulk transfer of taxable fuel to a terminal or refinery if the party removing or entering the taxable fuel and the

BACKGROUND

operator of the refinery are both registered under Code Sec. 4101. The tax is triggered by the involvement of an unregistered party in this transfer.

NEW LAW EXPLAINED

Registration requirements for deep-draft vessels.—The exclusion of deep-draft ocean-going vessels from the registration requirements under Code Sec. 4101 is eliminated. Therefore, on or after August 10, 2005, any vessel described in Code Sec. 4042(c)(1) must be registered with the IRS. However, an operator of a deep-draft ocean-going vessel that is used exclusively to enter taxable fuel need not register the vessel (Act Sec. 11166(a) of the SAFE Transportation Equity Act of 2005).

> **Comment:** The exclusion of deep-draft ocean-going vessels only appears in Reg. §48.4101-1(b)(8). Presumably, this section of the Highway Act is instructing the IRS to amend the regulation in order to limit the registration exception to only those deep-draft ocean-going vessels that are used exclusively for the bulk entry of fuels into the United States.

Exemption from tax. Vessels used for the bulk entry into the United States of taxable fuels are not required to register in order for the exemption from the excise tax on motor and aviation fuels to apply. Therefore, an unregistered, deep-draft, ocean-going vessel can make a bulk entry of taxable fuels for use, consumption or warehousing in the United States without triggering the tax imposed by Code Sec. 4081 (Code Sec. 4081(a)(1)(B), as amended by the Highway Act).

▶ **Effective date.** This provision is effective on August 10, 2005 (Act Sec. 11166(b)(2) of the SAFE Transportation Equity Act of 2005).

Law source: Law at ¶5290 and ¶7100. Committee Report at ¶15,310.
— Act Sec. 11166(a) of the SAFE Transportation Equity Act of 2005;
— Act Sec. 11166(b)(1), amending Code Sec. 4081(a)(1)(B);
— Act Sec. 11166(b)(2), providing the effective date.

Reporter references: For further information, consult the following CCH reporters.
— Excise Tax Reporter, ETR ¶10,945.02

¶780 Motor Fuel Tax Enforcement Advisory Commission

BACKGROUND

Revenues from motor fuel and other highway use taxes flow into the Highway Trust Fund (HTF) to provide financing for the nation's highway and transit systems. Motor fuel tax evasion, however, has been an on-going problem causing loss of revenues. The federal and state governments are addressing the problem through motor fuel tax compliance and enforcement programs. The Highway Use Tax Evasion program (23 USC § 143) supports state and federal efforts to enhance motor fuel tax enforce-

BACKGROUND

ment, and HTF resources administered by the Federal Highway Administration have been used to support joint enforcement efforts of federal and state agencies in combating the motor fuel tax evasion.

NEW LAW EXPLAINED

Motor Fuel Tax Enforcement Advisory Commission established.—The SAFE Transportation Equity Act of 2005 establishes a Motor Fuel Tax Enforcement Advisory Commission (the "Commission") (Act Sec. 11141(a) of the Highway Act). The Commission will be funded by the Highway Trust Fund and will terminate on September 30, 2009 (Act Sec. 11141(d) and (g) of the Highway Act). The Commission will perform the following functions:

(1) review motor fuel revenue collections, both historical and current;

(2) review the progress of investigations related to motor fuel taxes;

(3) develop and review legislative proposals with respect to motor fuel taxes;

(4) monitor the progress of administrative regulation projects relating to motor fuel taxes;

(5) review the results of federal and state agency cooperative efforts regarding motor fuel taxes;

(6) review the results of federal interagency cooperative efforts regarding motor fuel taxes; and

(7) evaluate and make recommendations to the President and Congress regarding the effectiveness of existing federal enforcement programs on motor fuel taxes, enforcement personnel allocation, and proposals for regulatory projects, legislation, and funding (Act Sec. 11141(b) of the Highway Act).

Membership. The Commission will be composed of the following government and private sector representatives appointed by the chairmen and ranking members of the Senate Finance Committee and the House Ways and Means Committee:

(1) at least one representative from the Department of Homeland Security, the Department of Transportation's Office of Inspector General, the Federal Highway Administration, the Department of Defense, and the Department of Justice;

(2) at least one representative from the Federation of State Tax Administrators;

(3) at least one representative from any state department of transportation;

(4) two representatives from the highway construction industry;

(5) six representatives from industries relating to fuel distribution—two from refiners, one from distributors, one from pipelines, and two from terminal operators;

(6) one representative from the retail fuel industry; and

(7) two representatives from the staff of the Senate Finance Committee and two from the House Ways and Means Committee staff.

¶780

NEW LAW EXPLAINED

Members will be appointed for the life of the Commission and any vacancies will be filled in the manner in which the original appointment was made. The members will elect the chairman of the Commission (Act Sec. 11141(c) of the Highway Act).

Obtaining data and assistance. The Commission is authorized to secure directly from any U.S. department or agency nonconfidential information necessary to carry out its duties. The Commission is also authorized to gather evidence by other appropriate means, including hearings and public comment solicitation (Act Sec. 11141(f) of the Highway Act). Moreover, the Commission may request a consultation from the IRS that will assist it in carrying out its duties (Act Sec. 11141(e) of the Highway Act).

▶ **Effective date.** No specific effective date is provided by the SAFE Transportation Equity Act of 2005. The provision is, therefore, considered effective on August 10, 2005.

Law source: Law at ¶7065. Committee Report at ¶15,150.

— Act Sec. 11141 of the SAFE Transportation Equity Act of 2005.

LUST TAX AND TECHNICAL CORRECTIONS

¶785 Leaking Underground Storage Tank Trust Fund

BACKGROUND

The Leaking Underground Storage Tank (LUST) Trust Fund was created by the Superfund Revenue Act of 1986 (P.L. 99-499) to pay cleanup and related costs of petroleum storage tanks that have no solvent owner, as well as tanks whose owner or operator refuses or is unable to comply with an urgent corrective order. The LUST Trust Fund is financed by a 0.1 cent-per-gallon excise tax on the manufacture, sale or use of gasoline, diesel, kerosene or special motor fuels (other than liquefied petroleum gas or other liquefied natural gas), including use on an inland waterway (Code Secs. 4041(d), 4042 and 4081(a)). The tax expires on September 30, 2005.

> **Comment:** The LUST tax is reduced to 0.05 cent per gallon on the sale or use of "qualified methanol or ethanol fuel" (liquid fuel which is at least 85-percent methanol, ethanol or other alcohol produced from coal, including peat) for a motor vehicle or motorboat (Code Sec. 4041(b)(2)(A)(ii) and (D)).

> **Comment:** Under the Taxpayer Relief Act of 1997 (P.L. 105-34), the LUST tax was imposed through April 1, 2005. It was subsequently extended to October 1, 2005 (P.L. 109-6).

Exemptions. Gasoline, diesel, kerosene and special motor fuels may be exempt from the manufacturers and retail sale excise taxes if they are destined for a nontaxable use (Code Secs. 4041 and 4082). Among other things, nontaxable use includes the following: use in a school or local bus; "off-highway" business use; for farming purposes; as supplies for vessels or aircraft; use by certain aircraft museums; use with a helicopter or fixed-winged aircraft; or the exclusive use by a State in the operation of an essential government function. An exemption from the excise tax on retail sales of diesel fuel and kerosene is also available if the fuel was previously subject to the

BACKGROUND

manufacturers excise tax (but not refunded or credited). These exemptions apply to the LUST portion of any excise tax payable since the LUST tax is imposed "in addition to" any fuel excise tax. An exemption from the LUST tax is also expressly allowed for liquids sold for use in an off-highway business use.

Refunds and credits. Generally, refunds and income tax credits that are available for fuel excise taxes imposed on gasoline, diesel, kerosene and special motor fuels are also available for the LUST tax, unless expressly disallowed. For example, a refund or credit is allowed for the manufacturers excise tax and LUST tax imposed by Code Sec. 4081 on gasoline for use on a farm or other nontaxable purposes (e.g., off-highway business use, etc.) (Code Secs. 6420 and 6421). A refund or credit of the LUST tax, however, is not available if the gasoline is used as a fuel in an aircraft in commercial aviation or as a fuel in a train (Code Secs. 6421(f) and 6427(l)).

NEW LAW EXPLAINED

LUST tax extended.—The Energy Tax Incentives Act of 2005 has extended the Leaking Underground Storage Tank (LUST) Trust Fund financing rate (the LUST tax) through September 30, 2011 (Code Sec. 4081(d)(3), as amended by the Energy Act).

Exemptions limited. The Energy Act also eliminates most situations where fuel would have been exempt from the LUST tax. For example, diesel and kerosene (including dyed fuel) destined for nontaxable use (i.e., such as use in a train) will no longer be exempt from the LUST tax (Code Sec. 4082(a), as amended by the Energy Act) even though the rest of the tax is exempt. The LUST tax exemption for liquids sold for an off-highway business use has also been eliminated (Code Sec. 4041(b)(1)(A), as amended by the Energy Act).

In addition, the LUST tax will be applied if the fuel in question is destined for the following nontaxable uses: farming purposes; as supplies for vessels or aircraft; use by certain aircraft museums; use with a helicopter or fixed-winged aircraft; or the exclusive use by a State in the operation of an essential government function (Code Sec. 4041(d)(5), as added by the Energy Act). A taxpayer will continue, however, to be exempt from the LUST tax with respect to the sale of any liquid for export or shipment to a possession of the United States.

No refunds or credits of LUST tax. The Energy Act greatly limits the availability of refunds or credits of LUST taxes. No refund or credit, or payments by the IRS to a taxpayer will be made for any LUST tax paid, except for fuels destined for export (Code Sec. 6430, as added by the Energy Act).

> **Compliance Tip:** Refunds or credits for LUST taxes that were allowed *prior* to the Energy Act may still be available for fuel entered, removed, or sold on or before September 30, 2005. Credit claims should be made on Form 4136, "Credit for Federal Tax Paid on Fuels." Refund claims should be made on Form 8849, "Claim for Refund of Excise Taxes."

For a discussion regarding authorized expenditures from the LUST Trust Fund, see ¶1035.

NEW LAW EXPLAINED

▶ **Effective date.** Generally, the amendments made by this section shall take effect on October 1, 2005 (Act Sec. 1362(d)(1) of the Energy Tax Incentives Act of 2005). However, the amendments eliminating certain exemptions, refunds and credits for the LUST tax apply to fuel entered, removed, or sold after September 30, 2005 (Act Sec. 1362(d)(2) of the Energy Act).

Law source: Law at ¶5265, ¶5290, ¶5295, ¶5435 and ¶5495. Committee Report at ¶10,360.

— Act Sec. 1362(a) of the Energy Tax Incentives Act of 2005, amending Code Sec. 4081(d)(3);

— Act Sec. 1362(b), amending Code Secs. 4041(a)(1)(B), (a)(2)(A), (b)(1)(A), (c)(2), and 4082(a), and adding new Code Secs. 4041(d)(5) and 6430;

— Act Sec. 1362(d), providing the effective date.

Reporter references: For further information, consult the following CCH reporters.

— Federal Tax Guide, 2005FTG ¶21,020

— Excise Tax Reporter, ETR ¶5700.0129, ¶8915.02 and ¶9215.02

¶787 Gasohol Refund Claims Repealed

BACKGROUND

Prior to the American Jobs Act of 2004 (P.L. 108-357), fuel mixtures containing alcohol were taxed at lower rates. Generally, the higher the alcohol content of the mixture, the lower the rate of tax. Under these former rules, a credit or refund was available for taxable fuels mixed with alcohol and for noncommercial aviation fuel mixed with alcohol.

The 2004 Jobs Act repealed the reduced rates of tax on fuels containing alcohol under Code Secs. 4081(c) and 4091(c). In place of the reduced rates, the 2004 Jobs Act created a credit for alcohol fuel that is claimed against the excise tax imposed by Code Sec. 4081 on certain removals, entries and sales of taxable fuels (Code Secs. 40 and 6426). The 2004 Jobs Act did not remove the credit and refund provisions of the Code related to the taxation of fuel mixtures containing alcohol at reduced rates.

NEW LAW EXPLAINED

Gasohol refund provisions conformed.—The SAFE Transportation Equity Act of 2005 removes the credit and refund provisions related to the repeal of the reduced rates on taxable fuel mixtures containing alcohol. As a result, the credit and refund provisions of Code Sec. 6427 are now conformed to the current method of taxing fuels containing alcohol (Code Sec. 6427, as amended by the SAFE Transportation Equity Act of 2005).

▶ **Effective date.** In the case of fuel described in former Code Sec. 4081(c), the provision applies to fuel sold or used after December 31, 2004. In the case of fuel described in former Code Sec. 4091(c), the provision applies to fuel, removed, entered, or sold after December

NEW LAW EXPLAINED

31, 2004 (Act Sec. 11151(f)(1) of the SAFE Transportation Equity Act of 2005; Act Secs. 301(d) and 853(e) of the American Jobs Creation Act of 2004 (P.L. 108-357)).

Law source: Law at ¶5430. Committee Report at ¶15,220.

— Act Sec. 11151(a) of the SAFE Transportation Equity Act of 2005, striking Code Sec. 6427(f) and (o), and redesignating Code Sec. 6427(p) as (o);

— Act Sec. 11151(f)(1), providing the effective date.

Reporter references: For further information, consult the following CCH reporters.

— Excise Tax Reporter, ETR ¶49,685.09

¶790 Reduced Tax Rate for Aviation Fuel Used by Registrants

BACKGROUND

The rate of tax on aviation-grade kerosene is 21.8 cents per gallon unless the fuel is used in commercial aviation (Code Sec. 4081(a)(2)(A)(iv)). In that case, the rate of tax is 4.3 cents per gallon (Code Sec. 4081(a)(2)(C)). In addition, both commercial and noncommercial aviation fuel is subject to a 0.1 cent Leaking Underground Storage Tank (LUST) Trust Fund tax (Code Sec. 4081(a)(2)(B)).

The American Jobs Creation Act of 2004 (P.L. 108-357) moved the incidence of taxation on aviation-grade kerosene to its removal from a refinery or terminal, or upon its entry into the United States, similar to the way gasoline, diesel fuel, and non-aviation grade kerosene are taxed. The 2004 Jobs Act did not change the rate of tax on aviation fuel, it simply changed where in the chain of distribution the tax was imposed.

Prior to the enactment of the 2004 Jobs Act, aviation fuel was taxed upon its sale by a producer or importer (Code Sec. 4091, prior to repeal by P.L. 108-357). In addition, in order to qualify for the reduced 4.3 cent rate of tax, persons engaged in commercial aviation fuel must have been registered with the IRS. This registration allowed the IRS to track the flow of fuel and thus combat fraud by those seeking to obtain fuel at the lower tax rate.

When the 2004 Jobs Act moved the incidence of taxation of aviation-grade kerosene, it inadvertently failed to stupulate that *only* commercial aviation fuel *registrants* could obtain the reduced 4.3 rate of tax.

NEW LAW EXPLAINED

Reduced tax rate applies to commercial aviation fuel if user is registered.—The SAFE Transportation Equity Act of 2005 clarifies that in order for users of aviation fuel in commercial aviation to pay the reduced 4.3 cent per gallon tax, they must be registered with the IRS (Code Sec. 4081(a)(2)(C), as amended by the Highway Act).

NEW LAW EXPLAINED

Comment: This clarification should come as no surprise to those required to report fuel transactions and pay the attendant taxes. The IRS's position was clearly announced in Notice 2005-4, I.R.B. 2005-2, 298. The notice spells out that buyers of reduced rate aviation-grade kerosene must register with the IRS, and it provides the procedures for doing so.

The Highway Act also makes other changes related to aviation fuel. See ¶740. In addition, the Highway Act makes some conforming changes to Code Sec. 6421(f)(2) to correspond to changes made by the 2004 Jobs Act.

▶ **Effective date.** The provision applies to aviation-grade kerosene removed, entered or sold after December 31, 2004 (Act Sec. 11151(f)(1) of the SAFE Transportation Equity Act of 2005; Act Sec. 853(e) of the American Jobs Creation Act of 2004 (P.L. 108-357)).

Law source: Law at ¶5290 and ¶5420. Committee Report at ¶15,230.

— Act Sec. 11151(b)(1) of the SAFE Transportation Equity Act of 2005, amending Code Sec. 4081(a)(2)(C);

— Act Sec. 11151(b)(3), amending Code Sec. 6421(f)(2);

— Act Sec. 11151(f)(1), providing the effective date.

Reporter references: For further information, consult the following CCH reporters.

— Federal Tax Guide, 2005FTG ¶21,050

— Excise Tax Reporter, ETR ¶8919.02 and ¶49,685.13

¶795 Termination Date for Tax on Aviation-Grade Kerosene

BACKGROUND

The rate of tax on aviation-grade kerosene is 21.8 cents per gallon unless the fuel is used in commercial aviation (Code Sec. 4081(a)(2)(A)(iv)). In that case, the rate of tax is 4.3 cents per gallon (Code Sec. 4081(a)(2)(C)). In addition to both rates of tax, there is also a 0.1 cent Leaking Underground Storage Tank (LUST) Trust Fund tax on aviation-grade kerosene (Code Sec. 4081(a)(2)(B)).

The taxes collected (other than the LUST tax) are transferred to the Airport and Airway Trust Fund and used to fund certain appropriations relating to airports as well as funding air traffic control, air navigation, communications and other support services for the airway system (Code Sec. 9502(d)). Currently the tax on aviation gasoline is set to expire on October 1, 2007. Similarly, funds from the Airport and Airway Trust Fund can be appropriated until October 1, 2007.

The American Jobs Creation Act of 2004 (P.L. 108-357) moved the incidence of taxation on aviation-grade kerosene to its removal from a refinery or terminal, or upon its entry into the United States, similar to the way gasoline, diesel fuel, and non-aviation grade kerosene are taxed. Prior to these changes, Code Sec. 4091(c)(5), repealed by P.L. 108-357, provided that the tax on aviation fuel would not apply after

BACKGROUND

September 30, 2007. When the 2004 Jobs Act moved the incidence of tax on aviation-grade kerosene, it inadvertently failed to provide an expiration date for the tax.

NEW LAW EXPLAINED

Clarification of termination date for aviation fuel.—In a technical correction, the SAFE Transportation Equity Act of 2005 provides that the termination date for the tax on aviation-grade kerosene mirrors the termination date for the tax on aviation gasoline—that is, the tax terminates on October 1, 2007 (Code Sec. 4081(d)(2), as amended Act Sec. 11152(b)(2) of the Highway Act but prior to amendment by Act Sec. 11161(a)(4)(D) of the Highway Act).

Comment: A similar provision in the Highway bill also provides for this date.

▶ **Effective date.** The provision applies to aviation-grade kerosene removed, entered or sold after December 31, 2004 (Act Sec. 11151(f)(1) of the SAFE Transportation Equity Act of 2005; Act Sec. 853(e) of the American Jobs Creation Act of 2004 (P.L. 108-357)).

Law source: Law at ¶5290. Committee Report at ¶15,230.

— Act Sec. 11151(b)(2) of the SAFE Transportation Equity Act of 2005, amending Code Sec. 4081(d)(2) prior to amendment by Act Sec. 11161(a)(4)(D);

— Act Sec. 11151(f)(1), providing the effective date.

Reporter references: For further information, consult the following CCH reporters.

— Excise Tax Reporter, ETR ¶8919.01

¶797 Small Engine Fuel Taxes to Fund Coastal Wetlands Protection

BACKGROUND

Code Sec. 9503(c)(5)(A) provides that amounts received from small-engine fuel taxes and originally deposited into the Highway Trust Fund will be transferred to the Sport Fish Restoration Account under Code Sec. 9504(b). One of the purposes for which expenditures from the Sport Fish Restoration Account can be used is to carry out the purposes of the Coastal Wetlands Planning, Protection and Restoration Act. "Small engine fuel taxes" are those collected under Code Sec. 4081 on gasoline used as a fuel in small-engine outdoor power equipment (and the use is nonbusiness related) (Code Sec. 9503(c)(5)(B)).

The Transportation Equity Act for the 21st Century (P.L. 105-178) redesignated Code Sec. 9504(b)(2)(B), relating to the Coastal Wetlands Planning, Protection and Restoration Act, as Code Sec. 9504(b)(2)(C). However, Congress did not fix the cross reference in the last sentence of Code Sec. 9504(b)(2) concerning the limitation of using small-engine fuel taxes for Coastal Wetlands only.

NEW LAW EXPLAINED

Appropriation of taxes collected on small-engine outdoor power equipment.—The SAFE Transportation Equity Act of 2005 clarifies that amounts collected from small-engine fuel taxes that are deposited into the Sport Fish Restoration Account may only be used to carry out the purpose of the Coastal Wetlands Planning, Protection and Restoration Act (Code Sec. 9504(b)(2), as amended by the Highway Act).

> **Comment:** The Highway Act merged the Boat Safety Account and the Sport Fish Restoration Account into the new Sport Fish Restoration and Boating Trust Fund. See ¶1030 for more details.

▶ **Effective date.** The clarification is effective as of June 9, 1998, the date P.L. 105-178 was enacted (Act Sec. 11151(f)(2) of the SAFE Transportation Equity Act of 2005 and Act Sec. 9005(e) of the Transportation Equity Act for the 21st Century (P.L. 105-178)).

Law source: Law at ¶5490. Committee Report at ¶15,240.

— Act Sec. 11151(c) of the SAFE Transportation Equity Act of 2005, amending Code Sec. 9504(b)(2);

— Act Sec. 11151(f)(2), providing the effective date.

¶797

Other Excise Taxes

AIR AND WATER TRANSPORTATION

¶805 Modification of rural airport definition
¶810 Ticket tax exemption for seaplane transportation
¶815 Sightseeing flights exempt from taxes on air transportation
¶820 Fuel excise tax exemptions clarified for crop dusters
¶822 Fixed-wing aircraft engaged in forestry operations exempt from ticket taxes
¶825 Repeal of harbor maintenance tax on exports

ALCOHOL

¶830 Small alcohol excise taxpayers
¶835 Income tax credit for distilled spirits
¶840 Occupational taxes on producers and marketers of alcoholic beverages

SPORTING GOODS

¶845 Excise tax on fishing rods and poles
¶850 Custom gunsmiths

AIR AND WATER TRANSPORTATION

¶805 Modification of Rural Airport Definition

BACKGROUND

Air passenger transportation is subject to an excise tax equal to 7.5 percent of the fare plus $3.20 (in 2005) per domestic flight segment (Code Sec. 4261(a) and (b)). The excise tax on flight segments ("airline ticket segment tax") does not apply to a domestic segment beginning or ending at a rural airport. A "rural airport" is any airport during a calendar year year that had fewer than 100,000 commercial passengers departing in the second preceding year and is (1) not within 75 miles of an

BACKGROUND

airport that had at least 100,000 commercial passengers departing in the second preceding calendar year or (2) receiving essential air subsidies as of August 5, 1997 (Code Sec. 4261(e)(1)(B)).

Domestic flight segments beginning or ending at a rural airport are exempt from the airline ticket segment tax because the tax was primarily intended to cover increased security costs for airports servicing international flights and serving large aircrafts. Most rural airports are at least 75 miles away from the larger airports. However, in some states (e.g., Alaska), there are small community airports that are within 75 miles of the larger airports but are not connected by paved roads. Passengers who need to go to the larger airport cannot drive but have to fly to get there, thus, they end up paying the airline ticket segment tax at least twice.

NEW LAW EXPLAINED

Rural airport definition modified.—The term "rural airport" for any calendar year is expanded to include an airport that (1) is not connected by paved roads to another airport and (2) had fewer than 100,000 commercial air passengers on flight segments of at least 100 miles during the second preceding calendar year (Code Sec. 4261(e)(1)(B), as amended by the SAFE Transportation Equity Act of 2005).

> **Comment:** According to the IRS, taxpayers may rely on the list of rural airports published by the U.S. Department of Transportation to determine whether an airport is a "rural airport" for purposes of determining whether or not the airline ticket segment tax will apply. The list, found at http://ostpxweb.dot.gov/aviation/domav/ruralair.pdf, is periodically updated but is not separately published by the IRS. The IRS also provides the list on its web site at www.irs.gov/businesses/small/topic/index.html under the Excise Tax link. Any airport not listed may still qualify for the rural airport exception to the airline ticket segment tax if it meets the requirements of Code Sec. 4261(e)(1)(B) (Rev. Proc. 2005-45, I.R.B. 2005-30, 141).

▶ **Effective date.** The provision is effective on October 1, 2005 (Act Sec. 11122(b) of the SAFE Transportation Equity Act of 2005).

Law source: Law at ¶5325. Committee Report at ¶15,080.

— Act Sec. 11122(a) of the SAFE Transportation Equity Act of 2005, amending Code Sec. 4261(e)(1)(B);

— Act Sec. 11122(b), providing the effective date.

Reporter references: For further information, consult the following CCH reporters.

— Federal Tax Guide, 2005FTG ¶21,240

— Excise Tax Reporter, ETR ¶19,305.0148

¶805

¶810 Ticket Tax Exemption for Seaplane Transportation

BACKGROUND

Air passenger transportation is generally subject to an excise tax ("air passenger tax") equal to 7.5 percent of the fare plus $3.20 (in 2005) per domestic segment (Code Sec. 4261(a) and (b)). A "domestic flight segment" is any segment of air transportation consisting of a single takeoff and a single landing (Code Sec. 4261(b)(2)). Passengers are liable for the tax, and air carriers are responsible for collecting and remitting the tax to the government.

A 6.25-percent tax ("air cargo tax") is imposed on amounts paid to persons engaged in the business of transporting property by air for hire for any taxable transportation of property by air (Code Sec. 4271(a)). The term "taxable transportation" refers to air transportation that begins and ends in the United States (Code Sec. 4272(a)). Thus, the air cargo tax applies to amounts paid to an air carrier by a freight forwarder or express company for the transportation of property by air.

After collection, both taxes are transferred to the Airport and Airway Trust Fund to finance a portion of the cost of programs administered by the Federal Aviation Administration, including the Airport Improvement Program (AIP), which provides for the maintenance and improvement of airports. In several states, these taxes were also collected from seaplane operators for flights that land on and take off from open waters and not from facilities using AIP funds.

Aviation fuel is taxed at a rate of 21.9 cents per gallon when used in noncommercial aviation and at 4.4 cents per gallon when used in commercial aviation (Code Sec. 4081(a)(2)(A), as amended by SAFE Transportation Equity Act of 2005). The rates include a 0.1 cent per gallon Leaking Underground Storage Tank (LUST) Trust Fund tax (Code Sec. 4081(a)(2)(B)). "Commercial aviation" is any use of an aircraft in the business of transporting persons or property for compensation or hire by air (Code Sec. 4083(b)). It does not include aircraft used for skydiving, small aircraft on nonestablished lines, or transportation for affiliated group members. Fuel for commercial planes are taxed at a lower rate because ticket taxes are also imposed on air transportation.

NEW LAW EXPLAINED

Seaplanes exempted from ticket taxes.—Under the new law, the Code Sec. 4261 air passenger tax and the Code Sec. 4271 air cargo tax will not apply to transportation by a seaplane for any segment consisting of a takeoff from, and a landing on, water (Code Sec. 4261(i), as added by Act Sec. 11123(a) of the SAFE Transportation Equity Act of 2005). Seaplanes are aircraft equipped with flotation gear that are designed to take off and land from the water's surface. The places where the takeoff and landing occur must not have received and may not be receiving financial assistance from the Airport and Airway Trust Fund in order for the exemption to apply.

NEW LAW EXPLAINED

Seaplanes excluded from definition of commercial aviation. Transportation by seaplanes is also excluded from the definition of "commercial aviation" (Code Sec. 4083(b), as amended by the Highway Act). Thus, fuel for seaplanes is taxed at the higher noncommercial aviation fuel rate.

▶ **Effective date.** The amendments apply to transportation beginning after September 30, 2005 (Act Sec. 11123(c) of the SAFE Transportation Equity Act of 2005).

Law source: Law at ¶5300 and ¶5325. Committee Report at ¶15,080.

— Act Sec. 11123(a) of the SAFE Transportation Equity Act of 2005, redesignating Code Sec. 4261(i) as 4261(j) and adding new Code Sec. 4261(i);

— Act Sec. 11123(b), amending Code Sec. 4083(b);

— Act Sec. 11123(c), providing the effective date.

Reporter references: For further information, consult the following CCH reporters.

— Federal Tax Guide, 2005FTG ¶21,240

— Excise Tax Reporter, ETR ¶19,305.013 and ¶20,115.01

¶815 Sightseeing Flights Exempt From Taxes on Air Transportation

BACKGROUND

An aircraft having a maximum certificated takeoff weight of 6,000 pounds or less is not subject to the taxes on air freight and passenger air transportation unless the aircraft is operated on an established line (Code Sec. 4281). The transportation taxes on persons and/or property are applicable if the aircraft is operated on an established line.

> **Comment:** Being "operated on an established line" means operated with some degree of regularity between definite points. The determination of whether an aircraft is operating on an established line is based on the facts and circumstances. It does not necessarily mean that strict regularity of schedule is maintained, that a full run is always made, that a particular route is followed, or that intermediate stops are restricted. The term implies that the person providing the service maintains and exercises control over the direction, route, time, number of passengers carried, etc.

The exemption does not apply, however, to unscheduled flights by an airline operating a regularly scheduled air service between the same two points (Rev. Rul. 72-219, 1972-1 CB 350).

NEW LAW EXPLAINED

Sightseeing exemption from air transportation tax.—An aircraft operated with the sole purpose of sightseeing will not be considered as operated on an established line

NEW LAW EXPLAINED

for purposes of the exemption from taxes on air transportation for small aircraft operated on nonestablished lines (Code Sec. 4281, as amended by the SAFE Transportation Equity Act of 2005).

▶ **Effective date.** The provision applies to transportation beginning after September 30, 2005, and does not apply to any amount paid before that date for such transportation (Act Sec. 11124 of the SAFE Transportation Equity Act of 2005).

Law source: Law at ¶5335. Committee Report at ¶15,100.

— Act Sec. 11124(a) of the SAFE Transportation Equity Act of 2005, amending Code Sec. 4281;

— Act Sec. 11124(b), providing the effective date.

Reporter references: For further information, consult the following CCH reporters.

— Federal Tax Guide, 2005FTG ¶21,240

— Excise Tax Reporter, ETR ¶20,375.01

¶820 Fuel Excise Tax Exemptions Clarified for Crop Dusters

BACKGROUND

Aviation fuel is taxed upon its removal from a refinery or terminal, or upon its entry into the United States, similar to gasoline, diesel fuel and kerosene (Code Sec. 4081(a)(2)(A)(iv)). The rate of tax is 4.4 cents per gallon for fuel used in commercial aviation and 21.9 cents per gallon for any other use.

Among the nontaxable uses of aviation fuel are: (1) use on a farm for farming purposes and (2) use as fuel in a helicopter or a fixed-wing aircraft under certain circumstances. In order to qualify for these exemptions, the buyer of the fuel must provide the seller with a written exemption certificate. If previously taxed fuel is used for nontaxable purposes, the user ("ultimate purchaser") may claim a refund for the tax previously paid (Code Sec. 6427(i)(1)).

Farm use exemption. If gasoline is used on a farm for farming purposes, the ultimate purchaser is entitled to a credit for excise taxes included in the price of the gasoline (Code Sec. 6420(a); Reg. §48.6420-1(a)). The ultimate purchaser includes a person who is a farm owner, tenant or operator (Reg. §48.6420-4(j)). The credit or payment is not allowed for gasoline used for nonfarming purposes, or gasoline used off a farm, regardless of the nature of the use. If a vehicle or other equipment is used both on a farm and off the farm, or if it is used on a farm both for farming and non-farming purposes, the credit or payment is allowed only with respect to that portion of the gasoline which was "used on a farm for farming purposes." The actual use of the equipment or vehicle and the place where it is used are material. For example, if a truck used on a farm for farming purposes is also used on the highways, gasoline used in connection with operating the truck on the highways is not taken into account in computing the credit or payment. Likewise, fuel consumed by a crop

BACKGROUND

duster traveling to and from the farm is also not exempt from tax (Reg. § 48.6420-1(d)).

Farming purposes. Gasoline is used "for farming purposes" when it is used by the farm owner, tenant, or operator in connection with the operation, management, conservation, improvement, or maintenance of the farm and its tools and equipment. Covered activities are those which contribute in any way to the conduct of the farm, as distinguished from any other enterprise in which the owner, tenant, or operator may be engaged. Since the gasoline must be used by the farm owner, tenant, or operator to which the operations relate, gasoline used by an organization which contracts with a farmer to renovate his farm properties is not considered used for farming purposes (Reg. § 48.6420-4(g)).

Farming use other than by owner. The farm owner, tenant, or operator is ordinarily treated as the user and ultimate purchaser of gasoline, except where (1) the ultimate purchaser and user of the gasoline is an aerial or other applicator (i.e., crop duster) of fertilizers or other substances, and (2) the farm owner, tenant, or operator waives his right to be treated as the ultimate purchaser and user of the gasoline (Code Sec. 6420(c)(4); Reg. § 48.6420-4(k)-(l)). In such instances, a crop duster is treated as having used such gasoline on a farm for farming purposes.

Waiver. To waive the right to be treated as a user and ultimate purchaser of gasoline used on a farm by a crop duster, the farm owner, tenant or operator who is otherwise entitled to treatment as the ultimate purchaser must execute an irrevocable written agreement. The waiver must clearly evidence that the farm owner, tenant or operator knowingly gives up the right to receive a payment and the period covered by the waiver (Reg. § 48.6420-4(l)(2); a sample waiver is located in Reg. § 48.6420-4(l)(6)). Copies of the waiver do not need to be filed with the IRS, unless the IRS requests a copy (Reg. § 48.6420-4(l)(4)). Crop dusters must retain copies of all waivers, and a copy of each waiver must be supplied by the crop duster to the farm owner, tenant or operator who waives his or her right to receive payment.

NEW LAW EXPLAINED

Crop dusters no longer need waiver for aerial fuel excise tax exemption.—For purposes of the aerial fuel excise tax exemption, the new law treats agricultural aerial applicators (i.e., crop dusters), as having used gasoline on a farm for farming purposes, provided they are the ultimate purchaser of the gasoline, without having to obtain a written waiver from the farm owner, tenant, or operator (Code Sec. 6420(c)(4)(B), as amended by the SAFE Transportation Equity Act of 2005). In addition, the term "farming use" is expanded to include fuel used for the direct flight between the airfield and one or more farms (Code Sec. 6420(c)(4), as amended by the Highway Act).

> **Comment:** The Senate Finance Committee believes that significant simplification and reduction of administration burden will be achieved by eliminating the requirements that crop dusters obtain written consent from the farm owner for exempt fuel use and by allowing exempt fuel use to extend to fuel consumed when flying between the farms where chemicals are applied and the airport

NEW LAW EXPLAINED

where the airplane takes off and lands (Senate Finance Committee Report (S. Rpt. No. 109-82)).

▶ **Effective date.** The new law applies to fuel use or air transportation after September 30, 2005 (Act Sec. 11121(d) of the SAFE Transportation Equity Act of 2005).

Law source: Law at ¶5415. Committee Report at ¶15,070.

— Act Sec. 11121(a) of the SAFE Transportation Equity Act of 2005, amending Code Sec. 6420(c)(4)(B);

— Act Sec. 11121(b), amending Code Sec. 6420(c)(4);

— Act Sec. 11121(d), providing the effective date.

Reporter references: For further information, consult the following CCH reporters.

— Federal Tax Guide, 2005FTG ¶21,140

— Excise Tax Reporter, ETR ¶48,695.01 and ¶48,695.02

¶822 Fixed-Wing Aircraft Engaged in Forestry Operations Exempt from Ticket Taxes

BACKGROUND

Air passenger transportation is subject to a 7.5 percent tax on the amount paid for transportation plus a domestic flight segment tax of $3.20 (in 2005). The flight segment tax is adjusted annually for inflation (Code Sec. 4261(e)(4)). An exemption from these taxes applies to a helicopter or fixed-wing aircraft (collectively, "eligible aircraft") while engaged in hard-mineral exploration or development or certain timber operations (Code Sec. 4261(f)). The aircraft must not take off from, or land at, a facility eligible for assistance under the Airport and Airway Development Act of 1970, or otherwise use services provided under the Airport and Airway System Development Act of 1982. The exemption also applies to eligible aircraft engaged in the exploration of oil or gas (Code Sec. 4041(l)). In addition, it applies to eligible aircraft taking off and landing at any airport (including aviation facilities that receive federal assistance) that provides emergency medical transportation, as well as to eligible aircraft dedicated to acute emergency medical services as described in Code Sec. 4261(g).

NEW LAW EXPLAINED

Exemption extended to fixed-wing aircraft engaged in forestry operations.—The new law adds fixed-wing aircraft to the exemption from tax on air transportation of persons by helicopters engaged in forestry purposes (Code Sec. 4261(f)(2), as amended by the SAFE Transportation Equity Act of 2005). Exempt uses include the planting, cultivation, cutting, transporting, or caring for trees, including logging operations.

NEW LAW EXPLAINED

> **Comment:** The exemption under Code Sec. 4261(f)(1), which applies to the transportation by helicopter of individuals, equipment, or supplies in the exploration for, or the development or removal of, hard minerals, oil, or gas, was not similarly expanded to fixed-wing aircraft.

To qualify for the exemption, the helicopter or fixed-wing aircraft must not take off from, or land at federally assisted facilities or services (i.e., a facility eligible for assistance under the Airport and Airway Development Act of 1970, or otherwise use services provided pursuant to section 44509 or 44913(b) or subchapter I of chapter 471 of title 49, United States Code), during such use. For helicopter transportation described in Code Sec. 4261(f)(1), each segment of the flight is treated as a separate flight in order to determine if the flight is exempt from excise tax.

> **Comment:** According to the Senate Finance Committee, it is appropriate to extend the current exemption for helicopters engaged in timber operations to fixed-wing aircraft when not using a Federally funded airport and airway services, since the purpose of the aviation excise taxes is to generate revenue for the Airport Improvement Program, which builds new, and retrofits and expands existing, public airports (Senate Finance Committee Report (S. Rpt. No. 109-82)).

▶ **Effective date.** The new law applies to fuel use or air transportation after September 30, 2005 (Act Sec. 11121(d) of the SAFE Transportation Equity Act of 2005).

Law source: Law at ¶5325. Committee Report at ¶15,070.

— Act Sec. 11121(c), amending Code Sec. 4261(f);

— Act Sec. 11121(d), providing the effective date.

Reporter references: For further information, consult the following CCH reporters.

— Federal Tax Guide, 2005FTG ¶21,140

— Excise Tax Reporter, ETR ¶19,305.05

¶825 Repeal of Harbor Maintenance Tax on Exports

BACKGROUND

A 0.125 percent harbor maintenance tax (HMT) is imposed on the value of most commercial cargo loaded or unloaded at U.S. ports (Code Sec. 4461(b)). The tax is deposited into the Harbor Maintenance Trust Fund for use in sharing the cost of financing various harbor and water projects (Code Sec. 9505(b)). The harbor maintenance port use tax is administered and enforced by the U.S. Customs Service in a manner similar to customs duties.

Article I, Section 9, Clause 5 of the United States Constitution prohibits the government from taxing exports. The United States Supreme Court in *United States Shoe Corp.*, (98-1 USTC ¶70,091) held that the HMT was unconstitutional as it applied to exports. The court held that the tax did not bear a reasonable relationship to the cost of the use of the port. As a result, it was not a fair approximation of port services

BACKGROUND

rendered because the tax is calculated based on the value of the exported cargo as opposed to the size, weight or depth of the vessel using the harbor.

NEW LAW EXPLAINED

Exports not subject to HMT.—The SAFE Transportation Equity Act of 2005 codifies the Supreme Court's decision in *U.S. Shoe Corp.*, and exempts exported commercial cargo from the harbor maintenance tax (Code Sec. 4462(d), as amended by the Highway Act). The tax remains in effect for imported cargo.

▶ **Effective date.** The provision is effective before, on, and after August 10, 2005 (Act Sec. 11116(c) of the SAFE Transportation Equity Act of 2005).

Law source: Law at ¶5340 and ¶5345. Committee Report at ¶15,060.

— Act Sec. 11116(a) of the SAFE Transportation Equity Act 2005, amending Code Sec. 4462(d);

— Act Sec. 11116(b), amending Code Sec. 4461(c)(1) and (2);

— Act Sec. 11116(c), providing the effective date.

Reporter references: For further information, consult the following CCH reporters.

— Federal Tax Guide, 2005FTG ¶21,180

— Excise Tax Reporter, ETR ¶28,175.01

ALCOHOL

¶830 Small Alcohol Excise Taxpayers

BACKGROUND

Excise taxes that are imposed on distilled spirits, wine and beer are collected on the basis of a tax return. Regulations prescribe when the returns must be filed and the taxes paid (Code Sec. 5061(a)).

Liquor taxes are generally payable by excise tax returns that are filed on a semi-monthly basis. The first semi-monthly period in each month generally runs from the first through the 15th day of the month, and the second semi-monthly period generally runs from the 16th through the last day of the month (27 CFR §19.522 (spirits), §24.271 (wine) and §25.164 (beer)). The return must be filed and the tax must be paid within 14 days after the end of the semi-monthly period in which:

- the spirit, wine or beer is withdrawn under a bond for deferred payment of tax;
- imported spirit, wine or beer (other than in bulk containers) enters into U.S. Customs territory; or
- imported spirits, wine or beer that was entered into the United States for warehousing is removed from the first warehouse (Code Sec. 5061(d)).

¶830

BACKGROUND

Under the Uruguay Round Agreements Act (P.L. 103-465), the tax on spirits, wine and beer for the period beginning on September 16 and ending on September 26 of any year must be paid by September 29. A safe harbor provides that this requirement is met if the payment made by September 29 is equal to at least $^{11}/_{15}$ of the tax on spirits, wine and beer for the period beginning on September 1 and ending on September 15 of any year (Code Sec. 5061(d)(4)). Returns and taxes for the period from September 27 through September 30 are due by October 14 (27 CFR § 19.522 (spirits), § 24.271 (wine) and § 25.164 (beer)).

Regulations permit small wine producers to file excise tax returns and pay tax on an annual, rather than a semi-monthly basis. This exception applies to a producer who has not been given a deferred payment bond, if the producer paid less than $1,000 in wine excise taxes for the previous year, or has a newly established bonded wine premises and expects to pay less than $1,000 in wine excise taxes for the current calendar year (27 CFR § 24.273(a)).

NEW LAW EXPLAINED

Small amounts of liquor taxes are paid on a quarterly basis.—Beginning in 2006, small importers and domestic producers of distilled spirits, wines and beers will pay certain liquor excise taxes on a quarterly, rather than a semi-monthly, basis (Code Sec. 5061(d)(4), as amended by the SAFE Transportation Equity Act of 2005).

> **Comment:** The amended statute addresses only tax payments, not returns. However, since liquor excise taxes are collected on the basis of returns and regulations prescribe when the returns must be filed, new regulations will likely be issued providing that taxpayers who pay their liquor taxes on a quarterly basis may also file their returns on a quarterly basis.

Requirements. The quarterly payment schedule applies when the following tests are satisfied:

(1) the taxes are imposed on the spirits, wine or beer upon the withdrawal, removal or entry (or articles brought into the United States from Puerto Rico) under deferred payment bonds;

(2) the taxpayer's total liability for all liquor excise taxes during the preceding calendar year must have been $50,000 or less; and

(3) the taxpayer reasonably expects to be liable for no more than $50,000 in total liquor taxes for the current calendar year (Code Sec. 5061(d)(4)(A), as amended by the Highway Act).

> **Comment:** These rules are written in mandatory, not permissive terms. Thus, taxpayers who satisfy these tests *must* pay the taxes on a quarterly basis.

Liquor taxes that are payable on the quarterly schedule are due within 14 days after the end of the quarter (Code Sec. 5061(d)(4)(A), as amended by the Highway Act). Quarters end on March 31, June 30, September 30 and December 31 (Code Sec. 5061(d)(4)(C), as amended by the Highway Act).

¶830

NEW LAW EXPLAINED

The quarterly payment schedule does not apply to any taxes that are not related to deferred payment bonds. Thus, the semi-monthly payment schedule continues to apply to taxes that are imposed when imported liquor enters U.S. Customs territory or is removed from the first warehouse. Although these taxes cannot be paid on a quarterly schedule, they are taken into account in determining whether a taxpayer meets the $50,000 liquor tax test for making quarterly payments (Conference Committee Report (H.R. Conf. Rep. No. 109-203)). A taxpayer that reverts to a semi-monthly schedule, and must make the next tax payment within 14 days after the end of the semi-monthly period in which the taxpayer's liquor tax liability first exceeds $50,000 (Code Sec. 5061(d)(4)(B), as amended by the Highway Act).

According to the Conference Committee Report, the rules that accelerate tax payments for the second half of September do not apply to the quarterly payment schedule. Also, qualified small wine producers may still file returns and pay tax on an annual basis (H.R. Conf. Rep. No. 109-203).

▶ **Effective date.** The provision applies with respect to quarterly periods beginning on and after January 1, 2006 (Act Sec. 11127(c) of the SAFE Transportation Equity Act of 2005).

Law source: Law at ¶5375. Committee Report at ¶15,130.

— Act Sec. 11127(a) of the SAFE Transportation Equity Act of 2005, redesignating Code Sec. 5061(d)(4)-(5) as (d)(5)-(6), respectively, and adding new Code Sec. 5061(d)(4);

— Act Sec. 11127(b), amending Code Sec. 5061(d)(6) as redesignated by Act Sec. 11127(a);

— Act Sec. 11127(c), providing the effective date.

Reporter references: For further information, consult the following CCH reporters.

— Excise Tax Reporter, ETR ¶36,610.02

¶835 Income Tax Credit for Distilled Spirits

BACKGROUND

An excise tax is imposed on all distilled spirits produced in or imported into the United States. The tax is imposed at a rate of $13.50 on each proof gallon (Code Sec. 5001(a)(1)).

> **Comment:** The term "distilled spirits" means "that substance known as ethyl alcohol, ethanol, or spirits of wine in any form" (Code Sec. 5002(a)(8)). Separate excise taxes are imposed on wines (Code Sec. 5041) and beer (Code Sec. 5051). Wines containing more than 24 percent of alcohol by volume are taxed as distilled spirits (Code Secs. 5001(a)(3) and 5041(a)).

Like most other federal excise taxes, the excise tax on distilled spirits is imposed before the product reaches the consumer. For distilled spirits produced in the United States, the excise tax is imposed when the distilled spirits are removed from the plant where they are produced. For distilled spirits that are bottled before being imported into the United States, the excise tax is imposed when the distilled spirits are removed from the first U.S. customs bonded warehouse to which they are landed. Distilled spirits imported in bulk containers for later bottling in the United States

BACKGROUND

may be transferred to a domestic distilled spirits plant without payment of the excise tax. Such distilled spirits are then later taxed in the same manner as domestically produced distilled spirits (i.e., upon removal from the plant).

Under current law, no tax credits are provided for business costs that are associated with having tax-paid products (such as distilled spirits) in inventory. The excise tax that is included in the purchase price of a product is treated the same as any other component of the product cost (i.e., it is deductible as a cost of goods sold).

NEW LAW EXPLAINED

Distilled spirits income tax credit created.—A new income tax credit for the cost of carrying tax-paid distilled spirits in inventory has been created (Code Sec. 5011(a), as added by the SAFE Transportation Equity Act of 2005). The distilled spirits credit, which is treated as a general business credit (Code Sec. 38(b)), is available to (1) any eligible wholesaler or (2) any person subject to Code Sec. 5005 (generally, a distiller or importer of distilled spirits) that is not an eligible wholesaler (Code Sec. 5011(a), as added by the Highway Act).

> **Comment:** The credit is designed to approximate the interest charge (or "float") that results from carrying tax-paid distilled spirits in inventory.

> **Comment:** The credit is in addition to current rules that allow tax included in inventory costs to be deducted as a cost of goods sold (Conference Committee Report (H.R. Conf. Rep. No. 109-203)).

Computation of credit—eligible wholesaler. In the case of an eligible wholesaler, the amount of the distilled spirits credit for any tax year is the amount equal to the product of:

(1) the number of cases of bottled distilled spirits that were bottled in the United States and which are purchased by the wholesaler during the tax year directly from the bottler of the spirits, and

(2) the "average tax-financing cost per case" for the most recent calendar year ending before the beginning of such tax year (Code Sec. 5011(a), as added by the Highway Act).

> **Comment:** Distilled spirits that are imported in bulk and then bottled domestically are considered to have been bottled in the United States (Conference Committee Report (H.R. Conf. Rep. No. 109-203)).

Computation of credit—person who is not an eligible wholesaler. In the case of a person subject to Code Sec. 5005 that is not an eligible wholesaler, the amount of the distilled spirits credit for any tax year is the amount equal to the product of:

(1) the number of cases of bottled distilled spirits that are stored in a warehouse operated by (or on behalf of) a state or political subdivision of a state, or an agency of either, on which title has not passed unconditionally, and

(2) the "average tax-financing cost per case" for the most recent calendar year ending before the beginning of such tax year (Code Sec. 5011(a), as added by the Highway Act).

NEW LAW EXPLAINED

Comment: The credit for persons that are not eligible wholesalers applies to distilled spirits bottled both domestically and abroad (Conference Committee Report (H.R. Conf. Rep. No. 109-203)).

Eligible wholesaler defined. An "eligible wholesaler" is any person that holds a permit under the Federal Alcohol Administration Act as a wholesaler of distilled spirits that is not a state or political subdivision of a state, or an agency of either (Code Sec. 5011(b), as added by the Highway Act).

Average tax-financing cost defined. The "average tax-financing cost per case" for any tax year is the amount of interest that would accrue at the deemed financing rate during a 60-day period on an amount equal to the deemed federal excise tax per case (Code Sec. 5011(c)(1), as added by the Highway Act). The "deemed federal excise tax per case" is $25.68 (Code Sec. 5011(c)(3), as added by the Highway Act). The "deemed financing rate" for any calendar year is defined as the average of the Code Sec. 6621(a)(1) corporate overpayment rates for calendar quarters of such year. (The average of the corporate overpayment rates is determined without regard to the last sentence of Code Sec. 6621(a)(1), relating to corporate overpayments that exceed $10,000 (Code Sec. 5011(c)(2), as added by the Highway Act)).

Comment: The overpayment rate under Code Sec. 6621(a)(1) is the sum of the federal short-term rate plus three percentage points (two percentage points in the case of a corporation). This rate is determined on a quarterly basis. See, for example, Rev. Rul. 2005-35, I.R.B. 2005-24, 1214 (setting the corporate overpayment rate at 5.0 percent for the calendar quarter beginning on July 1, 2005).

Case defined. A case consists of twelve 80-proof 750-milliliter bottles (Code Sec. 5011(d)(1), as added by the Highway Act). The number of cases in any lot of distilled spirits is equal to the number of liters in the lot divided by nine (Code Sec. 5011(d)(2), as added by the Highway Act).

Comment: Thus, stated slightly differently, the average tax-financing cost per case is the amount of interest that would accrue at corporate overpayment rates for a 60-day holding period on as assumed tax rate of $25.68 per case of 12 80-proof 750-milliliter bottles.

▶ **Effective date.** The provisions apply to tax years beginning after September 30, 2005 (Act Sec. 11126(d), of the SAFE Transportation Equity Act of 2005).

Law source: Law at ¶5040 and ¶5370. Committee Report at ¶15,120.

— Act Sec. 11126(a) of the SAFE Transportation Equity Act of 2005, adding new Code Sec. 5011;

— Act Sec. 11126(b), adding new Code Sec. 38(b)(20);

— Act Sec. 11126(c), amending table of sections for chapter 51;

— Act Sec. 11126(d), providing the effective date.

Reporter references: For further information, consult the following CCH reporters.

— Standard Federal Tax Reporter, 2005FED ¶4251.01

— Federal Tax Service, FTS § G:24.20

— Excise Tax Reporter, ETR ¶36,610.04

¶835

¶840 Occupational Taxes on Producers and Marketers of Alcoholic Beverages

BACKGROUND

Federal liquor taxes are both regulatory and revenue-producing. They are of two classes: (1) excise taxes on distilled spirits, wines, and fermented malt liquors (beer) (Code Secs. 5001–5067); and (2) so-called special taxes (occupational taxes) imposed on certain manufacturers and on retail and wholesale dealers (Code Secs. 5081–5149). The special occupational taxes are due July 1 of each year.

Prior to July 1, 2005, the special occupational taxes, generally, were as follows:

(1) for producers of distilled spirits and wines (Code Sec. 5081), $1,000 per year, per premise and a similar fee for brewers (Code Sec. 5091);

(2) for wholesale dealers of liquors, wines, or beer (Code Sec. 5111), $500 per year;

(3) for retail dealers of liquors, wines, or beer (Code Sec. 5121), $250 per year;

(4) for nonbeverage use of distilled spirits (Code Sec. 5131), $500 per year; and

(5) for industrial use of distilled spirits (Code Sec. 5276), $250 per year.

Reduced rates apply for small proprietors (as defined in Code Secs. 5081(b) and 5091(b)). A manufacturer who has used distilled spirits for nonbeverage purposes and has paid the special tax on such use is eligible for a refund, referred to as a drawback (Code Sec. 5131).

Wholesale or retail dealers in liquors, wine or beer are required to register their name, place of residence, trade or business, and place where that trade or business is conducted with the Secretary of the Treasury (Code Secs. 5141 and 7011) and keep records of their transactions (Code Secs. 5114 and 5124). Producers engaged in the industrial use of distilled spirits and proprietors of distilled spirits plants are also subject to recordkeeping requirements (Code Secs. 5207 and 5275), and penalties apply for noncompliance with the recordkeeping rules (Code Sec. 5603). These records must be available for inspection.

In addition, dealers may only purchase their liquor stock that is intended for resale from certain parties (Code Sec. 5117). Violation of this restriction is punishable by $1,000 fine, imprisonment of one year, or both (Code Sec. 5687). A violation also subjects the alcohol to seizure and forfeiture (Code Sec. 7302).

The American Jobs Creation Act of 2004 (P.L. 108-357) suspended the special occupational tax for the period beginning July 1, 2005, through June 30, 2008 (Code Sec. 5148).

NEW LAW EXPLAINED

Special occupational taxes repealed.—The special occupational taxes on producers and marketers of alcoholic beverages are repealed effective on July 1, 2008 (Act Sec. 11125(a) of the SAFE Transportation Equity Act of 2005). Conforming amendments have also been made to strike references to the special occupational taxes in certain

NEW LAW EXPLAINED

provisions, including those regarding manufacturers of stills, nonbeverage domestic drawback claimants, and recordkeeping by dealers (Act Sec. 11125(b) of the Highway Act).

> **Comment:** Although the effective date is July 1, 2008, the tax is not currently in effect due to its suspension by the 2004 Jobs Act from July 1, 2005, through June 30, 2008.

Who is affected. A "dealer" is any person who sells, or offers for sale, any distilled spirits, wines, or beer. "Wholesale dealers in liquors" are defined as dealers who (other than wholesale dealers in beer) sell or offer for sale, distilled spirits, wines, or beer, to another dealer; "wholesale dealers in beer" refers to dealers who sell, or offer for sale, beer, but not distilled spirits or wines, to another dealer. There is a rebuttable presumption that a person who sells or offers for sale, distilled spirits, wines, or beer, in quantities of 20 wine gallons or more to the same person at the same time is carrying on the business of a wholesale dealer. The presumption may be overcome by evidence satisfactorily demonstrating that the sale or offer for sale was made to a person other than a dealer (Code Sec. 5114(c), as amended by the Highway Act).

Further, a "retail dealer in liquors" is defined as any dealer (other than a dealer in beer or a limited retail dealer) who sells, or offers for sale, distilled spirits, wines, or beer to any person other than a dealer (Code Sec. 5124(c), as amended by the Highway Act). Similarly, a "retail dealer in beer" refers to a dealer (other than a limited retail dealer) who sells, or offers for sale, beer, but not distilled spirits or wines, to any person other than a dealer. A "limited retail dealer" is any fraternal, civic, church, labor, charitable, benevolent, or ex-servicemen's organization making sales of distilled spirits, wine, or beer on the occasion of any kind of entertainment, dance, picnic, bazaar, or festival held by it, or any person making sales of distilled spirits, wine or beer to the members, guests, or patrons of bona fide fairs, reunions, picnics, carnivals, or other similar outings, if the organization or person is not otherwise engaged in business as a dealer.

A "brewer" is defined as any person who brews beer or produces beer for sale (Code Sec. 5132, as added by the Highway Act). This definition does not include a person who produces only beer and who is exempt from tax under Code Sec. 5053(e).

Registration, recordkeeping and inspection. The Highway Act retains the registration, recordkeeping and inspection requirements, specifying that every dealer register with the Secretary of the Treasury its name or style, place of residence, trade or business, and place where the trade or business is conducted. With respect to the recordkeeping requirements, the Highway Act specifies that it is unlawful for a dealer to purchase distilled spirits for resale from any person other than a wholesale dealer in liquors who is required to keep records. However, a limited retail dealer may lawfully purchase distilled spirits for resale from a retail dealer in liquors.

Existing criminal penalties for failure to comply with the records requirements have also been retained.

▶ **Effective date.** The provision takes effect on July 1, 2008, but does not apply to taxes imposed for periods before this date (Act Sec. 11125(c) of the SAFE Transportation Equity Act of 2005).

¶840

NEW LAW EXPLAINED

Law source: Law at ¶5390, ¶5460, ¶5475, and ¶7060. Committee Report at ¶15,110.

— Act Sec. 11125(a)-(b) of the SAFE Transportation Equity Act of 2005, amending, redesignating and repealing portions of part II of subchapter A of chapter 51, repealing part V of subchapter J of chapter 51, and amending Code Secs. 6071(c), 7012 and 7652(g).

— Act Sec. 11125(c), providing the effective date.

Reporter references: For further information, consult the following CCH reporters.

— Excise Tax Reporter, ETR ¶36,610.03

SPORTING GOODS

¶845 Excise Tax on Fishing Rods and Poles

BACKGROUND

A manufacturers excise tax is imposed on the sale or use of certain sports equipment. A 10 percent sales tax is imposed on sport fishing equipment sold by the manufacturer, producer or importer (Code Sec. 4161(a)(1)). Electric outboard motors and fishing tackle boxes are taxed at the reduced rate of three percent (Code Secs. 4161(a)(2)(A) and 4161(a)(3)).

> **Comment:** Sport fishing equipment taxable at the 10-percent rate includes fishing rods and poles, fishing reels, fly fishing lines, other fishing lines not exceeding 130 pound test, fishing spears, spear guns, spear tips, fish stringers, creels, bags, baskets, other containers designed to hold fish, portable bait containers, fishing vests, landing nets, gaff hooks, fishing hook disgorgers, dressing for fishing lines, artificial flies, fishing tip-ups and tilts, fishing rod belts, fishing rod holders, fishing harnesses, fish fighting chairs, fishing outriggers and downriggers, and tackle items including leaders, artificial lures, baits, flies, fishing hooks, bobbers, sinkers, snaps, drayles and swivels.

Prior to the enactment of the American Jobs Creation Act, a three-percent rate of tax also applied to sonar devices suitable for finding fish ("fish finders"), but the tax could not exceed $30. The 2004 Jobs Act repealed this tax effective after December 31, 2004. In an apparent oversight, however, Congress did not remove the reference to the reduced rate of tax in Code Sec. 4161(a)(2)(A) or the $30 limit on that tax in Code Sec. 4161(a)(2)(B).

Revenues from the excise tax on fishing equipment are deposited in the Sport Fish Restoration Account of the Aquatic Resources Trust Fund and are intended to support Federal-State sport fish enhancement and safety programs (but see ¶1030 for a discussion of the elimination of the Aquatic Resources Trust Fund).

NEW LAW EXPLAINED

Excise tax on fishing rods and poles cannot exceed $10.—Effective for sales after September 30, 2005, the 10-percent excise tax imposed on any fishing rod or pole may

NEW LAW EXPLAINED

not exceed $10 (Code Sec. 4161(a)(1), as amended by the SAFE Transportation Equity Act of 2005). Electric outboard motors and fishing tackle boxes continue to be taxed at the reduced rate of three percent (Code Sec. 4161(a)(2)(A) and (a)(3), as amended by the Highway Act).

> **Comment:** The Highway Act makes a conforming amendment to Code Sec. 4161(a)(2) to account for the new $10 limitation. As noted in the background to this provision, however, Code Sec. 4161(a)(2) should have been removed or amended as part of the changes made by the 2004 Jobs Act to remove fish finders from the list of taxable fishing equipment.

▶ **Effective date.** The provision applies to articles sold by the manufacturer, producer, or importer after September 30, 2005 (Act Sec. 11117(c) of the SAFE Transportation Equity Act of 2005).

Law source: Law at ¶5310. Committee Report at ¶15,065.

— Act Sec. 11117(a) of the SAFE Transportation Equity Act of 2005, amending Code Sec. 4161(a)(1);

— Act Sec. 11117(b), amending Code Sec. 4161(a)(2);

— Act Sec. 11117(c), providing the effective date.

Reporter references: For further information, consult the following CCH reporters.

— Excise Tax Reporter, ETR ¶13,105.02

¶850 Custom Gunsmiths

BACKGROUND

A manufacturer's excise tax is imposed upon the sale by the manufacturer, producer or importer of certain firearms and ammunition (Code Sec. 4181). Pistols and revolvers are taxed at 10 percent. Firearms (other than pistols and revolvers), shells, and cartridges are taxed at 11 percent. This tax does not apply to machine guns and short-barrelled firearms, which instead are taxed under Code Sec. 5811.

> **Comment:** Congressional testimony indicates that a custom gunmaker typically does not actually build a new gun, but takes an existing rifle action and completely rebuilds it into a unique firearm for an individual, updating and upgrading it.

The IRS has ruled that for Code Sec. 4181 purposes, a gunsmith's customer is considered the manufacturer of a rifle if the customer supplies the parts used by the gunsmith in the fabrication of the rifle. If the transaction is not a regular practice of the customer and the rifle is produced for the customer's personal use, the customer is exempt from tax by reason of Reg. § 48.4218-2 (Rev. Rul. 84-116, 1984-2 C.B. 203).

NEW LAW EXPLAINED

Small manufacturers exempt from firearms excise tax.—The SAFE Transportation Equity Act of 2005 exempts pistols, revolvers and firearms that are manufactured, produced, or imported by a person who manufactures, produces, and imports less than 50 of such articles during the calendar year from the Code Sec. 4181 tax.

In applying the exemption, all persons treated as a single employer for purposes of Code Sec. 52(a) or (b) are treated as one person. Thus, all employees of trades or business (whether or not incorporated) that are under common control are treated as employed by a single employer. Further, all employees of corporations that are members of the same controlled group of corporations are treated as employed by a single employer. For these purposes, the term "controlled group of corporations" has the meaning given to it by Code Sec. 1563(a), except "more than 50 percent" is substituted for "at least 80 percent" and Code Sec. 1563(a)(4) and (e)(3)(C) are not applicable.

> **Caution Note:** The Highway Act specifically states that no inference is intended from this provision as to the proper treatment of pre-effective date sales (Act Sec. 11131(b)(2) of the Highway Act).

▶ **Effective date.** The provision applies to articles sold by the manufacturer, producer, or importer after September 30, 2005 (Act Sec. 11131(b)(1) of the SAFE Transportation Equity Act of 2005).

Law source: Law at ¶5315. Committee Report at ¶15,140.

— Act Sec. 11131(a) of the SAFE Transportation Equity Act of 2005, redesignating Code Sec. 4182(c) as (d) and adding new Code Sec. 4182(c);

— Act Sec. 11131(b), providing the effective date.

Reporter references: For further information, consult the following CCH reporters.

— Excise Tax Reporter, ETR ¶13,775.02 and ¶13,775.03

Highways and Railroads

¶905 Extension of taxes and trust fund
¶910 Tax treatment of state ownership of railroad real estate investment trust
¶915 Tax-exempt bond financing for highway projects and rail-truck transfer facilities
¶920 National surface transportation infrastructure financing commission

¶905 Extension of Taxes and Trust Fund

BACKGROUND

Six separate excise taxes are imposed to finance the Federal Highway Trust Fund program. Three of these taxes are imposed on highway motor fuels. The other three include a retail sales tax on heavy highway vehicles, a manufacturers' excise tax on heavy vehicle tires and an annual use tax on heavy vehicles. The three motor fuel taxes and three nonfuel excise taxes are:

(1) 18.3 cents per gallon tax on gasoline,

(2) 24.3 cents per gallon tax on diesel fuel (including transmix) and kerosene,

(3) 18.3 cents per gallon generally on special motor fuels,

(4) a 12 percent excise tax imposed on the first retail sale of heavy highway vehicles, tractors and trailers (generally, trucks having a gross vehicle weight in excess of 33,000 pounds and trailers having such a weight in excess of 26,000 pounds) (Code Sec. 4051),

(5) an excise tax imposed on highway tires with a rated load capacity exceeding 3,500 pounds, generally at a rate of 9.45 cents per 10 pounds of excess (Code Sec. 4071(a)), and

(6) an annual use tax imposed on highway vehicles having a taxable gross weight of 55,000 pounds or more (Code Sec. 4481). (The maximum rate for this tax is $550 per year, imposed on vehicles having a taxable gross weight over 75,000 pounds.)

¶905

BACKGROUND

Most of the taxes are scheduled to expire after September 30, 2005. Exceptions include the heavy vehicle use tax (HVUT), 4.3 cents per gallon of the Highway Trust Fund fuel tax rate and a portion of the tax on certain special motor fuel. The 4.3-cents-per-gallon portion of the fuels tax rates is permanent. The HVUT is scheduled to expire on October 1, 2006.

Present law includes many exemptions for certain uses of taxable fuels and for specified fuels. Since fuel taxes generally are imposed before the end use of the fuel is known, many exemptions are realized through refunds to end users because the tax was paid by a taxpayer earlier in the distribution chain. Exempt uses and fuels include:

(1) use in state and local government and nonprofit educational organization highway vehicles;

(2) use in buses engaged in transporting students and employees of schools;

(3) use in local mass transit buses having a seating capacity of at least 20 adults (exclusive of the driver) when the buses operate under contract with, or are subsidized by, a state or local governmental unit to furnish the transportation; and

(4) use in intercity buses serving the general public along scheduled routes. (Such use is totally exempt from the gasoline excise tax and is exempt from 17 cents per gallon of the diesel fuel tax.)

Fuels used in off-highway business use or on a farm for farming purposes generally are also exempt from these motor fuels taxes. The Highway Trust Fund does not receive excise taxes imposed on fuel used in off-highway activities. Taxes imposed on off-highway use fuel consumption are used to finance other trust funds or are retained in the General Fund.

Code Sec. 9503 governs the dedication of excise tax revenues to the Highway Trust Fund and expenditures from the Fund. The Code authorizes expenditures (subject to appropriations) from the Fund through August 14, 2005. Revenues from the highway excise taxes generally are dedicated to the Highway Trust Fund. Under Code Sec. 9503(c)(2), however, certain transfers are made from the Highway Trust Fund into the General Fund. These transfers consist of amounts paid in respect of gasoline used on farms, amounts paid in respect of gasoline used for certain nonhighway purposes or by local transit systems, amounts relating to fuels not used for taxable purposes and income tax credits for certain uses of fuels.

The Highway Trust Fund has a subaccount for Mass Transit. Both the Trust Fund and its subaccount are funding sources for specific programs. The Highway Trust Fund's Mass Transit subaccount receives 2.86 cents per gallon of the highway motor fuels excise taxes (Code Sec. 9503(e)).

Since establishment of the Highway Trust Fund in 1956, expenditure purposes of the Fund have been revised with each authorizing Act. In general, expenditures authorized under those Acts (as the Acts were in effect on the date of enactment of the most recent authorizing Act) are authorized under the Code as Highway Trust Fund expenditure purposes. Consequently, no Highway Trust Fund monies may be spent for a purpose not approved by the tax-writing committees of Congress. Since the

¶905

BACKGROUND

authority to make expenditures from the Highway Trust Fund expires after August 14, 2005, no Highway Trust Fund expenditure may occur after that date.

The tax code also contains a special enforcement provision to prevent expenditure of Highway Trust Fund monies for unauthorized purposes (Code Sec. 9503(b)(5)(A)). Should unapproved expenditures occur, no further excise tax receipts will be transferred to the Highway Trust Fund. Taxes will continue to be imposed, but receipts will be retained in the General Fund. The enforcement provision applies not only to unauthorized expenditures under the current Code provisions, but also to expenditures pursuant to future legislation that does not amend the Code Sec. 9503 expenditure authorization provisions or otherwise authorize the expenditure as part of a revenue Act. An exception to this provision exists for expenditures to liquidate contracts entered into before July 31, 2005 (Code Sec. 9503(b)(6)(B)).

Aquatic Resources Trust Fund. The Aquatic Resources Trust Fund, which consists of two accounts—the Boat Safety Account and the Sport Fish Restoration Account, is funded by a portion of the receipts from the excise tax imposed on motorboat gasoline and special motor fuels, as well as small-engine fuel taxes, that are first deposited into the Highway Trust Fund. Hence, transfers to the Aquatic Resources Trust Fund are governed in part by Highway Trust Fund provisions (Code Sec. 9503(c)(4) and (5)).

Transfers to the Boat Safety Account are limited to $70 million per year and subject to an overall annual limit equal to an amount that will not cause the Account to have an unobligated balance in excess of $45 million (Code Sec. 9503(c)(4)(A)). If there is any excess, the next $1 million of motorboat fuel taxes is transferred from the Highway Trust Fund to the Land and Water Conservation Fund provided for in Title I of the Land and Water Conservation Fund Act of 1965 (Code Sec. 9503(c)(4)(B)).

The Sport Fish Restoration Account receives the balance of the motorboat gasoline and special motor fuels receipts from the Highway Trust Fund (Code Sec. 9503(c)(4)(C)). In addition, this Account receives 13 cents per gallon of the revenues from the tax imposed on gasoline used as a fuel in the nonbusiness use of small-engine outdoor power equipment (Code Sec. 9503(c)(5)). This Account also is funded with receipts from an ad valorem manufacturer's excise tax on sport fishing equipment (Code Sec. 9504(b)(1)).

Expenditures from the Aquatic Resources Trust Fund may be made only to the extent permitted by Code Sec. 9504 (Code Sec. 9504(d)(1)). An exception to this provision exists for expenditures to liquidate contracts entered into before July 31, 2005 (Code Sec. 9504(d)(2)).

Expenditures from the Boat Safety Account must be specifically appropriated. Expenditures from this Account were authorized through August 14, 2005, as provided by appropriation acts (Code Sec. 9504(c)). The Sport Fish Restoration Account has operated under a permanent appropriations act, approved in 1950 (Code Sec. 9504(b)(2)(A)).

¶905

NEW LAW EXPLAINED

Extension of highway-related taxes and trust funds.—The SAFE Transportation Equity Act of 2005 generally provides for a six-year extension of the Highway Trust Fund excise taxes scheduled to expire in 2005. Conforming amendments are made to floor stock taxes and tax exemptions. Provisions in the Highway Act extending highway-related taxes are:

Tax on heavy trucks and trailers. The scheduled October 1, 2005, termination date of the 12-percent excise tax on heavy trucks and trailers is extended until October 1, 2011 (Code Sec. 4051(c), as amended by the Highway Act).

Heavy vehicle use tax. The expiration of the excise tax on highway motor vehicles with a taxable gross weight of at least 55,000 pounds is delayed from uses on or after October 1, 2006, to uses on or after October 1, 2011 (Code Secs. 4481(f), 4482(c)(4) and 4482(d), as amended by the Highway Act).

Tax on heavy tires. The scheduled October 1, 2005, termination date of the excise tax on tires is delayed until October 1, 2011 (Code Sec. 4071(d), as amended by the Highway Act).

Special motor fuels. The reduction of the tax rates applicable to special motor fuels used in motor vehicles and motorboats is delayed from sales and uses after September 30, 2005, to sales and uses after September 30, 2011 (Code Sec. 4041(a)(2)(B), as amended by the Highway Act).

Diesel fuel used in certain buses. The reduction of the 7.3 cents per gallon tax on diesel fuel used in public and school buses to 4.3 cents per gallon is delayed to cover sales after September 30, 2011. Previously, the reduction related to sales after September 30, 2005 (Code Sec. 4041(a)(1)(C)(iii)(I), as amended by the Highway Act).

Alcohol fuel. The reduction in the rate of tax imposed on partially exempt methanol fuel (9.15 cents per gallon to 2.15 cents per gallon) or ethanol (11.3 cents per gallon to 4.3 cents per gallon) sold or used after September 30, 2005, is delayed to sales and uses after September 30, 2011 (Code Sec. 4041(m)(1), as amended by the Highway Act).

Gasoline, diesel fuel, and kerosene. Code Sec. 4081 imposes a tax on gasoline, diesel fuel, and kerosene removed from terminals and refineries, imported into the United States, or sold to certain unregistered persons. The scheduled reduction of the 18.3 cents per gallon tax on gasoline (other than aviation fuel) to 4.3 cents per gallon after September 30, 2005, is delayed until after September 30, 2011. The scheduled reduction of the 24.3 cents per gallon tax on diesel fuel or kerosene to 4.3 cents per gallon after September 30, 2005, is delayed until after September 30, 2011 (Code Sec. 4081(d)(1), as amended by the Highway Act).

Floor stocks refunds. Floor stock refunds with respect to the tire tax imposed by Code Sec. 4071 and the fuels tax imposed by Code Sec. 4081 on certain removals, entries, and sales to unregistered persons will be determined with reference to tax-paid articles held by a dealer on or after October 1, 2011, rather than October 1, 2005 (Code Sec. 6412(a)(1), as amended by the Highway Act).

Extension of exemptions for extended taxes. The expiration of the exemption from the tire tax (Code Sec. 4071) and the tax on heavy trucks and trailers sold at retail (Code Sec.

NEW LAW EXPLAINED

4051) for sales to state and local governments and tax-exempt organizations is delayed from October 1, 2005, to October 1, 2011 (Code Sec. 4221(a), as amended by the Highway Act).

The expiration of the exemption from the HVUT on highway motor vehicles with a gross weight of at least 55,000 pounds (Code Sec. 4481) used by state and local governments and certain transit buses is delayed from October 1, 2006 to October 1, 2011 (Code Sec. 4483(h), as amended by the Highway Act).

Extension of Highway Trust Fund deposits and withdrawals. The transfer of excise taxes to the Highway Trust Fund is extended to include taxes received in the Treasury before October 1, 2011, rather than taxes received in the Treasury before October 1, 2005 (Code Sec. 9503(b), as amended by the Highway Act). The authorization of transfers from the Highway Trust Fund to the general fund of the Treasury for excise tax repayments and credits is extended to amounts paid before July 1, 2012; previously, it covered amounts paid before July 1, 2006 (Code Sec. 9503(c)(2) and(3), as amended by the Highway Act). Authorization for the transfers of motorboat fuel taxes and small engine fuel taxes from the Highway Trust Fund to the Aquatic Resources Trust Fund (Code Sec. 9504) is extended from amounts received before October 1, 2005, to amounts received before October 1, 2011 (Code Sec. 9503(c)(4) and (5), as amended by the Highway Act).

Extension and expansion of expenditures from Highway Trust Fund and Mass Transit Account. The Highway Act extends authority for transferring amounts from the Highway Trust Fund to pay for federal-aid highway programs from expenditures incurred before August 15, 2005, to expenditures incurred before September 30, 2009 (October 1, 2009 in the case of expenditures for administrative expenses). The Highway Trust Fund is available for making expenditures to meet the obligations of the United States incurred in the past and in the future which are authorized to be paid out of the Highway Trust Fund under the Highway Act or any other provision referred to in Code Sec. 9503(c)(1), before August 10, 2005, and as in effect on that date (Code Sec. 9503(c)(1), as amended by the Highway Act).

The Highway Act also extends the authority to make expenditures from the Mass Transit Account of the Highway Trust Fund to expenditures before October 1, 2009. Previously, the authority related to expenditures before August 15, 2005. The Mass Transit Account may be used to pay for expenditures made in accordance with the Highway Act or any other provision of law which was referred to in Code Sec. 9503(e)(3) before August 10, 2005, and as in effect on that date (Code Sec. 9503(e)(3), as amended by the Highway Act).

The Highway Act also extends the exception to the special enforcement provision to prevent expenditure of Highway Trust Fund monies for purposes not authorized in Code Sec. 9503. Under the Highway Act, an exception exists for expenditures to liquidate contracts entered into before September 30, 2009 (October 1, 2009 in the case of expenditures for administrative expenses). Previously, the exception existed for expenditures entered into before July 31, 2005 (Code Sec. 9503(b)(6)(B), as amended by the Highway Act).

NEW LAW EXPLAINED

The expenditure purposes of the Sport Fish Restoration Account have been amended to conform to the purposes in the authorizing provisions. (See ¶1030 regarding the transformation of the Sport Fish Restoration Account.)

The exception to the provision that expenditures from the Sport Fish Restoration and Boating Trust Fund may be made only to the extent permitted by Code Sec. 9504 has been extended to expenditures to liquidate contracts entered into before October 1, 2009 (Code Sec. 9504(d)(2), as amended by the Highway Act). (See ¶1030 regarding the elimination of the Aquatic Resources Trust Fund and the transformation of the Sport Fish Restoration Account.)

▶ **Effective date.** The extensions are effective on August 10, 2005 (Act Sec. 11101(e) of the SAFE Transportation Equity Act of 2005).

Law source: Law at ¶5265, ¶5270, ¶5280, ¶5290, ¶5320, ¶5350, ¶5355, ¶5360, ¶5405, ¶5485, ¶5490, and ¶7050. Committee Report at ¶15,010.

— Act Sec. 11101(a) of the SAFE Transportation Equity Act of 2005, amending Code Secs. 4041(a), 4041(m)(1), 4051(c), 4071(d), 4081(d)(1), 4481(f), 4482 and 6412(a)(1);

— Act Sec. 11101(b), amending Code Secs. 4221(a) and 4483(h);

— Act Sec. 11101(c), amending Code Sec. 9503(b) and (c), and 16 U.S.C. § 460l-11(b);

— Act Sec. 11101(d), amending Code Secs. 9503(c)(1), 9503(e)(3), 9503(b)(6)(B), 9504(b)(2), and 9504(d)(2).

— Act Sec. 11101(e), providing the effective date.

Reporter references: For further information, consult the following CCH reporters.

— Excise Tax Reporter, ETR ¶5700.01, ¶5700.33, ¶5700.065, ¶6325.01, ¶8045.01, ¶8915.02, ¶15,555.01, ¶15,565.01, ¶29,545.01, ¶29,735.01, ¶29,975.01 and ¶46,535.01

¶910 Tax Treatment of State Ownership of Railroad Real Estate Investment Trust

BACKGROUND

Gross income does not include income accruing to a state or territory, or any political subdivision thereof, or the District of Columbia, which is derived from the exercise of any essential governmental function or from any public utility (Code Sec. 115).

A corporation, trust, or association that specializes in investments in real estate and real estate mortgages that meets certain status requirements as to ownership and purpose, and satisfies the gross income and asset diversification requirements may elect to be taxed as a real estate investment trust (REIT). If an organization meets the REIT requirements, it will be taxed only on its undistributed income and capital gains. Distributed income is taxed directly to the shareowners.

An organization must meet the following ownership and purpose requirements to qualify as a REIT:

BACKGROUND

(1) Beneficial ownership in the organization must be held by at least 100 persons for at least 335 days during a 12-month tax year or for a proportionate part of a tax year of less than 12 months (Code Secs. 856(a)(5) and 856(b)).

(2) The beneficial ownership must be evidenced by transferable shares or transferable certificates of beneficial interest (Code Sec. 856(a)(2)).

(3) The organization's management must be in the hands of one or more trustees or directors, with the trustees generally holding legal title to the organization's property and having exclusive authority over management (Code Sec. 856(a)(1)).

(4) The organization, in addition to central management, must also possess all other necessary attributes that would, except for the REIT Code provisions, cause it to be taxed as a corporation (Code Sec. 856(a)(3)).

(5) Five or fewer individuals may not directly or indirectly own more than half of the value of the organization's stock during the last six months of the organization's tax year (Code Sec. 856(a)(6) and (h)).

(6) The organization may be neither a financial institution referred to in Code Sec. 582(c)(5), nor an insurance company to which subchapter L applies (Code Sec. 856(a)(4)).

A corporation generally recognizes gain or loss upon a distribution of property in complete liquidation as if it had sold the property to the distributee at its fair market value (Code Sec. 336(a)). There is an exception to the general rule requiring recognition of gain or loss for complete liquidations of subsidiaries (Code Sec. 337).

Code Sec. 103 provides the basic framework for state and local governmental bonds. It recognizes the principle that when bond proceeds are used exclusively for traditional governmental purposes the interest earned on the bonds is excludable from gross income. It also provides general limitations on the receipt of tax-exempt interest. Bond interest is not tax-free when it is derived from (a) state or local bonds that have not been issued in registered form, (b) arbitrage bonds, or (c) private activity bonds that are not exempt as qualified bonds. Under two special provisions, non-governmental entities may issue obligations that will be treated similar to bonds that have been issued for traditional governmental purposes. Such obligations include qualified scholarship funding bonds and volunteer fire department bonds (Code Sec. 150).

NEW LAW EXPLAINED

Income accrues to a state.—Income of a qualified corporation from its railroad transportation and economic development activities is treated as accruing to the state under Code Sec. 115, to the extent the activities are of a type that are essential government functions (Act Sec. 11146(a) of the SAFE Transportation Equity Act of 2005). All of the stock of a qualified corporation must be owned by the state and the corporation:

(1) is a real estate investment trust on August 10, 2005;

(2) is a non-operating class III railroad; and

NEW LAW EXPLAINED

(3) substantiality all of its activities must consist of the ownership, leasing, and operation by the corporation of facilities, equipment, and other property used by the corporation or other persons for railroad transportation and for economic development for the benefit of a state and its citizens.

Conversions. No gain or loss is recognized under Code Secs. 336 or 337 from the deemed conversion of a REIT to a qualified corporation. In addition, no change in property basis will occur (Act Sec. 11146(b) of the Highway Act).

Tax-exempt financing. Any obligation issued by a qualified corporation is treated as a state or local bond for purposes of applying the tax-exempt bond provisions if at least 95 percent of the net proceeds of the obligation are to be used to provide for the acquisition, construction, or improvement of railroad transportation infrastructure (including railroad terminal facilities) (Act Sec. 11146(c) of the Highway Act). In addition, the obligation is not treated as a private activity bond solely because of the ownership or use of such railroad infrastructure by the corporation. All other present law provisions relating to tax-exempt bonds continue to apply to and govern bonds issued by the corporation.

> **Comment:** A private business's use of railroad property financed with bond proceeds issued by a qualified corporation may cause the bonds to be taxable activity bonds.

Real estate investment trust. "Real estate investment trust" has the meaning given under Code Sec. 856(a) (Act Sec. 11146(d)(1) of the Highway Act).

Non-operating class III railroad. A non-operating class III railroad has the same meaning as under Title 49, subtitle IV, part A (49 U.S.C. § 10101; Act Sec. 11146(d)(2) of the Highway Act).

> **Comment:** Class III railroads are generally local, serving a small number of towns or industries.

State. A "state" includes the District of Columbia, any possession of the United States, and any authority, agency, or public corporation of a state (Act Sec. 11146(d)(3) of the Highway Act).

▶ **Effective date.** The provision applies on and after the date a state becomes the owner of all the outstanding stock of a qualified corporation through action of the corporation's board of directors, provided that the state becomes owner of all the voting stock of the corporation on or before December 31, 2003, and becomes the owner of all the outstanding stock of the corporation on or before December 31, 2006 (Act Sec. 11146(e) of the SAFE Transportation Equity Act of 2005).

Law source: Law at ¶7085. Committee Report at ¶15,200.

— Act Sec. 11146(a)–(d) of the SAFE Transportation Equity Act of 2005;
— Act Sec. 11146(e), providing the effective date.

Reporter references: For further information, consult the following CCH reporters.

— Standard Federal Tax Reporter, 2005FED ¶7142.01 and ¶26,512.021
— Federal Tax Service, FTS § F:9.40

¶910

¶915 Tax-exempt Bond Financing for Highway Projects and Rail-Truck Transfer Facilities

BACKGROUND

Many large public construction projects are paid for with contributions from both the federal and the state or local government. Bonds may be issued to finance the local contribution. Bonds used to finance the activities of private persons are not tax-exempt unless a specific exception applies. Private activity bonds that are exempt include exempt facility bonds. Exempt facility bonds can be issued to finance certain transportation facilities, including airports, ports, mass commuting, and high-speed intercity rail facilities, as well as low-income residential rental property, certain utility facilities, certain educational facilities, and some other types of facilities (Code Sec. 142(a)). An annual limit restricts the amount of private activity bonds that can be issued in each state each year. However, some types of these bonds are excluded from the annual state limit, typically because they are subject to some other limit.

NEW LAW EXPLAINED

Highway projects and rail-truck transfer facilities can be financed with exempt facility bonds.—The new law adds "qualified highway or surface freight transfer facilities" to the list of facilities that can be financed with exempt facility bonds (Code Sec. 142(a)(15), as added by the SAFE Transportation Equity Act of 2005). A national limit of $15 billion is placed on the total face value of these surface transportation bonds (Code Sec. 142(m)(2)(A), as added by the Highway Act). The Secretary of Transportation has discretion to allocate that limit among projects. The state volume limitations generally applicable to private activity bonds, including exempt facility bonds, do not apply to these bonds (Code Sec. 146(g)(3), as amended by the Highway Act).

Qualified highway or surface freight transfer facilities. "Qualified highway or surface freight transfer facilities" include:

- any surface transportation project which receives federal assistance under the highways title of the United States Code (Title 23),
- any international bridge or tunnel project for which an international entity authorized under federal or state law is responsible and which receives federal assistance under Title 23, and
- any facility for the transfer of freight from truck to rail or rail to truck (including related temporary storage facilities) which receives federal assistance under Title 23 or the transportation title of the United States Code (Title 49) (Code Sec. 142(m)(1), as added by the Highway Act).

    Comment: The Treasury Department has stated that eligible surface freight transfer facilities would include cranes, loading docks, and computer-controlled equipment that are integral to freight transfers. Lodging, retail, industrial or manufacturing facilities would not be qualified. Source: http://www.treas.gov/offices/tax-policy/library/bluebk04.pdf.

NEW LAW EXPLAINED

Spending requirement. At least 95 percent of the net proceeds of a surface transportation bond issue must be spent on qualified facilities within the 5-year period beginning on the date of issuance. The IRS can extend the period at the issuer's request if the issuer establishes that the failure to meet the spending requirement was due to circumstances beyond the issuer's control. If the issuer does not receive an extension, it must use all unspent proceeds to redeem bonds of the issue within 90 days after the end of the five-year period (Code Sec. 142(m)(3), as added by the Highway Act).

Enforcement of limitation allocation. The Secretary of Transportation will allocate portions of the $15 billion national limit to various facilities. An issue will not be treated as an exempt facility bond for the financing of qualified highway or surface freight transfer facilities if the face amount of bonds issued in that issue for a particular facility, when aggregated with amounts previously issued for that facility, exceed the amount allocated to the facility (Code Sec. 142(m)(2)(B), as added by the Highway Act).

An issuer can issue new bonds to replace an existing issue without having to count the new bonds against the allocated limitation. Bonds issued to refund a previously issued surface transportation bond do not count against the limitation if the average maturity date of the new issue is not later than the average maturity date of the bonds being replaced, the amount of the new bonds does not exceed the amount of the old bonds outstanding, and the old bonds are redeemed no later than 90 days after the issuance of the new bonds (Code Sec. 142(m)(4), as added by the Highway Act).

> **Comment:** The Conference Committee Report for the Highway Act (H.R. Conf. Rep. No. 109-203) includes a statement that "The conference agreement on this provision is not intended to expand the scope of any federal requirement beyond its application under present law and does not broaden the application of any federal requirement under present law in Title 49." Presumably this refers to federal prevailing wage requirements under the Davis-Bacon Act and various other restrictions that may be imposed on projects financed with federal funds, and suggests that those requirements will not apply to any project merely because it is funded with exempt facility bonds.

▶ **Effective date.** The provision applies to bonds issued after August 10, 2005 (Act Sec. 11143(d) of the SAFE Transportation Equity Act of 2005).

Law source: Law at ¶5145 and ¶5150. Committee Report at ¶15,170.

— Act Sec. 11143(a) of the SAFE Transportation Equity Act of 2005, adding new Code Sec. 142(a)(15);

— Act Sec. 11143(b), adding new Code Sec. 142(m);

— Act Sec. 11143(c), amending Code Sec. 146(g)(3);

— Act Sec. 11143(d), providing the effective date.

Reporter references: For further information, consult the following CCH reporters.

— Standard Federal Tax Reporter, 2005FED ¶7752.01 and ¶7854.066

— Federal Tax Service, FTS § E:17.60

¶915

¶920 National Surface Transportation Infrastructure Financing Commission

BACKGROUND

The Highway Trust Fund (HTF), which was created by the Highway Revenue Act of 1956 (P.L. 84-627), provides federal funding for the nation's highway and mass transit systems. Financing for the HTF is derived from a variety of highway user taxes, including excise taxes on motor fuels and truck-related taxes on truck tires, sales of trucks and trailers, and the use of heavy vehicles. A stable flow of revenues to the HTF is crucial for maintaining the highway and transit systems and providing infrastructure funding to the states. However, the increased use of ethanol and the increased production of fuel efficient vehicles and vehicles powered by alternative fuels have raised concerns about a potential loss of revenues to the HTF.

NEW LAW EXPLAINED

National Surface Transportation Infrastructure Financing Commission established.—The SAFE Transportation Equity Act of 2005 establishes a National Surface Transportation Infrastructure Financing Commission (the "Commission") to study highway and transit financing needs and prepare a final report with recommendations. The Commission will hold its first meeting within 90 days of the appointment of its eighth member, and submit its final report no later than two years after that first meeting (Act Secs. 11142(a) and 11142(h) of the Highway Act). The Commission will be funded by the Treasury Department and Department of Transportation (Act Sec. 11142(e) of the Highway Act).

Membership. The Commission will have 15 members drawn from among individuals knowledgeable in the fields of public transportation finance or highway and transit programs, policy, and needs. The members may include representatives of interested parties, such as state and local governments or other public transportation authorities or agencies, representatives of the transportation construction industry, transportation labor, transportation providers, the financial community, and users of highway and transit systems.

The Secretary of Transportation, in consultation with the Secretary of the Treasury, will appoint seven of the Commission members. The chairman and the ranking minority member of the House Ways and Means Committee will each appoint two members, and the chairman and the ranking minority member of the Senate Finance Committee will each appoint two members. The members will elect the chairman of the Commission. All members will be appointed for the life of the Commission and any vacancies will be filled in the manner in which the original appointments were made. In addition, the members will serve without compensation but will be entitled to travel expenses (Act Sec. 11142(c) of the Highway Act).

Functions. With respect to the period beginning on August 10, 2005, and ending before 2016, the Commission will perform the following functions:

NEW LAW EXPLAINED

(1) thoroughly investigate and study the revenues flowing into the Highway Trust Fund (HTF) under current law, including the individual components of the overall revenue flow;

(2) consider whether the amount of such revenues is likely to increase, decline, or remain unchanged, absent changes in the law;

(3) consider alternative approaches to generating revenue for the HTF, and the level of revenues that those alternatives would yield;

(4) consider highway and transit needs and whether additional revenues into the HTF, or other federal revenues dedicated to highway and transit infrastructure, would be required to meet such needs;

(5) consider a program that would exempt all or a portion of gasoline or other motor fuels used in a state from federal excise tax if such state elects not to receive all or a portion of federal transportation funding, including: (a) whether such state should be required to increase state gasoline or other motor fuels taxes by the amount of the decrease in the federal excise tax on such gasoline or other motor fuels, (b) whether any federal transportation funding should not be reduced or eliminated for states participating in such program, and (c) whether there are any compliance problems related to enforcement of federal transportation-related excise taxes under such program; and

(6) study other appropriate matters closely related to the above subjects (Act Sec. 11142(b)(1) of the Highway Act).

Preparation of final report. Based on its investigation and study, the Commission will prepare a final report. The report must include recommendations indicating the policies that should be adopted to achieve various levels of annual revenue for the HTF and to enable the HTF to receive revenues sufficient to meet highway and transit needs. The recommendations must address, among other matters:

(1) what levels of revenue are required by the HTF to maintain and improve the condition and performance of the nation's highway and transit systems;

(2) what levels of revenue are required by the HTF to ensure that federal levels of investment in highways and transit do not decline in real terms; and

(3) the extent, if any, to which the HTF should be augmented by other mechanisms or funds as a federal means of financing highway and transit infrastructure investments (Act Sec. 11142(b)(2) of the Highway Act).

Within two years of its first meeting, the Commission will submit its final report, including recommendations, to the Secretary of Transportation, the Secretary of the Treasury, the House Ways and Means Committee, the Senate Finance Committee, the House Committee on Transportation and Infrastructure, the Senate Committee on Environment and Public Works, and the Senate Committee on Banking, Housing, and Urban Affairs (Act Sec. 11142(h) of the Highway Act).

Obtaining data and assistance. The Commission is authorized to secure directly from any U.S. department or agency nonconfidential information necessary to carry out its duties. The Commission is also authorized to gather evidence through other appropriate means, including hearings and public comment solicitation (Act Sec. 11142(g)

¶920

NEW LAW EXPLAINED

of the Highway Act). Further, the Commission may seek assistance from the personnel of any federal agency (Act Sec. 11142(f) of the Highway Act).

Termination. The Commission will terminate on the 180th day after the submission of its final report (Act Sec. 11142(i) of the Highway Act).

▶ **Effective date.** No specific effective date is provided by the SAFE Transportation Equity Act of 2005. The provision is, therefore, considered effective on August 10, 2005.

Law source: Law at ¶7070. Committee Report at ¶15,160.

— Act Sec. 11142 of the SAFE Transportation Equity Act of 2005.

Reports, Studies and Funding

REPORTS AND STUDIES

¶1005 National Academy of Sciences study and report
¶1010 Energy savings through recycling to be studied
¶1015 Study of highway fuels used by trucks for nontransportation purposes
¶1020 Study on the collection of excise tax on taxable tires

GOVERNMENT FUNDING

¶1025 Modification of adjustments and apportionments
¶1030 Elimination of Aquatic Resources Trust Fund and transformation of Sport Fish Restoration Account
¶1035 Transfers from Leaking Underground Storage Tank Trust Fund

REPORTS AND STUDIES

¶1005 National Academy of Sciences Study and Report

BACKGROUND

The production and consumption of energy has many external costs and benefits associated with it that may not be fully known. Congress wants to determine these costs as they relate to health, environment, security, and infrastructure of the United States. Further, Congress wants to determine if these external costs and benefits are fully incorporated into the market price of energy. The law currently does not provide for a study of external costs and benefits.

NEW LAW EXPLAINED

National Academy of Sciences to study external costs of energy production and consumption.—The Secretary of the Treasury is directed to enter into an agreement with the National Academy of Sciences, within 60 days of August 8, 2005, to conduct

NEW LAW EXPLAINED

a study to define and evaluate the external costs and benefits that are associated with the production and consumption of energy (Act Sec. 1352 of the Energy Tax Incentives Act of 2005). The study should evaluate the health, environmental, security, and infrastructure external costs and benefits that may not be included in the market price of the energy. In addition, the study should evaluate the external costs and benefits of a federal tax, fee, or other applicable revenue measure related to the consumption or production of energy. The National Academy of Sciences will submit a report of the study to Congress no later than two years after the date on which the agreement with the Secretary of Treasury is entered into.

▶ **Effective date.** No specific date is provided by the Act. The provision is, therefore, considered effective on August 8, 2005.

Law source: Law at ¶7015. Committee Report at ¶10,330.

— Act Sec. 1352 of the Energy Tax Incentives Act of 2005.

¶1010 Energy Savings Through Recycling to be Studied

BACKGROUND

As a way to reduce energy needs, Congress is looking into the recycling of glass, paper, plastic, steel, aluminum, and electronic devices. Congress would like to determine if there are any energy savings to be made by recycling these items. Congress would also like to determine if tax incentives would cause consumers and/or companies to recycle these items.

NEW LAW EXPLAINED

Treasury and Energy to study energy savings through recycling and identify tax incentives to encourage recycling.—The Secretary of the Treasury, in consultation with the Secretary of the Energy is required to conduct a study to determine energy savings gained by recycling glass, paper, plastic, steel, aluminum, and electronic devices (Act Sec. 1353 of the Energy Tax Incentives Act of 2005). The study should identify any tax incentives that would encourage the recycling of these materials. The Secretary of the Treasury must submit a report on this study to Congress no later than one year after August 8, 2005.

> **Comment:** The Senate version of the Energy Act included a provision that provided for a 15-percent tax credit for the cost of qualified recycling equipment placed into service or leased by the taxpayer. Qualified recycling equipment is equipment that is used in sorting or processing residential and commercial recycling materials, or equipment that has a primary purpose of shredding and processing electronic waste. This provision was not included in the final version of the bill.

NEW LAW EXPLAINED

State Tax Consequences: Many states provide energy incentives through personal and corporate income tax credits. See ¶195 for a state-by-state summary of available credits.

▶ **Effective date.** No specific date is provided by the Act. The provision is, therefore, considered effective on August 8, 2005.

Law source: Law at ¶7020. Committee Report at ¶10,340.

— Act Sec. 1353 of the Energy Tax Incentives Act of 2005.

¶1015 Study of Highway Fuels Used by Trucks for Nontransportation Purposes

BACKGROUND

Generally, large commercial trucks driven on interstate highways idle about six hours overnight while the drivers sleep. It is estimated that about 20 million barrels of diesel fuel are consumed each year by idling long-haul trucks. The United States government and the truck industry have initiated a program to develop technologies that would reduce fuel use by idling trucks. However, current law does not provide a study of fuel used by trucks.

NEW LAW EXPLAINED

Treasury required to study use of highway fuels by trucks for nontransportation purposes.—The Secretary of the Treasury is required to study the use of highway motor fuel by trucks that is not used for the propulsion of the vehicle. The Secretary must report the findings of the study to the Committee on Finance of the Senate and the Committee on Ways and Means of the House of Representatives by no later than January 1, 2007.

In the case of vehicles carrying equipment that is unrelated to the vehicles' transportation function, the study will determine the average annual amount of tax-paid fuel consumed per vehicle carrying equipment that is unrelated to its transportation function by type of vehicle used by the propulsion engine to provide the power to operate the equipment attached to the highway vehicle. In addition, the study will review the technical and administrative feasibility of exempting such nonpropulsive use of highway fuels from the highway motor fuels excise taxes. If determined feasible, the Secretary will propose options for implementing such exemptions for (1) mobile machinery whose non-propulsive fuel use exceeds 50 percent, and (2) any highway vehicle that consumes fuel for both transportation and nontransportation-related equipment using a single motor.

> **Comment:** According to the Conference Committee Report for the Highway Act (H.R. Conf. Rep. No. 109-203), the Secretary should consider such factors as whether the fuel use for nontransportation equipment by the vehicle operator is

NEW LAW EXPLAINED

significantly relative both to transportation-related fuel consumption of the vehicle and to the vehicle operator's business. The Secretary should also take into account variations in fuel use among the different types of vehicles, such as concrete mixers, refuse collection vehicles, tow trucks, mobile drills and other vehicles (Conference Committee Report).

In the case of nontransportation equipment run by a separate motor, the study will determine the annual average amount of fuel exempted from tax in the use of nontransportation equipment run on a separate motor by equipment type, and will review any administrative and compliance issues related to the present-law exemption for such fuel use. Additionally, the Secretary will estimate the amount of taxable fuel consumed by trucks and the emission of various pollutants due to the long-term idling of diesel engines, and will determine the cost of reducing such idling through the use of plug-ins at truck stops, auxiliary power units or other technologies.

▶ **Effective date.** No specific effective date is provided by the Act. The provision is therefore, considered effective on August 10, 2005.

Law source: Law at ¶7075. Committee Report at ¶15,180.

— Act Sec. 11144 of the SAFE Transportation Equity Act of 2005.

Reporter references: For further information, consult the following CCH reporters.

— Excise Tax Reporter, ETR ¶58,425.01

¶1020 Study on the Collection of Excise Tax on Taxable Tires

BACKGROUND

The term "highway-type tire" was renamed "taxable tire" and the computation of the tax was changed by the American Jobs Creation Act of 2004 (P.L. 108-357). The excise tax on tires based on tire weight was replaced with rates based on the load capacity of a tire. The administration of the excise tax on tires was simplified because both the tire manufacturers and the IRS can forego the tedious process of weighing the different types of tires to determine the tax. Instead, the tax is based on the tire load capacity stamped on the side of the taxable tires as required by the Department of Transportation.

Comment: No study on the collection of excise tax on taxable tires and the number of tires in each class on which tax is imposed was conducted when the change in the method of computing was applied to sales beginning on or after January 1, 2005.

NEW LAW EXPLAINED

IRS required to conduct a study.—The IRS is required to conduct a study to determine the amount of excise tax on taxable tires collected for each class of tire

NEW LAW EXPLAINED

under Code Sec. 4071 (e.g. biasply, super single, or other) during a one-year period beginning January 1, 2006. The study must also include the number of tires in each class on which tax is imposed during the same period. The IRS must submit a report on the study to Congress not later than July 1, 2007.

> **Comment:** The IRS is directed by the Joint Committee on Taxation, Description and Technical Explanation of the Energy Tax Incentives Act of 2005 (JCX-60-05), to revise Form 720, Quarterly Federal Excise Tax Return, to collect the information necessary to conduct the study and prepare the report.

▶ **Effective date.** No specific effective date is provided by the Act. The provision is, therefore, considered effective on August 8, 2005.

Law source: Law at ¶7025. Committee Report at ¶10,380.

— Act Sec.1364(c) of the Energy Tax Incentives Act of 2005.

Reporter references: For further information, consult the following CCH reporters.

— Excise Tax Reporter, ETR ¶8,045.01

GOVERNMENT FUNDING

¶1025 Modification of Adjustments of Apportionments

BACKGROUND

Since highway projects can take multiple years to complete, the Highway Trust Fund carries positive unexpended balances, a large portion of which are reserved to cover existing obligations. Anti-deficit provisions limit Highway Trust Fund spending. Under the "Harry Byrd rule", the Treasury Department must determine quarterly the amount (if any) by which unfunded highway authorizations at the close of the next fiscal year exceed projected net Highway Trust Fund tax receipts for the 24-month period beginning at the close of that fiscal year (Code Sec. 9503(d)). If unfunded authorizations exceed projected 24-month receipts, apportionments to the states for specified programs funded by the relevant Trust Fund Account are to be reduced proportionately (Code Sec. 9503(d)(3)). Similar rules apply to unfunded Mass Transit Account authorizations, with respect to a 12-month period (Code Sec. 9503(e)(4)). As a consequence of the Harry Byrd rule, taxes dedicated to the Highway Trust Fund typically are scheduled to expire at least 24 months after current authorizing acts.

Under a temporary rule (in effect through August 14, 2005), for purposes of determining 24 months of projected revenues for the anti-deficit provisions, the Secretary of the Treasury is instructed to treat each expiring provision relating to appropriations and transfers to the Highway Trust Fund as having been extended through the end of the 24-month period. In addition, the Secretary of the Treasury is to assume that the rate of tax during that 24-month period remains at the same rate in effect on the date of enactment of the provision (Surface Transportation Extension Act of 2005, Part V (P.L. 109-14), extended the rule to August 14, 2005).

NEW LAW EXPLAINED

Anti-deficit provisions modified.—The "Harry Byrd rule" is changed from a 24-month period to a 48-month period (Code Sec. 9503(d)(1)(B), as amended by the SAFE Transportation Equity Act of 2005). Thus, the rule now requires the Treasury Department to determine, on a quarterly basis, the amount (if any) by which unfunded highway authorizations exceed projected net Highway Trust Fund tax receipts for the 48-month period beginning at the close of each fiscal year.

> **Comment:** The Highway Act does not increase the 12-month receipt rule with respect to the Mass Transit Account (Code Sec. 9503(e)(4)).

Measurement of net highway receipts. The temporary rule for determining projected revenues has also been made permanent (Code Sec. 9503(d)(6), as added by the Highway Act). Under the rule, each expiring provision relating to appropriations and transfers to the Highway Trust Fund will be assumed to have been extended through the end of the 48-month period, and the rate of tax during that 48-month period is assumed to remain at the same rate that was in effect on August 10, 2005.

▶ **Effective date.** The provision takes effect on August 10, 2005 (Act Sec. 11102(c) of the SAFE Transportation Equity Act of 2005).

Law source: Law at ¶5485. Committee Report at ¶15,010.

— Act Sec. 11102(a) of the SAFE Transportation Equity Act of 2005, amending Code Sec. 9503(d)(1)(B) and 9503(d)(3);

— Act Sec. 11102(b), redesignating Code Sec. 9503(d)(6) as (d)(7), and adding new Code Sec. 9503(d)(6);

— Act Sec. 11102(c), providing the effective date.

¶1030 Elimination of Aquatic Resources Trust Fund and Transformation of Sport Fish Restoration Account

BACKGROUND

A tax equal to 18.4 cents per gallon is imposed on gasoline and special motor fuels used in motorboats, and on gasoline used in the nonbusiness use of small-engine outdoor power equipment (Code Sec. 4081(a)(2)). The Leaking Underground Storage Tank Trust Fund receives 0.1 cent per gallon of this tax rate. Of the remaining 18.3 cents per gallon, tax collected in excess of 13.5 cents per gallon (4.8 cents per gallon) is retained in the General Fund of the Treasury. The balance is transferred to the Highway Trust Fund and then retransferred (except for amounts transferred to the fund for land and water conservation) to the Aquatic Resources Trust Fund.

The Aquatic Resources Trust Fund is made up of two accounts. First, the Boat Safety Account is funded by a portion of the receipts from the tax imposed on motorboat gasoline and special motor fuels. No more than $70 million per year may be transferred to the Boat Safety Account. In addition, transfers to the Account are

BACKGROUND

subject to an overall annual limit equal to an amount that will not cause the Boat Safety Account to have an unobligated balance in excess of $70 million.

Second, the Sport Fish Restoration Account receives the balance of the motorboat gasoline and special motor fuels receipts that are transferred to the Aquatic Resources Trust Fund. The Sport Fish Restoration Account is also funded from an excise tax imposed on sport-fishing equipment sold by the manufacturer, producer or importer. The excise tax rate is 10 percent on the sale price of sport-fishing equipment (Code Sec. 4161(a)). A reduced rate of 3 percent applies to electric outboard motors and fishing tackle boxes. Examples of sport-fishing equipment subject to the 10-percent excise tax include:

(1) fishing rods and poles;

(2) fishing reels;

(3) fly fishing lines and certain other fishing lines;

(4) fishing spears and spear tips;

(5) spear guns;

(6) items of terminal tackle;

(7) fishing vests;

(8) landing nets; and

(9) portable bait containers.

Import duties on certain fishing tackle, yachts and pleasure craft are also transferred into the Sport Fish Restoration Account.

Taxes on gasoline used as a fuel in the nonbusiness use of small-engine outdoor power equipment that are retransferred from the Highway Trust Fund to the Aquatic Resources Trust Fund are directed to the Coastal Wetlands Sub-Account, a separate sub-account of the Sport Fish Restoration Account.

Amounts expended from the Boat Safety Account are subject to annual appropriations. Amounts transferred, paid or credited to the Sport Fish Restoration Account (including the Coastal Wetlands Sub-Account) are to be appropriated for the uses authorized in the expenditure provisions.

NEW LAW EXPLAINED

Sport Fish Restoration and Boating Trust Fund.—The Aquatic Resources Trust Fund has been eliminated along with future transfers to the Boat Safety Account. The Sport Fish Restoration Account has been transformed into the Sport Fish Restoration and Boating Trust Fund (Code Sec. 9504(a), as amended by the SAFE Transportation Equity Act of 2005). After the Land and Water Conservation Fund has been funded in an amount not to exceed $1 million during any fiscal year, the balance of the taxes on motorboat fuels is transferred from the Highway Trust Fund into the Sport Fish Restoration and Boating Trust Fund (Code Sec. 9503(c)(4), as added by the Highway Act). The amounts subject to the transfer are equivalent to the motorboat fuel taxes received on or after October 1, 2005, and before October 1, 2011. In addition, the

NEW LAW EXPLAINED

transfers from the Highway Trust Fund to the Sport Fish Restoration and Boating Trust Fund of taxes on gasoline used as a fuel in the nonbusiness use of small-engine outdoor power equipment are extended through September 30, 2011 (Code Sec. 9503(c)(5)(A) as amended by the Highway Act).

Amounts remaining in the Boat Safety Account on October 1, 2005, plus accrued interest on the account's interest-bearing obligations, are available for making expenditures before October 1, 2010, to carry out the purposes of section 15 of the Dingell-Johnson Sport Fish Restoration Act. The expenditure provisions also authorize the appropriation of amounts in the Sport Fish Restoration and Boating Trust Fund, including for boating safety, for uses authorized in the expenditure provisions (Code Sec. 9504(c), as amended by Sec. 11115(c) of the Highway Act).

▶ **Effective date.** The amendments made by this section take effect on October 1, 2005 (Act Sec. 11115(d) of the SAFE Transportation Equity Act of 2005).

Law source: Law at ¶5485, ¶5490 and ¶7055. Committee Report at ¶15,050.

— Act Sec. 11115(a) of the SAFE Transportation Equity Act of 2005, amending Code Sec. 9503(c)(4);

— Act Sec. 11115(b), amending Code Sec. 9504(a), (b), (d) and (e);

— Act Sec. 11115(c), amending Code Sec. 9504(c);

— Act Sec. 11115(d), providing the effective date.

¶1035 Transfers from Leaking Underground Storage Tank Trust Fund

BACKGROUND

The Leaking Underground Storage Tank (LUST) Trust Fund was created by the Superfund Revenue Act of 1986 (P.L. 99-499). The LUST Trust Fund is financed by a 0.1 cent per gallon excise tax on the manufacture, sale or use of gasoline, diesel, kerosene or special motor fuels (other than liquefied petroleum gas or other liquefied natural gas), including use on an inland waterway (Code Secs. 4041(d), 4042 and 4081(a)). The LUST Trust Fund is also financed with amounts collected under section 9003(h)(6) of the Solid Waste Disposal Act (Code Sec. 9508(b)).

Monies in the LUST Trust Fund are available to pay cleanup and related costs of petroleum storage tanks that have no solvent owner, as well as tanks whose owner or operator refuses or is unable to comply with an urgent corrective order (section 9003(h)(6) of the Solid Waste Disposal Act) (Code Sec. 9508(c)). The funds are also available to provide grants to the states for carrying out these purposes (Code Sec. 9508(c); Committee Report on P.L. 99-499).

The LUST Trust Fund is required to reimburse the General Fund of the Treasury for tax refunds paid and credits allowed for certain uses of fuel (Code Sec. 9508(c)(2)). Specifically, reimbursements are required for refunds paid with respect to gasoline used on farms, gasoline used for certain nonhighway purposes or by local transit

BACKGROUND

systems, and fuels not used for taxable purposes (Code Secs. 6420, 6421, 6427 and 9508(c)(2)(A)(i)). Reimbursements are also required for credits allowed for retail sales and uses excise taxes under Code Sec. 4041 and the manufacturers excise tax under Code Sec. 4081, to the extent attributable to the LUST tax (Code Secs. 34 and 9508(c)(2)(A)(ii)).

NEW LAW EXPLAINED

Transfers from LUST Trust Fund limited.—The SAFE Transportation Equity Act of 2005 has added a special enforcement provision to the LUST Trust Fund similar to that for the Highway Trust Fund set forth in Code Sec. 9503(b)(6). This new provision is intended to prevent LUST Trust Fund monies from being spent for unauthorized purposes (Conference Committee Report (H.R. Conf. Rep. No. 109-203)).

Under the new provision, no amount may be appropriated from the LUST Trust Fund on and after the date of any expenditure which is not permitted under Code Sec. 9508. Whether or not an expenditure is permitted is determined without regard to: (1) any provision of law not contained or referenced in the Internal Revenue Code or in a Revenue Act; and (2) whether that provision of law is a subsequently enacted provision or directly or indirectly seeks to waive the application of the enforcement provision (Code Sec. 9508(e)(1), as added by the Highway Act). This enforcement provision does not apply to any expenditure from the LUST Trust Fund to liquidate any contract entered into, or for any amount otherwise obligated, before October 1, 2011 (Code Sec. 9508(e)(2), as added by the Highway Act).

> **Comment:** If unapproved expenditures from the LUST Trust Fund occur, it is assumed that LUST tax receipts will be treated in the manner as are Highway Trust Fund tax receipts when an unapproved expenditure from that fund occurs: the LUST taxes will continue to be imposed but receipts will be retained in the General Fund of the Treasury (Conference Committee Report (H.R. Conf. Rep. No. 109-203)).

Under the Energy Tax Incentives Act of 2005, the LUST Trust Fund is also no longer required to reimburse the General Fund of the Treasury for claims and credits attributable to nontaxable uses of fuel (Code Sec. 9508(c), as amended by the Energy Act).

> **Comment:** The Energy Act has extended the excise tax used to finance the LUST Trust Fund through September 30, 2011. In addition, exemptions from the tax have been greatly limited, as has the ability to obtain a refund or credit for LUST excise taxes paid (see ¶785).

▶ **Effective date.** The amendment limiting the expenditure of LUST Trust Fund monies shall take effect on August 10, 2005 (Act Sec. 11147(b) of the SAFE Transportation Equity Act of 2005). The amendment eliminating the reimbursement of the General Fund from the LUST Trust Fund for certain refund and credit claims shall take effect on October 1, 2005 (Act Sec. 1362(d) of the Energy Tax Incentives Act of 2005).

NEW LAW EXPLAINED

Law source: Law at ¶5495. Committee Report at ¶10,360 and ¶15,210.

— Act Sec. 11147(a) of the SAFE Transportation Equity Act of 2005, adding new Code Sec. 9508(e);

— Act Sec. 1362(c) of the Energy Tax Incentives Act of 2005, amending Code Sec. 9508(c);

— Act Sec. 11147(b) of the Highway Act and Act Sec. 1362(d) of the Energy Act, providing the effective dates.

Code Sections Added, Amended or Repealed

[¶ 5001]

INTRODUCTION.

The Internal Revenue Code provisions amended by the Energy Tax Incentives Act of 2005 (H.R. 6) and the Safe, Accountable, Flexible, Efficient Transportation Equity Act: A Legacy for Users (H.R. 3), as passed by the House and Senate and signed by President Bush, are shown in the following paragraphs. Deleted Code material or the text of the Code Section prior to amendment appears in the amendment notes following each amended Code provision. *Any changed or added material is set out in italics.*

[¶ 5005] CODE SEC. 23. ADOPTION EXPENSES.

* * *

>>>→ *Caution: H.R. 6 amended Code Sec. 23(c). However, the amendment cannot be made to the version of Code Sec. 23(c), below, as in effect on January 1, 2006.*

(c) CARRYFORWARDS OF UNUSED CREDIT.—If the credit allowable under subsection (a) for any taxable year exceeds the limitation imposed by subsection (b)(4) for such taxable year, such excess shall be carried to the succeeding taxable year and added to the credit allowable under subsection (a) for such taxable year. No credit may be carried forward under this subsection to any taxable year following the fifth taxable year after the taxable year in which the credit arose. For purposes of the preceding sentence, credits shall be treated as used on a first-in first-out basis.

* * *

[CCH Explanation at ¶ 210. Committee Reports at ¶ 10,230.]

Amendments

• **2005, Energy Tax Incentives Act of 2005 (H.R. 6)**

H.R. 6, § 1335(b)(1):

Amended Code Sec. 23(c) by striking "this section and section 1400C" and inserting "this section, section 25D, and section 1400C". **Effective** for property placed in service after 12-31-2005, in tax years ending after such date. [Note, this amendment cannot be made to the version of Code Sec. 23(c) as in effect on January 1, 2006.—CCH.]

[¶ 5010] CODE SEC. 25. INTEREST ON CERTAIN HOME MORTGAGES.

* * *

(e) SPECIAL RULES AND DEFINITIONS.—For purposes of this section—

(1) CARRYFORWARD OF UNUSED CREDIT.—

* * *

>>>→ *Caution: H.R. 6 amended Code Sec. 25(e)(1)(C). However, the amendment cannot be made to the version of Code Sec. 25(e)(1)(C), below, as in effect on January 1, 2006.*

(C) APPLICABLE TAX LIMIT.—For purposes of this paragraph, the term "applicable tax limit" means the limitation imposed by section 26(a) for the taxable year reduced by the sum of the credits allowable under this subpart (other than this section and sections 23, 24, 25B, and 1400C).

* * *

[CCH Explanation at ¶210. Committee Reports at ¶10,230.]

Amendments

• 2005, Energy Tax Incentives Act of 2005 (H.R. 6)

H.R. 6, §1335(b)(2):

Amended Code Sec. 25(e)(1)(C) by striking "this section and sections 23 and 1400C" and inserting "other than this section, section 23, section 25D, and section 1400C". **Effective** for property placed in service after 12-31-2005, in tax years ending after such date. [Note, this amendment cannot be made to the version of Code Sec. 25(e)(1)(C), as in effect on January 1, 2006.—CCH.]

⟫⟶ *Caution: Code Sec. 25C, below, as added by H.R. 6, applies to property placed in service after December 31, 2005.*

[¶5015] **CODE SEC. 25C. NONBUSINESS ENERGY PROPERTY.**

(a) ALLOWANCE OF CREDIT.—In the case of an individual, there shall be allowed as a credit against the tax imposed by this chapter for the taxable year an amount equal to the sum of—

(1) 10 percent of the amount paid or incurred by the taxpayer for qualified energy efficiency improvements installed during such taxable year, and

(2) the amount of the residential energy property expenditures paid or incurred by the taxpayer during such taxable year.

(b) LIMITATIONS.—

(1) LIFETIME LIMITATION.—The credit allowed under this section with respect to any taxpayer for any taxable year shall not exceed the excess (if any) of $500 over the aggregate credits allowed under this section with respect to such taxpayer for all prior taxable years.

(2) WINDOWS.—In the case of amounts paid or incurred for components described in subsection (c)(3)(B) by any taxpayer for any taxable year, the credit allowed under this section with respect to such amounts for such year shall not exceed the excess (if any) of $200 over the aggregate credits allowed under this section with respect to such amounts for all prior taxable years.

(3) LIMITATION ON RESIDENTIAL ENERGY PROPERTY EXPENDITURES.—The amount of the credit allowed under this section by reason of subsection (a)(2) shall not exceed—

(A) $50 for any advanced main air circulating fan,

(B) $150 for any qualified natural gas, propane, or oil furnace or hot water boiler, and

(C) $300 for any item of energy-efficient building property.

(c) QUALIFIED ENERGY EFFICIENCY IMPROVEMENTS.—For purposes of this section—

(1) IN GENERAL.—The term "qualified energy efficiency improvements" means any energy efficient building envelope component which meets the prescriptive criteria for such component established by the 2000 International Energy Conservation Code, as such Code (including supplements) is in effect on the date of the enactment of this section (or, in the case of a metal roof with appropriate pigmented coatings which meet the Energy Star program requirements), if—

(A) such component is installed in or on a dwelling unit located in the United States and owned and used by the taxpayer as the taxpayer's principal residence (within the meaning of section 121),

(B) the original use of such component commences with the taxpayer, and

(C) such component reasonably can be expected to remain in use for at least 5 years.

(2) BUILDING ENVELOPE COMPONENT.—The term "building envelope component" means—

(A) any insulation material or system which is specifically and primarily designed to reduce the heat loss or gain of a dwelling unit when installed in or on such dwelling unit,

(B) exterior windows (including skylights),

(C) exterior doors, and

(D) any metal roof installed on a dwelling unit, but only if such roof has appropriate pigmented coatings which are specifically and primarily designed to reduce the heat gain of such dwelling unit.

(3) MANUFACTURED HOMES INCLUDED.—The term "dwelling unit" includes a manufactured home which conforms to Federal Manufactured Home Construction and Safety Standards (section 3280 of title 24, Code of Federal Regulations).

(d) RESIDENTIAL ENERGY PROPERTY EXPENDITURES.—For purposes of this section—

(1) IN GENERAL.—The term "residential energy property expenditures" means expenditures made by the taxpayer for qualified energy property which is—

(A) installed on or in connection with a dwelling unit located in the United States and owned and used by the taxpayer as the taxpayer's principal residence (within the meaning of section 121), and

(B) originally placed in service by the taxpayer.

Such term includes expenditures for labor costs properly allocable to the onsite preparation, assembly, or original installation of the property.

(2) QUALIFIED ENERGY PROPERTY.—

(A) IN GENERAL.—The term "qualified energy property" means—

(i) energy-efficient building property,

(ii) a qualified natural gas, propane, or oil furnace or hot water boiler, or

(iii) an advanced main air circulating fan.

(B) PERFORMANCE AND QUALITY STANDARDS.—Property described under subparagraph (A) shall meet the performance and quality standards, and the certification requirements (if any), which—

(i) have been prescribed by the Secretary by regulations (after consultation with the Secretary of Energy or the Administrator of the Environmental Protection Agency, as appropriate), and

(ii) are in effect at the time of the acquisition of the property, or at the time of the completion of the construction, reconstruction, or erection of the property, as the case may be.

(C) REQUIREMENTS FOR STANDARDS.—The standards and requirements prescribed by the Secretary under subparagraph (B)—

(i) in the case of the energy efficiency ratio (EER) for central air conditioners and electric heat pumps—

(I) shall require measurements to be based on published data which is tested by manufacturers at 95 degrees Fahrenheit, and

(II) may be based on the certified data of the Air Conditioning and Refrigeration Institute that are prepared in partnership with the Consortium for Energy Efficiency, and

(ii) in the case of geothermal heat pumps—

(I) shall be based on testing under the conditions of ARI/ISO Standard 13256-1 for Water Source Heat Pumps or ARI 870 for Direct Expansion GeoExchange Heat Pumps (DX), as appropriate, and

(II) shall include evidence that water heating services have been provided through a desuperheater or integrated water heating system connected to the storage water heater tank.

(3) ENERGY-EFFICIENT BUILDING PROPERTY.—The term "energy-efficient building property" means—

(A) an electric heat pump water heater which yields an energy factor of at least 2.0 in the standard Department of Energy test procedure,

(B) an electric heat pump which has a heating seasonal performance factor (HSPF) of at least 9, a seasonal energy efficiency ratio (SEER) of at least 15, and an energy efficiency ratio (EER) of at least 13,

(C) a geothermal heat pump which—

(i) in the case of a closed loop product, has an energy efficiency ratio (EER) of at least 14.1 and a heating coefficient of performance (COP) of at least 3.3,

(ii) in the case of an open loop product, has an energy efficiency ratio (EER) of at least 16.2 and a heating coefficient of performance (COP) of at least 3.6, and

(iii) in the case of a direct expansion (DX) product, has an energy efficiency ratio (EER) of at least 15 and a heating coefficient of performance (COP) of at least 3.5,

(D) a central air conditioner which achieves the highest efficiency tier established by the Consortium for Energy Efficiency, as in effect on January 1, 2006, and

(E) a natural gas, propane, or oil water heater which has an energy factor of at least 0.80.

(4) QUALIFIED NATURAL GAS, PROPANE, OR OIL FURNACE OR HOT WATER BOILER.—The term "qualified natural gas, propane, or oil furnace or hot water boiler" means a natural gas, propane, or oil furnace or hot water boiler which achieves an annual fuel utilization efficiency rate of not less than 95.

(5) ADVANCED MAIN AIR CIRCULATING FAN.—The term "advanced main air circulating fan" means a fan used in a natural gas, propane, or oil furnace and which has an annual electricity use of no more than 2 percent of the total annual energy use of the furnace (as determined in the standard Department of Energy test procedures).

(e) SPECIAL RULES.—For purposes of this section—

(1) APPLICATION OF RULES.—Rules similar to the rules under paragraphs (4), (5), (6), (7), (8), and (9) of section 25D(e) shall apply.

(2) JOINT OWNERSHIP OF ENERGY ITEMS.—

(A) IN GENERAL.—Any expenditure otherwise qualifying as an expenditure under this section shall not be treated as failing to so qualify merely because such expenditure was made with respect to two or more dwelling units.

(B) LIMITS APPLIED SEPARATELY.—In the case of any expenditure described in subparagraph (A), the amount of the credit allowable under subsection (a) shall (subject to paragraph (1)) be computed separately with respect to the amount of the expenditure made for each dwelling unit.

(f) BASIS ADJUSTMENTS.—For purposes of this subtitle, if a credit is allowed under this section for any expenditure with respect to any property, the increase in the basis of such property which would (but for this subsection) result from such expenditure shall be reduced by the amount of the credit so allowed.

(g) TERMINATION.—This section shall not apply with respect to any property placed in service after December 31, 2007.

[CCH Explanation at ¶ 205. Committee Reports at ¶ 10,210.]

Amendments

• 2005, Energy Tax Incentives Act of 2005 (H.R. 6)

H.R. 6, § 1333(a):

Amended subpart A of part IV of subchapter A of chapter 1 by inserting after Code Sec. 25B a new Code Sec. 25C.
Effective for property placed in service after 12-31-2005.

⟶ *Caution: Code Sec. 25D, below, as added by H.R. 6, applies to property placed in service after December 31, 2005, in tax years ending after such date.*

[¶ 5020] CODE SEC. 25D. RESIDENTIAL ENERGY EFFICIENT PROPERTY.

(a) ALLOWANCE OF CREDIT.—In the case of an individual, there shall be allowed as a credit against the tax imposed by this chapter for the taxable year an amount equal to the sum of—

(1) 30 percent of the qualified photovoltaic property expenditures made by the taxpayer during such year,

(2) 30 percent of the qualified solar water heating property expenditures made by the taxpayer during such year, and

(3) 30 percent of the qualified fuel cell property expenditures made by the taxpayer during such year.

(b) LIMITATIONS.—

(1) MAXIMUM CREDIT.—The credit allowed under subsection (a) for any taxable year shall not exceed—

(A) $2,000 with respect to any qualified photovoltaic property expenditures,

(B) $2,000 with respect to any qualified solar water heating property expenditures, and

(C) $500 with respect to each half kilowatt of capacity of qualified fuel cell property (as defined in section 48(c)(1)) for which qualified fuel cell property expenditures are made.

(2) CERTIFICATION OF SOLAR WATER HEATING PROPERTY.—No credit shall be allowed under this section for an item of property described in subsection (d)(1) unless such property is certified for performance by the non-profit Solar Rating Certification Corporation or a comparable entity endorsed by the government of the State in which such property is installed.

(c) CARRYFORWARD OF UNUSED CREDIT.—If the credit allowable under subsection (a) exceeds the limitation imposed by section 26(a) for such taxable year reduced by the sum of the credits allowable under this subpart (other than this section), such excess shall be carried to the succeeding taxable year and added to the credit allowable under subsection (a) for such succeeding taxable year.

(d) DEFINITIONS.—For purposes of this section—

(1) QUALIFIED SOLAR WATER HEATING PROPERTY EXPENDITURE.—The term "qualified solar water heating property expenditure" means an expenditure for property to heat water for use in a dwelling unit located in the United States and used as a residence by the taxpayer if at least half of the energy used by such property for such purpose is derived from the sun.

(2) QUALIFIED PHOTOVOLTAIC PROPERTY EXPENDITURE.—The term "qualified photovoltaic property expenditure" means an expenditure for property which uses solar energy to generate electricity for use in a dwelling unit located in the United States and used as a residence by the taxpayer.

(3) QUALIFIED FUEL CELL PROPERTY EXPENDITURE.—The term "qualified fuel cell property expenditure" means an expenditure for qualified fuel cell property (as defined in section 48(c)(1)) installed on or in connection with a dwelling unit located in the United States and used as a principal residence (within the meaning of section 121) by the taxpayer.

(e) SPECIAL RULES.—For purposes of this section—

(1) LABOR COSTS.—Expenditures for labor costs properly allocable to the onsite preparation, assembly, or original installation of the property described in subsection (d) and for piping or wiring to interconnect such property to the dwelling unit shall be taken into account for purposes of this section.

(2) SOLAR PANELS.—No expenditure relating to a solar panel or other property installed as a roof (or portion thereof) shall fail to be treated as property described in paragraph (1) or (2) of subsection (d) solely because it constitutes a structural component of the structure on which it is installed.

(3) SWIMMING POOLS, ETC., USED AS STORAGE MEDIUM.—Expenditures which are properly allocable to a swimming pool, hot tub, or any other energy storage medium which has a function other than the function of such storage shall not be taken into account for purposes of this section.

(4) DOLLAR AMOUNTS IN CASE OF JOINT OCCUPANCY.—In the case of any dwelling unit which is jointly occupied and used during any calendar year as a residence by two or more individuals the following rules shall apply:

(A) The amount of the credit allowable, under subsection (a) by reason of expenditures (as the case may be) made during such calendar year by any of such individuals with respect to such dwelling unit shall be determined by treating all of such individuals as 1 taxpayer whose taxable year is such calendar year.

(B) There shall be allowable, with respect to such expenditures to each of such individuals, a credit under subsection (a) for the taxable year in which such calendar year ends in an amount which bears the same ratio to the amount determined under subparagraph (A) as the amount of such expenditures made by such individual during such calendar year bears to the aggregate of such expenditures made by all of such individuals during such calendar year.

(C) Subparagraphs (A) and (B) shall be applied separately with respect to expenditures described in paragraphs (1), (2), and (3) of subsection (d).

(5) TENANT-STOCKHOLDER IN COOPERATIVE HOUSING CORPORATION.—In the case of an individual who is a tenant-stockholder (as defined in section 216) in a cooperative housing corporation (as defined in such section), such individual shall be treated as having made his tenant-stockholder's proportionate share (as defined in section 216(b)(3)) of any expenditures of such corporation.

(6) CONDOMINIUMS.—

(A) IN GENERAL.—In the case of an individual who is a member of a condominium management association with respect to a condominium which the individual owns, such individual shall be treated as having made the individual's proportionate share of any expenditures of such association.

(B) CONDOMINIUM MANAGEMENT ASSOCIATION.—For purposes of this paragraph, the term "condominium management association" means an organization which meets the requirements of paragraph (1) of section 528(c) (other than subparagraph (E) thereof) with respect to a condominium project substantially all of the units of which are used as residences.

(7) ALLOCATION IN CERTAIN CASES.—If less than 80 percent of the use of an item is for nonbusiness purposes, only that portion of the expenditures for such item which is properly allocable to use for nonbusiness purposes shall be taken into account.

(8) WHEN EXPENDITURE MADE; AMOUNT OF EXPENDITURE.—

(A) IN GENERAL.—Except as provided in subparagraph (B), an expenditure with respect to an item shall be treated as made when the original installation of the item is completed.

(B) EXPENDITURES PART OF BUILDING CONSTRUCTION.—In the case of an expenditure in connection with the construction or reconstruction of a structure, such expenditure shall be treated as made when the original use of the constructed or reconstructed structure by the taxpayer begins.

(9) PROPERTY FINANCED BY SUBSIDIZED ENERGY FINANCING.—For purposes of determining the amount of expenditures made by any individual with respect to any dwelling unit, there shall not be taken into account expenditures which are made from subsidized energy financing (as defined in section 48(a)(4)(C)).

(f) BASIS ADJUSTMENTS.—For purposes of this subtitle, if a credit is allowed under this section for any expenditure with respect to any property, the increase in the basis of such property which would (but for this subsection) result from such expenditure shall be reduced by the amount of the credit so allowed.

(g) TERMINATION.—The credit allowed under this section shall not apply to property placed in service after December 31, 2007.

[CCH Explanation at ¶ 210. Committee Reports at ¶ 10,230.]

Amendments

- **2005, Energy Tax Incentives Act of 2005 (H.R. 6)**

H.R. 6, § 1335(a):

Amended subpart A of part IV of subchapter A of chapter 1, as amended by this Act, by inserting after Code Sec. 25C a

new Code Sec. 25D. **Effective** for property placed in service after 12-31-2005, in tax years ending after such date.

[¶ 5025] CODE SEC. 30. CREDIT FOR QUALIFIED ELECTRIC VEHICLES.

* * *

(b) LIMITATIONS.—

* * *

(3) APPLICATION WITH OTHER CREDITS.—The credit allowed by subsection (a) for any taxable year shall not exceed the excess (if any) of—

⇒→ *Caution: Code Sec. 30(b)(3)(A), as amended by H.R. 6, applies to credits determined under the Internal Revenue Code of 1986 for tax years ending after December 31, 2005.*

(A) the regular tax for the taxable year reduced by the sum of the credits allowable under subpart A and *section 27*, over—

(B) the tentative minimum tax for the taxable year.

* * *

[CCH Explanation at ¶610 and ¶615. Committee Reports at ¶10,110.]

Amendments

- **2005, Energy Tax Incentives Act of 2005 (H.R. 6)**

H.R. 6, §1322(a)(3)(A):

Amended Code Sec. 30(b)(3)(A) by striking "sections 27 and 29" and inserting "section 27". **Effective** for credits determined under the Internal Revenue Code of 1986 for tax years ending after 12-31-2005.

⇒→ *Caution: Code Sec. 30B, below, as added by H.R. 6, applies to property placed in service after December 31, 2005, in tax years ending after such date.*

[¶5030] CODE SEC. 30B. ALTERNATIVE MOTOR VEHICLE CREDIT.

(a) ALLOWANCE OF CREDIT.—There shall be allowed as a credit against the tax imposed by this chapter for the taxable year an amount equal to the sum of—

(1) the new qualified fuel cell motor vehicle credit determined under subsection (b),

(2) the new advanced lean burn technology motor vehicle credit determined under subsection (c),

(3) the new qualified hybrid motor vehicle credit determined under subsection (d), and

(4) the new qualified alternative fuel motor vehicle credit determined under subsection (e).

(b) NEW QUALIFIED FUEL CELL MOTOR VEHICLE CREDIT.—

(1) IN GENERAL.—For purposes of subsection (a), the new qualified fuel cell motor vehicle credit determined under this subsection with respect to a new qualified fuel cell motor vehicle placed in service by the taxpayer during the taxable year is—

(A) $8,000 ($4,000 in the case of a vehicle placed in service after December 31, 2009), if such vehicle has a gross vehicle weight rating of not more than 8,500 pounds,

(B) $10,000, if such vehicle has a gross vehicle weight rating of more than 8,500 pounds but not more than 14,000 pounds,

(C) $20,000, if such vehicle has a gross vehicle weight rating of more than 14,000 pounds but not more than 26,000 pounds, and

(D) $40,000, if such vehicle has a gross vehicle weight rating of more than 26,000 pounds.

(2) INCREASE FOR FUEL EFFICIENCY.—

(A) IN GENERAL.—The amount determined under paragraph (1)(A) with respect to a new qualified fuel cell motor vehicle which is a passenger automobile or light truck shall be increased by—

(i) $1,000, if such vehicle achieves at least 150 percent but less than 175 percent of the 2002 model year city fuel economy,

(ii) $1,500, if such vehicle achieves at least 175 percent but less than 200 percent of the 2002 model year city fuel economy,

(iii) $2,000, if such vehicle achieves at least 200 percent but less than 225 percent of the 2002 model year city fuel economy,

(iv) $2,500, if such vehicle achieves at least 225 percent but less than 250 percent of the 2002 model year city fuel economy,

(v) $3,000, if such vehicle achieves at least 250 percent but less than 275 percent of the 2002 model year city fuel economy,

(vi) $3,500, if such vehicle achieves at least 275 percent but less than 300 percent of the 2002 model year city fuel economy, and

(vii) $4,000, if such vehicle achieves at least 300 percent of the 2002 model year city fuel economy.

(B) 2002 MODEL YEAR CITY FUEL ECONOMY.—For purposes of subparagraph (A), the 2002 model year city fuel economy with respect to a vehicle shall be determined in accordance with the following tables:

(i) In the case of a passenger automobile:

If vehicle inertia weight class is:	The 2002 model year city fuel economy is:
1,500 or 1,750 lbs	45.2 mpg
2,000 lbs	39.6 mpg
2,250 lbs	35.2 mpg
2,500 lbs	31.7 mpg
2,750 lbs	28.8 mpg
3,000 lbs	26.4 mpg
3,500 lbs	22.6 mpg
4,000 lbs	19.8 mpg
4,500 lbs	17.6 mpg
5,000 lbs	15.9 mpg
5,500 lbs	14.4 mpg
6,000 lbs	13.2 mpg
6,500 lbs	12.2 mpg
7,000 to 8,500 lbs	11.3 mpg.

(ii) In the case of a light truck:

If vehicle inertia weight class is:	The 2002 model year city fuel economy is:
1,500 or 1,750 lbs	39.4 mpg
2,000 lbs	35.2 mpg
2,250 lbs	31.8 mpg
2,500 lbs	29.0 mpg
2,750 lbs	26.8 mpg
3,000 lbs	24.9 mpg
3,500 lbs	21.8 mpg
4,000 lbs	19.4 mpg
4,500 lbs	17.6 mpg
5,000 lbs	16.1 mpg
5,500 lbs	14.8 mpg
6,000 lbs	13.7 mpg
6,500 lbs	12.8 mpg
7,000 to 8,500 lbs	12.1 mpg.

(C) VEHICLE INERTIA WEIGHT CLASS.—For purposes of subparagraph (B), the term "vehicle inertia weight class" has the same meaning as when defined in regulations prescribed by the Administrator of the Environmental Protection Agency for purposes of the administration of title II of the Clean Air Act (42 U.S.C. 7521 et seq.).

(3) NEW QUALIFIED FUEL CELL MOTOR VEHICLE.—For purposes of this subsection, the term "new qualified fuel cell motor vehicle" means a motor vehicle—

(A) which is propelled by power derived from 1 or more cells which convert chemical energy directly into electricity by combining oxygen with hydrogen fuel which is stored on board the vehicle in any form and may or may not require reformation prior to use,

(B) which, in the case of a passenger automobile or light truck, has received on or after the date of the enactment of this section a certificate that such vehicle meets or exceeds the Bin 5 Tier II emission level established in regulations prescribed by the Administrator of the Environmental Protection Agency under section 202(i) of the Clean Air Act for that make and model year vehicle,

(C) the original use of which commences with the taxpayer,

(D) which is acquired for use or lease by the taxpayer and not for resale, and

(E) which is made by a manufacturer.

(c) NEW ADVANCED LEAN BURN TECHNOLOGY MOTOR VEHICLE CREDIT.—

(1) IN GENERAL.—For purposes of subsection (a), the new advanced lean burn technology motor vehicle credit determined under this subsection for the taxable year is the credit amount determined under paragraph (2) with respect to a new advanced lean burn technology motor vehicle placed in service by the taxpayer during the taxable year.

(2) CREDIT AMOUNT.—

(A) FUEL ECONOMY.—

(i) IN GENERAL.—The credit amount determined under this paragraph shall be determined in accordance with the following table:

In the case of a vehicle which achieves a fuel economy (expressed as a percentage of the 2002 model year city fuel economy) of—	The credit amount is—
At least 125 percent but less than 150 percent	$400
At least 150 percent but less than 175 percent	$800
At least 175 percent but less than 200 percent	$1,200
At least 200 percent but less than 225 percent	$1,600
At least 225 percent but less than 250 percent	$2,000
At least 250 percent	$2,400.

(ii) 2002 MODEL YEAR CITY FUEL ECONOMY.—For purposes of clause (i), the 2002 model year city fuel economy with respect to a vehicle shall be determined on a gasoline gallon equivalent basis as determined by the Administrator of the Environmental Protection Agency using the tables provided in subsection (b)(2)(B) with respect to such vehicle.

(B) CONSERVATION CREDIT.—The amount determined under subparagraph (A) with respect to a new advanced lean burn technology motor vehicle shall be increased by the conservation credit amount determined in accordance with the following table:

In the case of a vehicle which achieves a lifetime fuel savings (expressed in gallons of gasoline) of—	The conservation credit amount is—
At least 1,200 but less than 1,800	$250
At least 1,800 but less than 2,400	$500
At least 2,400 but less than 3,000	$750
At least 3,000	$1,000.

(3) NEW ADVANCED LEAN BURN TECHNOLOGY MOTOR VEHICLE.—For purposes of this subsection, the term "new advanced lean burn technology motor vehicle" means a passenger automobile or a light truck—

(A) with an internal combustion engine which—

(i) is designed to operate primarily using more air than is necessary for complete combustion of the fuel,

(ii) incorporates direct injection,

(iii) achieves at least 125 percent of the 2002 model year city fuel economy,

(iv) for 2004 and later model vehicles, has received a certificate that such vehicle meets or exceeds—

(I) in the case of a vehicle having a gross vehicle weight rating of 6,000 pounds or less, the Bin 5 Tier II emission standard established in regulations prescribed by the Administrator of the Environmental Protection Agency under section 202(i) of the Clean Air Act for that make and model year vehicle, and

(II) in the case of a vehicle having a gross vehicle weight rating of more than 6,000 pounds but not more than 8,500 pounds, the Bin 8 Tier II emission standard which is so established,

(B) the original use of which commences with the taxpayer,

(C) which is acquired for use or lease by the taxpayer and not for resale, and

(D) which is made by a manufacturer.

(4) LIFETIME FUEL SAVINGS.—For purposes of this subsection, the term "lifetime fuel savings" means, in the case of any new advanced lean burn technology motor vehicle, an amount equal to the excess (if any) of—

(A) 120,000 divided by the 2002 model year city fuel economy for the vehicle inertia weight class, over

(B) 120,000 divided by the city fuel economy for such vehicle.

(d) NEW QUALIFIED HYBRID MOTOR VEHICLE CREDIT.—

(1) IN GENERAL.—For purposes of subsection (a), the new qualified hybrid motor vehicle credit determined under this subsection for the taxable year is the credit amount determined under paragraph (2) with respect to a new qualified hybrid motor vehicle placed in service by the taxpayer during the taxable year.

(2) CREDIT AMOUNT.—

(A) CREDIT AMOUNT FOR PASSENGER AUTOMOBILES AND LIGHT TRUCKS.—In the case of a new qualified hybrid motor vehicle which is a passenger automobile or light truck and which has a gross vehicle weight rating of not more than 8,500 pounds, the amount determined under this paragraph is the sum of the amounts determined under clauses (i) and (ii).

(i) FUEL ECONOMY.—The amount determined under this clause is the amount which would be determined under subsection (c)(2)(A) if such vehicle were a vehicle referred to in such subsection.

(ii) CONSERVATION CREDIT.—The amount determined under this clause is the amount which would be determined under subsection (c)(2)(B) if such vehicle were a vehicle referred to in such subsection.

(B) CREDIT AMOUNT FOR OTHER MOTOR VEHICLES.—

(i) IN GENERAL.—In the case of any new qualified hybrid motor vehicle to which subparagraph (A) does not apply, the amount determined under this paragraph is the amount equal to the applicable percentage of the qualified incremental hybrid cost of the vehicle as certified under clause (v).

(ii) APPLICABLE PERCENTAGE.—For purposes of clause (i), the applicable percentage is—

(I) 20 percent if the vehicle achieves an increase in city fuel economy relative to a comparable vehicle of at least 30 percent but less than 40 percent,

(II) 30 percent if the vehicle achieves such an increase of at least 40 percent but less than 50 percent, and

(III) 40 percent if the vehicle achieves such an increase of at least 50 percent.

(iii) QUALIFIED INCREMENTAL HYBRID COST.—For purposes of this subparagraph, the qualified incremental hybrid cost of any vehicle is equal to the amount of the excess of the manufacturer's suggested retail price for such vehicle over such price for a comparable vehicle, to the extent such amount does not exceed—

(I) $7,500, if such vehicle has a gross vehicle weight rating of not more than 14,000 pounds,

(II) $15,000, if such vehicle has a gross vehicle weight rating of more than 14,000 pounds but not more than 26,000 pounds, and

(III) $30,000, if such vehicle has a gross vehicle weight rating of more than 26,000 pounds.

(iv) COMPARABLE VEHICLE.—For purposes of this subparagraph, the term "comparable vehicle" means, with respect to any new qualified hybrid motor vehicle, any vehicle which is powered solely by a gasoline or diesel internal combustion engine and which is comparable in weight, size, and use to such vehicle.

(v) CERTIFICATION.—A certification described in clause (i) shall be made by the manufacturer and shall be determined in accordance with guidance prescribed by the Secretary. Such guidance shall specify procedures and methods for calculating fuel economy savings and incremental hybrid costs.

(3) NEW QUALIFIED HYBRID MOTOR VEHICLE.—For purposes of this subsection—

(A) IN GENERAL.—The term "new qualified hybrid motor vehicle" means a motor vehicle—

(i) which draws propulsion energy from onboard sources of stored energy which are both—

(I) an internal combustion or heat engine using consumable fuel, and

(II) a rechargeable energy storage system,

(ii) which, in the case of a vehicle to which paragraph (2)(A) applies, has received a certificate of conformity under the Clean Air Act and meets or exceeds the equivalent qualifying California low emission vehicle standard under section 243(e)(2) of the Clean Air Act for that make and model year, and

(I) in the case of a vehicle having a gross vehicle weight rating of 6,000 pounds or less, the Bin 5 Tier II emission standard established in regulations prescribed by the Administrator of the Environmental Protection Agency under section 202(i) of the Clean Air Act for that make and model year vehicle, and

(II) in the case of a vehicle having a gross vehicle weight rating of more than 6,000 pounds but not more than 8,500 pounds, the Bin 8 Tier II emission standard which is so established,

(iii) which has a maximum available power of at least—

(I) 4 percent in the case of a vehicle to which paragraph (2)(A) applies,

(II) 10 percent in the case of a vehicle which has a gross vehicle weight rating of more than 8,500 pounds and not more than 14,000 pounds, and

(III) 15 percent in the case of a vehicle in excess of 14,000 pounds,

(iv) which, in the case of a vehicle to which paragraph (2)(B) applies, has an internal combustion or heat engine which has received a certificate of conformity under the Clean Air Act as meeting the emission standards set in the regulations prescribed by the Administrator of the Environmental Protection Agency for 2004 through 2007 model year diesel heavy duty engines or ottocycle heavy duty engines, as applicable,

(v) the original use of which commences with the taxpayer,

(vi) which is acquired for use or lease by the taxpayer and not for resale, and

(vii) which is made by a manufacturer.

Such term shall not include any vehicle which is not a passenger automobile or light truck if such vehicle has a gross vehicle weight rating of less than 8,500 pounds.

(B) CONSUMABLE FUEL.—For purposes of subparagraph (A)(i)(I), the term "consumable fuel" means any solid, liquid, or gaseous matter which releases energy when consumed by an auxiliary power unit.

(C) MAXIMUM AVAILABLE POWER.—

(i) CERTAIN PASSENGER AUTOMOBILES AND LIGHT TRUCKS.—In the case of a vehicle to which paragraph (2)(A) applies, the term "maximum available power" means the maximum power available from the rechargeable energy storage system, during a standard 10 second pulse power or equivalent test, divided by such maximum power and the SAE net power of the heat engine.

(ii) OTHER MOTOR VEHICLES.—In the case of a vehicle to which paragraph (2)(B) applies, the term "maximum available power" means the maximum power available from the rechargeable energy storage system, during a standard 10 second pulse power or equivalent test, divided by the vehicle's total traction power. For purposes of the preceding sentence, the term "total traction power" means the sum of the peak power from the rechargeable energy storage system and the heat engine peak power of the vehicle, except that if such storage system is the sole means by which the vehicle can be driven, the total traction power is the peak power of such storage system.

(e) NEW QUALIFIED ALTERNATIVE FUEL MOTOR VEHICLE CREDIT.—

(1) ALLOWANCE OF CREDIT.—Except as provided in paragraph (5), the new qualified alternative fuel motor vehicle credit determined under this subsection is an amount equal to the applicable percentage of the incremental cost of any new qualified alternative fuel motor vehicle placed in service by the taxpayer during the taxable year.

(2) APPLICABLE PERCENTAGE.—For purposes of paragraph (1), the applicable percentage with respect to any new qualified alternative fuel motor vehicle is—

(A) 50 percent, plus

(B) 30 percent, if such vehicle—

(i) has received a certificate of conformity under the Clean Air Act and meets or exceeds the most stringent standard available for certification under the Clean Air Act for that make and model year vehicle (other than a zero emission standard), or

(ii) has received an order certifying the vehicle as meeting the same requirements as vehicles which may be sold or leased in California and meets or exceeds the most stringent standard available for certification under the State laws of California (enacted in accordance with a waiver granted under section 209(b) of the Clean Air Act) for that make and model year vehicle (other than a zero emission standard).

For purposes of the preceding sentence, in the case of any new qualified alternative fuel motor vehicle which weighs more than 14,000 pounds gross vehicle weight rating, the most stringent standard available shall be such standard available for certification on the date of the enactment of the Energy Tax Incentives Act of 2005.

(3) INCREMENTAL COST.—For purposes of this subsection, the incremental cost of any new qualified alternative fuel motor vehicle is equal to the amount of the excess of the manufacturer's suggested retail price for such vehicle over such price for a gasoline or diesel fuel motor vehicle of the same model, to the extent such amount does not exceed—

(A) $5,000, if such vehicle has a gross vehicle weight rating of not more than 8,500 pounds,

(B) $10,000, if such vehicle has a gross vehicle weight rating of more than 8,500 pounds but not more than 14,000 pounds,

(C) $25,000, if such vehicle has a gross vehicle weight rating of more than 14,000 pounds but not more than 26,000 pounds, and

(D) $40,000, if such vehicle has a gross vehicle weight rating of more than 26,000 pounds.

(4) NEW QUALIFIED ALTERNATIVE FUEL MOTOR VEHICLE.—For purposes of this subsection—

(A) IN GENERAL.—The term "new qualified alternative fuel motor vehicle" means any motor vehicle—

(i) which is only capable of operating on an alternative fuel,

(ii) the original use of which commences with the taxpayer,

(iii) which is acquired by the taxpayer for use or lease, but not for resale, and

(iv) which is made by a manufacturer.

(B) ALTERNATIVE FUEL.—The term "alternative fuel" means compressed natural gas, liquefied natural gas, liquefied petroleum gas, hydrogen, and any liquid at least 85 percent of the volume of which consists of methanol.

(5) CREDIT FOR MIXED-FUEL VEHICLES.—

(A) IN GENERAL.—In the case of a mixed-fuel vehicle placed in service by the taxpayer during the taxable year, the credit determined under this subsection is an amount equal to—

(i) in the case of a 75/25 mixed-fuel vehicle, 70 percent of the credit which would have been allowed under this subsection if such vehicle was a qualified alternative fuel motor vehicle, and

(ii) in the case of a 90/10 mixed-fuel vehicle, 90 percent of the credit which would have been allowed under this subsection if such vehicle was a qualified alternative fuel motor vehicle.

(B) MIXED-FUEL VEHICLE.—For purposes of this subsection, the term "mixed-fuel vehicle" means any motor vehicle described in subparagraph (C) or (D) of paragraph (3), which—

(i) is certified by the manufacturer as being able to perform efficiently in normal operation on a combination of an alternative fuel and a petroleum-based fuel,

(ii) either—

(I) has received a certificate of conformity under the Clean Air Act, or

(II) has received an order certifying the vehicle as meeting the same requirements as vehicles which may be sold or leased in California and meets or exceeds the low emission vehicle standard under section 88.105-94 of title 40, Code of Federal Regulations, for that make and model year vehicle,

(iii) the original use of which commences with the taxpayer,

(iv) which is acquired by the taxpayer for use or lease, but not for resale, and

(v) which is made by a manufacturer.

(C) 75/25 MIXED-FUEL VEHICLE.—For purposes of this subsection, the term "75/25 mixed-fuel vehicle" means a mixed-fuel vehicle which operates using at least 75 percent alternative fuel and not more than 25 percent petroleum-based fuel.

(D) 90/10 MIXED-FUEL VEHICLE.—For purposes of this subsection, the term "90/10 mixed-fuel vehicle" means a mixed-fuel vehicle which operates using at least 90 percent alternative fuel and not more than 10 percent petroleum-based fuel.

(f) LIMITATION ON NUMBER OF NEW QUALIFIED HYBRID AND ADVANCED LEAN-BURN TECHNOLOGY VEHICLES ELIGIBLE FOR CREDIT.—

(1) IN GENERAL.—In the case of a qualified vehicle sold during the phaseout period, only the applicable percentage of the credit otherwise allowable under subsection (c) or (d) shall be allowed.

(2) PHASEOUT PERIOD.—For purposes of this subsection, the phaseout period is the period beginning with the second calendar quarter following the calendar quarter which includes the first date on which the number of qualified vehicles manufactured by the manufacturer of the vehicle referred to in paragraph (1) sold for use in the United States after December 31, 2005, is at least 60,000.

(3) APPLICABLE PERCENTAGE.—For purposes of paragraph (1), the applicable percentage is—

(A) 50 percent for the first 2 calendar quarters of the phaseout period,

(B) 25 percent for the 3d and 4th calendar quarters of the phaseout period, and

(C) 0 percent for each calendar quarter thereafter.

(4) CONTROLLED GROUPS.—

(A) IN GENERAL.—For purposes of this subsection, all persons treated as a single employer under subsection (a) or (b) of section 52 or subsection (m) or (o) of section 414 shall be treated as a single manufacturer.

(B) INCLUSION OF FOREIGN CORPORATIONS.—For purposes of subparagraph (A), in applying subsections (a) and (b) of section 52 to this section, section 1563 shall be applied without regard to subsection (b)(2)(C) thereof.

(5) QUALIFIED VEHICLE.—For purposes of this subsection, the term "qualified vehicle"' means any new qualified hybrid motor vehicle (described in subsection (d)(2)(A)) and any new advanced lean burn technology motor vehicle.

(g) APPLICATION WITH OTHER CREDITS.—

(1) BUSINESS CREDIT TREATED AS PART OF GENERAL BUSINESS CREDIT.—So much of the credit which would be allowed under subsection (a) for any taxable year (determined without regard to this subsection) that is attributable to property of a character subject to an allowance for depreciation shall be treated as a credit listed in section 38(b) for such taxable year (and not allowed under subsection (a)).

(2) PERSONAL CREDIT.—The credit allowed under subsection (a) (after the application of paragraph (1)) for any taxable year shall not exceed the excess (if any) of—

(A) the regular tax reduced by the sum of the credits allowable under subpart A and sections 27 and 30, over

(B) the tentative minimum tax for the taxable year.

(h) OTHER DEFINITIONS AND SPECIAL RULES.—For purposes of this section—

(1) MOTOR VEHICLE.—The term "motor vehicle" has the meaning given such term by section 30(c)(2).

(2) CITY FUEL ECONOMY.—The city fuel economy with respect to any vehicle shall be measured in a manner which is substantially similar to the manner city fuel economy is measured in accordance with procedures under part 600 of subchapter Q of chapter I of title 40, Code of Federal Regulations, as in effect on the date of the enactment of this section.

(3) OTHER TERMS.—The terms "automobile", "passenger automobile", "medium duty passenger vehicle", "light truck", and "manufacturer" have the meanings given such terms in regulations prescribed by the Administrator of the Environmental Protection Agency for purposes of the administration of title II of the Clean Air Act (42 U.S.C. 7521 et seq.).

(4) REDUCTION IN BASIS.—For purposes of this subtitle, the basis of any property for which a credit is allowable under subsection (a) shall be reduced by the amount of such credit so allowed (determined without regard to subsection (g)).

(5) NO DOUBLE BENEFIT.—The amount of any deduction or other credit allowable under this chapter—

(A) for any incremental cost taken into account in computing the amount of the credit determined under subsection (e) shall be reduced by the amount of such credit attributable to such cost, and

(B) with respect to a vehicle described under subsection (b) or (c), shall be reduced by the amount of credit allowed under subsection (a) for such vehicle for the taxable year.

(6) PROPERTY USED BY TAX-EXEMPT ENTITY.—In the case of a vehicle whose use is described in paragraph (3) or (4) of section 50(b) and which is not subject to a lease, the person who sold such vehicle to the person or entity using such vehicle shall be treated as the taxpayer that placed such vehicle in service, but only if such person clearly discloses to such person or entity in a document the amount of any credit allowable under subsection (a) with respect to such vehicle (determined without regard to subsection (g)).

(7) PROPERTY USED OUTSIDE UNITED STATES, ETC., NOT QUALIFIED.—No credit shall be allowable under subsection (a) with respect to any property referred to in section 50(b)(1) or with respect to the portion of the cost of any property taken into account under section 179.

(8) RECAPTURE.—The Secretary shall, by regulations, provide for recapturing the benefit of any credit allowable under subsection (a) with respect to any property which ceases to be property eligible for such credit (including recapture in the case of a lease period of less than the economic life of a vehicle).

(9) ELECTION TO NOT TAKE CREDIT.—No credit shall be allowed under subsection (a) for any vehicle if the taxpayer elects to not have this section apply to such vehicle.

(10) INTERACTION WITH AIR QUALITY AND MOTOR VEHICLE SAFETY STANDARDS.—Unless otherwise provided in this section, a motor vehicle shall not be considered eligible for a credit under this section unless such vehicle is in compliance with—

   (A) the applicable provisions of the Clean Air Act for the applicable make and model year of the vehicle (or applicable air quality provisions of State law in the case of a State which has adopted such provision under a waiver under section 209(b) of the Clean Air Act), and

   (B) the motor vehicle safety provisions of sections 30101 through 30169 of title 49, United States Code.

(i) REGULATIONS.—

   (1) IN GENERAL.—Except as provided in paragraph (2), the Secretary shall promulgate such regulations as necessary to carry out the provisions of this section.

   (2) COORDINATION IN PRESCRIPTION OF CERTAIN REGULATIONS.—The Secretary of the Treasury, in coordination with the Secretary of Transportation and the Administrator of the Environmental Protection Agency, shall prescribe such regulations as necessary to determine whether a motor vehicle meets the requirements to be eligible for a credit under this section.

(j) TERMINATION.—This section shall not apply to any property purchased after—

   (1) in the case of a new qualified fuel cell motor vehicle (as described in subsection (b)), December 31, 2014,

   (2) in the case of a new advanced lean burn technology motor vehicle (as described in subsection (c)) or a new qualified hybrid motor vehicle (as described in subsection (d)(2)(A)), December 31, 2010,

   (3) in the case of a new qualified hybrid motor vehicle (as described in subsection (d)(2)(B)), December 31, 2009, and

   (4) in the case of a new qualified alternative fuel vehicle (as described in subsection (e)), December 31, 2010.

[CCH Explanation at ¶305, ¶310, ¶315, ¶320, ¶325 and ¶330. Committee Reports at ¶10,260.]

Amendments

• **2005, Energy Tax Incentives Act of 2005 (H.R. 6)**

H.R. 6, §1341(a):

Amended subpart B of part IV of subchapter A of chapter 1 by adding at the end a new Code Sec. 30B. **Effective** for property placed in service after 12-31-2005, in tax years ending after such date.

⟫⟫→ *Caution: Code Sec. 30C, below, as added by H.R. 6, applies to property placed in service after December 31, 2005, in tax years ending after such date.*

[¶ 5035] CODE SEC. 30C. ALTERNATIVE FUEL VEHICLE REFUELING PROPERTY CREDIT.

(a) CREDIT ALLOWED.—There shall be allowed as a credit against the tax imposed by this chapter for the taxable year an amount equal to 30 percent of the cost of any qualified alternative fuel vehicle refueling property placed in service by the taxpayer during the taxable year.

(b) LIMITATION.—The credit allowed under subsection (a) with respect to any alternative fuel vehicle refueling property shall not exceed—

(1) $30,000 in the case of a property of a character subject to an allowance for depreciation, and

(2) $1,000 in any other case.

(c) QUALIFIED ALTERNATIVE FUEL VEHICLE REFUELING PROPERTY.—

(1) IN GENERAL.—Except as provided in paragraph (2), the term "qualified alternative fuel vehicle refueling property" has the meaning given to such term by section 179A(d), but only with respect to any fuel—

(A) at least 85 percent of the volume of which consists of one or more of the following: ethanol, natural gas, compressed natural gas, liquefied natural gas, liquefied petroleum gas, or hydrogen, or

(B) any mixture of biodiesel (as defined in section 40A(d)(1)) and diesel fuel (as defined in section 4083(a)(3)), determined without regard to any use of kerosene and containing at least 20 percent biodiesel.

(2) RESIDENTIAL PROPERTY.—In the case of any property installed on property which is used as the principal residence (within the meaning of section 121) of the taxpayer, paragraph (1) of section 179A(d) shall not apply.

(d) APPLICATION WITH OTHER CREDITS.—

(1) BUSINESS CREDIT TREATED AS PART OF GENERAL BUSINESS CREDIT.—So much of the credit which would be allowed under subsection (a) for any taxable year (determined without regard to this subsection) that is attributable to property of a character subject to an allowance for depreciation shall be treated as a credit listed in section 38(b) for such taxable year (and not allowed under subsection (a)).

(2) PERSONAL CREDIT.—The credit allowed under subsection (a) (after the application of paragraph (1)) for any taxable year shall not exceed the excess (if any) of—

(A) the regular tax reduced by the sum of the credits allowable under subpart A and sections 27, 30, and 30B, over

(B) the tentative minimum tax for the taxable year.

(e) SPECIAL RULES.—For purposes of this section—

(1) BASIS REDUCTION.—The basis of any property shall be reduced by the portion of the cost of such property taken into account under subsection (a).

(2) PROPERTY USED BY TAX-EXEMPT ENTITY.—In the case of any qualified alternative fuel vehicle refueling property the use of which is described in paragraph (3) or (4) of section 50(b) and which is not subject to a lease, the person who sold such property to the person or entity using such property shall be treated as the taxpayer that placed such property in service, but only if such person clearly discloses to such person or entity in a document the amount of any credit allowable under subsection (a) with respect to such property (determined without regard to subsection (d)).

(3) PROPERTY USED OUTSIDE UNITED STATES NOT QUALIFIED.—No credit shall be allowable under subsection (a) with respect to any property referred to in section 50(b)(1) or with respect to the portion of the cost of any property taken into account under section 179.

(4) ELECTION NOT TO TAKE CREDIT.—No credit shall be allowed under subsection (a) for any property if the taxpayer elects not to have this section apply to such property.

(5) RECAPTURE RULES.—Rules similar to the rules of section 179A(e)(4) shall apply.

(f) REGULATIONS.—The Secretary shall prescribe such regulations as necessary to carry out the provisions of this section.

(g) TERMINATION.—This section shall not apply to any property placed in service—

(1) in the case of property relating to hydrogen, after December 31, 2014, and

(2) in the case of any other property, after December 31, 2009.

[CCH Explanation at ¶730. Committee Reports at ¶10,270.]

Amendments

• **2005, Energy Tax Incentives Act of 2005 (H.R. 6)**

H.R. 6, §1342(a):

Amended subpart B of part IV of subchapter A of chapter 1, as amended by this Act, by adding at the end a new Code

Sec. 30C. **Effective** for property placed in service after 12-31-2005, in tax years ending after such date.

[¶5040] CODE SEC. 38. GENERAL BUSINESS CREDIT.

* * *

(b) CURRENT YEAR BUSINESS CREDIT.—For purposes of this subpart, the amount of the current year business credit is the sum of the following credits determined for the taxable year:

* * *

(17) the biodiesel fuels credit determined under section 40A(a),

(18) the low sulfur diesel fuel production credit determined under section 45H(a),

(19) the marginal oil and gas well production credit determined under section 45I(a),

(20) the distilled spirits credit determined under section 5011(a),

(21) the advanced nuclear power facility production credit determined under section 45J(a),

⟫→ *Caution: Code Sec. 38(b)(22)-(26), below, as added by H.R. 6, apply generally after December 31, 2005.*

(22) the nonconventional source production credit determined under section 45K(a),

(23) the new energy efficient home credit determined under section 45L(a),

(24) the energy efficient appliance credit determined under section 45M(a),

(25) the portion of the alternative motor vehicle credit to which section 30B(g)(1) applies, and

(26) the portion of the alternative fuel vehicle refueling property credit to which section 30C(d)(1) applies.

* * *

[CCH Explanation at ¶220, ¶225, ¶305, ¶440, ¶615, ¶730 and ¶835. Committee Reports at ¶10,050, ¶10,110, ¶10,200, ¶10,220, ¶10,260, ¶10,270, ¶15,120 and ¶15,250.]

Amendments

• **2005, Safe, Accountable, Flexible, Efficient Transportation Equity Act: A Legacy for Users (H.R. 3)**

H.R. 3, §11126(b):

Amended Code Sec. 38(b) by striking "plus" at the end of paragraph (18), by striking the period at the end of paragraph (19) and inserting ", plus", and by adding at the end a new paragraph (20). **Effective** for tax years beginning after 9-30-2005. For a special rule, see H.R. 3, Act Sec. 11151(d)(2), below.

H.R. 3, §11151(d)(2), provides:

(2) If the Energy Policy Act of 2005 is enacted before the date of the enactment of this Act, for purposes of executing any amendments made by the Energy Policy Act of 2005 to section 38(b) of the Internal Revenue Code of 1986, the amendments made by section 1126(b) of this Act shall be treated as having been executed before such amendments made by the Energy Policy Act of 2005.

- 2005, Energy Tax Incentives Act of 2005 (H.R. 6)

H.R. 6, § 1306(b):

Amended Code Sec. 38(b), as amended by the Safe, Accountable, Flexible, Efficient Transportation Equity Act: A Legacy for Users, by striking "plus" at the end of paragraph (19), by striking the period at the end of paragraph (20) and inserting ", plus", and by adding at the end a new paragraph (21). **Effective** for production in tax years beginning after 8-8-2005. For a special rule, see H.R. 3, Act Sec. 11151(d)(2).

H.R. 6, § 1322(a)(2):

Amended Code Sec. 38(b), as amended by this Act, by striking "plus" at the end of paragraph (20), by striking the period at the end of paragraph (21) and inserting ", plus", and by adding at the end a new paragraph (22). **Effective** for credits determined under the Internal Revenue Code of 1986 for tax years ending after 12-31-2005.

H.R. 6, § 1332(b):

Amended Code Sec. 38(b), as amended by this Act, by striking "plus" at the end of paragraph (21), by striking the period at the end of paragraph (22) and inserting ", plus", and by adding at the end a new paragraph (23). **Effective** for qualified new energy efficient homes acquired after 12-31-2005, in tax years ending after such date.

H.R. 6, § 1334(b):

Amended Code Sec. 38(b), as amended by this Act, by striking "plus" at the end of paragraph (22), by striking the period at the end of paragraph (23) and inserting ", plus", and by adding at the end a new paragraph (24). **Effective** for appliances produced after 12-31-2005.

H.R. 6, § 1341(b)(1):

Amended Code Sec. 38(b), as amended by this Act, by striking "plus" at the end of paragraph (23), by striking the period at the end of paragraph (24) and inserting ", and", and by adding at the end a new paragraph (25). **Effective** for property placed in service after 12-31-2005, in tax years ending after such date.

H.R. 6, § 1342(b)(1):

Amended Code Sec. 38(b), as amended by this Act, by striking "plus" at the end of paragraph (24), by striking the period at the end of paragraph (25) and inserting ", and", and by adding at the end a new paragraph (26). **Effective** for property placed in service after 12-31-2005, in tax years ending after such date.

[¶ 5045] CODE SEC. 40. ALCOHOL USED AS FUEL.

* * *

(g) DEFINITIONS AND SPECIAL RULES FOR ELIGIBLE SMALL ETHANOL PRODUCER CREDIT.—For purposes of this section—

(1) ELIGIBLE SMALL ETHANOL PRODUCER.—The term "eligible small ethanol producer" means a person who, at all times during the taxable year, has a productive capacity for alcohol (as defined in subsection (d)(1)(A) without regard to clauses (i) and (ii)) not in excess of *60,000,000* gallons.

(2) AGGREGATION RULE.—For purposes of the 15,000,000 gallon limitation under subsection (b)(4)(C) and the *60,000,000* gallon limitation under paragraph (1), all members of the same controlled group of corporations (within the meaning of section 267(f)) and all persons under common control (within the meaning of section 52(b) but determined by treating an interest of more than 50 percent as a controlling interest) shall be treated as 1 person.

* * *

(5) REGULATIONS.—The Secretary may prescribe such regulations as may be necessary—

(A) to prevent the credit provided for in subsection (a)(3) from directly or indirectly benefiting any person with a direct or indirect productive capacity of more than *60,000,000* gallons of alcohol during the taxable year, or

(B) to prevent any person from directly or indirectly benefiting with respect to more than 15,000,000 gallons during the taxable year.

(6) ALLOCATION OF SMALL ETHANOL PRODUCER CREDIT TO PATRONS OF COOPERATIVE.—

(A) ELECTION TO ALLOCATE.—

(i) IN GENERAL.—In the case of a cooperative organization described in section 1381(a), any portion of the credit determined under subsection (a)(3) for the taxable year may, at the election of the organization, be apportioned pro rata among patrons of the organization on the basis of the quantity or value of business done with or for such patrons for the taxable year.

(ii) FORM AND EFFECT OF ELECTION.—An election under clause (i) for any taxable year shall be made on a timely filed return for such year. Such election, once made, shall be irrevocable for such taxable year. *Such election shall not take effect unless the organization designates the apportionment as such in a written notice mailed to its patrons during the payment period described in section 1382(d).*

* * *

[CCH Explanation at ¶715 and ¶735. Committee Reports at ¶10,290 and ¶10,310.]

Amendments

- **2005, Energy Tax Incentives Act of 2005 (H.R. 6)**

H.R. 6, §1347(a):

Amended Code Sec. 40(g) by striking "30,000,000" each place it appears and inserting "60,000,000". **Effective** for tax years ending after 8-8-2005.

H.R. 6, §1347(b):

Amended Code Sec. 40(g)(6)(A)(ii) by adding at the end a new sentence. **Effective** for tax years ending after 8-8-2005.

⇒ *Caution: The heading for Code Sec. 40A, below, as amended by H.R. 6, applies with respect to fuel sold or used after December 31, 2005.*

[¶5050] CODE SEC. 40A. BIODIESEL *AND RENEWABLE DIESEL* USED AS FUEL.

(a) GENERAL RULE.—*For purposes of section 38, the biodiesel fuels credit determined under this section for the taxable year is an amount equal to the sum of—*

(1) *the biodiesel mixture credit, plus*

(2) *the biodiesel credit, plus*

(3) *in the case of an eligible small agri-biodiesel producer, the small agri-biodiesel producer credit.*

[CCH Explanation at ¶705, ¶710 and ¶715. Committee Reports at ¶10,290 and ¶10,300.]

Amendments

- **2005, Energy Tax Incentives Act of 2005 (H.R. 6)**

H.R. 6, §1345(a):

Amended Code Sec. 40A(a). **Effective** for tax years ending after 8-8-2005. Prior to amendment, Code Sec. 40A(a) read as follows:

(a) GENERAL RULE.—For purposes of section 38, the biodiesel fuels credit determined under this section for the taxable year is an amount equal to the sum of—

(1) the biodiesel mixture credit, plus

(2) the biodiesel credit.

H.R. 6, §1346(b)(1):

Amended the heading for Code Sec. 40A by inserting "AND RENEWABLE DIESEL" after "BIODIESEL". **Effective** with respect to fuel sold or used after 12-31-2005.

(b) DEFINITION OF BIODIESEL MIXTURE CREDIT, *BIODIESEL CREDIT, AND SMALL AGRI-BIODIESEL PRODUCER CREDIT.*—For purposes of this section—

* * *

(4) CERTIFICATION FOR BIODIESEL.—No credit shall be allowed under *paragraph (1) or (2) of subsection (a)* unless the taxpayer obtains a certification (in such form and manner as prescribed by the Secretary) from the producer or importer of the biodiesel which identifies the product produced and the percentage of biodiesel and agri-biodiesel in the product.

(5) SMALL AGRI-BIODIESEL PRODUCER CREDIT.—

(A) IN GENERAL.—The small agri-biodiesel producer credit of any eligible small agribiodiesel producer for any taxable year is 10 cents for each gallon of qualified agri-biodiesel production of such producer.

(B) QUALIFIED AGRI-BIODIESEL PRODUCTION.—For purposes of this paragraph, the term "qualified agri-biodiesel production" means any agri-biodiesel (determined without regard to the last sentence of subsection (d)(2)) which is produced by an eligible small agri-biodiesel producer, and which during the taxable year—

(i) is sold by such producer to another person—

(I) for use by such other person in the production of a qualified biodiesel mixture in such other person's trade or business (other than casual off-farm production),

(II) for use by such other person as a fuel in a trade or business, or

(III) who sells such agri-biodiesel at retail to another person and places such agri-biodiesel in the fuel tank of such other person, or

(ii) is used or sold by such producer for any purpose described in clause (i).

(C) LIMITATION.—The qualified agri-biodiesel production of any producer for any taxable year shall not exceed 15,000,000 gallons.

* * *

[CCH Explanation at ¶710. Committee Reports at ¶10,300.]

Amendments

• 2005, Energy Tax Incentives Act of 2005 (H.R. 6)

H.R. 6, §1345(b):

Amended Code Sec. 40A(b) by adding at the end a new paragraph (5). **Effective** for tax years ending after 8-8-2005.

H.R. 6, §1345(d)(1):

Amended Code Sec. 40A(b)(4) by striking "this section" and inserting "paragraph (1) or (2) of subsection (a)". **Effective** for tax years ending after 8-8-2005.

H.R. 6, §1345(d)(2):

Amended the heading of Code Sec. 40A(b) by striking "and Biodiesel Credit" and inserting ", Biodiesel Credit, and Small Agri-biodiesel Producer Credit". **Effective** for tax years ending after 8-8-2005.

(d) DEFINITIONS AND SPECIAL RULES.—For purposes of this section—

* * *

(3) MIXTURE OR BIODIESEL NOT USED AS A FUEL, ETC.—

* * *

(C) PRODUCER CREDIT.—If—

(i) any credit was determined under subsection (a)(3), and

(ii) any person does not use such fuel for a purpose described in subsection (b)(5)(B), then there is hereby imposed on such person a tax equal to 10 cents a gallon for each gallon of such agri-biodiesel.

(D) APPLICABLE LAWS.—All provisions of law, including penalties, shall, insofar as applicable and not inconsistent with this section, apply in respect of any tax imposed under subparagraph (A) or (B) as if such tax were imposed by section 4081 and not by this chapter.

(4) PASS-THRU IN THE CASE OF ESTATES AND TRUSTS.—Under regulations prescribed by the Secretary, rules similar to the rules of subsection (d) of section 52 shall apply.

[CCH Explanation at ¶710. Committee Reports at ¶10,300.]

Amendments

• 2005, Energy Tax Incentives Act of 2005 (H.R. 6)

H.R. 6, §1345(d)(3):

Amended Code Sec. 40A(d)(3) by redesignating subparagraph (C) as subparagraph (D) and by inserting after subparagraph (B) a new subparagraph (C). **Effective** for tax years ending after 8-8-2005.

(e) DEFINITIONS AND SPECIAL RULES FOR SMALL AGRI-BIODIESEL PRODUCER CREDIT.—For purposes of this section—

(1) ELIGIBLE SMALL AGRI-BIODIESEL PRODUCER.—The term "eligible small agri-biodiesel producer" means a person who, at all times during the taxable year, has a productive capacity for agri-biodiesel not in excess of 60,000,000 gallons.

(2) AGGREGATION RULE.—For purposes of the 15,000,000 gallon limitation under subsection (b)(5)(C) and the 60,000,000 gallon limitation under paragraph (1), all members of the same controlled group of corporations (within the meaning of section 267(f)) and all persons under common control (within the meaning of section 52(b) but determined by treating an interest of more than 50 percent as a controlling interest) shall be treated as 1 person.

(3) PARTNERSHIP, S CORPORATION, AND OTHER PASS-THRU ENTITIES.—In the case of a partnership, trust, S corporation, or other pass-thru entity, the limitations contained in subsection (b)(5)(C) and paragraph (1) shall be applied at the entity level and at the partner or similar level.

(4) ALLOCATION.—For purposes of this subsection, in the case of a facility in which more than 1 person has an interest, productive capacity shall be allocated among such persons in such manner as the Secretary may prescribe.

(5) REGULATIONS.—The Secretary may prescribe such regulations as may be necessary—

(A) to prevent the credit provided for in subsection (a)(3) from directly or indirectly benefiting any person with a direct or indirect productive capacity of more than 60,000,000 gallons of agri-biodiesel during the taxable year, or

(B) to prevent any person from directly or indirectly benefiting with respect to more than 15,000,000 gallons during the taxable year.

(6) ALLOCATION OF SMALL AGRI-BIODIESEL CREDIT TO PATRONS OF COOPERATIVE.—

(A) ELECTION TO ALLOCATE.—

(i) IN GENERAL.—In the case of a cooperative organization described in section 1381(a), any portion of the credit determined under subsection (a)(3) for the taxable year may, at the election of the organization, be apportioned pro rata among patrons of the organization on the basis of the quantity or value of business done with or for such patrons for the taxable year.

(ii) FORM AND EFFECT OF ELECTION.—An election under clause (i) for any taxable year shall be made on a timely filed return for such year. Such election, once made, shall be irrevocable for such taxable year. Such election shall not take effect unless the organization designates the apportionment as such in a written notice mailed to its patrons during the payment period described in section 1382(d).

(B) TREATMENT OF ORGANIZATIONS AND PATRONS.—

(i) ORGANIZATIONS.—The amount of the credit not apportioned to patrons pursuant to subparagraph (A) shall be included in the amount determined under subsection (a)(3) for the taxable year of the organization.

(ii) PATRONS.—The amount of the credit apportioned to patrons pursuant to subparagraph (A) shall be included in the amount determined under such subsection for the first taxable year of each patron ending on or after the last day of the payment period (as defined in section 1382(d)) for the taxable year of the organization or, if earlier, for the taxable year of each patron ending on or after the date on which the patron receives notice from the cooperative of the apportionment.

(iii) SPECIAL RULES FOR DECREASE IN CREDITS FOR TAXABLE YEAR.—If the amount of the credit of the organization determined under such subsection for a taxable year is less than the amount of such credit shown on the return of the organization for such year, an amount equal to the excess of—

(I) such reduction, over

(II) the amount not apportioned to such patrons under subparagraph (A) for the taxable year, shall be treated as an increase in tax imposed by this chapter on the organization. Such increase shall not be treated as tax imposed by this chapter for purposes of determining the amount of any credit under this chapter or for purposes of section 55.

[CCH Explanation at ¶705. Committee Reports at ¶10,290.]

Amendments

- 2005, Energy Tax Incentives Act of 2005 (H.R. 6)

H.R. 6, § 1345(c):

Amended Code Sec. 40A by redesignating subsection (e) as subsection (f) and by inserting after subsection (d) a new subsection (e). **Effective** for tax years ending after 8-8-2005.

⟫⟶ *Caution: Code Sec. 40A(f), below, as added by H.R. 6, applies with respect to fuel sold or used after December 31, 2005.*

(f) RENEWABLE DIESEL.—For purposes of this title—

(1) TREATMENT IN THE SAME MANNER AS BIODIESEL.—Except as provided in paragraph (2), renewable diesel shall be treated in the same manner as biodiesel.

(2) EXCEPTIONS.—

(A) RATE OF CREDIT.—Subsections (b)(1)(A) and (b)(2)(A) shall be applied with respect to renewable diesel by substituting "$1.00" for "50 cents".

(B) NONAPPLICATION OF CERTAIN CREDITS.—Subsections (b)(3) and (b)(5) shall not apply with respect to renewable diesel.

(3) RENEWABLE DIESEL DEFINED.—The term "renewable diesel" means diesel fuel derived from biomass (as defined in section 45K(c)(3)) using a thermal depolymerization process which meets—

(A) the registration requirements for fuels and fuel additives established by the Environmental Protection Agency under section 211 of the Clean Air Act (42 U.S.C. 7545), and

(B) the requirements of the American Society of Testing and Materials D975 or D396.

[CCH Explanation at ¶710 and ¶715. Committee Reports at ¶10,290 and ¶10,300.]

Amendments

• **2005, Energy Tax Incentives Act of 2005 (H.R. 6)**

H.R. 6, §1346(a):

Amended Code Sec. 40A, as amended by this Act, by redesignating subsection (f) as subsection (g) and by inserting after subsection (e) a new subsection (f). **Effective** with respect to fuel sold or used after 12-31-2005.

⟫⟶ *Caution: Former Code Sec. 40A(e) was redesignated as Code Sec. 40A(g), below, by H.R. 6, applicable with respect to fuel sold or used after December 31, 2005.*

(g) TERMINATION.—This section shall not apply to any sale or use after December 31, *2008*.

[CCH Explanation at ¶710 and ¶715. Committee Reports at ¶10,290 and ¶10,300.]

Amendments

• **2005, Energy Tax Incentives Act of 2005 (H.R. 6)**

H.R. 6, §1344(a):

Amended Code Sec. 40A(e) by striking "2006" and inserting "2008". **Effective** 8-8-2005.

H.R. 6, §1345(c):

Amended Code Sec. 40A by redesignating subsection (e) as subsection (f). **Effective** for tax years ending after 8-8-2005.

H.R. 6, §1346(a):

Amended Code Sec. 40A, as amended by this Act, by redesignating subsection (f) as subsection (g). **Effective** with respect to fuel sold or used after 12-31-2005.

[¶5055] CODE SEC. 41. CREDIT FOR INCREASING RESEARCH ACTIVITIES.

(a) GENERAL RULE.—For purposes of section 38, the research credit determined under this section for the taxable year shall be an amount equal to the sum of—

(1) 20 percent of the excess (if any) of—

(A) the qualified research expenses for the taxable year, over

(B) the base amount,

(2) 20 percent of the basic research payments determined under subsection (e)(1)(A) , *and*

(3) *20 percent of the amounts paid or incurred by the taxpayer in carrying on any trade or business of the taxpayer during the taxable year (including as contributions) to an energy research consortium.*

Law Added, Amended or Repealed

[CCH Explanation at ¶ 235. Committee Reports at ¶ 10,320.]

Amendments

• **2005, Energy Tax Incentives Act of 2005 (H.R. 6)**

H.R. 6, § 1351(a)(1):

Amended Code Sec. 41(a) by striking "and" at the end of paragraph (1), by striking the period at the end of paragraph (2) and inserting ", and", and by adding at the end a new paragraph (3). **Effective** for amounts paid or incurred after 8-8-2005, in tax years ending after such date.

(b) QUALIFIED RESEARCH EXPENSES.—For purposes of this section—

* * *

(3) CONTRACT RESEARCH EXPENSES.—

* * *

(C) AMOUNTS PAID TO CERTAIN RESEARCH CONSORTIA.—

* * *

(ii) QUALIFIED RESEARCH CONSORTIUM.—The term "qualified research consortium" means any organization *(other than an energy research consortium)* which—

(I) is described in section 501(c)(3) or 501(c)(6) and is exempt from tax under section 501(a),

(II) is organized and operated primarily to conduct scientific research, and

(III) is not a private foundation.

(D) AMOUNTS PAID TO ELIGIBLE SMALL BUSINESSES, UNIVERSITIES, AND FEDERAL LABORATORIES.—

(i) IN GENERAL.—In the case of amounts paid by the taxpayer to—

(I) an eligible small business,

(II) an institution of higher education (as defined in section 3304(f)), or

(III) an organization which is a Federal laboratory,

for qualified research which is energy research, subparagraph (A) shall be applied by substituting "100 percent" for "65 percent".

(ii) ELIGIBLE SMALL BUSINESS.—For purposes of this subparagraph, the term "eligible small business" means a small business with respect to which the taxpayer does not own (within the meaning of section 318) 50 percent or more of—

(I) in the case of a corporation, the outstanding stock of the corporation (either by vote or value), and

(II) in the case of a small business which is not a corporation, the capital and profits interests of the small business.

(iii) SMALL BUSINESS.—For purposes of this subparagraph—

(I) IN GENERAL.—The term "small business" means, with respect to any calendar year, any person if the annual average number of employees employed by such person during either of the 2 preceding calendar years was 500 or fewer. For purposes of the preceding sentence, a preceding calendar year may be taken into account only if the person was in existence throughout the year.

(II) STARTUPS, CONTROLLED GROUPS, AND PREDECESSORS.—Rules similar to the rules of subparagraphs (B) and (D) of section 220(c)(4) shall apply for purposes of this clause.

(iv) FEDERAL LABORATORY.—For purposes of this subparagraph, the term "Federal laboratory" has the meaning given such term by section 4(6) of the Stevenson-Wydler Technology Innovation Act of 1980 (15 U.S.C. 3703(6)), as in effect on the date of the enactment of the Energy Tax Incentives Act of 2005.

* * *

[CCH Explanation at ¶ 235. Committee Reports at ¶ 10,320.]

Amendments

• **2005, Energy Tax Incentives Act of 2005 (H.R. 6)**

H.R. 6, § 1351(a)(3):

Amended Code Sec. 41(b)(3)(C) by inserting "(other than an energy research consortium)" after "organization". **Effective** for amounts paid or incurred after 8-8-2005, in tax years ending after such date.

H.R. 6, § 1351(b):

Amended Code Sec. 41(b)(3) by adding at the end a new subparagraph (D). **Effective** for amounts paid or incurred after 8-8-2005, in tax years ending after such date.

(f) SPECIAL RULES.—For purposes of this section—

* * *

(6) ENERGY RESEARCH CONSORTIUM.—

(A) IN GENERAL.—The term "energy research consortium" means any organization—

(i) which is—

(I) described in section 501(c)(3) and is exempt from tax under section 501(a) and is organized and operated primarily to conduct energy research, or

(II) organized and operated primarily to conduct energy research in the public interest (within the meaning of section 501(c)(3)),

(ii) which is not a private foundation,

(iii) to which at least 5 unrelated persons paid or incurred during the calendar year in which the taxable year of the organization begins amounts (including as contributions) to such organization for energy research, and

(iv) to which no single person paid or incurred (including as contributions) during such calendar year an amount equal to more than 50 percent of the total amounts received by such organization during such calendar year for energy research.

(B) TREATMENT OF PERSONS.—All persons treated as a single employer under subsection (a) or (b) of section 52 shall be treated as related persons for purposes of subparagraph (A)(iii) and as a single person for purposes of subparagraph (A)(iv).

* * *

[CCH Explanation at ¶ 235. Committee Reports at ¶ 10,320.]

Amendments

• **2005, Energy Tax Incentives Act of 2005 (H.R. 6)**

H.R. 6, § 1351(a)(2):

Amended Code Sec. 41(f) by adding at the end a new paragraph (6). **Effective** for amounts paid or incurred after 8-8-2005, in tax years ending after such date.

[¶ 5060] CODE SEC. 43. ENHANCED OIL RECOVERY CREDIT.

* * *

(b) PHASE-OUT OF CREDIT AS CRUDE OIL PRICES INCREASE.—

* * *

⇛ *Caution: Code Sec. 43(b)(2), below, as amended by H.R. 6, applies to credits determined after December 31, 2005.*

(2) REFERENCE PRICE.—For purposes of this subsection, the term "reference price" means, with respect to any calendar year, the reference price determined for such calendar year under section 45K(d)(2)(C).

* * *

[CCH Explanation at ¶615. Committee Reports at ¶10,110.]

Amendments

- **2005, Energy Tax Incentives Act of 2005 (H.R. 6)**

H.R. 6, §1322(a)(3)(B):

Amended Code Sec. 43(b)(2) by striking "section 29(d)(2)(C)" and inserting "section 45K(d)(2)(C)". **Effective** for credits determined under the Internal Revenue Code of 1986 for tax years ending after 12-31-2005.

[¶5065] CODE SEC. 45. ELECTRICITY PRODUCED FROM CERTAIN RENEWABLE RESOURCES, etc. [sic]

* * *

(b) LIMITATIONS AND ADJUSTMENTS.—

* * *

(4) CREDIT RATE AND PERIOD FOR ELECTRICITY PRODUCED AND SOLD FROM CERTAIN FACILITIES.—

(A) CREDIT RATE.—In the case of electricity produced and sold in any calendar year after 2003 at any qualified facility described in paragraph (3), (5), (6), *(7), or (9)* of subsection (d), the amount in effect under subsection (a)(1) for such calendar year (determined before the application of the last sentence of paragraph (2) of this subsection) shall be reduced by one-half.

(B) CREDIT PERIOD.—

(i) IN GENERAL.—Except as provided in clause (ii) *or clause (iii)*, in the case of any facility described in paragraph (3), (4), (5), (6), or (7) of subsection (d), the 5-year period beginning on the date the facility was originally placed in service shall be substituted for the 10-year period in subsection (a)(2)(A)(ii).

(ii) CERTAIN OPEN-LOOP BIOMASS FACILITIES.—In the case of any facility described in subsection (d)(3)(A)(ii) placed in service before the date of the enactment of this paragraph, the 5-year period beginning on *January 1, 2005,* shall be substituted for the 10-year period in subsection (a)(2)(A)(ii).

(iii) TERMINATION.—Clause (i) shall not apply to any facility placed in service after the date of the enactment of this clause.

[CCH Explanation at ¶405, ¶410 and ¶415. Committee Reports at ¶10,010.]

Amendments

- **2005, Energy Tax Incentives Act of 2005 (H.R. 6)**

H.R. 6, §1301(b)(1)-(2):

Amended Code Sec. 45(b)(4)(B) by inserting "or clause (iii)" after "clause (ii)" in clause (i), and by adding at the end a new clause (iii). **Effective** 8-8-2005.

H.R. 6, §1301(c)(2):

Amended Code Sec. 45(b)(4)(A) by striking "or (7)" and inserting "(7), or (9)". **Effective** 8-8-2005.

H.R. 6, §1301(f)(1):

Amended Code Sec. 45(b)(4)(B)(ii) by striking "the date of the enactment of this Act" and inserting "January 1, 2005,". **Effective** as if included in the amendments made by section 710 of P.L. 108-357 [**effective** generally for electricity produced and sold after 12-31-2004, in tax years ending after such date.—CCH].

(c) RESOURCES.—For purposes of this section:

(1) IN GENERAL.—The term "qualified energy resources" means—

(A) wind,

(B) closed-loop biomass,

(C) open-loop biomass,

(D) geothermal energy,

(E) solar energy,

(F) small irrigation power,

(G) municipal solid waste, *and*

(H) *qualified hydropower production.*

(2) CLOSED-LOOP BIOMASS.—The term "closed-loop biomass" means any organic material from a plant which is planted exclusively for purposes of being used at a qualified facility to produce electricity.

(3) OPEN-LOOP BIOMASS.—

(A) IN GENERAL.—The term "open-loop biomass" means—

(i) any agricultural livestock waste nutrients, or

(ii) any solid, nonhazardous, cellulosic waste material *or any nonhazardous lignin waste material* which is segregated from other waste materials and which is derived from—

(I) any of the following forestrelated resources: mill and harvesting residues, precommercial thinnings, slash, and brush,

(II) solid wood waste materials, including waste pallets, crates, dunnage, manufacturing and construction wood wastes (other than pressure-treated, chemically-treated, or painted wood wastes), and landscape or right-of-way tree trimmings, but not including municipal solid waste, gas derived from the biodegradation of solid waste, or paper which is commonly recycled, or

(III) agriculture sources, including orchard tree crops, vineyard, grain, legumes, sugar, and other crop by-products or residues.

Such term shall not include closed-loop biomass or biomass burned in conjunction with fossil fuel (cofiring) beyond such fossil fuel required for startup and flame stabilization.

* * *

(8) QUALIFIED HYDROPOWER PRODUCTION.—

(A) IN GENERAL.—The term "qualified hydropower production" means—

(i) in the case of any hydroelectric dam which was placed in service on or before the date of the enactment of this paragraph, the incremental hydropower production for the taxable year, and

(ii) in the case of any nonhydroelectric dam described in subparagraph (C), the hydropower production from the facility for the taxable year.

(B) DETERMINATION OF INCREMENTAL HYDROPOWER PRODUCTION.—

(i) IN GENERAL.—For purposes of subparagraph (A), incremental hydropower production for any taxable year shall be equal to the percentage of average annual hydropower production at the facility attributable to the efficiency improvements or additions of capacity placed in service after the date of the enactment of this paragraph, determined by using the same water flow information used to determine an historic average annual hydropower production baseline for such facility. Such percentage and baseline shall be certified by the Federal Energy Regulatory Commission.

(ii) OPERATIONAL CHANGES DISREGARDED.—For purposes of clause (i), the determination of incremental hydropower production shall not be based on any operational changes at such facility not directly associated with the efficiency improvements or additions of capacity.

(C) NONHYDROELECTRIC DAM.—For purposes of subparagraph (A), a facility is described in this subparagraph if—

(i) the facility is licensed by the Federal Energy Regulatory Commission and meets all other applicable environmental, licensing, and regulatory requirements,

(ii) the facility was placed in service before the date of the enactment of this paragraph and did not produce hydroelectric power on the date of the enactment of this paragraph, and

(iii) turbines or other generating devices are to be added to the facility after such date to produce hydroelectric power, but only if there is not any enlargement of the diversion structure, or construction or enlargement of a bypass channel, or the impoundment or any withholding of any additional water from the natural stream channel.

(9) INDIAN COAL.—

(A) IN GENERAL.—The term "Indian coal" means coal which is produced from coal reserves which, on June 14, 2005—

(i) were owned by an Indian tribe, or

(ii) were held in trust by the United States for the benefit of an Indian tribe or its members.

(B) INDIAN TRIBE.—For purposes of this paragraph, the term "Indian tribe" has the meaning given such term by section 7871(c)(3)(E)(ii).

[CCH Explanation at ¶405, ¶410 and ¶415. Committee Reports at ¶10,010.]

Amendments

- **2005, Energy Tax Incentives Act of 2005 (H.R. 6)**

H.R. 6, §1301(c)(1):

Amended Code Sec. 45(c)(1) by striking "and" at the end of subparagraph (F), by striking the period at the end of subparagraph (G) and inserting ", and", and by adding at the end a new subparagraph (H). **Effective** 8-8-2005.

H.R. 6, §1301(c)(3):

Amended Code Sec. 45(c) by adding at the end a new paragraph (8). **Effective** 8-8-2005.

H.R. 6, §1301(d)(2):

Amended Code Sec. 45(c), as amended by this Act, by adding at the end a new paragraph (9). **Effective** 8-8-2005.

H.R. 6, §1301(d)(4):

Amended the heading for Code Sec. 45(c) by striking "QUALIFIED ENERGY RESOURCES AND REFINED COAL" and inserting "RESOURCES". **Effective** 8-8-2005.

H.R. 6, §1301(f)(2):

Amended Code Sec. 45(c)(3)(A)(ii) by inserting "or any nonhazardous lignin waste material" after "cellulosic waste material". **Effective** as if included in the amendments made by section 710 of P.L. 108-357 [**effective** generally for electricity produced and sold after 10-22-2004, in tax years ending after such date.—CCH].

(d) QUALIFIED FACILITIES.—For purposes of this section:

(1) WIND FACILITY.—In the case of a facility using wind to produce electricity, the term "qualified facility" means any facility owned by the taxpayer which is originally placed in service after December 31, 1993, and before *January 1, 2008*.

(2) CLOSED-LOOP BIOMASS FACILITY.—

(A) IN GENERAL.—In the case of a facility using closed-loop biomass to produce electricity, the term "qualified facility" means any facility—

(i) owned by the taxpayer which is originally placed in service after December 31, 1992, and before *January 1, 2008*, or

(ii) owned by the taxpayer which before *January 1, 2008*, is originally placed in service and modified to use closed-loop biomass to co-fire with coal, with other biomass, or with both, but only if the modification is approved under the Biomass Power for Rural Development Programs or is part of a pilot project of the Commodity Credit Corporation as described in 65 Fed. Reg. 63052.

* * *

(3) OPEN-LOOP BIOMASS FACILITIES.—

(A) IN GENERAL.—In the case of a facility using open-loop biomass to produce electricity, the term "qualified facility" means any facility owned by the taxpayer which—

(i) in the case of a facility using agricultural livestock waste nutrients—

(I) is originally placed in service after the date of the enactment of this subclause and before *January 1, 2008*, and

(II) the nameplate capacity rating of which is not less than 150 kilowatts, and

(ii) in the case of any other facility, is originally placed in service before *January 1, 2008*.

(B) CREDIT ELIGIBILITY.—In the case of any facility described in subparagraph (A), if the owner of such facility is not the producer of the electricity, the person eligible for the credit allowable under subsection (a) shall be the lessee or the operator of such facility.

(4) GEOTHERMAL OR SOLAR ENERGY FACILITY.—In the case of a facility using geothermal or solar energy to produce electricity, the term "qualified facility" means any facility owned by the taxpayer which is originally placed in service after the date of the enactment of this paragraph and before *January 1, 2008 (January 1, 2006, in the case of a facility using solar energy)*. Such term shall not include any property described in section 48(a)(3) the basis of which is taken into account by the taxpayer for purposes of determining the energy credit under section 48.

(5) SMALL IRRIGATION POWER FACILITY.—In the case of a facility using small irrigation power to produce electricity, the term "qualified facility" means any facility owned by the taxpayer which is originally placed in service after the date of the enactment of this paragraph and before *January 1, 2008*.

(6) LANDFILL GAS FACILITIES.—In the case of a facility producing electricity from gas derived from the biodegradation of municipal solid waste, the term "qualified facility" means any facility owned by the taxpayer which is originally placed in service after the date of the enactment of this paragraph and before *January 1, 2008*.

(7) TRASH COMBUSTION FACILITIES.—In the case of a facility which burns municipal solid waste to produce electricity, the term "qualified facility" means any facility owned by the taxpayer which is originally placed in service after the date of the enactment of this paragraph and before *January 1, 2008. Such term shall include a new unit placed in service in connection with a facility placed in service on or before the date of the enactment of this paragraph, but only to the extent of the increased amount of electricity produced at the facility by reason of such new unit*.

(8) REFINED COAL PRODUCTION FACILITY.—The term "refined coal production facility" means a facility which is placed in service after the date of the enactment of this paragraph and before January 1, 2009.

(9) QUALIFIED HYDROPOWER FACILITY.—*In the case of a facility producing qualified hydroelectric production described in subsection (c)(8), the term "qualified facility" means—*

(A) in the case of any facility producing incremental hydropower production, such facility but only to the extent of its incremental hydropower production attributable to efficiency improvements or additions to capacity described in subsection (c)(8)(B) placed in service after the date of the enactment of this paragraph and before January 1, 2008, and

(B) any other facility placed in service after the date of the enactment of this paragraph and before January 1, 2008.

(C) CREDIT PERIOD.—In the case of a qualified facility described in subparagraph (A), the 10-year period referred to in subsection (a) shall be treated as beginning on the date the efficiency improvements or additions to capacity are placed in service.

(10) INDIAN COAL PRODUCTION FACILITY.—The term "Indian coal production facility" means a facility which is placed in service before January 1, 2009.

[CCH Explanation at ¶405 and ¶410. Committee Reports at ¶10,010.]

Amendments

• 2005, Energy Tax Incentives Act of 2005 (H.R. 6)

H.R. 6, §1301(a)(1)-(2):

Amended Code Sec. 45(d) by striking "January 1, 2006" each place it appears in paragraphs (1), (2), (3), (5), (6), and (7) and inserting "January 1, 2008", and by striking "January 1, 2006" in paragraph (4) and inserting "January 1, 2008 (January 1, 2006, in the case of a facility using solar energy)". **Effective** 8-8-2005.

H.R. 6, §1301(c)(4):

Amended Code Sec. 45(d) by adding at the end a new paragraph (9). **Effective** 8-8-2005.

¶5065 Code Sec. 45(d)(3)(A)(ii)

Law Added, Amended or Repealed   **295**

H.R. 6, § 1301(d)(3):

Amended Code Sec. 45(d), as amended by this Act, by adding at the end a new paragraph (10). **Effective** 8-8-2005.

H.R. 6, § 1301(e):

Amended Code Sec. 45(d)(7) by adding at the end a new sentence. **Effective** as if included in the amendments made by section 710 of P.L. 108-357 [**effective** generally for electricity produced and sold after 10-22-2004, in tax years ending after such date.—CCH].

(e) DEFINITIONS AND SPECIAL RULES.—For purposes of this section—

* * *

(6) [*Stricken.*]

* * *

(8) REFINED COAL PRODUCTION FACILITIES.—

* * *

(C) APPLICATION OF RULES.—Rules similar to the rules of the subsection (b)(3) and paragraphs (1) through (5) of this subsection shall apply for purposes of determining the amount of any increase under this paragraph.

⟫⟶ *Caution: Code Sec. 45(e)(9), below, as amended by H.R. 6, §1301(f)(4)(A), but prior to amendment by H.R. 6, §1322(a)(3)(C)(i)-(ii), applies to credits determined under the Internal Revenue Code of 1986 for tax years ending on or before December 31, 2005.*

(9) COORDINATION WITH CREDIT FOR PRODUCING FUEL FROM A NONCONVENTIONAL SOURCE.—

(A) IN GENERAL.—The term "qualified facility" shall not include any facility which produces electricity from gas derived from the biodegradation of municipal solid waste if such biodegradation occurred in a facility (within the meaning of section 29) the production from which is allowed as a credit under section 29 for the taxable year or any prior taxable year.

(B) REFINED COAL FACILITIES.—The term "refined coal production facility" shall not include any facility the production from which is allowed as a credit under section 29 for the taxable year or any prior taxable year.

⟫⟶ *Caution: Code Sec. 45(e)(9), below, as amended by H.R. 6, §1301(f)(4)(A), and further amended by H.R. 6, §1322(a)(3)(C)(i)-(ii), applies to credits determined under the Internal Revenue Code of 1986 for tax years ending after December 31, 2005.*

(9) COORDINATION WITH CREDIT FOR PRODUCING FUEL FROM A NONCONVENTIONAL SOURCE.—

(A) IN GENERAL.—The term "qualified facility" shall not include any facility which produces electricity from gas derived from the biodegradation of municipal solid waste if such biodegradation occurred in a facility (within the meaning of section 45K) the production from which is allowed as a credit under section 45K for the taxable year or any prior taxable year.

(B) REFINED COAL FACILITIES.—The term "refined coal production facility" shall not include any facility the production from which is allowed as a credit under section 45K for the taxable year or any prior taxable year (or under section 29, as in effect on the day before the date of enactment of the Energy Tax Incentives Act of 2005, for any prior taxable year).

(10) INDIAN COAL PRODUCTION FACILITIES.—

(A) DETERMINATION OF CREDIT AMOUNT.—In the case of a producer of Indian coal, the credit determined under this section (without regard to this paragraph) for any taxable year shall be increased by an amount equal to the applicable dollar amount per ton of Indian coal—

(i) produced by the taxpayer at an Indian coal production facility during the 7-year period beginning on January 1, 2006, and

(ii) sold by the taxpayer—

(I) to an unrelated person, and

(II) during such 7-year period and such taxable year.

Code Sec. 45(e)(10)(A)(ii)(II)   ¶5065

(B) APPLICABLE DOLLAR AMOUNT.—

(i) IN GENERAL.—The term "applicable dollar amount" for any taxable year beginning in a calendar year means—

(I) $1.50 in the case of calendar years 2006 through 2009, and

(II) $2.00 in the case of calendar years beginning after 2009.

(ii) INFLATION ADJUSTMENT.—In the case of any calendar year after 2006, each of the dollar amounts under clause (i) shall be equal to the product of such dollar amount and the inflation adjustment factor determined under paragraph (2)(B) for the calendar year, except that such paragraph shall be applied by substituting "2005" for "1992".

(C) APPLICATION OF RULES.—Rules similar to the rules of the subsection (b)(3) and paragraphs (1), (3), (4), and (5) of this subsection shall apply for purposes of determining the amount of any increase under this paragraph.

(D) TREATMENT AS SPECIFIED CREDIT.—The increase in the credit determined under subsection (a) by reason of this paragraph with respect to any facility shall be treated as a specified credit for purposes of section 38(c)(4)(A) during the 4-year period beginning on the later of January 1, 2006, or the date on which such facility is placed in service by the taxpayer.

(11) ALLOCATION OF CREDIT TO PATRONS OF AGRICULTURAL COOPERATIVE.—

(A) ELECTION TO ALLOCATE.—

(i) IN GENERAL.—In the case of an eligible cooperative organization, any portion of the credit determined under subsection (a) for the taxable year may, at the election of the organization, be apportioned among patrons of the organization on the basis of the amount of business done by the patrons during the taxable year.

(ii) FORM AND EFFECT OF ELECTION.—An election under clause (i) for any taxable year shall be made on a timely filed return for such year. Such election, once made, shall be irrevocable for such taxable year. Such election shall not take effect unless the organization designates the apportionment as such in a written notice mailed to its patrons during the payment period described in section 1382(d).

(B) TREATMENT OF ORGANIZATIONS AND PATRONS.—The amount of the credit apportioned to any patrons under subparagraph (A)—

(i) shall not be included in the amount determined under subsection (a) with respect to the organization for the taxable year, and

(ii) shall be included in the amount determined under subsection (a) for the first taxable year of each patron ending on or after the last day of the payment period (as defined in section 1382(d)) for the taxable year of the organization or, if earlier, for the taxable year of each patron ending on or after the date on which the patron receives notice from the cooperative of the apportionment.

(C) SPECIAL RULES FOR DECREASE IN CREDITS FOR TAXABLE YEAR.—If the amount of the credit of a cooperative organization determined under subsection (a) for a taxable year is less than the amount of such credit shown on the return of the cooperative organization for such year, an amount equal to the excess of—

(i) such reduction, over

(ii) the amount not apportioned to such patrons under subparagraph (A) for the taxable year,

shall be treated as an increase in tax imposed by this chapter on the organization. Such increase shall not be treated as tax imposed by this chapter for purposes of determining the amount of any credit under this chapter.

(D) ELIGIBLE COOPERATIVE DEFINED.—For purposes of this section the term "eligible cooperative" means a cooperative organization described in section 1381(a) which is owned more than 50 percent

Law Added, Amended or Repealed

by agricultural producers or by entities owned by agricultural producers. For this purpose an entity owned by an agricultural producer is one that is more than 50 percent owned by agricultural producers.

[CCH Explanation at ¶ 405, ¶ 420, and ¶ 615. Committee Reports at ¶ 10,010 and ¶ 10,110.]

Amendments

• **2005, Energy Tax Incentives Act of 2005 (H.R. 6)**

H.R. 6, § 1301(d)(1):

Amended Code Sec. 45(e) by adding at the end a new paragraph (10). **Effective** 8-8-2005.

H.R. 6, § 1301(f)(3):

Amended Code Sec. 45(e) by striking paragraph (6). **Effective** as if included in the amendments made by section 710 of P.L. 108-357 [**effective** generally for electricity produced and sold after 10-22-2004, in tax years ending after such date.—CCH]. Prior to being stricken, Code Sec. 45(e)(6) read as follows:

(6) CREDIT ELIGIBILITY IN THE CASE OF GOVERNMENT-OWNED FACILITIES USING POULTRY WASTE.—In the case of a facility using poultry waste to produce electricity and owned by a governmental unit, the person eligible for the credit under subsection (a) is the lessee or the operator of such facility.

H.R. 6, § 1301(f)(4)(A):

Amended Code Sec. 45(e)(9). **Effective** as if included in the amendments made by section 710 of P.L. 108-357 [**effective** generally for electricity produced and sold after 10-22-2004, in tax years ending after such date.—CCH]. Prior to amendment, Code Sec. 45(e)(9) read as follows:

(9) COORDINATION WITH CREDIT FOR PRODUCING FUEL FROM A NONCONVENTIONAL SOURCE.—The term "qualified facility" shall not include any facility the production from which is allowed as a credit under section 29 for the taxable year or any prior taxable year.

H.R. 6, § 1301(f)(4)(B):

Amended Code Sec. 45(e)(8)(C) by striking "and (9)" after "through (5)". **Effective** as if included in the amendments made by section 710 of P.L. 108-357 [**effective** generally for electricity produced and sold after 10-22-2004, in tax years ending after such date.—CCH].

H.R. 6, § 1302(a):

Amended Code Sec. 45(c), as amended by this Act, by adding at the end a new paragraph (11). **Effective** for tax years of cooperative organizations ending after 8-8-2005.

H.R. 6, § 1322(a)(3)(C)(i)-(ii):

Amended Code Sec. 45(e)(9), as added [amended] by this Act, by striking "section 29" each place it appears and inserting "section 45K", and by inserting "(or under section 29, as in effect on the day before the date of enactment of the Energy Tax Incentives Act of 2005, for any prior taxable year)" before the period at the end thereof. **Effective** for credits determined under the Internal Revenue Code of 1986 for tax years ending after 12-31-2005.

[¶ 5070] CODE SEC. 45I. CREDIT FOR PRODUCING OIL AND GAS FROM MARGINAL WELLS.

* * *

(b) CREDIT AMOUNT.—For purposes of this section—

(1) IN GENERAL.—The credit amount is—

(A) $3 per barrel of qualified crude oil production, and

(B) 50 cents per 1,000 cubic feet of qualified natural gas production.

(2) REDUCTION AS OIL AND GAS PRICES INCREASE.—

* * *

(C) REFERENCE PRICE.—For purposes of this paragraph, the term "reference price" means, with respect to any calendar year—

⟫→ *Caution: Code Sec. 45I(b)(2)(C)(i), below, as amended by H.R. 6, applies to credits determined under the Internal Revenue Code of 1986 for tax years ending after December 31, 2005.*

(i) in the case of qualified crude oil production, the reference price determined under *section 45K(d)(2)(C)*, and

(ii) in the case of qualified natural gas production, the Secretary's estimate of the annual average wellhead price per 1,000 cubic feet for all domestic natural gas.

[CCH Explanation at ¶ 615. Committee Reports at ¶ 10,110.]

Amendments

• **2005, Energy Tax Incentives Act of 2005 (H.R. 6)**

H.R. 6, § 1322(a)(3)(B):

Amended Code Sec. 45I(b)(2)(C)(i) by striking "section 29(d)(2)(C)" and inserting "section 45K(d)(2)(C)". **Effective** for credits determined under the Internal Revenue Code of 1986 for tax years ending after 12-31-2005.

(c) QUALIFIED CRUDE OIL AND NATURAL GAS PRODUCTION.—For purposes of this section—

(1) IN GENERAL.—The terms "qualified crude oil production" and "qualified natural gas production" mean domestic crude oil or natural gas which is produced from a qualified marginal well.

(2) LIMITATION ON AMOUNT OF PRODUCTION WHICH MAY QUALIFY.—

➤➤➤ *Caution: Code Sec. 45I(c)(2)(A), below, as amended by H.R. 6, applies to credits determined under the Internal Revenue Code of 1986 for tax years ending after December 31, 2005.*

(A) IN GENERAL.—Crude oil or natural gas produced during any taxable year from any well shall not be treated as qualified crude oil production or qualified natural gas production to the extent production from the well during the taxable year exceeds 1,095 barrels or barrel-of-oil equivalents (as defined in *section 45K(d)(5)*).

* * *

[CCH Explanation at ¶ 615. Committee Reports at ¶ 10,110.]

Amendments

• **2005, Energy Tax Incentives Act of 2005 (H.R. 6)**

H.R. 6, § 1322(a)(3)(D)(i):

Amended Code Sec. 45I(c)(2)(A) by striking "section 29(d)(5)" and inserting "section 45K(d)(5))". **Effective** for credits determined under the Internal Revenue Code of 1986 for tax years ending after 12-31-2005.

(d) OTHER RULES.—

* * *

➤➤➤ *Caution: Code Sec. 45I(d)(3), below, as amended by H.R. 6, applies to credits determined under the Internal Revenue Code of 1986 for tax years ending after December 31, 2005.*

(3) PRODUCTION FROM NONCONVENTIONAL SOURCES EXCLUDED.—In the case of production from a qualified marginal well which is eligible for the credit allowed under *section 45K* for the taxable year, no credit shall be allowable under this section unless the taxpayer elects not to claim the credit under *section 45K* with respect to the well.

[CCH Explanation at ¶ 615. Committee Reports at ¶ 10,110.]

Amendments

• **2005, Energy Tax Incentives Act of 2005 (H.R. 6)**

H.R. 6, § 1322(a)(3)(D)(ii):

Amended Code Sec. 45I(d)(3) by striking "section 29" both places it appears and inserting "section 45K". **Effective** for credits determined under the Internal Revenue Code of 1986 for tax years ending after 12-31-2005.

[¶ 5075] CODE SEC. 45J. CREDIT FOR PRODUCTION FROM ADVANCED NUCLEAR POWER FACILITIES.

(a) GENERAL RULE.—For purposes of section 38, the advanced nuclear power facility production credit of any taxpayer for any taxable year is equal to the product of—

(1) 1.8 cents, multiplied by

(2) the kilowatt hours of electricity—

(A) produced by the taxpayer at an advanced nuclear power facility during the 8-year period beginning on the date the facility was originally placed in service, and

(B) sold by the taxpayer to an unrelated person during the taxable year.

(b) NATIONAL LIMITATION.—

(1) IN GENERAL.—The amount of credit which would (but for this subsection and subsection (c)) be allowed with respect to any facility for any taxable year shall not exceed the amount which bears the same ratio to such amount of credit as—

(A) the national megawatt capacity limitation allocated to the facility, bears to

(B) the total megawatt nameplate capacity of such facility.

(2) AMOUNT OF NATIONAL LIMITATION.—The national megawatt capacity limitation shall be 6,000 megawatts.

(3) ALLOCATION OF LIMITATION.—The Secretary shall allocate the national megawatt capacity limitation in such manner as the Secretary may prescribe.

(4) REGULATIONS.—Not later than 6 months after the date of the enactment of this section, the Secretary shall prescribe such regulations as may be necessary or appropriate to carry out the purposes of this subsection. Such regulations shall provide a certification process under which the Secretary, after consultation with the Secretary of Energy, shall approve and allocate the national megawatt capacity limitation.

(c) OTHER LIMITATIONS.—

(1) ANNUAL LIMITATION.—The amount of the credit allowable under subsection (a) (after the application of subsection (b)) for any taxable year with respect to any facility shall not exceed an amount which bears the same ratio to $125,000,000 as—

(A) the national megawatt capacity limitation allocated under subsection (b) to the facility, bears to

(B) 1,000.

(2) OTHER LIMITATIONS.—Rules similar to the rules of section 45(b)(1) shall apply for purposes of this section.

(d) ADVANCED NUCLEAR POWER FACILITY.—For purposes of this section—

(1) IN GENERAL.—The term "advanced nuclear power facility" means any advanced nuclear facility—

(A) which is owned by the taxpayer and which uses nuclear energy to produce electricity, and

(B) which is placed in service after the date of the enactment of this paragraph and before January 1, 2021.

(2) ADVANCED NUCLEAR FACILITY.—For purposes of paragraph (1), the term "advanced nuclear facility" means any nuclear facility the reactor design for which is approved after December 31, 1993, by the Nuclear Regulatory Commission (and such design or a substantially similar design of comparable capacity was not approved on or before such date).

(e) OTHER RULES TO APPLY.—Rules similar to the rules of paragraphs (1), (2), (3), (4), and (5) of section 45(e) shall apply for purposes of this section.

[CCH Explanation at ¶440. Committee Reports at ¶10,050.]

Amendments
• 2005, Energy Tax Incentives Act of 2005 (H.R. 6)

Effective for production in tax years beginning after 8-8-2005.

H.R. 6, §1306(a):

Amended subpart D of part IV of subchapter A of chapter 1 by adding after Code Sec. 45I a new Code Sec. 45J.

⟫⟶ *Caution: Former Code Sec. 29 was amended and redesignated as Code Sec. 45K, below, by H.R. 6, generally applicable to tax years ending after December 31, 2005.*

[¶5080] CODE SEC. 45K. CREDIT FOR PRODUCING FUEL FROM A NONCONVENTIONAL SOURCE.

(a) ALLOWANCE OF CREDIT.—For purposes of section 38, if the taxpayer elects to have this section apply, the nonconventional source production credit determined under this section for the taxable year is an amount equal to—

(1) $3, multiplied by

(2) the barrel-of-oil equivalent of qualified fuels—

(A) sold by the taxpayer to an unrelated person during the taxable year, and

(B) the production of which is attributable to the taxpayer.

[CCH Explanation at ¶615. Committee Reports at ¶10,110.]

Amendments

- **2005, Energy Tax Incentives Act of 2005 (H.R. 6)**

H.R. 6, §1322(a)(1):

Amended the Internal Revenue Code of 1986 by redesignating Code Sec. 29 as Code Sec. 45K and by moving Code Sec. 45K (as so redesignated) from subpart B of part IV of subchapter A of chapter 1 to the end of subpart D of part IV of subchapter A of chapter 1. **Effective** for credits determined under the Internal Revenue Code of 1986 for tax years ending after 12-31-2005.

H.R. 6, §1322(a)(3)(E):

Amended Code Sec. 45K(a), as redesignated by Act Sec. 1322(a)(1), by striking "There shall be allowed as a credit against the tax imposed by this chapter for the taxable year" and inserting "For purposes of section 38, if the taxpayer elects to have this section apply, the nonconventional source production credit determined under this section for the taxable year is". **Effective** for credits determined under the Internal Revenue Code of 1986 for tax years ending after 12-31-2005.

(b) LIMITATIONS AND ADJUSTMENTS.—

* * *

(6) [Stricken.]

[CCH Explanation at ¶615. Committee Reports at ¶10,110.]

Amendments

- **2005, Energy Tax Incentives Act of 2005 (H.R. 6)**

H.R. 6, §1322(a)(1):

Amended the Internal Revenue Code of 1986 by redesignating Code Sec. 29 as Code Sec. 45K and by moving Code Sec. 45K (as so redesignated) from subpart B of part IV of subchapter A of chapter 1 to the end of subpart D of part IV of subchapter A of chapter 1. **Effective** for credits determined under the Internal Revenue Code of 1986 for tax years ending after 12-31-2005.

H.R. 6, §1322(a)(3)(F):

Amended Code Sec. 45K(b), as redesignated by Act Sec. 1322(a)(1), by striking paragraph (6). **Effective** for credits determined under the Internal Revenue Code of 1986 for tax years ending after 12-31-2005. Prior to being stricken, Code Sec. 45K(b)(6) read as follows:

(6) APPLICATION WITH OTHER CREDITS.—The credit allowed by subsection (a) for any taxable year shall not exceed the excess (if any) of—

(A) the regular tax for the taxable year reduced by the sum of the credits allowable under subpart A and section 27, over

(B) the tentative minimum tax for the taxable year.

(c) DEFINITION OF QUALIFIED FUELS.—For purposes of this section—

* * *

(2) GAS FROM GEOPRESSURED BRINE, ETC.—

(A) IN GENERAL.—Except as provided in subparagraph (B), the determination of whether any gas is produced from geopressured brine, Devonian shale, coal seams, or a tight formation shall be made in accordance with section 503 of the Natural Gas Policy Act of 1978 (as in effect before the repeal of such section).

* * *

[CCH Explanation at ¶615. Committee Reports at ¶10,110.]

Amendments

- **2005, Energy Tax Incentives Act of 2005 (H.R. 6)**

H.R. 6, §1322(a)(1):

Amended the Internal Revenue Code of 1986 by redesignating Code Sec. 29 as Code Sec. 45K and by moving Code Sec. 45K (as so redesignated) from subpart B of part IV of subchapter A of chapter 1 to the end of subpart D of part IV of subchapter A of chapter 1. **Effective** for credits determined under the Internal Revenue Code of 1986 for tax years ending after 12-31-2005.

H.R. 6, §1322(b)(1)(A):

Amended Code Sec. 29(c)(2)(A), before redesignation as Code Sec. 45K by Act Sec. 1322(a), by inserting "(as in effect before the repeal of such section)" after "1978". **Effective** 8-8-2005.

(e) APPLICATION OF SECTION.—This section shall apply with respect to qualified fuels—

Law Added, Amended or Repealed

(1) which are—

(A) produced from a well drilled after December 31, 1979, and before January 1, 1993, or

(B) produced in a facility placed in service after December 31, 1979, and before January 1, 1993, and

(2) which are sold before January 1, 2003.

[CCH Explanation at ¶ 615. Committee Reports at ¶ 10,110.]

Amendments

- **2005, Energy Tax Incentives Act of 2005 (H.R. 6)**

H.R. 6, § 1322(b)(1)(B):

Amended Code Sec. 29(c)(2)(A) [Code Sec. 29], before redesignation as Code Sec. 45K by Act Sec. 1322(a) and as amended by Act Sec. 1321, by striking subsection (e) and redesignating subsections (f), (g), and (h) as subsections (e), (f), and (g), respectively. **Effective** 8-8-2005. Prior to being stricken, Code Sec. 29(e) read as follows:

(e) APPLICATION WITH THE NATURAL GAS POLICY ACT OF 1978.—

(1) NO CREDIT IF SECTION 107 OF THE NATURAL GAS POLICY ACT OF 1978 IS UTILIZED.—Subsection (a) shall apply with respect to any natural gas described in subsection (c)(1)(B)(i) which is sold during the taxable year only if such natural gas is sold at a lawful price which is determined without regard to the provisions of section 107 of the Natural Gas Policy Act of 1978 and subtitle B of title I of such Act.

(2) TREATMENT OF THIS SECTION.—For purposes of section 107(d) of the Natural Gas Policy Act of 1978, this section shall not be treated as allowing any credit, exemption, deduction, or comparable adjustment applicable to the computation of any Federal tax.

(f) EXTENSION FOR CERTAIN FACILITIES.—

(1) IN GENERAL.—In the case of a facility for producing qualified fuels described in subparagraph (B)(ii) or (C) of subsection (c)(1)—

(A) for purposes of *subsection (e)(1)(B)*, such facility shall be treated as being placed in service before January 1, 1993, if such facility is placed in service before July 1, 1998, pursuant to a binding written contract in effect before January 1, 1997, and

(B) if such facility is originally placed in service after December 31, 1992, paragraph (2) of *subsection (e)* shall be applied with respect to such facility by substituting "January 1, 2008" for "January 1, 2003".

(2) SPECIAL RULE.—Paragraph (1) shall not apply to any facility which produces coke or coke gas unless the original use of the facility commences with the taxpayer.

[CCH Explanation at ¶ 615. Committee Reports at ¶ 10,110.]

Amendments

- **2005, Energy Tax Incentives Act of 2005 (H.R. 6)**

H.R. 6, § 1322(a)(1):

Amended the Internal Revenue Code of 1986 by redesignating Code Sec. 29 as Code Sec. 45K and by moving Code Sec. 45K (as so redesignated) from subpart B of part IV of subchapter A of chapter 1 to the end of subpart D of part IV of subchapter A of chapter 1. **Effective** for credits determined under the Internal Revenue Code of 1986 for tax years ending after 12-31-2005.

H.R. 6, § 1322(b)(1)(B):

Amended Code Sec. 29(c)(2)(A) [Code Sec. 29], before redesignation as Code Sec. 45K by Act Sec. 1322(a) and as amended by Act Sec. 1321, by redesignating subsection (g) as subsection (f). **Effective** 8-8-2005.

H.R. 6, § 1322(b)(2)(A)-(B):

Amended Code Sec. 29(g)(1), before redesignation by Act Sec. 1322(a) and Act Sec. 1322(b)(1), by striking "subsection (f)(1)(B)" and inserting "subsection (e)(1)(B)" in subparagraph (A), and by striking "subsection (f)" and inserting "subsection (e)" in subparagraph (B). **Effective** 8-8-2005.

(g) EXTENSION FOR FACILITIES PRODUCING COKE OR COKE GAS.—Notwithstanding subsection (f)—

(1) IN GENERAL.—In the case of a facility for producing coke or coke gas which was placed in service before January 1, 1993, or after June 30, 1998, and before January 1, 2010, this section shall apply with respect to coke and coke gas produced in such facility and sold during the period—

(A) beginning on the later of January 1, 2006, or the date that such facility is placed in service, and

(B) ending on the date which is 4 years after the date such period began.

(2) SPECIAL RULES.—In determining the amount of credit allowable under this section solely by reason of this subsection—

(A) DAILY LIMIT.—The amount of qualified fuels sold during any taxable year which may be taken into account by reason of this subsection with respect to any facility shall not exceed an average barrel-of-oil equivalent of 4,000 barrels per day. Days before the date the facility is placed in service shall not be taken into account in determining such average.

(B) EXTENSION PERIOD TO COMMENCE WITH UNADJUSTED CREDIT AMOUNT.—For purposes of applying subsection (b)(2) to the $3 amount in subsection (a), in the case of fuels sold after 2005, subsection (d)(2)(B) shall be applied by substituting "2004" for "1979".

(C) DENIAL OF DOUBLE BENEFIT.—This subsection shall not apply to any facility producing qualified fuels for which a credit was allowed under this section for the taxable year or any preceding taxable year by reason of subsection (g).

[CCH Explanation at ¶615. Committee Reports at ¶10,110.]

Amendments

- **2005, Energy Tax Incentives Act of 2005 (H.R. 6)**

H.R. 6, §1321(a):

Amended Code Sec. 29 by adding at the end a new subsection (h). **Effective** for fuel produced and sold after 12-31-2005, in tax years ending after such date.

H.R. 6, §1322(a)(1):

Amended the Internal Revenue Code of 1986 by redesignating Code Sec. 29 as Code Sec. 45K and by moving Code Sec. 45K (as so redesignated) from subpart B of part IV of subchapter A of chapter 1 to the end of subpart D of part IV of subchapter A of chapter 1. **Effective** for credits determined under the Internal Revenue Code of 1986 for tax years ending after 12-31-2005.

H.R. 6, §1322(b)(1)(B):

Amended Code Sec. 29(c)(2)(A) [Code Sec. 29], before redesignation by Act Sec. 1322(a) and as amended by Act Sec. 1321, by redesignating subsection (h) as subsection (g). **Effective** 8-8-2005.

>>>→ **Caution:** Code Sec. 45L, below, as added by H.R. 6, applies to qualified new energy efficient homes acquired after December 31, 2005, in tax years ending after such date.

[¶5085] CODE SEC. 45L. NEW ENERGY EFFICIENT HOME CREDIT.

(a) ALLOWANCE OF CREDIT.—

(1) IN GENERAL.—For purposes of section 38, in the case of an eligible contractor, the new energy efficient home credit for the taxable year is the applicable amount for each qualified new energy efficient home which is—

(A) constructed by the eligible contractor, and

(B) acquired by a person from such eligible contractor for use as a residence during the taxable year.

(2) APPLICABLE AMOUNT.—For purposes of paragraph (1), the applicable amount is an amount equal to—

(A) in the case of a dwelling unit described in paragraph (1) or (2) of subsection (c), $2,000, and

(B) in the case of a dwelling unit described in paragraph (3) of subsection (c), $1,000.

(b) DEFINITIONS.—For purposes of this section—

(1) ELIGIBLE CONTRACTOR.—The term "eligible contractor" means—

(A) the person who constructed the qualified new energy efficient home, or

(B) in the case of a qualified new energy efficient home which is a manufactured home, the manufactured home producer of such home.

(2) QUALIFIED NEW ENERGY EFFICIENT HOME.—The term "qualified new energy efficient home" means a dwelling unit—

(A) located in the United States,

(B) the construction of which is substantially completed after the date of the enactment of this section, and

(C) which meets the energy saving requirements of subsection (c).

(3) CONSTRUCTION.—The term "construction" includes substantial reconstruction and rehabilitation.

(4) ACQUIRE.—The term "acquire" includes purchase.

(c) ENERGY SAVING REQUIREMENTS.—A dwelling unit meets the energy saving requirements of this subsection if such unit is—

(1) certified—

(A) to have a level of annual heating and cooling energy consumption which is at least 50 percent below the annual level of heating and cooling energy consumption of a comparable dwelling unit—

(i) which is constructed in accordance with the standards of chapter 4 of the 2003 International Energy Conservation Code, as such Code (including supplements) is in effect on the date of the enactment of this section, and

(ii) for which the heating and cooling equipment efficiencies correspond to the minimum allowed under the regulations established by the Department of Energy pursuant to the National Appliance Energy Conservation Act of 1987 and in effect at the time of completion of construction, and

(B) to have building envelope component improvements account for at least $1/5$ of such 50 percent,

(2) a manufactured home which conforms to Federal Manufactured Home Construction and Safety Standards (section 3280 of title 24, Code of Federal Regulations) and which meets the requirements of paragraph (1), or

(3) a manufactured home which conforms to Federal Manufactured Home Construction and Safety Standards (section 3280 of title 24, Code of Federal Regulations) and which—

(A) meets the requirements of paragraph (1) applied by substituting "30 percent" for "50 percent" both places it appears therein and by substituting "$1/3$" for "$1/5$" in subparagraph (B) thereof, or

(B) meets the requirements established by the Administrator of the Environmental Protection Agency under the Energy Star Labeled Homes program.

(d) CERTIFICATION.—

(1) METHOD OF CERTIFICATION.—A certification described in subsection (c) shall be made in accordance with guidance prescribed by the Secretary, after consultation with the Secretary of Energy. Such guidance shall specify procedures and methods for calculating energy and cost savings.

(2) FORM.—Any certification described in subsection (c) shall be made in writing in a manner which specifies in readily verifiable fashion the energy efficient building envelope components and energy efficient heating or cooling equipment installed and their respective rated energy efficiency performance.

(e) BASIS ADJUSTMENT.—For purposes of this subtitle, if a credit is allowed under this section in connection with any expenditure for any property, the increase in the basis of such property which would (but for this subsection) result from such expenditure shall be reduced by the amount of the credit so determined.

(f) COORDINATION WITH INVESTMENT CREDIT.—For purposes of this section, expenditures taken into account under section 47 or 48(a) shall not be taken into account under this section.

(g) TERMINATION.—This section shall not apply to any qualified new energy efficient home acquired after December 31, 2007.

[CCH Explanation at ¶ 220. Committee Reports at ¶ 10,200.]

Amendments

• **2005, Energy Tax Incentives Act of 2005 (H.R. 6)**

H.R. 6, § 1332(a):

Amended subpart D of part IV of subchapter A of chapter 1, as amended by this Act, by adding at the end a new Code Sec. 45L. **Effective** for qualified new energy efficient homes acquired after 12-31-2005, in tax years ending after such date.

⇛→ *Caution: Code Sec. 45M, below, as added by H.R. 6, applies to appliances produced after December 31, 2005.*

[¶ 5090]   CODE SEC. 45M. ENERGY EFFICIENT APPLIANCE CREDIT.

(a) GENERAL RULE.—

(1) IN GENERAL.—For purposes of section 38, the energy efficient appliance credit determined under this section for any taxable year is an amount equal to the sum of the credit amounts determined under paragraph (2) for each type of qualified energy efficient appliance produced by the taxpayer during the calendar year ending with or within the taxable year.

(2) CREDIT AMOUNTS.—The credit amount determined for any type of qualified energy efficient appliance is—

(A) the applicable amount determined under subsection (b) with respect to such type, multiplied by

(B) the eligible production for such type.

(b) APPLICABLE AMOUNT.—

(1) IN GENERAL.—For purposes of subsection (a)—

(A) DISHWASHERS.—The applicable amount is the energy savings amount in the case of a dishwasher which—

(i) is manufactured in calendar year 2006 or 2007, and

(ii) meets the requirements of the Energy Star program which are in effect for dishwashers in 2007.

(B) CLOTHES WASHERS.—The applicable amount is $100 in the case of a clothes washer which—

(i) is manufactured in calendar year 2006 or 2007, and

(ii) meets the requirements of the Energy Star program which are in effect for clothes washers in 2007.

(C) REFRIGERATORS.—

(i) 15 PERCENT SAVINGS.—The applicable amount is $75 in the case of a refrigerator which—

(I) is manufactured in calendar year 2006, and

(II) consumes at least 15 percent but not more than 20 percent less kilowatt hours per year than the 2001 energy conservation standards.

(ii) 20 PERCENT SAVINGS.—The applicable amount is $125 in the case of a refrigerator which—

(I) is manufactured in calendar year 2006 or 2007, and

(II) consumes at least 20 percent but not more than 25 percent less kilowatt hours per year than the 2001 energy conservation standards.

(iii) 25 PERCENT SAVINGS.—The applicable amount is $175 in the case of a refrigerator which—

(I) is manufactured in calendar year 2006 or 2007, and

(II) consumes at least 25 percent less kilowatt hours per year than the 2001 energy conservation standards.

(2) ENERGY SAVINGS AMOUNT.—For purposes of paragraph (1)(A)—

(A) IN GENERAL.—The energy savings amount is the lesser of—

(i) the product of—

(I) $3, and

(II) 100 multiplied by the energy savings percentage, or

(ii) $100.

(B) ENERGY SAVINGS PERCENTAGE.—For purposes of subparagraph (A), the energy savings percentage is the ratio of—

(i) the EF required by the Energy Star program for dishwashers in 2007 minus the EF required by the Energy Star program for dishwashers in 2005, to

(ii) the EF required by the Energy Star program for dishwashers in 2007.

(c) ELIGIBLE PRODUCTION.—

(1) IN GENERAL.—Except as provided in paragraphs [sic] (2), the eligible production in a calendar year with respect to each type of energy efficient appliance is the excess of—

(A) the number of appliances of such type which are produced by the taxpayer in the United States during such calendar year, over

(B) the average number of appliances of such type which were produced by the taxpayer (or any predecessor) in the United States during the preceding 3-calendar year period.

(2) SPECIAL RULE FOR REFRIGERATORS.—The eligible production in a calendar year with respect to each type of refrigerator described in subsection (b)(1)(C) is the excess of—

(A) the number of appliances of such type which are produced by the taxpayer in the United States during such calendar year, over

(B) 110 percent of the average number of appliances of such type which were produced by the taxpayer (or any predecessor) in the United States during the preceding 3-calendar year period.

(d) TYPES OF ENERGY EFFICIENT APPLIANCE.—For purposes of this section, the types of energy efficient appliances are—

(1) dishwashers described in subsection (b)(1)(A),

(2) clothes washers described in subsection (b)(1)(B),

(3) refrigerators described in subsection (b)(1)(C)(i),

(4) refrigerators described in subsection (b)(1)(C)(ii), and

(5) refrigerators described in subsection (b)(1)(C)(iii).

(e) LIMITATIONS.—

(1) AGGREGATE CREDIT AMOUNT ALLOWED.—The aggregate amount of credit allowed under subsection (a) with respect to a taxpayer for any taxable year shall not exceed $75,000,000 reduced by the amount of the credit allowed under subsection (a) to the taxpayer (or any predecessor) for all prior taxable years.

(2) AMOUNT ALLOWED FOR 15 PERCENT SAVINGS REFRIGERATORS.—In the case of refrigerators described in subsection (b)(1)(C)(i), the aggregate amount of the credit allowed under subsection (a) with respect to a taxpayer for any taxable year shall not exceed $20,000,000.

(3) LIMITATION BASED ON GROSS RECEIPTS.—The credit allowed under subsection (a) with respect to a taxpayer for the taxable year shall not exceed an amount equal to 2 percent of the average annual gross receipts of the taxpayer for the 3 taxable years preceding the taxable year in which the credit is determined.

(4) GROSS RECEIPTS.—For purposes of this subsection, the rules of paragraphs (2) and (3) of section 448(c) shall apply.

(f) DEFINITIONS.—For purposes of this section—

(1) QUALIFIED ENERGY EFFICIENT APPLIANCE.—The term "qualified energy efficient appliance" means—

　　(A) any dishwasher described in subsection (b)(1)(A),

　　(B) any clothes washer described in subsection (b)(1)(B), and

　　(C) any refrigerator described in subsection (b)(1)(C).

(2) DISHWASHER.—The term "dishwasher" means a residential dishwasher subject to the energy conservation standards established by the Department of Energy.

(3) CLOTHES WASHER.—The term "clothes washer" means a residential model clothes washer, including a residential style coin operated washer.

(4) REFRIGERATOR.—The term "refrigerator" means a residential model automatic defrost refrigerator-freezer which has an internal volume of at least 16.5 cubic feet.

(5) EF.—The term "EF" means the energy factor established by the Department of Energy for compliance with the Federal energy conservation standards.

(6) PRODUCED.—The term "produced" includes manufactured.

(7) 2001 ENERGY CONSERVATION STANDARD.—The term "2001 energy conservation standard" means the energy conservation standards promulgated by the Department of Energy and effective July 1, 2001.

(g) SPECIAL RULES.—For purposes of this section—

(1) IN GENERAL.—Rules similar to the rules of subsections (c), (d), and (e) of section 52 shall apply.

(2) CONTROLLED GROUP.—

　　(A) IN GENERAL.—All persons treated as a single employer under subsection (a) or (b) of section 52 or subsection (m) or (o) of section 414 shall be treated as a single producer.

　　(B) INCLUSION OF FOREIGN CORPORATIONS.—For purposes of subparagraph (A), in applying subsections (a) and (b) of section 52 to this section, section 1563 shall be applied without regard to subsection (b)(2)(C) thereof.

(3) VERIFICATION.—No amount shall be allowed as a credit under subsection (a) with respect to which the taxpayer has not submitted such information or certification as the Secretary, in consultation with the Secretary of Energy, determines necessary.

[CCH Explanation at ¶ 225. Committee Reports at ¶ 10,220.]

Amendments

• 2005, Energy Tax Incentives Act of 2005 (H.R. 6)

Sec. 45M. **Effective** for appliances produced after 12-31-2005.

H.R. 6, § 1334(a):

Amended Subpart D of part IV of subchapter A of chapter 1, as amended by this Act, by adding at the end a new Code

[¶ 5095] CODE SEC. 46. AMOUNT OF CREDIT.

For purposes of section 38, the amount of the investment credit determined under this section for any taxable year shall be the sum of—

　　(1) the rehabilitation credit,

　　(2) the energy credit [,]

　　(3) the qualifying advanced coal project credit, and

　　(4) the qualifying gasification project credit.

[CCH Explanation at ¶605. Committee Reports at ¶10,060.]

Amendments

• **2005, Energy Tax Incentives Act of 2005 (H.R. 6)**

H.R. 6, §1307(a):

Amended Code Sec. 46 by striking "and" at the end of paragraph (1), by striking the period at the end of paragraph (2), and by adding at the end new paragraphs (3) and (4). **Effective** for periods after 8-8-2005, under rules similar to the rules of Code Sec. 48(m) (as in effect on the day before the date of the enactment of P.L. 101-508 [11-4-90—CCH]).

[¶5100] CODE SEC. 48. ENERGY CREDIT.

(a) ENERGY CREDIT.—

⇒ *Caution: Code Sec. 48(a)(1), below, as amended by H.R. 6, applies generally to periods after December 31, 2005.*

(1) IN GENERAL.—For purposes of section 46, *except as provided in paragraph (1)(B) or (2)(B) of subsection (d),* the energy credit for any taxable year is the energy percentage of the basis of each energy property placed in service during such taxable year.

(2) ENERGY PERCENTAGE.—

⇒ *Caution: Code Sec. 48(a)(2)(A), below, as amended by H.R. 6, applies generally to periods after December 31, 2005.*

(A) IN GENERAL.—*The energy percentage is—*

(i) *30 percent in the case of—*

(I) *qualified fuel cell property,*

(II) *energy property described in paragraph (3)(A)(i) but only with respect to periods ending before January 1, 2008, and*

(III) *energy property described in paragraph (3)(A)(ii), and*

(ii) *in the case of any energy property to which clause (i) does not apply, 10 percent.*

(B) COORDINATION WITH REHABILITATION CREDIT.—The energy percentage shall not apply to that portion of the basis of any property which is attributable to qualified rehabilitation expenditures.

(3) ENERGY PROPERTY.—For purposes of this subpart, the term "energy property" means any property—

⇒ *Caution: Code Sec. 48(a)(3)(A), below, as amended by H.R. 6, applies generally to periods after December 31, 2005.*

(A) which is—

(i) equipment which uses solar energy to generate electricity, to heat or cool (or provide hot water for use in) a structure, or to provide solar process heat, *excepting property used to generate energy for the purposes of heating a swimming pool,*

(ii) *equipment which uses solar energy to illuminate the inside of a structure using fiber-optic distributed sunlight but only with respect to periods ending before January 1, 2008, or* [sic]

(iii) equipment used to produce, distribute, or use energy derived from a geothermal deposit (within the meaning of section 613(e)(2)), but only, in the case of electricity generated by geothermal power, up to (but not including) the electrical transmission stage, *or*

(iii)[(iv)] qualified fuel cell property or qualified microturbine property,

(B)(i) the construction, reconstruction, or erection of which is completed by the taxpayer, or

(ii) which is acquired by the taxpayer if the original use of such property commences with the taxpayer,

(C) with respect to which depreciation (or amortization in lieu of depreciation) is allowable, and

(D) which meets the performance and quality standards (if any) which—

(i) have been prescribed by the Secretary by regulations (after consultation with the Secretary of Energy), and

(ii) are in effect at the time of the acquisition of the property.

The term "energy property" shall not include any property which is public utility property (as defined in section 46(f)(5) as in effect on the day before the date of the enactment of the Revenue Reconciliation Act of 1990. Such term shall not include any property which is part of a facility the production from which is allowed as a credit under section 45 for the taxable year or any prior taxable year.

* * *

[CCH Explanation at ¶ 230 and ¶ 240. Committee Reports at ¶ 10,240 and ¶ 10,250.]

Amendments

- **2005, Energy Tax Incentives Act of 2005 (H.R. 6)**

H.R. 6, § 1336(a):

Amended Code Sec. 48(a)(3)(A) by striking "or" at the end of clause (i), by adding "or" at the end of clause (ii), and by inserting after clause (ii) a new clause (iii). **Effective** for periods after 12-31-2005, in tax years ending after such date, under rules similar to the rules of Code Sec. 48(m) (as in effect on the day before the date of the enactment of P.L. 101-508 [11-4-90.—CCH]).

H.R. 6, § 1336(c):

Amended Code Sec. 48(a)(2)(A). **Effective** for periods after 12-31-2005, in tax years ending after such date, under rules similar to the rules of Code Sec. 48(m) (as in effect on the day before the date of the enactment of P.L. 101-508 [11-4-90.—CCH]). Prior to amendment, Code Sec. 48(a)(2)(A) read as follows:

(A) IN GENERAL.—The energy percentage is 10 percent.

H.R. 6, § 1336(d):

Amended Code Sec. 48(a)(1) by inserting "except as provided in paragraph (1)(B) or (2)(B) of subsection (d)," before "the energy credit". **Effective** for periods after 12-31-2005, in tax years ending after such date, under rules similar to the rules of Code Sec. 48(m) (as in effect on the day before the date of the enactment of P.L. 101-508 [11-4-90.—CCH]).

H.R. 6, § 1337(a):

Amended Code Sec. 48(a)(2)(A), as amended by this Act. **Effective** for periods after 12-31-2005, in tax years ending after such date, under rules similar to the rules of Code Sec. 48(m) (as in effect on the day before the date of the enactment of P.L. 101-508 [11-4-90.—CCH]). Prior to amendment, Code Sec. 48(a)(2)(A) read as follows:

(A) IN GENERAL.—The energy percentage is—

(i) in the case of qualified fuel cell property, 30 percent, and

(ii) in the case of any other energy property, 10 percent.

H.R. 6, § 1337(b):

Amended Code Sec. 48(a)(3)(A) by striking "or" at the end of clause (i), by redesignating clause (ii) as clause (iii), and by inserting after clause (i) a new clause (ii). [Note: Act Sec. 1336(a) already struck "or" at the end of clause (i). Therefore, this amendment cannot be made. —CCH.] **Effective** for periods after 12-31-2005, in tax years ending after such date, under rules similar to the rules of Code Sec. 48(m) (as in effect on the day before the date of the enactment of P.L. 101-508 [11-4-90.—CCH]).

H.R. 6, § 1337(c):

Amended Code Sec. 48(a)(3)(A)(i) by inserting "excepting property used to generate energy for the purposes of heating a swimming pool," after "solar process heat,". **Effective** for periods after 12-31-2005, in tax years ending after such date, under rules similar to the rules of Code Sec. 48(m) (as in effect on the date before the date of the enactment of P.L. 101-508 [11-4-90.—CCH]).

⇒ *Caution: Code Sec. 48(c), below, as added by H.R. 6, applies generally to periods after December 31, 2005.*

(c) QUALIFIED FUEL CELL PROPERTY; QUALIFIED MICROTURBINE PROPERTY.—For purposes of this subsection—

(1) QUALIFIED FUEL CELL PROPERTY.—

(A) IN GENERAL.—The term "qualified fuel cell property" means a fuel cell power plant which—

(i) has a nameplate capacity of at least 0.5 kilowatt of electricity using an electrochemical process, and

(ii) has an electricity-only generation efficiency greater than 30 percent.

(B) LIMITATION.—In the case of qualified fuel cell property placed in service during the taxable year, the credit otherwise determined under paragraph (1) for such year with respect to such property shall not exceed an amount equal to $500 for each 0.5 kilowatt of capacity of such property.

(C) FUEL CELL POWER PLANT.—The term "fuel cell power plant" means an integrated system comprised of a fuel cell stack assembly and associated balance of plant components which converts a fuel into electricity using electrochemical means.

(D) SPECIAL RULE.—The first sentence of the matter in subsection (a)(3) which follows subparagraph (D) thereof shall not apply to qualified fuel cell property which is used predominantly in the trade or business of the furnishing or sale of telephone service, telegraph service by means of domestic telegraph operations, or other telegraph services (other than international telegraph services).

(E) TERMINATION.—The term "qualified fuel cell property" shall not include any property for any period after December 31, 2007.

(2) QUALIFIED MICROTURBINE PROPERTY.—

(A) IN GENERAL.—The term "qualified microturbine property" means a stationary microturbine power plant which—

(i) has a nameplate capacity of less than 2,000 kilowatts, and

(ii) has an electricity-only generation efficiency of not less than 26 percent at International Standard Organization conditions.

(B) LIMITATION.—In the case of qualified microturbine property placed in service during the taxable year, the credit otherwise determined under paragraph (1) for such year with respect to such property shall not exceed an amount equal $200 for each kilowatt of capacity of such property.

(C) STATIONARY MICROTURBINE POWER PLANT.—The term "stationary microturbine power plant" means an integrated system comprised of a gas turbine engine, a combustor, a recuperator or regenerator, a generator or alternator, and associated balance of plant components which converts a fuel into electricity and thermal energy. Such term also includes all secondary components located between the existing infrastructure for fuel delivery and the existing infrastructure for power distribution, including equipment and controls for meeting relevant power standards, such as voltage, frequency, and power factors.

(D) SPECIAL RULE.—The first sentence of the matter in subsection (a)(3) which follows subparagraph (D) thereof shall not apply to qualified microturbine property which is used predominantly in the trade or business of the furnishing or sale of telephone service, telegraph service by means of domestic telegraph operations, or other telegraph services (other than international telegraph services).

(E) TERMINATION.—The term "qualified microturbine property" shall not include any property for any period after December 31, 2007.

[CCH Explanation at ¶240. Committee Reports at ¶10,240.]

- **2005, Energy Tax Incentives Act of 2005 (H.R. 6)**

H.R. 6, §1336(b):

Amended Code Sec. 48 by adding at the end a new subsection (c). **Effective** for periods after 12–31–2005, in tax years ending after such date, under rules similar to the rules of Code Sec. 48(m) (as in effect on the day before the date of the enactment of P.L. 101-508 [11-4-90.—CCH]).

[¶5105] CODE SEC. 48A. QUALIFYING ADVANCED COAL PROJECT CREDIT.

(a) IN GENERAL.—For purposes of section 46, the qualifying advanced coal project credit for any taxable year is an amount equal to—

(1) 20 percent of the qualified investment for such taxable year in the case of projects described in subsection (d)(3)(B)(i), and

(2) 15 percent of the qualified investment for such taxable year in the case of projects described in subsection (d)(3)(B)(ii).

(b) QUALIFIED INVESTMENT.—

(1) IN GENERAL.—For purposes of subsection (a), the qualified investment for any taxable year is the basis of eligible property placed in service by the taxpayer during such taxable year which is part of a qualifying advanced coal project—

(A)(i) the construction, reconstruction, or erection of which is completed by the taxpayer, or

(ii) which is acquired by the taxpayer if the original use of such property commences with the taxpayer, and

(B) with respect to which depreciation (or amortization in lieu of depreciation) is allowable.

(2) SPECIAL RULE FOR CERTAIN SUBSIDIZED PROPERTY.—Rules similar to section 48(a)(4) shall apply for purposes of this section.

(3) CERTAIN QUALIFIED PROGRESS EXPENDITURES RULES MADE APPLICABLE.—Rules similar to the rules of subsections (c)(4) and (d) of section 46 (as in effect on the day before the enactment of the Revenue Reconciliation Act of 1990) shall apply for purposes of this section.

(c) DEFINITIONS.—For purposes of this section—

(1) QUALIFYING ADVANCED COAL PROJECT.—The term "qualifying advanced coal project" means a project which meets the requirements of subsection (e).

(2) ADVANCED COAL-BASED GENERATION TECHNOLOGY.—The term "advanced coal-based generation technology" means a technology which meets the requirements of subsection (f).

(3) ELIGIBLE PROPERTY.—The term "eligible property" means—

(A) in the case of any qualifying advanced coal project using an integrated gasification combined cycle, any property which is a part of such project and is necessary for the gasification of coal, including any coal handling and gas separation equipment, and

(B) in the case of any other qualifying advanced coal project, any property which is a part of such project.

(4) COAL.—The term "coal" means anthracite, bituminous coal, subbituminous coal, lignite, and peat.

(5) GREENHOUSE GAS CAPTURE CAPABILITY.—The term "greenhouse gas capture capability" means an integrated gasification combined cycle technology facility capable of adding components which can capture, separate on a long-term basis, isolate, remove, and sequester greenhouse gases which result from the generation of electricity.

(6) ELECTRIC GENERATION UNIT.—The term "electric generation unit" means any facility at least 50 percent of the total annual net output of which is electrical power, including an otherwise eligible facility which is used in an industrial application.

(7) INTEGRATED GASIFICATION COMBINED CYCLE.—The term "integrated gasification combined cycle" means an electric generation unit which produces electricity by converting coal to synthesis gas which is used to fuel a combined-cycle plant which produces electricity from both a combustion turbine (including a combustion turbine/fuel cell hybrid) and a steam turbine.

(d) QUALIFYING ADVANCED COAL PROJECT PROGRAM.—

(1) ESTABLISHMENT.—Not later than 180 days after the date of enactment of this section, the Secretary, in consultation with the Secretary of Energy, shall establish a qualifying advanced coal project program for the deployment of advanced coal-based generation technologies.

(2) CERTIFICATION.—

(A) APPLICATION PERIOD.—Each applicant for certification under this paragraph shall submit an application meeting the requirements of subparagraph (B). An applicant may only submit an application during the 3-year period beginning on the date the Secretary establishes the program under paragraph (1).

(B) REQUIREMENTS FOR APPLICATIONS FOR CERTIFICATION.—An application under subparagraph (A) shall contain such information as the Secretary may require in order to make a determination to accept or reject an application for certification as meeting the requirements under subsection (e)(1). Any information contained in the application shall be protected as provided in section 552(b)(4) of title 5, United States Code.

(C) TIME TO ACT UPON APPLICATIONS FOR CERTIFICATION.—The Secretary shall issue a determination as to whether an applicant has met the requirements under subsection (e)(1) within 60 days following the date of submittal of the application for certification.

(D) TIME TO MEET CRITERIA FOR CERTIFICATION.—Each applicant for certification shall have 2 years from the date of acceptance by the Secretary of the application during which to provide to the Secretary evidence that the criteria set forth in subsection (e)(2) have been met.

(E) PERIOD OF ISSUANCE.—An applicant which receives a certification shall have 5 years from the date of issuance of the certification in order to place the project in service and if such project is not placed in service by that time period then the certification shall no longer be valid.

(3) AGGREGATE CREDITS.—

(A) IN GENERAL.—The aggregate credits allowed under subsection (a) for projects certified by the Secretary under paragraph (2) may not exceed $1,300,000,000.

(B) PARTICULAR PROJECTS.—Of the dollar amount in subparagraph (A), the Secretary is authorized to certify—

(i) $800,000,000 for integrated gasification combined cycle projects, and

(ii) $500,000,000 for projects which use other advanced coal-based generation technologies.

(4) REVIEW AND REDISTRIBUTION.—

(A) REVIEW.—Not later than 6 years after the date of enactment of this section, the Secretary shall review the credits allocated under this section as of the date which is 6 years after the date of enactment of this section.

(B) REDISTRIBUTION.—The Secretary may reallocate credits available under clauses (i) and (ii) of paragraph (3)(B) if the Secretary determines that—

(i) there is an insufficient quantity of qualifying applications for certification pending at the time of the review, or

(ii) any certification made pursuant to subsection paragraph (2) has been revoked pursuant to subsection paragraph (2)(D) because the project subject to the certification has been delayed as a result of third party opposition or litigation to the proposed project.

(C) REALLOCATION.—If the Secretary determines that credits under clause (i) or (ii) of paragraph (3)(B) are available for reallocation pursuant to the requirements set forth in paragraph (2), the Secretary is authorized to conduct an additional program for applications for certification.

(e) QUALIFYING ADVANCED COAL PROJECTS.—

(1) REQUIREMENTS.—For purposes of subsection (c)(1), a project shall be considered a qualifying advanced coal project that the Secretary may certify under subsection (d)(2) if the Secretary determines that, at a minimum—

(A) the project uses an advanced coalbased generation technology—

(i) to power a new electric generation unit; or

(ii) to retrofit or repower an existing electric generation unit (including an existing natural gas-fired combined cycle unit);

(B) the fuel input for the project, when completed, is at least 75 percent coal;

(C) the project, consisting of one or more electric generation units at one site, will have a total nameplate generating capacity of at least 400 megawatts;

(D) the applicant provides evidence that a majority of the output of the project is reasonably expected to be acquired or utilized;

(E) the applicant provides evidence of ownership or control of a site of sufficient size to allow the proposed project to be constructed and to operate on a long-term basis; and

(F) the project will be located in the United States.

(2) REQUIREMENTS FOR CERTIFICATION.—For the purpose of subsection (d)(2)(D), a project shall be eligible for certification only if the Secretary determines that—

(A) the applicant for certification has received all Federal and State environmental authorizations or reviews necessary to commence construction of the project; and

(B) the applicant for certification, except in the case of a retrofit or repower of an existing electric generation unit, has purchased or entered into a binding contract for the purchase of the main steam turbine or turbines for the project, except that such contract may be contingent upon receipt of a certification under subsection (d)(2).

(3) PRIORITY FOR INTEGRATED GASIFICATION COMBINED CYCLE PROJECTS.—In determining which qualifying advanced coal projects to certify under subsection (d)(2), the Secretary shall—

(A) certify capacity, in accordance with the procedures set forth in subsection (d), in relatively equal amounts to—

(i) projects using bituminous coal as a primary feedstock,

(ii) projects using subbituminous coal as a primary feedstock, and

(iii) projects using lignite as a primary feedstock, and

(B) give high priority to projects which include, as determined by the Secretary—

(i) greenhouse gas capture capability,

(ii) increased by-product utilization, and

(iii) other benefits.

(f) ADVANCED COAL-BASED GENERATION TECHNOLOGY.—

(1) IN GENERAL.—For the purpose of this section, an electric generation unit uses advanced coal-based generation technology if—

(A) the unit—

(i) uses integrated gasification combined cycle technology, or

(ii) except as provided in paragraph (3), has a design net heat rate of 8530 Btu/kWh (40 percent efficiency), and

(B) the unit is designed to meet the performance requirements in the following table:

Performance characteristic:	Design level for project:
SO_2 (percent removal)	99 percent
NO_x (emissions)	0.07 lbs/MMBTU
PM* (emissions)	0.015 lbs/MMBTU
Hg (percent removal)	90 percent

(2) DESIGN NET HEAT RATE.—For purposes of this subsection, design net heat rate with respect to an electric generation unit shall—

(A) be measured in Btu per kilowatt hour (higher heating value),

(B) be based on the design annual heat input to the unit and the rated net electrical power, fuels, and chemicals output of the unit (determined without regard to the cogeneration of steam by the unit),

(C) be adjusted for the heat content of the design coal to be used by the unit—

Law Added, Amended or Repealed   313

(i) *if the heat content is less than 13,500 Btu per pound, but greater than 7,000 Btu per pound, according to the following formula: design net heat rate = unit net heat rate × [1-[((13,500-design coal heat content, Btu per pound)/1,000)* 0.013]], and*

(ii) *if the heat content is less than or equal to 7,000 Btu per pound, according to the following formula: design net heat rate = unit net heat rate × [1-[((13,500-design coal heat content, Btu per pound)/1,000)* 0.018]], and*

(D) *be corrected for the site reference conditions of—*

(i) *elevation above sea level of 500 feet,*

(ii) *air pressure of 14.4 pounds per square inch absolute,*

(iii) *temperature, dry bulb of 63°F,*

(iv) *temperature, wet bulb of 54°F, and*

(v) *relative humidity of 55 percent.*

(3) EXISTING UNITS.—*In the case of any electric generation unit in existence on the date of the enactment of this section, such unit uses advanced coal-based generation technology if, in lieu of the requirements under paragraph (1)(A)(ii), such unit achieves a minimum efficiency of 35 percent and an overall thermal design efficiency improvement, compared to the efficiency of the unit as operated, of not less than—*

(A) *7 percentage points for coal of more than 9,000 Btu,*

(B) *6 percentage points for coal of 7,000 to 9,000 Btu, or*

(C) *4 percentage points for coal of less than 7,000 Btu.*

(g) APPLICABILITY.—*No use of technology (or level of emission reduction solely by reason of the use of the technology), and no achievement of any emission reduction by the demonstration of any technology or performance level, by or at one or more facilities with respect to which a credit is allowed under this section, shall be considered to indicate that the technology or performance level is—*

(1) *adequately demonstrated for purposes of section 111 of the Clean Air Act (42 U.S. C. 7411);*

(2) *achievable for purposes of section 169 of that Act (42 U.S. C. 7479); or*

(3) *achievable in practice for purposes of section 171 of such Act (42 U.S.C. 7501).*

[CCH Explanation at ¶ 605. Committee Reports at ¶ 10,060.]

Amendments

• **2005, Energy Tax Incentives Act of 2005 (H.R. 6)**

H.R. 6, § 1307(b):

Amended subpart E of part IV of subchapter A of chapter 1 by inserting after Code Sec. 48 new Code Secs. 48A-48B.

Effective for periods after 8-8-2005, under rules similar to the rules of Code Sec. 48(m) (as in effect on the day before the date of enactment of P.L. 101-508 [11-4-90.—CCH].

[¶ 5110] CODE SEC. 48B. QUALIFYING GASIFICATION PROJECT CREDIT.

(a) IN GENERAL.—*For purposes of section 46, the qualifying gasification project credit for any taxable year is an amount equal to 20 percent of the qualified investment for such taxable year.*

(b) QUALIFIED INVESTMENT.—

(1) IN GENERAL.—*For purposes of subsection (a), the qualified investment for any taxable year is the basis of eligible property placed in service by the taxpayer during such taxable year which is part of a qualifying gasification project—*

(A)(i) *the construction, reconstruction, or erection of which is completed by the taxpayer, or*

(ii) *which is acquired by the taxpayer if the original use of such property commences with the taxpayer, and*

(B) *with respect to which depreciation (or amortization in lieu of depreciation) is allowable.*

(2) SPECIAL RULE FOR CERTAIN SUBSIDIZED PROPERTY.—*Rules similar to section 48(a)(4) shall apply for purposes of this section.*

(3) CERTAIN QUALIFIED PROGRESS EXPENDITURES RULES MADE APPLICABLE.—Rules similar to the rules of subsections (c)(4) and (d) of section 46 (as in effect on the day before the enactment of the Revenue Reconciliation Act of 1990) shall apply for purposes of this section.

(c) DEFINITIONS.—For purposes of this section—

(1) QUALIFYING GASIFICATION PROJECT.—The term "qualifying gasification project" means any project which—

(A) employs gasification technology,

(B) will be carried out by an eligible entity, and

(C) any portion of the qualified investment of which is certified under the qualifying gasification program as eligible for credit under this section in an amount (not to exceed $650,000,000) determined by the Secretary.

(2) GASIFICATION TECHNOLOGY.—The term "gasification technology" means any process which converts a solid or liquid product from coal, petroleum residue, biomass, or other materials which are recovered for their energy or feedstock value into a synthesis gas composed primarily of carbon monoxide and hydrogen for direct use or subsequent chemical or physical conversion.

(3) ELIGIBLE PROPERTY.—The term "eligible property" means any property which is a part of a qualifying gasification project and is necessary for the gasification technology of such project.

(4) BIOMASS.

(A) IN GENERAL.—The term "biomass" means any—

(i) agricultural or plant waste,

(ii) byproduct of wood or paper mill operations, including lignin in spent pulping liquors, and

(iii) other products of forestry maintenance.

(B) EXCLUSION.—The term "biomass" does not include paper which is commonly recycled.

(5) CARBON CAPTURE CAPABILITY.—The term "carbon capture capability" means a gasification plant design which is determined by the Secretary to reflect reasonable consideration for, and be capable of, accommodating the equipment likely to be necessary to capture carbon dioxide from the gaseous stream, for later use or sequestration, which would otherwise be emitted in the flue gas from a project which uses a nonrenewable fuel.

(6) COAL.—The term "coal" means anthracite, bituminous coal, subbituminous coal, lignite, and peat.

(7) ELIGIBLE ENTITY.—The term "eligible entity" means any person whose application for certification is principally intended for use in a domestic project which employs domestic gasification applications related to—

(A) chemicals,

(B) fertilizers,

(C) glass,

(D) steel,

(E) petroleum residues,

(F) forest products, and

(G) agriculture, including feedlots and dairy operations.

(8) PETROLEUM RESIDUE.—The term "petroleum residue" means the carbonized product of highboiling hydrocarbon fractions obtained in petroleum processing.

(d) Qualifying Gasification Project Program.—

(1) In general.—Not later than 180 days after the date of the enactment of this section, the Secretary, in consultation with the Secretary of Energy, shall establish a qualifying gasification project program to consider and award certifications for qualified investment eligible for credits under this section to qualifying gasification project sponsors under this section. The total amounts of credit that may be allocated under the program shall not exceed $350,000,000 under rules similar to the rules of section 48A(d)(4).

(2) Period of issuance.—A certificate of eligibility under paragraph (1) may be issued only during the 10-fiscal year period beginning on October 1, 2005.

(3) Selection criteria.—The Secretary shall not make a competitive certification award for qualified investment for credit eligibility under this section unless the recipient has documented to the satisfaction of the Secretary that—

(A) the award recipient is financially viable without the receipt of additional Federal funding associated with the proposed project,

(B) the recipient will provide sufficient information to the Secretary for the Secretary to ensure that the qualified investment is spent efficiently and effectively,

(C) a market exists for the products of the proposed project as evidenced by contracts or written statements of intent from potential customers,

(D) the fuels identified with respect to the gasification technology for such project will comprise at least 90 percent of the fuels required by the project for the production of chemical feedstocks, liquid transportation fuels, or coproduction of electricity,

(E) the award recipient's project team is competent in the construction and operation of the gasification technology proposed, with preference given to those recipients with experience which demonstrates successful and reliable operations of the technology on domestic fuels so identified, and

(F) the award recipient has met other criteria established and published by the Secretary.

(e) Denial of Double Benefit.—A credit shall not be allowed under this section for any qualified investment for which a credit is allowed under section 48A.

[CCH Explanation at ¶605. Committee Reports at ¶10,060.]

Amendments

• 2005, Energy Tax Incentives Act of 2005 (H.R. 6)

H.R. 6, §1307(b):

Amended subpart E of part IV of subchapter A of chapter 1 by inserting after Code Sec. 48 new Code Secs. 48A-48B.

Effective for periods after 8-8-2005, under rules similar to the rules of Code Sec. 48(m) (as in effect on the day before the date of enactment of P.L. 101-508 [11-4-90.—CCH]).

[¶5115] CODE SEC. 49. AT-RISK RULES.

(a) General Rule.—

(1) Certain nonrecourse financing excluded from credit base.—

* * *

(C) Credit base defined.—For purposes of this paragraph, the term "credit base" means—

(i) the portion of the basis of any qualified rehabilitated building attributable to qualified rehabilitation expenditures,

(ii) the basis of any energy property,

(iii) the basis of any property which is part of a qualifying advanced coal project under section 48A, and

(iv) the basis of any property which is part of a qualifying gasification project under section 48B.

* * *

[CCH Explanation at ¶605. Committee Reports at ¶10,060.]

Amendments

- **2005, Energy Tax Incentives Act of 2005 (H.R. 6)**

H.R. 6, §1307(c)(1):

Amended Code Sec. 49(a)(1)(C) by striking "and" at the end of clause (ii), by striking clause (iii), and by adding after clause (ii) new clauses (iii)-(iv). **Effective** for periods after 8-8-2005, under rules similar to the rules of Code Sec. 48(m) (as in effect on the day before the date of enactment of P.L. 101-508 [11-4-90.—CCH]). Prior to being stricken, Code Sec. 49(a)(1)(C)(iii) read as follows:

(iii) the amortizable basis of any qualified timber property.

[¶5120] CODE SEC. 53. CREDIT FOR PRIOR YEAR MINIMUM TAX LIABILITY.

* * *

(d) DEFINITIONS.—For purposes of this section—

(1) NET MINIMUM TAX.—

(A) IN GENERAL.—The term "net minimum tax" means the tax imposed by section 55.

(B) CREDIT NOT ALLOWED FOR EXCLUSION PREFERENCES.—

* * *

⇶→ *Caution: Code Sec. 53(d)(1)(B)(iii), below, as amended by H.R. 6, applies to credits determined under the Internal Revenue Code of 1986 for tax years ending after December 31, 2005.*

(iii) SPECIAL RULE.—The adjusted net minimum tax for the taxable year shall be increased by the amount of the credit not allowed under section 30 solely by reason of the application of section 30(b)(3)(B).

* * *

[CCH Explanation at ¶610 and ¶615. Committee Reports at ¶10,110.]

Amendments

- **2005, Energy Tax Incentives Act of 2005 (H.R. 6)**

H.R. 6, §1322(a)(3)(G):

Amended Code Sec. 53(d)(1)(B)(iii) by striking "under section 29" and all that follows through "or not allowed,". **Effective** for credits determined under the Internal Revenue Code of 1986 for tax years ending after 12-31-2005. Prior to amendment, Code Sec. 53(d)(1)(B)(iii) read as follows:

(iii) SPECIAL RULE.—The adjusted net minimum tax for the taxable year shall be increased by the amount of the credit not allowed under section 29 (relating to credit for producing fuel from a nonconventional source) solely by reason of the application of section 29(b)(6)(B) or not allowed under section 30 solely by reason of the application of section 30(b)(3)(B).

⇶→ *Caution: Code Sec. 54, below, as added by H.R. 6, applies to bonds issued after December 31, 2005.*

[¶5125] CODE SEC. 54. CREDIT TO HOLDERS OF CLEAN RENEWABLE ENERGY BONDS.

(a) ALLOWANCE OF CREDIT.—If a taxpayer holds a clean renewable energy bond on one or more credit allowance dates of the bond occurring during any taxable year, there shall be allowed as a credit against the tax imposed by this chapter for the taxable year an amount equal to the sum of the credits determined under subsection (b) with respect to such dates.

(b) AMOUNT OF CREDIT.—

(1) IN GENERAL.—The amount of the credit determined under this subsection with respect to any credit allowance date for a clean renewable energy bond is 25 percent of the annual credit determined with respect to such bond.

(2) ANNUAL CREDIT.—The annual credit determined with respect to any clean renewable energy bond is the product of—

(A) the credit rate determined by the Secretary under paragraph (3) for the day on which such bond was sold, multiplied by

(B) the outstanding face amount of the bond.

(3) DETERMINATION.—For purposes of paragraph (2), with respect to any clean renewable energy bond, the Secretary shall determine daily or cause to be determined daily a credit rate which shall apply to the first day on which there is a binding, written contract for the sale or exchange of the bond. The credit rate for any day is the credit rate which the Secretary or the Secretary's designee estimates will permit the issuance of clean renewable energy bonds with a specified maturity or redemption date without discount and without interest cost to the qualified issuer.

(4) CREDIT ALLOWANCE DATE.—For purposes of this section, the term "credit allowance date" means—

    (A) March 15,

    (B) June 15,

    (C) September 15, and

    (D) December 15.

Such term also includes the last day on which the bond is outstanding.

(5) SPECIAL RULE FOR ISSUANCE AND REDEMPTION.—In the case of a bond which is issued during the 3-month period ending on a credit allowance date, the amount of the credit determined under this subsection with respect to such credit allowance date shall be a ratable portion of the credit otherwise determined based on the portion of the 3-month period during which the bond is outstanding. A similar rule shall apply when the bond is redeemed or matures.

(c) LIMITATION BASED ON AMOUNT OF TAX.—The credit allowed under subsection (a) for any taxable year shall not exceed the excess of—

    (1) the sum of the regular tax liability (as defined in section 26(b)) plus the tax imposed by section 55, over

    (2) the sum of the credits allowable under this part (other than subpart C and this section).

(d) CLEAN RENEWABLE ENERGY BOND.—For purposes of this section—

    (1) IN GENERAL.—The term "clean renewable energy bond" means any bond issued as part of an issue if—

        (A) the bond is issued by a qualified issuer pursuant to an allocation by the Secretary to such issuer of a portion of the national clean renewable energy bond limitation under subsection (f)(2),

        (B) 95 percent or more of the proceeds of such issue are to be used for capital expenditures incurred by qualified borrowers for one or more qualified projects,

        (C) the qualified issuer designates such bond for purposes of this section and the bond is in registered form, and

        (D) the issue meets the requirements of subsection (h).

    (2) QUALIFIED PROJECT; SPECIAL USE RULES.—

        (A) IN GENERAL.—The term "qualified project" means any qualified facility (as determined under section 45(d) without regard to paragraph (10) and to any placed in service date) owned by a qualified borrower.

        (B) REFINANCING RULES.—For purposes of paragraph (1)(B), a qualified project may be refinanced with proceeds of a clean renewable energy bond only if the indebtedness being refinanced (including any obligation directly or indirectly refinanced by such indebtedness) was originally incurred by a qualified borrower after the date of the enactment of this section.

        (C) REIMBURSEMENT.—For purposes of paragraph (1)(B), a clean renewable energy bond may be issued to reimburse a qualified borrower for amounts paid after the date of the enactment of this section with respect to a qualified project, but only if—

            (i) prior to the payment of the original expenditure, the qualified borrower declared its intent to reimburse such expenditure with the proceeds of a clean renewable energy bond,

(ii) not later than 60 days after payment of the original expenditure, the qualified issuer adopts an official intent to reimburse the original expenditure with such proceeds, and

(iii) the reimbursement is made not later than 18 months after the date the original expenditure is paid.

(D) TREATMENT OF CHANGES IN USE.—For purposes of paragraph (1)(B), the proceeds of an issue shall not be treated as used for a qualified project to the extent that a qualified borrower or qualified issuer takes any action within its control which causes such proceeds not to be used for a qualified project. The Secretary shall prescribe regulations specifying remedial actions that may be taken (including conditions to taking such remedial actions) to prevent an action described in the preceding sentence from causing a bond to fail to be a clean renewable energy bond.

(e) MATURITY LIMITATIONS.—

(1) DURATION OF TERM.—A bond shall not be treated as a clean renewable energy bond if the maturity of such bond exceeds the maximum term determined by the Secretary under paragraph (2) with respect to such bond.

(2) MAXIMUM TERM.—During each calendar month, the Secretary shall determine the maximum term permitted under this paragraph for bonds issued during the following calendar month. Such maximum term shall be the term which the Secretary estimates will result in the present value of the obligation to repay the principal on the bond being equal to 50 percent of the face amount of such bond. Such present value shall be determined without regard to the requirements of subsection (l)(6) and using as a discount rate the average annual interest rate of tax-exempt obligations having a term of 10 years or more which are issued during the month. If the term as so determined is not a multiple of a whole year, such term shall be rounded to the next highest whole year.

(f) LIMITATION ON AMOUNT OF BONDS DESIGNATED.—

(1) NATIONAL LIMITATION.—There is a national clean renewable energy bond limitation of $800,000,000.

(2) ALLOCATION BY SECRETARY.—The Secretary shall allocate the amount described in paragraph (1) among qualified projects in such manner as the Secretary determines appropriate, except that the Secretary may not allocate more than $500,000,000 of the national clean renewable energy bond limitation to finance qualified projects of qualified borrowers which are governmental bodies.

(g) CREDIT INCLUDED IN GROSS INCOME.—Gross income includes the amount of the credit allowed to the taxpayer under this section (determined without regard to subsection (c)) and the amount so included shall be treated as interest income.

(h) SPECIAL RULES RELATING TO EXPENDITURES.—

(1) IN GENERAL.—An issue shall be treated as meeting the requirements of this subsection if, as of the date of issuance, the qualified issuer reasonably expects—

(A) at least 95 percent of the proceeds of such issue are to be spent for one or more qualified projects within the 5-year period beginning on the date of issuance of the clean energy bond,

(B) a binding commitment with a third party to spend at least 10 percent of the proceeds of such issue will be incurred within the 6-month period beginning on the date of issuance of the clean energy bond or, in the case of a clean energy bond the proceeds of which are to be loaned to two or more qualified borrowers, such binding commitment will be incurred within the 6-month period beginning on the date of the loan of such proceeds to a qualified borrower, and

(C) such projects will be completed with due diligence and the proceeds of such issue will be spent with due diligence.

(2) EXTENSION OF PERIOD.—Upon submission of a request prior to the expiration of the period described in paragraph (1)(A), the Secretary may extend such period if the qualified issuer establishes that the failure to satisfy the 5-year requirement is due to reasonable cause and the related projects will continue to proceed with due diligence.

(3) Failure to spend required amount of bond proceeds within 5 years.—To the extent that less than 95 percent of the proceeds of such issue are expended by the close of the 5-year period beginning on the date of issuance (or if an extension has been obtained under paragraph (2), by the close of the extended period), the qualified issuer shall redeem all of the nonqualified bonds within 90 days after the end of such period. For purposes of this paragraph, the amount of the nonqualified bonds required to be redeemed shall be determined in the same manner as under section 142.

(i) Special Rules Relating to Arbitrage.—A bond which is part of an issue shall not be treated as a clean renewable energy bond unless, with respect to the issue of which the bond is a part, the qualified issuer satisfies the arbitrage requirements of section 148 with respect to proceeds of the issue.

(j) Cooperative Electric Company; Qualified Energy Tax Credit Bond Lender; Governmental Body; Qualified Borrower.—For purposes of this section—

(1) Cooperative electric company.—The term "cooperative electric company" means a mutual or cooperative electric company described in section 501(c)(12) or section 1381(a)(2)(C), or a not-for-profit electric utility which has received a loan or loan guarantee under the Rural Electrification Act.

(2) Clean renewable energy bond lender.—The term "clean renewable energy bond lender" means a lender which is a cooperative which is owned by, or has outstanding loans to, 100 or more cooperative electric companies and is in existence on February 1, 2002, and shall include any affiliated entity which is controlled by such lender.

(3) Governmental body.—The term "governmental body" means any State, territory, possession of the United States, the District of Columbia, Indian tribal government, and any political subdivision thereof.

(4) Qualified issuer.—The term "qualified issuer" means—

(A) a clean renewable energy bond lender,

(B) a cooperative electric company, or

(C) a governmental body.

(5) Qualified borrower.—The term "qualified borrower" means—

(A) a mutual or cooperative electric company described in section 501(c)(12) or 1381(a)(2)(C), or

(B) a governmental body.

(k) Special Rules Relating to Pool Bonds.—No portion of a pooled financing bond may be allocable to any loan unless the borrower has entered into a written loan commitment for such portion prior to the issue date of such issue.

(l) Other Definitions and Special Rules.—For purposes of this section—

(1) Bond.—The term "bond" includes any obligation.

(2) Pooled financing bond.—The term "pooled financing bond" shall have the meaning given such term by section 149(f)(4)(A).

(3) Partnership; s corporation; and other pass-thru entities.—

(A) In general.—Under regulations prescribed by the Secretary, in the case of a partnership, trust, S corporation, or other pass-thru entity, rules similar to the rules of section 41(g) shall apply with respect to the credit allowable under subsection (a).

(B) No basis adjustment.—In the case of a bond held by a partnership or an S corporation, rules similar to the rules under section 1397E(i) shall apply.

(4) Bonds held by regulated investment companies.—If any clean renewable energy bond is held by a regulated investment company, the credit determined under subsection (a) shall be allowed to shareholders of such company under procedures prescribed by the Secretary.

(5) TREATMENT FOR ESTIMATED TAX PURPOSES.—Solely for purposes of sections 6654 and 6655, the credit allowed by this section (determined without regard to subsection (c)) to a taxpayer by reason of holding a clean renewable energy bond on a credit allowance date shall be treated as if it were a payment of estimated tax made by the taxpayer on such date.

(6) RATABLE PRINCIPAL AMORTIZATION REQUIRED.—A bond shall not be treated as a clean renewable energy bond unless it is part of an issue which provides for an equal amount of principal to be paid by the qualified issuer during each calendar year that the issue is outstanding.

(7) REPORTING.—Issuers of clean renewable energy bonds shall submit reports similar to the reports required under section 149(e).

(m) TERMINATION.—This section shall not apply with respect to any bond issued after December 31, 2007.

[CCH Explanation at ¶455. Committee Reports at ¶10,020.]

Amendments

- **2005, Energy Tax Incentives Act of 2005 (H.R. 6)**

H.R. 6, §1303(a):

Amended part IV of subchapter A of chapter 1 by adding at the end a new subpart H (Code Sec. 54). **Effective** for bonds issued after 12-31-2005.

[¶5130] CODE SEC. 55. ALTERNATIVE MINIMUM TAX IMPOSED.

* * *

(c) REGULAR TAX.—

(1) IN GENERAL.—For purposes of this section, the term "regular tax" means the regular tax liability for the taxable year (as defined in section 26(b)) reduced by the foreign tax credit allowable under section 27(a), the section 936 credit allowable under section 27(b), and the Puerto Rico economic activity credit under section 30A. Such term shall not include any increase in tax under section *45(e)(11)(C)*, 49(b) or 50(a) or subsection (j) or (k) of section 42.

* * *

⇒→ *Caution: Code Sec. 55(c)(3), below, as amended by H.R. 6, applies to credits determined under the Internal Revenue Code of 1986 for tax years ending after December 31, 2005.*

(3) CROSS REFERENCES.—

For provisions providing that certain credits are not allowable against the tax imposed by this section, see sections 26(a), 30(b)(3), and 38(c).

* * *

[CCH Explanation at ¶305, ¶420, ¶615 and ¶730. Committee Reports at ¶10,010, ¶10,110, ¶10,260, and ¶10,270.]

Amendments

- **2005, Energy Tax Incentives Act of 2005 (H.R. 6)**

H.R. 6, §1302(b):

Amended the last sentence of Code Sec. 55(c)(1), by inserting "45(e)(11)(C)," after "section" [and before "49(b)"]. **Effective** for tax years of cooperative organizations ending after 8-8-2005.

H.R. 6, §1322(a)(3)(H):

Amended Code Sec. 55(c)(3) by striking "29(b)(6)," following "sections 26(a),". **Effective** for credits determined under the Internal Revenue Code of 1986 for tax years ending after 12-31-2005.

H.R. 6, §1341(b)(3):

Amended Code Sec. 55(c)(2), as amended by this Act, by inserting "30B(g)(2)," after "30(b)(2),". [Note: The amendment to Code Sec. 55(c)(2) does not contain the text "30(b)(2)". Therefore this amendment cannot be made.—CCH.] **Effective** for property placed in service after 12-31-2005, in tax years ending after such date.

H.R. 6, §1342(b)(3):

Amended Code Sec. 55(c)(2), as amended by this Act, by inserting "30C(d)(2)," after "30B(g)(2),". [Note: The amendment to Code Sec. 55(c)(2) by Act Sec. 1341(b)(3) could not be made. Consequently, Code Sec. 55(c)(2) does not contain the text "30B(g)(2)," to be amended by Act Sec. 1342(b)(3).—CCH] **Effective** for property placed in service after 12-31-2005, in tax years ending after such date.

[¶ 5135] CODE SEC. 56. ADJUSTMENTS IN COMPUTING ALTERNATIVE MINIMUM TAXABLE INCOME.

(a) ADJUSTMENTS APPLICABLE TO ALL TAXPAYERS.—In determining the amount of the alternative minimum taxable income for any taxable year the following treatment shall apply (in lieu of the treatment applicable for purposes of computing the regular tax):

(1) DEPRECIATION.—

* * *

(B) EXCEPTION FOR CERTAIN PROPERTY.—This paragraph shall not apply to property described in paragraph (1), (2), (3), or (4) of section 168(f), *or in section 168(e)(3)(C)(iv)*.

* * *

[CCH Explanation at ¶ 520. Committee Reports at ¶ 10,150.]

Amendments

• **2005, Energy Tax Incentives Act of 2005 (H.R. 6)**

H.R. 6, § 1326(d):

Amended Code Sec. 56(a)(1)(B) by inserting ", or in section 168(e)(3)(C)(iv)" before the period. **Effective** for property placed in service after 4-11-2005. For an exception, see Act Sec. 1326(e)(2), below.

H.R. 6, § 1326(e)(2), provides:

(2) EXCEPTION.—The amendments made by this section shall not apply to any property with respect to which the taxpayer or a related party has entered into a binding contract for the construction thereof on or before April 11, 2005, or, in the case of self-constructed property, has started construction on or before such date.

[¶ 5140] CODE SEC. 141. PRIVATE ACTIVITY BOND; QUALIFIED BOND.

* * *

(c) PRIVATE LOAN FINANCING TEST.—

* * *

(2) EXCEPTION FOR TAX ASSESSMENT, ETC., LOANS.—For purposes of paragraph (1), a loan is described in this paragraph if such loan—

(A) enables the borrower to finance any governmental tax or assessment of general application for a specific essential governmental function,

(B) is a nonpurpose investment (within the meaning of section 148(f)(6)(A)) *, or*

(C) is a qualified natural gas supply contract (as defined in section 148(b)(4)).

[CCH Explanation at ¶ 530. Committee Reports at ¶ 10,160.]

Amendments

• **2005, Energy Tax Incentives Act of 2005 (H.R. 6)**

H.R. 6, § 1327(b):

Amended Code Sec. 141(c)(2) by striking "or" at the end of subparagraph (A), by striking the period at the end of subparagraph (B) and inserting ", or", and by adding at the end a new subparagraph (C). **Effective** for obligations issued after 8-8-2005.

(d) CERTAIN ISSUES USED TO ACQUIRE NONGOVERNMENTAL OUTPUT PROPERTY TREATED AS PRIVATE ACTIVITY BONDS.—

* * *

(7) EXCEPTION FOR QUALIFIED ELECTRIC AND NATURAL GAS SUPPLY CONTRACTS.—The term "nongovernmental output property" shall not include any contract for the prepayment of electricity or natural gas which is not investment property under section 148(b)(2).

* * *

[CCH Explanation at ¶ 530. Committee Reports at ¶ 10,160.]

Amendments

- **2005, Energy Tax Incentives Act of 2005 (H.R. 6)**

H.R. 6, §1327(c):

Amended Code Sec. 141(d) by adding at the end a new paragraph (7). **Effective** for obligations issued after 8-8-2005.

[¶ 5145] CODE SEC. 142. EXEMPT FACILITY BOND.

(a) GENERAL RULE.—For purposes of this part, the term "exempt facility bond" means any bond issued as part of an issue 95 percent or more of the net proceeds of which are to be used to provide—

(1) airports,

(2) docks and wharves,

(3) mass commuting facilities,

(4) facilities for the furnishing of water,

(5) sewage facilities,

(6) solid waste disposal facilities,

(7) qualified residential rental projects,

(8) facilities for the local furnishing of electric energy or gas,

(9) local district heating or cooling facilities,

(10) qualified hazardous waste facilities,

(11) high-speed intercity rail facilities,

(12) environmental enhancements of hydroelectric generating facilities,

(13) qualified public educational facilities,

(14) qualified green building and sustainable design projects *, or*

(15) *qualified highway or surface freight transfer facilities.*

* * *

[CCH Explanation at ¶ 915. Committee Reports at ¶ 15,170.]

Amendments

- **2005, Safe, Accountable, Flexible, Efficient Transportation Equity Act: A Legacy for Users (H.R. 3)**

H.R. 3, §11143(a):

Amended Code Sec. 142(a) by striking "or" at the end of paragraph (13), by striking the period at the end of paragraph (14) and inserting ", or", and by adding at the end a new paragraph (15). **Effective** for bonds issued after 8-10-2005.

(m) QUALIFIED HIGHWAY OR SURFACE FREIGHT TRANSFER FACILITIES.—

(1) IN GENERAL.—For purposes of subsection (a)(15), the term "qualified highway or surface freight transfer facilities" means—

(A) any surface transportation project which receives Federal assistance under title 23, United States Code (as in effect on the date of the enactment of this subsection)

(B) any project for an international bridge or tunnel for which an international entity authorized under Federal or State law is responsible and which receives Federal assistance under title 23, United States Code (as so in effect), or

(C) any facility for the transfer of freight from truck to rail or rail to truck (including any temporary storage facilities directly related to such transfers) which receives Federal assistance under either title 23 or title 49, United States Code (as so in effect).

(2) NATIONAL LIMITATION ON AMOUNT OF TAX-EXEMPT FINANCING FOR FACILITIES.—

(A) NATIONAL LIMITATION.—The aggregate amount allocated by the Secretary of Transportation under subparagraph (C) shall not exceed $15,000,000,000.

(B) ENFORCEMENT OF NATIONAL LIMITATION.—An issue shall not be treated as an issue described in subsection (a)(15) if the aggregate face amount of bonds issued pursuant to such issue for any qualified highway or surface freight transfer facility (when added to the aggregate face amount of bonds previously so issued for such facility) exceeds the amount allocated to such facility under subparagraph (C).

(C) ALLOCATION BY SECRETARY OF TRANSPORTATION.—The Secretary of Transportation shall allocate the amount described in subparagraph (A) among qualified highway or surface freight transfer facilities in such manner as the Secretary determines appropriate.

(3) EXPENDITURE OF PROCEEDS.—An issue shall not be treated as an issue described in subsection (a)(15) unless at least 95 percent of the net proceeds of the issue is expended for qualified highway or surface freight transfer facilities within the 5-year period beginning on the date of issuance. If at least 95 percent of such net proceeds is not expended within such 5-year period, an issue shall be treated as continuing to meet the requirements of this paragraph if the issuer uses all unspent proceeds of the issue to redeem bonds of the issue within 90 days after the end of such 5-year period. The Secretary, at the request of the issuer, may extend such 5-year period if the issuer establishes that any failure to meet such period is due to circumstances beyond the control of the issuer.

(4) EXCEPTION FOR CURRENT REFUNDING BONDS.—Paragraph (2) shall not apply to any bond (or series of bonds) issued to refund a bond issued under subsection (a)(15) if—

(A) the average maturity date of the issue of which the refunding bond is a part is not later than the average maturity date of the bonds to be refunded by such issue,

(B) the amount of the refunding bond does not exceed the outstanding amount of the refunded bond, and

(C) the refunded bond is redeemed not later than 90 days after the date of the issuance of the refunding bond.

For purposes of subparagraph (A), average maturity shall be determined in accordance with section 147(b)(2)(A).

[CCH Explanation at ¶915. Committee Reports at ¶15,170.]

Amendments
- **2005, Safe, Accountable, Flexible, Efficient Transportation Equity Act: A Legacy for Users (H.R. 3)**

H.R. 3, §11143(b):

Amended Code Sec. 142 by adding at the end a new subsection (m). **Effective** for bonds issued after 8-10-2005.

[¶5150] CODE SEC. 146. VOLUME CAP.

* * *

(g) EXCEPTION FOR CERTAIN BONDS.—Only for purposes of this section, the term "private activity bond" shall not include—

* * *

(3) any exempt facility bond issued as part of an issue described in paragraph (1), (2), (12), (13), (14), or (15) of section 142(a), and

* * *

[CCH Explanation at ¶915. Committee Reports at ¶15,170.]

Amendments

- **2005, Safe, Accountable, Flexible, Efficient Transportation Equity Act: A Legacy for Users (H.R. 3)**

H.R. 3, §11143(c):

Amended Code Sec. 146(g)(3) by striking "or 14" and all that follows through the end of the paragraph and inserting "(14), or (15) or section 142(a), and". **Effective** for bonds issued after 8-10-2005. Prior to amendment, Code Sec. 146(g)(3) read as follows:

(3) any exempt facility bond issued as part of an issue described in paragraph (1), (2), (12), (13), or (14) of section 142(a) (relating to airports, docks and wharves, environmental enhancements of hydroelectric generating facilities, qualified public educational facilities, and qualified green building and sustainable design projects), and

[¶5155] CODE SEC. 148. ARBITRAGE.

* * *

(b) HIGHER YIELDING INVESTMENTS.—For purposes of this section—

* * *

(4) SAFE HARBOR FOR PREPAID NATURAL GAS.—

(A) IN GENERAL.—The term "investment-type property" does not include a prepayment under a qualified natural gas supply contract.

(B) QUALIFIED NATURAL GAS SUPPLY CONTRACT.—For purposes of this paragraph, the term "qualified natural gas supply contract" means any contract to acquire natural gas for resale by a utility owned by a governmental unit if the amount of gas permitted to be acquired under the contract by the utility during any year does not exceed the sum of—

(i) the annual average amount during the testing period of natural gas purchased (other than for resale) by customers of such utility who are located within the service area of such utility, and

(ii) the amount of natural gas to be used to transport the prepaid natural gas to the utility during such year.

(C) NATURAL GAS USED TO GENERATE ELECTRICITY.—Natural gas used to generate electricity shall be taken into account in determining the average under subparagraph (B)(i)—

(i) only if the electricity is generated by a utility owned by a governmental unit, and

(ii) only to the extent that the electricity is sold (other than for resale) to customers of such utility who are located within the service area of such utility.

(D) ADJUSTMENTS FOR CHANGES IN CUSTOMER BASE.—

(i) NEW BUSINESS CUSTOMERS.—If—

(I) after the close of the testing period and before the date of issuance of the issue, the utility owned by a governmental unit enters into a contract to supply natural gas (other than for resale) for a business use at a property within the service area of such utility, and

(II) the utility did not supply natural gas to such property during the testing period or the ratable amount of natural gas to be supplied under the contract is significantly greater than the ratable amount of gas supplied to such property during the testing period,

then a contract shall not fail to be treated as a qualified natural gas supply contract by reason of supplying the additional natural gas under the contract referred to in subclause (I).

(ii) LOST CUSTOMERS.—The average under subparagraph (B)(i) shall not exceed the annual amount of natural gas reasonably expected to be purchased (other than for resale) by persons who are located within the service area of such utility and who, as of the date of issuance of the issue, are customers of such utility.

(E) RULING REQUESTS.—The Secretary may increase the average under subparagraph (B)(i) for any period if the utility owned by the governmental unit establishes to the satisfaction of the Secretary that, based on objective evidence of growth in natural gas consumption or population, such average would otherwise be insufficient for such period.

(F) ADJUSTMENT FOR NATURAL GAS OTHERWISE ON HAND.—

(i) IN GENERAL.—The amount otherwise permitted to be acquired under the contract for any period shall be reduced by—

(I) the applicable share of natural gas held by the utility on the date of issuance of the issue, and

(II) the natural gas (not taken into account under subclause (I)) which the utility has a right to acquire during such period (determined as of the date of issuance of the issue).

(ii) APPLICABLE SHARE.—For purposes of the clause (i), the term "applicable share" means, with respect to any period, the natural gas allocable to such period if the gas were allocated ratably over the period to which the prepayment relates.

(G) INTENTIONAL ACTS.—Subparagraph (A) shall cease to apply to any issue if the utility owned by the governmental unit engages in any intentional act to render the volume of natural gas acquired by such prepayment to be in excess of the sum of—

(i) the amount of natural gas needed (other than for resale) by customers of such utility who are located within the service area of such utility, and

(ii) the amount of natural gas used to transport such natural gas to the utility.

(H) TESTING PERIOD.—For purposes of this paragraph, the term "testing period" means, with respect to an issue, the most recent 5 calendar years ending before the date of issuance of the issue.

(I) SERVICE AREA.—For purposes of this paragraph, the service area of a utility owned by a governmental unit shall be comprised of—

(i) any area throughout which such utility provided at all times during the testing period—

(I) in the case of a natural gas utility, natural gas transmission or distribution services, and

(II) in the case of an electric utility, electricity distribution services,

(ii) any area within a county contiguous to the area described in clause (i) in which retail customers of such utility are located if such area is not also served by another utility providing natural gas or electricity services, as the case may be, and

(iii) any area recognized as the service area of such utility under State or Federal law.

* * *

[CCH Explanation at ¶530. Committee Reports at ¶10,160.]
Amendments
• **2005, Energy Tax Incentives Act of 2005 (H.R. 6)**
H.R. 6, § 1327(a):

Amended Code Sec. 148(b) by adding at the end a new paragraph (4). **Effective** for obligations issued after 8-8-2005.

[¶5160] CODE SEC. 167. DEPRECIATION.

* * *

(h) AMORTIZATION OF GEOLOGICAL AND GEOPHYSICAL EXPENDITURES.—

(1) IN GENERAL.—Any geological and geophysical expenses paid or incurred in connection with the exploration for, or development of, oil or gas within the United States (as defined in section 638) shall be allowed as a deduction ratably over the 24-month period beginning on the date that such expense was paid or incurred.

(2) HALF-YEAR CONVENTION.—For purposes of paragraph (1), any payment paid or incurred during the taxable year shall be treated as paid or incurred on the mid-point of such taxable year.

(3) EXCLUSIVE METHOD.—Except as provided in this subsection, no depreciation or amortization deduction shall be allowed with respect to such payments.

(4) TREATMENT UPON ABANDONMENT.—If any property with respect to which geological and geophysical expenses are paid or incurred is retired or abandoned during the 24-month period described in paragraph (1), no deduction shall be allowed on account of such retirement or abandonment and the amortization deduction under this subsection shall continue with respect to such payment.

[CCH Explanation at ¶525. Committee Reports at ¶10,180.]
Amendments
- **2005, Energy Tax Incentives Act of 2005 (H.R. 6)**

H.R. 6, §1329(a):

Amended Code Sec. 167 by redesignating subsection (h) as subsection (i) and by inserting after subsection (g) a new subsection (h). **Effective** for amounts paid or incurred in tax years beginning after 8-8-2005.

(i) CROSS REFERENCES.—

(1) For additional rule applicable to depreciation of improvements in the case of mines, oil and gas wells, other natural deposits, and timber, see section 611.

(2) For amortization of goodwill and certain other intangibles, see section 197.

[CCH Explanation at ¶525. Committee Reports at ¶10,180.]
Amendments
- **2005, Energy Tax Incentives Act of 2005 (H.R. 6)**

H.R. 6, §1329(a):

Amended Code Sec. 167 by redesignating subsection (h) as subsection (i). **Effective** for amounts paid or incurred in tax years beginning after 8-8-2005.

[¶5165] CODE SEC. 168. ACCELERATED COST RECOVERY SYSTEM.

* * *

(e) CLASSIFICATION OF PROPERTY.—For purposes of this section—

* * *

(3) CLASSIFICATION OF CERTAIN PROPERTY.—

* * *

(B) 5-YEAR PROPERTY.—The term "5-year property" includes—

(i) any automobile or light general purpose truck,

(ii) any semi-conductor manufacturing equipment,

(iii) any computer-based telephone central office switching equipment,

(iv) any qualified technological equipment,

(v) any section 1245 property used in connection with research and experimentation, and

(vi) any property which—

(I) is described in subparagraph (A) of section 48(a)(3) (or would be so described if "solar and wind" were substituted for "solar" in clause (i) thereof and the last sentence of such section did not apply to such subparagraph),

* * *

(C) 7-YEAR PROPERTY.—The term "7-year property" includes—

(i) any railroad track,

(ii) any motorsports entertainment complex,

(iii) any Alaska natural gas pipeline,

(iv) *any natural gas gathering line the original use of which commences with the taxpayer after April 11, 2005, and*

(v) any property which—

(I) does not have a class life, and

(II) is not otherwise classified under paragraph (2) or this paragraph.

* * *

(E) 15-YEAR PROPERTY.—The term "15-year property" includes—

(i) any municipal wastewater treatment plant,

(ii) any telephone distribution plant and comparable equipment used for 2-way exchange of voice and data communications,

(iii) any section 1250 property which is a retail motor fuels outlet (whether or not food or other convenience items are sold at the outlet),

(iv) any qualified leasehold improvement property placed in service before January 1, 2006,

(v) any qualified restaurant property placed in service before January 1, 2006,

(vi) initial clearing and grading land improvements with respect to gas utility property,

(vii) any section 1245 property (as defined in section 1245(a)(3)) used in the transmission at 69 or more kilovolts of electricity for sale and the original use of which commences with the taxpayer after April 11, 2005, and

(viii) any natural gas distribution line the original use of which commences with the taxpayer after April 11, 2005, and which is placed in service before January 1, 2011.

* * *

[CCH Explanation at ¶405, ¶425, ¶515 and ¶520. Committee Reports at ¶10,010, ¶10,070, ¶10,140 and ¶10,150.]

Amendments

- **2005, Energy Tax Incentives Act of 2005 (H.R. 6)**

H.R. 6, §1301(f)(5):

Amended Code Sec. 168(e)(3)(B)(vi)(I). **Effective** as if included in the amendments made by section 710 of P.L. 108-357 ([**effective** generally for electricity produced and sold after 10-22-2004, in tax years ending after such date.—CCH.]). Prior to amendment, Code Sec. 168(e)(3)(B)(vi)(I) read as follows:

(I) is described in subparagraph (A) of section 48(a)(3) (or would be so described if "solar and wind" were substituted for "solar" in clause (i) thereof,

H.R. 6, §1308(a):

Amended Code Sec. 168(e)(3)(E) by striking "and" at the end of clause (v), by striking the period at the end of clause (vi) and inserting ", and", and by adding at the end a new clause (vii). **Effective** generally for property placed in service after 4-11-2005. For an exception, see Act Sec. 1308(c)(2), below.

H.R. 6, §1308(c)(2), provides:

(2) EXCEPTION.—The amendments made by this section shall not apply to any property with respect to which the taxpayer or a related party has entered into a binding contract for the construction thereof on or before April 11, 2005, or, in the case of self-constructed property, has started construction on or before such date.

H.R. 6, §1325(a):

Amended Code Sec. 168(e)(3)(E), as amended by Act Sec. 1308(a), by striking "and" at the end of clause (vi), by striking the period at the end of clause (vii) and inserting ", and", and by adding at the end a new clause (viii). **Effective** generally for property placed in service after 4-11-2005. For an exception, see Act Sec. 1325(c)(2), below.

H.R. 6, §1325(c)(2), provides:

(2) EXCEPTION—The amendments made by this section shall not apply to any property with respect to which the taxpayer or a related party has entered into a binding contract for the construction thereof on or before April 11, 2005, or, in the case of self-constructed property, has started construction on or before such date.

H.R. 6, §1326(a):

Amended Code Sec. 168(e)(3)(C) by striking "and" at the end of clause (iii), by redesignating clause (iv) as clause (v), and by inserting after clause (iii) a new clause (iv). **Effective** generally for property placed in service after 4-11-2005. For an exception, see Act Sec. 1326(e)(2), below.

H.R. 6, §1362(e)(2), provides:

(2) EXCEPTION—The amendments made by this section shall not apply to any property with respect to which the taxpayer or a related party has entered into a binding contract for the construction thereof on or before April 11, 2005, or, in the case of self-constructed property, has started construction on or before such date.

(g) Alternative Depreciation System for Certain Property.—

* * *

(3) Special rules for determining class life.—

* * *

(B) Special rule for certain property assigned to classes.—For purposes of paragraph (2), in the case of property described in any of the following subparagraphs of subsection (e)(3), the class life shall be determined as follows:

If property is described in subparagraph:	The class life is:
(A)(iii)	4
(B)(ii)	5
(B)(iii)	9.5
(C)(i)	10
(C)(iii)	22
(C)(iv)	*14*
(D)(i)	15
(D)(ii)	20
(E)(i)	24
(E)(ii)	24
(E)(iii)	20
(E)(iv)	39
(E)(v)	39
(E)(vi)	20
(E)(vii)	*30*
(E)(viii)	*35*
(F)	25

* * *

[CCH Explanation at ¶425 and ¶515 and ¶520. Committee Reports at ¶10,070, ¶10,140 and ¶10,150.]

Amendments

• 2005, Energy Tax Incentives Act of 2005 (H.R. 6)

H.R. 6, §1308(b):

Amended the table contained in Code Sec. 168(g)(3)(B) by inserting after the item relating to subparagraph (E)(vi) a new item relating to subparagraph (E)(vii). **Effective** generally for property placed in service after 4-11-2005. For an exception, see Act Sec. 1308(c)(2), below.

H.R. 6, §1308(c)(2), provides:

(2) Exception—The amendments made by this section shall not apply to any property with respect to which the taxpayer or a related party has entered into a binding contract for the construction thereof on or before April 11, 2005, or, in the case of self-constructed property, has started construction on or before such date.

H.R. 6, §1325(b):

Amended the table contained in Code Sec. 168(g)(3)(B), as amended by this Act, by inserting after the item relating to subparagraph (E)(vii) a new item relating to subparagraph (E)(viii). **Effective** generally for property placed in service after 4-11-2005. For an exception, see Act Sec. 1325(c)(2), below.

H.R. 6, §1325(c)(2), provides:

(2) Exception—The amendments made by this section shall not apply to any property with respect to which the taxpayer or a related party has entered into a binding contract for the construction thereof on or before April 11, 2005, or, in the case of self-constructed property, has started construction on or before such date.

H.R. 6, §1326(c):

Amended the table contained in Code Sec. 168(g)(3)(B), as amended by this Act, by inserting after the item relating to subparagraph (C)(iii) a new item relating to subparagraph (C)(iv). **Effective** generally for property placed in service after 4-11-2005. For an exception, see Act Sec. 1326(e)(2), below.

H.R. 6, §1326(e)(2), provides:

(2) Exception—The amendments made by this section shall not apply to any property with respect to which the taxpayer or a related party has entered into a binding contract for the construction thereof on or before April 11, 2005, or, in the case of self-constructed property, has started construction on or before such date.

(i) DEFINITIONS AND SPECIAL RULES.—For purposes of this section—

* * *

(17) NATURAL GAS GATHERING LINE.—The term "natural gas gathering line" means—

(A) the pipe, equipment, and appurtenances determined to be a gathering line by the Federal Energy Regulatory Commission, and

(B) the pipe, equipment, and appurtenances used to deliver natural gas from the wellhead or a commonpoint to the point at which such gas first reaches—

(i) a gas processing plant,

(ii) an interconnection with a transmission pipeline for which a certificate as an interstate transmission pipeline has been issued by the Federal Energy Regulatory Commission,

(iii) an interconnection with an intrastate transmission pipeline, or

(iv) a direct interconnection with a local distribution company, a gas storage facility, or an industrial consumer.

[CCH Explanation at ¶ 520. Committee Reports at ¶ 10,150.]

Amendments

- **2005, Energy Tax Incentives Act of 2005 (H.R. 6)**

H.R. 6, § 1326(b):

Amended Code Sec. 168(i) by inserting after paragraph (16) a new paragraph (17). **Effective** generally for property placed in service after 4-11-2005. For an exception, see Act Sec. 1326(e)(2), below.

H.R. 6, § 1326(e)(2), provides:

(2) EXCEPTION—The amendments made by this section shall not apply to any property with respect to which the taxpayer or a related party has entered into a binding contract for the construction thereof on or before April 11, 2005, or, in the case of self-constructed property, has started construction on or before such date.

[¶ 5170] CODE SEC. 169. AMORTIZATION OF POLLUTION CONTROL FACILITIES.

* * *

(d) DEFINITIONS *AND SPECIAL RULES.*—For purposes of this section—

* * *

(3) FEDERAL CERTIFYING AUTHORITY.—The term "Federal certifying authority" means, in the case of water pollution, the Secretary of the Interior and, in the case of air pollution, the Secretary of *Health and Human Services.*

(4) NEW IDENTIFIABLE TREATMENT FACILITY.—

(A) IN GENERAL.—For purposes of paragraph (1), the term "new identifiable treatment facility" includes only tangible property (not including a building and its structural components, other than a building which is exclusively a treatment facility) which is of a character subject to the allowance for depreciation provided in section 167, which is identifiable as a treatment facility, and which is property—

(i) the construction, reconstruction, or erection of which is completed by the taxpayer after December 31, 1968, or

(ii) acquired after December 31, 1968, if the original use of the property commences with the taxpayer and commences after such date.

In applying this section in the case of property described in clause (i) there shall be taken into account only that portion of the basis which is properly attributable to construction, reconstruction, or erection after December 31, 1968.

(B) CERTAIN FACILITIES PLACED IN OPERATION AFTER APRIL *11, 2005.—In the case of any facility described in paragraph (1) solely by reason of paragraph (5), subparagraph (A) shall be applied by substituting "April 11, 2005" for "December 31, 1968" each place it appears therein.*

(5) SPECIAL RULE RELATING TO CERTAIN ATMOSPHERIC POLLUTION CONTROL FACILITIES.—*In the case of any atmospheric pollution control facility which is placed in service after April 11, 2005, and used in connection with an electric generation plant or other property which is primarily coal fired—*

(A) paragraph (1) shall be applied without regard to the phrase "in operation before January 1, 1976", and

(B) this section shall be applied by substituting "84" for "60" each place it appears in subsections (a) and (b).

* * *

[CCH Explanation at ¶620. Committee Reports at ¶10,080.]

Amendments

- **2005, Energy Tax Incentives Act of 2005 (H.R. 6)**

H.R. 6, §1309(a):

Amended Code Sec. 169(d) by adding at the end a new paragraph (5). **Effective** for facilities placed in service after 4-11-2005.

H.R. 6, §1309(b):

Amended Code Sec. 169(d)(4)(B). **Effective** for facilities placed in service after 4-11-2005. Prior to amendment, Code Sec. 169(d)(4)(B) read as follows:

(B) CERTAIN PLANTS, ETC., PLACED IN OPERATION AFTER 1968.—In the case of any treatment facility used in connection with any plant or other property not in operation before January 1, 1969, the preceding sentence shall be applied by substituting December 31, 1975, for December 31, 1968.

H.R. 6, §1309(c):

Amended the heading for Code Sec. 169(d) by inserting "AND SPECIAL RULES" after "DEFINITIONS". **Effective** for facilities placed in service after 4-11-2005.

H.R. 6, §1309(d):

Amended Code Sec. 169(d)(3) by striking "Health, Education, and Welfare" and inserting "Health and Human Services". **Effective** for facilities placed in service after 4-11-2005.

[¶5175] CODE SEC. 172. NET OPERATING LOSS DEDUCTION.

* * *

(b) NET OPERATING LOSS CARRYBACKS AND CARRYOVERS.—

(1) YEARS TO WHICH LOSS MAY BE CARRIED.—

* * *

(I) TRANSMISSION PROPERTY AND POLLUTION CONTROL INVESTMENT.—

(i) IN GENERAL.—At the election of the taxpayer in any taxable year ending after December 31, 2005, and before January 1, 2009, in the case of a net operating loss in a taxable year ending after December 31, 2002, and before January 1, 2006, there shall be a net operating loss carryback to each of the 5 years preceding the taxable year of such loss to the extent that such loss does not exceed 20 percent of the sum of electric transmission property capital expenditures and pollution control facility capital expenditures of the taxpayer for the taxable year preceding the taxable year in which such election is made.

(ii) LIMITATIONS.—For purposes of this subsection—

(I) not more than one election may be made under clause (i) with respect to any net operating loss in a taxable year, and

(II) an election may not be made under clause (i) for more than 1 taxable year beginning in any calendar year.

(iii) COORDINATION WITH ORDERING RULE.—For purposes of applying subsection (b)(2), the portion of any loss which is carried back 5 years by reason of clause (i) shall be treated in a manner similar to the manner in which a specified liability loss is treated.

(iv) APPLICATION FOR ADJUSTMENT.—In the case of any portion of a net operating loss to which an election under clause (i) applies, an application under section 6411(a) with respect to such loss shall not fail to be treated as timely filed if filed within 24 months after the due date specified under such section.

(v) SPECIAL RULES RELATING TO REFUND.—For purposes of a net operating loss to which an election under clause (i) applies, references in sections 6501(h), 6511(d)(2)(A), and 6611(f)(1) to the taxable year in which such net operating loss arises or result in a net loss carryback shall be treated as references to the taxable year in which such election occurs.

(vi) DEFINITIONS.—For purposes of this subparagraph—

(I) ELECTRIC TRANSMISSION PROPERTY CAPITAL EXPENDITURES.—The term "electric transmission property capital expenditures" means any expenditure, chargeable to capital account, made by the taxpayer which is attributable to electric transmission property used by the taxpayer in the transmission at 69 or more kilovolts of electricity for sale. Such term shall not include any expenditure which may be refunded or the purpose of which may be modified at the option of the taxpayer so as to cease to be treated as an expenditure within the meaning of such term.

(II) POLLUTION CONTROL FACILITY CAPITAL EXPENDITURES.—The term "pollution control facility capital expenditures" means any expenditure, chargeable to capital account, made by an electric utility company (as defined in section 2(3) of the Public Utility Holding Company Act (15 U.S.C. 79b(3)), as in effect on the day before the date of the enactment of the Energy Tax Incentives Act of 2005) which is attributable to a facility which will qualify as a certified pollution control facility as determined under section 169(d)(1) by striking "before January 1, 1976," and by substituting "an identifiable" for "a new identifiable". Such term shall not include any expenditure which may be refunded or the purpose of which may be modified at the option of the taxpayer so as to cease to be treated as an expenditure within the meaning of such term.

* * *

[CCH Explanation at ¶430. Committee Reports at ¶10,100.]

Amendments

- 2005, Energy Tax Incentives Act of 2005 (H.R. 6)

H.R. 6, §1311:

Amended Code Sec. 172(b)(1) by adding at the end a new subparagraph (I). **Effective** 8-8-2005.

[¶5180] CODE SEC. 179A. DEDUCTION FOR CLEAN-FUEL VEHICLES AND CERTAIN REFUELING PROPERTY.

* * *

(f) TERMINATION.—This section shall not apply to any property placed in service after *December 31, 2005*.

[CCH Explanation at ¶330. Committee Reports at ¶10,260.]

Amendments

- 2005, Energy Tax Incentives Act of 2005 (H.R. 6)

H.R. 6, §1348:

Amended Code Sec. 179A(f) by striking "December 31, 2006" and inserting "December 31, 2005". **Effective** 8-8-2005.

[¶5185] CODE SEC. 179B. DEDUCTION FOR CAPITAL COSTS INCURRED IN COMPLYING WITH ENVIRONMENTAL PROTECTION AGENCY SULFUR REGULATIONS.

* * *

(e) ELECTION TO ALLOCATE DEDUCTION TO COOPERATIVE OWNER.—

(1) IN GENERAL.—If—

(A) a small business refiner to which subsection (a) applies is an organization to which part I of subchapter T applies, and

(B) one or more persons directly holding an ownership interest in the refiner are organizations to which part I of subchapter T apply,

the refiner may elect to allocate all or a portion of the deduction allowable under subsection (a) to such persons. Such allocation shall be equal to the person's ratable share of the total amount allocated, determined on the basis of the person's ownership interest in the taxpayer. The taxable income of the refiner shall not be reduced under section 1382 by reason of any amount to which the preceding sentence applies.

(2) FORM AND EFFECT OF ELECTION.—An election under paragraph (1) for any taxable year shall be made on a timely filed return for such year. Such election, once made, shall be irrevocable for such taxable year.

(3) WRITTEN NOTICE TO OWNERS.—If any portion of the deduction available under subsection (a) is allocated to owners under paragraph (1), the cooperative shall provide any owner receiving an allocation written notice of the amount of the allocation. Such notice shall be provided before the date on which the return described in paragraph (2) is due.

[CCH Explanation at ¶ 535. Committee Reports at ¶ 10,130.]

Amendments

• 2005, Energy Tax Incentives Act of 2005 (H.R. 6)

H.R. 6, § 1324(a):

Amended Code Sec. 179B by adding at the end a new subsection (e). **Effective** as if included in the amendment made by section 338(a) of P.L. 108-357 [**effective** for expenses paid or incurred after 12-31-2002, in tax years ending after such date.—CCH].

[¶ 5190] CODE SEC. 179C. ELECTION TO EXPENSE CERTAIN REFINERIES.

(a) TREATMENT AS EXPENSES.—A taxpayer may elect to treat 50 percent of the cost of any qualified refinery property as an expense which is not chargeable to capital account. Any cost so treated shall be allowed as a deduction for the taxable year in which the qualified refinery property is placed in service.

(b) ELECTION.—

(1) IN GENERAL.—An election under this section for any taxable year shall be made on the taxpayer's return of the tax imposed by this chapter for the taxable year. Such election shall be made in such manner as the Secretary may by regulations prescribe.

(2) ELECTION IRREVOCABLE.—Any election made under this section may not be revoked except with the consent of the Secretary.

(c) QUALIFIED REFINERY PROPERTY.—

(1) IN GENERAL.—The term "qualified refinery property" means any portion of a qualified refinery—

(A) the original use of which commences with the taxpayer,

(B) which is placed in service by the taxpayer after the date of the enactment of this section and before January 1, 2012,

(C) in the case any portion of a qualified refinery (other than a qualified refinery which is separate from any existing refinery), which meets the requirements of subsection (e),

(D) which meets all applicable environmental laws in effect on the date such portion was placed in service,

(E) no written binding contract for the construction of which was in effect on or before June 14, 2005, and

(F)(i) the construction of which is subject to a written binding construction contract entered into before January 1, 2008,

(ii) which is placed in service before January 1, 2008, or

(iii) in the case of self-constructed property, the construction of which began after June 14, 2005, and before January 1, 2008.

(2) SPECIAL RULE FOR SALE-LEASEBACKS.—For purposes of paragraph (1)(A), if property is—

(A) originally placed in service after the date of the enactment of this section by a person, and

(B) sold and leased back by such person within 3 months after the date such property was originally placed in service, such property shall be treated as originally placed in service not earlier than the date on which such property is used under the leaseback referred to in subparagraph (B).

(3) EFFECT OF WAIVER UNDER CLEAN AIR ACT.—A waiver under the Clean Air Act shall not be taken into account in determining whether the requirements of paragraph (1)(D) are met.

(d) QUALIFIED REFINERY.—For purposes of this section, the term "qualified refinery" means any refinery located in the United States which is designed to serve the primary purpose of processing liquid fuel from crude oil or qualified fuels (as defined in section 45K(c)).

(e) PRODUCTION CAPACITY.—The requirements of this subsection are met if the portion of the qualified refinery—

(1) enables the existing qualified refinery to increase total volume output (determined without regard to asphalt or lube oil) by 5 percent or more on an average daily basis, or

(2) enables the existing qualified refinery to process qualified fuels (as defined in section 45K(c)) at a rate which is equal to or greater than 25 percent of the total throughput of such qualified refinery on an average daily basis.

(f) INELIGIBLE REFINERY PROPERTY.—No deduction shall be allowed under subsection (a) for any qualified refinery property—

(1) the primary purpose of which is for use as a topping plant, asphalt plant, lube oil facility, crude or product terminal, or blending facility, or

(2) which is built solely to comply with consent decrees or projects mandated by Federal, State, or local governments.

(g) ELECTION TO ALLOCATE DEDUCTION TO COOPERATIVE OWNER.—

(1) IN GENERAL.—If—

(A) a taxpayer to which subsection (a) applies is an organization to which part I of subchapter T applies, and

(B) one or more persons directly holding an ownership interest in the taxpayer are organizations to which part I of subchapter T apply,

the taxpayer may elect to allocate all or a portion of the deduction allowable under subsection (a) to such persons. Such allocation shall be equal to the person's ratable share of the total amount allocated, determined on the basis of the person's ownership interest in the taxpayer. The taxable income of the taxpayer shall not be reduced under section 1382 by reason of any amount to which the preceding sentence applies.

(2) FORM AND EFFECT OF ELECTION.—An election under paragraph (1) for any taxable year shall be made on a timely filed return for such year. Such election, once made, shall be irrevocable for such taxable year.

(3) WRITTEN NOTICE TO OWNERS.—If any portion of the deduction available under subsection (a) is allocated to owners under paragraph (1), the cooperative shall provide any owner receiving an allocation written notice of the amount of the allocation. Such notice shall be provided before the date on which the return described in paragraph (2) is due.

(h) REPORTING.—No deduction shall be allowed under subsection (a) to any taxpayer for any taxable year unless such taxpayer files with the Secretary a report containing such information with respect to the operation of the refineries of the taxpayer as the Secretary shall require.

[CCH Explanation at ¶ 505. Committee Reports at ¶ 10,120.]
Amendments
- **2005, Energy Tax Incentives Act of 2005 (H.R. 6)**

H.R. 6, § 1323(a):

Amended part VI of subchapter B of chapter 1 by inserting after Code Sec. 179B a new Code Sec. 179C. **Effective** for properties placed in service after 8-8-2005.

➤ *Caution: Code Sec. 179D, below, as added by H.R. 6, applies to property placed in service after December 31, 2005.*

[¶ 5195] CODE SEC. 179D. ENERGY EFFICIENT COMMERCIAL BUILDINGS DEDUCTION.

(a) IN GENERAL.—There shall be allowed as a deduction an amount equal to the cost of energy efficient commercial building property placed in service during the taxable year.

(b) MAXIMUM AMOUNT OF DEDUCTION.—The deduction under subsection (a) with respect to any building for any taxable year shall not exceed the excess (if any) of—

(1) the product of—

(A) $1.80, and

(B) the square footage of the building, over

(2) the aggregate amount of the deductions under subsection (a) with respect to the building for all prior taxable years.

(c) DEFINITIONS.—For purposes of this section—

(1) ENERGY EFFICIENT COMMERCIAL BUILDING PROPERTY.—The term "energy efficient commercial building property" means property—

(A) with respect to which depreciation (or amortization in lieu of depreciation) is allowable,

(B) which is installed on or in any building which is—

(i) located in the United States, and

(ii) within the scope of Standard 90.1-2001,

(C) which is installed as part of—

(i) the interior lighting systems,

(ii) the heating, cooling, ventilation, and hot water systems, or

(iii) the building envelope, and

(D) which is certified in accordance with subsection (d)(6) as being installed as part of a plan designed to reduce the total annual energy and power costs with respect to the interior lighting systems, heating, cooling, ventilation, and hot water systems of the building by 50 percent or more in comparison to a reference building which meets the minimum requirements of Standard 90.1-2001 using methods of calculation under subsection (d)(2).

(2) STANDARD 90.1-2001.—The term "Standard 90.1-2001" means Standard 90.1-2001 of the American Society of Heating, Refrigerating, and Air Conditioning Engineers and the Illuminating Engineering Society of North America (as in effect on April 2, 2003).

(d) SPECIAL RULES.—

(1) PARTIAL ALLOWANCE.—

(A) IN GENERAL.—Except as provided in subsection (f), if—

(i) the requirement of subsection (c)(1)(D) is not met, but

(ii) there is a certification in accordance with paragraph (6) that any system referred to in subsection (c)(1)(C) satisfies the energy-savings targets established by the Secretary under subparagraph (B) with respect to such system,

then the requirement of subsection (c)(1)(D) shall be treated as met with respect to such system, and the deduction under subsection (a) shall be allowed with respect to energy efficient commercial building property installed as part of such system and as part of a plan to meet such targets, except that subsection (b) shall be applied to such property by substituting "$.60" for "$1.80".

(B) REGULATIONS.—The Secretary, after consultation with the Secretary of Energy, shall establish a target for each system described in subsection (c)(1)(C) which, if such targets were met for all such systems, the building would meet the requirements of subsection (c)(1)(D).

(2) METHODS OF CALCULATION.—The Secretary, after consultation with the Secretary of Energy, shall promulgate regulations which describe in detail methods for calculating and verifying energy and power consumption and cost, based on the provisions of the 2005 California Nonresidential Alternative Calculation Method Approval Manual.

(3) COMPUTER SOFTWARE.—

(A) IN GENERAL.—Any calculation under paragraph (2) shall be prepared by qualified computer software.

(B) QUALIFIED COMPUTER SOFTWARE.—For purposes of this paragraph, the term "qualified computer software" means software—

(i) for which the software designer has certified that the software meets all procedures and detailed methods for calculating energy and power consumption and costs as required by the Secretary,

(ii) which provides such forms as required to be filed by the Secretary in connection with energy efficiency of property and the deduction allowed under this section, and

(iii) which provides a notice form which documents the energy efficiency features of the building and its projected annual energy costs.

(4) ALLOCATION OF DEDUCTION FOR PUBLIC PROPERTY.—In the case of energy efficient commercial building property installed on or in property owned by a Federal, State, or local government or a political subdivision thereof, the Secretary shall promulgate a regulation to allow the allocation of the deduction to the person primarily responsible for designing the property in lieu of the owner of such property. Such person shall be treated as the taxpayer for purposes of this section.

(5) NOTICE TO OWNER.—Each certification required under this section shall include an explanation to the building owner regarding the energy efficiency features of the building and its projected annual energy costs as provided in the notice under paragraph (3)(B)(iii).

(6) CERTIFICATION.—

(A) IN GENERAL.—The Secretary shall prescribe the manner and method for the making of certifications under this section.

(B) PROCEDURES.—The Secretary shall include as part of the certification process procedures for inspection and testing by qualified individuals described in subparagraph (C) to ensure compliance of buildings with energy-savings plans and targets. Such procedures shall be comparable, given the difference between commercial and residential buildings, to the requirements in the Mortgage Industry National Accreditation Procedures for Home Energy Rating Systems.

(C) QUALIFIED INDIVIDUALS.—Individuals qualified to determine compliance shall be only those individuals who are recognized by an organization certified by the Secretary for such purposes.

(e) BASIS REDUCTION.—For purposes of this subtitle, if a deduction is allowed under this section with respect to any energy efficient commercial building property, the basis of such property shall be reduced by the amount of the deduction so allowed.

(f) INTERIM RULES FOR LIGHTING SYSTEMS.—Until such time as the Secretary issues final regulations under subsection (d)(1)(B) with respect to property which is part of a lighting system—

(1) IN GENERAL.—The lighting system target under subsection (d)(1)(A)(ii) shall be a reduction in lighting power density of 25 percent (50 percent in the case of a warehouse) of the minimum requirements in Table 9.3.1.1 or Table 9.3.1.2 (not including additional interior lighting power allowances) of Standard 90.1-2001.

(2) REDUCTION IN DEDUCTION IF REDUCTION LESS THAN 40 PERCENT.—

(A) IN GENERAL.—If, with respect to the lighting system of any building other than a warehouse, the reduction in lighting power density of the lighting system is not at least 40 percent, only the applicable percentage of the amount of deduction otherwise allowable under this section with respect to such property shall be allowed.

(B) APPLICABLE PERCENTAGE.—For purposes of subparagraph (A), the applicable percentage is the number of percentage points (not greater than 100) equal to the sum of—

(i) 50, and

(ii) the amount which bears the same ratio to 50 as the excess of the reduction of lighting power density of the lighting system over 25 percentage points bears to 15.

(C) EXCEPTIONS.—This subsection shall not apply to any system—

(i) the controls and circuiting of which do not comply fully with the mandatory and prescriptive requirements of Standard 90.1-2001 and which do not include provision for bilevel switching in all occupancies except hotel and motel guest rooms, store rooms, restrooms, and public lobbies, or

(ii) which does not meet the minimum requirements for calculated lighting levels as set forth in the Illuminating Engineering Society of North America Lighting Handbook, Performance and Application, Ninth Edition, 2000.

(g) REGULATIONS.—The Secretary shall promulgate such regulations as necessary—

(1) to take into account new technologies regarding energy efficiency and renewable energy for purposes of determining energy efficiency and savings under this section, and

(2) to provide for a recapture of the deduction allowed under this section if the plan described in subsection (c)(1)(D) or (d)(1)(A) is not fully implemented.

(h) TERMINATION.—This section shall not apply with respect to property placed in service after December 31, 2007.

* * *

[CCH Explanation at ¶ 215. Committee Reports at ¶ 10,190.]

Amendments

• **2005, Energy Tax Incentives Act of 2005 (H.R. 6)**

H.R. 6, § 1331(a):

Amended part VI of subchapter B of chapter 1, as amended by this Act, by inserting after Code Sec. 179C a

new Code Sec. 179D. **Effective** for property placed in service after 12-31-2005.

[¶ 5200] CODE SEC. 196. DEDUCTION FOR CERTAIN UNUSED BUSINESS CREDITS.

* * *

(c) QUALIFIED BUSINESS CREDITS.—For purposes of this section, the term "qualified business credits" means—

* * *

(11) the biodiesel fuels credit determined under section 40A(a),

(12) the low sulfur diesel fuel production credit determined under section 45H(a), *and*

⟫⟫→ *Caution: Code Sec. 196(c)(13), below, as added by H.R. 6, applies to qualified new energy efficient homes acquired after December 31, 2005, in tax years ending after such date.*

(13) the new energy efficient home credit determined under section 45L(a).

* * *

[CCH Explanation at ¶220. Committee Reports at ¶10,200.]

Amendments

- **2005, Energy Tax Incentives Act of 2005 (H.R. 6)**

H.R. 6, §1332(d):

Amended Code Sec. 196(c) by striking "and" at the end of paragraph (11), by striking the period at the end of paragraph (12) and inserting ", and", and by adding at the end a new paragraph (13). **Effective** for qualified new energy efficient homes acquired after 12-31-2005, in tax years ending after such date.

[¶5205] CODE SEC. 263. CAPITAL EXPENDITURES.

(a) GENERAL RULE.—No deduction shall be allowed for—

(1) Any amount paid out for new buildings or for permanent improvements or betterments made to increase the value of any property or estate. This paragraph shall not apply to—

(A) expenditures for the development of mines or deposits deductible under section 616,

(B) research and experimental expenditures deductible under section 174,

(C) soil and water conservation expenditures deductible under section 175,

(D) expenditures by farmers for fertilizer, etc., deductible under section 180,

(E) expenditures for removal of architectural and transportation barriers to the handicapped and elderly which the taxpayer elects to deduct under section 190,

(F) expenditures for tertiary injectants with respect to which a deduction is allowed under section 193;

(G) expenditures for which a deduction is allowed under section 179;

(H) expenditures for which a deduction is allowed under section 179A,

(I) expenditures for which a deduction is allowed under section 179B,

(J) *expenditures for which a deduction is allowed under section 179C, or*

⟫⟫→ *Caution: Code Sec. 263(a)(1)(K), below, as added by H.R. 6, applies to property placed in service after December 31, 2005.*

(K) *expenditures for which a deduction is allowed under section 179D.*

* * *

[CCH Explanation at ¶215 and ¶505. Committee Reports at ¶10,120 and ¶10,190.]

Amendments

- **2005, Energy Tax Incentives Act of 2005 (H.R. 6)**

H.R. 6, §1323(b)(2):

Amended Code Sec. 263(a)(1) by striking "or" at the end of subparagraph (H), by striking the period at the end of subparagraph (I) and inserting ", or", and by inserting after subparagraph (I) a new subparagraph (J). **Effective** for properties placed in service after 8-8-2005.

H.R. 6, §1331(b)(4):

Amended Code Sec. 263(a)(1), as amended by this Act, by striking "or" at the end of subparagraph (I), by striking the period at the end of subparagraph (J) and inserting ", or", and by inserting after subparagraph (J) a new subparagraph (K). **Effective** for property placed in service after 12-31-2005.

[¶5207] CODE SEC. 263A. CAPITALIZATION AND INCLUSION IN INVENTORY COSTS OF CERTAIN EXPENSES.

* * *

(c) GENERAL EXCEPTIONS.—

* * *

(3) CERTAIN DEVELOPMENT AND OTHER COSTS OF OIL AND GAS WELLS OR OTHER MINERAL PROPERTY.—This section shall not apply to any cost allowable as a deduction under section *167(h)*, 179B, 263(c), 263(i), 291(b)(2), 616, or 617.

* * *

[CCH Explanation at ¶ 525. Committee Reports at ¶ 10,180.]

Amendments

- **2005, Energy Tax Incentives Act of 2005 (H.R. 6)**

H.R. 6, § 1329(b):

Amended Code Sec. 263A(c)(3) by inserting "167(h)" after "under section". **Effective** for amounts paid or incurred in tax years beginning after 8-8-2005.

[¶ 5210] CODE SEC. 312. EFFECT ON EARNINGS AND PROFITS.

* * *

(k) EFFECT OF DEPRECIATION ON EARNINGS AND PROFITS.—

* * *

(3) EXCEPTION FOR TANGIBLE PROPERTY.—

* * *

⟫→ *Caution: Code Sec. 312(k)(3)(B), below, as amended by H.R. 6, §1323(b)(3), but prior to amendment by §1331(b)(5), applies to property placed in service on or before December 31, 2005.*

(B) TREATMENT OF AMOUNTS DEDUCTIBLE UNDER SECTION *179, 179A, 179B, or 179C*.—For purposes of computing the earnings and profits of a corporation, any amount deductible under section *179, 179A, 179B, or 179C* shall be allowed as a deduction ratably over the period of 5 taxable years (beginning with the taxable year for which such amount is deductible under section *179, 179A, 179B, or 179C*, as the case may be).

⟫→ *Caution: Code Sec. 312(k)(3)(B), below, as amended by H.R. 6, §1323(b)(3) and further amended by §1331(b)(5), applies to property placed in service after December 31, 2005.*

(B) TREATMENT OF AMOUNTS DEDUCTIBLE UNDER SECTION *179, 179A, 179B, 179C, or 179D*.—For purposes of computing the earnings and profits of a corporation, any amount deductible under section *179, 179A, 179B, 179C, or 179D* shall be allowed as a deduction ratably over the period of 5 taxable years (beginning with the taxable year for which such amount is deductible under section *179, 179A, 179B, 179C, or 179D*, as the case may be).

* * *

[CCH Explanation at ¶ 215, ¶ 505 and ¶ 525. Committee Reports at ¶ 10,120 and ¶ 10,190.]

Amendments

- **2005, Energy Tax Incentives Act of 2005 (H.R. 6)**

H.R. 6, § 1323(b)(3):

Amended Code Sec. 312(k)(3)(B) by striking "179 179A, or 179B" each place it appears in the heading and text and inserting "179, 179A, 179B, or 179C". **Effective** for properties placed in service after 8-8-2005.

H.R. 6, § 1331(b)(5):

Amended Code Sec. 312(k)(3)(B), as amended by this Act, by striking "179, 179A, 179B, or 179C" each place it appears in the heading and text and inserting "179, 179A, 179B, 179C, or 179D". **Effective** for property placed in service after 12-31-2005.

[¶ 5215] CODE SEC. 451. GENERAL RULE FOR TAXABLE YEAR OF INCLUSION.

* * *

(i) SPECIAL RULE FOR SALES OR DISPOSITIONS TO IMPLEMENT FEDERAL ENERGY REGULATORY COMMISSION OR STATE ELECTRIC RESTRUCTURING POLICY.—

* * *

¶ 5210 Code Sec. 263A(c)(3)

(3) QUALIFYING ELECTRIC TRANSMISSION TRANSACTION.—For purposes of this subsection, the term "qualifying electric transmission transaction" means any sale or other disposition before January 1, *2008*, of—

    (A) property used in the trade or business of providing electric transmission services, or

    (B) any stock or partnership interest in a corporation or partnership, as the case may be, whose principal trade or business consists of providing electric transmission services,

but only if such sale or disposition is to an independent transmission company.

(4) INDEPENDENT TRANSMISSION COMPANY.—For purposes of this subsection, the term "independent transmission company" means—

* * *

    (B) a person—

* * *

        (ii) whose transmission facilities to which the election under this subsection applies are under the operational control of a Federal Energy Regulatory Commission-approved independent transmission provider before the close of the period specified in such authorization, but not later than *December 31, 2007*, or

* * *

[CCH Explanation at ¶435. Committee Reports at ¶10,040.]

Amendments

- **2005, Energy Tax Incentives Act of 2005 (H.R. 6)**

H.R. 6, §1305(a):

Amended Code Sec. 451(i)(3) by striking "2007" and inserting "2008". **Effective** for transactions occurring after 8-8-2005.

H.R. 6, §1305(b):

Amended Code Sec. 451(i)(4)(B)(ii) by striking "the close of the period applicable under subsection (a)(2)(B) as extended under paragraph (2)" and inserting "December 31, 2007". **Effective** as if included in the amendments made by section 909 of P.L. 108-357 [**effective** for transactions occurring after 10-22-2004, in tax years ending after such date.—CCH].

[¶5220] CODE SEC. 468A. SPECIAL RULES FOR NUCLEAR DECOMMISSIONING COSTS.

* * *

⟩⟩⟩→ *Caution: Code Sec. 468A(b), below, as amended by H.R. 6, applies to tax years beginning after December 31, 2005.*

(b) LIMITATION ON AMOUNTS PAID INTO FUND.—The amount which a taxpayer may pay into the Fund for any taxable year shall not exceed the ruling amount applicable to such taxable year.

* * *

[CCH Explanation at ¶445. Committee Reports at ¶10,090.]

Amendments

- **2005, Energy Tax Incentives Act of 2005 (H.R. 6)**

H.R. 6, §1310(a):

Amended Code Sec. 468A(b). **Effective** for tax years beginning after 12-31-2005. Prior to amendment, Code Sec. 468A(b) read as follows:

(b) LIMITATION ON AMOUNTS PAID INTO FUND.—The amount which a taxpayer may pay into the Fund for any taxable year shall not exceed the lesser of—

(1) the amount of nuclear decommissioning costs allocable to the Fund which is included in the taxpayer's cost of service for ratemaking purposes for such taxable year, or

(2) the ruling amount applicable to such taxable year.

(d) RULING AMOUNT.—For purposes of this section—

»»→ Caution: *Code Sec. 468A(d)(1), below, as amended by H.R. 6, applies to tax years beginning after December 31, 2005.*

(1) REQUEST REQUIRED.—No deduction shall be allowed for any payment to the Fund unless the taxpayer requests, and receives, from the Secretary a schedule of ruling amounts. *For purposes of the preceding sentence, the taxpayer shall request a schedule of ruling amounts upon each renewal of the operating license of the nuclear powerplant.*

(2) RULING AMOUNT.—The term "ruling amount" means, with respect to any taxable year, the amount which the Secretary determines under paragraph (1) to be necessary to—

»»→ Caution: *Code Sec. 468A(d)(2)(A), below, as amended by H.R. 6, applies to tax years beginning after December 31, 2005.*

(A) fund the total nuclear decommissioning costs with respect to such power plant over the estimated useful life of such power plant, and

(B) prevent any excessive funding of such costs or the funding of such costs at a rate more rapid than level funding, taking into account such discount rates as the Secretary deems appropriate.

* * *

[CCH Explanation at ¶ 445. Committee Reports at ¶ 10,090.]

Amendments

• **2005, Energy Tax Incentives Act of 2005 (H.R. 6)**

H.R. 6, § 1310(b)(2):

Amended Code Sec. 468A(d)(2)(A). **Effective** for tax years beginning after 12-31-2005. Prior to amendment, Code Sec. 468A(d)(2)(A) read as follows:

(A) fund that portion of the nuclear decommissioning costs of the taxpayer with respect to the nuclear powerplant which bears the same ratio to the total nuclear decommissioning costs with respect to such nuclear powerplant as the period for which the Fund is in effect bears to the estimated useful life of such nuclear powerplant, and

H.R. 6, § 1310(c):

Amended Code Sec. 468A(d)(1) by adding at the end a new sentence. **Effective** for tax years beginning after 12-31-2005.

(e) NUCLEAR DECOMMISSIONING RESERVE FUND.—

(1) IN GENERAL.—Each taxpayer who elects the application of this section shall establish a Nuclear Decommissioning Reserve Fund with respect to each nuclear powerplant to which such election applies.

»»→ Caution: *Code Sec. 468A(e)(2), below, as amended by H.R. 6, applies to tax years beginning after December 31, 2005.*

(2) TAXATION OF FUND.—

(A) IN GENERAL.—There is hereby imposed on the gross income of the Fund for any taxable year a tax at the *rate of 20 percent*, except that—

(i) there shall not be included in the gross income of the Fund any payment to the Fund with respect to which a deduction is allowable under subsection (a), and

(ii) there shall be allowed as a deduction to the Fund any amount paid by the Fund which is described in paragraph (4)(B) (other than an amount paid to the taxpayer) and which would be deductible under this chapter for purposes of determining the taxable income of a corporation.

(B) TAX IN LIEU OF OTHER TAXATION.—The tax imposed by subparagraph (A) shall be in lieu of any other taxation under this subtitle of the income from assets in the Fund.

(C) FUND TREATED AS CORPORATION.—For purposes of subtitle F—

(i) the Fund shall be treated as if it were a corporation, and

(ii) any tax imposed by this paragraph shall be treated as a tax imposed by section 11.

»»→ **Caution:** *Code Sec. 468A(e)(3), below, as amended by H.R. 6, applies to tax years beginning after December 31, 2005.*

(3) CONTRIBUTIONS TO FUND.—Except as provided in subsection (f), the Fund shall not accept any payments (or other amounts) other than payments with respect to which a deduction is allowable under subsection (a).

* * *

[CCH Explanation at ¶445. Committee Reports at ¶10,090.]

Amendments

• **2005, Energy Tax Incentives Act of 2005 (H.R. 6)**

H.R. 6, §1310(d):

Amended Code Sec. 468A(e)(3) by striking "The Fund" and inserting "Except as provided in subsection (f), the Fund". **Effective** for tax years beginning after 12-31-2005.

H.R. 6, §1310(e)(1)-(3):

Amended Code Sec. 468A(e)(2) by striking "rate set forth in subparagraph (B)" in subparagraph (A) and inserting "rate of 20 percent", by striking subparagraph (B), and by redesignating subparagraphs (C) and (D) as subparagraphs (B) and (C), respectively. **Effective** for tax years beginning after 12-31-2005. Prior to being stricken, Code Sec. 468A(e)(2)(B) read as follows:

(B) RATE OF TAX.—For purposes of subparagraph (A), the rate set forth in this subparagraph is—

(i) 22 percent in the case of taxable years beginning in calendar year 1994 or 1995, and

(ii) 20 percent in the case of taxable years beginning after December 31, 1995.

»»→ **Caution:** *Code Sec. 468A(f), below, as added by H.R. 6, applies to tax years beginning after December 31, 2005.*

(f) TRANSFERS INTO QUALIFIED FUNDS.—

(1) IN GENERAL.—Notwithstanding subsection (b), any taxpayer maintaining a Fund to which this section applies with respect to a nuclear power plant may transfer into such Fund not more than an amount equal to the present value of the portion of the total nuclear decommissioning costs with respect to such nuclear power plant previously excluded for such nuclear power plant under subsection (d)(2)(A) as in effect immediately before the date of the enactment of this subsection.

(2) DEDUCTION FOR AMOUNTS TRANSFERRED.—

(A) IN GENERAL.—Except as provided in subparagraph (C), the deduction allowed by subsection (a) for any transfer permitted by this subsection shall be allowed ratably over the remaining estimated useful life (within the meaning of subsection (d)(2)(A)) of the nuclear power plant beginning with the taxable year during which the transfer is made.

(B) DENIAL OF DEDUCTION FOR PREVIOUSLY DEDUCTED AMOUNTS.—No deduction shall be allowed for any transfer under this subsection of an amount for which a deduction was previously allowed to the taxpayer (or a predecessor) or a corresponding amount was not included in gross income of the taxpayer (or a predecessor). For purposes of the preceding sentence, a ratable portion of each transfer shall be treated as being from previously deducted or excluded amounts to the extent thereof.

(C) TRANSFERS OF QUALIFIED FUNDS.—If—

(i) any transfer permitted by this subsection is made to any Fund to which this section applies, and

(ii) such Fund is transferred thereafter,

any deduction under this subsection for taxable years ending after the date that such Fund is transferred shall be allowed to the transferor for the taxable year which includes such date.

(D) SPECIAL RULES.—

(i) GAIN OR LOSS NOT RECOGNIZED ON TRANSFERS TO FUND.—No gain or loss shall be recognized on any transfer described in paragraph (1).

(ii) TRANSFERS OF APPRECIATED PROPERTY TO FUND.—If appreciated property is transferred in a transfer described in paragraph (1), the amount of the deduction shall not exceed the adjusted basis of such property.

(3) NEW RULING AMOUNT REQUIRED.—Paragraph (1) shall not apply to any transfer unless the taxpayer requests from the Secretary a new schedule of ruling amounts in connection with such transfer.

(4) NO BASIS IN QUALIFIED FUNDS.—Notwithstanding any other provision of law, the taxpayer's basis in any Fund to which this section applies shall not be increased by reason of any transfer permitted by this subsection.

[CCH Explanation at ¶445. Committee Reports at ¶10,090.]
Amendments
- **2005, Energy Tax Incentives Act of 2005 (H.R. 6)**

H.R. 6, §1310(b)(1):

Amended Code Sec. 468A by redesignating subsections (f) and (g) as subsections (g) and (h), respectively, and by inserting after subsection (e) a new subsection (f). **Effective** for tax years beginning after 12-31-2005.

>>→ *Caution: Former Code Sec. 468A(f) was redesignated as Code Sec. 468A(g), below, by H.R. 6, applicable to tax years beginning after December 31, 2005.*

(g) NUCLEAR POWERPLANT.—For purpose of this section, the term "nuclear powerplant" includes any unit thereof.

[CCH Explanation at ¶445. Committee Reports at ¶10,090.]
Amendments
- **2005, Energy Tax Incentives Act of 2005 (H.R. 6)**

H.R. 6, §1310(b)(1):

Amended Code Sec. 468A by redesignating subsection (f) as subsection (g). **Effective** for tax years beginning after 12-31-2005.

>>→ *Caution: Former Code Sec. 468A(g) was redesignated as Code Sec. 468A(h), below, by H.R. 6, applicable to tax years beginning after December 31, 2005.*

(h) TIME WHEN PAYMENTS DEEMED MADE.—For purposes of this section, a taxpayer shall be deemed to have made a payment to the Fund on the last day of a taxable year if such payment is made on account of such taxable year and is made within $2^1/_2$ months after the close of such taxable year.

[CCH Explanation at ¶445. Committee Reports at ¶10,090.]
Amendments
- **2005, Energy Tax Incentives Act of 2005 (H.R. 6)**

H.R. 6, §1310(b)(1):

Amended Code Sec. 468A by redesignating subsection (g) as subsection (h). **Effective** for tax years beginning after 12-31-2005.

[¶5225] CODE SEC. 501. EXEMPTION FROM TAX ON CORPORATIONS, CERTAIN TRUSTS, ETC.

* * *

(c) LIST OF EXEMPT ORGANIZATIONS.—The following organizations are referred to in subsection (a):

* * *

(12)(C) In the case of a mutual or cooperative electric company, subparagraph (A) shall be applied without taking into account any income received or accrued—

(i) from qualified pole rentals, or

(ii) from any provision or sale of electric energy transmission services or ancillary services if such services are provided on a nondiscriminatory open access basis under an open access transmission tariff approved or accepted by FERC or under an independent transmission provider agreement approved or accepted by FERC (other than income received or accrued directly or indirectly from a member),

(iii) from the provision or sale of electric energy distribution services or ancillary services if such services are provided on a nondiscriminatory open access basis to distribute electric energy not owned by the mutual or electric cooperative company—

(I) to end-users who are served by distribution facilities not owned by such company or any of its members (other than income received or accrued directly or indirectly from a member), or

(II) generated by a generation facility not owned or leased by such company or any of its members and which is directly connected to distribution facilities owned by such company or any of its members (other than income received or accrued directly or indirectly from a member),

(iv) from any nuclear decommissioning transaction, or

(v) from any asset exchange or conversion transaction.

* * *

(H)(i) In the case of a mutual or cooperative electric company described in this paragraph or an organization described in section 1381(a)(2)(C), income received or accrued from a load loss transaction shall be treated as an amount collected from members for the sole purpose of meeting losses and expenses.

* * *

(x) [*Stricken.*]

* * *

[CCH Explanation at ¶450. Committee Reports at ¶10,030.]

Amendments   H.R. 6, §1304(b):

• **2005, Energy Tax Incentives Act of 2005 (H.R. 6)**

H.R. 6, §1304(a):

Amended Code Sec. 501(c)(12)(C) by striking the last sentence. **Effective** 8-8-2005. Prior to being stricken, the last sentence of Code Sec. 501(c)(12)(C) read as follows:

Clauses (ii) through (v) shall not apply to taxable years beginning after December 31, 2006.

Amended Code Sec. 501(c)(12)(H) by striking clause (x). **Effective** 8-8-2005. Prior to being stricken, Code Sec. 501(c)(12)(H)(x) read as follows:

(x) This subparagraph shall not apply to taxable years beginning after December 31, 2006.

[¶5230] CODE SEC. 613A. LIMITATIONS ON PERCENTAGE DEPLETION IN CASE OF OIL AND GAS WELLS.

* * *

(c) Exemption for Independent Producers and Royalty Owners.—

* * *

(6) Oil and Natural Gas Produced From Marginal Properties.—

* * *

⇒ *Caution: Code Sec. 613A(c)(6)(C), below, as amended by H.R. 6, applies to credits determined under the Internal Revenue Code of 1986 for tax years ending after December 31, 2005.*

(C) Applicable percentage.—For purposes of subparagraph (A), the term "applicable percentage" means the percentage (not greater than 25 percent) equal to the sum of—

(i) 15 percent, plus

(ii) 1 percentage point for each whole dollar by which $20 exceeds the reference price for crude oil for the calendar year preceding the calendar year in which the taxable year begins.

For purposes of this paragraph, the term "reference price" means, with respect to any calendar year, the reference price determined for such calendar year under *section 45K(d)(2)(C)*.

* * *

[CCH Explanation at ¶ 615. Committee Reports at ¶ 10,110.]

Amendments

• **2005, Energy Tax Incentives Act of 2005 (H.R. 6)**

H.R. 6, § 1322(a)(3)(B):

Amended Code Sec. 613A(c)(6)(C) by striking "section 29(d)(2)(C)" and inserting "section 45K(d)(2)(C)". **Effective** for credits determined under the Internal Revenue Code of 1986 for tax years ending after 12-31-2005.

(d) LIMITATIONS ON APPLICATION OF SUBSECTION (c).—

* * *

(4) CERTAIN REFINERS EXCLUDED.—If the taxpayer or 1 or more related persons engages in the refining of crude oil, subsection (c) shall not apply to the taxpayer for a taxable year if the average daily refinery runs of the taxpayer and such persons for the taxable year exceed 75,000 barrels. For purposes of this paragraph, the average daily refinery runs for any taxable year shall be determined by dividing the aggregate refinery runs for the taxable year by the number of days in the taxable year.

* * *

[CCH Explanation at ¶ 510. Committee Reports at ¶ 10,170.]

Amendments

• **2005, Energy Tax Incentives Act of 2005 (H.R. 6)**

H.R. 6, § 1328(a):

Amended Code Sec. 613A(d)(4). **Effective** for tax years ending after 8-8-2005. Prior to amendment, Code Sec. 613A(d)(4) read as follows:

(4) CERTAIN REFINERS EXCLUDED.—If the taxpayer or a related person engages in the refining of crude oil, subsection (c) shall not apply to such taxpayer if on any day during the taxable year the refinery runs of the taxpayer and such person exceed 50,000 barrels.

[¶ 5235] CODE SEC. 772. SIMPLIFIED FLOW-THROUGH.

(a) GENERAL RULE.—In determining the income tax of a partner of an electing large partnership, such partner shall take into account separately such partner's distributive share of the partnership's—

* * *

(9) foreign income taxes, *and*

⋙→ *Caution: Former Code Sec. 772(a)(11) was redesignated as Code Sec. 772(a)(10), below, by H.R. 6, applicable to credits determined under the Internal Revenue Code of 1986 for tax years ending after December 31, 2005.*

(10) other items to the extent that the Secretary determines that the separate treatment of such items is appropriate.

* * *

[CCH Explanation at ¶ 615. Committee Reports at ¶ 10,110.]

Amendments

• **2005, Energy Tax Incentives Act of 2005 (H.R. 6)**

H.R. 6, § 1322(a)(3)(I):

Amended Code Sec. 772(a) by inserting "and" at the end of paragraph (9), by striking paragraph (10), and by redesignating paragraph (11) as paragraph (10). **Effective** for credits determined under the Internal Revenue Code of 1986 for tax years ending after 12-31-2005. Prior to being stricken, Code Sec. 772(a)(10) read as follows:

(10) the credit allowable under section 29, and

(d) OPERATING RULES.—For purposes of this section—

* * *

⋙→ *Caution: Code Sec. 772(d)(5), below, as amended by H.R. 6, applies to credits determined under the Internal Revenue Code of 1986 for tax years ending after December 31, 2005.*

(5) GENERAL CREDITS.—The term "general credits" means any credit other than the low-income housing credit, the rehabilitation credit, *and the foreign tax credit.*

* * *

[CCH Explanation at ¶615. Committee Reports at ¶10,110.]

Amendments

• **2005, Energy Tax Incentives Act of 2005 (H.R. 6)**

H.R. 6, §1322(a)(3)(J):

Amended Code Sec. 772(d)(5) by striking "the foreign tax credit, and the credit allowable under section 29" and inserting "and the foreign tax credit". **Effective** for credits determined under the Internal Revenue Code of 1986 for tax years ending after 12-31-2005.

[¶5240] CODE SEC. 1016. ADJUSTMENTS TO BASIS.

(a) GENERAL RULE. Proper adjustment in respect of the property shall in all cases be made—

* * *

(30) to the extent provided in section 179B(c),

(31) in the case of a facility with respect to which a credit was allowed under section 45H, to the extent provided in section 45H(d),

⋙→ *Caution: Code Sec. 1016(a)(32)-(37), below, as added by H.R. 6, applies generally after December 31, 2005.*

(32) *to the extent provided in section 179D(e),*

(33) *to the extent provided in section 45L(e), in the case of amounts with respect to which a credit has been allowed under section 45L,*

(34) *to the extent provided in section 25C(e), in the case of amounts with respect to which a credit has been allowed under section 25C,*

(35) *to the extent provided in section 25D(f), in the case of amounts with respect to which a credit has been allowed under section 25D,*

(36) *to the extent provided in section 30B(h)(4), and*

(37) *to the extent provided in section 30C(f).*

* * *

[CCH Explanation at ¶205, ¶210, ¶215, ¶220, ¶305 and ¶730. Committee Reports at ¶10,190, ¶10,200, ¶10,210, ¶10,230, ¶10,260 and ¶10,270.]

Amendments

• **2005, Energy Tax Incentives Act of 2005 (H.R. 6)**

H.R. 6, §1331(b)(1):

Amended Code Sec. 1016(a) by striking "and" at the end of paragraph (30), by striking the period at the end of paragraph (31) and inserting ", and", and by adding at the end a new paragraph (32). **Effective** for property placed in service after 12-31-2005.

H.R. 6, §1332(c):

Amended Code Sec. 1016(a), as amended by this Act, by striking "and" at the end of paragraph (32), by striking the period at the end of paragraph (32) and inserting ", and", and by adding at the end a new paragraph (33). **Effective** for qualified new energy efficient homes acquired after 12-31-2005, in tax years ending after such date.

H.R. 6, §1333(b)(1):

Amended Code Sec. 1016(a), as amended by this Act, by striking "and" at the end of paragraph (32), by striking the period at the end of paragraph (33) and inserting ", and", and by adding at the end a new paragraph (34). **Effective** for property placed in service after 12-31-2005.

H.R. 6, §1335(b)(4):

Amended Code Sec. 1016(a), as amended by this Act, by striking "and" at the end of paragraph (33), by striking the period at the end of paragraph (34) and inserting ", and", and by adding at the end a new paragraph (35). **Effective** for property placed in service after 12-31-2005, in tax years ending after such date.

H.R. 6, §1341(b)(2):

Amended Code Sec. 1016(a), as amended by this Act, by striking "and" at the end of paragraph (34), by striking the period at the end of paragraph (35) and inserting ", and", and by adding at the end a new paragraph (36). **Effective** for property placed in service after 12-31-2005, in tax years ending after such date.

H.R. 6, § 1342(b)(2):

Amended Code Sec. 1016(a), as amended by this Act, by striking "and" at the end of paragraph (35), by striking the period at the end of paragraph (36) and inserting ", and", and by adding at the end a new paragraph (37). **Effective** for property placed in service after 12-31-2005, in tax years ending after such date.

[¶ 5245] CODE SEC. 1245. GAIN FROM DISPOSITIONS OF CERTAIN DEPRECIABLE PROPERTY.

(a) GENERAL RULE.—

* * *

(2) RECOMPUTED BASIS.—For purposes of this section—

* * *

(C) CERTAIN DEDUCTIONS TREATED AS AMORTIZATION.—Any deduction allowable under section 179, 179A, 179B, *179C, 179D,* 190, or 193 shall be treated as if it were a deduction allowable for amortization.

(3) SECTION 1245 PROPERTY.—For purposes of this section, the term "section 1245 property" means any property which is or has been property of a character subject to the allowance for depreciation provided in section 167 and is either—

* * *

(C) so much of any real property (other than any property described in subparagraph B)) which has an adjusted basis in which there are reflected adjustments for amortization under section 169, 179, 179A, 179B, *179C, 179D,* 185, 188 (as in effect before its repeal by the Revenue Reconciliation Act of 1990), 190, 193, or 194,

* * *

[CCH Explanation at ¶ 215 and ¶ 505. Committee Reports at ¶ 10,120 and ¶ 10,190.]

Amendments

- **2005, Energy Tax Incentives Act of 2005 (H.R. 6)**

H.R. 6, § 1323(b)(1):

Amended Code Sec. 1245(a) by inserting "179C," after "179B," both places it appears in paragraphs (2)(C) and (3)(C). **Effective** for properties placed in service after 8-8-2005.

H.R. 6, § 1331(b)(2):

Amended Code Sec. 1245(a), as amended by this Act, by inserting "179D," after "179C," both places it appears in paragraphs (2)(C) and (3)(C). **Effective** for property placed in service after 12-31-2005.

(b) EXCEPTIONS AND LIMITATIONS.—

* * *

(9) DISPOSITION OF AMORTIZABLE SECTION *197 INTANGIBLES.*—

(A) IN GENERAL.—If a taxpayer disposes of more than 1 amortizable section 197 intangible (as defined in section 197(c)) in a transaction or a series of related transactions, all such amortizable 197 intangibles shall be treated as 1 section 1245 property for purposes of this section.

(B) EXCEPTION.—Subparagraph (A) shall not apply to any amortizable section 197 intangible (as so defined) with respect to which the adjusted basis exceeds the fair market value.

* * *

[CCH Explanation at ¶ 245. Committee Reports at ¶ 10,370.]

Amendments

- **2005, Energy Tax Incentives Act of 2005 (H.R. 6)**

H.R. 6, § 1363(a):

Amended Code Sec. 1245(b) by adding at the end a new paragraph (9). **Effective** for dispositions of property after 8-8-2005.

[¶ 5250] CODE SEC. 1250. GAIN FROM DISPOSITIONS OF CERTAIN DEPRECIABLE REALTY.

* * *

(b) ADDITIONAL DEPRECIATION DEFINED.—For purposes of this section—

* * *

>>>→ *Caution: Code Sec. 1250(b)(3), below, as amended by H.R. 6, applies to property placed in service after December 31, 2005.*

(3) DEPRECIATION ADJUSTMENTS.—The term "depreciation adjustments" means, in respect of any property, all adjustments attributable to periods after December 31, 1963, reflected in the adjusted basis of such property on account of deductions (whether in respect of the same or other property) allowed or allowable to the taxpayer or to any other person for exhaustion, wear and tear, obsolescence, or amortization (other than amortization under section 168 (as in effect before its repeal by the Tax Reform Act of 1976), 169, 185 (as in effect before its repeal by the Tax Reform Act of 1986), 188 (as in effect before its repeal by the Revenue Reconciliation Act of 1990), 190, or 193 *or by section 179D*. For purposes of the preceding sentence, if the taxpayer can establish by adequate records or other sufficient evidence that the amount allowed as a deduction for any period was less than the amount allowable, the amount taken into account for such period shall be the amount allowed.

* * *

[CCH Explanation at ¶ 215. Committee Reports at ¶ 10,190.]

Amendments

• **2005, Energy Tax Incentives Act of 2005 (H.R. 6)**

H.R. 6, § 1331(b)(3):

Amended Code Sec. 1250(b)(3) by inserting before the period at the end of the first sentence "or by section 179D". **Effective** for property placed in service after 12-31-2005.

[¶ 5255] CODE SEC. 1397E. CREDIT TO HOLDERS OF QUALIFIED ZONE ACADEMY BONDS.

* * *

(c) LIMITATION BASED ON AMOUNT OF TAX.—The credit allowed under subsection (a) for any taxable year shall not exceed the excess of—

(1) the sum of the regular tax liability (as defined in section 26(b)) plus the tax imposed by section 55, over

>>>→ *Caution: Code Sec. 1397E(c)(2), below, as amended by H.R. 6, applies to bonds issued after December 31, 2005.*

(2) the sum of the credits allowable under part IV of subchapter A (other than subpart C thereof, relating to refundable credits, *and subpart H thereof*).

* * *

[CCH Explanation at ¶ 455. Committee Reports at ¶ 10,020.]

Amendments

• **2005, Energy Tax Incentives Act of 2005 (H.R. 6)**

H.R. 6, § 1303(c)(2):

Amended Code Sec. 1397E(c)(2) by inserting ", and subpart H thereof" after "refundable credits". **Effective** for bonds issued after 12-31-2005.

»»→ *Caution: Code Sec. 1397E(h), below, as amended by H.R. 6, applies to bonds issued after December 31, 2005.*

(h) CREDIT TREATED AS NONREFUNDABLE BONDHOLDER CREDIT.—For purposes of this title, the credit allowed by this section shall be treated as a credit allowable under subpart H of part IV of subchapter A of this chapter.

* * *

[CCH Explanation at ¶ 455. Committee Reports at ¶ 10,020.]

Amendments

• **2005, Energy Tax Incentives Act of 2005 (H.R. 6)**

H.R. 6, § 1303(c)(3):

Amended Code Sec. 1397E(h). **Effective** for bonds issued after 12-31-2005. Prior to amendment, Code Sec. 1397E(h) read as follows:

(h) CREDIT TREATED AS ALLOWED UNDER PART IV OF SUBCHAPTER A.—For purposes of subtitle F, the credit allowed by this section shall be treated as a credit allowable under part IV of subchapter A of this chapter.

[¶ 5260] CODE SEC. 1400C. FIRST-TIME HOMEBUYER CREDIT FOR DISTRICT OF COLUMBIA.

* * *

»»→ *Caution: H.R. 6 amended Code Sec. 1400C(d), but the effective date of the amendment as it relates to the statutory language applicable at that time cannot be reconciled.*

(d) CARRYOVER OF CREDIT.—If the credit allowable under subsection (a) exceeds the limitation imposed by section 26(a) for such taxable year reduced by the sum of the credits allowable under subpart A of part IV of subchapter A (other than *this section and section 25D*), such excess shall be carried to the succeeding taxable year and added to the credit allowable under subsection (a) for such taxable year.

* * *

[CCH Explanation at ¶ 210. Committee Reports at ¶ 10,230.]

Amendments

• **2005, Energy Tax Incentives Act of 2005 (H.R. 6)**

H.R. 6, § 1335(b)(3):

Amended Code Sec. 1400C(d) by striking "this section" and inserting "this section and section 25D". **Effective** for

property placed in service after 12-31-2005, in tax years ending after such date. [Note, this amendment cannot be made to the version of Code Sec. 1400C(d) in effect on January 1, 2006.—CCH.]

[¶ 5265] CODE SEC. 4041. IMPOSITION OF TAX.

(a) DIESEL FUEL AND SPECIAL MOTOR FUELS.—

(1) TAX ON DIESEL FUEL AND KEROSENE IN CERTAIN CASES.—

* * *

(B) EXEMPTION FOR PREVIOUSLY TAXED FUEL.—No tax shall be imposed by this paragraph on the sale or use of any liquid if tax was imposed on such liquid under section 4081 *(other than such tax at the Leaking Underground Storage Tank Trust Fund financing rate)* and the tax thereon was not credited or refunded.

(C) RATE OF TAX.—

* * *

(iii) RATE OF TAX ON CERTAIN BUSES.—

(I) IN GENERAL.—Except as provided in subclause (II), in the case of fuel sold for use or used in a use described in section 6427(b)(1) (after the application of section 6427(b)(3)), the rate of tax imposed by this paragraph shall be 7.3 cents per gallon (4.3 cents per gallon after September 30, *2011*).

* * *

≫→ *Caution: Code Sec. 4041(a)(2), below, as amended by H.R. 6 and H.R. 3, §11101(a)(1)(B), but prior to amendment by H.R. 3, §§11113(a) and 11151(e)(2), applies to any sale or use for any period on or before September 30, 2006.*

(2) SPECIAL MOTOR FUELS.—

(A) IN GENERAL.—There is hereby imposed a tax on any liquid (other than gas oil, fuel oil, or any product taxable under section 4081 *(other than such tax at the Leaking Underground Storage Tank Trust Fund financing rate))*—

(i) sold by any person to an owner, lessee, or other operator of a motor vehicle or motorboat for use as a fuel in such motor vehicle or motorboat, or

(ii) used by any person as a fuel in a motor vehicle or motorboat unless there was a taxable sale of such liquid under clause (i).

(B) RATE OF TAX.—The rate of the tax imposed by this paragraph shall be—

(i) except as otherwise provided in this subparagraph, the rate of tax specified in section 4081(a)(2)(A)(i) which is in effect at the time of such sale or use,

(ii) 13.6 cents per gallon in the case of liquefied petroleum gas, and

(iii) 11.9 cents per gallon in the case of liquefied natural gas.

In the case of any sale or use after September 30, *2011*, clause (ii) shall be applied by substituting "3.2 cents" for "13.6 cents", and clause (iii) shall be applied by substituting "2.8 cents" for "11.9 cents".

≫→ *Caution: Code Sec. 4041(a)(2), below, as amended by H.R. 6 and H.R. 3, §§11113(a) and 11151(e)(2), applies to any sale or use for any period after September 30, 2006.*

(2) ALTERNATIVE FUELS.—

(A) IN GENERAL.—There is hereby imposed a tax on any liquid (other than gas oil, fuel oil, or any product taxable under section 4081 *(other than such tax at the Leaking Underground Storage Tank Trust Fund financing rate))*—

(i) sold by any person to an owner, lessee, or other operator of a motor vehicle or motorboat for use as a fuel in such motor vehicle or motorboat, or

(ii) used by any person as a fuel in a motor vehicle or motorboat unless there was a taxable sale of such liquid under clause (i).

(B) RATE OF TAX.—The rate of the tax imposed by this paragraph shall be—

(i) except as otherwise provided in this subparagraph, the rate of tax specified in section 4081(a)(2)(A)(i) which is in effect at the time of such sale or use, *and*

(ii) in the case of liquefied natural gas, any liquid fuel (other than ethanol and methanol) derived from coal (including peat), and liquid hydrocarbons derived from biomass (as defined in section 45K(c)(3)), 24.3 cents per gallon.

(3) COMPRESSED NATURAL GAS.—

≫→ *Caution: Code Sec. 4041(a)(3)(A), below, as amended by H.R. 3, applies to any sale or use for any period after September 30, 2006.*

(A) IN GENERAL.—There is hereby imposed a tax on compressed natural gas—

(i) sold by any person to an owner, lessee, or other operator of a motor vehicle or motorboat for use as a fuel in such motor vehicle or motorboat, or

(ii) used by any person as a fuel in a motor vehicle or motorboat unless there was a taxable sale of such gas under clause (i).

The rate of the tax imposed by this paragraph shall be *18.3 cents per energy equivalent of a gallon of gasoline.*

* * *

⟫⟫→ *Caution: Code Sec. 4041(a)(3)(C), below, as amended by H.R. 3, applies to any sale or use for any period after September 30, 2006.*

(C) ADMINISTRATIVE PROVISIONS.—For purposes of applying this title with respect to the taxes imposed by this subsection, references to any liquid subject to tax under this subsection shall be treated as including references to compressed natural gas subject to tax under this paragraph, and references to gallons shall be treated as including references to *energy equivalent of a gallon of gasoline* with respect to such gas.

[CCH Explanation at ¶725, ¶740, ¶785 and ¶905. Committee Reports at ¶10,360, ¶15,010, ¶15,040 and ¶15,260.]

Amendments

- **2005, Safe, Accountable, Flexible, Efficient Transportation Equity Act: A Legacy for Users (H.R. 3)**

H.R. 3, §11101(a)(1)(A):

Amended Code Sec. 4041(a)(1)(C)(iii)(I) by striking "2005" and inserting "2011". **Effective** 8-10-2005.

H.R. 3, §11101(a)(1)(B):

Amended Code Sec. 4041(a)(2)(B) by striking "2005" and inserting "2011". **Effective** 8-10-2005.

H.R. 3, §11113(a)(1)(A)-(D):

Amended Code Sec. 4041(a)(2)(B) by adding "and" at the end of clause (i), by striking clauses (ii) and (iii), by striking the last sentence, and by adding after clause (i) a new clause (ii). **Effective** for any sale or use for any period after 9-30-2006. Prior to amendment, Code Sec. 4041(a)(2)(B) read as follows:

(B) RATE OF TAX.—The rate of the tax imposed by this paragraph shall be—

(i) except as otherwise provided in this subparagraph, the rate of tax specified in section 4081(a)(2)(A)(i) which is in effect at the time of such sale or use,

(ii) 13.6 cents per gallon in the case of liquefied petroleum gas, and

(iii) 11.9 cents per gallon in the case of liquefied natural gas.

In the case of any sale or use after September 30, 2011, clause (ii) shall be applied by substituting "3.2 cents" for "13.6 cents", and clause (iii) shall be applied by substituting "2.8 cents" for "11.9 cents".

H.R. 3, §11113(a)(2)(A)-(B):

Amended Code Sec. 4041(a)(3) by striking "48.54 cents per MCF (determined at standard temperature and pressure)" in subparagraph (A) and inserting "18.3 cents per energy equivalent of a gallon of gasoline", and by striking "MCF" in subparagraph (C) and inserting "energy equivalent of a gallon of gasoline". **Effective** for any sale or use for any period after 9-30-2006.

H.R. 3, §11113(a)(3):

Amended the heading for Code Sec. 4041(a)(2) by striking "SPECIAL MOTOR FUELS" and inserting "ALTERNATIVE FUELS". **Effective** for any sale or use for any period after 9-30-2006.

H.R. 3, §11151(e)(2):

Amended Code Sec. 4041(a)(2)(B)(ii) by striking "section 29(c)(3)" and inserting "section 45K(c)(3)". **Effective** as if included in the provision of the Energy Tax Incentives Act of 2005 to which it relates [**effective** for fuel entered, removed or sold after 9-30-2005.—CCH].

H.R. 3, §11161(b)(3)(A):

Amended Code Sec. 4041(a)(1)(B) by striking the last sentence. **Effective** for fuels or liquids removed, entered, or sold after 9-30-2005. Prior to being stricken, the last sentence of Code Sec. 4041(a)(1)(B) read as follows:

This subparagraph shall not apply to aviation-grade kerosene.

- **2005, Energy Tax Incentives Act of 2005 (H.R. 6)**

H.R. 6, §1362(b)(2)(A):

Amended Code Sec. 4041(a)(1)(B) and (2)(A) by inserting "(other than such tax at the Leaking Underground Storage Tank Trust Fund financial rate)" after "section 4081". **Effective** for fuel entered, removed, or sold after 9-30-2005.

(b) EXEMPTION FOR OFF-HIGHWAY BUSINESS USE; REDUCTION IN TAX FOR QUALIFIED METHANOL AND ETHANOL FUEL.—

(1) EXEMPTION FOR OFF-HIGHWAY BUSINESS USE.—

(A) IN GENERAL.—No tax shall be imposed by subsection (a) on liquids sold for use or used in an off-highway business use.

* * *

[CCH Explanation at ¶740 and ¶785. Committee Reports at ¶10,360.]

Amendments

- **2005, Energy Tax Incentives Act of 2005 (H.R. 6)**

H.R. 6, §1362(b)(2)(B):

Amended Code Sec. 4041(b)(1)(A) by striking "or (d)(1))" after "(a)" [Note: The second parenthesis does not appear in the text.—CCH]. **Effective** for fuel entered, removed, or sold after 9-30-2005.

(c) CERTAIN LIQUIDS USED AS A FUEL IN AVIATION.—

(1) IN GENERAL.—There is hereby imposed a tax upon *any liquid for use as a fuel other than aviation gasoline* —

(A) sold by any person to an owner, lessee, or other operator of an aircraft for use in such aircraft, or

(B) used by any person in an aircraft unless there was a taxable sale of such fuel under subparagraph (A).

(2) EXEMPTION FOR PREVIOUSLY TAXED FUEL.—No tax shall be imposed by this subsection on the sale or use of any *liquid for use as a fuel other than aviation gasoline* if tax was imposed on such liquid under section 4081 *(other than such tax at the Leaking Underground Storage Tank Trust Fund financing rate)* and the tax thereon was not credited or refunded.

(3) RATE OF TAX.—*The rate of tax imposed by this subsection shall be 21.8 cents per gallon (4.3 cents per gallon with respect to any sale or use for commercial aviation).*

[CCH Explanation at ¶785. Committee Reports at ¶10,360.]
Amendments

• **2005, Safe, Accountable, Flexible, Efficient Transportation Equity Act: A Legacy for Users (H.R. 3)**

H.R. 3, §11161(b)(1)(A)-(D):

Amended Code Sec. 4041(c) by striking "aviation-grade kerosene" in paragraph (1) and inserting "any liquid for use as a fuel other than aviation gasoline", by striking "aviation-grade kerosene" in paragraph (2) and inserting "liquid for use as a fuel other than aviation gasoline", by striking paragraph (3) and inserting a new paragraph (3), and by striking "AVIATION-GRADE KEROSENE" in the heading and inserting "CERTAIN LIQUIDS USED AS A FUEL IN AVIATION". **Effective** for fuels or liquids removed, entered, or sold after 9-30-2005. Prior to being stricken, Code Sec. 4041(c)(3) read as follows:

(3) RATE OF TAX.—The rate of tax imposed by this subsection shall be the rate of tax applicable under section 4081(a)(2)(A)(iv) which is in effect at the time of such sale or use.

• **2005, Energy Tax Incentives Act of 2005 (H.R. 6)**

H.R. 6, §1362(b)(2)(A):

Amended Code Sec. 4041(c)(2) by inserting "(other than such tax at the Leaking Underground Storage Tank Trust Fund financial rate)" after "section 4081". **Effective** for fuel entered, removed, or sold after 9-30-2005.

(d) ADDITIONAL TAXES TO FUND LEAKING UNDERGROUND STORAGE TANK TRUST FUND.—

* * *

(5) NONAPPLICATION OF EXEMPTIONS OTHER THAN FOR EXPORTS.—*For purposes of this section, the tax imposed under this subsection shall be determined without regard to subsections (f), (g) (other than with respect to any sale for export under paragraph (3) thereof), (h), and (l).*

* * *

[CCH Explanation at ¶785. Committee Reports at ¶10,360.]
Amendments

• **2005, Energy Tax Incentives Act of 2005 (H.R. 6)**

H.R. 6, §1362(b)(2)(C):

Amended Code Sec. 4041(d) by adding at the end a new paragraph (5). **Effective** for fuel entered, removed, or sold after 9-30-2005.

(m) CERTAIN ALCOHOL FUELS.—

(1) IN GENERAL.—In the case of the sale or use of any partially exempt methanol or ethanol fuel the rate of the tax imposed by subsection (a)(2) shall be—

(A) after September 30, 1997, and before October 1, *2011* —

(i) in the case of fuel none of the alcohol in which consists of ethanol, 9.15 cents per gallon, and

(ii) in any other case, 11.3 cents per gallon, and

(B) after September 30, *2011* —

(i) in the case of fuel none of the alcohol in which consists of ethanol, 2.15 cents per gallon, and

(ii) in any other case, 4.3 cents per gallon.

* * *

[CCH Explanation at ¶ 905. Committee Reports at ¶ 15,010.]
Amendments

- **2005, Safe, Accountable, Flexible, Efficient Transportation Equity Act: A Legacy for Users (H.R. 3)**

H.R. 3, § 11101(a)(1)(C):

Amended Code Sec. 4041(m)(1) by striking "2005" each place it appears and inserting "2011". **Effective** 8-10-2005.

[¶ 5270] CODE SEC. 4051. IMPOSITION OF TAX ON HEAVY TRUCKS AND TRAILERS SOLD AT RETAIL.

(a) IMPOSITION OF TAX.—

* * *

(4) EXCLUSION FOR TRACTORS WEIGHING 19,500 POUNDS OR LESS.—*The tax imposed by paragraph (1) shall not apply to tractors of the kind chiefly used for highway transportation in combination with a trailer or semitrailer if—*

(A) *such tractor has a gross vehicle weight of 19,500 pounds or less (as determined by the Secretary), and*

(B) *such tractor, in combination with a trailer or semitrailer, has a gross combined weight of 33,000 pounds or less (as determined by the Secretary).*

(5) SALE OF TRUCKS, ETC., TREATED AS SALE OF CHASSIS AND BODY.—For purposes of this subsection, a sale of an automobile truck or truck trailer or semitrailer shall be considered to be a sale of a chassis and of a body described in paragraph (1).

* * *

[CCH Explanation at ¶ 340. Committee Reports at ¶ 15,030.]
Amendments

- **2005, Safe, Accountable, Flexible, Efficient Transportation Equity Act: A Legacy for Users (H.R. 3)**

H.R. 3, § 11112(a):

Amended Code Sec. 4051(a) by redesignating paragraph (4) as paragraph (5) and by inserting after paragraph (3) a new paragraph (4). **Effective** for sales after 9-30-2005.

(c) TERMINATION.—On and after October 1, *2011*, the taxes imposed by this section shall not apply.

* * *

[CCH Explanation at ¶ 905. Committee Reports at ¶ 15,010.]
Amendments

- **2005, Safe, Accountable, Flexible, Efficient Transportation Equity Act: A Legacy for Users (H.R. 3)**

H.R. 3, § 11101(a)(1)(D):

Amended Code Sec. 4051(c) by striking "2005" and inserting "2011". **Effective** 8-10-2005.

[¶ 5275] CODE SEC. 4064. GAS GUZZLER[S] TAX.

* * *

(b) DEFINITIONS.—For purposes of this section—

(1) AUTOMOBILE.—

(A) IN GENERAL.—The term "automobile" means any 4-wheeled vehicle propelled by fuel—

(i) which is manufactured primarily for use on public streets, roads, and highways (except any vehicle operated exclusively on a rail or rails), and

(ii) which is rated at 6,000 pounds unloaded gross vehicle weight or less.

* * *

In the case of a limousine, the preceding sentence shall be applied without regard to clause (ii).

[CCH Explanation at ¶ 335. Committee Reports at ¶ 15,020.]

Amendments

• 2005, Safe, Accountable, Flexible, Efficient Transportation Equity Act: A Legacy for Users (H.R. 3)

H.R. 3, § 11111(a):

Amended Code Sec. 4064(b)(1)(A) by striking the second sentence. **Effective** 10-1-2005. Prior to being stricken, the second sentence of Code Sec. 4064(b)(1)(A) read as follows:

[¶ 5280] CODE SEC. 4071. IMPOSITION OF TAX.

* * *

(d) TERMINATION.—On and after October 1, *2011*, the taxes imposed by subsection (a) shall not apply.

[CCH Explanation at ¶ 905. Committee Reports at ¶ 15,010.]

Amendments

• 2005, Safe, Accountable, Flexible, Efficient Transportation Equity Act: A Legacy for Users (H.R. 3)

H.R. 3, § 11101(a)(1)(E):

Amended Code Sec. 4071(d) by striking "2005" and inserting "2011". **Effective** 8-10-2005.

[¶ 5285] CODE SEC. 4072. DEFINITIONS.

* * *

(e) SUPER SINGLE TIRE.—For purposes of this part, the term "super single tire" means a single tire greater than 13 inches in cross section width designed to replace 2 tires in a dual fitment. *Such term shall not include any tire designed for steering.*

[CCH Explanation at ¶ 345. Committee Reports at ¶ 10,380.]

Amendments

• 2005, Energy Tax Incentives Act of 2005 (H.R. 6)

H.R. 6, § 1364(a):

Amended Code Sec. 4072(e) by adding at the end a new sentence. **Effective** as if included in Act Sec. 869 of P.L.

108-357 [**effective** for sales in calendar years beginning more than 30 days after 10-22-2004.—CCH].

[¶ 5290] CODE SEC. 4081. IMPOSITION OF TAX.

(a) TAX IMPOSED.—

(1) TAX ON REMOVAL, ENTRY, OR SALE.—

* * *

(B) EXEMPTION FOR BULK TRANSFERS TO REGISTERED TERMINALS OR REFINERIES.—

(i) IN GENERAL.—The tax imposed by this paragraph shall not apply to any removal or entry of a taxable fuel transferred in bulk by pipeline or vessel to a terminal or refinery if the person removing or entering the taxable fuel, the operator of such pipeline or vessel (except as provided in clause (ii)), and the operator of such terminal or refinery are registered under section 4101.

(ii) NONAPPLICATION OF REGISTRATION TO VESSEL OPERATORS ENTERING BY DEEP-DRAFT VESSEL.—For purposes of clause (i), a vessel operator is not required to be registered with respect to the entry of a taxable fuel transferred in bulk by a vessel described in section 4042(c)(1).

(2) RATES OF TAX.—

(A) IN GENERAL.—The rate of the tax imposed by this section is—

(i) in the case of gasoline other than aviation gasoline, 18.3 cents per gallon,

(ii) in the case of aviation gasoline, 19.3 cents per gallon, *and*

(iii) in the case of diesel fuel or kerosene, 24.3 cents per gallon.

(B) LEAKING UNDERGROUND STORAGE TANK TRUST FUND TAX.—The rates of tax specified in subparagraph (A) shall each be increased by 0.1 cent per gallon. The increase in tax under this subparagraph shall in this title be referred to as the Leaking Underground Storage Tank Trust Fund financing rate.

(C) TAXES IMPOSED ON FUEL USED IN AVIATION.—In the case of kerosene which is removed from any refinery or terminal directly into the fuel tank of an aircraft for use in aviation, the rate of tax under subparagraph (A)(iii) shall be—

(i) in the case of use for commercial aviation by a person registered for such use under section 4101, 4.3 cents per gallon, and

(ii) in the case of use for aviation not described in clause (i), 21.8 cents per gallon.

➤➤➤ Caution: Code Sec. 4081(a)(2)(D), below, as added by H.R. 6, is effective January 1, 2006.

(D) DIESEL-WATER FUEL EMULSION.—In the case of diesel-water fuel emulsion at least 14 percent of which is water and with respect to which the emulsion additive is registered by a United States manufacturer with the Environmental Protection Agency pursuant to section 211 of the Clean Air Act (as in effect on March 31, 2003), subparagraph (A)(iii) shall be applied by substituting "19.7 cents" for "24.3 cents". The preceding sentence shall not apply to the removal, sale, or use of diesel-water fuel emulsion unless the person so removing, selling, or using such fuel is registered under section 4101.

(3) CERTAIN REFUELER TRUCKS, TANKERS, AND TANK WAGONS TREATED AS TERMINAL.—

(A) IN GENERAL.—For purposes of paragraph (2)(C), a refueler truck, tanker, or tank wagon shall be treated as part of a terminal if—

(i) such terminal is located within an airport,

(ii) any kerosene which is loaded in such truck, tanker, or wagon at such terminal is for delivery only into aircraft at the airport in which such terminal is located,

(iii) such truck, tanker, or wagon meets the requirements of subparagraph (B) with respect to such terminal, and

(iv) except in the case of exigent circumstances identified by the Secretary in regulations, no vehicle registered for highway use is loaded with kerosene at such terminal.

* * *

(D) APPLICABLE RATE.—For purposes of paragraph (2)(C), in the case of any kerosene treated as removed from a terminal by reason of this paragraph—

(i) the rate of tax specified in paragraph (2)(C)(i) in the case of use described in such paragraph shall apply if such terminal is located within a secured area of an airport, and

(ii) the rate of tax specified in paragraph (2)(C)(ii) shall apply in all other cases.

(4) LIABILITY FOR TAX ON KEROSENE USED IN COMMERCIAL AVIATION.—For purposes of *paragraph (2)(C)(i)*, the person who uses the fuel for commercial aviation shall pay the tax imposed under such paragraph. For purposes of the preceding sentence, fuel shall be treated as used when such fuel is removed into the fuel tank.

* * *

[CCH Explanation at ¶720, ¶740, ¶775 and ¶790. Committee Reports at ¶10,280, ¶15,230, ¶15,260 and ¶15,310.]

Amendments

• **2005, Safe, Accountable, Flexible, Efficient Transportation Equity Act: A Legacy for Users (H.R. 3)**

H.R. 3, §11151(b)(1):

Amended Code Sec. 4081(a)(2)(C) by striking "for use in commercial aviation" and inserting "for use in commercial aviation by a person registered for such use under section 4101". **Effective** as if included in the provision of P.L. 108-357 to which it relates [**effective** for aviation-grade kerosene removed, entered, or sold after 12-31-2004.—CCH].

H.R. 3, §11161(a)(1):

Amended Code Sec. 4081(a)(2)(A) by adding "and" at the end of clause (ii), by striking ", and" at the end of clause (iii) and inserting a period, and by striking clause (iv). **Effective** for fuels or liquids removed, entered, or sold after 9-30-2005. Prior to being stricken, Code Sec. 4081(a)(2)(A)(iv) read as follows:

(iv) in the case of aviation-grade kerosene, 21.8 cents per gallon.

H.R. 3, §11161(a)(2):

Amended Code Sec. 4081(a)(2)(C). **Effective** for fuels or liquids removed, entered, or sold after 9-30-2005. Prior to amendment, Code Sec. 4081(a)(2)(C) read as follows:

(C) TAXES IMPOSED ON FUEL USED IN COMMERCIAL AVIATION.—In the case of aviation-grade kerosene which is removed from any refinery or terminal directly into the fuel tank of an aircraft for use in commercial aviation by a person registered for such use under section 4101, the rate of tax under subparagraph (A)(iv) shall be 4.3 cents per gallon.

H.R. 3, §11161(a)(3)(A)-(B):

Amended Code Sec. 4081(a)(3) by striking "a secured area of" in subparagraph (A)(i) before "an airport", and by adding at the end a new subparagraph (D). **Effective** for fuels or liquids removed, entered, or sold after 9-30-2005.

H.R. 3, §11161(a)(4)(A):

Amended Code Sec. 4081(a)(3)(A) by striking "aviation-grade" each place it appears. **Effective** for fuels or liquids removed, entered, or sold after 9-30-2005. Prior to amendment, Code Sec. 4081(a)(3)(A) read as follows:

(A) IN GENERAL.—For purposes of paragraph (2)(C), a refueler truck, tanker, or tank wagon shall be treated as part of a terminal if—

(i) such terminal is located within an airport,

(ii) any aviation-grade kerosene which is loaded in such truck, tanker, or wagon at such terminal is for delivery only into aircraft at the airport in which such terminal is located,

(iii) such truck, tanker, or wagon meets the requirements of subparagraph (B) with respect to such terminal, and

(iv) except in the case of exigent circumstances identified by the Secretary in regulations, no vehicle registered for highway use is loaded with aviation-grade kerosene at such terminal.

H.R. 3, §11161(a)(4)(B):

Amended Code Sec. 4081(a)(4) by striking "paragraph (2)(C)" and inserting "paragraph (2)(C)(i)". **Effective** for fuels or liquids removed, entered, or sold after 9-30-2005.

H.R. 3, §11161(a)(4)(C):

Amended the heading for Code Sec. 4081(a)(4) by striking "AVIATION-GRADE" before KEROSENE. **Effective** for fuels or liquids removed, entered, or sold after 9-30-2005.

H.R. 3, §11166(b)(1):

Amended Code Sec. 4081(a)(1)(B). **Effective** 8-10-2005. Prior to amendment, Code Sec. 4081(a)(1)(B) read as follows:

(B) EXEMPTION FOR BULK TRANSFERS TO REGISTERED TERMINALS OR REFINERIES.—The tax imposed by this paragraph shall not apply to any removal or entry of a taxable fuel transferred in bulk by pipeline or vessel to a terminal or refinery if the person removing or entering the taxable fuel, the operator of such pipeline or vessel, and the operator of such terminal or refinery are registered under section 4101.

• **2005, Energy Tax Incentives Act of 2005 (H.R. 6)**

H.R. 6, §1343(a):

Amended Code Sec. 4081(a)(2) by adding at the end a new subparagraph (D). **Effective** 1-1-2006.

➤ *Caution: Code Sec. 4081(c), below, as added by H.R. 6, is effective January 1, 2006.*

(c) LATER SEPARATION OF FUEL FROM DIESEL-WATER FUEL EMULSION.—If any person separates the taxable fuel from a diesel-water fuel emulsion on which tax was imposed under subsection (a) at a rate determined under subsection (a)(2)(D) (or with respect to which a credit or payment was allowed or made by reason of section 6427), such person shall be treated as the refiner of such taxable fuel. The amount of tax imposed on any removal of such fuel by such person shall be reduced by the amount of tax imposed (and not credited or refunded) on any prior removal or entry of such fuel.

[CCH Explanation at ¶720. Committee Reports at ¶10,280.]
Amendments

• **2005, Energy Tax Incentives Act of 2005 (H.R. 6)**

H.R. 6, §1343(b)(2):

Amended Code Sec. 4081 by inserting after subsection (b) a new subsection (c). **Effective** 1-1-2006.

(d) TERMINATION.—

(1) IN GENERAL.—The rates of tax specified in clauses (i) and (iii) of subsection (a)(2)(A) shall be 4.3 cents per gallon after September 30, *2011*.

(2) AVIATION FUELS.—The rates of tax specified in subsections (a)(2)(A)(ii) and (a)(2)(C)(ii) shall be 4.3 cents per gallon—

(A) after December 31, 1996, and before the date which is 7 days after the date of the enactment of the Airport and Airway Trust Fund Tax Reinstatement Act of 1997, and

(B) after September 30, 2007.

(3) LEAKING UNDERGROUND STORAGE TANK TRUST FUND FINANCING RATE.—The Leaking Underground Storage Tank Trust Fund financing rate under subsection (a)(2) shall apply after September 30, 1997, and before October 1, *2011*.

* * *

[CCH Explanation at ¶740, ¶785, ¶795 and ¶905. Committee Reports at ¶10,360, ¶15,010, ¶15,230 and ¶15,260.]
Amendments

• **2005, Safe, Accountable, Flexible, Efficient Transportation Equity Act: A Legacy for Users (H.R. 3)**

H.R. 3, §11101(a)(1)(F):

Amended Code Sec. 4081(d)(1) by striking "2005" and inserting "2011". **Effective** 8-10-2005.

H.R. 3, §11151(b)(2):

Amended so much of Code Sec. 4081(d)(2) as precedes subparagraph (A). **Effective** as if included in the provision of P.L. 108-357 to which it relates [effective for aviation-grade kerosene removed, entered, or sold after 12-31-2004.—CCH]. Prior to amendment, the matter preceding Code Sec. 4081(d)(2)(A) read as follows:

(2) AVIATION GASOLINE.—The rate of tax specified in subsection (a)(2)(A)(ii) shall be 4.3 cents per gallon—

H.R. 3, §11161(a)(4)(D):

Amended Code Sec. 4081(d)(2) by striking so much as precedes subparagraph (A) and inserting new text beginning with "(2)". **Effective** for fuels or liquids removed, entered, or sold after 9-30-2005. Prior to being stricken, so much of Code Sec. 4081(d)(2) as precedes subparagraph (A) read as follows:

(2) AVIATION FUELS.—The rates of tax specified in clauses (ii) and (iv) of subsection (a)(2)(A) shall be 4.3 cents per gallon—

• **2005, Energy Tax Incentives Act of 2005 (H.R. 6)**

H.R. 6, §1362(a):

Amended Code Sec. 4081(d)(3) by striking "2005" and inserting "2011". **Effective** 10-1-2005.

[¶5295] CODE SEC. 4082. EXEMPTIONS FOR DIESEL FUEL AND KEROSENE.

(a) IN GENERAL.—The tax imposed by section 4081 *(other than such tax at the Leaking Underground Storage Tank Trust Fund financing rate imposed in all cases other than for export)* shall not apply to diesel fuel and kerosene—

(1) which the Secretary determines is destined for a nontaxable use,

(2) which is indelibly dyed by mechanical injection in accordance with regulations which the Secretary shall prescribe, and

(3) which meets such marking requirements (if any) as may be prescribed by the Secretary in regulations.

Such regulations shall allow an individual choice of dye color approved by the Secretary or chosen from any list of approved dye colors that the Secretary may publish.

[CCH Explanation at ¶785. Committee Reports at ¶10,360.]
Amendments

• **2005, Energy Tax Incentives Act of 2005 (H.R. 6)**

H.R. 6, §1362(b)(1):

Amended Code Sec. 4082(a) by inserting "(other than such tax at the Leaking Underground Storage Tank Trust Fund financing rate imposed in all cases other than for export)" after "section 4081". **Effective** for fuel entered, removed, or sold after 9-30-2005.

(b) NONTAXABLE USE.—For purposes of this section, the term "nontaxable use" means—

(1) any use which is exempt from the tax imposed by section 4041(a)(1) other than by reason of a prior imposition of tax,

(2) any use in a train, and

(3) any use described in section 4041(a)(1)(C)(iii)(II).

The term "nontaxable use" does not include the use of kerosene in an aircraft and such term shall not include any use described in section 6421(e)(2)(C).

* * *

[CCH Explanation at ¶740. Committee Reports at ¶15,260.]
Amendments

• **2005, Safe, Accountable, Flexible, Efficient Transportation Equity Act: A Legacy for Users (H.R. 3)**

H.R. 3, §11161(a)(4)(A):

Amended Code Sec. 4082(b) by striking "aviation-grade" before "kerosene". **Effective** for fuels or liquids removed, entered, or sold after 9-30-2005.

(d) ADDITIONAL EXCEPTIONS TO DYEING REQUIREMENTS FOR KEROSENE.—

* * *

(2) WHOLESALE DISTRIBUTORS.—To the extent provided in regulations, subsection (a)(2) shall not apply to kerosene received by a wholesale distributor of kerosene if such distributor—

* * *

(B) sells kerosene exclusively to ultimate vendors described in *section 6427(l)(6)(B)* with respect to kerosene.

[CCH Explanation at ¶740. Committee Reports at ¶15,260.]
Amendments

• **2005, Safe, Accountable, Flexible, Efficient Transportation Equity Act: A Legacy for Users (H.R. 3)**

H.R. 3, §11161(b)(3)(C):

Amended Code Sec. 4082(d)(2)(B) by striking "section 6427(l)(5)(B)" and inserting "section 6427(l)(6)(B)". **Effective** for fuels or liquids removed, entered, or sold after 9-30-2005.

(e) KEROSENE REMOVED INTO AN AIRCRAFT.—In the case of kerosene which is exempt from the tax imposed by section 4041(c) (other than by reason of a prior imposition of tax) and which is removed from any refinery or terminal directly into the fuel tank of an aircraft, the rate of tax under *section*

4081(a)(2)(A)(iii) shall be zero. For purposes of this subsection, any removal described in section 4081(a)(3)(A) shall be treated as a removal from a terminal but only if such terminal is located within a secure area of an airport.

* * *

[CCH Explanation at ¶ 740. Committee Reports at ¶ 15,260.]

Amendments

• **2005, Safe, Accountable, Flexible, Efficient Transportation Equity Act: A Legacy for Users (H.R. 3)**

H.R. 3, § 11161(a)(4)(E)(i)-(iv):

Amended Code Sec. 4082(e) by striking "aviation-grade", by striking "section 4081(a)(2)(A)(iv)" and inserting "section 4081(a)(2)(A)(iii)", by adding at the end a new sentence, and by striking "AVIATION-GRADE KEROSENE" in the heading thereof and inserting "KEROSENE REMOVED INTO AN AIRCRAFT". **Effective** for fuels or liquids removed, entered, or sold after 9-30-2005. Prior to amendment, Code Sec. 4082(e) read as follows:

(e) AVIATION-GRADE KEROSENE.—In the case of aviation-grade kerosene which is exempt from the tax imposed by section 4041(c) (other than by reason of a prior imposition of tax) and which is removed from any refinery or terminal directly into the fuel tank of an aircraft, the rate of tax under section 4081(a)(2)(A)(iv) shall be zero.

[¶ 5300] CODE SEC. 4083. DEFINITIONS; SPECIAL RULE; ADMINISTRATIVE AUTHORITY.

* * *

(b) COMMERCIAL AVIATION.—For purposes of this subpart, the term "commercial aviation" means any use of an aircraft in a business of transporting persons or property for compensation or hire by air, unless properly allocable to any transportation exempt from the taxes imposed by sections 4261 and 4271 by reason of section 4281 or 4282 or by reason of *subsection (h) or (i) of section 4261*.

* * *

[CCH Explanation at ¶ 810. Committee Reports at ¶ 15,090.]

Amendments

• **2005, Safe, Accountable, Flexible, Efficient Transportation Equity Act: A Legacy for Users (H.R. 3)**

H.R. 3, § 11123(b):

Amended Code Sec. 4083(b) by striking "section 4261(h)" and inserting "subsection (h) or (i) of section 4261". **Effective** for transportation beginning after 9-30-2005.

[¶ 5305] CODE SEC. 4101. REGISTRATION AND BOND.

(a) REGISTRATION.—

⇛ *Caution: Code Sec. 4101(a)(1), below, as amended by H.R. 3, applies to any sale or use for any period after September 30, 2006.*

(1) IN GENERAL.—Every person required by the Secretary to register under this section with respect to the tax imposed by section *4041(a)* or 4081 and every person producing or importing biodiesel (as defined in section 40A(d)(1)) or alcohol (as defined in section 6426(b)(4)(A)) shall register with the Secretary at such time, in such form and manner, and subject to such terms and conditions, as the Secretary may by regulations prescribe. A registration under this section may be used only in accordance with regulations prescribed under this section.

* * *

⇛ *Caution: Code Sec. 4101(a)(4), below, as added by H.R. 3, applies to sales after December 31, 2005.*

(4) REGISTRATION OF PERSONS EXTENDING CREDIT ON CERTAIN EXEMPT SALES OF FUEL.—The Secretary shall require registration by any person which—

(A) extends credit by credit card to any ultimate purchaser described in subparagraph (C) or (D) of section 6416(b)(2) for the purchase of taxable fuel upon which tax has been imposed under section 4041 or 4081, and

(B) does not collect the amount of such tax from such ultimate purchaser.

(4)[(5)] REREGISTRATION IN EVENT OF CHANGE IN OWNERSHIP.—*Under regulations prescribed by the Secretary, a person (other than a corporation the stock of which is regularly traded on an established securities market) shall be required to reregister under this section if after a transaction (or series of related transactions) more than 50 percent of ownership interests in, or assets of, such person are held by persons other than persons (or persons related thereto) who held more than 50 percent of such interests or assets before the transaction (or series of related transactions).*

* * *

[CCH Explanation at ¶ 725, ¶ 745 and ¶ 755. Committee Reports at ¶ 15,040, ¶ 15,280 and ¶ 15,290.]

Amendments

- **2005, Safe, Accountable, Flexible, Efficient Transportation Equity Act: A Legacy for Users (H.R. 3)**

H.R. 3, § 11113(c):

Amended Code Sec. 4101(a)(1) by striking "4041(a)(1)" and inserting "4041(a)". **Effective** for any sale or use for any period after 9-30-2006.

H.R. 3, § 11163(a):

Amended Code Sec. 4101(a) by adding at the end a new paragraph (4). **Effective** for sales after 12-31-2005.

H.R. 3, § 11164(a):

Amended Code Sec. 4101(a) by adding at the end a new paragraph (4)[(5)]. **Effective** for actions, or failures to act, after 8-10-2005.

[¶ 5310] CODE SEC. 4161. IMPOSITION OF TAX.

(a) SPORT FISHING EQUIPMENT.—

    (1) IMPOSITION OF TAX.—

        (A) IN GENERAL.—*There is hereby imposed on the sale of any article of sport fishing equipment by the manufacturer, producer, or importer a tax equal to 10 percent of the price for which so sold.*

        (B) LIMITATION ON TAX IMPOSED ON FISHING RODS AND POLES.—*The tax imposed by subparagraph (A) on any fishing rod or pole shall not exceed $10.*

    (2) 3 PERCENT RATE OF TAX FOR ELECTRIC OUTBOARD MOTORS AND SONAR DEVICES SUITABLE FOR FINDING FISH.—

        (A) IN GENERAL.—*In the case of an electric outboard motor or a sonar device suitable for finding fish, paragraph (1)(A) shall be applied by substituting "3 percent" for "10 percent".*

        (B) $30 LIMITATION ON TAX IMPOSED ON SONAR DEVICES SUITABLE FOR FINDING FISH.—*The tax imposed by paragraph (1)(A) on any sonar device suitable for finding fish shall not exceed $30.*

* * *

[CCH Explanation at ¶ 845. Committee Reports at ¶ 15,065.]

Amendments

- **2005, Safe, Accountable, Flexible, Efficient Transportation Equity Act: A Legacy for Users (H.R. 3)**

H.R. 3, § 11117(a):

Amended Code Sec. 4161(a)(1). **Effective** for articles sold by the manufacturer, producer, or importer after 9-30-2005. Prior to amendment, Code Sec. 4161(a)(1), read as follows:

(1) IMPOSITION OF TAX.—There is hereby imposed on the sale of any article of sport fishing equipment by the manufacturer, producer, or importer a tax equal to 10 percent of the price for which so sold.

H.R. 3, § 11117(b):

Amended Code Sec. 4161(a)(2) by striking "paragraph (1)" both places it appears and inserting "paragraph (1)(A)". **Effective** for articles sold by the manufacturer, producer, or importer after 9-30-2005.

[¶ 5315] CODE SEC. 4182. EXEMPTIONS.

* * *

(c) SMALL MANUFACTURERS, ETC.—

    (1) IN GENERAL.—*The tax imposed by section 4181 shall not apply to any pistol, revolver, or firearm described in such section if manufactured, produced, or imported by a person who manufactures, produces, and imports less than an aggregate of 50 of such articles during the calendar year.*

(2) CONTROLLED GROUPS.—*All persons treated as a single employer for purposes of subsection (a) or (b) of section 52 shall be treated as one person for purposes of paragraph (1).*

[CCH Explanation at ¶ 850. Committee Reports at ¶ 15,140.]

Amendments

- **2005, Safe, Accountable, Flexible, Efficient Transportation Equity Act: A Legacy for Users (H.R. 3)**

H.R. 3, § 11131(a):

Amended Code Sec. 4182 by redesignating subsection (c) as subsection (d) and by inserting after subsection (b) a new subsection (c). **Effective** for articles sold by the manufacturer, producer, or importer after 9-30-2005. For a special rule, see Act Sec. 11131(b)(2), below.

H.R. 3, § 11131(b)(2), provides:

(2) NO INFERENCE.—Nothing in the amendments made by this section shall be construed to create any inference with respect to the proper tax treatment of any sales before the effective date of such amendments.

(d) RECORDS.—Notwithstanding the provisions of sections 922(b)(5) and 923(g) of title 18, United States Code, no person holding a Federal license under chapter 44 of title 18, United States Code, shall be required to record the name, address, or other information about the purchaser of shotgun ammunition, ammunition suitable for use only in rifles generally available in commerce, or component parts for the aforesaid types of ammunition.

[CCH Explanation at ¶ 850. Committee Reports at ¶ 15,140.]

Amendments

- **2005, Safe, Accountable, Flexible, Efficient Transportation Equity Act: A Legacy for Users (H.R. 3)**

H.R. 3, § 11131(a):

Amended Code Sec. 4182 by redesignating subsection (c) as subsection (d). **Effective** for articles sold by the manufacturer, producer, or importer after 9-30-2005. For a special rule, see Act Sec. 11131(b)(2), below.

H.R. 3, § 11131(b)(2), provides:

(2) NO INFERENCE.—Nothing in the amendments made by this section shall be construed to create any inference with respect to the proper tax treatment of any sales before the effective date of such amendments.

[¶ 5320] CODE SEC. 4221. CERTAIN TAX-FREE SALES.

(a) GENERAL RULE.—Under regulations prescribed by the Secretary, no tax shall be imposed under this chapter (other than under section 4121 or 4081) on the sale by the manufacturer (or under subchapter A or C of chapter 31 on the first retail sale) of an article—

(1) for use by the purchaser for further manufacture, or for resale by the purchaser to a second purchaser for use by such second purchaser in further manufacture,

(2) for export, or for resale by the purchaser to a second purchaser for export,

(3) for use by the purchaser as supplies for vessels or aircraft,

(4) to a State or local government for the exclusive use of a State or local government, or

(5) to a nonprofit educational organization for its exclusive use,

but only if such exportation or use is to occur before any other use. Paragraphs (4) and (5) shall not apply to the tax imposed by section 4064. In the case of taxes imposed by section 4051 or 4071, paragraphs (4) and (5) shall not apply on and after October 1, *2011*. In the case of the tax imposed by section 4131, paragraphs (3), (4), and (5) shall not apply and paragraph (2) shall apply only if the use of the exported vaccine meets such requirements as the Secretary may by regulations prescribe. In the case of taxes imposed by subchapter A of chapter 31, paragraphs (1), (3), (4), and (5) shall not apply.

[CCH Explanation at ¶ 905. Committee Reports at ¶ 15,010.]

Amendments

• 2005, Safe, Accountable, Flexible, Efficient Transportation Equity Act: A Legacy for Users (H.R. 3)

H.R. 3, § 11101(b)(1):

Amended Code Sec. 4221(a) by striking "2005" and inserting "2011". **Effective** 8-10-2005.

[¶ 5325] CODE SEC. 4261. IMPOSITION OF TAX.

* * *

(e) SPECIAL RULES.—

(1) SEGMENTS TO AND FROM RURAL AIRPORTS.—

* * *

(B) RURAL AIRPORT.—For purposes of this paragraph, the term "rural airport" means, with respect to any calendar year, any airport if—

(i) there were fewer than 100,000 commercial passengers departing by air *(in the case of any airport described in clause (ii)(III), on flight segments of at least 100 miles)* during the second preceding calendar year from such airport, and

(ii) such airport—

(I) is not located within 75 miles of another airport which is not described in clause (i),

(II) is receiving essential air service subsidies as of the date of the enactment of this paragraph, *or*

(III) is not connected by paved roads to another airport.

* * *

[CCH Explanation at ¶ 805. Committee Reports at ¶ 15,080.]

Amendments

• 2005, Safe, Accountable, Flexible, Efficient Transportation Equity Act: A Legacy for Users (H.R. 3)

H.R. 3, § 11122(a)(1)-(2):

Amended Code Sec. 4261(e)(1)(B) by inserting "(in the case of any airport described in clause (ii)(III), on flight segments of at least 100 miles)" after "by air" in clause (i), and by striking "or" at the end of subclause (I) of clause (ii), by striking the period at the end of subclause (II) of clause (ii) and inserting ", or", and by adding at the end of clause (ii) a new subclause (III). **Effective** 10-1-2005.

(f) EXEMPTION FOR CERTAIN USES.—No tax shall be imposed under subsection (a) or (b) on air transportation—

(1) by helicopter for the purpose of transporting individuals, equipment, or supplies in the exploration for, or the development or removal of, hard minerals, oil, or gas, or

(2) by helicopter or by fixed-wing aircraft for the purpose of the planting, cultivation, cutting, or transportation of, or caring for, trees (including logging operations),

but only if the helicopter or fixed-wing aircraft does not take off from, or land at, a facility eligible for assistance under the Airport and Airway Development Act of 1970, or otherwise use services provided pursuant to section 44509 or 44913(b) or subchapter I of chapter 471 of title 49, United States Code, during such use. In the case of helicopter transportation described in paragraph (1), this subsection shall be applied by treating each flight segment as a distinct flight.

* * *

[CCH Explanation at ¶ 820. Committee Reports at ¶ 15,070.]

Amendments

- 2005, Safe, Accountable, Flexible, Efficient Transportation Equity Act: A Legacy for Users (H.R. 3)

H.R. 3, § 11121(c):

Amended Code Sec. 4261(f). **Effective** for fuel use or air transportation after 9-30-2005. Prior to amendment, Code Sec. 4261(f) read as follows:

(f) EXEMPTION FOR CERTAIN HELICOPTER USES.—No tax shall be imposed under subsection (a) or (b) on air transportation by helicopter for the purpose of—

(1) transporting individuals, equipment, or supplies in the exploration for, or the development or removal of, hard minerals, oil, or gas, or

(2) the planting, cultivation, cutting, or transportation of, or caring for, trees (including logging operations),

but only if the helicopter does not take off from, or land at, a facility eligible for assistance under the Airport and Airway Development Act of 1970, or otherwise use services provided pursuant to section 44509 or 44913(b) or subchapter I of chapter 471 of title 49, United States Code, during such use. In the case of helicopter transportation described in paragraph (1), this subsection shall be applied by treating each flight segment as a distinct flight.

(i) EXEMPTION FOR SEAPLANES.—No tax shall be imposed by this section or section 4271 on any air transportation by a seaplane with respect to any segment consisting of a takeoff from, and a landing on, water, but only if the places at which such takeoff and landing occur have not received and are not receiving financial assistance from the Airport and Airways Trust Fund.

[CCH Explanation at ¶ 810. Committee Reports at ¶ 15,090.]

Amendments

- 2005, Safe, Accountable, Flexible, Efficient Transportation Equity Act: A Legacy for Users (H.R. 3)

H.R. 3, § 11123(a):

Amended Code Sec. 4261 by redesignating subsection (i) as subsection (j) and by inserting after subsection (h) a new subsection (i). **Effective** for transportation beginning after 9-30-2005.

(j) APPLICATION OF TAXES.—

* * *

[CCH Explanation at ¶ 810. Committee Reports at ¶ 15,090.]

Amendments

- 2005, Safe, Accountable, Flexible, Efficient Transportation Equity Act: A Legacy for Users (H.R. 3)

H.R. 3, § 11123(a):

Amended Code Sec. 4261 by redesignating subsection (i) as subsection (j). **Effective** for transportation beginning after 9-30-2005.

[¶ 5335] CODE SEC. 4281. SMALL AIRCRAFT ON NONESTABLISHED LINES.

The taxes imposed by sections 4261 and 4271 shall not apply to transportation by an aircraft having a maximum certificated takeoff weight of 6,000 pounds or less, except when such aircraft is operated on an established line. For purposes of the preceding sentence, the term "maximum certificated takeoff weight" means the maximum such weight contained in the type certificate or airworthiness certificate. *For purposes of this section, an aircraft shall not be considered as operated on an established line at any time during which such aircraft is being operated on a flight the sole purpose of which is sightseeing.*

[CCH Explanation at ¶ 815. Committee Reports at ¶ 15,100.]

Amendments

- 2005, Safe, Accountable, Flexible, Efficient Transportation Equity Act: A Legacy for Users (H.R. 3)

H.R. 3, § 11124(a):

Amended Code Sec. 4281 by adding at the end a new sentence. **Effective** with respect to transportation beginning after 9-30-2005, but shall not apply to any amount paid before such date for such transportation.

[¶ 5340] CODE SEC. 4461. IMPOSITION OF TAX.

* * *

(c) LIABILITY AND TIME OF IMPOSITION OF TAX.—

(1) LIABILITY.—The tax imposed by subsection (a) shall be paid by—

(A) in the case of cargo entering the United States, the importer, *or*

(B) in any other case, the shipper.

(2) TIME OF IMPOSITION.—Except as provided by regulations, the tax imposed by subsection (a) shall be *imposed* at the time of unloading.

[CCH Explanation at ¶ 825. Committee Reports at ¶ 15,060.]

Amendments

• 2005, Safe, Accountable, Flexible, Efficient Transportation Equity Act: A Legacy for Users (H.R. 3)

H.R. 3, § 11116(b)(1):

Amended Code Sec. 4461(c)(1) by adding "or" at the end of subparagraph (A), by striking subparagraph (B), and by redesignating subparagraph (C) as subparagraph (B). **Effective** before, on, and after 8-10-2005. Prior to being stricken, Code Sec. 4461(c)(1)(B) read as follows:

(B) in the case of cargo to be exported from the United States, the exporter, or

H.R. 3, § 11116(b)(2):

Amended Code Sec. 4461(c)(2) by striking "imposed—" and all that follows through "in any other case," and inserting "imposed". **Effective** before, on, and after 8-10-2005. Prior to amendment, Code Sec. 4461(c)(2) read as follows:

(2) TIME OF IMPOSITION.—Except as provided by regulations, the tax imposed by subsection (a) shall be imposed—

(A) in the case of cargo to be exported from the United States, at the time of loading, and

(B) in any other case, at the time of unloading.

[¶ 5345] CODE SEC. 4462. DEFINITIONS AND SPECIAL RULES.

* * *

(d) NONAPPLICABILITY OF TAX TO EXPORTS.—The tax imposed by section 4461(a) shall not apply to any port use with respect to any commercial cargo to be exported from the United States.

* * *

[CCH Explanation at ¶ 825. Committee Reports at ¶ 15,060.]

Amendments

• 2005, Safe, Accountable, Flexible, Efficient Transportation Equity Act: A Legacy for Users (H.R. 3)

H.R. 3, § 11116(a):

Amended Code Sec. 4462(d). **Effective** before, on, and after 8-10-2005. Prior to amendment, Code Sec. 4462(d) read as follows:

(d) NONAPPLICABILITY OF TAX TO CERTAIN CARGO.—

(1) IN GENERAL.—Subject to paragraph (2), the tax imposed by section 4461(a) shall not apply to bonded commercial cargo entering the United States for transportation and direct exportation to a foreign country.

(2) IMPOSITION OF CHARGES.—Paragraph (1) shall not apply to any cargo exported to Canada or Mexico—

(A) during the period—

(i) after the date on which the Secretary determines that the Government of Canada or Mexico (as the case may be) has imposed a substantially equivalent tax, fee, or charge on commercial vessels or commercial cargo utilizing ports of such country, and

(ii) subject to subparagraph (B), before the date on which the Secretary determines that such tax, fee, charge has been discontinued by such country, and

(B) with respect to a particular United States port (or to any transaction or class of transactions at any such port) to the extent that the study made pursuant to section 1407(a) of the Water Resources Development Act of 1986 (or a review thereof pursuant to section 1407(b) of such Act) finds that—

(i) the imposition of the tax imposed by this subchapter at such port (or to any transaction or class of transactions at such port) is not likely to divert a significant amount of cargo from such port to a port in a country contiguous to the United States, or that any such diversion is not likely to result in significant economic loss to such port, or

(ii) the nonapplicability of such tax at such port (or to any transaction or class of transactions at such port) is likely to result in significant economic loss to any other United States port.

[¶ 5350] CODE SEC. 4481. IMPOSITION OF TAX.

* * *

(f) PERIOD TAX IN EFFECT.—The tax imposed by this section shall apply only to use before October 1, *2011.*

[CCH Explanation at ¶ 905. Committee Reports at ¶ 15,010.]
Amendments
- 2005, Safe, Accountable, Flexible, Efficient Transportation Equity Act: A Legacy for Users (H.R. 3)

H.R. 3, § 11101(a)(2)(A):

Amended Code Sec. 4481(f) by striking "2006" and inserting "2011". **Effective** 8-10-2005.

[¶ 5355] CODE SEC. 4482. DEFINITIONS.

* * *

(c) OTHER DEFINITIONS AND SPECIAL RULE.—For purposes of this subchapter—

* * *

(4) TAXABLE PERIOD.—The term "taxable period" means any year beginning before July 1, *2011*, and the period which begins on July 1, *2011*, and ends at the close of September 30, *2011*.

* * *

[CCH Explanation at ¶ 905. Committee Reports at ¶ 15,010.]
Amendments
- 2005, Safe, Accountable, Flexible, Efficient Transportation Equity Act: A Legacy for Users (H.R. 3)

H.R. 3, § 11101(a)(2)(B):

Amended Code Sec. 4482(c)(4) by striking "2006" each place it appears and inserting "2011". **Effective** 8-10-2005.

(d) SPECIAL RULE FOR TAXABLE PERIOD IN WHICH TERMINATION DATE OCCURS.—In the case of the taxable period which ends on September 30, *2011*, the amount of the tax imposed by section 4481 with respect to any highway motor vehicle shall be determined by reducing each dollar amount in the table contained in section 4481(a) by 75 percent.

[CCH Explanation at ¶ 905. Committee Reports at ¶ 15,010.]
Amendments
- 2005, Safe, Accountable, Flexible, Efficient Transportation Equity Act: A Legacy for Users (H.R. 3)

H.R. 3, § 11101(a)(2)(C):

Amended Code Sec. 4482(d) by striking "2006" and inserting "2011". **Effective** 8-10-2005.

[¶ 5360] CODE SEC. 4483. EXEMPTIONS.

* * *

(h) TERMINATION OF EXEMPTIONS.—Subsections (a) and (c) shall not apply on and after October 1, *2011*.

[CCH Explanation at ¶ 905. Committee Reports at ¶ 15,010.]
Amendments
- 2005, Safe, Accountable, Flexible, Efficient Transportation Equity Act: A Legacy for Users (H.R. 3)

H.R. 3, § 11101(b)(2):

Amended Code Sec. 4483(h) by striking "2006" and inserting "2011". **Effective** 8-10-2005.

[¶ 5365] CODE SEC. 4611. IMPOSITION OF TAX.

* * *

(f) APPLICATION OF OIL SPILL LIABILITY TRUST FUND FINANCING RATE.—

(1) IN GENERAL.—Except as provided in paragraphs (2) and (3), the Oil Spill Liability Trust Fund financing rate under subsection (c) shall apply on and after April 1, 2006, or if later, the date which is 30 days after the last day of any calendar quarter for which the Secretary estimates that, as of the close of that quarter, the unobligated balance in the Oil Spill Liability Trust Fund is less than $2,000,000,000.

(2) FUND BALANCE.—The Oil Spill Liability Trust Fund financing rate shall not apply during a calendar quarter if the Secretary estimates that, as of the close of the preceding calendar quarter, the unobligated balance in the Oil Spill Liability Trust Fund exceeds $2,700,000,000.

(3) TERMINATION.—The Oil Spill Liability Trust Fund financing rate shall not apply after December 31, 2014.

[CCH Explanation at ¶ 540. Committee Reports at ¶ 10,350.]

Amendments

- **2005, Energy Tax Incentives Act of 2005 (H.R. 6)**

H.R. 6, § 1361:

Amended Code Sec. 4611(f). **Effective** 8-8-2005. Prior to amendment, Code Sec. 4611(f) read as follows:

(f) APPLICATION OF OIL SPILL LIABILITY TRUST FUND FINANCING RATE.—

(1) IN GENERAL.—Except as provided in paragraph (2), the Oil Spill Liability Trust Fund financing rate under subsection (c) shall apply after December 31, 1989, and before January 1, 1995.

(2) NO TAX IF UNOBLIGATED BALANCE IN FUND EXCEEDS $1,000,000,000.—The Oil Spill Liability Trust Fund financing rate shall not apply during any calendar quarter if the Secretary estimates that as of the close of the preceding calendar quarter the unobligated balance in the Oil Spill Liability Trust Fund exceeds $1,000,000,000.

[¶ 5370] CODE SEC. 5011. INCOME TAX CREDIT FOR AVERAGE COST OF CARRYING EXCISE TAX.

(a) IN GENERAL.—For purposes of section 38, the amount of the distilled spirits credit for any taxable year is the amount equal to the product of—

(1) in the case of—

(A) any eligible wholesaler, the number of cases of bottled distilled spirits—

(i) which were bottled in the United States, and

(ii) which are purchased by such wholesaler during the taxable year directly from the bottler of such spirits, or

(B) any person which is subject to section 5005 and which is not an eligible wholesaler, the number of cases of bottled distilled spirits which are stored in a warehouse operated by, or on behalf of, a State or political subdivision thereof, or an agency of either, on which title has not passed on an unconditional sale basis, and

(2) the average tax-financing cost per case for the most recent calendar year ending before the beginning of such taxable year.

(b) ELIGIBLE WHOLESALER.—For purposes of this section, the term "eligible wholesaler" means any person which holds a permit under the Federal Alcohol Administration Act as a wholesaler of distilled spirits which is not a State or political subdivision thereof, or an agency of either.

(c) AVERAGE TAX-FINANCING COST.—

(1) IN GENERAL.—For purposes of this section, the average tax-financing cost per case for any calendar year is the amount of interest which would accrue at the deemed financing rate during a 60-day period on an amount equal to the deemed Federal excise tax per case.

(2) DEEMED FINANCING RATE.—For purposes of paragraph (1), the deemed financing rate for any calendar year is the average of the corporate overpayment rates under paragraph (1) of section 6621(a) (determined without regard to the last sentence of such paragraph) for calendar quarters of such year.

(3) DEEMED FEDERAL EXCISE TAX PER CASE.—For purposes of paragraph (1), the deemed Federal excise tax per case is $25.68.

(d) OTHER DEFINITIONS AND SPECIAL RULES.—For purposes of this section—

(1) CASE.—The term "case" means 12 80-proof 750-milliliter bottles.

(2) NUMBER OF CASES IN LOT.—The number of cases in any lot of distilled spirits shall be determined by dividing the number of liters in such lot by 9.

[CCH Explanation at ¶ 835. Committee Reports at ¶ 15,120.]

Amendments

• 2005, Safe, Accountable, Flexible, Efficient Transportation Equity Act: A Legacy for Users (H.R. 3)

H.R. 3, § 11126(a):

Amended subpart A of part I of subchapter A of chapter 51 by adding at the end a new Code Sec. 5011. **Effective** for tax years beginning after 9-30-2005.

[¶ 5375] CODE SEC. 5061. METHOD OF COLLECTING TAX.

* * *

(d) TIME FOR COLLECTING TAX ON DISTILLED SPIRITS, WINES, AND BEER.—

* * *

⋙→ Caution: Code Sec. 5061(d)(4), below, as added by H.R. 3, applies with respect to quarterly periods beginning on and after January 1, 2006.

(4) TAXPAYERS LIABLE FOR TAXES OF NOT MORE THAN $50,000.—

(A) IN GENERAL.—In the case of any taxpayer who reasonably expects to be liable for not more than $50,000 in taxes imposed with respect to distilled spirits, wines, and beer under subparts A, C, and D and section 7652 for the calendar year and who was liable for not more than $50,000 in such taxes in the preceding calendar year, the last day for the payment of tax on withdrawals, removals, and entries (and articles brought into the United States from Puerto Rico) under bond for deferred payment shall be the 14th day after the last day of the calendar quarter during which the action giving rise to the imposition of such tax occurs.

(B) NO APPLICATION AFTER LIMIT EXCEEDED.—Subparagraph (A) shall not apply to any taxpayer for any portion of the calendar year following the first date on which the aggregate amount of tax due under subparts A, C, and D and section 7652 from such taxpayer during such calendar year exceeds $50,000, and any tax under such subparts which has not been paid on such date shall be due on the 14th day after the last day of the semimonthly period in which such date occurs.

(C) CALENDAR QUARTER.—For purposes of this paragraph, the term "calendar quarter" means the three-month period ending on March 31, June 30, September 30, or December 31.

⋙→ Caution: Former Code Sec. 5061(d)(4) was redesignated as Code Sec. 5061(d)(5), below, by H.R. 3, applicable with respect to quarterly periods beginning on and after January 1, 2006.

(5) SPECIAL RULE FOR TAX DUE IN SEPTEMBER.—

(A) IN GENERAL.—Notwithstanding the preceding provisions of this subsection, the taxes on distilled spirits, wines, and beer for the period beginning on September 16 and ending on September 26 shall be paid not later than September 29.

(B) SAFE HARBOR.—The requirement of subparagraph (A) shall be treated as met if the amount paid not later than September 29 is not less than $11/15$ of the taxes on distilled spirits, wines, and beer for the period beginning on September 1 and ending on September 15.

(C) TAXPAYERS NOT REQUIRED TO USE ELECTRONIC FUNDS TRANSFER.— In the case of payments not required to be made by electronic funds transfer, subparagraphs (A) and (B) shall be applied by substituting "September 25" for "September 26", September 28" for September 29", and "$^2/_3$" for "$^{11}/_{15}$".

⟫➔ *Caution: Code Sec. 5061(d)(6) was redesignated and amended by H.R. 3, applicable with respect to quarterly periods beginning on and after January 1, 2006.*

(6) SPECIAL RULE WHERE DUE DATE FALLS ON SATURDAY, SUNDAY, OR HOLIDAY.—Notwithstanding section 7503, if, but for this paragraph, the due date under this subsection for payment of tax would fall on a Saturday, Sunday, or a legal holiday (within the meaning of section 7503), such due date shall be the immediately preceding day which is not a Saturday, Sunday, or such a holiday (or the immediately following day where the due date described in *paragraph (5)* falls on a Sunday).

[CCH Explanation at ¶ 830. Committee Reports at ¶ 15,130.]

Amendments
- **2005, Safe, Accountable, Flexible, Efficient Transportation Equity Act: A Legacy for Users (H.R. 3)**

H.R. 3, § 11127(a):

Amended Code Sec. 5061(d) by redesignating paragraphs (4) and (5) as paragraphs (5) and (6), respectively, and by inserting after paragraph (3) a new paragraph (4). **Effective** with respect to quarterly periods beginning on and after 1-1-2006.

H.R. 3, § 11127(b):

Amended Code Sec. 5061(d)(6), as redesignated by Act Sec. 11127(a), by striking "paragraph (4)" and inserting "paragraph (5)". **Effective** with respect to quarterly periods beginning on and after 1-1-2006.

[¶ 5385] CODE SEC. 6049. RETURNS REGARDING PAYMENTS OF INTEREST.

* * *

(d) DEFINITIONS AND SPECIAL RULES.—For purposes of this section—

* * *

⟫➔ *Caution: Code Sec. 6049(d)(8), below, as added by H.R. 6, applies to bonds issued after December 31, 2005.*

(8) REPORTING OF CREDIT ON CLEAN RENEWABLE ENERGY BONDS.—

(A) IN GENERAL.—*For purposes of subsection (a), the term "interest" includes amounts includible in gross income under section 54(g) and such amounts shall be treated as paid on the credit allowance date (as defined in section 54(b)(4)).*

(B) REPORTING TO CORPORATIONS, ETC.—*Except as otherwise provided in regulations, in the case of any interest described in subparagraph (A), subsection (b)(4) shall be applied without regard to subparagraphs (A), (H), (I), (J), (K), and (L)(i) of such subsection.*

(C) REGULATORY AUTHORITY.—*The Secretary may prescribe such regulations as are necessary or appropriate to carry out the purposes of this paragraph, including regulations which require more frequent or more detailed reporting.*

[CCH Explanation at ¶ 455. Committee Reports at ¶ 10,020.]

Amendments
- **2005, Energy Tax Incentives Act of 2005 (H.R. 6)**

H.R. 6, § 1303(b):

Amended Code Sec. 6049(d) by adding at the end a new paragraph (8). **Effective** for bonds issued after 12-31-2005.

[¶ 5390] CODE SEC. 6071. TIME FOR FILING RETURNS AND OTHER DOCUMENTS.

* * *

>>→ *Caution: Code Sec. 6071(c), below, as amended by H.R. 3, is effective July 1, 2008, but shall not apply to taxes imposed for periods before such date.*

(c) SPECIAL TAXES.—For payment of special taxes before engaging in certain trades and businesses, see section 4901 and *section 5732*.

[CCH Explanation at ¶ 840. Committee Reports at ¶ 15,110.]

Amendments

- **2005, Safe, Accountable, Flexible, Efficient Transportation Equity Act: A Legacy for Users (H.R. 3)**

H.R. 3, § 11125(b)(21):

Amended Code Sec. 6071(c) by striking "section 5142" and inserting "section 5732". **Effective** 7-1-2008, but shall not apply to taxes imposed for periods before such date.

>>→ *Caution: Code Sec. 6206, below, as amended by H.R. 3, applies to sales after December 31, 2005.*

[¶ 5395] CODE SEC. 6206. SPECIAL RULES APPLICABLE TO EXCESSIVE CLAIMS UNDER *CERTAIN SECTIONS*.

Any portion of a refund made under section 6416(a)(4) and any portion of a payment made under section 6420, 6421, or 6427 which constitutes an excessive amount (as defined in section 6675(b)), and any civil penalty provided by section 6675, may be assessed and collected as if it were a tax imposed by section 4081 (with respect to *refunds under section 6416(a)(4) and payments under sections 6420* and 6421), or 4041 or 4081 (with respect to payments under section 6427) and as if the person who made the claim were liable for such tax. The period for assessing any such portion, and for assessing any such penalty, shall be 3 years from the last day prescribed for the filing of the claim under *section 6416(a)(4), 6420*, 6421, or 6427 as the case may be.

[CCH Explanation at ¶ 745. Committee Reports at ¶ 15,280.]

Amendments

- **2005, Safe, Accountable, Flexible, Efficient Transportation Equity Act: A Legacy for Users (H.R. 3)**

H.R. 3, § 11163(d)(1)(A)-(D):

Amended Code Sec. 6206 by striking "Any portion" in the first sentence and inserting "Any portion of a refund made under section 6416(a)(4) and any portion", by striking "payments under sections 6420" in the first sentence and inserting "refunds under section 6416(a)(4) and payments under sections 6420", by striking "section 6420" in the second sentence and inserting "section 6416(a)(4), 6420", and by striking "**SECTIONS 6420, 6421, AND 6427**" in the heading thereof and inserting "**CERTAIN SECTIONS**". **Effective** for sales after 12-31-2005.

[¶ 5400] CODE SEC. 6401. AMOUNTS TREATED AS OVERPAYMENTS.

* * *

(b) EXCESSIVE CREDITS.—

>>→ *Caution: Code Sec. 6401(b)(1), below, as amended by H.R. 6, applies to bonds issued after December 31, 2005.*

(1) IN GENERAL.—If the amount allowable as credits under subpart C of part IV of subchapter A of chapter 1 (relating to refundable credits) exceeds the tax imposed by subtitle A (reduced by the credits allowable under subparts A, B, D, *G, and H* of such part IV), the amount of such excess shall be considered an overpayment.

* * *

[CCH Explanation at ¶ 455. Committee Reports at ¶ 10,020.]

Amendments

• **2005, Energy Tax Incentives Act of 2005 (H.R. 6)**

H.R. 6, § 1303(c)(4):

Amended Code Sec. 6401(b)(1) by striking "and G" and inserting "G, and H". **Effective** for bonds issued after 12-31-2005.

[¶ 5405] CODE SEC. 6412. FLOOR STOCKS REFUNDS.

(a) IN GENERAL.—

(1) TIRES AND TAXABLE FUEL.—Where before October 1, *2011*, any article subject to the tax imposed by section 4071 or 4081 has been sold by the manufacturer, producer, or importer and on such date is held by a dealer and has not been used and is intended for sale, there shall be credited or refunded (without interest) to the manufacturer, producer, or importer an amount equal to the difference between the tax paid by such manufacturer, producer, or importer on his sale of the article and the amount of tax made applicable to such article on and after October 1, *2011*, if claim for such credit or refund is filed with the Secretary on or before March 31, *2012*, based upon a request submitted to the manufacturer, producer, or importer before January 1, *2012*, by the dealer who held the article in respect of which the credit or refund is claimed, and, on or before March 31, *2012*, reimbursement has been made to such dealer by such manufacturer, producer, or importer for the tax reduction on such article or written consent has been obtained from such dealer to allowance of such credit or refund. No credit or refund shall be allowable under this paragraph with respect to taxable fuel in retail stocks held at the place where intended to be sold at retail, nor with respect to taxable fuel held for sale by a producer or importer of taxable fuel.

* * *

[CCH Explanation at ¶ 905. Committee Reports at ¶ 15,010.]

Amendments

• **2005, Safe, Accountable, Flexible, Efficient Transportation Equity Act: A Legacy for Users (H.R. 3)**

H.R. 3, § 11101(a)(3)(A)-(B):

Amended Code Sec. 6412(a)(1) by striking "2005" each place it appears and inserting "2011", and by striking "2006" each place it appears and inserting "2012". **Effective** 8-10-2005.

[¶ 5410] CODE SEC. 6416. CERTAIN TAXES ON SALES AND SERVICES.

(a) CONDITION TO ALLOWANCE.—

* * *

⟫➔ *Caution: Code Sec. 6416(a)(4), below, as amended by H.R. 3, applies to sales after December 31, 2005.*

(4) REGISTERED ULTIMATE VENDOR OR CREDIT CARD ISSUER TO ADMINISTER CREDITS AND REFUNDS OF GASOLINE TAX.—

(A) IN GENERAL.—For purposes of this subsection, *except as provided in subparagraph (B)*, if an ultimate vendor purchases any gasoline on which tax imposed by section 4081 has been paid and sells such gasoline to an ultimate purchaser described in subparagraph (C) or (D) of subsection (b)(2) (and such gasoline is for a use described in such subparagraph), such ultimate vendor shall be treated as the person (and the only person) who paid such tax, but only if such ultimate vendor is registered under section 4101.

(B) CREDIT CARD ISSUER.—*For purposes of this subsection, if the purchase of gasoline described in subparagraph (A) (determined without regard to the registration status of the ultimate vendor) is made by means of a credit card issued to the ultimate purchaser, paragraph (1) shall not apply and the* person extending the credit to the ultimate purchaser shall be treated as the person (and the only person) who paid the tax, but only if such person—

(i) is registered under section 4101,

(ii) has established, under regulations prescribed by the Secretary, that such person—

(I) has not collected the amount of the tax from the person who purchased such article, or

(II) has obtained the written consent from the ultimate purchaser to the allowance of the credit or refund, and

(iii) has so established that such person—

(I) has repaid or agreed to repay the amount of the tax to the ultimate vendor,

(II) has obtained the written consent of the ultimate vendor to the allowance of the credit or refund, or

(III) has otherwise made arrangements which directly or indirectly provides the ultimate vendor with reimbursement of such tax.

If clause (i), (ii), or (iii) is not met by such person extending the credit to the ultimate purchaser, then such person shall collect an amount equal to the tax from the ultimate purchaser and only such ultimate purchaser may claim such credit or payment.

(C) TIMING OF CLAIMS.—The procedure and timing of any claim under *subparagraph (A) or (B)* shall be the same as for claims under section 6427(i)(4), except that the rules of section 6427(i)(3)(B) regarding electronic claims shall not apply unless the ultimate vendor *or credit card issuer* has certified to the Secretary for the most recent quarter of the taxable year that all ultimate purchasers of the vendor are certified and entitled to a refund under subparagraph (C) or (D) of subsection (b)(2).

[CCH Explanation at ¶745. Committee Reports at ¶15,280.]

Amendments

- **2005, Safe, Accountable, Flexible, Efficient Transportation Equity Act: A Legacy for Users (H.R. 3)**

H.R. 3, §11163(b)(1)(A)-(E):

Amended Code Sec. 6416(a)(4) by inserting "except as provided in subparagraph (B)," after "For purposes of this subsection," in subparagraph (A), by redesignating subparagraph (B) as subparagraph (C) and by inserting after subparagraph (A) a new subparagraph (B), by striking "subparagraph (A)" in subparagraph (C), as redesignated by Act Sec. 11163(b)(2) [Act Sec. 11163(b)(1)(B)], and inserting "subparagraph (A) or (B)", by inserting "or credit card issuer" after "vendor" in subparagraph (C), as so redesignated, and by inserting "OR CREDIT CARD ISSUER" after "VENDOR" in the heading thereof. **Effective** for sales after 12-31-2005.

(b) SPECIAL CASES IN WHICH TAX PAYMENTS CONSIDERED OVERPAYMENTS.—Under regulations prescribed by the Secretary, credit or refund (without interest) shall be allowed or made in respect of the overpayments determined under the following paragraphs:

* * *

⇒ *Caution: Code Sec. 6416(b)(2), below, as amended by H.R. 3, applies to sales after December 31, 2005.*

(2) SPECIFIED USES AND RESALES.—The tax paid under chapter 32 (or under subsection (a) or (d) of section 4041 in respect of sales or under section 4051) in respect of any article shall be deemed to be an overpayment if such article was, by any person—

(A) exported;

(B) used or sold for use as supplies for vessels or aircraft;

(C) sold to a State or local government for the exclusive use of a State or local government;

(D) sold to a nonprofit educational organization for its exclusive use;

(E) in the case of any tire taxable under section 4071(a), sold to any person for use as described in section 4221(e)(3); or

(F) in the case of gasoline, used or sold for use in the production of special fuels referred to in section 4041.

Subparagraphs (C) and (D) shall not apply in the case of any tax paid under section 4064. This paragraph shall not apply in the case of any tax imposed under section 4041(a)(1) or 4081 on diesel fuel or kerosene and any tax paid under section 4121. In the case of the tax imposed by section 4131, subparagraphs (B), (C), and (D) shall not apply and subparagraph (A) shall apply only if the use of the exported vaccine meets such requirements as the Secretary may by regulations prescribe. *Subparagraphs (C) and (D) shall not apply in the case of any tax imposed on gasoline under section 4081 if the requirements of subsection (a)(4) are not met.*

* * *

[CCH Explanation at ¶745. Committee Reports at ¶15,280.]

Amendments

• 2005, Safe, Accountable, Flexible, Efficient Transportation Equity Act: A Legacy for Users (H.R. 3)

H.R. 3, §11163(b)(2):

Amended Code Sec. 6416(b)(2) by adding at the end a new sentence. **Effective** for sales after 12-31-2005.

[¶5415] CODE SEC. 6420. GASOLINE USED ON FARMS.

* * *

(c) MEANING OF TERMS.—For purposes of this section—

* * *

(4) CERTAIN FARMING USE OTHER THAN BY OWNER, ETC.—In applying paragraph (3)(A) to a use on a farm for any purpose described in paragraph (3)(A) by any person other than the owner, tenant, or operator of such farm—

(A) the owner, tenant, or operator of such farm shall be treated as the user and ultimate purchaser of the gasoline, except that

(B) if the person so using the gasoline is an aerial or other applicator of fertilizers or other substances and is the ultimate purchaser of the gasoline, then subparagraph (A) of this paragraph shall not apply and the aerial or other applicator shall be treated as having used such gasoline on a farm for farming purposes.

In the case of an aerial applicator, gasoline shall be treated as used on a farm for farming purposes if the gasoline is used for the direct flight between the airfield and one or more farms.

(5) GASOLINE.—The term "gasoline" has the meaning given to such term by section 4083(a).

[CCH Explanation at ¶820. Committee Reports at ¶15,070.]

Amendments

• 2005, Safe, Accountable, Flexible, Efficient Transportation Equity Act: A Legacy for Users (H.R. 3)

H.R. 3, §11121(a):

Amended Code Sec. 6420(c)(4)(B). **Effective** for fuel use or air transportation after 9-30-2005. Prior to amendment, Code Sec. 6420(c)(4)(B) read as follows:

(B) if—

(i) the person so using the gasoline is an aerial or other applicator of fertilizers or other substances and is the ultimate purchaser of the gasoline, and

(ii) the person described in subparagraph (A) waives (at such time and in such form and manner as the Secretary shall prescribe) his right to be treated as the user and ultimate purchaser of the gasoline,

then subparagraph (A) of this paragraph shall not apply and the aerial or other applicator shall be treated as having used such gasoline on a farm for farming purposes.

H.R. 3, §11121(b):

Amended Code Sec. 6420(c)(4), as amended by Act Sec. 11121(a), by adding at the end a new flush sentence. **Effective** for fuel use or air transportation after 9-30-2005.

[¶ 5420] CODE SEC. 6421. GASOLINE USED FOR CERTAIN NONHIGHWAY PURPOSES, USED BY LOCAL TRANSIT SYSTEMS, OR SOLD FOR CERTAIN EXEMPT PURPOSES.

* * *

(f) EXEMPT SALES; OTHER PAYMENTS OR REFUNDS AVAILABLE.—

* * *

(2) GASOLINE USED IN AVIATION.—This section shall not apply in respect of gasoline which is used as a fuel in an aircraft—

(A) in *aviation which is not commercial aviation (as defined in section 4083(b))*, or

(B) in *commercial aviation* (as so defined) with respect to the tax imposed by section 4081 at the Leaking Underground Storage Tank Trust Fund financing rate and, in the case of fuel purchased after September 30, 1995, at so much of the rate specified in section 4081(a)(2)(A) as does not exceed 4.3 cents per gallon.

* * *

[CCH Explanation at ¶ 790. Committee Reports at ¶ 15,230.]

Amendments

- 2005, Safe, Accountable, Flexible, Efficient Transportation Equity Act: A Legacy for Users (H.R. 3)

H.R. 3, § 11151(b)(3)(A)-(B):

Amended Code Sec. 6421(f)(2) by striking "noncommercial aviation (as defined in section 4041(c)(2))" in subparagraph (A) and inserting "aviation which is not commercial aviation (as defined in section 4083(b))", and by striking "aviation which is not noncommercial aviation" in subparagraph (B) and inserting "commercial aviation". **Effective** as if included in the provision of P.L. 108-357 to which it relates [**effective** for aviation-grade kerosene removed, entered or sold after 12-31-2004.—CCH].

»»→ *Caution: The heading for Code Sec. 6426, below, as amended by H.R. 3, applies to any sale or use for any period after September 30, 2006.*

[¶ 5425] CODE SEC. 6426. CREDIT FOR *ALCOHOL FUEL, BIODIESEL, AND ALTERNATIVE FUEL.*

»»→ *Caution: Code Sec. 6426(a), below, as amended by H.R. 3, applies to any sale or use for any period after September 30, 2006.*

(a) ALLOWANCE OF CREDITS.—There shall be allowed as a credit—

(1) against the tax imposed by section 4081 an amount equal to the sum of the credits described in subsections (b), (c), and (e), and

(2) against the tax imposed by section 4041 an amount equal to the sum of the credits described in subsection (d).

No credit shall be allowed in the case of the credits described in subsections (d) and (e) unless the taxpayer is registered under section 4101.

* * *

[CCH Explanation at ¶ 725. Committee Reports at ¶ 15,040.]

Amendments

- 2005, Safe, Accountable, Flexible, Efficient Transportation Equity Act: A Legacy for Users (H.R. 3)

H.R. 3, § 11113(b)(1):

Amended Code Sec. 6426(a). **Effective** for any sale or use for any period after 9-30-2006. Prior to amendment, Code Sec. 6426(a) read as follows:

(a) ALLOWANCE OF CREDITS.—There shall be allowed as a credit against the tax imposed by section 4081 an amount equal to the sum of—

(1) the alcohol fuel mixture credit, plus

(2) the biodiesel mixture credit.

H.R. 3, § 11113(b)(3)(A):

Amended the heading for Code Sec. 6426 by striking "ALCOHOL FUEL AND BIODIESEL" and inserting "ALCOHOL FUEL, BIODIESEL, AND ALTERNATIVE FUEL". **Effective** for any sale or use for any period after 9-30-2006.

(c) BIODIESEL MIXTURE CREDIT.—

* * *

(6) TERMINATION.—This subsection shall not apply to any sale, use, or removal for any period after December 31, *2008.*

[CCH Explanation at ¶705. Committee Reports at ¶10,290.]

Amendments

- **2005, Energy Tax Incentives Act of 2005 (H.R. 6) (H.R. 6)**

H.R. 6, §1344(a):

Amended Code Sec. 6426(c)(6) by striking "2006" and inserting "2008". **Effective** 8-8-2005.

⋙→ *Caution: Code Sec. 6426(d), below, as added by H.R. 3, applies to any sale or use for any period after September 30, 2006.*

(d) ALTERNATIVE FUEL CREDIT.—

(1) IN GENERAL.—For purposes of this section, the alternative fuel credit is the product of 50 cents and the number of gallons of an alternative fuel or gasoline gallon equivalents of a nonliquid alternative fuel sold by the taxpayer for use as a fuel in a motor vehicle or motorboat, or so used by the taxpayer.

(2) ALTERNATIVE FUEL.—For purposes of this section, the term "alternative fuel" means—

(A) liquefied petroleum gas,

(B) P Series Fuels (as defined by the Secretary of Energy under section 13211(2) of title 42, United States Code),

(C) compressed or liquefied natural gas,

(D) liquefied hydrogen,

(E) any liquid fuel derived from coal (including peat) through the Fischer-Tropsch process, and

(F) liquid hydrocarbons derived from biomass (as defined in section 45K(c)(3)). Such term does not include ethanol, methanol, or biodiesel.

(3) GASOLINE GALLON EQUIVALENT.—For purposes of this subsection, the term "gasoline gallon equivalent" means, with respect to any nonliquid alternative fuel, the amount of such fuel having a Btu content of 124,800 (higher heating value).

(4) TERMINATION.—This subsection shall not apply to any sale or use for any period after September 30, 2009 (September 30, 2014, in the case of any sale or use involving liquefied hydrogen).

[CCH Explanation at ¶725. Committee Reports at ¶15,040.]

Amendments

- **2005, Safe, Accountable, Flexible, Efficient Transportation Equity Act: A Legacy for Users (H.R. 3)**

H.R. 3, §11113(b)(2):

Amended Code Sec. 6426 by redesignating subsections (d) and (e) as subsections (f) and (g) and by inserting after subsection (c) new subsections (d) and (e). **Effective** for any sale or use for any period after 9-30-2006.

H.R. 3, §11151(e)(2):

Amended Code Sec. 6426(d)(2)(F) [as added by Act Sec. 11113(b)(2)], by striking "section 29(c)(3)" and inserting "section 45K(c)(3)". **Effective** as if included in the provision of the Energy Tax Incentives Act of 2005 to which it relates [**effective** for credits determined under the Internal Revenue Code of 1986 for tax years ending after 12-31-2005.—CCH].

⋙→ *Caution: Code Sec. 6426(e), below, as added by H.R. 3, applies to any sale or use for any period after September 30, 2006.*

(e) ALTERNATIVE FUEL MIXTURE CREDIT.—

(1) IN GENERAL.—For purposes of this section, the alternative fuel mixture credit is the product of 50 cents and the number of gallons of alternative fuel used by the taxpayer in producing any alternative fuel mixture for sale or use in a trade or business of the taxpayer.

(2) ALTERNATIVE FUEL MIXTURE.—For purposes of this section, the term "alternative fuel mixture" means a mixture of alternative fuel and taxable fuel (as defined in subparagraph (A), (B), or (C) of section 4083(a)(1)) which—

(A) is sold by the taxpayer producing such mixture to any person for use as fuel, or

(B) is used as a fuel by the taxpayer producing such mixture.

(3) TERMINATION.—This subsection shall not apply to any sale or use for any period after September 30, 2009 (September 30, 2014, in the case of any sale or use involving liquefied hydrogen).

[CCH Explanation at ¶ 725. Committee Reports at ¶ 15,040.]

Amendments

• **2005, Safe, Accountable, Flexible, Efficient Transportation Equity Act: A Legacy for Users (H.R. 3)**

H.R. 3, § 11113(b)(2):

Amended Code Sec. 6426 by redesignating subsections (d) and (e) as subsections (f) and (g) and by inserting after subsection (c) new subsections (d) and (e). **Effective** for any sale or use for any period after 9-30-2006.

⋙→ *Caution: Former Code Sec. 6426(d) was redesignated as Code Sec. 6426(f), below, by H.R. 3, applicable to any sale or use for any period after September 30, 2006.*

(f) MIXTURE NOT USED AS A FUEL, ETC.—

(1) IMPOSITION OF TAX.—If—

(A) any credit was determined under this section with respect to alcohol or biodiesel used in the production of any alcohol fuel mixture or biodiesel mixture, respectively, and

(B) any person—

(i) separates the alcohol or biodiesel from the mixture, or

(ii) without separation, uses the mixture other than as a fuel,

then there is hereby imposed on such person a tax equal to the product of the applicable amount and the number of gallons of such alcohol or biodiesel.

(2) APPLICABLE LAWS.—All provisions of law, including penalties, shall, insofar as applicable and not inconsistent with this section, apply in respect of any tax imposed under paragraph (1) as if such tax were imposed by section 4081 and not by this section.

[CCH Explanation at ¶ 725. Committee Reports at ¶ 15,040.]

Amendments

• **2005, Safe, Accountable, Flexible, Efficient Transportation Equity Act: A Legacy for Users (H.R. 3)**

H.R. 3, § 11113(b)(2):

Amended Code Sec. 6426 by redesignating subsection (d) as subsection (f). **Effective** for any sale or use for any period after 9-30-2006.

¶ 5425 Code Sec. 6426(e)

⟫⟫→ *Caution: Former Code Sec. 6426(e) was redesignated as Code Sec. 6426(g), below, by H.R. 3, applicable to any sale or use for any period after September 30, 2006.*

(g) COORDINATION WITH EXEMPTION FROM EXCISE TAX.—Rules similar to the rules under section 40(c) shall apply for purposes of this section.

[CCH Explanation at ¶725. Committee Reports at ¶15,040.]

Amendments

- **2005, Safe, Accountable, Flexible, Efficient Transportation Equity Act: A Legacy for Users (H.R. 3)**

H.R. 3, §11113(b)(2):

Amended Code Sec. 6426 by redesignating subsection (e) as subsection (g). **Effective** for any sale or use for any period after 9-30-2006.

[¶5430] CODE SEC. 6427. FUELS NOT USED FOR TAXABLE PURPOSES.

* * *

(e) ALCOHOL OR BIODIESEL USED TO PRODUCE ALCOHOL FUEL AND BIODIESEL MIXTURES.—Except as provided in subsection (k)—

* * *

(3) TERMINATION.—This subsection shall not apply with respect to—

(A) any alcohol fuel mixture (as defined in section 6426(b)(3)) sold or used after December 31, 2010, and

(B) any biodiesel mixture (as defined in section 6426(c)(3)) sold or used after December 31, *2008*.

[CCH Explanation at ¶705, ¶725 and ¶787. Committee Reports at ¶10,290, ¶15,040 and ¶15,220.]

Amendments

- **2005, Energy Tax Incentives Act of 2005 (H.R. 6)**

H.R. 6, §1344(a):

Amended Code Sec. 6427(e)(4)[(3)](B) by striking "2006" and inserting "2008". **Effective** 8-8-2005.

(f) [*Stricken.*]

[CCH Explanation at ¶787. Committee Reports at ¶15,220.]

Amendments

- **2005, Safe, Accountable, Flexible, Efficient Transportation Equity Act: A Legacy for Users (H.R. 3)**

H.R. 3, §11151(a)(1):

Amended Code Sec. 6427 by striking subsection (f). **Effective** as if included in the provision of P.L. 108-357 to which it relates [**effective** for fuel sold or used after 12-31-2004.—CCH]. Prior to being stricken, Code Sec. 6427(f) read as follows:

(f) GASOLINE, DIESEL FUEL, KEROSENE, AND AVIATION FUEL USED TO PRODUCE CERTAIN ALCOHOL FUELS.—

(1) IN GENERAL.—Except as provided in subsection (k), if any gasoline, diesel fuel, kerosene, or aviation fuel on which tax was imposed by section 4081 or 4091 at the regular tax rate is used by any person in producing a mixture described in section 4081(c) or 4091(c)(1)(A) (as the case may be) which is sold or used in such person's trade or business the Secretary shall pay (without interest) to such person an amount equal to the excess of the regular tax rate over the incentive tax rate with respect to such fuel.

(2) DEFINITIONS.—For purposes of paragraph (1)—

(A) REGULAR TAX RATE.—The term "regular tax rate" means—

(i) in the case of gasoline, diesel fuel, or kerosene the aggregate rate of tax imposed by section 4081 determined without regard to subsection (c) thereof, and

(ii) in the case of aviation fuel, the aggregate rate of tax imposed by section 4091 determined without regard to subsection (c) thereof.

(B) INCENTIVE TAX RATE.—The term "incentive tax rate" means—

(i) in the case of gasoline, diesel fuel, or kerosene the aggregate rate of tax imposed by section 4081 with respect to fuel described in subsection (c)(2) thereof, and

(ii) in the case of aviation fuel, the aggregate rate of tax imposed by section 4091 with respect to fuel described in subsection (c)(2) thereof.

(3) COORDINATION WITH OTHER REPAYMENT PROVISIONS.—No amount shall be payable under paragraph (1) with respect to any gasoline, diesel fuel, kerosene, or aviation fuel with respect to which an amount is payable under subsection (d) or (1) of this section or under section 6420 or 6421.

(4) TERMINATION.—This subsection shall not apply with respect to any mixture sold or used after September 30, 2007.

(i) TIME FOR FILING CLAIMS; PERIOD COVERED.—

⇛→ *Caution: Code Sec. 6427(i)(1), below, as amended by H.R. 6, is effective January 1, 2006.*

(1) GENERAL RULE.—Except as otherwise provided in this subsection, not more than one claim may be filed under subsection (a), (b), (d), (h), (l), *(m)*, or (o) by any person with respect to fuel used during his taxable year; and no claim shall be allowed under this paragraph with respect to fuel used during any taxable year unless filed by the purchaser not later than the time prescribed by law for filing a claim for credit or refund of overpayment of income tax for such taxable year. For purposes of this paragraph, a person's taxable year shall be his taxable year for purposes of subtitle A.

⇛→ *Caution: Code Sec. 6427(i)(2), below, as amended by H.R. 6, is effective January 1, 2006.*

(2) EXCEPTIONS.—

(A) IN GENERAL.—If, at the close of any quarter of the taxable year of any person, at least $750 is payable in the aggregate under subsections (a), (b), (d), (h), (l), *(m)*, and (o) of this section and section 6421 to such person with respect to fuel used during—

(i) such quarter, or

(ii) any prior quarter (for which no other claim has been filed) during such taxable year,

a claim may be filed under this section with respect to such fuel.

(B) TIME FOR FILING CLAIM.—No claim filed under this paragraph shall be allowed unless filed during the first quarter following the last quarter included in the claim.

(C) NONAPPLICATION OF PARAGRAPH.—This paragraph shall not apply to any fuel used solely in any off-highway business use described in section 6421(e)(2)(C).

* * *

(4) SPECIAL RULE FOR VENDOR REFUNDS.—

(A) IN GENERAL.—A claim may be filed under subsections (b)(4) and *paragraph (4)(B), (5), or (6)* of subsection (l) by any person with respect to fuel sold by such person for any period—

(i) for which $200 or more ($100 or more in the case of kerosene) is payable under *paragraph (4)(B), (5), or (6)* of subsection (l), and

(ii) which is not less than 1 week.

Notwithstanding subsection (l)(1), paragraph (3)(B) shall apply to claims filed under *subsections (b)(4), (l)(5), and (l)(6)*.

* * *

[CCH Explanation at ¶720 and ¶740. Committee Reports at ¶10,280 and ¶15,260.]

Amendments

• **2005, Safe, Accountable, Flexible, Efficient Transportation Equity Act: A Legacy for Users (H.R. 3)**

H.R. 3, §11161(b)(3)(D)(i)-(ii):

Amended Code Sec. 6427(i)(4)(A) by striking "paragraph (4)(B) or (5)" both places it appears and inserting "paragraph (4)(B), (5), or (6)", and by striking "subsection (b)(4) and subsection (l)(5)" in the last sentence and inserting "subsections (b)(4), (l)(5), and (l)(6)". **Effective** for fuels or liquids removed, entered, or sold after 9-30-2005.

• **2005, Energy Tax Incentives Act of 2005 (H.R. 6)**

H.R. 6, §1343(b)(3):

Amended Code Sec. 6427(i)(1) and (2) by inserting "(m)," after "(l),". **Effective** 1-1-2006.

¶5430 Code Sec. 6427(i)

(l) NONTAXABLE USES OF DIESEL FUEL *AND KEROSENE*.—

* * *

(2) NONTAXABLE USE.—*For purposes of this subsection, the term "nontaxable use" means any use which is exempt from the tax imposed by section 4041(a)(1) other than by reason of a prior imposition of tax.*

* * *

(4) REFUNDS FOR *KEROSENE USED IN COMMERCIAL AVIATION*.—

(A) NO REFUND OF CERTAIN TAXES ON FUEL USED IN COMMERCIAL AVIATION.—In the case of kerosene used in commercial aviation (as defined in section 4083(b)) (other than supplies for vessels or aircraft within the meaning of section 4221(d)(3)), paragraph (1) shall not apply to so much of the tax imposed by section 4081 as is attributable to—

(i) the Leaking Underground Storage Tank Trust Fund financing rate imposed by such section, and

(ii) so much of the rate of tax specified in *section 4081(a)(2)[A](iii)* as does not exceed 4.3 cents per gallon.

(B) PAYMENT TO ULTIMATE, REGISTERED VENDOR.—With respect to *kerosene used in commercial aviation as described in subparagraph (A)*, if the ultimate purchaser of such kerosene waives (at such time and in such form and manner as the Secretary shall prescribe) the right to payment under paragraph (1) and assigns such right to the ultimate vendor, then the Secretary shall pay the amount which would be paid under paragraph (1) to such ultimate vendor, but only if such ultimate vendor—

(i) is registered under section 4101, and

(ii) meets the requirements of subparagraph (A), (B), or (D) of section 6416(a)(1).

(5) REFUNDS FOR *KEROSENE USED IN NONCOMMERCIAL AVIATION*.—

(A) IN GENERAL.—*In the case of kerosene used in aviation not described in paragraph (4)(A) (other than any use which is exempt from the tax imposed by section 4041(c) other than by reason of a prior imposition of tax), paragraph (1) shall not apply to so much of the tax imposed by section 4081 as is attributable to*—

(i) *the Leaking Underground Storage Tank Trust Fund financing rate imposed by such section, and*

(ii) *so much of the rate of tax specified in section 4081(a)(2)(A)(iii) as does not exceed the rate specified in section 4081(a)(2)(C)(ii).*

(B) PAYMENT TO ULTIMATE, REGISTERED VENDOR.—*The amount which would be paid under paragraph (1) with respect to any kerosene shall be paid only to the ultimate vendor of such kerosene. A payment shall be made to such vendor if such vendor*—

(i) *is registered under section 4101, and*

(ii) *meets the requirements of subparagraph (A), (B), or (D) of section 6416(a)(1).*

(6) REGISTERED VENDORS TO ADMINISTER CLAIMS FOR REFUND OF DIESEL FUEL OR KEROSENE SOLD TO STATE AND LOCAL GOVERNMENTS.—

(A) IN GENERAL.—*Paragraph (1) shall not apply to diesel fuel or kerosene used by a State or local government.*

(B) SALES OF KEROSENE NOT FOR USE IN MOTOR FUEL.—Paragraph (1) shall not apply to kerosene (other than *kerosene used in aviation*) sold by a vendor—

(i) for any use if such sale is from a pump which (as determined under regulations prescribed by the Secretary) is not suitable for use in fueling any diesel-powered highway vehicle or train, or

Code Sec. 6427(l)(6)(B)(i) ¶5430

(ii) to the extent provided by the Secretary, for blending with heating oil to be used during periods of extreme or unseasonable cold.

»» *Caution: Code Sec. 6427(l)(6)(C), below, as amended by H.R. 3, applies to sales after December 31, 2005.*

(C) PAYMENT TO ULTIMATE, REGISTERED VENDOR.—*Except as provided in subparagraph (D), the amount* which would (but for subparagraph (A) or (B)) have been paid under paragraph (1) with respect to any fuel shall be paid to the ultimate vendor of such fuel, if such vendor—

(i) is registered under section 4101, and

(ii) meets the requirements of subparagraph (A), (B), or (D) of section 6416(a)(1).

»» *Caution: Code Sec. 6427(l)(6)(D), below, as added by H.R. 3, applies to sales after December 31, 2005.*

(D) CREDIT CARD ISSUER.—*For purposes of this paragraph, if the purchase of any fuel described in subparagraph (A) (determined without regard to the registration status of the ultimate vendor) is made by means of a credit card issued to the ultimate purchaser, the Secretary shall pay to the person extending the credit to the ultimate purchaser the amount which would have been paid under paragraph (1) (but for subparagraph (A)), but only if such person meets the requirements of clauses (i), (ii), and (iii) of section 6416(a)(4)(B). If such clause (i), (ii), or (iii) is not met by such person extending the credit to the ultimate purchaser, then such person shall collect an amount equal to the tax from the ultimate purchaser and only such ultimate purchaser may claim such amount.*

[CCH Explanation at ¶740, ¶745 and ¶750. Committee Reports at ¶15,260, ¶15,270 and ¶15,280.]

Amendments

- **2005, Safe, Accountable, Flexible, Efficient Transportation Equity Act: A Legacy for Users (H.R. 3)**

H.R. 3, §11161(b)(2)(A):

Amended Code Sec. 6427(l)(2). **Effective** for fuels or liquids removed, entered, or sold after 9-30-2005. Prior to amendment, Code Sec. 6427(l)(2) read as follows:

(2) NONTAXABLE USE.—For purposes of this subsection, the term "nontaxable use" means—

(A) in the case of diesel fuel or kerosene, any use which is exempt from the tax imposed by section 4041(a)(1) other than by reason of a prior imposition of tax, and

(B) in the case of aviation-grade kerosene—

(i) any use which is exempt from the tax imposed by section 4041(c) other than by reason of a prior imposition of tax, or

(ii) any use in commercial aviation (within the meaning of section 4083(b)).

H.R. 3, §11161(b)(2)(B):

Amended Code Sec. 6427(l) by redesignating paragraph (5) as paragraph (6) and by inserting after paragraph (4) a new paragraph (5). **Effective** for fuels or liquids removed, entered, or sold after 9-30-2005.

H.R. 3, §11161(b)(3)(B):

Amended the heading for Code Sec. 6427(l) by striking ", KEROSENE AND AVIATION FUEL" and inserting "AND KEROSENE". **Effective** for fuels or liquids removed, entered, or sold after 9-30-2005.

H.R. 3, §11161(b)(3)(E)(i)-(iv):

Amended Code Sec. 6427(l)(4) by striking "aviation-grade" before "kerosene" in subparagraph (A), by striking "section 4081(a)(2)(A)(iv)" and inserting "section 4081(a)(2)[A](iii)", by striking "aviation-grade kerosene" in subparagraph (B) and inserting "kerosene used in commercial aviation as described in subparagraph (A)", and by striking "AVIATION-GRADE KEROSENE" in the heading thereof and inserting "KEROSENE USED IN COMMERCIAL AVIATION". **Effective** for fuels or liquids removed, entered, or sold after 9-30-2005.

H.R. 3, §11161(b)(3)(F):

Amended Code Sec. 6427(l)(6)(B), as redesignated by Act Sec. 11161(b)(2)(B), by striking "aviation-grade kerosene" and inserting "kerosene used in aviation". **Effective** for fuels or liquids removed, entered, or sold after 9-30-2005.

H.R. 3, §11162(a):

Amended Code Sec. 6427(l)(6)(A), as redesignated by Act Sec. 11161. **Effective** for sales after 9-30-2005. Prior to amendment, Code Sec. 6427(l)(6)(A) read as follows:

(A) IN GENERAL.—Paragraph (1) shall not apply to diesel fuel or kerosene used—

(i) on a farm for farming purposes (within the meaning of section 6420(c)), or

(ii) by a State or local government.

H.R. 3, §11162(b):

Amended the heading of Code Sec. 6427(l)(6), as redesignated by Act Sec. 11161, by striking "FARMERS AND" before "STATE AND LOCAL". **Effective** for sales after 9-30-2005.

H.R. 3, §11163(c)(1)-(2):

Amended Code Sec. 6427(l)(6), as redesignated by Act Sec. 11161, by striking "The amount" in subparagraph (C), inserting "Except as provided in subparagraph (D), the amount", and by adding at the end a new subparagraph (D). **Effective** for sales after 12-31-2005.

➤➤➤ *Caution: Code Sec. 6427(m), below, as added by H.R. 6, is effective January 1, 2006.*

(m) DIESEL FUEL USED TO PRODUCE EMULSION.—

(1) IN GENERAL.—Except as provided in subsection (k), if any diesel fuel on which tax was imposed by section 4081 at the regular tax rate is used by any person in producing an emulsion described in section 4081(a)(2)(D) which is sold or used in such person's trade or business, the Secretary shall pay (without interest) to such person an amount equal to the excess of the regular tax rate over the incentive tax rate with respect to such fuel.

(2) DEFINITIONS.—For purposes of paragraph (1)—

(A) REGULAR TAX RATE.—The term "regular tax rate" means the aggregate rate of tax imposed by section 4081 determined without regard to section 4081(a)(2)(D).

(B) INCENTIVE TAX RATE.—The term "incentive tax rate" means the aggregate rate of tax imposed by section 4081 determined with regard to section 4081(a)(2)(D).

[CCH Explanation at ¶720. Committee Reports at ¶10,280.]
Amendments

• **2005, Energy Tax Incentives Act of 2005 (H.R. 6)**

H.R. 6, §1343(b)(1):

Amended Code Sec. 6427 by redesignating subsections (m) through (p) as subsections (n) through (q), respectively, and by inserting after subsection (l) a new subsection (m). **Effective** 1-1-2006.

➤➤➤ *Caution: Former Code Sec. 6427(m) was redesignated as Code Sec. 6427(n), below, by H.R. 6, effective January 1, 2006.*

(n) REGULATIONS.—The Secretary may by regulations prescribe the conditions, not inconsistent with the provisions of this section, under which payments may be made under this section.

[CCH Explanation at ¶720. Committee Reports at ¶10,280.]
Amendments

• **2005, Energy Tax Incentives Act of 2005 (H.R. 6)**

H.R. 6, §1343(b)(1):

Amended Code Sec. 6427 by redesignating subsection (m) as subsection (n). **Effective** 1-1-2006.

➤➤➤ *Caution: Former Code Sec. 6427(n) was redesignated as Code Sec. 6427(o), below, by H.R. 6, effective January 1, 2006.*

(o) PAYMENTS FOR TAXES IMPOSED BY SECTION 4041(d).—For purposes of subsections (a), (b), and (c), the taxes imposed by section 4041(d) shall be treated as imposed by section 4041(a).

[CCH Explanation at ¶720. Committee Reports at ¶10,280.]
Amendments

• **2005, Safe, Accountable, Flexible, Efficient Transportation Equity Act: A Legacy for Users (H.R. 3)**

H.R. 3, §11151(a)(2):

Amended Code Sec. 6427 by striking subsection (o) and redesignating subsection (p) as subsection (o). **Effective** as if included in the provision of P.L. 108-357 to which it relates [**effective** for fuel sold or used after 12-31-2004.—CCH]. Prior to being stricken, Code Sec. 6427(o) read as follows:

(o) GASOHOL USED IN NONCOMMERCIAL AVIATION.—Except as provided in subsection (k), if—

(1) any tax is imposed by section 4081 at a rate determined under subsection (c) thereof on gasohol (as defined in such subsection), and

(2) such gasohol is used as a fuel in any aircraft in noncommercial aviation (as defined in section 4041(c)(2)),

the Secretary shall pay (without interest) to the ultimate purchaser of such gasohol an amount equal to 1.4 cents (2 cents in the case of a mixture none of the alcohol in which consists of ethanol) multiplied by the number of gallons of gasohol so used.

• **2005, Energy Tax Incentives Act of 2005 (H.R. 6)**

H.R. 6, §1343(b)(1):

Amended Code Sec. 6427 by redesignating subsection (n) as subsection (o). **Effective** 1-1-2006.

(q)[(p)] CROSS REFERENCES.—

(1) For civil penalty for excessive claims under this section, see section 6675.

(2) For fraud penalties, etc., see chapter 75 (section 7201 and following, relating to crimes, other offenses, and forfeitures).

(3) For treatment of an Indian tribal government as a State (and a subdivision of an Indian tribal government as a political subdivision of a State), see section 7871.

[CCH Explanation at ¶787. Committee Reports at ¶15,220.]

Amendments

• **2005, Safe, Accountable, Flexible, Efficient Transportation Equity Act: A Legacy for Users (H.R. 3)**

H.R. 3, §11151(a)(2):

Amended Code Sec. 6427 by redesignating subsection (p) as subsection (o). [Note, however, subsection (p) was redesignated as subsection (q) by H.R. 6, **effective** 1-1-2006.—CCH.] **Effective** as if included in the provision of P.L. 108-357 to which it relates [**effective** for fuel sold or used after 12-31-2004.—CCH].

• **2005, Energy Tax Incentives Act of 2005 (H.R. 6)**

H.R. 6, §1343(b)(1):

Amended Code Sec. 6427 by redesignating subsection (p) as subsection (q). [This amendment did not account for the striking of Code Sec. 6427(o) by H.R. 3. As a result, the redesignation by H.R. 6 in the manner provided for by Congress is alphabetically incorrect.—CCH.] **Effective** 1-1-2006.

[¶5435] CODE SEC. 6430. TREATMENT OF TAX IMPOSED AT LEAKING UNDERGROUND STORAGE TANK TRUST FUND FINANCING RATE.

No refunds, credits, or payments shall be made under this subchapter for any tax imposed at the Leaking Underground Storage Tank Trust Fund financing rate, except in the case of fuels destined for export.

[CCH Explanation at ¶785. Committee Reports at ¶10,360.]

Amendments

• **2005, Energy Tax Incentives Act of 2005 (H.R. 6)**

H.R. 6, §1362(b)(3)(A):

Amended subchapter B of chapter 65 by adding at the end a new Code Sec. 6430. **Effective** for fuel entered, removed, or sold after 9-30-2005.

[¶5440] CODE SEC. 6501. LIMITATIONS ON ASSESSMENT AND COLLECTION.

* * *

⟫→ *Caution: Code Sec. 6501(m), below, as amended by H.R. 6, applies to property placed in service after December 31, 2005, in tax years ending after such date.*

(m) DEFICIENCIES ATTRIBUTABLE TO ELECTION OF CERTAIN CREDITS.—The period for assessing a deficiency attributable to any election under section 30(d)(4), 30B(h)(9), 30C(e)(5), 40(f), 43, 45B, 45C(d)(4), or 51(j) (or any revocation thereof) shall not expire before the date 1 year after the date on which the Secretary is notified of such election (or revocation).

* * *

[CCH Explanation at ¶305 and ¶730. Committee Reports at ¶10,260 and ¶10,270.]

Amendments

• **2005, Energy Tax Incentives Act of 2005 (H.R. 6)**

H.R. 6, §1341(b)(4):

Amended Code Sec. 6501(m) by inserting "30B(h)(9)," after "30(d)(4),". **Effective** for property placed in service after 12-31-2005, in tax years ending after such date.

H.R. 6, §1342(b)(4):

Amended Code Sec. 6501(m) by inserting "30C(e)(5)," after "30B(h)(9),". **Effective** for property placed in service after 12-31-2005, in tax years ending after such date.

[¶ 5445] CODE SEC. 6675. EXCESSIVE CLAIMS WITH RESPECT TO THE USE OF CERTAIN FUELS.

⟹ *Caution: Code Sec. 6675(a), below, as amended by H.R. 3, applies to sales after December 31, 2005.*

(a) CIVIL PENALTY.—In addition to any criminal penalty provided by law, if a claim is made under *section 6416(a)(4) (relating to certain sales of gasoline)*, section 6420 (relating to gasoline used on farms), 6421 (relating to gasoline used for certain nonhighway purposes or by local transit systems), or 6427 (relating to fuels not used for taxable purposes) for an excessive amount, unless it is shown that the claim for such excessive amount is due to reasonable cause, the person making such claim shall be liable to a penalty in an amount equal to whichever of the following is the greater:

(1) Two times the excessive amount; or

(2) $10.

[CCH Explanation at ¶ 745. Committee Reports at ¶ 15,280.]

Amendments

• 2005, Safe, Accountable, Flexible, Efficient Transportation Equity Act: A Legacy for Users (H.R. 3)

H.R. 3, § 11163(d)(2):

Amended Code Sec. 6675(a) by inserting "section 6416(a)(4) (relating to certain sales of gasoline)," after "made under". **Effective** for sales after 12-31-2005.

(b) EXCESSIVE AMOUNT DEFINED.—For purposes of this section, the term "excessive amount" means in the case of any person the amount by which—

⟹ *Caution: Code Sec. 6675(b)(1), below, as amended by H.R. 3, applies to sales after December 31, 2005.*

(1) the amount claimed under section *6416(a)(4)*, 6420, 6421, or 6427, as the case may be, for any period, exceeds

(2) the amount allowable under such section for such period.

* * *

[CCH Explanation at ¶ 745. Committee Reports at ¶ 15,280.]

Amendments

• 2005, Safe, Accountable, Flexible, Efficient Transportation Equity Act: A Legacy for Users (H.R. 3)

H.R. 3, § 11163(d)(3):

Amended Code Sec. 6675(b)(1) by inserting "6416(a)(4)," after "under section". **Effective** for sales after 12-31-2005.

[¶ 5450] CODE SEC. 6719. FAILURE TO REGISTER *OR REREGISTER*.

(a) FAILURE TO REGISTER *OR REREGISTER*.—Every person who is required to register *or reregister* under section 4101 and fails to do so shall pay a penalty in addition to the tax (if any).

[CCH Explanation at ¶ 755. Committee Reports at ¶ 15,290.]

Amendments

• 2005, Safe, Accountable, Flexible, Efficient Transportation Equity Act: A Legacy for Users (H.R. 3)

H.R. 3, § 11164(b)(1)(A)-(C):

Amended Code Sec. 6719 by inserting "or reregister" after "register" each place it appears, by inserting "OR REREGISTER" after "REGISTER" in the heading for subsection (a), and by inserting "OR REREGISTER" after "REGISTER" in the heading thereof. **Effective** for actions, or failures to act, after 8-10-2005.

(b) AMOUNT OF PENALTY.—The amount of the penalty under subsection (a) shall be—

(1) $10,000 for each initial failure to register *or reregister*, and

(2) $1,000 for each day thereafter such person fails to register *or reregister*.

* * *

[CCH Explanation at ¶ 755. Committee Reports at ¶ 15,290.]

Amendments

• **2005, Safe, Accountable, Flexible, Efficient Transportation Equity Act: A Legacy for Users (H.R. 3)**

H.R. 3, § 11164(b)(1)(A):

Amended Code Sec. 6719 by inserting "or reregister" after "register" each place it appears. **Effective** for actions, or failures to act, after 8-10-2005.

[¶ 5455] CODE SEC. 6720A. PENALTY WITH RESPECT TO CERTAIN ADULTERATED FUELS.

(a) IN GENERAL.—Any person who knowingly transfers for resale, sells for resale, or holds out for resale any liquid for use in a diesel-powered highway vehicle or a diesel-powered train which does not meet applicable EPA regulations (as defined in section 45H(c)(3)), shall pay a penalty of $10,000 for each such transfer, sale, or holding out for resale, in addition to the tax on such liquid (if any).

(b) PENALTY IN THE CASE OF RETAILERS.—Any person who knowingly holds out for sale (other than for resale) any liquid described in subsection (a), shall pay a penalty of $10,000 for each such holding out for sale, in addition to the tax on such liquid (if any).

[CCH Explanation at ¶ 765. Committee Reports at ¶ 15,320.]

Amendments

• **2005, Safe, Accountable, Flexible, Efficient Transportation Equity Act: A Legacy for Users (H.R. 3)**

H.R. 3, § 11167(a):

Amended part I of subchapter B of chapter 68 by adding at the end a new Code Sec. 6720A. **Effective** for any transfer, sale, or holding out for sale or resale occurring after 8-10-2005.

[¶ 5460] CODE SEC. 7012. CROSS REFERENCES.

(1) For provisions relating to registration in connection with firearms, see sections 5802, 5841, and 5861.

(2) For special rules with respect to registration by persons engaged in receiving wagers, see section 4412.

(3) For provisions relating to registration in relation to the taxes on gasoline and diesel fuel, see section 4101.

>>> *Caution: Code Sec. 7012(4), below, as added by H.R. 3, is effective July 1, 2008, but does not apply to taxes imposed for periods before such date.*

(4) For provisions relating to registration by dealers in distilled spirits, wines, and beer, see section 5124.

>>> *Caution: Former Code Sec. 7012(4) was redesignated as Code Sec. 7012(5), below, by H.R. 3, effective July 1, 2008.*

(5) For penalty for failure to register, see section 7272.

>>> *Caution: Former Code Sec. 7012(5) was redesignated as Code Sec. 7012(6), below, by H.R. 3, effective July 1, 2008.*

(6) For other penalties for failure to register with respect to wagering, see section 7262.

[CCH Explanation at ¶ 840. Committee Reports at ¶ 15,110.]

Amendments

- 2005, Safe, Accountable, Flexible, Efficient Transportation Equity Act: A Legacy for Users (H.R. 3)

H.R. 3, § 11125(b)(9):

Amended Code Sec. 7012 by redesignating paragraphs (4) and (5) as paragraphs (5) and (6), respectively, and by inserting after paragraph (3) a new paragraph (4). **Effective** 7-1-2008, but not applicable to taxes imposed for periods before such date.

[¶ 5465] CODE SEC. 7232. FAILURE TO REGISTER *OR REREGISTER* UNDER SECTION 4101, FALSE REPRESENTATIONS OF REGISTRATION STATUS, ETC.

Every person who fails to register *or reregister* as required by section 4101, or who in connection with any purchase of any taxable fuel (as defined in section 4083), or aviation fuel falsely represents himself to be registered as provided by section 4101, or who willfully makes any false statement in an application for registration *or reregistration* under section 4101, shall, upon conviction thereof, be fined not more than $10,000, or imprisoned not more than 5 years, or both, together with the costs of prosecution.

[CCH Explanation at ¶ 755. Committee Reports at ¶ 15,290.]

Amendments

- 2005, Safe, Accountable, Flexible, Efficient Transportation Equity Act: A Legacy for Users (H.R. 3)

H.R. 3, § 11164(b)(2)(A)-(C):

Amended Code Sec. 7232 by inserting "or reregister" after "register", by inserting "or reregistration" after "registration", and by inserting "OR REREGISTER" after "REGISTER" in the heading. **Effective** for actions, or failures to act, after 8-10-2005.

[¶ 5470] CODE SEC. 7272. PENALTY FOR FAILURE TO REGISTER *OR REREGISTER*.

(a) IN GENERAL.—Any person (other than persons required to register under subtitle E, or persons engaging in a trade or business on which a special tax is imposed by such subtitle) who fails to register with the Secretary as required by this title or by regulations issued thereunder shall be liable to a penalty of $50 ($10,000 in the case of a failure to register *or reregister* under section 4101).

* * *

[CCH Explanation at ¶ 755. Committee Reports at ¶ 15,290.]

Amendments

- 2005, Safe, Accountable, Flexible, Efficient Transportation Equity Act: A Legacy for Users (H.R. 3)

H.R. 3, § 11164(b)(3)(A)-(B):

Amended Code Sec. 7272 by inserting "or reregister" after "failure to register" in subsection (a), and by inserting "OR REREGISTER" after "REGISTER" in the heading. **Effective** for actions, or failures to act, after 8-10-2005.

[¶ 5475] CODE SEC. 7652. SHIPMENTS TO THE UNITED STATES.

* * *

(g) DRAWBACK FOR MEDICINAL ALCOHOL, ETC.—In the case of medicines, medicinal preparations, food products, flavors, flavoring extracts, or perfume containing distilled spirits, which are unfit for beverage purposes and which are brought into the United States from Puerto Rico or the Virgin Islands—

>>>→ *Caution: Code Sec. 7652(g)(1), below, as amended by H.R. 3, is effective July 1, 2008, but does not apply to taxes imposed for periods before such date.*

(1) *subpart B of part II of subchapter A of chapter 51 shall be applied as if—*

(A) *the use and tax determination described in section 5111 had occurred in the United States by a United States person at the time the article is brought into the United States, and*

(B) *the rate of tax were the rate applicable under subsection (f) of this section, and*

(2) no amount shall be covered into the treasuries of Puerto Rico or the Virgin Islands.

* * *

[CCH Explanation at ¶ 840. Committee Reports at ¶ 15,110.]

Amendments

- **2005, Safe, Accountable, Flexible, Efficient Transportation Equity Act: A Legacy for Users (H.R. 3)**

H.R. 3, § 11125(b)(22)(A)-(B):

Amended Code Sec. 7652(g)(1) by striking "subpart F" and inserting "subpart B", and by striking "section 5131(a)" and inserting "section 5111". **Effective** 7-1-2008, but does not apply to taxes imposed for periods before such date.

[¶ 5480] CODE SEC. 9502. AIRPORT AND AIRWAY TRUST FUND.

(a) CREATION OF TRUST FUND.—There is established in the Treasury of the United States a trust fund to be known as the "Airport and Airway Trust Fund", consisting of such amounts as may be *appropriated, credited, or paid into the Airport and Airway Trust Fund as provided in this section, section 9503(c)(7), or section 9602(b).*

[CCH Explanation at ¶ 740. Committee Reports at ¶ 15,260.]

Amendments

- **2005, Safe, Accountable, Flexible, Efficient Transportation Equity Act: A Legacy for Users (H.R. 3)**

H.R. 3, § 11161(c)(2)(A):

Amended Code Sec. 9502(a) by striking "appropriated or credited to the Airport and Airway Trust Fund as provided in this section or section 9602(b)" and inserting "appropriated, credited, or paid into the Airport and Airway Trust Fund as provided in this section, section 9503(c)(7), or section 9602(b)". **Effective** for fuels or liquids removed, entered, or sold after 9-30-2005.

(b) TRANSFERS TO AIRPORT AND AIRWAY TRUST FUND.—There are hereby appropriated to the Airport and Airway Trust Fund amounts equivalent to—

(1) the taxes received in the Treasury under—

(A) *section 4041(c)* (relating to aviation fuels),

(B) sections 4261 and 4271 (relating to transportation by air), and

(C) section 4081 with respect to aviation gasoline *and kerosene to the extent attributable to the rate specified in section 4081(a)(2)(C),* and

(2) the amounts determined by the Secretary of the Treasury to be equivalent to the amounts of civil penalties collected under section 47107(n) of title 49, United States Code.

* * *

[CCH Explanation at ¶740. Committee Reports at ¶15,260.]

Amendments

- **2005, Safe, Accountable, Flexible, Efficient Transportation Equity Act: A Legacy for Users (H.R. 3)**

H.R. 3, §11161(c)(2)(B)(i)-(ii):

Amended Code Sec. 9502(b)(1) by striking "subsections (c) and (e) of section 4041" in subparagraph (A) and inserting "section 4041(c)", and by striking "and aviation-grade kerosene" in subparagraph (C) and inserting "and kerosene to the extent attributable to the rate specified in section 4081(a)(2)(C)". **Effective** for fuels or liquids removed, entered, or sold after 9-30-2005.

(d) EXPENDITURES FROM AIRPORT AND AIRWAY TRUST FUND.—

* * *

(2) TRANSFERS FROM AIRPORT AND AIRWAY TRUST FUND ON ACCOUNT OF CERTAIN REFUNDS.—The Secretary of the Treasury shall pay from time to time from the Airport and Airway Trust Fund into the general fund of the Treasury amounts equivalent to the amounts paid after August 31, 1982, in respect of fuel used in aircraft, under section 6420 (relating to amounts paid in respect of gasoline used on farms), 6421 (relating to amounts paid in respect of gasoline used for certain nonhighway purposes), or 6427 (relating to fuels not used for taxable purposes) *(other than subsection (l)(4) and (l)(5) thereof)*.

(3) TRANSFERS FROM THE AIRPORT AND AIRWAY TRUST FUND ON ACCOUNT OF CERTAIN SECTION 34 CREDITS.—The Secretary of the Treasury shall pay from time to time from the Airport and Airway Trust Fund into the general fund of the Treasury amounts equivalent to the credits allowed under section 34 *(other than payments made by reason of paragraph (4) or (5) of section 6427(l))* with respect to fuel used after August 31, 1982. Such amounts shall be transferred on the basis of estimates by the Secretary of the Treasury, and proper adjustments shall be made in amounts subsequently transferred to the extent prior estimates were in excess of or less than the credits allowed.

* * *

[CCH Explanation at ¶740. Committee Reports at ¶15,260.]

Amendments

- **2005, Safe, Accountable, Flexible, Efficient Transportation Equity Act: A Legacy for Users (H.R. 3)**

H.R. 3, §11161(d)(1):

Amended Code Sec. 9502(d)(2) by inserting "(other than subsection (l)(4) and (l)(5) thereof)" after "or 6427 (relating to fuels not used for taxable purposes)". **Effective** for fuels or liquids removed, entered, or sold after 9-30-2005.

H.R. 3, §11161(d)(2):

Amended Code Sec. 9502(d)(3) by inserting "(other than payments made by reason of paragraph (4) or (5) of section 6427(l))" after "section 34". **Effective** for fuels or liquids removed, entered, or sold after 9-30-2005.

[¶5485] CODE SEC. 9503. HIGHWAY TRUST FUND.

* * *

(b) TRANSFER TO HIGHWAY TRUST FUND OF AMOUNTS EQUIVALENT TO CERTAIN TAXES AND PENALTIES.—

(1) CERTAIN TAXES.—There are hereby appropriated to the Highway Trust Fund amounts equivalent to the taxes received in the Treasury before October 1, *2011*, under the following provisions—

(A) section 4041 (relating to taxes on diesel fuels and special motor fuels),

(B) section 4051 (relating to retail tax on heavy trucks and trailers),

(C) section 4071 (relating to tax on tires),

(D) section 4081 (relating to tax on gasoline, diesel fuel, and kerosene), and

(E) section 4481 (relating to tax on use of certain vehicles).

For purposes of this paragraph, taxes received under sections 4041 and 4081 shall be determined without reduction for credits under section 6426.

(2) LIABILITIES INCURRED BEFORE OCTOBER 1, *2011*.—There are hereby appropriated to the Highway Trust Fund amounts equivalent to the taxes which are received in the Treasury after

September 30, *2011*, and before July 1, *2012*, and which are attributable to liability for tax incurred before October 1, *2011*, under the provisions described in paragraph (1).

(3) [*Stricken.*]

* * *

(5) CERTAIN PENALTIES.—There are hereby appropriated to the Highway Trust Fund amounts equivalent to the penalties paid under sections 6715, 6715A, 6717, 6718, 6719, *6720A,* 6725, 7232, and 7272 (but only with regard to penalties under such section related to failure to register under section 4101).

(6) LIMITATION ON TRANSFERS TO HIGHWAY TRUST FUND.—

* * *

(B) EXCEPTION FOR PRIOR OBLIGATIONS.—Subparagraph (A) shall not apply to any expenditure to liquidate any contract entered into (or for any amount otherwise obligated) before *September 30, 2009 (October 1, 2009, in the case of expenditures for administrative expenses)*, in accordance with the provisions of this section.

[CCH Explanation at ¶ 740, ¶ 765 and ¶ 905. Committee Reports at ¶ 15,010, ¶ 15,260 and ¶ 15,320.]

Amendments

• **2005, Safe, Accountable, Flexible, Efficient Transportation Equity Act: A Legacy for Users (H.R. 3)**

H.R. 3, § 11101(c)(1)(A)-(B):

Amended Code Sec. 9503(b)(1)-(2) by striking "2005" each place it appears and inserting "2011", and by striking "2006" and inserting "2012". **Effective** 8-10-2005.

H.R. 3, § 11101(d)(1)(C):

Amended Code Sec. 9503(b)(6)(B) by striking "July 31, 2005" and inserting "September 30, 2009 (October 1, 2009, in the case of expenditures for administrative expenses)". **Effective** 8-10-2005.

H.R. 3, § 11161(c)(2)(C):

Amended Code Sec. 9503(b) by striking paragraph (3). **Effective** for fuels or liquids removed, entered, or sold after 9-30-2005. Prior to being stricken, Code Sec. 9503(b)(3) read as follows:

(3) ADJUSTMENTS FOR AVIATION USES.—The amounts described in paragraph (1) and (2) with respect to any period shall (before the application of this subsection) be reduced by appropriate amounts to reflect any amounts transferred to the Airport and Airway Trust Fund under section 9502(b) with respect to such period.

H.R. 3, § 11167(b):

Amended Code Sec. 9503(b)(5) by inserting "6720A," after "6719,". **Effective** for any transfer, sale, or holding out for sale or resale occurring after 8-10-2005.

(c) EXPENDITURES FROM HIGHWAY TRUST FUND.—

(1) FEDERAL-AID HIGHWAY PROGRAM.—Except as provided in subsection (e), amounts in the Highway Trust Fund shall be available, as provided by appropriation Acts, for making expenditures before September 30, 2009 (October 1, 2009, in the case of expenditures for administrative expenses), to meet those obligations of the United States heretofore or hereafter incurred which are authorized to be paid out of the Highway Trust Fund under the Safe, Accountable, Flexible, Efficient Transportation Equity Act: A Legacy for Users or any other provision of law which was referred to in this paragraph before the date of the enactment of such Act (as such Act and provisions of law are in effect on the date of the enactment of such Act).

(2) TRANSFERS FROM HIGHWAY TRUST FUND FOR CERTAIN REPAYMENTS AND CREDITS.—

(A) IN GENERAL.—The Secretary shall pay from time to time from the Highway Trust Fund into the general fund of the Treasury amounts equivalent to—

(i) the amounts paid before July 1, *2012*, under—

(I) section 6420 (relating to amounts paid in respect of gasoline used on farms),

(II) section 6421 (relating to amounts paid in respect of gasoline used for certain nonhighway purposes or by local transit systems), and

(III) section 6427 (relating to fuels not used for taxable purposes), on the basis of claims filed for periods ending before October 1, *2011*, and

(ii) the credits allowed under section 34 (relating to credit for certain uses of fuel) with respect to fuel used before October 1, 2011.

* * *

(3) FLOOR STOCKS REFUNDS.—The Secretary shall pay from time to time from the Highway Trust Fund into the general fund of the Treasury amounts equivalent to the floor stocks refunds made before July 1, 2012, under section 6412(a).

(4) TRANSFERS FROM THE TRUST FUND FOR MOTORBOAT FUEL TAXES.—

(A) TRANSFER TO LAND AND WATER CONSERVATION FUND.—

(i) IN GENERAL.—The Secretary shall pay from time to time from the Highway Trust Fund into the land and water conservation fund provided for in title I of the Land and Water Conservation Fund Act of 1965 amounts (as determined by the Secretary) equivalent to the motorboat fuel taxes received on or after October 1, 2005, and before October 1, 2011.

(ii) LIMITATION.—The aggregate amount transferred under this subparagraph during any fiscal year shall not exceed $1,000,000.

(B) EXCESS FUNDS TRANSFERRED TO SPORT FISH RESTORATION AND BOATING TRUST FUND.—Any amounts in the Highway Trust Fund—

(i) which are attributable to motorboat fuel taxes, and

(ii) which are not transferred from the Highway Trust Fund under subparagraph (A),

shall be transferred by the Secretary from the Highway Trust Fund into the Sport Fish Restoration and Boating Trust Fund.

(C) MOTORBOAT FUEL TAXES.—For purposes of this paragraph, the term "motorboat fuel taxes" means the taxes under section 4041(a)(2) with respect to special motor fuels used as fuel in motorboats and under section 4081 with respect to gasoline used as fuel in motorboats, but only to the extent such taxes are deposited into the Highway Trust Fund.

(D) DETERMINATION.—The amount of payments made under this paragraph after October 1, 1986 shall be determined by the Secretary in accordance with the methodology described in the Treasury Department's Report to Congress of June 1986 entitled "Gasoline Excise Tax Revenues Attributable to Fuel Used in Recreational Motorboats."

(5) TRANSFERS FROM THE TRUST FUND FOR SMALL-ENGINE FUEL TAXES.—

(A) IN GENERAL.—The Secretary shall pay from time to time from the Highway Trust Fund into the Sport Fish Restoration *and Boating* Trust Fund amounts (as determined by him) equivalent to the small-engine fuel taxes received on or after December 1, 1990, and before October 1, 2011.

(B) SMALL-ENGINE FUEL TAXES.—For purposes of this paragraph, the term "small-engine fuel taxes" means the taxes under section 4081 with respect to gasoline used as a fuel in the nonbusiness use of small-engine outdoor power equipment, but only to the extent such taxes are deposited into the Highway Trust Fund.

(7)[(6)] TRANSFERS FROM THE TRUST FUND FOR CERTAIN AVIATION FUEL TAXES.—The Secretary shall pay at least monthly from the Highway Trust Fund into the Airport and Airway Trust Fund amounts (as determined by the Secretary) equivalent to the taxes received on or after October 1, 2005, and before October 1, 2011, under section 4081 with respect to so much of the rate of tax as does not exceed—

(A) 4.3 cents per gallon of kerosene with respect to which a payment has been made by the Secretary under section 6427(l)(4), and

(B) 21.8 cents per gallon of kerosene with respect to which a payment has been made by the Secretary under section 6427(l)(5).

Transfers under the preceding sentence shall be made on the basis of estimates by the Secretary, and proper adjustments shall be made in the amounts subsequently transferred to the extent prior estimates were in excess of or less than the amounts required to be transferred. Any amount allowed as a credit under section 34 by reason of paragraph (4) or (5) of section 6427(l) shall be treated for purposes of subparagraphs (A) and (B) as a payment made by the Secretary under such paragraph.

[CCH Explanation at ¶740, ¶905 and ¶1030. Committee Reports at ¶15,010, ¶15,050 and ¶15,260.]

Amendments

- **2005, Safe, Accountable, Flexible, Efficient Transportation Equity Act: A Legacy for Users (H.R. 3)**

H.R. 3, §11101(c)(1)(A)-(B):

Amended Code Sec. 9503(c)(2)-(3) by striking "2005" each place it appears and inserting "2011", and by striking "2006" each place it appears and inserting "2012". **Effective** 8-10-2005.

H.R. 3, §11101(c)(2)(A):

Amended Code Sec. 9503(c)(5)(A) by striking "2005" and inserting "2011". **Effective** 8-10-2005.

H.R. 3, §11101(d)(1)(A):

Amended Code Sec. 9503(c)(1). **Effective** 8-10-2005. Prior to amendment, Code Sec. 9503(c)(1) read as follows:

(1) FEDERAL-AID HIGHWAY PROGRAM.—Except as provided in subsection (e), amounts in the Highway Trust Fund shall be available, as provided by appropriation Acts, for making expenditures before August 15, 2005, to meet those obligations of the United States heretofore or hereafter incurred which are—

(A) authorized by law to be paid out of the Highway Trust Fund established by section 209 of the Highway Revenue Act of 1956,

(B) authorized to be paid out of the Highway Trust Fund under title I or II of the Surface Transportation Assistance Act of 1982,

(C) authorized to be paid out of the Highway Trust Fund under the Surface Transportation and Uniform Relocation Assistance Act of 1987,

(D) authorized to be paid out of the Highway Trust Fund under the Intermodal Surface Transportation Efficiency Act of 1991,

(E) authorized to be paid out of the Highway Trust Fund under the Transportation Equity Act for the 21st Century,

(F) authorized to be paid out of the Highway Trust Fund under the Surface Transportation Extension Act of 2003,

(G) authorized to be paid out of the Highway Trust Fund under the Surface Transportation Extension Act of 2004,

(H) authorized to be paid out of the Highway Trust Fund under the Surface Transportation Extension Act of 2004, Part II,

(I) authorized to be paid out of the Highway Trust Fund under the Surface Transportation Extension Act of 2004, Part III,

(J) authorized to be paid out of the Highway Trust Fund under the Surface Transportation Extension Act of 2004, Part IV,

(K) authorized to be paid out of the Highway Trust Fund under the Surface Transportation Extension Act of 2004, Part V,

(L) authorized to be paid out of the Highway Trust Fund under the Surface Transportation Extension Act of 2005,

(M) authorized to be paid out of the Highway Trust Fund under the Surface Transportation Extension Act of 2005, Part II,

(N) authorized to be paid out of the Highway Trust Fund under the Surface Transportation Extension Act of 2005, Part III,

(O) authorized to be paid out of the Highway Trust Fund under the Surface Transportation Extension Act of 2005, Part IV,

(P) authorized to be paid out of the Highway Trust Fund under the Surface Transportation Extension Act of 2005, Part V, or

(Q) authorized to be paid out of the Highway Trust Fund under the Surface Transportation Extension Act of 2005, Part VI.

In determining the authorizations under the Acts referred to in the preceding subparagraphs, such Acts shall be applied as in effect on the date of enactment of the Surface Transportation Extension Act of 2005, Part VI.

H.R. 3, §11115(a)(1)(A)-(C):

Amended Code Sec. 9503(c)(4) by striking so much of paragraph (4) as precedes subparagraph (D), by redesignating subparagraphs (D) and (E) as subparagraphs (C) and (D), respectively, and by inserting before subparagraph (C), as so redesignated, new subparagraphs (A) and (B). **Effective** 10-1-2005. Prior to amendment, Code Sec. 9503(c)(4) read as follows:

(4) TRANSFERS FROM THE TRUST FUND FOR MOTORBOAT FUEL TAXES.—

(A) TRANSFER TO BOAT SAFETY ACCOUNT.—

(i) IN GENERAL.—The Secretary shall pay from time to time from the Highway Trust Fund into the Boat Safety Account in the Aquatic Resources Trust Fund amounts (as determined by him) equivalent to the motorboat fuel taxes received on or after October 1, 1980, and before October 1, 2005.

(ii) LIMITATIONS.—

(I) LIMIT ON TRANSFERS DURING ANY FISCAL YEAR.—The aggregate amount transferred under this subparagraph during any fiscal year shall not exceed $60,000,000 for each of fiscal years 1989 and 1990 and $70,000,000 for each fiscal year thereafter.

(II) LIMIT ON AMOUNT IN FUND.—No amount shall be transferred under this subparagraph if the Secretary determines that such transfer would result in increasing the amount in the Boat Safety Account to a sum in excess of $60,000,000 for Fiscal Year 1987 only and $45,000,000 for each fiscal year thereafter.

In making the determination under subclause (II) for any fiscal year, the Secretary shall not take into account any amount appropriated from the Boat Safety Account in any preceding fiscal year but not distributed.

(B) $1,000,000 PER YEAR OF EXCESS TRANSFERRED TO LAND AND WATER CONSERVATION FUND.—

(i) IN GENERAL.—Any amount received in the Highway Trust Fund—

(I) which is attributable to motorboat fuel taxes, and

(II) which is not transferred from the Highway Trust Fund under subparagraph (A),

shall be transferred (subject to the limitation of clause (ii)) by the Secretary from the Highway Trust Fund into the land

¶5485 Code Sec. 9503(c)(7)[(6)](B)

and water conservation fund provided for in title I of the Land and Water Conservation Fund Act of 1965.

(ii) LIMITATION.—The aggregate amount transferred under this subparagraph during any fiscal year shall not exceed $1,000,000.

(C) EXCESS FUNDS TRANSFERRED TO SPORT FISH RESTORATION ACCOUNT.—Any amount received in the Highway Trust Fund—

(i) which is attributable to motorboat fuel taxes, and

(ii) which is not transferred from the Highway Trust Fund under subparagraph (A) or (B),

shall be transferred by the Secretary from the Highway Trust Fund into the Sport Fish Restoration Account in the Aquatic Resources Trust Fund.

(D) MOTORBOAT FUEL TAXES.—For purposes of this paragraph, the term "motorboat fuel taxes" means the taxes under section 4041(a)(2) with respect to special motor fuels used as fuel in motorboats and under section 4081 with respect to gasoline used as fuel in motorboats, but only to the extent such taxes are deposited into the Highway Trust Fund.

(E) DETERMINATION.—The amount of payments made under this paragraph after October 1, 1986 shall be determined by the Secretary in accordance with the methodology described in the Treasury Department's Report to Congress of June 1986 entitled "Gasoline Excise Tax Revenues Attributable to Fuel Used in Recreational Motorboats."

H.R. 3, § 11115(a)(2):

Amended Code Sec. 9503(c)(5)(A) by striking "Account in the Aquatic Resources" and inserting "and Boating". **Effective** 10-1-2005.

H.R. 3, § 11161(c)(1):

Amended Code Sec. 9503(c) by adding at the end a new paragraph (7)[(6)]. **Effective** for fuels or liquids removed, entered, or sold after 9-30-2005.

(d) ADJUSTMENTS OF APPORTIONMENTS.—

(1) ESTIMATES OF UNFUNDED HIGHWAY AUTHORIZATIONS AND NET HIGHWAY RECEIPTS.—The Secretary of the Treasury, not less frequently than once in each calendar quarter, after consultation with the Secretary of Transportation, shall estimate—

(A) the amount which would (but for this subsection) be the unfunded highway authorizations at the close of the next fiscal year, and

(B) the net highway receipts for the *48-month* period beginning at the close of such fiscal year.

* * *

(3) ADJUSTMENT OF APPORTIONMENTS WHERE UNFUNDED AUTHORIZATIONS EXCEED *4 YEARS* RECEIPTS.—

* * *

(6) MEASUREMENT OF NET HIGHWAY RECEIPTS.—*For purposes of making any estimate under paragraph (1) of net highway receipts for periods ending after the date specified in subsection (b)(1), the Secretary shall treat—*

(A) each expiring provision of subsection (b) which is related to appropriations or transfers to the Highway Trust Fund to have been extended through the end of the 48-month period referred to in paragraph (1)(B), and

(B) with respect to each tax imposed under the sections referred to in subsection (b)(1), the rate of such tax during the 48-month period referred to in paragraph (1)(B) to be the same as the rate of such tax as in effect on the date of such estimate.

(7) REPORTS.—Any estimate under paragraph (1) and any determination under paragraph (2) shall be reported by the Secretary of the Treasury to the Committee on Ways and Means of the House of Representatives, the Committee on Finance of the Senate, the Committees on the Budget of both Houses, the Committee on Public Works and Transportation of the House of Representatives, and the Committee on Environment and Public Works of the Senate.

[CCH Explanation at ¶ 1025. Committee Reports at ¶ 15,010.]

Amendments

- **2005, Safe, Accountable, Flexible, Efficient Transportation Equity Act: A Legacy for Users (H.R. 3)**

H.R. 3, § 11102(a)(1)-(2):

Amended Code Sec. 9503(d) by striking "24-month" in paragraph (1)(B) and inserting "48-month", and by striking "2 YEARS" in the heading for paragraph (3) and inserting "4 YEARS". **Effective** 8-10-2005.

H.R. 3, § 11102(b):

Amended Code Sec. 9503(d) by redesignating paragraph (6) as paragraph (7) and by inserting after paragraph (5) a new paragraph (6). **Effective** 8-10-2005.

(e) ESTABLISHMENT OF MASS TRANSIT ACCOUNT.—

* * *

(3) EXPENDITURES FROM ACCOUNT.—Amounts in the Mass Transit Account shall be available, as provided by appropriation Acts, for making capital or capital related expenditures (including capital expenditures for new projects) before October 1, 2009, in accordance with the Safe, Accountable, Flexible, Efficient Transportation Equity Act: A Legacy for Users or any other provision of law which was referred to in this paragraph before the date of the enactment of such Act (as such Act and provisions of law are in effect on the date of the enactment of such Act).

* * *

[CCH Explanation at ¶ 905. Committee Reports at ¶ 15,010.]

Amendments

- **2005, Safe, Accountable, Flexible, Efficient Transportation Equity Act: A Legacy for Users (H.R. 3)**

H.R. 3, § 11101(d)(1)(B):

Amended Code Sec. 9503(e)(3). **Effective** 8-10-2005. Prior to amendment, Code Sec. 9503(e)(3) read as follows:

(3) EXPENDITURES FROM ACCOUNT.—Amounts in the Mass Transit Account shall be available, as provided by appropriation Acts, for making capital or capital-related expenditures before August 15, 2005 (including capital expenditures for new projects) in accordance with—

(A) section 5338(a)(1) or (b)(1) of title 49,

(B) the Intermodal Surface Transportation Efficiency Act of 1991,

(C) the Transportation Equity Act for the 21st Century,

(D) the Surface Transportation Extension Act of 2003,

(E) the Surface Transportation Extension Act of 2004,

(F) the Surface Transportation Extension Act of 2004, Part II,

(G) the Surface Transportation Extension Act of 2004, Part III,

(H) the Surface Transportation Extension Act of 2004, Part IV,

(I) the Surface Transportation Extension Act of 2004, Part V,

(J) the Surface Transportation Extension Act of 2005,

(K) the Surface Transportation Extension Act of 2005, Part II,

(L) the Surface Transportation Extension Act of 2005, Part III,

(M) the Surface Transportation Extension Act of 2005, Part IV,

(N) the Surface Transportation Extension Act of 2005, Part V, or

(O) the Surface Transportation Extension Act of 2005, Part VI,

as such section and Acts are in effect on the date of enactment of the Surface Transportation Extension Act of 2005, Part VI.

[¶ 5490] CODE SEC. 9504. SPORT FISH RESTORATION AND BOATING TRUST FUND.

(a) CREATION OF TRUST FUND.—There is hereby established in the Treasury of the United States a trust fund to be known as the "Sport Fish Restoration and Boating Trust Fund". Such Trust Fund shall consist of such amounts as may be appropriated, credited, or paid to it as provided in this section, section 9503(c)(4), section 9503(c)(5), or section 9602(b).

[CCH Explanation at ¶ 1030. Committee Reports at ¶ 15,050.]

Amendments

- **2005, Safe, Accountable, Flexible, Efficient Transportation Equity Act: A Legacy for Users (H.R. 3)**

H.R. 3, § 11115(b)(1):

Amended Code Sec. 9504(a). **Effective** 10-1-2005. Prior to amendment, Code Sec. 9504(a) read as follows:

(a) CREATION OF TRUST FUND.—

(1) IN GENERAL.—There is hereby established in the Treasury of the United States a trust fund to be known as the "Aquatic Resources Trust Fund".

(2) ACCOUNTS IN TRUST FUND.—The Aquatic Resources Trust Fund shall consist of—

(A) a Sport Fish Restoration Account, and

(B) a Boat Safety Account.

Each such Account shall consist of such amounts as may be appropriated, credited, or paid to it as provided in this section, section 9503(c)(4), section 9503(c)(5) or section 9602(b).

H.R. 3, § 11115(b)(2)(D):

Amended Code Sec. 9504 by striking "AQUATIC RESOURCES" in the heading and inserting "SPORT FISH RESTORATION AND BOATING". **Effective** 10-1-2005.

(b) SPORT FISH RESTORATION *AND BOATING TRUST FUND.*—

(1) TRANSFER OF CERTAIN TAXES TO *TRUST FUND.*—There is hereby appropriated to the Sport Fish Restoration *and Boating Trust Fund* amounts equivalent to the following amounts received in the Treasury on or after October 1, 1984—

(A) the taxes imposed by section 4161(a) (relating to sport fishing equipment), and

(B) the import duties imposed on fishing tackle under heading 9507 of the Harmonized Tariff Schedule of the United States (19 U.S.C. 1202) and on yachts and pleasure craft under chapter 89 of the Harmonized Tariff Schedule of the United States.

(2) EXPENDITURES FROM *TRUST FUND.*—Amounts in the Sport Fish Restoration *and Boating Trust Fund* shall be available, as provided by appropriation Acts, for making expenditures—

(A) to carry out the purposes of *the Dingell-Johnson Sport Fish Restoration Act* (as in effect on the date of the enactment of the *Safe, Accountable, Flexible, Efficient Transportation Equity Act: A Legacy for Users*),

(B) to carry out the purposes of section 7404(d) of the Transportation Equity Act for the 21st Century (as in effect on the date of the enactment of the *Safe, Accountable, Flexible, Efficient Transportation Equity Act: A Legacy for Users*), and

(C) to carry out the purposes of the Coastal Wetlands Planning Protection and Restoration Act (as in effect on the date of the enactment of the *Safe, Accountable, Flexible, Efficient Transportation Equity Act: A Legacy for Users*).

Amounts transferred to such account under section 9503(c)(5) may be used only for making expenditures described in *subparagraph (C)* of this paragraph.

[CCH Explanation at ¶ 797, ¶ 905 and ¶ 1030. Committee Reports at ¶ 15,010, ¶ 15,050 and ¶ 15,240.]

Amendments

- **2005, Safe, Accountable, Flexible, Efficient Transportation Equity Act: A Legacy for Users (H.R. 3)**

H.R. 3, § 11101(d)(2)(A):

Amended Code Sec. 9504(b)(2) by striking "Surface Transportation Extension Act of 2005, Part V" each place it appears and inserting "Safe, Accountable, Flexible, Efficient Transportation Equity Act: A Legacy for Users". **Effective** 8-10-2005.

H.R. 3, § 11115(b)(2)(A)(i)-(iii):

Amended Code Sec. 9504(b), as amended by Act Sec. 11101, by striking "ACCOUNT" in the heading and inserting "AND BOATING TRUST FUND", by striking "Account" both places it appears in paragraphs (1) and (2) and inserting "and Boating Trust Fund", and by striking "ACCOUNT" both places it appears in the headings for paragraphs (1) and (2) and inserting "TRUST FUND". **Effective** 10-1-2005.

H.R. 3, § 11151(c):

Amended Code Sec. 9504(b)(2) by striking in the last sentence "subparagraph (B)" and inserting "subparagraph (C)". **Effective** as if included in the provision of the Transportation Equity Act for the 21st Century to which it relates [effective 6-9-98.—CCH].

H.R. 3, § 11151(e)(1):

Amended Code Sec. 9504(b)(2)(A) by striking "the Act entitled 'An Act to provide that the United States shall aid the States in fish restoration and management projects, and for other purposes', approved August 9, 1950" and inserting "the Dingell-Johnson Sport Fish Restoration Act". **Effective** 8-10-2005.

(c) EXPENDITURES FROM BOAT SAFETY ACCOUNT.—*Amounts remaining in the Boat Safety Account on October 1, 2005, and amounts thereafter credited to the Account under section 9602(b), shall be available, without further appropriation, for making expenditures before October 1, 2010, to carry out the purposes of section 15 of the Dingell-Johnson Sport Fish Restoration Act (as in effect on the date of the enactment of the Safe, Accountable, Flexible, Efficient Transportation Equity Act: A Legacy for Users). For purposes of section 9602, the Boat Safety Account shall be treated as a Trust Fund established by this subchapter.*

[CCH Explanation at ¶1030. Committee Reports at ¶15,050.]

Amendments

• 2005, Safe, Accountable, Flexible, Efficient Transportation Equity Act: A Legacy for Users (H.R. 3)

H.R. 3, §11115(c):

Amended Code Sec. 9504(c). **Effective** 10-1-2005. Prior to amendment, Code Sec. 9504(c) read as follows:

(c) EXPENDITURES FROM BOAT SAFETY ACCOUNT.—Amounts in the Boat Safety Account shall be available, as provided by appropriation Acts, for making expenditures before August 15, 2005, to carry out the purposes of section 13106 of title 46, United States Code (as in effect on the date of the enactment of the Surface Transportation Extension Act of 2005, Part VI).

(d) LIMITATION ON TRANSFERS TO TRUST FUND.—

(1) IN GENERAL.—Except as provided in paragraph (2), no amount may be appropriated or paid to *the Sport Fish Restoration and Boating* Trust Fund on and after the date of any expenditure from *such Trust Fund* which is not permitted by this section. The determination of whether an expenditure is so permitted shall be made without regard to—

(A) any provision of law which is not contained or referenced in this title or in a revenue Act, and

(B) whether such provision of law is a subsequently enacted provision or directly or indirectly seeks to waive the application of this subsection.

(2) EXCEPTION FOR PRIOR OBLIGATIONS.—Paragraph (1) shall not apply to any expenditure to liquidate any contract entered into (or for any amount otherwise obligated) before *October 1, 2009*, in accordance with the provisions of this section.

[CCH Explanation at ¶905 and ¶1030. Committee Reports at ¶15,010 and ¶15,050.]

Amendments

• 2005, Safe, Accountable, Flexible, Efficient Transportation Equity Act: A Legacy for Users (H.R. 3)

H.R. 3, §11101(d)(2)(B):

Amended Code Sec. 9504(d)(2) by striking "July 31, 2005" and inserting "October 1, 2009". **Effective** 8-10-2005.

H.R. 3, §11115(b)(2)(B)(i)-(iii):

Amended Code Sec. 9504(d), as amended by Act Sec. 11101, by striking "AQUATIC RESOURCES" before "TRUST FUND" in the heading, by striking "any Account in the Aquatic Resources" in paragraph (1) and inserting "the Sport Fish Restoration and Boating", and by striking "any such Account" in paragraph (1) and inserting "such Trust Fund". **Effective** 10-1-2005.

(e) CROSS REFERENCE.—

For provision transferring motorboat fuels taxes to *Sport Fish Restoration and Boating Trust Fund*, see section 9503(c)(4).

[CCH Explanation at ¶1030. Committee Reports at ¶15,050.]

Amendments

• 2005, Safe, Accountable, Flexible, Efficient Transportation Equity Act: A Legacy for Users (H.R. 3)

H.R. 3, §11115(b)(2)(C):

Amended Code Sec. 9504(e) by striking "Boat Safety Account and Sport Fish Restoration Account" and inserting "Sport Fish Restoration and Boating Trust Fund". **Effective** 10-1-2005.

[¶5495] CODE SEC. 9508. LEAKING UNDERGROUND STORAGE TANK TRUST FUND.

* * *

(c) EXPENDITURES.—Amounts in the Leaking Underground Storage Tank Trust Fund shall be available, as provided in appropriation Acts, only for purposes of making expenditures to carry out section 9003(h) of the Solid Waste Disposal Act as in effect on the date of the enactment of the Superfund Amendments and Reauthorization Act of 1986.

* * *

[CCH Explanation at ¶ 785. Committee Reports at ¶ 10,360.]
Amendments

• **2005, Energy Tax Incentives Act of 2005 (H.R. 6)**

H.R. 6, § 1362(c):

Amended Code Sec. 9508(c). **Effective** 10-1-2005. Prior to amendment, Code Sec. 9508(c) read as follows:

(c) EXPENDITURES.—

(1) IN GENERAL.—Except as provided in paragraph (2), amounts in the Leaking Underground Storage Tank Trust Fund shall be available, as provided in appropriation Acts, only for purposes of making expenditures to carry out section 9003(h) of the Solid Waste Disposal Act as in effect on the date of the enactment of the Superfund Amendments and Reauthorization Act of 1986.

(2) TRANSFERS FROM TRUST FUND FOR CERTAIN REPAYMENTS AND CREDITS.—

(A) IN GENERAL.—The Secretary shall pay from time to time from the Leaking Underground Storage Tank Trust Fund into the general fund of the Treasury amounts equivalent to—

(i) amounts paid under—

(I) section 6420 (relating to amounts paid in respect of gasoline used on farms),

(II) section 6421 (relating to amounts paid in respect of gasoline used for certain nonhighway purposes or by local transit systems), and

(III) section 6427 (relating to fuels not used for taxable purposes), and

(ii) credits allowed under section 34, with respect to the taxes imposed by section 4041(d) or by section 4081 (to the extent attributable to the Leaking Underground Storage Tank Trust Fund financing rate under such sections).

(B) TRANSFERS BASED ON ESTIMATES.—Transfers under subparagraph (A) shall be made on the basis of estimates by the Secretary, and proper adjustments shall be made in amounts subsequently transferred to the extent prior estimates were in excess of or less than the amounts required to be transferred.

(e) LIMITATION ON TRANSFERS TO LEAKING UNDERGROUND STORAGE TANK TRUST FUND.—

(1) IN GENERAL.—Except as provided in paragraph (2), no amount may be appropriated to the Leaking Underground Storage Tank Trust Fund on and after the date of any expenditure from the Leaking Underground Storage Tank Trust Fund which is not permitted by this section. The determination of whether an expenditure is so permitted shall be made without regard to—

(A) any provision of law which is not contained or referenced in this title or in a revenue Act, and

(B) whether such provision of law is a subsequently enacted provision or directly or indirectly seeks to waive the application of this paragraph.

(2) EXCEPTION FOR PRIOR OBLIGATIONS.—Paragraph (1) shall not apply to any expenditure to liquidate any contract entered into (or for any amount otherwise obligated) before October 1, 2011, in accordance with the provisions of this section.

[CCH Explanation at ¶ 1035. Committee Reports at ¶ 10,360 and ¶ 15,210 .]
Amendments

• **2005, Safe, Accountable, Flexible, Efficient Transportation Equity Act: A Legacy for Users (H.R. 3)**

H.R. 3, § 11147(a):

Amended Code Sec. 9508 by adding at the end a new subsection (e). **Effective** 8-10-2005.

Act Sections Not Amending Code Sections

ENERGY POLICY ACT OF 2005

TITLE XIII—ENERGY POLICY TAX INCENTIVES

[¶ 7003] ACT SECTION 1300. SHORT TITLE; AMENDMENT OF 1986 CODE.

(a) SHORT TITLE.—This title may be cited as the "Energy Tax Incentives Act of 2005".

(b) AMENDMENT OF 1986 CODE.—Except as otherwise expressly provided, whenever in this title an amendment or repeal is expressed in terms of an amendment to, or repeal of, a section or other provision, the reference shall be considered to be made to a section or other provision of the Internal Revenue Code of 1986.

Subtitle A—Electricity Infrastructure

[¶ 7005] ACT SEC. 1301. EXTENSION AND MODIFICATION OF RENEWABLE ELECTRICITY PRODUCTION CREDIT.

* * *

(f) ADDITIONAL TECHNICAL AMENDMENTS RELATED TO SECTION 710 OF THE AMERICAN JOBS CREATION ACT OF 2004.—

* * *

(6) Paragraph (4) of section 710(g) of the American Jobs Creation Act of 2004 is amended by striking "January 1, 2004" and inserting "January 1, 2005".

- • *2004 JOBS ACT ACT SEC. 710(g)(4) AS AMENDED*——————————————

ACT SEC. 710. EXPANSION OF CREDIT FOR ELECTRICITY PRODUCED FROM CERTAIN RENEWABLE RESOURCES.

* * *

(g) EFFECTIVE DATES.—

* * *

(4) NONAPPLICATION OF AMENDMENTS TO PREEFFECTIVE DATE POULTRY WASTE FACILITIES.— The amendments made by this section shall not apply with respect to any poultry waste facility (within the meaning of section 45(c)(3)(C), as in effect on the day before the date of the enactment of this act) placed in service before *January 1, 2005*.

* * *

(g) EFFECTIVE DATES.—

* * *

(2) TECHNICAL AMENDMENTS.—. The amendments made by subsections (e) and (f) shall take effect as if included in the amendments made by section 710 of the American Jobs Creation Act of 2004.

* * *

[CCH Explanation at ¶ 405. Committee Reports at ¶ 10,010.]

[¶ 7010] ACT SEC. 1303. CLEAN RENEWABLE ENERGY BONDS.

* * *

(d) ISSUANCE OF REGULATIONS.—The Secretary of Treasury shall issue regulations required under section 54 of the Internal Revenue Code of 1986 (as added by this section) not later than 120 days after the date of the enactment of this Act.

* * *

[CCH Explanation at ¶ 455. Committee Reports at ¶ 10,020.]

Subtitle E—Additional Energy Tax Incentives

* * *

[¶ 7015] ACT SEC. 1352. NATIONAL ACADEMY OF SCIENCES STUDY AND REPORT.

(a) STUDY.—Not later than 60 days after the date of the enactment of this Act, the Secretary of the Treasury shall enter into an agreement with the National Academy of Sciences under which the National Academy of Sciences shall conduct a study to define and evaluate the health, environmental, security, and infrastructure external costs and benefits associated with the production and consumption of energy that are not or may not be fully incorporated into the market price of such energy, or into the Federal tax or fee or other applicable revenue measure related to such production or consumption.

(b) REPORT.—Not later than 2 years after the date on which the agreement under subsection (a) is entered into, the National Academy of Sciences shall submit to Congress a report on the study conducted under subsection (a).

[CCH Explanation at ¶ 1005. Committee Reports at ¶ 10,330.]

[¶ 7020] ACT SEC. 1353. RECYCLING STUDY.

(a) STUDY.—The Secretary of the Treasury, in consultation with the Secretary of Energy, shall conduct a study—

(1) to determine and quantify the energy savings achieved through the recycling of glass, paper, plastic, steel, aluminum, and electronic devices, and

(2) to identify tax incentives which would encourage recycling of such material.

(b) REPORT.—Not later than 1 year after the date of the enactment of this Act, the Secretary of the Treasury shall submit to Congress a report on the study conducted under subsection (a).

[CCH Explanation at ¶ 1010. Committee Reports at ¶ 10,340.]

Subtitle F—Revenue Raising Provisions

* * *

[¶ 7025] ACT SEC. 1364. CLARIFICATION OF TIRE EXCISE TAX.

* * *

(c) STUDY.—

(1) IN GENERAL.—With respect to the 1-year period beginning on January 1, 2006, the Secretary of the Treasury shall conduct a study to determine—

(A) the amount of tax collected during such period under section 4071 of the Internal Revenue Code of 1986 with respect to each class of tire, and

(B) the number of tires in each such class on which tax is imposed under such section during such period.

(2) REPORT.—Not later than July 1, 2007, the Secretary of the Treasury shall submit to Congress a report on the study conducted under paragraph (1).

[CCH Explanation at ¶1020. Committee Reports at ¶10,380.]

SAFE, ACCOUNTABLE, FLEXIBLE, EFFICIENT TRANSPORTATION EQUITY ACT: A LEGACY FOR USERS

TITLE XI—HIGHWAY REAUTHORIZATION AND EXCISE TAX SIMPLIFICATION

[¶7045] ACT SEC. 11100. AMENDMENT OF 1986 CODE.

Except as otherwise expressly provided, whenever in this title an amendment or repeal is expressed in terms of an amendment to, or repeal of, a section or other provision, the reference shall be considered to be made to a section or other provision of the Internal Revenue Code of 1986.

Subtitle A—Trust Fund Reauthorization

[¶7050] ACT SEC. 11101. EXTENSION OF HIGHWAY-RELATED TAXES AND TRUST FUNDS.

* * *

(c) EXTENSION OF TRANSFERS OF CERTAIN TAXES.—

* * *

(2) MOTORBOAT AND SMALL-ENGINE FUEL TAX TRANSFERS.—

* * *

(B) CONFORMING AMENDMENTS TO LAND AND WATER CONSERVATION FUND.—Section 201(b) of the Land and Water Conservation Fund Act of 1965 (16 U.S.C. 460l-11(b)) is amended—

(i) by striking "2003" and inserting "2011", and

(ii) by striking "2004" each place it appears and inserting "2012".

* * *

(e) EFFECTIVE DATE.—The amendments made by this section shall take effect on the date of the enactment of this Act.

* * *

[CCH Explanation at ¶905. Committee Reports at ¶15,010.]

Subtitle B—Excise Tax Reform and Simplification

PART 2—AQUATIC EXCISE TAXES

[¶7055] ACT SEC. 11115. ELIMINATION OF AQUATIC RESOURCES TRUST FUND AND TRANSFORMATION OF SPORT FISH RESTORATION ACCOUNT.

* * *

(b) MERGING OF ACCOUNTS.—

* * *

(2) CONFORMING AMENDMENTS.—

* * *

(F) Paragraph (2) of section 1511(e) of the Homeland Security Act of 2002 (6 U.S.C. 551(e)) is amended by striking "Aquatic Resources Trust Fund of the Highway Trust Fund" and inserting "Sport Fish Restoration and Boating Trust Fund".

* * *

(d) EFFECTIVE DATE.—The amendments made by this section shall take effect on October 1, 2005.

* * *

[CCH Explanation at ¶ 1030. Committee Reports at ¶ 15,050.]

PART 4—TAXES RELATING TO ALCOHOL

[¶ 7060] ACT SEC. 11125. REPEAL OF SPECIAL OCCUPATIONAL TAXES ON PRODUCERS AND MARKETERS OF ALCOHOLIC BEVERAGES.

(a) REPEAL OF OCCUPATIONAL TAXES.—

(1) IN GENERAL.—The following provisions of part II of subchapter A of chapter 51 (relating to occupational taxes) are hereby repealed:

(A) Subpart A (relating to proprietors of distilled spirits plants, bonded wine cellars, etc.).

(B) Subpart B (relating to brewer).

(C) Subpart D (relating to wholesale dealers) (other than sections 5114 and 5116).

(D) Subpart E (relating to retail dealers) (other than section 5124).

(E) Subpart G (relating to general provisions) (other than sections 5142, 5143, 5145, and 5146).

(2) NONBEVERAGE DOMESTIC DRAWBACK.—Section 5131 is amended by striking ", on payment of a special tax per annum,".

(3) INDUSTRIAL USE OF DISTILLED SPIRITS.—Section 5276 is hereby repealed.

(b) CONFORMING AMENDMENTS.—

(1)(A) The heading for part II of subchapter A of chapter 51 and the table of subparts for such part are amended to read as follows:

"PART II—MISCELLANEOUS PROVISIONS

"Subpart A. Manufacturers of stills.

"Subpart B. Nonbeverage domestic drawback claimants.

"Subpart C. Recordkeeping by dealers.

"Subpart D. Other provisions.".

(B) The table of parts for such subchapter A is amended by striking the item relating to part II and inserting the following new item:

"Part II. Miscellaneous provisions.".

(2) Subpart C of part II of such subchapter (relating to manufacturers of stills) is redesignated as subpart A.

(3)(A) Subpart F of such part II (relating to nonbeverage domestic drawback claimants) is redesignated as subpart B and sections 5131 through 5134 are redesignated as sections 5111 through 5114, respectively.

(B) The table of sections for such subpart B, as so redesignated, is amended—

(i) by redesignating the items relating to sections 5131 through 5134 as relating to sections 5111 through 5114, respectively, and

(ii) by striking "and rate of tax" in the item relating to section 5111, as so redesignated.

(C) Section 5111, as redesignated by subparagraph (A), is amended—

(i) by striking "AND RATE OF TAX" in the section heading,

(ii) by striking the subsection heading for subsection (a), and

(iii) by striking subsection (b).

(4) Part II of subchapter A of chapter 51 is amended by adding after subpart B, as redesignated by paragraph (3), the following new subpart:

"Subpart C—Recordkeeping and Registration by Dealers

"Sec. 5121. Recordkeeping by wholesale dealers.

"Sec. 5122. Recordkeeping by retail dealers.

"Sec. 5123. Preservation and inspection of records, and entry of premises for inspection.

"Sec. 5124. Registration by dealers.".

(5)(A) Section 5114 (relating to records) is moved to subpart C of such part II and inserted after the table of sections for such subpart.

(B) Section 5114 is amended—

(i) by striking the section heading and inserting the following new heading:

"SEC. 5432. RECORDKEEPING BY WHOLESALE DEALERS.";

and

(ii) by redesignating subsection (c) as subsection (d) and by inserting after subsection (b) the following new subsection:

"(c) WHOLESALE DEALERS.—For purposes of this part—

"(1) WHOLESALE DEALER IN LIQUORS.—The term 'wholesale dealer in liquors' means any dealer (other than a wholesale dealer in beer) who sells, or offers for sale, distilled spirits, wines, or beer, to another dealer.

"(2) WHOLESALE DEALER IN BEER.—The term 'wholesale dealer in beer' means any dealer who sells, or offers for sale, beer, but not distilled spirits or wines, to another dealer.

"(3) DEALER.—The term 'dealer' means any person who sells, or offers for sale, any distilled spirits, wines, or beer.

"(4) PRESUMPTION IN CASE OF SALE OF 20 WINE GALLONS OR MORE.—The sale, or offer for sale, of distilled spirits, wines, or beer, in quantities of 20 wine gallons or more to the same person at the same time, shall be presumptive evidence that the person making such sale, or offer for sale, is engaged in or carrying on the business of a wholesale dealer in liquors or a wholesale dealer in beer, as the case may be. Such presumption may be overcome by evidence satisfactorily showing that such sale, or offer for sale, was made to a person other than a dealer.".

(C) Paragraph (3) of section 5121(d), as so redesignated, is amended by striking "section 5146" and inserting "section 5123".

(6)(A) Section 5124 (relating to records) is moved to subpart C of part II of subchapter A of chapter 51 and inserted after section 5121.

(B) Section 5124 is amended—

(i) by striking the section heading and inserting the following new heading:

"SEC. 5122. RECORDKEEPING BY RETAIL DEALERS.",

(ii) by striking "section 5146" in subsection (c) and inserting "section 5123", and

(iii) by redesignating subsection (c) as subsection (d) and inserting after subsection (b) the following new subsection:

"(c) RETAIL DEALERS.—For purposes of this section—

"(1) RETAIL DEALER IN LIQUORS.—The term 'retail dealer in liquors' means any dealer (other than a retail dealer in beer or a limited retail dealer) who sells, or offers for sale, distilled spirits, wines, or beer, to any person other than a dealer.

"(2) RETAIL DEALER IN BEER.—The term 'retail dealer in beer' means any dealer (other than a limited retail dealer) who sells, or offers for sale, beer, but not distilled spirits or wines, to any person other than a dealer.

"(3) LIMITED RETAIL DEALER.—The term 'limited retail dealer' means any fraternal, civic, church, labor, charitable, benevolent, or ex-servicemen's organization making sales of distilled spirits, wine or beer on the occasion of any kind of entertainment, dance, picnic, bazaar, or festival held by it, or any person making sales of distilled spirits, wine or beer to the members, guests, or patrons of bona fide fairs, reunions, picnics, carnivals, or other similar outings, if such organization or person is not otherwise engaged in business as a dealer.

"(4) DEALER.—The term 'dealer' has the meaning given such term by section 5121(c)(3).".

(7) Section 5146 is moved to subpart C of part II of subchapter A of chapter 51, inserted after section 5122, and redesignated as section 5123.

(8) Subpart C of part II of subchapter A of chapter 51, as amended by paragraph (7), is amended by adding at the end the following new section:

"SEC. 5124. REGISTRATION BY DEALERS.

"Every dealer who is subject to the recordkeeping requirements under section 5121 or 5122 shall register with the Secretary such dealer's name or style, place of residence, trade or business, and the place where such trade or business is to be carried on. In the case of a firm or company, the names of the several persons constituting the same, and the places of residence, shall be so registered."

(9) Section 7012 is amended by redesignating paragraphs (4) and (5) as paragraphs (5) and (6), respectively, and by inserting after paragraph (3) the following new paragraph:

"(4) For provisions relating to registration by dealers in distilled spirits, wines, and beer, see section 5124.".

(10) Part II of subchapter A of chapter 51 is amended by inserting after subpart C the following new subpart:

"Subpart D. Other Provisions

"Sec. 5131. Packaging distilled spirits for industrial uses.

"Sec. 5132. Prohibited purchases by dealers.".

(11) Section 5116 is moved to subpart D of part II of subchapter A of chapter 51, inserted after the table of sections, redesignated as section 5131, and amended by inserting "(as defined in section 5121(c))" after "dealer" in subsection (a).

(12) Subpart D of part II of subchapter A of chapter 51 is amended by adding at the end the following new section:

"SEC. 5132. PROHIBITED PURCHASES BY DEALERS.

"(a) IN GENERAL.—Except as provided in regulations prescribed by the Secretary, it shall be unlawful for a dealer to purchase distilled spirits for resale from any person other than a wholesale dealer in liquors who is required to keep the records prescribed by section 5121.

"(b) LIMITED RETAIL DEALERS.—A limited retail dealer may lawfully purchase distilled spirits for resale from a retail dealer in liquors.

"(c) PENALTY AND FORFEITURE.—

"For penalty and forfeiture provisions applicable to violations of subsection (a), see sections 5687 and 7302.".

(13) Subsection (b) of section 5002 is amended—

(A) by striking "section 5112(a)" and inserting "section 5121(c)(3)",

(B) by striking "section 5112" and inserting "section 5121(c)", and

(C) by striking "section 5122" and inserting "section 5122(c)".

(14) Subparagraph (A) of section 5010(c)(2) is amended by striking "section 5134" and inserting "section 5114".

(15) Subsection (d) of section 5052 is amended to read as follows:

"(d) BREWER.—For purposes of this chapter, the term 'brewer' means any person who brews beer or produces beer for sale. Such term shall not include any person who produces only beer exempt from tax under section 5053(e).".

(16) The text of section 5182 is amended to read as follows:

¶7060 Act Sec. 1125(b)(7)

"For provisions requiring recordkeeping by wholesale liquor dealers, see section 5112, and by retail liquor dealers, see section 5122.".

(17) Subsection (b) of section 5402 is amended by striking "section 5092" and inserting "section 5052(d)".

(18) Section 5671 is amended by striking "or 5091".

(19)(A) Part V of subchapter J of chapter 51 is hereby repealed.

(B) The table of parts for such subchapter J is amended by striking the item relating to part V.

(20)(A) Sections 5142, 5143, and 5145 are moved to subchapter D of chapter 52, inserted after section 5731, redesignated as sections 5732, 5733, and 5734, respectively, and amended by striking "this part" each place it appears and inserting "this subchapter".

(B) Section 5732, as redesignated by subparagraph (A), is amended by striking "(except the tax imposed by section 5131)" each place it appears.

(C) Paragraph (2) of section 5733(c), as redesignated by subparagraph (A), is amended by striking "liquors" both places it appears and inserting "tobacco products and cigarette papers and tubes".

(D) The table of sections for subchapter D of chapter 52 is amended by adding at the end the following:

"Sec. 5732. Payment of tax.

"Sec. 5733. Provisions relating to liability for occupational taxes.

"Sec. 5734. Application of State laws.".

(E) Section 5731 is amended by striking subsection (c) and by redesignating subsection (d) as subsection (c).

(21) Subsection (c) of section 6071 is amended by striking "section 5142" and inserting "section 5732".

(22) Paragraph (1) of section 7652(g) is amended—

(A) by striking "subpart F" and inserting "subpart B", and

(B) by striking "section 5131(a)" and inserting "section 5111".

(c) EFFECTIVE DATE.—The amendments made by this section shall take effect on July 1, 2008, but shall not apply to taxes imposed for periods before such date.

* * *

[CCH Explanation at ¶ 840. Committee Reports at ¶ 15,110.]

Subtitle C—Miscellaneous Provisions

[¶ 7065] ACT SEC. 11141. MOTOR FUEL TAX ENFORCEMENT ADVISORY COMMISSION.

(a) ESTABLISHMENT.—There is established a Motor Fuel Tax Enforcement Advisory Commission (in this section referred to as the "Commission").

(b) FUNCTION.—The Commission shall—

(1) review motor fuel revenue collections, historical and current;

(2) review the progress of investigations with respect to motor fuel taxes;

(3) develop and review legislative proposals with respect to motor fuel taxes;

(4) monitor the progress of administrative regulation projects relating to motor fuel taxes;

(5) review the results of Federal and State agency cooperative efforts regarding motor fuel taxes;

(6) review the results of Federal interagency cooperative efforts regarding motor fuel taxes; and

(7) evaluate and make recommendations to the President and Congress regarding—

(A) the effectiveness of existing Federal enforcement programs regarding motor fuel taxes,

(B) enforcement personnel allocation, and

(C) proposals for regulatory projects, legislation, and funding.

(c) MEMBERSHIP.—

(1) APPOINTMENT.—The Commission shall be composed of the following representatives appointed by the Chairmen and the Ranking Members of the Committee on Finance of the Senate and the Committee on Ways and Means of the House of Representatives:

(A) At least one representative from each of the following Federal entities: the Department of Homeland Security, the Department of Transportation—Office of Inspector General, the Federal Highway Administration, the Department of Defense, and the Department of Justice.

(B) At least one representative from the Federation of State Tax Administrators.

(C) At least one representative from any State department of transportation.

(D) two representatives from the highway construction industry.

(E) six representatives from industries relating to fuel distribution — refiners (two representatives), distributors (one representative), pipelines (one representative), and terminal operators (two representatives).

(F) one representative from the retail fuel industry.

(G) two representatives from the staff of the Committee on Finance of the Senate and two representatives from the staff of the Committee on Ways and Means of the House of Representatives.

(2) TERMS.—Members shall be appointed for the life of the Commission.

(3) VACANCIES.—A vacancy in the Commission shall be filled in the manner in which the original appointment was made.

(4) TRAVEL EXPENSES.—Members shall serve without pay but shall receive travel expenses, including per diem in lieu of subsistence, in accordance with sections 5702 and 5703 of title 5, United States Code.

(5) CHAIRMAN.—The Chairman of the Commission shall be elected by the members.

(d) FUNDING.—Such sums as are necessary shall be available from the Highway Trust fund for the expenses of the Commission.

(e) CONSULTATION.—Upon request of the Commission, representatives of the Department of the Treasury and the Internal Revenue Service shall be available for consultation to assist the Commission in carrying out its duties under this section.

(f) OBTAINING DATA.—The Commission may secure directly from any department or agency of the United States, information (other than information required by any law to be kept confidential by such department or agency) necessary for the Commission to carry out its duties under this section. Upon request of the Commission, the head of that department or agency shall furnish such nonconfidential information to the Commission. The Commission shall also gather evidence through such means as it may deem appropriate, including through holding hearings and soliciting comments by means of Federal Register notices.

(g) TERMINATION.—The Commission shall terminate as of the close of September 30, 2009.

[CCH Explanation at ¶ 780. Committee Reports at ¶ 15,150.]

[¶ 7070] ACT SEC. 11142. NATIONAL SURFACE TRANSPORTATION INFRASTRUCTURE FINANCING COMMISSION.

(a) ESTABLISHMENT.—There is established a National Surface Transportation Infrastructure Financing Commission (in this section referred to as the "Commission"). The Commission shall hold its first meeting within 90 days of the appointment of the eighth individual to be named to the Commission.

(b) FUNCTION.—

(1) IN GENERAL.—The Commission shall, with respect to the period beginning on the date of the enactment of this Act and ending before 2016—

(A) make a thorough investigation and study of revenues flowing into the Highway Trust Fund under current law, including the individual components of the overall flow of such revenues;

(B) consider whether the amount of such revenues is likely to increase, decline, or remain unchanged, absent changes in the law, particularly by taking into account the impact of possible changes in public vehicular choice, fuel use, or travel alternatives that could be expected to reduce or increase revenues into the Highway Trust Fund;

(C) consider alternative approaches to generating revenues for the Highway Trust Fund, and the level of revenues that such alternatives would yield;

(D) consider highway and transit needs and whether additional revenues into the Highway Trust Fund, or other Federal revenues dedicated to highway and transit infrastructure, would be required in order to meet such needs;

(E) consider a program that would exempt all or a portion of gasoline or other motor fuels used in a State from the Federal excise tax on such gasoline or other motor fuels if such State elects not to receive all or a portion of Federal transportation funding, including—

(i) whether such State should be required to increase State gasoline or other motor fuels taxes by the amount of the decrease in the Federal excise tax on such gasoline or other motor fuels;

(ii) whether any Federal transportation funding should not be reduced or eliminated for States participating in such program; and

(iii) whether there are any compliance problems related to enforcement of Federal transportation-related excise taxes under such program; and

(F) study such other matters closely related to the subjects described in the preceding subparagraphs as it may deem appropriate.

(2) PREPARATION OF REPORT.—Based on such investigation and study, the Commission shall develop a final report, with recommendations and the bases for those recommendations, indicating policies that should be adopted, or not adopted, to achieve various levels of annual revenue for the Highway Trust Fund and to enable the Highway Trust Fund to receive revenues sufficient to meet highway and transit needs. Such recommendations shall address, among other matters as the Commission may deem appropriate—

(A) what levels of revenue are required by the Federal Highway Trust Fund in order for it to meet needs to maintain and improve the condition and performance of the Nation's highway and transit systems;

(B) what levels of revenue are required by the Federal Highway Trust Fund in order to ensure that Federal levels of investment in highways and transit do not decline in real terms; and

(C) the extent, if any, to which the Highway Trust Fund should be augmented by other mechanisms or funds as a Federal means of financing highway and transit infrastructure investments.

(c) MEMBERSHIP.—

(1) APPOINTMENT.—The Commission shall be composed of fifteen members, appointed as follows:

(A) seven members appointed by the Secretary of Transportation, in consultation with the Secretary of the Treasury.

(B) two members appointed by the Chairman of the Committee on Ways and Means of the House of Representatives.

(C) two members appointed by the Ranking Minority Member of the Committee on Ways and Means of the House of Representatives.

(D) two members appointed by the Chairman of the Committee on Finance of the Senate.

(E) two members appointed by the Ranking Minority Member of the Committee on Finance of the Senate.

(2) QUALIFICATIONS.—Members appointed pursuant to paragraph (1) shall be appointed from among individuals knowledgeable in the fields of public transportation finance or highway and transit programs, policy, and needs, and may include representatives of interested parties, such as State and local governments or other public transportation authorities or agencies, representatives of the transportation construction industry (including suppliers of technology, machinery, and materials), transportation labor (including construction and providers), transportation providers, the financial community, and users of highway and transit systems.

(3) TERMS.—Members shall be appointed for the life of the Commission.

(4) VACANCIES.—A vacancy in the Commission shall be filled in the manner in which the original appointment was made.

(5) TRAVEL EXPENSES.—Members shall serve without pay but shall receive travel expenses, including per diem in lieu of subsistence, in accordance with sections 5702 and 5703 of title 5, United States Code.

(6) CHAIRMAN.—The Chairman of the Commission shall be elected by the members.

(d) STAFF.—The Commission may appoint and fix the pay of such personnel as it considers appropriate.

(e) FUNDING.—Funding for the Commission shall be provided by the Secretary of the Treasury and by the Secretary of Transportation, out of funds available to those agencies for administrative and policy functions.

(f) STAFF OF FEDERAL AGENCIES.—Upon request of the Commission, the head of any department or agency of the United States may detail any of the personnel of that department or agency to the Commission to assist in carrying out its duties under this section.

(g) OBTAINING DATA.—The Commission may secure directly from any department or agency of the United States, information (other than information required by any law to be kept confidential by such department or agency) necessary for the Commission to carry out its duties under this section. Upon request of the Commission, the head of that department or agency shall furnish such nonconfidential information to the Commission. The Commission shall also gather evidence through such means as it may deem appropriate, including through holding hearings and soliciting comments by means of Federal Register notices.

(h) REPORT.—Not later than 2 years after the date of its first meeting, the Commission shall transmit its final report, including recommendations, to the Secretary of Transportation, the Secretary of the Treasury, and the Committee on Ways and Means of the House of Representatives, the Committee on Finance of the Senate, the Committee on Transportation and Infrastructure of the House of Representatives, the Committee on Environment and Public Works of the Senate, and the Committee on Banking, Housing, and Urban Affairs of the Senate.

(i) TERMINATION.—The Commission shall terminate on the 180th day following the date of transmittal of the report under subsection (h). All records and papers of the Commission shall thereupon be delivered to the Administrator of General Services for deposit in the National Archives.

* * *

[CCH Explanation at ¶ 920. Committee Reports at ¶ 15,160.]

[¶ 7075] ACT SEC. 11144. TREASURY STUDY OF HIGHWAY FUELS USED BY TRUCKS FOR NON-TRANSPORTATION PURPOSES.

(a) STUDY.—The Secretary of the Treasury shall conduct a study regarding the use of highway motor fuel by trucks that is not used for the propulsion of the vehicle. As part of such study—

(1) in the case of vehicles carrying equipment that is unrelated to the transportation function of the vehicle—

(A) the Secretary of the Treasury, in consultation with the Secretary of Transportation, and with public notice and comment, shall determine the average annual amount of tax-paid fuel consumed per vehicle, by type of vehicle, used by the propulsion engine to provide the power to operate the equipment attached to the highway vehicle, and

(B) the Secretary of the Treasury shall review the technical and administrative feasibility of exempting such nonpropulsive use of highway fuels from the highway motor fuels excise taxes, and, if such exemptions are technically and administratively feasible, shall propose options for implementing such exemptions for—

(i) mobile machinery (as defined in section 4053(8) of the Internal Revenue Code of 1986) whose nonpropulsive fuel use exceeds 50 percent, and

(ii) any highway vehicle which consumes fuel for both transportation- and non-transportation-related equipment, using a single motor,

(2) in the case where non-transportation equipment is run by a separate motor—

(A) the Secretary of the Treasury shall determine the annual average amount of fuel exempted from tax in the use of such equipment by equipment type, and

(B) the Secretary of the Treasury shall review issues of administration and compliance related to the present-law exemption provided for such fuel use, and

(3) the Secretary of the Treasury shall—

(A) estimate the amount of taxable fuel consumed by trucks and the emissions of various pollutants due to the long-term idling of diesel engines, and

(B) determine the cost of reducing such long-term idling through the use of plug-ins at truck stops, auxiliary power units, or other technologies.

(b) REPORT.—Not later than January 1, 2007, the Secretary of the Treasury shall report the findings of the study required under subsection (a) to the Committee on Finance of the Senate and the Committee on Ways and Means of the House of Representatives.

[CCH Explanation at ¶1015. Committee Reports at ¶15,180.]

[¶7080] ACT SEC. 11145. DIESEL FUEL TAX EVASION REPORT.

Not later than 360 days after the date of the enactment of this Act, the Commissioner of the Internal Revenue shall report to the Committees on Finance and Environment and Public Works of the Senate and the Committees on Ways and Means and Transportation and Infrastructure of the House of Representatives on—

(1) the availability of new technologies, including forensic or chemical molecular markers, that can be employed to enhance collections of the excise tax on diesel fuel and the plans of the Internal Revenue Service to employ such technologies,

(2) the design of a test to place forensic or chemical molecular markers in any excluded liquid (as defined in section 48.4081-1(b) of title 26, Code of Federal Regulations),

(3) the design of a test, in consultation with the Department of Defense, to place forensic or chemical molecular markers in all nonstrategic bulk fuel deliveries of diesel fuel to the military, and

(4) the design of a test to place forensic or chemical molecular markers in all diesel fuel bound for export utilizing the Gulf of Mexico.

[CCH Explanation at ¶760. Committee Reports at ¶15,190.]

[¶7085] ACT SEC. 11146. TAX TREATMENT OF STATE OWNERSHIP OF RAILROAD REAL ESTATE INVESTMENT TRUST.

(a) IN GENERAL.—If a State owns all of the outstanding stock of a corporation—

(1) which is a real estate investment trust on the date of the enactment of this Act,

(2) which is a non-operating class III railroad, and

(3) substantially all of the activities of which consist of the ownership, leasing, and operation by such corporation of facilities, equipment, and other property used by the corporation or other persons for railroad transportation and for economic development purposes for the benefit of the State and its citizens, then, to the extent such activities are of a type which are an essential governmental function within the meaning of section 115 of the Internal Revenue Code of 1986, income derived from such activities by the corporation shall be treated as accruing to the State for purposes of section 115 of such Code.

(b) GAIN OR LOSS NOT RECOGNIZED ON CONVERSION.—Notwithstanding section 337(d) of the Internal Revenue Code of 1986—

(1) no gain or loss shall be recognized under section 336 or 337 of such Code, and

(2) no change in basis of the property of such corporation shall occur, because of any change of status of a corporation to a tax-exempt entity by reason of the application of subsection (a).

(c) TAX-EXEMPT FINANCING.—

(1) IN GENERAL.—Any obligation issued by a corporation described in subsection (a) at least 95 percent of the net proceeds (as defined in section 150(a) of the Internal Revenue Code of 1986) of which are to be used to provide for the acquisition, construction, or improvement of railroad transportation infrastructure (including railroad terminal facilities)—

(A) shall be treated as a State or local bond (within the meaning of section 103(c) of such Code), and

(B) shall not be treated as a private activity bond (within the meaning of section 103(b)(1) of such Code) solely by reason of the ownership or use of such railroad transportation infrastructure by the corporation.

(2) NO INFERENCE.—Except as provided in paragraph (1), nothing in this subsection shall be construed to affect the treatment of the private use of proceeds or property financed with obligations issued by the corporation for purposes of section 103 of the Internal Revenue Code of 1986 and part IV of subchapter B of such Code.

(d) DEFINITIONS.—For purposes of this section:

(1) REAL ESTATE INVESTMENT TRUST.—The term "real estate investment trust" has the meaning given such term by section 856(a) of the Internal Revenue Code of 1986.

(2) NON-OPERATING CLASS III RAILROAD.—The term "non-operating class III railroad" has the meaning given such term by part A of subtitle IV of title 49, United States Code (49 U.S.C. 10101 et seq.), and the regulations thereunder.

(3) STATE.—The term "State" includes—

(A) the District of Columbia and any possession of the United States, and

(B) any authority, agency, or public corporation of a State.

(e) APPLICABILITY.—

(1) IN GENERAL.—Except as provided in paragraph (2), this section shall apply on and after the date on which a State becomes the owner of all of the outstanding stock of a corporation described in subsection (a) through action of such corporation's board of directors.

(2) EXCEPTION.—This section shall not apply to any State which—

(A) becomes the owner of all of the voting stock of a corporation described in subsection (a) after December 31, 2003, or

(B) becomes the owner of all of the outstanding stock of a corporation described in subsection (a) after December 31, 2006.

* * *

[CCH Explanation at ¶910. Committee Reports at ¶15,200.]

Subtitle D—Highway-Related Technical Corrections

[¶7090] ACT SEC. 11151. HIGHWAY-RELATED TECHNICAL CORRECTIONS.

* * *

(d) AMENDMENT RELATED TO SECTION 1306 OF THE ENERGY POLICY ACT OF 2005.—

* * *

(1) Subsection (b) of section 1306 of the Energy Tax Incentives Act of 2005 is amended by striking "Transportation Equity Act: A Legacy for Users" and inserting "Safe, Accountable, Flexible, Efficient Transportation Equity Act: A Legacy for Users".

(2) If the Energy Policy Act of 2005 is enacted before the date of the enactment of this Act, for purposes of executing any amendments made by the Energy Policy Act of 2005 to section 38(b) of the Internal Revenue Code of 1986, the amendments made by section 11126(b) of this Act shall be treated as having been executed before such amendments made by the Energy Policy Act of 2005.

* * *

(f) EFFECTIVE DATES.—

* * *

(3) The amendments made by subsections (d)(1) and (e)(2) shall take effect as if included in the provision of the Energy Tax Incentives Act of 2005 to which they relate.

* * *

[Committee Reports at ¶15,250.]

Subtitle E—Preventing Fuel Fraud

* * *

[¶7095] ACT SEC. 11165. RECONCILIATION OF ON-LOADED CARGO TO ENTERED CARGO.

(a) IN GENERAL.—Subsection (a) of section 343 of the Trade Act of 2002 is amended by inserting at the end the following new paragraph:

"(4) TRANSMISSION OF DATA.—Pursuant to paragraph (2), not later than 1 year after the date of enactment of this paragraph, the Secretary of Homeland Security, after consultation with the Secretary of the Treasury, shall establish an electronic data interchange system through which the United States Customs and Border Protection shall transmit to the Internal Revenue Service information pertaining to cargoes of any taxable fuel (as defined in section 4083 of the Internal Revenue Code of 1986) that the United States Customs and Border Protection has obtained electronically under its regulations adopted in accordance with paragraph (1). For this purpose, not later than 1 year after the date of enactment of this paragraph, all filers of required cargo information for such taxable fuels (as so defined) must provide such information to the United States Customs and Border Protection through such electronic data interchange system.".

(b) EFFECTIVE DATE.—The amendments made by this section shall take effect on the date of the enactment of this Act.

[CCH Explanation at ¶770. Committee Reports at ¶15,300.]

[¶7100] ACT SEC. 11166. TREATMENT OF DEEP-DRAFT VESSELS.

(a) IN GENERAL.—On and after the date of the enactment of this Act, the Secretary of the Treasury shall require that a vessel described in section 4042(c)(1) of the Internal Revenue Code of 1986 be considered a vessel for purposes of the registration of the operator of such vessel under section 4101 of such Code, unless such operator uses such vessel exclusively for purposes of the entry of taxable fuel.

* * *

[CCH Explanation at ¶775. Committee Reports at ¶15,310.]

Committee Reports

Energy Tax Incentives Act of 2005

¶10,001 Introduction

The committee reports and the description and technical explanation of the conference agreement prepared by the Staff of the Joint Committee on Taxation for the Energy Tax Incentives Act of 2005 (Title XIII of the Energy Policy Act of 2005, H.R. 6) explain the intent of Congress regarding the revenue-related provisions of the Act. Reports of the Joint Committee on Taxation are included in this section to aid in the reader's understanding of the relevant provisions, but may not be cited as the official Senate or Conference Committee Reports accompanying the 2005 Act. Likewise, portions of H.R. REP. NO. 109-45 are included to aid in the reader's understanding of the relevant provisions, but may not be cited as the controlling Committee Report accompanying the 2005 Act. Subscribers to the electronic version can link from these references to the corresponding material. *The pertinent sections of these reports appear in Act Section order beginning at ¶10,010.*

¶10,005 Background

The Energy Policy Act of 2005 (H.R. 6) was introduced in the House of Representatives on April 18, 2005. On April 21, 2005, the House passed H.R. 6 by a vote of 249 to 183. On June 28, 2005, the Senate passed H.R. 6 with an amendment by a vote of 85 to 12.

A conference report on H.R. 6 was filed on July 27, 2005 (H.R. CONF. REP. NO. 109-190). The conference report did not contain a statement of managers. The House agreed to the conference report on July 28, 2005, by a vote of 275 to 156. On July 29, 2005, the Senate agreed to the conference report by a vote of 74 to 26.

On July 28, 2005, House Ways and Means Committee Chairman Bill Thomas (R-Cal.), inserted a letter into the Congressional Record to explain why there is no Statement of Managers for H.R. 6. He stated:

> Mr. Speaker, the need to complete this comprehensive energy bill leads us to consider it without the normal accompanying statement of managers used to clarify and enhance understanding of the legislative text. Our colleagues, the chairman of the Committee on Finance and the ranking minority member of that committee, agree with me that those who follow tax legislation can and should use the Joint Committee on Taxation's publication, "Description and Technical Explanation of the Conference Agreement on H.R. 6, Title XIII, Energy Tax Incentives Act of 2005," JCX-60-05, as the functional equivalent of a statement of managers for the purposes of completing their understanding of what the tax incentives provide.

The following material includes the pertinent texts of the committee reports and the description and technical explanation of the conference agreement prepared by the Staff of the Joint Committee on Taxation for the Energy Tax Incentives Act of 2005

(Title XIII of the Energy Policy Act of 2005, H.R. 6) that explain the intent of Congress regarding the revenue-related provisions of the Act. Omissions of text are indicated by asterisks (* * *). References are to the following reports:

• The Enhanced Energy Infrastructure and Technology Tax Policy Act of 2005 (H.R. 1541), House Ways and Means Committee Report, as reported on April 18, 2005, is referred to as House Committee Report (H.R. REP. NO. 109-45). Excerpts from this report are included to assist the reader's understanding. H.R. 1541 contained the tax portions of the Energy Policy Bill of 2005, but was never voted on by the House as a standalone bill. Its provisions, however, were included in the larger energy bill (H.R. 6) that passed the House on April 21, 2005. The Committee did not issue a separate report on H.R. 6.

• The Joint Committee on Taxation, Description of the "Energy Policy Tax Incentives Act of 2005" (JCX-44-05) (H.R. 6, June 14, 2005) is referred to as Joint Committee on Taxation (J.C.T. REP. NO. JCX-44-05).

• The Joint Committee on Taxation, Description of the Chairman's Modification to the Provisions of the "Energy Policy Tax Incentives Act of 2005" (JCX-46-05) (H.R. 6, June 16, 2005) is referred to as Joint Committee on Taxation (J.C.T. REP. NO. JCX-46-05).

• The Joint Committee on Taxation, Description and Technical Explanation of the Conference Agreement of H.R. 6, Title XIII, the "Energy Tax Incentives Act of 2005" (JCX-60-05) (H.R. 6, June 16, 2005) is referred to as Joint Committee on Taxation (J.C.T. REP. NO. JCX-60-05).

[¶10,010] Act Secs. 1301 and 1302. Extension and modification of renewable electricity production credit

Joint Committee on Taxation (J.C.T. REP. NO. JCX-44-05)

⟫→ *Caution: The Technical Explanation of the "Energy Policy Tax Incentives Act of 2005" (JCX-44-05), below, is included to assist the reader's understanding but may not be cited as the official Senate Committee Report to H.R. 6—CCH.*

[Code Sec. 45]

Present Law

In general

An income tax credit is allowed for the production of electricity from qualified facilities sold by the taxpayer to an unrelated person (sec. 45). Qualified facilities comprise wind energy facilities, closed-loop biomass facilities, open-loop biomass (including agricultural livestock waste nutrients) facilities, geothermal energy facilities, solar energy facilities, small irrigation power facilities, landfill gas facilities, and trash combustion facilities. In addition, an income tax credit is allowed for the production of refined coal.

Credit amounts and credit period

In general

The base amount of the credit is 1.5 cents per kilowatt-hour (indexed for inflation) of electricity produced. The amount of the credit is 1.9 cents per kilowatt-hour for 2005. A taxpayer may claim credit for the 10-year period commencing with the date the qualified facility is placed in service. The credit is reduced for grants, tax-exempt bonds, subsidized energy financing, and other credits. The amount of credit a taxpayer may claim is phased out as the market price of electricity (or refined coal in the case of the refined coal production credit) exceeds certain threshold levels.

Reduced credit amounts and credit periods

In the case of open-loop biomass facilities (including agricultural livestock waste nutrient facilities), geothermal energy facilities, solar energy facilities, small irrigation power facilities, landfill gas facilities, and trash combustion facilities, the 10-year credit period is reduced to five years commencing on the date the facility is placed in service. In general, for eligible preexisting facilities and other facilities placed in service prior to January 1, 2005, the credit period commences on January 1, 2005. In the case of a closed-loop biomass facility modified to co-fire with coal, to co-fire with other biomass, or to co-fire with coal and other biomass, the credit period begins no earlier than October 22, 2004.

In the case of open-loop biomass facilities (including agricultural livestock waste nutrient facilities), small irrigation power facilities, landfill gas facilities, and trash combustion facilities, the otherwise allowable credit amount is 0.75 cent per kilowatt-hour, indexed for inflation measured after 1992.

Credit applicable to refined coal

The amount of the credit for refined coal is $4.375 per ton (also indexed for inflation after 1992 and equaling $5.481 per ton for 2005).

Other limitations on credit claimants and credit amounts

In general, in order to claim the credit, a taxpayer must own the qualified facility and sell the electricity produced by the facility (or refined coal in the case of the refined coal production credit) to an unrelated party. Also, in general, the amount of credit a taxpayer may claim is reduced by reason of grants, tax-exempt bonds, subsidized energy financing, and other credits. The reduction cannot exceed 50 percent of the otherwise allowable credit.[2]

The credit for electricity produced from renewable sources is a component of the general business credit (sec. 38(b)(8)). Generally, the general business credit for any taxable year may not exceed the amount by which the taxpayer's net income tax exceeds the greater of the tentative minimum tax or so much of the net regular tax liability as exceeds $25,000. Excess credits may be carried back one year and forward up to 20 years.

A taxpayer's tentative minimum tax is treated as being zero for purposes of determining the tax liability limitation with respect to the section 45 credit for electricity produced from a

---

[2] In the case of closed-loop biomass facilities modified to co-fire with coal, to co-fire with other biomass, or to co-fire with coal and other biomass, there is no reduction in credit by reason of grants, tax-exempt bonds, subsidized energy financing, and other credits.

facility (placed in service after October 22, 2004) during the first four years of production beginning on the date the facility is placed in service.

Summary of credit rate and credit period by facility type

Table 1.—Summary of Section 45 Credit for Electricity Produced from Certain Renewable Resources and Refined Coal

Electricity produced from renewable resources	Credit amount for 2005 (cents per kilowatt-hour; dollars per ton)	Credit period (years from placed-in-service date) [1]
Wind	1.9	10
Closed-loop biomass	1.9	10
Open-loop biomass (including agricultural livestock waste nutrient facilities)	0.9	5
Geothermal	1.9	5
Solar	1.9	5
Small irrigation power	0.9	5
Municipal solid waste (including landfill gas facilities and trash combustion facilities)	0.9	5
Refined Coal	5.481	10

[1] For eligible pre-existing facilities and other facilities placed in service prior to January 1, 2005, the credit period commences on January 1, 2005. In the case of certain co-firing closed-loop facilities, the credit period begins no earlier than October 22, 2004.

Periods for which credit allowable

In order to be a qualified facility—

Wind energy facility

A wind energy facility must be placed in service after December 31, 1993, and before January 1, 2006.

Closed-loop biomass facility

A closed-loop biomass facility must be placed in service after December 31, 1992, and before January 1, 2006. In the case of a facility using closed-loop biomass but also co-firing the closed-loop biomass with coal, other biomass, or coal and other biomass, a qualified facility must be originally placed in service and modified to co-fire the closed-loop biomass at any time before January 1, 2006.

Open-loop biomass (including agricultural livestock waste nutrients) facility

An open-loop biomass facility must be placed in service after October 22, 2004 and before January 1, 2006, in the case of a facility using agricultural livestock waste nutrients and must be placed in service at any time prior to January 1, 2006 in the case of a facility using other open-loop biomass.

Geothermal, solar, small irrigation, landfill gas, and trash combustion facilities

To be a qualifying facility, a geothermal, solar, small irrigation, landfill gas, or trash combustion facility must be placed in service after October 22, 2004 and before January 1, 2006.

Refined coal facility

A refined coal facility must be placed in service after October 22, 2004 and before January 1, 2009.

Description of Proposal

The proposal extends the placed-in-service date by three years (through December 31, 2008) for the following qualifying facilities: wind facilities; closed-loop biomass facilities (including a facility co-firing the closed-loop biomass with coal, other biomass, or coal and other biomass); open-loop biomass facilities; geothermal facilities; small irrigation power facilities; landfill gas facilities; and trash combustion facilities. The proposal does not extend the placed-in-service date for solar facilities (December 31, 2005) or refined coal facilities (December 31, 2008).

The proposal adds one new qualifying energy resource, fuel cells. A qualifying fuel cell facility is an integrated system comprised of a fuel cell stack assembly and associated balance of plant components that convert a fuel into electricity using electrochemical means, and which has an electricity-only generation efficiency of greater than 30 percent and generates at least 0.5 megawatts of electricity, and which is placed in service after December 31, 2005, and before January 1, 2009. The taxpayer can claim the 1.5 cents-per-kilowatt-hour (indexed for inflation) credit for a five-year period commencing on the date the facility is placed in service.

Joint Committee on Taxation (J.C.T. Rep. No. JCX-60-05)

>>>→ *Caution: The Description and Technical Explanation of the Conference Agreement of H.R. 6, Title XIII, the "Energy Tax Incentives Act of 2005" (JCX-60-05), below, is included to assist the reader's understanding, but may not be cited as the official Conference Committee Report to H.R. 6—CCH.*

Present Law

* * *

Taxation of cooperatives and their patrons

For Federal income tax purposes, a cooperative generally computes its income as if it were a taxable corporation, with one exception—the cooperative may exclude from its taxable income distributions of patronage dividends. Generally, cooperatives that are subject to the cooperative tax rules of subchapter T of the Code[25] are permitted a deduction for patronage dividends from their taxable income only to the extent of net income that is derived from transactions with patrons who are members of the cooperative.[26] The availability of such deductions from taxable income has the effect of allowing the cooperative to be treated like a conduit with respect to profits derived from transactions with patrons who are members of the cooperative. Present law does not permit cooperatives to pass any portion of the income tax credit for electricity production through to their patrons.

House Bill

No provision.

Conference Agreement

The conference agreement follows the Senate amendment with modifications.

Extension of placed-in-service date for qualifying facilities

The conference agreement extends the placed-in-service date by two years (through December 31, 2007) for the following qualifying facilities: wind facilities; closed-loop biomass facilities (including a facility co-firing the closed-loop biomass with coal, other biomass, or coal and other biomass); open-loop biomass facilities; geothermal facilities; small irrigation power facilities; landfill gas facilities; and trash combustion facilities. The conference agreement does not alter the terminating placed-in-service date for solar facilities (December 31, 2005) or refined coal facilities (December 31, 2008).

New qualifying energy resources

The conference agreement adds two new qualifying energy resources: hydropower; and Indian coal.

Hydropower

The conference agreement follows the Senate amendment with respect to hydropower.

Indian coal

The conference agreement adds Indian coal as a new energy source. The taxpayer may claim a credit for sales of coal to an unrelated third party from a qualified facility for the seven-year period beginning on January 1, 2006, and ending after December 31, 2012. The value of the credit is $1.50 per ton for the first four years of the seven-year period and $2.00 per ton for the last three years of the seven-year period. The credit amounts are indexed for inflation. A qualified Indian coal facility is a facility that produces coal from reserves that on June 14, 2005, were owned by a Federally recognized tribe of Indians or were held in trust by the United States for a tribe or its members.

Equalization of credit period for all qualifying renewable resources

The conference agreement follows the Senate amendment with respect to equalization of the credit period for qualifying open-loop biomass facilities (including agricultural livestock waste nutrient facilities), geothermal facilities, solar facilities, small irrigation power facilities, landfill gas facilities, trash combustion facilities, and hydropower facilities. The conference agreement provides a seven-year credit period for Indian coal facilities, as explained above.

Clarification of units added to pre-existing trash combustion facilities

The conference agreement follows the Senate amendment with respect to clarification of units added to pre-existing trash combustion facilities.

Taxation of cooperatives and their patrons

The conference agreement follows the Senate amendment with respect to the taxation of cooperatives and their patrons.

---

[25] Sec. 1381, et seq.

[26] Sec. 1382.

Effective Date

The provision generally is effective on the date of enactment. With respect to the taxation of cooperatives and their patrons, the provision applies to taxable years ending after the date of enactment.

[Law at ¶ 5065, ¶ 5130, ¶ 5165 and ¶ 7005. CCH Explanation at ¶ 405, ¶ 410, ¶ 415 and ¶ 420.]

[¶ 10,020] Act Sec. 1303. Clean renewable energy bonds

Joint Committee on Taxation (J.C.T. Rep. No. JCX-44-05)

⇛ *Caution: The Technical Explanation of the "Energy Policy Tax Incentives Act of 2005" (JCX-44-05), below, is included to assist the reader's understanding but may not be cited as the official Senate Committee Report to H.R. 6— CCH.*

[New Code Sec. 54]

Present law

Tax-exempt bonds

Interest on State and local government bonds generally is excluded from gross income for Federal income tax purposes if the proceeds of the bonds are used to finance direct activities of these governmental units or if the bonds are repaid with revenues of the governmental units. Activities that can be financed with these tax-exempt bonds include the financing of electric power facilities (i.e., generation, transmission, distribution, and retailing).

Interest on State or local bonds to finance activities of private persons ("private activity bonds") is taxable unless a specific exception is contained in the Code (or in a non-Code provision of a revenue Act). The term "private person" generally includes the Federal Government and all other individuals and entities other than States or local governments. The Code includes exceptions permitting States or local governments to act as conduits providing tax-exempt financing for certain private activities. In most cases, the aggregate volume of these tax-exempt private activity bonds is restricted by annual aggregate volume limits imposed on bonds issued by issuers within each State. For calendar year 2005, the State volume cap is the greater of $80 per resident or $239 million. The Code imposes several additional restrictions on tax-exempt private activity bonds that do not apply to bonds for governmental activities.

The tax exemption for State and local bonds does not apply to any arbitrage bond.[3] A bond is defined as an arbitrage bond if any proceeds of the issue are reasonably expected to be used (or intentionally are used) to acquire higher yielding investments or to replace funds that are used to acquire higher yielding investments.[4] In general, arbitrage profits may be earned only during specified periods (e.g., defined "temporary periods") before funds are needed for the purpose of the borrowing or on specified types of investments (e.g., "reasonably required reserve or replacement funds"). Subject to limited exceptions, investment profits that are earned during these periods or on such investments must be rebated to the Federal Government.

An issuer of State or local bonds must file with the IRS certain information about the bonds in order for such bonds to be tax-exempt.[5] Generally, this information return is required to be filed no later than the 15th day of the second month after the close of the calendar quarter in which the bonds were issued.

Qualified zone academy bonds

As an alternative to traditional tax-exempt bonds, States and local governments may issue "qualified zone academy bonds."[6] "Qualified zone academy bonds" are defined as any bond issued by a State or local government, provided that (1) at least 95 percent of the proceeds are used for the purpose of renovating, providing equipment to, developing course materials for use at, or training teachers and other school personnel in a "qualified zone academy" and (2) private entities have promised to contribute to the qualified zone academy certain equipment, technical assistance or training, employee services, or other property or services with a value equal to at least 10 percent of the bond proceeds. A school is a "qualified zone academy" if (1) the school is a public school that provides education and training below the college level, (2) the school operates a special academic program in cooperation with businesses to enhance the academic curriculum and increase graduation and employment rates, and (3) either (a) the school is located in an empowerment zone or enterprise community designated under the Code, or (b) it

---

[3] Secs. 103(a) and (b)(2).
[4] Sec. 148.
[5] Sec. 149(e).
[6] Sec. 1397E.

is reasonably expected that at least 35 percent of the students at the school will be eligible for free or reduced-cost lunches under the school lunch program established under the National School Lunch Act.

Financial institutions that hold qualified zone academy bonds are entitled to a nonrefundable tax credit in an amount equal to a credit rate multiplied by the face amount of the bond. The Treasury Department sets the credit rate at a rate estimated to allow issuance of qualified zone academy bonds without discount and without interest cost to the issuer. The credit is includable in gross income (as if it were a taxable interest payment on the bond), and may be claimed against regular income tax and AMT liability. The maximum term of the bond is determined by the Treasury Department, so that the present value of the obligation to repay the bond is 50 percent of the face value of the bond.

There is an annual limitation of $400 million on the amount of qualified zone academy bonds that may be issued in calendar years 1998 through 2005. The $400 million aggregate bond cap is allocated each year to the States according to their respective populations of individuals below the poverty line. Each State, in turn, allocates the credit authority to qualified zone academies within such State.

Tax credits for production of electricity from renewable sources

An income tax credit is allowed for the production of electricity from qualified facilities sold by the taxpayer to an unrelated person.[7] The base amount of the credit is 1.5 cents per kilowatt-hour (indexed for inflation) of electricity produced. The amount of the credit is 1.9 cents per kilowatt-hour for 2005. A taxpayer may claim credit for the 10-year period commencing with the date the qualified facility is placed in service. The credit is reduced for grants, tax-exempt bonds, subsidized energy financing, and other credits. The amount of credit a taxpayer may claim is phased out as the market price of electricity (or refined coal in the case of the refined coal production credit) exceeds certain threshold levels.

Qualified facilities comprise wind energy facilities, closed-loop biomass facilities, open-loop biomass (including agricultural livestock waste nutrients) facilities, geothermal energy facilities, solar energy facilities, small irrigation power facilities, landfill gas facilities, and trash combustion facilities. In addition, an income tax credit is allowed for the production of refined coal.

To be a qualified facility, a wind energy facility must be placed in service after December 31, 1993, and before January 1, 2006. A closed-loop biomass facility must be placed in service after December 31, 1992, and before January 1, 2006. In the case of a facility using closed-loop biomass but also co-firing the closed-loop biomass with coal, other biomass, or coal and other biomass, a qualified facility must be originally placed in service and modified to co-fire the closed-loop biomass at any time before January 1, 2006. An open-loop biomass facility must be placed in service after October 22, 2004 and before January 1, 2006, in the case of facility using agricultural livestock waste nutrients, and must be placed in service at any time prior to January 1, 2006 in the case of a facility using other open-loop biomass. Geothermal, solar, small irrigation, landfill gas, and trash combustion facilities all must be placed in service after October 22, 2004 and before January 1, 2006. In addition, a qualifying refined coal facility is a facility producing refined coal that is placed in service after October 22, 2004 and before January 1, 2009.

Description of Proposal

The proposal creates a new category of tax credit bonds, "Clean Renewable Energy Bonds." Clean Renewable Energy Bonds are defined as any bond issued by a qualified issuer if, in addition to the requirements discussed below, 95 percent or more of the proceeds of such bonds are used to finance capital expenditures incurred by qualified borrowers for facilities that qualify for the tax credit under section 45 ("qualified projects"), without regard to the placed in service date requirements of that section.

Like qualified zone academy bonds, Clean Renewable Energy Bonds are not interest-bearing obligations. Rather, the taxpayer holding a Clean Renewable Energy Bond on a credit allowance date would be entitled to a tax credit. The amount of the credit is determined by multiplying the bond's credit rate by the face amount on the holder's bond. The credit rate on the bonds is determined by the Secretary and is to be a rate that permits issuance of Clean Renewable Energy Bonds without discount and interest cost to the qualified issuer. The credit is includable in gross income (as if it were an interest payment on the bond), and can be claimed against regular income tax liability and alternative minimum tax liability.

The proposal also imposes a maximum maturity limitation on any Clean Renewable Energy

---

[7] Sec. 45.

Bond. The maximum maturity is the term which the Secretary estimates will result in the present value of the obligation to repay the principal on a Clean Renewable Energy Bond being equal to 50 percent of the face amount of such bond.

For purposes of the proposal, "qualified issuers" include governmental bodies; the Tennessee Valley Authority; mutual or cooperative electric companies (either described in section 501(c)(12) or section 1381(a)(2)(C)), or a not-for-profit electric utility which has received a loan or guarantee under the Rural Electrification Act); and clean energy bond lenders. A clean energy bond lender means a cooperative lending organization which is owned by, or has outstanding loans to, 100 or more cooperative electric companies and was in existence on February 1, 2002. The term "qualified borrower" includes a governmental body (including an Indian tribal government), the Tennessee Valley Authority, and a mutual or cooperative electric company.

Under the proposal, Clean Renewable Energy Bonds are subject to the arbitrage requirements of section 148 that apply to traditional tax-exempt bonds. In addition, to qualify as Clean Renewable Energy Bonds, 95 percent or more of the proceeds of such bonds must be spent on qualified projects within the five-year period that begins on the date of issuance. To the extent less than 95 percent of the proceeds are used to finance qualified projects during the five-year spending period, bonds will continue to qualify as Clean Renewable Energy Bonds if unspent proceeds are used within 90 days from the end of such five-year period to redeem an amount of outstanding bonds to satisfy the 95 percent expenditure test. The five-year spending period also may be extended by the Secretary upon the qualified issuer's request.

Unlike qualified zone academy bonds, the proposal requires issuers of Clean Renewable Energy Bonds to report issuance to the IRS in a manner similar to the information returns required for traditional tax-exempt bonds. Under the proposal, there is a national limitation of $1 billion of Clean Renewable Energy Bonds that the Secretary may allocate, in the aggregate, to qualified projects. The authority to issue Clean Renewable Energy Bonds expires December 31, 2008.

Effective Date

The proposal is effective for bonds issued after December 31, 2005.

Joint Committee on Taxation (J.C.T. REP. NO. JCX-60-05)

⇉→ *Caution: The Description and Technical Explanation of the Conference Agreement of H.R. 6, Title XIII, the "Energy Tax Incentives Act of 2005" (JCX-60-05), below, is included to assist the reader's understanding, but may not be cited as the official Conference Committee Report to H.R. 6—CCH.*

House Bill

No provision.

Conference Agreement

The conference agreement follows the Senate amendment with modifications. Under the conference agreement, the term "qualified issuers" includes (1) governmental bodies (including Indian tribal governments); (2) mutual or cooperative electric companies (described in section 501(c)(12) or section 1381(a)(2)(C), or a not-for-profit electric utility which has received a loan or guarantee under the Rural Electrification Act); and (3) clean energy bond lenders. The term "qualified borrower" includes a governmental body (including an Indian tribal government) and a mutual or cooperative electric company.

Under the conference agreement, there is a national limitation of $800 million of CREBs that the Secretary may allocate, in the aggregate, to qualified projects. Qualified projects are any "qualified facilities" within the meaning of section 45 (without regard to the placed-in-service date requirements of that section), other than Indian coal production facilities. In addition, the conference agreement provides that the authority to issue CREBs expires December 31, 2007. However, the Secretary shall not allocate more than $500 million of CREBs to finance qualified projects for qualified borrowers that are governmental bodies (as defined under the conference agreement).

[Law at ¶ 5125, ¶ 5255, ¶ 5340, ¶ 5385 and ¶ 7010. CCH Explanation at ¶ 455.]

¶ 10,020 Act Sec. 1303

[¶10,030] Act Sec. 1304. Treatment of income of certain electric cooperatives

Joint Committee on Taxation (J.C.T. Rep. No. JCX-44-05)

⇒ *Caution: The Technical Explanation of the "Energy Policy Tax Incentives Act of 2005" (JCX-44-05), below, is included to assist the reader's understanding but may not be cited as the official Senate Committee Report to H.R. 6— CCH.*

[Code Sec. 501(c)(12)]

Present Law

In general

Under present law, an entity must be operated on a cooperative basis in order to be treated as a cooperative for Federal income tax purposes. Although not defined by statute or regulation, the two principal criteria for determining whether an entity is operating on a cooperative basis are: (1) ownership of the cooperative by persons who patronize the cooperative; and (2) return of earnings to patrons in proportion to their patronage. The IRS requires that cooperatives must operate under the following principles: (1) subordination of capital in control over the cooperative undertaking and in ownership of the financial benefits from ownership; (2) democratic control by the members of the cooperative; (3) vesting in and allocation among the members of all excess of operating revenues over the expenses incurred to generate revenues in proportion to their participation in the cooperative (patronage); and (4) operation at cost (not operating for profit or below cost).[8]

In general, cooperative members are those who participate in the management of the cooperative and who share in patronage capital. As described below, income from the sale of electric energy by an electric cooperative may be member or non-member income to the cooperative, depending on the membership status of the purchaser. A municipal corporation may be a member of a cooperative.

For Federal income tax purposes, a cooperative generally computes its income as if it were a taxable corporation, with one exception—the cooperative may exclude from its taxable income distributions of patronage dividends. In general, patronage dividends are the profits of the cooperative that are rebated to its patrons pursuant to a pre-existing obligation of the cooperative to do so. The rebate must be made in some equitable fashion on the basis of the quantity or value of business done with the cooperative.

Except for tax-exempt farmers' cooperatives, cooperatives that are subject to the cooperative tax rules of subchapter T of the Code[9] are permitted a deduction for patronage dividends from their taxable income only to the extent of net income that is derived from transactions with patrons who are members of the cooperative.[10] The availability of such deductions from taxable income has the effect of allowing the cooperative to be treated like a conduit with respect to profits derived from transactions with patrons who are members of the cooperative.

Cooperatives that qualify as tax-exempt farmers' cooperatives are permitted to exclude patronage dividends from their taxable income to the extent of all net income, including net income that is derived from transactions with patrons who are not members of the cooperative, provided the value of transactions with patrons who are not members of the cooperative does not exceed the value of transactions with patrons who are members of the cooperative.[11]

Taxation of electric cooperatives exempt from subchapter T

In general, the cooperative tax rules of subchapter T apply to any corporation operating on a cooperative basis (except mutual savings banks, insurance companies, other tax-exempt organizations, and certain utilities), including tax-exempt farmers' cooperatives (described in sec. 521(b)). However, subchapter T does not apply to an organization that is "engaged in furnishing electric energy, or providing telephone service, to persons in rural areas."[12] Instead, electric cooperatives are taxed under rules that were generally applicable to cooperatives prior to the enactment of subchapter T in 1962. Under these rules, an electric cooperative can exclude patronage dividends from taxable income to the extent of all net income of the cooperative, including net income derived from

---

[8] Announcement 96-24, "Proposed Examination Guidelines Regarding Rural Electric Cooperatives," 1996-16 I.R.B. 35.
[9] Sec. 1381, et seq.
[10] Sec. 1382.
[11] Sec. 521.
[12] Sec. 1381(a)(2)(C).

transactions with patrons who are not members of the cooperative.[13]

Tax exemption of rural electric cooperatives

Section 501(c)(12) provides an income tax exemption for rural electric cooperatives if at least 85 percent of the cooperative's income consists of amounts collected from members for the sole purpose of meeting losses and expenses of providing service to its members. The IRS takes the position that rural electric cooperatives also must comply with the fundamental cooperative principles described above in order to qualify for tax exemption under section 501(c)(12).[14] The 85-percent test is determined without taking into account any income from: (1) qualified pole rentals; (2) open access electric energy transmission services; (3) open access electric energy distribution services; (4) any nuclear decommissioning transaction; (5) any asset exchange or conversion transaction.[15]

Income from open access transactions

Income received or accrued by a rural electric cooperative (other than income received or accrued directly or indirectly from a member of the cooperative) from the provision or sale of electric energy transmission services or ancillary services on a nondiscriminatory open access basis under an open access transmission tariff approved or accepted by Federal Energy Regulations Commission ("FERC") or under an independent transmission provider agreement approved or accepted by FERC (including an agreement providing for the transfer of control-but not ownership-of transmission facilities) is excluded in determining whether a rural electric cooperative satisfies the 85-percent test for tax exemption under section 501(c)(12).

In addition, income is excluded for purposes of the 85-percent test if it is received or accrued by a rural electric cooperative (other than income received or accrued directly or indirectly from a member of the cooperative) from the provision or sale of electric energy distribution services or ancillary services, provided such services are provided on a nondiscriminatory open access basis to distribute electric energy not owned by the cooperative: (1) to end-users who are served by distribution facilities not owned by the cooperative or any of its members; or (2) generated by a generation facility that is not owned or leased by the cooperative or any of its members and that is directly connected to distribution facilities owned by the cooperative or any of its members.

The exclusion for income from open access transactions does not apply to taxable years beginning after December 31, 2006.

Income from nuclear decommissioning transactions

Income received or accrued by a rural electric cooperative from any "nuclear decommissioning transaction" also is excluded in determining whether a rural electric cooperative satisfies the 85-percent test for tax exemption under section 501(c)(12). The term "nuclear decommissioning transaction" is defined as—

1. any transfer into a trust, fund, or instrument established to pay any nuclear decommissioning costs if the transfer is in connection with the transfer of the cooperative's interest in a nuclear powerplant or nuclear powerplant unit;

2. any distribution from a trust, fund, or instrument established to pay any nuclear decommissioning costs; or

3. any earnings from a trust, fund, or instrument established to pay any nuclear decommissioning costs.

The exclusion for income from nuclear decommissioning transactions does not apply to taxable years beginning after December 31, 2006.

Income from asset exchange or conversion transactions

Gain realized by a tax-exempt rural electric cooperative from a voluntary exchange or involuntary conversion of certain property is excluded in determining whether a rural electric cooperative satisfies the 85-percent test for tax exemption under section 501(c)(12). This provision only applies to the extent that: (1) the gain would qualify for deferred recognition under section 1031 (relating to exchanges of property held for productive use or investment) or section 1033 (relating to involuntary conversions); and (2) the replacement property that is acquired by the cooperative pursuant to section 1031 or section 1033 (as the case may be) constitutes property that is used, or to be used, for the purpose of generating, transmitting, distributing, or selling electricity or natural gas.

The exclusion for income from asset exchange or conversion transactions does not ap-

---

[13] See Rev. Rul. 83-135, 1983-2 C.B. 149.
[14] Rev. Rul. 72-36, 1972-1 C.B. 151.
[15] Sec. 501(c)(12)(C).

ply to taxable years beginning after December 31, 2006.

Treatment of income from load loss transactions

Tax-exempt rural electric cooperatives

Under present law, income received or accrued by a tax-exempt rural electric cooperative from a "load loss transaction" is treated under 501(c)(12) as income collected from members for the sole purpose of meeting losses and expenses of providing service to its members.[16] Therefore, income from load loss transactions is treated as member income in determining whether a rural electric cooperative satisfies the 85-percent test for tax exemption under section 501(c)(12). In addition, income from load loss transactions does not cause a tax-exempt electric cooperative to fail to be treated for Federal income tax purposes as a mutual or cooperative company under the fundamental cooperative principles described above.

The term "load loss transaction" is generally defined as any wholesale or retail sale of electric energy (other than to a member of the cooperative) to the extent that the aggregate amount of such sales during a seven-year period beginning with the "start-up year" does not exceed the reduction in the amount of sales of electric energy during such period by the cooperative to members. The "start-up year" is defined as the first year that the cooperative offers nondiscriminatory open access or, if later and at the election of the cooperative, 2004.

Present law also excludes income received or accrued by rural electric cooperatives from load loss transactions from the tax on unrelated trade or business income.

The special rule for income received or accrued by a tax-exempt rural electric cooperative from a load loss transaction does not apply to taxable years beginning after December 31, 2006.

Taxable electric cooperatives

The receipt or accrual of income from load loss transactions by taxable electric cooperatives is treated as income from patrons who are members of the cooperative.[17] Thus, income from a load loss transaction is excludible from the taxable income of a taxable electric cooperative if the cooperative distributes such income pursuant to a pre-existing contract to distribute the income to a patron who is not a member of the cooperative. In addition, income from load loss transactions does not cause a taxable electric cooperative to fail to be treated for Federal income tax purposes as a mutual or cooperative company under the fundamental cooperative principles described above.

The special rule for income received or accrued by a taxable electric cooperative from a load loss transaction does not apply to taxable years beginning after December 31, 2006.

Description of Proposal

The proposal eliminates the sunset date for the rules excluding income received or accrued by tax-exempt rural electric cooperatives from open access electric energy transmission or distribution services, any nuclear decommissioning transaction, and any asset exchange or conversion transaction for purposes of the 85-percent test under section 501(c)(12). The proposal also eliminates the sunset date for the rule that allows income from load loss transactions to be treated as member income in determining whether a rural electric cooperative satisfies the 85-percent test. In addition, the proposal eliminates the sunset date for the rule that permits taxable electric cooperatives to treat the receipt or accrual of income from load loss transactions as income from patrons who are members of the cooperative.

Effective Date

The proposal is effective on the date of enactment.

Joint Committee on Taxation (J.C.T. REP. NO. JCX-60-05)

⮞ *Caution: The Description and Technical Explanation of the Conference Agreement of H.R. 6, Title XIII, the "Energy Tax Incentives Act of 2005" (JCX-60-05), below, is included to assist the reader's understanding, but may not be cited as the official Conference Committee Report to H.R. 6—CCH.*

House Bill

No provision.

Conference Agreement

The conference agreement follows the Senate amendment.

[Law at ¶ 5225. CCH Explanation at ¶ 450.]

---

[16] Sec. 501(c)(12)(H).

[17] Sec. 501(c)(12)(H).

[¶10,040] Act Sec. 1305. Dispositions of transmission property to implement FERC restructuring policy

Joint Committee on Taxation (J.C.T. Rep. No. JCX-44-05)

>>> *Caution: The Technical Explanation of the "Energy Policy Tax Incentives Act of 2005" (JCX-44-05), below, is included to assist the reader's understanding but may not be cited as the official Senate Committee Report to H.R. 6—CCH.*

[Code Sec. 451]

Present Law

Generally, a taxpayer selling property recognizes gain to the extent the sales price (and any other consideration received) exceeds the seller's basis in the property. The recognized gain is subject to current income tax unless the gain is deferred or not recognized under a special tax provision.

One such special tax provision permits taxpayers to elect to recognize gain from qualifying electric transmission transactions ratably over an eight-year period beginning in the year of sale if the amount realized from such sale is used to purchase exempt utility property within the applicable period[18] (the "reinvestment property"). If the amount realized exceeds the amount used to purchase reinvestment property, any realized gain is recognized to the extent of such excess in the year of the qualifying electric transmission transaction.

A qualifying electric transmission transaction is the sale or other disposition of property used by the taxpayer in the trade or business of providing electric transmission services, or an ownership interest in such an entity, to an independent transmission company prior to January 1, 2007. In general, an independent transmission company is defined as: (1) an independent transmission provider[19] approved by the FERC; (2) a person (i) who the FERC determines under section 203 of the Federal Power Act (or by declaratory order) is not a "market participant" and (ii) whose transmission facilities are placed under the operational control of a FERC-approved independent transmission provider before the close of the period specified in such authorization, but not later than January 1, 2007; or (3) in the case of facilities subject to the jurisdiction of the Public Utility Commission of Texas, (i) a person which is approved by that Commission as consistent with Texas State law regarding an independent transmission organization, or (ii) a political subdivision, or affiliate thereof, whose transmission facilities are under the operational control of an organization described in (i).

Exempt utility property is defined as: (1) property used in the trade or business of generating, transmitting, distributing, or selling electricity or producing, transmitting, distributing, or selling natural gas, or (2) stock in a controlled corporation whose principal trade or business consists of the activities described in (1).

If a taxpayer is a member of an affiliated group of corporations filing a consolidated return, the reinvestment property may be purchased by any member of the affiliated group (in lieu of the taxpayer).

Description of Proposal

The proposal extends the deferral provision to sales or dispositions to an independent transmission company prior to January 1, 2008.

Effective Date

The proposal is effective for transactions occurring after the date of enactment. However, because the proposal is an extension of a present law provision which expires on December 31, 2006, only transactions occurring after December 31, 2006 and prior to January 1, 2008 will be affected.

---

[18] The applicable period for a taxpayer to reinvest the proceeds is four years after the close of the taxable year in which the qualifying electric transmission transaction occurs.

[19] For example, a regional transmission organization, an independent system operator, or and independent transmission company.

Joint Committee on Taxation (J.C.T. REP. NO. JCX-60-05)

⇒ *Caution: The Description and Technical Explanation of the Conference Agreement of H.R. 6, Title XIII, the "Energy Tax Incentives Act of 2005" (JCX-60-05), below, is included to assist the reader's understanding, but may not be cited as the official Conference Committee Report to H.R. 6—CCH.*

House Bill

No provision.

Conference Agreement

The conference agreement follows the Senate amendment.

[Law at ¶ 5215. CCH Explanation at ¶ 435.]

[¶ 10,050] Act Sec. 1306. Credit for production from advanced nuclear power facilities

Joint Committee on Taxation (J.C.T. REP. NO. JCX-44-05)

⇒ *Caution: The Technical Explanation of the "Energy Policy Tax Incentives Act of 2005" (JCX-44-05), below, is included to assist the reader's understanding but may not be cited as the official Senate Committee Report to H.R. 6—CCH*

[New Code Sec. 45J]

Present Law

An income tax credit is allowed for production of electricity from qualified facilities sold by the taxpayer to an unrelated person (sec. 45). Qualified facilities comprise wind energy facilities, closed-loop biomass facilities, open-loop biomass (including agricultural livestock waste nutrients) facilities, geothermal energy facilities, solar energy facilities, small irrigation power facilities, landfill gas facilities, and trash combustion facilities. The base amount of the credit is 1.5 cents per kilowatt-hour (indexed for inflation) of electricity produced. The amount of the credit is 1.9 cents per kilowatt-hour for 2005. However, electricity produced at open-loop biomass, small irrigation power, and municipal solid waste facilities receives only 50 percent of the credit, or 0.9 cents per kilowatt-hour for 2005. Generally, wind and closed-loop biomass facilities may claim this credit for 10 years from the placed-in-service date of the facility. Other qualified facilities may claim the credit for only five years from the placed-in-service date.

Present law does not provide a credit for electricity produced at advanced nuclear power facilities.

Description of Proposal

The proposal permits a taxpayer producing electricity at a qualifying advanced nuclear power facility to claim a credit equal to 1.8 cents per kilowatt-hour of electricity produced for the eight-year period starting when the facility is placed in service.[20] The aggregate amount of credit that a taxpayer may claim in any year during the eight-year period is subject to limitation based on allocated capacity and an annual limitation as described below.

A qualifying advanced nuclear facility is an advanced nuclear facility for which the taxpayer has received an allocation of megawatt capacity from the Secretary of Treasury, in consultation with the Secretary of Energy, and is placed in service before January 1, 2021. The taxpayer may only claim credit for production of electricity equal to the ratio of the allocated capacity that the taxpayer receives from the Secretary of Treasury to the rated nameplate capacity of the taxpayer's facility. For example, if the taxpayer receives an allocation of 750 megawatts of capacity from the Secretary and the taxpayer's facility has a rated nameplate capacity of 1,000 megawatts, then the taxpayer may claim three-quarters of the otherwise allowable credit, or 1.35 cents per kilowatt-hour, for each kilowatt-hour of electricity produced at the facility (subject to the annual limitation described below). The Secretary of Treasury may allocate up to 6,000 megawatts of capacity.

---

[20] The 1.8-cents credit amount is reduced, but not below zero, if the annual average contract price per kilowatt-hour of electricity generated from advanced nuclear power facilities in the preceding year exceeds eight cents per kilowatt-hour. The eight-cent price comparison level is indexed for inflation after 1992.

Act Sec. 1306 ¶ 10,050

A taxpayer operating a qualified facility may claim no more than $125 million in tax credits per 1,000 megawatts of allocated capacity in any one year of the eight-year credit period. If the taxpayer operates a 1,350 megawatt rated nameplate capacity system and has received an allocation from the Secretary for 1,350 megawatts of capacity eligible for the credit, the taxpayer's annual limitation on credits that may be claimed is equal to 1.35 times $125 million, or $168.75 million. If the taxpayer operates a facility with a nameplate rated capacity of 1,350 megawatts, but has received an allocation from the Secretary for 750 megawatts of credit eligible capacity, then the two limitations apply such that the taxpayer may claim a credit equal to 1.35 cents per kilowatt-hour of electricity produced (as described above) subject to an annual credit limitation of $93.75 million in credits (three-quarters of $125 million).

An advanced nuclear facility is any nuclear facility for the production of electricity, the reactor design for which was approved after 1993 by the Nuclear Regulatory Commission. For this purpose, a qualifying advanced nuclear facility does not include any facility for which a substantially similar design for a facility of comparable capacity was approved before 1994.

In addition, the credit allowable to the taxpayer is reduced by reason of grants, tax-exempt bonds, subsidized energy financing, and other credits, but such reduction cannot exceed 50 percent of the otherwise allowable credit. The credit is treated as part of the general business credit and, under a special transition rule may not be carried back to a taxable year ending before or on the effective date of the provision.

Effective Date

The proposal applies to electricity produced in taxable years beginning after the date of enactment.

Joint Committee on Taxation (J.C.T. REP. NO. JCX-60-05)

⟫→ *Caution: The Description and Technical Explanation of the Conference Agreement of H.R. 6, Title XIII, the "Energy Tax Incentives Act of 2005" (JCX-60-05), below, is included to assist the reader's understanding, but may not be cited as the official Conference Committee Report to H.R. 6—CCH*

House Bill

No provision.

Conference Agreement

The conference agreement follows the Senate amendment.

[Law at ¶5040 and ¶5075. CCH Explanation at ¶440.]

[¶10,060] Act Sec. 1307. Credit for investment in clean coal facilities

Joint Committee on Taxation (J.C.T. REP. NO. JCX-44-05)

⟫→ *Caution: The Technical Explanation of the "Energy Policy Tax Incentives Act of 2005" (JCX-44-05), below, is included to assist the reader's understanding but may not be cited as the official Senate Committee Report to H.R. 6—CCH*

[New Code Secs. 48A and 48B]

Present Law

Present law does not provide an investment credit for electricity production facilities property that uses coal as a fuel or for the gasification of coal or other materials. However, a nonrefundable, 10-percent investment tax credit ("energy credit") is allowed for the cost of new property that is equipment (1) that uses solar energy to generate electricity, to heat or cool a structure, or to provide solar process heat, or (2) that is used to produce, distribute, or use energy derived from a geothermal deposit, but only, in the case of electricity generated by geothermal power, up to the electric transmission stage (sec. 48). The energy credit is a component of the general business credit (sec. 38(b)(1)).

Description of Proposal

The proposal adds two new 20-percent investment tax credits to the energy credit. Both credits are available only to projects certified by the Secretary of Treasury, in consultation with the Secretary of Energy. Certifications are issued using a competitive bidding process.

With respect to the first investment tax credit, the proposal establishes a 10-year program to produce 6,500 megawatts of power generation capacity using integrated gasification combined cycle and other advanced coal-based electricity generation technologies. Qualified projects must be economically feasible and use the appropriate clean coal technologies. In determining which qualified projects to certify, the Secretary of Treasury shall give priority to projects that include carbon capture capability, increased by-product utilization and other benefits. The Secretary of Treasury, in consultation with the Secretary of Energy, must allocate up to 3,575 megawatts of power generation capacity to credit-eligible projects using an integrated gasification combined cycle technology. The remaining 2,925 megawatts of power generation capacity must be allocated to credit-eligible projects that use other advanced coal-based technologies.

With respect to the second investment tax credit, the proposal authorizes the certification of certain gasification projects. Qualified gasification projects convert coal, petroleum residue, biomass, or other materials recovered for their energy or feedstock value into a synthesis gas composed primarily of carbon monoxide and hydrogen for direct use or subsequent chemical or physical conversion. Under the proposal, certified gasification projects are eligible for the new 20 percent investment tax credit. The total value of credit-eligible expenditures on all certified gasification projects may not exceed $4 billion. In addition, no single project may claim a gasification investment tax credit in excess of $200 million.

Effective Date

The credits apply to periods after the date of enactment, under rules similar to the rules of section 48(m) (as in effect before its repeal).

Joint Committee on Taxation (J.C.T. REP. NO. JCX-60-05)

⋙→ *Caution: The Description and Technical Explanation of the Conference Agreement of H.R. 6, Title XIII, the "Energy Tax Incentives Act of 2005" (JCX-60-05), below, is included to assist the reader's understanding, but may not be cited as the official Conference Committee Report to H.R. 6—CCH.*

House Bill

No provision.

Conference Agreement

The conference agreement follows the Senate amendment with modifications. Under the conference agreement, the Secretary may allocate investment credits for projects using IGCC and other advanced coal-based technologies based on the amount invested, rather than on megawatts of power generation capacity. The Secretary may allocate $800 million of credits to IGCC projects and $500 million of credits to projects using other advanced coal-based technologies.

Under the agreement, the credit available to IGCC projects remains 20 percent of qualified investments; however, the credit for other advanced coal-based projects is reduced to 15 percent of qualified investments. With respect to IGCC projects, the conference agreement narrows the definition of credit-eligible investments to include only investments in property associated with the gasification of coal, including any coal handling and gas separation equipment. Thus, investments in equipment that could operate by drawing fuel directly from a natural gas pipeline do not qualify for the credit.

The conference agreement retains the 20 percent investment credit for certified gasification projects. The agreement, however, reduces the total amount of gasification credits allocable by the Secretary to $350 million. A maximum of $650 million of credit-eligible investment may be allocated to any single gasification project. The conference agreement also clarifies that only property which is part of a qualifying gasification project and necessary for the gasification technology of such project is eligible for the gasification credit.

[Law at ¶5095, ¶5105, ¶5110 and ¶5115. CCH Explanation at ¶605.]

[¶ 10,070] Act Sec. 1308. Transmission property treated as fifteen-year property

House Committee Report (H.R. Rep. No. 109-45)

⇉→ *Caution: Excerpts from H.R. Rep. No. 109-45, below, are included to assist the reader's understanding. H.R. Rep. No. 109-45 accompanies H.R. 1541, which was amended and reported favorably by the Committee on Ways and Means on April 18, 2005. H.R. 1541 contained the tax portions of the Energy Policy Bill of 2005, but was never voted on by the House as a standalone bill. Its provisions, however, were included in the larger energy bill (H.R. 6) that passed the House on April 21, 2005. The Committee did not issue a separate report on H.R. 6, but the provision described below is substantially similar to that contained in the Conference Report that accompanies H.R. 6.*

[Code Sec. 168]

Present Law

The applicable recovery period for assets placed in service under the Modified Accelerated Cost Recovery System is based on the "class life of the property." The class lives of assets placed in service after 1986 are generally set forth in Revenue Procedure 87-56.[6] Assets used in the transmission and distribution of electricity for sale and related land improvements are assigned a 20-year recovery period and a class life of 30 years.

Reasons for Change

The Committee recognizes the importance of modernizing our aging energy infrastructure to meet the demands of the twenty-first century, and the Committee also recognizes that both short-term and long-term solutions are required to meet this challenge. The Committee understands that investment in our electricity transmission infrastructure assets has not kept pace with the nation's needs. In light of this, the Committee believes it is appropriate to reduce the recovery period for investment in certain electricity transmission infrastructure property to encourage investment in such property.

Explanation of Provision

The provision establishes a statutory 15-year recovery period and a class life of 30 years for certain assets used in the transmission of electricity for sale and related land improvements. For purposes of the provision, section 1245 property used in the transmission at 69 or more kilovolts of electricity for sale, the original use of which commences with the taxpayer after April 11, 2005, will qualify for the new recovery period.

Effective Date

The provision is effective for property placed in service after April 11, 2005.

Joint Committee on Taxation (J.C.T. Rep. No. JCX-60-05)

⇉→ *Caution: The Description and Technical Explanation of the Conference Agreement of H.R. 6, Title XIII, the "Energy Tax Incentives Act of 2005" (JCX-60-05), below, is included to assist the reader's understanding, but may not be cited as the official Conference Committee Report to H.R. 6—CCH.*

Senate Amendment

No provision.

Conference Agreement

The conference agreement follows the House bill, except that the provision does not apply to property which is the subject of a binding contract on or before April 11, 2005.[8]

[Law at ¶ 5165. CCH Explanation at ¶ 425.]

---

[6] 1987-2 C.B. 674 (as clarified and modified by Rev. Proc. 88-22, 1988-1 C.B. 785).

[8] In the case of self-constructed property, the provision does not apply to property under construction on or before April 11, 2005.

[¶ 10,080] Act Sec. 1309. Amortization of atmospheric pollution control facilities

House Committee Report (H.R. Rep. No. 109-45)

⟫⟫→ *Caution: Excerpts from H.R. Rep. No. 109-45, below, are included to assist the reader's understanding. H.R. Rep. No. 109-45 accompanies H.R. 1541, which was amended and reported favorably by the Committee on Ways and Means on April 18, 2005. H.R. 1541 contained the tax portions of the Energy Policy Bill of 2005, but was never voted on by the House as a standalone bill. Its provisions, however, were included in the larger energy bill (H.R. 6) that passed the House on April 21, 2005. The Committee did not issue a separate report on H.R. 6, but the provision described below is substantially similar to that contained in the Conference Report that accompanies H.R. 6.*

[Code Sec. 169]

Present Law

In general, a taxpayer may elect to recover the cost of any certified pollution control facility over a period of 60 months.[8] A certified pollution control facility is defined as a new, identifiable treatment facility which (1) is used in connection with a plant in operation before January 1, 1976, to abate or control water or atmospheric pollution or contamination by removing, altering, disposing, storing, or preventing the creation or emission of pollutants, contaminants, wastes or heat; and (2) does not lead to a significant increase in output or capacity, a significant extension of useful life, a significant reduction in total operating costs for such plant or other property (or any unit thereof), or a significant alteration in the nature of a manufacturing production process or facility. Certification is required by appropriate State and Federal authorities that the facility complies with appropriate standards.

For a pollution control facility with a useful life greater than 15 years, only the portion of the basis attributable to the first 15 years is eligible to be amortized over a 60-month period.[9] In addition, a corporate taxpayer must reduce the amount of basis otherwise eligible for the 60-month recovery by 20 percent.[10] The amount of basis not eligible for 60-month amortization is depreciable under the regular tax rules for depreciation.

Reasons for Change

The Committee is concerned about the effects of atmospheric pollution created by coal-fired electric generation plants and recognizes that the present-law election is not available for pollution control facilities used in connection with such a plant which commenced operation after December 31, 1975. The Committee notes that the Environmental Protection Agency recently has promulgated new, stricter emissions standards for coal-fired, electric generation plants. The Committee believes that the present-law incentive to install pollution control facilities should be available to taxpayers that install atmospheric pollution control equipment in all such plants, regardless of when they commenced operation.

Explanation of Provision

The provision expands the provision allowing a taxpayer to recover the cost of certain certified air pollution control facilities (but not water pollution control facilities) over 60 months by repealing the requirement that only certified pollution control facilities used in connection with a plant in operation before January 1, 1976 qualify. Under the provision, a certified air pollution control facility which used in connection with a an electric generation plant which is primarily coal fired will be eligible for 60-month amortization regardless of whether the associated plant or other property was in operation prior to January 1, 1976. In the case a facility used in connection with a plant or other property not in operation before January 1, 1976, the facility must be property that either (i) the construction, reconstruction, or erection of which is completed by the taxpayer after April 11, 2005 (to the extent of the portion of the basis properly attributable to the construction, reconstruction, or erection after that date), or (ii) is acquired after April 11, 2005, if the original use of the

---

[8] Sec. 169. For purposes of computing alternative minimum taxable income, the depreciation deduction is determined using the straight-line method over the applicable regular tax recovery period.

[9] The amount attributable to the first 15 years is equal to an amount which bears the same ratio to the portion of the adjusted basis of the facility, which would be eligible for amortization but for the application of this rule, as 15 bears to the number of years of useful life of the facility.

[10] Sec. 291(a)(5).

property commences with the taxpayer after that date. The provision does not change the present-law rules relating to corporate taxpayers or to pollution control facilities with a useful life greater than 15 years, and the provision does not modify in any way the treatment of water pollution control facilities.

Joint Committee on Taxation (J.C.T. Rep. No. JCX-60-05)

⟫→ *Caution: The Description and Technical Explanation of the Conference Agreement of H.R. 6, Title XIII, the "Energy Tax Incentives Act of 2005" (JCX-60-05), below, is included to assist the reader's understanding, but may not be cited as the official Conference Committee Report to H.R. 6—CCH.*

Senate Amendment

No provision.

Effective Date

The provision is effective for air pollution control facilities placed in service after April 11, 2005.

Conference Agreement

The conference agreement follows the House bill, except that the amortization period is 84 months (rather than 60 months) for certified air pollution control facilities used in connection with an electric generation plant which is primarily coal fired and which was not in operation before January 1, 1976.

[Law at ¶ 5170. CCH Explanation at ¶ 620.]

[¶ 10,090] Act Sec. 1310. Modifications to special rules for nuclear decommissioning costs

House Committee Report (H.R. Rep. No. 109-45)

⟫→ *Caution: Excerpts from H.R. Rep. No. 109-45, below, are included to assist the reader's understanding. H.R. Rep. No. 109-45 accompanies H.R. 1541, which was amended and reported favorably by the Committee on Ways and Means on April 18, 2005. H.R. 1541 contained the tax portions of the Energy Policy Bill of 2005, but was never voted on by the House as a standalone bill. Its provisions, however, were included in the larger energy bill (H.R. 6) that passed the House on April 21, 2005. The Committee did not issue a separate report on H.R. 6, but the provision described below is substantially similar to that contained in the Conference Report that accompanies H.R. 6.*

[Code Sec. 468A]

Present Law

Overview

Special rules dealing with nuclear decommissioning reserve funds were enacted in the Deficit Reduction Act of 1984 ("1984 Act"), when tax issues regarding the time value of money were addressed generally. Under general tax accounting rules, a deduction for accrual basis taxpayers is deferred until there is economic performance for the item for which the deduction is claimed. However, the 1984 Act contains an exception under which a taxpayer responsible for nuclear powerplant decommissioning may elect to deduct contributions made to a qualified nuclear decommissioning fund for future decommissioning costs. Taxpayers who do not elect this provision are subject to general tax accounting rules.

Qualified nuclear decommissioning fund

A qualified nuclear decommissioning fund (a "qualified fund") is a segregated fund established by a taxpayer that is used exclusively for the payment of decommissioning costs, taxes on fund income, management costs of the fund, and for making investments. The income of the fund is taxed at a reduced rate of 20 percent for taxable years beginning after December 31, 1995.[10]

Contributions to a qualified fund are deductible in the year made to the extent that these amounts were collected as part of the cost of service to ratepayers (the "cost of service requirement").[11] Funds withdrawn by the tax-

---

[10] As originally enacted in 1984, a qualified fund paid tax on its earnings at the top corporate rate and, as a result, there was no present-value tax benefit of making deductible contributions to a qualified fund. Also, as originally enacted, the funds in the trust could be invested only in certain low risk investments. Subsequent amendments to the provision have reduced the rate of tax on a qualified fund to 20 percent and removed the restrictions on the types of permitted investments that a qualified fund can make.

[11] Taxpayers are required to include in gross income customer charges for decommissioning costs (sec. 88).

payer to pay for decommissioning costs are included in the taxpayer's income, but the taxpayer also is entitled to a deduction for decommissioning costs as economic performance for such costs occurs.

Accumulations in a qualified fund are limited to the amount required to fund decommissioning costs of a nuclear powerplant for the period during which the qualified fund is in existence (generally post-1984 decommissioning costs of a nuclear powerplant). For this purpose, decommissioning costs are considered to accrue ratably over a nuclear powerplant's estimated useful life. In order to prevent accumulations of funds over the remaining life of a nuclear powerplant in excess of those required to pay future decommissioning costs of such nuclear powerplant and to ensure that contributions to a qualified fund are not deducted more rapidly than level funding (taking into account an appropriate discount rate), taxpayers must obtain a ruling from the IRS to establish the maximum annual contribution that may be made to a qualified fund (the "ruling amount"). In certain instances (e.g., change in estimates), a taxpayer is required to obtain a new ruling amount to reflect updated information.

A qualified fund may be transferred in connection with the sale, exchange or other transfer of the nuclear powerplant to which it relates. If the transferee is a regulated public utility and meets certain other requirements, the transfer will be treated as a nontaxable transaction. No gain or loss will be recognized on the transfer of the qualified fund and the transferee will take the transferor's basis in the fund.[12] The transferee is required to obtain a new ruling amount from the IRS or accept a discretionary determination by the IRS.[13]

Nonqualified nuclear decommissioning funds

Federal and State regulators may require utilities to set aside funds for nuclear decommissioning costs in excess of the amount allowed as a deductible contribution to a qualified fund. In addition, taxpayers may have set aside funds prior to the effective date of the qualified fund rules.[14] The treatment of amounts set aside for decommissioning costs prior to 1984 varies. Some taxpayers may have received no tax benefit while others may have deducted such amounts or excluded such amounts from income. Since 1984, taxpayers have been required to include in gross income customer charges for decommissioning costs (sec. 88), and a deduction has not been allowed for amounts set aside to pay for decommissioning costs except through the use of a qualified fund. Income earned in a nonqualified fund is taxable to the fund's owner as it is earned.

Reasons for Change

The Committee recognizes the national importance of reserving funds to pay for decommissioning costs and the need for appropriate incentives to ensure that adequate funds are available for such costs. The Committee believes that it is appropriate to permit all decommissioning costs associated with a nuclear powerplant to be funded through a qualified fund. In addition, the Committee does not believe a utility should be denied the opportunity to contribute to a qualified fund simply because it operates in a deregulated environment.

Explanation of Provision

Repeal of cost of service requirement

The provision repeals the cost of service requirement for deductible contributions to a nuclear decommissioning fund. Thus, all taxpayers, including unregulated taxpayers, are allowed a deduction for amounts contributed to a qualified fund.

Permit contributions to a qualified fund for pre-1984 decommissioning costs

The provision also repeals the limitation that a qualified fund only accumulate an amount sufficient to pay for a nuclear powerplant's decommissioning costs incurred during the period that the qualified fund is in existence (generally post-1984 decommissioning costs). Thus, any taxpayer is permitted to accumulate an amount sufficient to cover the present value of 100 percent of a nuclear powerplant's estimated decommissioning costs in a qualified fund. The provision does not change the requirement that contributions to a qualified fund not be deducted more rapidly than level funding.

Exception to ruling amount for certain decommissioning costs

The provision permits a taxpayer to make contributions to a qualified fund in excess of the ruling amount in one circumstance. Specifically, a taxpayer is permitted to contribute up to the present value of total nuclear decommissioning costs with respect to a nuclear powerplant previ-

---

[12] Treas. reg. sec. 1.468A-6.
[13] Treas. reg. sec. 1.468A-6(f).

[14] These funds are generally referred to as "nonqualified funds."

ously excluded under section 468A(d)(2)(A).[15] It is anticipated that an amount that is permitted to be contributed under this special rule shall be determined using the estimate of total decommissioning costs used for purposes of determining the taxpayer's most recent ruling amount. Any amount transferred to the qualified fund under this special rule is allowed as a deduction over the remaining useful life of the nuclear powerplant.[16] If a qualified fund that has received amounts under this rule is transferred to another person, the transferor will be permitted a deduction for any remaining deductible amounts at the time of transfer.

Effective Date

The provision is effective for taxable years beginning after December 31, 2005.

Joint Committee on Taxation (J.C.T. Rep. No. JCX-60-05)

⇛ *Caution: The Description and Technical Explanation of the Conference Agreement of H.R. 6, Title XIII, the "Energy Tax Incentives Act of 2005" (JCX-60-05), below, is included to assist the reader's understanding, but may not be cited as the official Conference Committee Report to H.R. 6—CCH.*

Senate Bill

No provision.

Conference Agreement

The conference agreement follows the House bill, with the following modification. The conference agreement requires that a taxpayer apply for a new ruling amount with respect to a nuclear powerplant in any tax year in which the powerplant is granted a license renewal, extending its useful life.

[Law at ¶ 5220. CCH Explanation at ¶ 445.]

[¶ 10,100] Act Sec. 1311. Five-year carryback of net operating losses for certain electric utility companies

Joint Committee on Taxation (J.C.T. Rep. No. JCX-46-05)

⇛ *Caution: The Technical Explanation of the "Energy Policy Tax Incentives Act of 2005" (JCX-46-05), below, is included to assist the reader's understanding but may not be cited as the official Senate Committee Report to H.R. 6—CCH.*

[Code Sec. 172]

Present Law

A net operating loss ("NOL") is, generally, the amount by which a taxpayer's allowable deductions exceed the taxpayer's gross income. A carryback of an NOL generally results in the refund of Federal income tax for the carryback year. A carryforward of an NOL reduces Federal income tax for the carryforward year.

In general, an NOL may be carried back two years and carried forward 20 years to offset taxable income in such years.[3] Different rules apply with respect to NOLs arising in certain circumstances. For example, a three-year carryback applies with respect to NOLs (1) arising from casualty or theft losses of individuals, or (2) attributable to Presidentially declared disasters for taxpayers engaged in a farming business or a small business. A five-year carryback period applies to NOLs from a farming loss (regardless of whether the loss was incurred in a Presidentially declared disaster area). Special rules also apply to real estate investment trusts (no carryback), specified liability losses (10-year carryback), and excess interest losses (no carryback to any year preceding a corporate equity reduction transaction).

Section 202 of the Job Creation and Worker Assistance Act of 2002[4] ("JCWAA") provided a temporary extension of the general NOL carryback period to five years (from two years) for NOLs arising in taxable years ending in 2001 and 2002. In addition, the five-year carryback period

---

[15] For example, if $100 is the present value of the total decommissioning costs of a nuclear powerplant, and if under present law the qualified fund is only permitted to accumulate $75 of decommissioning costs over such plant's estimated useful life (because the qualified fund was not in existence during 25 percent of the estimated useful life of the nuclear powerplant), a taxpayer could contribute $25 to the qualified fund under this component of the provision.

[16] A taxpayer recognizes no gain or loss on the contribution of property to a qualified fund under this special rule.

The qualified fund will take a transferred (carryover) basis in such property. Correspondingly, a taxpayer's deduction (over the estimated life of the nuclear powerplant) is to be based on the adjusted tax basis of the property contributed rather than the fair market value of such property.

[3] Sec. 172.

[4] Pub. Law No. 107-147.

applies to NOLs from these years that qualify under present law for a three-year carryback period (i.e., NOLs arising from casualty or theft losses of individuals or attributable to certain Presidentially declared disaster areas).

A taxpayer can elect to forgo the five-year carryback period. The election to forgo the five-year carryback period is made in the manner prescribed by the Secretary of the Treasury and must be made by the due date of the return (including extensions) for the year of the loss. The election is irrevocable. If a taxpayer elects to forgo the five-year carryback period, then the losses are subject to the rules that otherwise would apply under section 172 absent the provision.

Description of Proposal

The proposal provides a temporary extension of the NOL carryback period to five years for NOLs of certain electric utility companies arising in taxable years ending in 2003, 2004, and 2005 ("eligible NOLs"). Regardless of the taxable year in which an eligible NOL arose, refund claims resulting from the extended carryback period can be made during any taxable year ending after December 31, 2005, and before December 31, 2008. However, the amount of the refund claimed during any one taxable year may not exceed the electric utility company's investment in electric transmission property and pollution control facilities in the preceding taxable year. Taxpayers may elect to forgo the five-year carryback period provided under the proposal if an election is filed before December 31, 2008.

Joint Committee on Taxation (J.C.T. REP. NO. JCX-60-05)

≫→ *Caution: The Description and Technical Explanation of the Conference Agreement of H.R. 6, Title XIII, the "Energy Tax Incentives Act of 2005" (JCX-60-05), below, is included to assist the reader's understanding, but may not be cited as the official Conference Committee Report to H.R. 6—CCH.*

House Bill

No provision.

Conference Agreement

The conference agreement follows the Senate amendment, with the following modifications. The conference agreement provides an election for certain electric utility companies to extend the carryback period to five years for a portion of NOLs arising in 2003, 2004, and 2005 ("loss years"). The election may be made during any taxable year ending after December 31, 2005, and before January 1, 2009 ("election years"). An electing taxpayer must specify to which loss year the election applies.

The portion of the loss year NOL to which the election may apply is limited to 20 percent of the amount of the taxpayer's qualifying investment in the taxable year prior to the year in which the election is made (the "qualifying investment limitation"). Rules similar to those applicable to specified liability losses apply, and any remaining portion of the loss year NOL remains subject to the present law NOL carryover rules. Only one election may be made in any election year, and elections may not be made for more than one election year beginning in the same calendar year. Thus, for example, a taxpayer with two short taxable years beginning in calendar year 2006 is eligible to make an election under this provision in only one of those two short taxable years. Once an election has been made with respect to a loss year, no subsequent election is available with respect to that loss year.

For purposes of calculating interest on overpayments, any overpayment resulting from a five-year NOL carryback elected under this provision is deemed not to have been made prior to the filing date for the taxable year in which the election is made. The statute of limitations for refund claims, and that for assessment of deficiencies, are also extended.

An election under this provision is made in such manner as the Secretary may prescribe. However, the conferees expect that the filing of a refund claim will be considered sufficient for making the election, provided that the taxpayer attaches to the refund claim a statement specifying the election year, the loss year, and the amount of qualifying investment in electric transmission property and pollution control facilities in the preceding taxable year.

Under the conference agreement, an investment in electric transmission property qualifies if it is a capital expenditure made by the taxpayer which is attributable to electric transmission property used by the taxpayer in the transmission at 69 or more kilovolts of electricity for sale. An investment in pollution control equipment qualifies if it is a capital expenditure, made by an electric utility company (as defined in the Public Utility Holding Company Act as in effect on the day before the date of enactment of the provision), which is attributable to a facility which will qualify as a certified pollution control facility, generally as defined under section 169(d)(1) but without regard to the requirements therein that the facility be new or that it be used in

Act Sec. 1311 ¶10,100

connection with a plant or other property in operation before January 1, 1976.

The conferees recognize that a significant amount of time may be required between the date of a capital expenditure for electric transmission property or pollution control equipment and the date the property is placed in service. Accordingly, there is no requirement that the transmission property or pollution control facilities be placed in service in the year in which the capital expenditures are incurred. However, it is intended that qualifying investment under the provision includes only capital expenditures to which the taxpayer is committed and with respect to property which the taxpayer intends to ultimately place in service in the taxpayer's trade or business. Under the conference agreement, capital expenditures which, at the taxpayer's option, are refundable or subject to material modification in a manner which would not meet the requirements of the provision, may not be taken into account. For example, if a taxpayer makes a cash deposit with respect to a contract for the purchase of electric transmission property, and the contract contains an option (or there is otherwise an understanding) under which the taxpayer may subsequently apply the deposit to the purchase of equipment other than electric transmission property, the deposit is not included in the taxpayer's qualifying investment. This rule is intended as an anti-abuse rule and should be interpreted to prevent a taxpayer from taking into account capital expenditures to which the taxpayer is not permanently committed.

Effective date

The conference agreement provision is effective for elections made in taxable years ending after December 31, 2005, and before January 1, 2009, with respect to net operating losses arising in taxable years ending in 2003, 2004, and 2005.

[Law at ¶ 5175. CCH Explanation at ¶ 430.]

[¶ 10,110] Act Secs.1321 and 1322. Modification of credit for producing fuel from a non-conventional source

House Committee Report (H.R. REP. NO. 109-45)

⇛→ *Caution: Excerpts from H.R. Rep. No. 109-45, below, are included to assist the reader's understanding. H.R. Rep. No. 109-45 accompanies H.R. 1541, which was amended and reported favorably by the Committee on Ways and Means on April 18, 2005. H.R. 1541 contained the tax portions of the Energy Policy Bill of 2005, but was never voted on by the House as a standalone bill. Its provisions, however, were included in the larger energy bill (H.R. 6) that passed the House on April 21, 2005. The Committee did not issue a separate report on H.R. 6, but the provision described below is substantially similar to that contained in the Conference Report that accompanies H.R. 6.*

[Code Sec. 29 and New Code Sec. 45K]

Present Law

Certain fuels produced from "non-conventional sources" and sold to unrelated parties are eligible for an income tax credit equal to $3 (generally adjusted for inflation)[8] per barrel or BTU oil barrel equivalent ("section 29 credit"). Qualified fuels must be produced within the United States.

Qualified fuels include:

1. oil produced from shale and tar sands;

2. gas produced from geopressured brine, Devonian shale, coal seams, tight formations, or biomass; and

3. liquid, gaseous, or solid synthetic fuels produced from coal (including lignite).

In general, the section 29 credit is available only with respect to fuels produced from wells drilled or facilities placed in service after December 31, 1979, and before January 1, 1993. An exception extends the January 1, 1993 expiration date for facilities producing gas from biomass and synthetic fuel from coal if the facility producing the fuel is placed in service before July 1, 1998, pursuant to a binding contract entered into before January 1, 1997.

The section 29 credit may be claimed for qualified fuels produced and sold before January 1, 2003 (in the case of non-conventional sources subject to the January 1, 1993 expiration date) or January 1, 2008 (in the case of biomass gas and synthetic fuel facilities eligible for the extension period).

The section 29 credit may not exceed the excess of the regular tax liability over the tenta-

---

[8] The value of the credit in 2004 was $6.56 per barrel of oil equivalent produced, which is approximately $1.16 per thousand cubic feet of natural gas.

¶ 10,110   Act Sec. 1321

tive minimum tax. Unused section 29 credits may not be carried forward or carried back to other taxable years. However, to the extent the section 29 credit is disallowed because of the tentative minimum tax, the minimum tax credit allowable in future years is increased by the amount so disallowed.

Other business credits are included in the general business credit (sec. 38). Generally, the general business credit may not exceed the excess of the taxpayer's net income tax over the greater of the taxpayer's tentative minimum tax or 25 percent of so much of the taxpayer's net regular tax liability as exceeds $25,000. General business credits in excess of this limitation may be carried back one year and forward up to 20 years. The section 29 credit is not part of the general business credit.

The section 29 credit includes definitional cross-references and a credit limitation relating to the Natural Gas Policy Act of 1978. The Natural Gas Policy Act of 1978 has been repealed.

Reasons for Change

The Committee recognizes that the section 29 credit is not part of the general business credits and therefore no carryback or carryforward is available for the credit. The Committee believes that the carryback and carryforward rules should apply to the credit, and therefore believes it is appropriate to treat the credit as part of the general business credits.

Explanation of Provision

The provision makes the credit for producing fuel from a non-conventional source part of the general business credit. Thus, the credit for producing fuel from a non-conventional source will be subject to the limitations applicable to the general business credit. Any unused credits may be carried back one year and forward 20 years.

The provision also makes certain clerical changes in cross-references to the Natural Gas Policy Act of 1978, which has been repealed.

Effective Date

The provision applies to credits determined for taxable years ending after December 31, 2005.[9] The clerical changes are effective on the date of enactment.

Joint Committee on Taxation (J.C.T. REP. NO. JCX-60-05)

⇶➔ *Caution: The Description and Technical Explanation of the Conference Agreement of H.R. 6, Title XIII, the "Energy Tax Incentives Act of 2005" (JCX-60-05), below, is included to assist the reader's understanding, but may not be cited as the official Conference Committee Report to H.R. 6—CCH.*

Senate Amendment

No provision.

Conference Agreement

The conference agreement follows the House provision with modifications. In addition to making the section 29 credit part of the general business credit, the conference agreement adds a production credit for qualified facilities that produce coke or coke gas. Qualified facilities must have been placed in service before January 1, 1993, or after June 30, 1998, and before January 1, 2010. The conferees understand that a single facility for the production of coke or coke gas is generally composed of multiple coke ovens or similar structures.

The production credit may be claimed with respect to coke and coke gas produced and sold during the period beginning on the later of January 1, 2006, or the date such facility is placed in service and ending on the date which is four years after such period began. The amount of credit-eligible coke produced may not exceed an average barrel-of-oil equivalent of 4,000 barrels per day. The $3.00 credit for coke or coke gas is indexed for inflation using 2004 as the base year instead of 1979. A facility that has claimed a credit under Code section 29(g) is not eligible to claim the new credit for producing coke or coke gas.

The conferees understand that the Internal Revenue Service has stopped issuing private letter rulings and other taxpayer-specific guidance regarding the section 29 credit. The conferees believe that the Internal Revenue Service should consider issuing such rulings and guidance on an expedited basis to those taxpayers who had pending ruling requests at the time the moratorium was implemented.

[Law at ¶5025, ¶5040, ¶5060, ¶5065, ¶5070, ¶5080, ¶5120, ¶5130, ¶5230 and ¶5235. CCH Explanation at ¶610 and ¶615.]

---

[9] The credit may not be carried back to a taxable year ending before January 1, 2006 (sec. 39(d)).

[¶10,120] Act Sec. 1323. Temporary expensing for equipment used in the refining of liquid fuels

Joint Committee on Taxation (J.C.T. Rep. No. JCX-44-05)

>>→ *Caution: The Technical Explanation of the "Energy Policy Tax Incentives Act of 2005" (JCX-44-05), below, is included to assist the reader's understanding but may not be cited as the official Senate Committee Report to H.R. 6— CCH.*

[New Code Sec. 179C]

Present Law

Depreciation of refinery assets

Under present law, depreciation allowances for property used in a trade or business generally are determined under the Modified Accelerated Cost Recovery System ("MACRS") of section 168 of the Internal Revenue Code. Under MACRS, petroleum refining assets are depreciated for regular tax purposes over a 10-year recovery period using the double declining balance method. Petroleum refining assets are assets used for distillation, fractionation, and catalytic cracking of crude petroleum into gasoline and its other components. Present law also provides a special expensing rule for small refiners for capital costs incurred in complying with Environmental Protection Agency sulfur regulations.

Taxation of cooperatives and their patrons

For Federal income tax purposes, a cooperative generally computes its income as if it were a taxable corporation, with one exception-the cooperative may exclude from its taxable income distributions of patronage dividends. In general, patronage dividends are the profits of the cooperative that are rebated to its patrons pursuant to a pre-existing obligation of the cooperative to do so. The rebate must be made in some equitable fashion on the basis of the quantity or value of business done with the cooperative.

Except for tax-exempt farmers' cooperatives, cooperatives that are subject to the cooperative tax rules of subchapter T of the Code[25] are permitted a deduction for patronage dividends from their taxable income only to the extent of net income that is derived from transactions with patrons who are members of the cooperative.[26] The availability of such deductions from taxable income has the effect of allowing the cooperative to be treated like a conduit with respect to profits derived from transactions with patrons who are members of the cooperative.

* * *

Description of Proposal

The proposal provides a temporary election to expense qualified refinery property. Qualified refinery property includes assets used in the refining of liquid fuels: (1) with respect to the construction of which there is a binding construction contract before January 1, 2008; (2) which is placed in service before January 1, 2012; (3) which increases the capacity of an existing refinery by at least five percent or increases throughput of qualified fuels (as defined in section 29(c)) by at least 25 percent; and (4) which meets all applicable environmental laws in effect when the property is placed in service.

The proposal also allows cooperatives to pass through to patrons the deduction permitted for qualified refinery property. To the extent the deduction for qualified refinery property is passed through to patrons, the cooperative is denied the deduction for such property or any depreciation deductions under sections 167 or 168 with respect to such property.

Effective Date

The proposal is effective for property placed in service after the date of enactment, the original use of which begins with the taxpayer, provided the property is not subject to a binding contract for construction as of June 14, 2005.

---

[25] Sec. 1381, et seq.

[26] Sec. 1382.

Joint Committee on Taxation (J.C.T. REP. NO. JCX-60-05)

>>>→ *Caution: The Description and Technical Explanation of the Conference Agreement of H.R. 6, Title XIII, the "Energy Tax Incentives Act of 2005" (JCX-60-05), below, is included to assist the reader's understanding, but may not be cited as the official Conference Committee Report to H.R. 6—CCH.*

House Bill

No provision.

Senate Amendment

The Senate amendment provision provides a temporary election to expense qualified refinery property.[55] Qualified refinery property includes assets, located in the United States, used in the refining of liquid fuels: (1) with respect to the construction of which there is a binding construction contract before January 1, 2008; (2) which are placed in service before January 1, 2012; (3) which increase the capacity of an existing refinery by at least five percent or increase the percentage of total throughput[56] attributable to qualified fuels (as defined in present law section 29(c), which is redesignated as section 45K(c) by section 1322(a)(1) of the Act)[57] such that it equals or exceeds 25 percent; and (4) which meet all applicable environmental laws in effect when the property is placed in service.[58]

* * *

* * * To the extent the deduction is passed through to owners, the cooperative is denied deductions it would otherwise be entitled with respect to qualified refinery property.

As a condition of eligibility for the expensing of equipment used in the refining of liquid fuels, the Senate amendment provision provides that a refinery must report to the IRS concerning its refinery operations (e.g. production and output).

Conference Agreement

The conference agreement follows the Senate amendment, with the following modifications. Under the conference agreement, the expensing election is limited to 50% of the taxpayer's qualifying expenditures. The remaining 50% is recovered as under present law.

Under the conference agreement, the five percent capacity requirement refers to the output capacity of the refinery, as measured by the volume of finished products other than asphalt and lube oil, rather than input capacity, as measured by rated capacity.

The conference agreement includes a clarification that the expensing election is not available with respect to identifiable refinery property built solely to comply with consent decrees or projects mandated by Federal, State, or local governments.

Finally, an exception to the original use requirement is provided for property which would meet the requirement but for a sale-leaseback transaction within the first three months after the property is originally placed in service.

Under the conference agreement, a cooperative organization electing to pass the expensing deduction through to its owners must make such an election on the tax return for the taxable year to which the deduction relates. Once made, the election is irrevocable. Moreover, the organization making the election must provide cooperative owners receiving an allocation of the deduction written notice of the amount of such allocation.

[Law at ¶ 5190, ¶ 5205, ¶ 5210 and ¶ 5245. CCH Explanation at ¶ 505.]

---

[55] For purposes of the provision, the term "refinery" refers to facilities the primary purpose of which is the processing of crude oil (whether or not previously refined) or qualified fuels (as defined in present law section 29(c), which is redesignated as section 45K(c) under section 1322(a)(1) of the Act). The limitation of present law section 29(d) (redesignated as section 45K(d) under the Act) requiring domestic production of qualified fuels is not applicable with respect to the definition of refinery under this provision; thus, otherwise qualifying refinery property will be eligible for the provision even if the primary purpose of the refinery is the processing of oil produced from shale and tar sands outside the United States. The term refinery would include a facility which processes coal via gas into liquid fuel.

[56] For purposes of the provision, the throughput of a refinery is measured on the basis of barrels per calendar day. Barrels per calendar day is the amount of fuels that a facility can process under usual operating conditions, expressed in terms of capacity during a 24-hour period and reduced to account for down time and other limitations.

[57] The limitation of present law section 29(d) (redesignated as section 45K(d) under section 1322(a)(1) of the Act) regarding domestic production is not applicable with respect to the definition of qualified fuels under this provision.

[58] The requirement to meet all applicable environmental laws applies specifically to the refinery or portion of a refinery placed in service after the date of enactment. A refinery's failure to meet applicable environmental laws with respect to a portion of the refinery which was in service prior to the effective date will not disqualify the taxpayer from making the election under the provision with respect to otherwise qualifying refinery property.

[¶ 10,130] Act Sec. 1324. Allow pass through to owners of deduction for capital costs incurred by small refiner cooperative in complying with Environmental Protection Agency sulfur regulations

Joint Committee on Taxation (J.C.T. Rep. No. JCX-44-05)

>>>→ *Caution: The Technical Explanation of the "Energy Policy Tax Incentives Act of 2005" (JCX-44-05), below, is included to assist the reader's understanding but may not be cited as the official Senate Committee Report to H.R. 6— CCH.*

[Code Sec. 179B]

Present Law

Expensing and credit for small refiners

Taxpayers generally may recover the costs of investments in refinery property through annual depreciation deductions. In addition, the Code permits small business refiners to immediately deduct as an expense up to 75 percent of the costs paid or incurred for the purpose of complying with the Highway Diesel Fuel Sulfur Control Requirements of the Environmental Protection Agency ("EPA"). Costs qualifying for the deduction are those costs paid or incurred with respect to any facility of a small business refiner during the period beginning on January 1, 2003 and ending on the earlier of the date that is one year after the date on which the taxpayer must comply with the applicable EPA regulations or December 31, 2009.

The Code also provides that a small business refiner may claim credit equal to five cents per gallon for each gallon of low sulfur diesel fuel produced during the taxable year that is in compliance with the Highway Diesel Fuel Sulfur Control Requirements. The total production credit claimed by the taxpayer is limited to 25 percent of the capital costs incurred to come into compliance with the EPA diesel fuel requirements. As with the deduction permitted under present law, costs qualifying for the credit are those costs paid or incurred with respect to any facility of a small business refiner during the period beginning on January 1, 2003 and ending on the earlier of the date that is one year after the date on which the taxpayer must comply with the applicable EPA regulations or December 31, 2009. The taxpayer's basis in property with respect to which the credit applies is reduced by the amount of production credit claimed.

For these purposes a small business refiner is a taxpayer who is within the business of refining petroleum products, employs not more than 1,500 employees directly in refining, and has less than 205,000 barrels per day (average) of total refinery capacity. The deduction is reduced, *pro rata*, for taxpayers with capacity in excess of 155,000 barrels per day.

In the case of a qualifying small business refiner that is owned by a cooperative, the cooperative is allowed to elect to pass any production credits to patrons of the organization. Present law does not permit cooperatives to pass through to members the deduction permitted for the costs paid or incurred for the purpose of complying with the Highway Diesel Fuel Sulfur Control Requirements.

Taxation of cooperatives and their patrons

For Federal income tax purposes, a cooperative generally computes its income as if it were a taxable corporation, with one exception-the cooperative may exclude from its taxable income distributions of patronage dividends. In general, patronage dividends are the profits of the cooperative that are rebated to its patrons pursuant to a pre-existing obligation of the cooperative to do so. The rebate must be made in some equitable fashion on the basis of the quantity or value of business done with the cooperative.

Except for tax-exempt farmers' cooperatives, cooperatives that are subject to the cooperative tax rules of subchapter T of the Code[28] are permitted a deduction for patronage dividends from their taxable income only to the extent of net income that is derived from transactions with patrons who are members of the cooperative.[29] The availability of such deductions from taxable income has the effect of allowing the cooperative to be treated like a conduit with respect to profits derived from transactions with patrons who are members of the cooperative.

Cooperatives that qualify as tax-exempt farmers' cooperatives are permitted to exclude patronage dividends from their taxable income to the extent of all net income, including net

---

[28] Sec. 1381, et seq.

[29] Sec. 1382.

income that is derived from transactions with patrons who are not members of the cooperative, provided the value of transactions with patrons who are not members of the cooperative does not exceed the value of transactions with patrons who are members of the cooperative.[30]

Description of Proposal

The proposal allows cooperatives to pass through to patrons the deduction permitted under section 179B for costs paid or incurred for the purpose of complying with the Highway Diesel Fuel Sulfur Control Requirements. To the extent the deduction is passed through to patrons, the cooperative is denied the deduction it would otherwise be entitled under section 179B or for depreciation deductions under sections 167 or 168 with respect to costs attributable to calculation of the patrons' allowable section 179B deduction.

Joint Committee on Taxation (J.C.T. Rep. No. JCX-60-05)

⇛→ *Caution: The Description and Technical Explanation of the Conference Agreement of H.R. 6, Title XIII, the "Energy Tax Incentives Act of 2005" (JCX-60-05), below, is included to assist the reader's understanding, but may not be cited as the official Conference Committee Report to H.R. 6—CCH.*

Effective Date

The provision is effective as if included in the amendments made by section 338(a) of the American Jobs Creation Act of 2004.[62]

House Bill

No provision.

Senate Amendment

The Senate amendment allows cooperatives to pass through to their owners the deduction permitted for costs paid or incurred for the purpose of complying with the Highway Diesel Fuel Sulfur Control Requirements. To the extent the deduction is passed through to owners, the cooperative is denied deductions it would otherwise be entitled with respect to costs attributable to complying with the Highway Diesel Fuel Sulfur Control Requirements.

Conference Agreement

The conference agreement follows the Senate amendment with modifications. The conference agreement clarifies the manner in which a cooperative organization may elect to pass through to cooperative owners the deduction for costs paid or incurred for the purpose of complying with the Highway Diesel Fuel Sulfur Control Requirements. Specifically, the election must be made on the tax return of the organization for the taxable year to which the deduction relates. Once made, the election is irrevocable. Moreover, the organization making such an election must provide cooperative owners receiving an allocation of the deduction written notice of the amount of such allocation. The written notice must be provided by the due date for the tax return on which the election is made.

[Law at ¶ 5185. CCH Explanation at ¶ 535.]

---

[30] Sec. 521.

[62] Pub. L. No. 108-357.

Act Sec. 1324   ¶10,130

[¶10,140] Act Sec. 1325. Natural gas distribution lines treated as fifteen-year property

House Committee Report (H.R. Rep. No. 109-45)

⇒ *Caution: Excerpts from H.R. Rep. No. 109-45, below, are included to assist the reader's understanding. H.R. Rep. No. 109-45 accompanies H.R. 1541, which was amended and reported favorably by the Committee on Ways and Means on April 18, 2005. H.R. 1541 contained the tax portions of the Energy Policy Bill of 2005, but was never voted on by the House as a standalone bill. Its provisions, however, were included in the larger energy bill (H.R. 6) that passed the House on April 21, 2005. The Committee did not issue a separate report on H.R. 6, but the provision described below is substantially similar to that contained in the Conference Report that accompanies H.R. 6.*

[Code Sec. 168]

Present Law

The applicable recovery period for assets placed in service under the Modified Accelerated Cost Recovery System is based on the "class life of the property." The class lives of assets placed in service after 1986 are generally set forth in Revenue Procedure 87-56.[3] Natural gas distribution pipelines are assigned a 20-year recovery period and a class life of 35 years.

Reasons for Change

The Committee recognizes the importance of modernizing our aging energy infrastructure to meet the demands of the twenty-first century, and the Committee also recognizes that both short-term and long-term solutions are required to meet this challenge. The Committee understands that investment in our energy infrastructure has not kept pace with the nation's needs. In light of this, the Committee believes it is appropriate to reduce the recovery period for investment in certain energy infrastructure property to encourage investment in such property.

Explanation of Provision

The provision establishes a statutory 15-year recovery period and a class life of 35 years for natural gas distribution lines.

The provision is effective for property placed in service after April 11, 2005.

Joint Committee on Taxation (J.C.T. Rep. No. JCX-60-05)

⇒ *Caution: The Description and Technical Explanation of the Conference Agreement of H.R. 6, Title XIII, the "Energy Tax Incentives Act of 2005" (JCX-60-05), below, is included to assist the reader's understanding, but may not be cited as the official Conference Committee Report to H.R. 6—CCH.*

Senate Amendment

The Senate amendment is the same as the House bill, except the Senate amendment requires that the original use of the property begin with the taxpayer and that the property be placed in service prior to January 1, 2008.

Conference Agreement

The conference agreement follows the House bill, with the following modifications. The conference agreement is effective for property, the original use of which begins with the taxpayer after April 11, 2005, which is placed in service after April 11, 2005 and before January 1, 2011. The provision does not apply to property subject to a binding contract on or before April 11, 2005.[5]

[Law at ¶5165. CCH Explanation at ¶515.]

---

[3] 1987-2 C.B. 674 (as clarified and modified by Rev. Proc. 88-22, 1988-1 C.B. 785).

[5] In the case of self-constructed property, the provision does not apply to property under construction on or before April 11, 2005.

[¶ 10,150] Act Sec. 1326. Natural gas gathering lines treated as seven-year property

House Committee Report (H.R. REP. NO. 109-45)

⇶→ *Caution: Excerpts from H.R. Rep. No. 109-45, below, are included to assist the reader's understanding. H.R. Rep. No. 109-45 accompanies H.R. 1541, which was amended and reported favorably by the Committee on Ways and Means on April 18, 2005. H.R. 1541 contained the tax portions of the Energy Policy Bill of 2005, but was never voted on by the House as a standalone bill. Its provisions, however, were included in the larger energy bill (H.R. 6) that passed the House on April 21, 2005. The Committee did not issue a separate report on H.R. 6, but the provision described below is substantially similar to that contained in the Conference Report that accompanies H.R. 6.*

[Code Sec. 168]

Present Law

The applicable recovery period for assets placed in service under the Modified Accelerated Cost Recovery System is based on the "class life of the property." The class lives of assets placed in service after 1986 are generally set forth in Revenue Procedure 87-56.[1] Revenue Procedure 87-56 includes two asset classes either of which could describe natural gas gathering lines owned by nonproducers of natural gas. Asset class 46.0, describing pipeline transportation, provides a class life of 22 years and a recovery period of 15 years. Asset class 13.2, describing assets used in the exploration for and production of petroleum and natural gas deposits, provides a class life of 14 years and a depreciation recovery period of seven years. The uncertainty regarding the appropriate recovery period of natural gas gathering lines has resulted in litigation between taxpayers and the IRS. In each of three recent cases, appellate courts have held that natural gas gathering lines owned by nonproducers fall within the scope of Asset class 13.2 (*i.e.*, seven-year recovery period).[2] The appellate court in each case reversed a lower court holding that natural gas gathering lines owned by nonproducers fall within the scope of Asset class 46.0 (*i.e.*, 15-year recovery period). The IRS has not yet indicated whether it acquiesces in the result in these three appellate decisions in cases arising in other circuits.

Reasons for Change

The Committee has noted the controversies between taxpayers and the IRS regarding the appropriate recovery period of natural gas gathering lines and believes it is important to provide clarity and certainty. The Committee notes that unprocessed gas in gathering lines is potentially more corrosive than interstate pipeline quality gas. The Committee concludes the appropriate recovery period for natural gas gathering lines is seven years. The Committee also believes a seven-year recovery period, and the certainty provided compared to present law, will foster investment in natural gas fields that will enhance the domestic supply of natural gas.

Explanation of Provision

The provision establishes a statutory seven-year recovery period and a class life of 14 years for natural gas gathering lines. In addition, no adjustment will be made to the allowable amount of depreciation with respect to this property for purposes of computing a taxpayer's alternative minimum taxable income. A natural gas gathering line is defined to include any pipe, equipment, and appurtenance that is (1) determined to be a gathering line by the Federal Energy Regulatory Commission, or (2) used to deliver natural gas from the wellhead or a common point to the point at which such gas first reaches (a) a gas processing plant, (b) an interconnection with an interstate transmission line, (c) an interconnection with an intrastate transmission line, or (d) a direct interconnection with a local distribution company, a gas storage facility, or an industrial consumer.

Effective Date

The provision is effective for property placed in service after April 11, 2005. No inference is intended as to the proper treatment of natural gas gathering lines placed in service on or before April 11, 2005.

---

[1] 1987-2 C.B. 674 (as clarified and modified by Rev. Proc. 88-22, 1988-1 C.B. 785).

[2] *Clajon Gas Co, L.P. v. Commissioner*, 354 F.3d 786 (8th Cir. 2004), *rev'g* 119 T.C. 197 (2002); *Saginaw Bay Pipeline Co. v. United States*, 338 F.3d 600 (6th Cir. 2003), *rev'g* 88 A.F.T.R.2d 2001-6019 (E.D. Mich. 2001); *Duke Energy v. Commissioner*, 172 F.3d 1255 (10th Cir. 1999), *rev'g* 109 T.C. 416 (1997).

House Floor Debate (151 CONG. REC. 105, H6953), July 28, 2005

⋙→ *Caution: [The following excerpt from the Congressional Record is included to assist the reader's understanding. The amendment discussed below on the floor of the Senate was renumbered in the final version of the bill.— CCH.]*

Mr. BARTON of Texas. Mr. Speaker, we thank the gentleman from Massachusetts (Mr. MARKEY) for using his chart once again.

Mr. Speaker, I yield 2 minutes to the gentleman from California (Mr. THOMAS), the distinguished chairman of the Ways and Means Committee.

Mr. THOMAS. Mr. Speaker,

* * *

I would also note, as a matter of clarification, section 1326 of the conference report, which provides for a 7-year depreciation peliod [sic] for natural gas gathering lines, is meant to prospectively clarify the depreciation of property meeting either of the two standards in subsection (b) of the section. This provision should not be interpreted as undermining any taxpayer's position versus the IRS in regard to current law, but instead as a clarification of the treatment of property meeting either of the standards described in subsection (b) after April 11, 2005.

* * *

Joint Committee on Taxation (J.C.T. REP. NO. JCX-60-05)

⋙→ *Caution: The Description and Technical Explanation of the Conference Agreement of H.R. 6, Title XIII, the "Energy Tax Incentives Act of 2005" (JCX-60-05), below, is included to assist the reader's understanding, but may not be cited as the official Conference Committee Report to H.R. 6—CCH.*

Senate Amendment

No provision.

Conference Agreement

The conference agreement follows the House bill, except that the provision requires that the original use of the property begin with the taxpayer. The provision does not apply to property with respect to which the taxpayer (or a related party) had a binding acquisition contract on or before April 11, 2005.

[Law at ¶ 5135 and ¶ 5165. CCH Explanation at ¶ 520.]

[¶ 10,160] Act Sec. 1327. Arbitrage rules not to apply to prepayments for natural gas

House Committee Report (H.R. REP. NO. 109-45)

⋙→ *Caution: Excerpts from H.R. Rep. No. 109-45, below, are included to assist the reader's understanding. H.R. Rep. No. 109-45 accompanies H.R. 1541, which was amended and reported favorably by the Committee on Ways and Means on April 18, 2005. H.R. 1541 contained the tax portions of the Energy Policy Bill of 2005, but was never voted on by the House as a standalone bill. Its provisions, however, were included in the larger energy bill (H.R. 6) that passed the House on April 21, 2005. The Committee did not issue a separate report on H.R. 6, but the provision described below is substantially similar to that contained in the Conference Report that accompanies H.R. 6.*

[Code Sec. 148]

Present Law

Arbitrage restrictions

Interest on bonds issued by States or local governments to finance activities carried out or paid for by those entities generally is exempt from income tax. Restrictions are imposed on the ability of States or local governments to invest the proceeds of these bonds for profit (the "arbitrage restrictions").[17] One such restriction limits the use of bond proceeds to acquire "investment-type property." The term investment-type property includes the acquisition of property in a

---

[17] Sec. 148.

transaction involving a prepayment if a principal purpose of the prepayment is to receive an investment return from the time the prepayment is made until the time payment otherwise would be made. A prepayment can produce prohibited arbitrage profits when the discount received for prepaying the costs exceeds the yield on the tax-exempt bonds. In general, prohibited prepayments include all prepayments that are not customary in an industry by both beneficiaries of tax-exempt bonds and other persons using taxable financing for the same transaction.

On August 4, 2003, the Treasury Department issued final regulations deeming to be customary, and not in violation of the arbitrage rules, certain prepayments for natural gas and electricity.[18] Generally, a qualified prepayment under the regulations requires that 90 percent of the natural gas or electricity purchased with the prepayment be used for a qualifying use. Generally, natural gas is used for a qualifying use if it is to be (1) furnished to retail gas customers of the issuing municipal utility who are located in the natural gas service area of the issuing municipal utility, however, gas used to produce electricity for sale is not included under this provision (2) used by the issuing municipal utility to produce electricity that will be furnished to retail electric service area customers of the issuing utility, (3) used by the issuing municipal utility to produce electricity that will be sold to a utility owned by a governmental person and furnished to the service area retail electric customers of the purchaser, (4) sold to a utility that is owned by a governmental person if the requirements of (1), (2) or (3) are satisfied by the purchasing utility (treating the purchaser as the issuing utility) or (5) used to fuel the pipeline transportation of the prepaid gas supply. Electricity is used for a qualifying use if it is to be (1) furnished to retail service area electric customers of the issuing municipal utility or (2) sold to a municipal utility and furnished to retail electric customers of the purchaser who are located in the electricity service area of the purchaser.

Private activity bond tests

State and local bonds may be classified as either governmental bonds or private activity bonds. Governmental bonds are bonds the proceeds of which are primarily used to finance governmental functions or the debt is repaid with governmental funds. Private activity bonds are bonds where the State or local government serves as a conduit providing financing to private businesses or individuals. A bond will be treated as a private activity bond if more than five percent of the proceeds of the bond issue, or, if less, more than $5,000,000 is used (directly or indirectly) to make or finance loans to persons other than governmental units (the "private loan financing test") or if it meets the requirements of a two-part private business test.[19]

The exclusion from income for State and local bonds does not apply to private activity bonds, unless the bonds are issued for certain purposes permitted by the Code. Section 141(d) of the Code provides that the term "private activity bond" includes any bond issued as part of an issue if the amount of the proceeds of the issue which are to be used (directly or indirectly) for the acquisition by a governmental unit of nongovernmental output property exceeds the lesser of five percent of such proceeds or $5 million. "Nongovernmental output property" generally means any property (or interest therein) which before such acquisition was used (or held for use) by a person other than a governmental unit in connection with an output facility (other than a facility for the furnishing of water). An exception applies to output property which is to be used in connection with an output facility 95 percent or more of the output of which will be consumed in (1) a qualified service area of the governmental unit acquiring the property, or (2) a qualified annexed area of such unit.

Reasons for Change

The Committee determined that it was appropriate to complement the Treasury regulations with a safe harbor that provides certainty on the date of issuance that prepayments for natural gas within the safe harbor will not violate the arbitrage rules. This provision will ensure adequate supplies of natural gas at predictable prices for natural gas utility customers without sacrificing to a great degree the appropriate present-law limitations regarding tax-exempt bond issuance for the purchase of investment property. The Committee believes that this proposal strikes an appropriate balance between these two competing policies. The creation of this safe harbor is not intended to limit the Secretary's regulatory authority to identify other situ-

---

[18] Treas. Reg. sec. 1.148-1(e)(2)(iii).

[19] Sec. 141(b) and (c). Under the private business test, a bond is a private activity bond if it is part of an issue in which: (1) more than 10 percent of the proceeds of the issue (including use of the bond-financed property) are to be used in the trade or business of any person other than a governmental unit ("private business use"); and (2) more than 10 percent of the payment of principal or interest on the issue is, directly or indirectly, (a) secured by property used or to be used for a private business use or (b) to be derived from payments in respect of property, or borrowed money, used or to be used for a private business use ("private payment test").

ations in which prepayments do not give rise to investment type property.

Explanation of Provision

In general

The provision creates a safe harbor exception to the general rule that tax-exempt bond-financed prepayments violate the arbitrage restrictions. The term "investment type property" does not include a prepayment under a qualified natural gas supply contract. The provision also provides that such prepayments are not treated as private loans for purposes of the private business tests.

Under the provision, a prepayment financed with tax-exempt bond proceeds for the purpose of obtaining a supply of natural gas for service area customers of a governmental utility is not treated as the acquisition of investment-type property. A contract is a qualified natural gas supply contract if the volume of natural gas secured for any year covered by the prepayment does not exceed the sum of (1) the average annual natural gas purchased (other than for resale) by customers of the utility within the service area of the utility ("retail natural gas consumption") during the testing period, and (2) the amount of natural gas that is needed to fuel transportation of the natural gas to the governmental utility. The testing period is the 5-calendar-year period immediately preceding the calendar year in which the bonds are issued. A retail customer is one who does not purchase natural gas for resale. Natural gas used to generate electricity by a utility owned by a governmental unit is counted as retail natural gas consumption if the electricity was sold to retail customers within the service area of the governmental electric utility.

Adjustments

The volume of gas permitted by the general rule is reduced by natural gas otherwise available on the date of issuance. Specifically, the amount of natural gas permitted to be acquired under a qualified natural gas supply contract for any period is to be reduced by the applicable share of natural gas held by the utility on the date of issuance of the bonds and natural gas that the utility has a right to acquire for the prepayment period (determined as of the date of issuance). For purposes of the preceding sentence, "applicable share" means, with respect to any period, the natural gas allocable to such period if the gas were allocated ratably over the period to which the prepayment relates.

For purposes of the safe harbor, if after the close of the testing period and before the issue date of the bonds (1) the government utility enters into a contract to supply natural gas (other than for resale) for a commercial person for use at a property within the service area of such utility and (2) the gas consumption for such property was not included in the testing period or the ratable amount of natural gas to be supplied under the contract is significantly greater than the ratable amount of gas supplied to such property during the testing period, then the amount of gas permitted to be purchased may be increased to accommodate the contract.

The calculation of average annual retail natural gas consumption for purposes of the safe harbor, however, is not to exceed the annual amount of natural gas reasonably expected to be purchased (other than for resale) by persons who are located within the service area of such utility and who, as of the date of issuance of the issue, are customers of such utility.

Intentional acts

The safe harbor does not apply if the utility engages in intentional acts to render (1) the volume of natural gas covered by the prepayment to be in excess of that needed for retail natural gas consumption, and (2) the amount of natural gas that is needed to fuel transportation of the natural gas to the governmental utility.

Definition of service area

Service area is defined as (1) any area throughout which the governmental utility provided (at all times during the testing period) in the case of a natural gas utility, natural gas transmission or distribution services, or in the case of an electric utility, electricity distribution services; (2) limited areas contiguous to such areas, and (3) any area recognized as the service area of the governmental utility under State or Federal law. Contiguous areas are limited to any area within a county contiguous to the area described in (1) in which retail customers of the utility are located if such area is not also served by another utility providing the same service.

Ruling request for higher prepayment amounts

Upon written request, the Secretary may allow an issuer to prepay for an amount of gas greater than that allowed by the safe harbor based on objective evidence of growth in gas consumption or population that demonstrates that the amount permitted by the exception is insufficient.

Nongovernmental output property restrictions

A qualified natural gas supply contract as defined in the provision is not nongovernmental output property for purposes of subsection (d) of section 141. Subsection (d) of section 141 does not apply to prepayment contracts for natural gas or electricity that either under the Treasury regulations or statutory safe harbor are not investment-type property for purposes of the arbitrage rules under section 148. No inference is intended regarding the application of subsection 141(d) to prepayment contracts not covered by the statutory safe harbor or Treasury regulations.

Application to joint action agencies

In a number of States, joint action agencies serve as purchasing agents for their member municipal gas utilities. The provision is intended to allow municipal utilities in a State to participate in such buying arrangements as established under State law, subject to the same limitations that would apply if an individual utility were to purchase gas directly. When acting on behalf of its municipal gas utility members, the total amount of gas that can be purchased by a joint action agency under the provision's exception to the arbitrage rules is the aggregate of what each such member could purchase for itself on a direct basis. Thus, with respect to qualified natural gas supply contracts entered into by joint action agencies for or on behalf of one or more member municipal utilities, the requirements of the safe harbor are tested at the individual municipal utility level based on the amount of gas that would be allocated to such member during any year covered by the contract.

Effective Date

The provision is effective for obligations issued after date of enactment.

Joint Committee on Taxation (J.C.T. REP. NO. JCX-60-05)

Senate Amendment

No provision.

Conference Agreement

The conference agreement follows the House bill.

[Law at ¶ 5140 and ¶ 5155. CCH Explanation at ¶ 530.]

[¶ 10,170] Act Sec. 1328. Determination of small refiner exception to oil depletion deduction

House Committee Report (H.R. REP. NO. 109-45)

⋙→ *Caution: Excerpts from H.R. Rep. No. 109-45, below, are included to assist the reader's understanding. H.R. Rep. No. 109-45 accompanies H.R. 1541, which was amended and reported favorably by the Committee on Ways and Means on April 18, 2005. H.R. 1541 contained the tax portions of the Energy Policy Bill of 2005, but was never voted on by the House as a standalone bill. Its provisions, however, were included in the larger energy bill (H.R. 6) that passed the House on April 21, 2005. The Committee did not issue a separate report on H.R. 6, but the provision described below is substantially similar to that contained in the Conference Report that accompanies H.R. 6.*

[Code Sec. 613A]

Present Law

Present law classifies oil and gas producers as independent producers or integrated companies. The Code provides special tax rules for operations by independent producers. One such rule allows independent producers to claim percentage depletion deductions rather than deducting the costs of their asset, a producing well, based on actual production from the well (i.e., cost depletion).

A producer is an independent producer only if its refining and retail operations are relatively small. For example, an independent producer may not have refining operations the runs from which exceed 50,000 barrels on any day in the taxable year during which independent producer status is claimed.[20] A refinery run is the volume of inputs of crude oil (excluding any product derived from oil) into the refining stream.[21]

---

[20] Sec. 613A(d)(4).

[21] Treas. Reg. sec. 1.613A-7(s).

Reasons for Change

The Committee notes that technological advances have permitted a number of small refineries to refine more petroleum without expanding their facilities. The Committee believes that the goal of present law, to identify producers without significant refining capacity, can be achieved while permitting more flexibility to refinery operations.

Explanation of Provision

The provision increases the current 50,000-barrel-per-day limitation to 75,000. In addition, the provision changes the refinery limitation on claiming independent producer status from a limit based on actual daily production to a limit based on average daily production for the taxable year. Accordingly, the average daily refinery runs for the taxable year may not exceed 75,000 barrels. For this purpose, the taxpayer calculates average daily refinery runs by dividing total refinery runs for the taxable year by the total number of days in the taxable year.

Effective Date

The provision is effective for taxable years ending after date of enactment.

Joint Committee on Taxation (J.C.T. Rep. No. JCX-60-05)

⇶→ *Caution: The Description and Technical Explanation of the Conference Agreement of H.R. 6, Title XIII, the "Energy Tax Incentives Act of 2005" (JCX-60-05), below, is included to assist the reader's understanding, but may not be cited as the official Conference Committee Report to H.R. 6—CCH.*

Conference Agreement

The conference agreement follows the House bill.

[Law at ¶ 5230. CCH Explanation at ¶ 510.]

[Code Sec. 613A]

Senate Amendment

No provision.

[¶ 10,180] Act Sec. 1329. Amortization of geological and geophysical expenditures

House Committee Report (H.R. Rep. No. 109-45)

⇶→ *Caution: Excerpts from H.R. Rep. No. 109-45, below, are included to assist the reader's understanding. H.R. Rep. No. 109-45 accompanies H.R. 1541, which was amended and reported favorably by the Committee on Ways and Means on April 18, 2005. H.R. 1541 contained the tax portions of the Energy Policy Bill of 2005, but was never voted on by the House as a standalone bill. Its provisions, however, were included in the larger energy bill (H.R. 6) that passed the House on April 21, 2005. The Committee did not issue a separate report on H.R. 6, but the provision described below is substantially similar to that contained in the Conference Report that accompanies H.R. 6.*

[Code Sec. 167]

Present Law

In general

Geological and geophysical expenditures ("G&G costs") are costs incurred by a taxpayer for the purpose of obtaining and accumulating data that will serve as the basis for the acquisition and retention of mineral properties by taxpayers exploring for minerals. A key issue with respect to the tax treatment of such expenditures is whether or not they are capital in nature. Capital expenditures are not currently deductible as ordinary and necessary business expenses, but are allocated to the cost of the property.[27]

Courts have held that G&G costs are capital, and therefore are allocable to the cost of the property[28] acquired or retained.[29] The costs attributable to such exploration are allocable to the cost of the property acquired or retained. As described further below, IRS administrative rulings have provided further guidance regarding the definition and proper tax treatment of G&G costs.

Revenue Ruling 77-188

In Revenue Ruling 77-188[30] (hereinafter referred to as the "1977 ruling"), the IRS provided guidance regarding the proper tax treatment of G&G costs. The ruling describes a typical geological and geophysical exploration program as containing the following elements:

• It is customary in the search for mineral producing properties for a taxpayer to conduct an exploration program in one or more identifiable project areas. Each project area encompasses a territory that the taxpayer determines can be explored advantageously in a single integrated operation. This determination is made after analyzing certain variables such as (1) the size and topography of the project area to be explored, (2) the existing information available with respect to the project area and nearby areas, and (3) the quantity of equipment, the number of personnel, and the amount of money available to conduct a reasonable exploration program over the project area.

• The taxpayer selects a specific project area from which geological and geophysical data are desired and conducts a reconnaissance-type survey utilizing various geological and geophysical exploration techniques. These techniques are designed to yield data that will afford a basis for identifying specific geological features with sufficient mineral potential to merit further exploration.

• Each separable, noncontiguous portion of the original project area in which such a specific geological feature is identified is a separate "area of interest." The original project area is subdivided into as many small projects as there are areas of interest located and identified within the original project area. If the circumstances permit a detailed exploratory survey to be conducted without an initial reconnaissance-type survey, the project area and the area of interest will be coextensive.

• The taxpayer seeks to further define the geological features identified by the prior reconnaissance-type surveys by additional, more detailed, exploratory surveys conducted with respect to each area of interest. For this purpose, the taxpayer engages in more intensive geological and geophysical exploration employing methods that are designed to yield sufficiently accurate sub-surface data to afford a basis for a decision to acquire or retain properties within or adjacent to a particular area of interest or to abandon the entire area of interest as unworthy of development by mine or well.

The 1977 ruling provides that if, on the basis of data obtained from the preliminary geological and geophysical exploration operations, only one area of interest is located and identified within the original project area, then the entire expenditure for those exploratory operations is to be allocated to that one area of interest and thus capitalized into the depletable basis of that area of interest. On the other hand, if two or more areas of interest are located and identified within the original project area, the entire expenditure for the exploratory operations is to be allocated equally among the various areas of interest.

If no areas of interest are located and identified by the taxpayer within the original project area, then the 1977 ruling states that the entire amount of the G&G costs related to the exploration is deductible as a loss under section 165. The loss is claimed in the taxable year in which that particular project area is abandoned as a potential source of mineral production.

---

[27] Under section 263, capital expenditures are defined generally as any amount paid for new buildings or for permanent improvements or betterments made to increase the value of any property or estate. Treasury regulations define capital expenditures to include amounts paid or incurred (1) to add to the value, or substantially prolong the useful life, of property owned by the taxpayer or (2) to adapt property to a new or different use. Treas. Reg. sec. 1.263(a)-1(b).

[28] "Property" means an interest in a property as defined in section 614 of the Code, and includes an economic interest in a tract or parcel of land notwithstanding that a mineral deposit has not been established or proved at the time the costs are incurred.

[29] See, e.g., Schermerhorn Oil Corporation v. Commissioner, 46 B.T.A. 151 (1942). By contrast, section 617 of the Code permits a taxpayer to elect to deduct certain expenditures incurred for the purpose of ascertaining the existence, location, extent, or quality of any deposit of ore or other mineral (but not oil and gas). These deductions are subject to recapture if the mine with respect to which the expenditures were incurred reaches the producing stage.

[30] 1977-1 C.B. 76.

A taxpayer may acquire or retain a property within or adjacent to an area of interest, based on data obtained from a detailed survey that does not relate exclusively to any discrete property within a particular area of interest. Generally, under the 1977 ruling, the taxpayer allocates the entire amount of G&G costs to the acquired or retained property as a capital cost under section 263(a). If more than one property is acquired, it is proper to determine the amount of the G&G costs allocable to each such property by allocating the entire amount of the costs among the properties on the basis of comparative acreage.

If, however, no property is acquired or retained within or adjacent to that area of interest, the entire amount of the G&G costs allocable to the area of interest is deductible as a loss under section 165 for the taxable year in which such area of interest is abandoned as a potential source of mineral production.

In 1983, the IRS issued Revenue Ruling 83-105,[31] which elaborates on the positions set forth in the 1977 ruling by setting forth seven factual situations and applying the principles of the 1977 ruling to those situations. In addition, Revenue Ruling 83-105 explains what constitutes "abandonment as a potential source of mineral production."

Reasons for Change

The Committee believes that substantial simplification for taxpayers, significant gains in taxpayer compliance, and reductions in administrative cost can be obtained by establishing a clear rule that all geological and geophysical costs may be amortized over two years, including the basis of abandoned property.

The Committee recognizes that, on average, a two-year amortization period accelerates recovery of geological and geophysical expenses. The Committee believes that more rapid recovery of such expenses will foster increased exploration for new sources of supply.

Explanation of Provision

The provision allows geological and geophysical amounts incurred in connection with oil and gas exploration in the United States to be amortized over two years. In the case of abandoned property, remaining basis may no longer be recovered in the year of abandonment of a property as all basis is recovered over the two-year amortization period.

Effective Date

The provision is effective for geological and geophysical costs paid or incurred in taxable years beginning after the date of enactment. No inference is intended from the prospective effective date of this provision as to the proper treatment of pre-effective date geological and geophysical costs.

Joint Committee on Taxation (J.C.T. Rep. No. JCX-60-05)

⇛→ *Caution: The Description and Technical Explanation of the Conference Agreement of H.R. 6, Title XIII, the "Energy Tax Incentives Act of 2005" (JCX-60-05), below, is included to assist the reader's understanding, but may not be cited as the official Conference Committee Report to H.R. 6—CCH.*

Senate Amendment

No provision.

Conference Agreement

The conference agreement follows the House bill.

[**Law at ¶5160 and ¶5205. CCH Explanation at ¶525.**]

---

[31] 1983-2 C.B. 51.

[¶ 10,190] Act Sec. 1331. Energy efficient commercial buildings deduction

Joint Committee on Taxation (J.C.T. REP. NO. JCX-44-05)

⟫→ *Caution: The Technical Explanation of the "Energy Policy Tax Incentives Act of 2005" (JCX-44-05), below, is included to assist the reader's understanding but may not be cited as the official Senate Committee Report to H.R. 6— CCH.*

[New Code Sec. 179D]

Present Law

No special deduction is currently provided for expenses incurred for energy-efficient commercial building property.

Description of Proposal

In general

The proposal provides a deduction equal to energy-efficient commercial building property expenditures made by the taxpayer. Energy-efficient commercial building property expenditures is defined as property: (1) which is installed on or in any building located in the United States, (2) which is installed as part of (i) the interior lighting systems, (ii) the heating, cooling, ventilation, and hot water systems, or (iii) the building envelope, and (3) which is certified as being installed as part of a plan designed to reduce the total annual energy and power costs with respect to the interior lighting systems, heating, cooling, ventilation, and hot water systems of the building by 50 percent or more in comparison to a reference building which meets the minimum requirements of Standard 90.1-2001 of the American Society of Heating, Refrigerating, and Air Conditioning Engineers and the Illuminating Engineering Society of North America ("ASHRAE/IESNA"). The deduction is limited to an amount equal to $2.25 per square foot of the property for which such expenditures are made. The deduction is allowed in the year in which the property is placed in service.

Eligible buildings may include any residential rental property, including any low-rise multifamily structure or single family housing property which is not within the scope of Standard 90.1-2001.

Certain certification requirements must be met in order to qualify for the deduction. The Secretary, in consultation with the Secretary of Energy, will promulgate regulations that describe methods of calculating and verifying energy and power costs using qualified computer software based on the provisions of the 2005 California Nonresidential Alternative Calculation Method Approval Manual or, in the case of residential property, the 2005 California Residential Alternative Calculation Method Approval Manual. The methods for calculation shall be fuel neutral, such that the same energy efficiency features shall qualify a building for the deduction under this subsection regardless of whether the heating source is a gas or oil furnace or boiler or an electric heat pump. The calculation methods shall provide appropriate calculated energy savings for design methods and technologies not otherwise credited in either Standard 90.1-2001 or in the 2005 California Nonresidential Alternative Calculation Method Approval Manual, including the following: (i) Natural ventilation, (ii) Evaporative cooling, (iii) Automatic lighting controls such as occupancy sensors, photocells, and timeclocks, (iv) Daylighting, (v) Designs utilizing semi-conditioned spaces which maintain adequate comfort conditions without air conditioning or without heating, (vi) Improved fan system efficiency, including reductions in static pressure, (vii) Advanced unloading mechanisms for mechanical cooling, such as multiple or variable speed compressors, (viii) The calculation methods may take into account the extent of commissioning in the building, and allow the taxpayer to take into account measured performance which exceeds typical performance, (ix) On-site generation of electricity, including combined heat and power systems, fuel cells, and renewable energy generation such as solar energy, and (x) Wiring with lower energy losses than wiring satisfying Standard 90.1-2001 requirements for building power distribution systems.

The Secretary shall prescribe procedures for the inspection and testing for compliance of buildings that are comparable, given the difference between commercial and residential buildings, to the requirements in the Mortgage Industry National Accreditation Procedures for Home Energy Rating Systems. Individuals qualified to determine compliance shall only be those recognized by one or more organizations certified by the Secretary for such purposes.

For energy-efficient commercial building property expenditures made by a public entity, such as public schools, the Secretary shall promulgate regulations that allow the deduction to be allocated to the person primarily responsible for designing the property in lieu of the public entity.

Partial allowance of deduction

In the case of a building that does not meet the overall building requirement of a 50-percent energy savings, a partial deduction is allowed with respect to each separate building system that comprises energy efficient property and which is certified by a qualified professional as meeting or exceeding the applicable system-specific savings targets established by the Secretary of the Treasury. The applicable system-specific savings targets to be established by the Secretary are those that would result in a total annual energy savings with respect to the whole building of 50 percent, if each of the separate systems met the system specific target. The separate building systems are (1) the interior lighting system, (2) the heating, cooling, ventilation and hot water systems, and (3) the building envelope. The maximum allowable deduction is $0.75 per square foot for each separate system.

In the case of system-specific partial deductions, in general no deduction is allowed until the Secretary establishes system-specific targets. However, in the case of lighting system retrofits, until such time as the Secretary issues final regulations, the system-specific energy savings target for the lighting system is deemed to be met by a reduction in Lighting Power Density of 40 percent (50 percent in the case of a warehouse) of the minimum requirements in Table 9.3.1.1 or Table 9.3.1.2 of ASHRAE/IESNA Standard 90.1-2001. Also, in the case of a lighting system that reduces lighting power density by 25 percent, a partial deduction of 37.5 cents per square foot is allowed. A pro-rated partial deduction is allowed in the case of a lighting system that reduces lighting power density between 25 percent and 40 percent. Certain lighting level and lighting control requirements must also be met in order to qualify for the partial lighting deductions.

Joint Committee on Taxation (J.C.T. REP. NO. JCX-60-05)

⮞⮞⮞ *Caution: The Description and Technical Explanation of the Conference Agreement of H.R. 6, Title XIII, the "Energy Tax Incentives Act of 2005" (JCX-60-05), below, is included to assist the reader's understanding, but may not be cited as the official Conference Committee Report to H.R. 6—CCH.*

House Bill

No provision.

Conference Agreement

The conference agreement follows the Senate amendment with modifications. The conference agreement provides that the deduction amount is reduced to $1.80 per square foot, and that the partial deduction for building subsystems is reduced to $0.60 per square foot. The conference agreement also modifies the effective date.

Effective Date

The provision is effective for property placed in service after December 31, 2005 and prior to January 1, 2008.

[**Law at** ¶ 5195, ¶ 5205, ¶ 5210, ¶ 5240, ¶ 5245 and ¶ 5250. CCH Explanation at ¶ 215.]

[¶ 10,200] Act Sec. 1332. Energy efficient new homes

Joint Committee on Taxation (J.C.T. REP. NO. JCX-44-05)

⮞⮞⮞ *Caution: The Technical Explanation of the "Energy Policy Tax Incentives Act of 2005" (JCX-44-05), below, is included to assist the reader's understanding but may not be cited as the official Senate Committee Report to H.R. 6—CCH.*

[New Code Sec. 45L]

Present Law

A nonrefundable, 10-percent business energy credit is allowed for the cost of new property that is equipment (1) that uses solar energy to generate electricity, to heat or cool a structure, or to provide solar process heat, or (2) used to produce, distribute, or use energy derived from a geothermal deposit, but only, in the case of electricity generated by geothermal power, up to the electric transmission stage.

The business energy tax credits are components of the general business credit (sec. 38(b)(1)). The business energy tax credits, when combined with all other components of the general business credit, generally may not exceed for any taxable year the excess of the taxpayer's net income tax over the greater of (1) 25 percent of net regular tax liability above $25,000 or (2) the tentative minimum tax. For credits arising in taxable years beginning after December 31, 1997, an unused general business credit generally may be carried back one year and carried forward 20 years (sec. 39).

¶ 10,200 Act Sec. 1332

A taxpayer may exclude from income the value of any subsidy provided by a public utility for the purchase or installation of an energy conservation measure. An energy conservation measure means any installation or modification primarily designed to reduce consumption of electricity or natural gas or to improve the management of energy demand with respect to a dwelling unit (sec. 136).

There is no present-law credit for the construction of new energy-efficient homes.

Description of Proposal

The proposal provides a credit to an eligible contractor * * * The credit cannot exceed $1,000 ($2,000) in the case of a new home that has a projected level of annual heating and cooling costs that is 30 percent (50 percent) less than a comparable dwelling constructed in accordance with the standards of chapter 4 of the 2003 International Energy Conservation Code as in effect (including supplements) on the date of enactment, and any applicable Federal minimum efficiency standards for equipment. With respect to homes that meet the 30-percent standard, 1/3 of such 30 percent savings must come from the building envelope, and with respect to homes that meet the 50-percent standard, 1/5 of such 50 percent savings must come from the building envelope.

The eligible contractor is the person who constructed the home, or in the case of a manufactured home, the producer of such home. * * *

To qualify as an energy-efficient new home, the home must be: (1) a dwelling located in the United States, (2) substantially completed after the date of enactment, and (3) certified in accordance with guidance prescribed by the Secretary to have a projected level of annual heating and cooling energy consumption that meets the standards for either the 30-percent or 50-percent reduction in energy usage.

Manufactured homes certified by a method prescribed by the Administrator of the Environmental Protection Agency under the Energy Star Labeled Homes program are eligible for the $1,000 credit provided criteria (1) and (2) are met.

The credit is part of the general business credit. No credits attributable to energy efficient homes can be carried back to any taxable year ending on or before the effective date of the credit. No deduction is allowed for that portion of expenses for a qualifying new home otherwise allowable as a deduction for the taxable year which is equal to the amount of the credit for such taxable year. If a credit is allowed for any expenditure, the basis of such property is reduced by the amount of the credit.

Joint Committee on Taxation (J.C.T. Rep. No. JCX-60-05)

⇶→ *Caution: The Description and Technical Explanation of the Conference Agreement of H.R. 6, Title XIII, the "Energy Tax Incentives Act of 2005" (JCX-60-05), below, is included to assist the reader's understanding, but may not be cited as the official Conference Committee Report to H.R. 6—CCH.*

Senate Amendment

* * *

The credit equals $1,000 in the case of a new home that meets the 30 percent standard and $2,000 in the case of a new home that meets the 50 percent standard.

* * * The Committee intends that the building envelope component means insulation materials or system specifically and primarily designed to reduce heat loss or gain, exterior windows (including skylights), doors, and any duct sealing and infiltration reduction measures.

Manufactured homes that conform to federal manufactured home construction and safety standards are eligible for the credit provided all the criteria for the credit are met. * * *

House Bill

No provision.

Conference Agreement

The conference agreement follows the Senate amendment with modifications. The conference agreement provides that the credit related to homes meeting the 30-percent efficiency standard applies only to manufactured homes. The conference agreement also modifies the effective date.

Effective Date

The credit applies to homes whose construction is substantially completed after December 31, 2005, and which are purchased after December 31, 2005 and prior to January 1, 2008.

[Law at ¶ 5040, ¶ 5085, ¶ 5200 and ¶ 5240. CCH Explanation at ¶ 220.]

Act Sec. 1332   ¶10,200

[¶10,210] Act Sec. 1333. Credit for certain nonbusiness energy property

Joint Committee on Taxation (J.C.T. REP. NO. JCX-60-05)

>>>→ *Caution: The Description and Technical Explanation of the Conference Agreement of H.R. 6, Title XIII, the "Energy Tax Incentives Act of 2005" (JCX-60-05), below, is included to assist the reader's understanding, but may not be cited as the official Conference Committee Report to H.R. 6—CCH.*

[New Code Sec. 25C]

Present Law

A taxpayer may exclude from income the value of any subsidy provided by a public utility for the purchase or installation of an energy conservation measure. An energy conservation measure means any installation or modification primarily designed to reduce consumption of electricity or natural gas or to improve the management of energy demand with respect to a dwelling unit (sec. 136).

There is no present law credit for energy efficiency improvements to existing homes.

House Bill

The provision provides a 20-percent credit for the purchase of qualified energy efficiency improvements to existing homes. The maximum credit for a taxpayer with respect to the same dwelling for all taxable years is $2,000. A qualified energy efficiency improvement is any energy efficiency building envelope component that meets or exceeds the prescriptive criteria for such a component established by the 2000 International Energy Conservation Code as supplemented and as in effect on the date of enactment (or, in the case of metal roofs with appropriate pigmented coatings, meets the Energy Star program requirements), and (1) that is installed in or on a dwelling located in the United States; (2) owned and used by the taxpayer as the taxpayer's principal residence; (3) the original use of which commences with the taxpayer; and (4) such component reasonably can be expected to remain in use for at least five years. The credit is nonrefundable.[86]

Building envelope components are: (1) insulation materials or systems which are specifically and primarily designed to reduce the heat loss or gain for a dwelling; (2) exterior windows (including skylights) and doors; and (3) metal roofs with appropriate pigmented coatings which are specifically and primarily designed to reduce the heat loss or gain for a dwelling.

The taxpayer's basis in the property is reduced by the amount of the credit. Special rules apply in the case of condominiums and tenant-stockholders in cooperative housing corporations.

In the case of expenditures that exceed $1,000, certain certification requirements must be met in order to qualify for the credit.

Senate Amendment

The provision provides a personal tax credit equal to the greater of (1) the total of the allowable credits for the purchase of certain property, or (2) the credit with respect to a highly energy-efficient principal residence.

The allowable credit for the purchase of certain property is (1) $50 for each advanced main air circulating fan, (2) $150 for each qualified natural gas, propane, or oil furnace or hot water boiler, and (3) $300 for each item of qualified energy efficient property.

An advanced main air circulating fan is a fan used in a natural gas, propane, or oil furnace originally placed in service by the taxpayer during the taxable year, and which has an annual electricity use of no more than two percent of the total annual energy use of the furnace (as determined in the standard Department of Energy test procedures).

A qualified natural gas, propane, or oil furnace or hot water boiler is a natural gas, propane, or oil furnace or hot water boiler with an annual fuel utilization efficiency rate of at least 95.

Qualified energy-efficient property is: (1) an electric heat pump water heater which yields an energy factor of at least 2.0 in the standard Department of Energy test procedure, (2) an electric heat pump which has a heating seasonal performance factor (HSPF) of at least 9, a seasonal energy efficiency ratio (SEER) of at least 15, and an energy efficiency ratio (EER) of at least 13, (3) a geothermal heat pump which (i) in the case of a closed loop product, has an energy efficiency ratio (EER) of at least 14.1 and a heating coefficient of performance (COP) of at least 3.3, (ii) in the case of an open loop product, has an energy

---

[86] Sec. 1321 of the House bill allows the credit to offset both the regular tax and the alternative minimum tax.

efficiency ratio (EER) of at least 16.2 and a heating coefficient of performance (COP) of at least 3.6, and (iii) in the case of a direct expansion (DX) product, has an energy efficiency ratio (EER) of at least 15 and a heating coefficient of performance (COP) of at least 3.5, (4) a central air conditioner which has a seasonal energy efficiency ratio (SEER) of at least 15 and an energy efficiency ratio (EER) of at least 13, and (5) a natural gas, propane, or oil water heater which has an energy factor of at least 0.80.

The credit with respect to a highly energy-efficient principal residence is $2,000 if the principal residence achieves a 50 percent reduction in energy costs relative to the original condition of the building. In the case of a new home, the original condition of the building is deemed to be a home constructed in accordance with the standards of chapter 4 of the 2003 International Energy Conservation Code as in effect (including supplements) on the date of enactment, and for which and any applicable Federal minimum efficiency standards for equipment are met. In the case of a principal residence that achieves a reduction in energy costs between 20 and 50 percent, the allowable credit is $4,000 times the percentage reduction. No credit is allowed in the case of energy cost savings of less than 20 percent.

The residence must be located in the United States, and, in the case of a new residence, not be acquired from a contractor eligible for a credit for the production of a new energy efficient home under Code section 45K (as added by the bill).

If a credit is allowed under Code section 25D (as added by the bill) relating to residential solar, photovoltaic and fuel cell property, for the purpose of measuring energy efficiency improvements under this provision, the original condition of the home, or the comparable building in the case of a new home, is determined assuming the building contains the property for which the credit is allowed. Additionally, if a credit is allowed under this provision for any expenditure, the increase in the basis of the property that would result from such expenditure is reduced by the amount of the credit.

In order to be eligible for the credit, the residence's energy savings must be demonstrated by performance-based compliance and be certified according to regulations established by the Secretary that follow various rules and procedures, including the use of computer software based on the 2005 California Residential Alternative Calculation Method Approval Manual. The determination of compliance may be provided by a local building regulatory authority, a utility, a manufactured home production inspection primary inspection agency (IPIA), or an accredited home energy rating system provider. All providers shall be accredited, or otherwise authorized to use approved energy performance measurement methods, by the Residential Energy Services Network (RESNET).

Special proration rules apply in the case of jointly owned property, condominiums, and tenant-stockholders in cooperative housing corporations. Certain restrictions and limitations apply with respect to property financed by subsidized energy financing or obtained through grant programs. If less than 80 percent of the property is used for nonbusiness purposes, only that portion of expenditures that is used for nonbusiness purposes is taken into account. If a credit is allowed under this provision with respect to any property, the basis of such property is reduced by the amount of the credit so allowed.

Conference Agreement

The conference agreement follows the House bill and the Senate amendment with modifications. The conference agreement follows the House bill with respect to energy efficient improvements to the building envelope, but the credit rate is reduced to 10 percent. The conference agreement includes the Senate amendment provisions related to (1) advanced main air circulating fans, (2) natural gas, propane, or oil furnace or hot water boilers and (3) qualified energy-efficient property, The conference agreement does not include the Senate amendment provision related to highly energy-efficient principal residences. The credit allowed under the conference agreement may not exceed $500 in total across all taxable years, and no more than $200 dollars of such credit may be attributable to expenditures on windows. There is no requirement for certification of expenditures.

The conference agreement modifies the energy efficiency requirements for qualifying central air conditioners to be the highest efficiency tier established by the Consortium for Energy Efficiency as in effect on Jan. 1, 2006.

The conference agreement also modifies the effective date.

Effective Date

The credit applies to property placed in service after December 31, 2005 and prior to January 1, 2008.

[Law at ¶ 5015 and ¶ 5240. CCH Explanation at ¶ 205.]

[¶ 10,220] Act Sec. 1334. Energy efficient appliances

Joint Committee on Taxation (J.C.T. REP. NO. JCX-44-05)

⟫⟶ *Caution: The Technical Explanation of the "Energy Policy Tax Incentives Act of 2005" (JCX-44-05), below, is included to assist the reader's understanding but may not be cited as the official Senate Committee Report to H.R. 6—CCH.*

[New Code Sec. 45M]

Present Law

A nonrefundable, 10-percent business energy credit is allowed for the cost of new property that is equipment: (1) that uses solar energy to generate electricity, to heat or cool a structure, or to provide solar process heat; or (2) used to produce, distribute, or use energy derived from a geothermal deposit, but only, in the case of electricity generated by geothermal power, up to the electric transmission stage.

The business energy tax credits are components of the general business credit (sec. 38(b)(1)). The business energy tax credits, when combined with all other components of the general business credit, generally may not exceed for any taxable year the excess of the taxpayer's net income tax over the greater of: (1) 25 percent of net regular tax liability above $25,000 or (2) the tentative minimum tax. For credits arising in taxable years beginning after December 31, 1997, an unused general business credit generally may be carried back one year and carried forward 20 years (sec. 39).

A taxpayer may exclude from income the value of any subsidy provided by a public utility for the purchase or installation of an energy conservation measure. An energy conservation measure means any installation or modification primarily designed to reduce consumption of electricity or natural gas or to improve the management of energy demand with respect to a dwelling unit (sec. 136).

There is no present-law credit for the manufacture of energy-efficient appliances.

Description of Proposal

The proposal provides a credit for the eligible production of certain energy-efficient dishwashers, clothes washers and refrigerators.

The credit for dishwashers applies to dishwashers produced in 2006 and 2007 that meet the Energy Star standards for 2007. The credit amount equals $3 multiplied by the percentage by which the efficiency of the 2007 standards (not yet known) exceeds that of the 2005 standards. The credit may not exceed $100 per dishwasher.

The credit for clothes washers equals (1) $50 for clothes washers manufactured in 2005 that have a modified energy factor (MEF) of at least 1.42, (2) $100 for clothes washers manufactured in 2005-2007 that meet the requirements of the Energy Star program which are in effect for clothes washers in 2007, or (3) the minimum of (i) $200 or (ii) $10 multiplied by the average of the energy and water savings percentages of the 2010 Energy Star standards relative to the 2007 Energy Star standards, for clothes washers manufactured in 2008-2010 that meet the requirements of the Energy Star program which are in effect for clothes washers in 2010.

The credit for refrigerators is based on energy savings and year of manufacture. The energy savings are determined relative to the energy conservation standards promulgated by the Department of Energy that took effect on July 1, 2001. Refrigerators that achieve a 15 to 20 percent energy saving and that are manufactured in 2005 or 2006 receive a $75 credit. Refrigerators that achieve a 20 to 25 percent energy saving receive a (i) $125 credit if manufactured in 2005-2007, or (ii) $100 credit if manufactured in 2008. Refrigerators that achieve at least a 25 percent energy saving receive a (i) $175 credit if manufactured in 2005-2007, or (ii) $150 credit if manufactured in 2008-2010.

Appliances eligible for the credit include only those that exceed the average amount of production from the 3 prior calendar years for each category of appliance. In the case of refrigerators, eligible production is production that exceeds 110 percent of the average amount of production from the three prior calendar years. Proration rules apply in the case of credits for 2005 production.

A dishwasher is any a residential dishwasher subject to the energy conservation standards established by the Department of Energy. A refrigerator must be an automatic defrost refrigerator-freezer with an internal volume of at least 16.5 cubic feet to qualify for the credit. A clothes washer is any residential clothes washer, including a residential style coin operated washer that satisfies the relevant efficiency standard.

The taxpayer may not claim credits in excess of $75 million for all taxable years, and may not claim credits in excess of $20 million with respect to clothes washers eligible for the $50 credit and refrigerators eligible for the $75 credit. A taxpayer may elect to increase the $20 million limitation described above to $25 million provided that the aggregate amount of credits with respect to such appliances, plus refrigerators eligible for the $100 and $125 credits, is limited to $50 million for all taxable years.

Additionally, the credit allowed for all appliances may not exceed two percent of the average annual gross receipts of the taxpayer for the three taxable years preceding the taxable year in which the credit is determined.

The credit is part of the general business credit.

Joint Committee on Taxation (J.C.T. REP. NO. JCX-60-05)

⇛→ *Caution: The Description and Technical Explanation of the Conference Agreement of H.R. 6, Title XIII, the "Energy Tax Incentives Act of 2005" (JCX-60-05), below, is included to assist the reader's understanding, but may not be cited as the official Conference Committee Report to H.R. 6—CCH.*

House Bill

No provision.

Conference Agreement

The conference agreement follows the Senate amendment, but only with respect to the provisions that cover production after December 31, 2005 and prior to January 1, 2008.

Effective Date

The credit applies to appliances produced after December 31, 2005 and prior to January 1, 2008.

[Law at ¶ 5040 and ¶ 5090. CCH Explanation at ¶ 225.]

[¶ 10,230] Act Sec. 1335. Credit for residential energy efficient property

Joint Committee on Taxation (J.C.T. REP. NO. JCX-60-05)

⇛→ *Caution: The Description and Technical Explanation of the Conference Agreement of H.R. 6, Title XIII, the "Energy Tax Incentives Act of 2005" (JCX-60-05), below, is included to assist the reader's understanding, but may not be cited as the official Conference Committee Report to H.R. 6—CCH.*

[New Code Sec. 25D]

Present Law

A taxpayer may exclude from income the value of any subsidy provided by a public utility for the purchase or installation of an energy conservation measure. An energy conservation measure means any installation or modification primarily designed to reduce consumption of electricity or natural gas or to improve the management of energy demand with respect to a dwelling unit (sec. 136).

There is no present-law credit for residential solar hot water, photovoltaic, or fuel cell property.

House Bill

The provision provides a personal tax credit for the purchase of qualified photovoltaic property and qualified solar water heating property that is used exclusively for purposes other than heating swimming pools and hot tubs. The credit is equal to 15 percent of qualified investment up to a maximum credit of $2,000 for solar water heating property and $2,000 for rooftop photovoltaic property. The provision also provides a 15-percent personal tax credit for the purchase of qualified fuel cell power plants. The credit may not exceed $500 for each 0.5 kilowatt of capacity. The credit is nonrefundable.[64] The taxpayer's ba-

---

[64] Sec. 1321 of the House bill allows the credit to offset both the regular tax and the alternative minimum tax.

sis in the property is reduced by the amount of the credit.

Qualifying solar water heating property is property that heats water for use in a dwelling unit if at least half of the energy used by such property for such purpose is derived from the sun. Qualified photovoltaic property is property that uses solar energy to generate electricity for use in a dwelling unit. A qualified fuel cell power plant is an integrated system comprised of a fuel cell stack assembly and associated balance of plant components that converts a fuel into electricity using electrochemical means, and which has an electricity-only generation efficiency of greater than 30 percent.

To qualify for the credit, the property must be installed on or in connection with a dwelling unit located in the United States and used as a residence by the taxpayer. If less than 80 percent of the use of an item is for nonbusiness purposes, only that portion of the expenditures for such item which is properly allocable to use for nonbusines purposes shall be taken into account. Certain equipment safety requirements need to be met to qualify for the credit. Special proration rules apply in the case of jointly owned property, condominiums, and tenant-stockholders in cooperative housing corporations.

Senate Amendment

The provision provides a personal tax credit for the purchase of qualified photovoltaic property and qualified solar water heating property that is used exclusively for purposes other than heating swimming pools and hot tubs. The credit is equal to 30 percent of qualifying expenditures, with a maximum credit for each of these systems of property of $2,000. The provision also provides a 30 percent credit for the purchase of qualified fuel cell power plants. The credit for any fuel cell may not exceed $500 for each 0.5 kilowatt of capacity.

Qualifying solar water heating property means an expenditure for property to heat water for use in a dwelling unit located in the United States and used as a residence if at least half of the energy used by such property for such purpose is derived from the sun. Qualified photovoltaic property is property that uses solar energy to generate electricity for use in a dwelling unit. A qualified fuel cell power plant is an integrated system comprised of a fuel cell stack assembly and associated balance of plant components that (1) converts a fuel into electricity using electrochemical means, (2) has an electricity-only generation efficiency of greater than 30 percent, and (3) generates at least 0.5 kilowatts of electricity. The qualified fuel cell power plant must be installed on or in connection with a dwelling unit located in the United States and used by the taxpayer as a principal residence.

The credit is nonrefundable, and the depreciable basis of the property is reduced by the amount of the credit. Expenditures for labor costs allocable to onsite preparation, assembly, or original installation of property eligible for the credit are eligible expenditures.

Certain equipment safety requirements need to be met to qualify for the credit. Special proration rules apply in the case of jointly owned property, condominiums, and tenant-stockholders in cooperative housing corporations. If less than 80 percent of the property is used for nonbusiness purposes, only that portion of expenditures that is used for nonbusiness purposes is taken into account.

Conference Agreement

The conference agreement follows the Senate amendment, but only for property placed in service prior to January 1, 2008.

Effective Date

The credit applies to property placed in service after December 31, 2005 and prior to January 1, 2008.

[Law at ¶5005, ¶5010, ¶5020, ¶5240 and ¶5260. CCH Explanation at ¶210.]

[¶10,240] Act Sec. 1336. Credit for business installation of qualified fuel cells and stationary microturbine power plants

Joint Committee on Taxation (J.C.T. Rep. No. JCX-44-05)

⇢ *Caution: The Technical Explanation of the "Energy Policy Tax Incentives Act of 2005" (JCX-44-05), below, is included to assist the reader's understanding but may not be cited as the official Senate Committee Report to H.R. 6— CCH.*

[Code Sec. 48]

Present Law

A nonrefundable, 10-percent business energy credit is allowed for the cost of new property that is equipment (1) that uses solar energy to generate electricity, to heat or cool a structure, or to provide solar process heat, or (2) used to produce, distribute, or use energy derived from a geothermal deposit, but only, in the case of electricity generated by geothermal power, up to the electric transmission stage.

The business energy tax credits are components of the general business credit (sec. 38(b)(1)). The business energy tax credits, when combined with all other components of the general business credit, generally may not exceed for any taxable year the excess of the taxpayer's net income tax over the greater of (1) 25 percent of net regular tax liability above $25,000 or (2) the tentative minimum tax. For credits arising in taxable years beginning after December 31, 1997, an unused general business credit generally may be carried back one year and carried forward 20 years (sec. 39).

There is no present-law credit for fuel cell or microturbine power plant property.

Description of Proposal

The proposal provides a 30 percent business energy credit for the purchase of qualified fuel cell power plants for businesses. A qualified fuel cell power plant is an integrated system comprised of a fuel cell stack assembly and associated balance of plant components that converts a fuel into electricity using electrochemical means, and which has an electricity-only generation efficiency of greater than 30 percent and generates at least 0.5 kilowatts of electricity. The credit for any fuel cell may not exceed $500 for each 0.5 kilowatts of capacity.

Additionally, the proposal provides a 10 percent credit for the purchase of qualifying stationary microturbine power plants. A qualified stationary microturbine power plant is an integrated system comprised of a gas turbine engine, a combustor, a recuperator or regenerator, a generator or alternator, and associated balance of plant components which converts a fuel into electricity and thermal energy. Such system also includes all secondary components located between the existing infrastructure for fuel delivery and the existing infrastructure for power distribution, including equipment and controls for meeting relevant power standards, such as voltage, frequency and power factors. Such system must have an electricity-only generation efficiency of not less that 26 percent at International Standard Organization conditions and a capacity of less than 2,000 kilowatts. The credit is limited to the lesser of 10 percent of the basis of the property or $200 for each kilowatt of capacity.

The credit is nonrefundable. The taxpayer's basis in the property is reduced by the amount of the credit claimed.

Joint Committee on Taxation (J.C.T. REP. NO. JCX-60-05)

➢➢➢ *Caution: The Description and Technical Explanation of the Conference Agreement of H.R. 6, Title XIII, the "Energy Tax Incentives Act of 2005" (JCX-60-05), below, is included to assist the reader's understanding, but may not be cited as the official Conference Committee Report to H.R. 6—CCH.*

Conference Agreement

The conference agreement follows the Senate amendment, but only for periods before January 1, 2008.

Effective Date

The credit applies to periods after December 31, 2005 and before January 1, 2008, for property placed in service in taxable years ending after December 31, 2005, under rules similar to rules of section 48(m) of the Internal Revenue Code of 1986 (as in effect on the day before the date of enactment of the Revenue Reconciliation Act of 1990).

[Law at ¶ 5100. CCH Explanation at ¶ 240.]

[¶ 10,250] Act Sec. 1337. Business solar investment tax credit

Joint Committee on Taxation (J.C.T. REP. NO. JCX-44-05)

➢➢➢ *Caution: The Technical Explanation of the "Energy Policy Tax Incentives Act of 2005" (JCX-44-05), below, is included to assist the reader's understanding but may not be cited as the official Senate Committee Report to H.R. 6— CCH.*

[Code Sec. 48]

Present Law

A nonrefundable, 10-percent business energy credit is allowed for the cost of new property that is equipment (1) that uses solar energy to generate electricity, to heat or cool a structure, or to provide solar process heat, or (2) used to produce, distribute, or use energy derived from a geothermal deposit, but only, in the case of electricity generated by geothermal power, up to the electric transmission stage.

The business energy tax credits are components of the general business credit (sec. 38(b)(1)). The business energy tax credits, when combined with all other components of the general business credit, generally may not exceed for any taxable year the excess of the taxpayer's net income tax over the greater of (1) 25 percent of net regular tax liability above $25,000 or (2) the tentative minimum tax. For credits arising in taxable years beginning after December 31, 1997, an unused general business credit generally may be carried back one year and carried forward 20 years (sec. 39).

Description of Proposal

The proposal increases the 10-percent credit to 30 percent in the case of solar energy property placed in service after December 31, 2005 and before January 1, 2010.

Joint Committee on Taxation (J.C.T. Rep. No. JCX-60-05)

⟫→ *Caution: The Description and Technical Explanation of the Conference Agreement of H.R. 6, Title XIII, the "Energy Tax Incentives Act of 2005" (JCX-60-05), below, is included to assist the reader's understanding, but may not be cited as the official Conference Committee Report to H.R. 6—CCH.*

House Bill

No provision.

Conference Agreement

The conference agreement follows the Senate amendment, but only for periods before January 1, 2008 with respect to the 30 percent credit and the fiber-optic distributed sunlight. The conference agreement makes permanent the provision that provides that property used to generate energy for the purposes of heating a swimming pool is not eligible solar energy property.

Effective Date

The provision with respect to the heating of swimming pools applies to periods after December 31, 2005. The increase in the credit rate and the provision related to fiber-optic distributed sunlight applies to periods after December 31, 2005 and before January 1, 2008 for property placed in service in taxable years ending after December 31, 2005, under rules similar to rules of section 48(m) of the Internal Revenue Code of 1986 (as in effect on the day before the date of enactment of the Revenue Reconciliation Act of 1990).

[Law at ¶ 5100. CCH Explanation at ¶ 230.]

[¶ 10,260] Act Secs. 1341 and 1348. Alternative technology vehicle credits

Joint Committee on Taxation (J.C.T. Rep. No. JCX-44-05)

⟫→ *Caution: The Technical Explanation of the "Energy Policy Tax Incentives Act of 2005" (JCX-44-05), below, is included to assist the reader's understanding but may not be cited as the official Senate Committee Report to H.R. 6—CCH.*

[Code Sec. 179A and New Code Sec. 30B]

Present Law

Certain costs of qualified clean-fuel vehicle may be expensed and deducted when such property is placed in service (sec. 179A). Qualified clean-fuel vehicle property includes motor vehicles that use certain clean-burning fuels (natural gas, liquefied natural gas, liquefied petroleum gas, hydrogen, electricity and any other fuel at least 85 percent of which is methanol, ethanol, any other alcohol or ether).[32] The maximum amount of the deduction is $50,000 for a truck or van with a gross vehicle weight over 26,000 pounds or a bus with seating capacities of at least 20 adults; $5,000 in the case of a truck or van with a gross vehicle weight between 10,000 and 26,000 pounds; and $2,000 in the case of any other motor vehicle. Qualified electric vehicles do not qualify for the clean-fuel vehicle deduction. The deduction is reduced to 25 percent of the otherwise allowable deduction in 2006 and is

---

[32] A hybrid-electric vehicle may qualify as a clean-fuel vehicle under present law.

unavailable for purchases after December 31, 2006.

Description of Proposal

Alternative motor vehicle credits

The proposal provides a credit for the purchase of a new qualified fuel cell motor vehicle, a new qualified hybrid motor vehicle, and a new qualified alternative fuel motor vehicle. In general the proposal provides that the buyer claims the credit, unless the buyer is a tax-exempt entity in which case the seller or lessor of the vehicle may claim the credit. The taxpayer may carry forward unused credits for 20 years or carry unused credits back for three years (but not to any taxable year beginning before the date of enactment). Qualified vehicles fuel cell motor vehicles are vehicles placed in service before 2015. Qualified hybrid motor vehicles are vehicles placed in service before 2010. Qualified alternative fuel motor vehicles are vehicles placed in service before 2011. Any deduction otherwise allowable under sec. 179A is reduced by the amount of credit allowable.

Fuel cell vehicles

A qualifying fuel cell vehicle is a motor vehicle that is propelled by power derived from one or more cells which convert chemical energy directly into electricity by combining oxygen with hydrogen fuel which is stored on board the vehicle and may or may not require reformation prior to use. The amount of credit for the purchase of a fuel cell vehicle is determined by a base credit amount that depends upon the weight class of the vehicle and, in the case of automobiles or light trucks, an additional credit amount that depends upon the rated fuel economy of the vehicle compared to a base fuel economy. For these purposes the base fuel economy is the 2002 model year city fuel economy rating for vehicles of various weight classes (see below). Table 2, below, shows the proposed base credit amounts.

Table 2.-Base Credit Amount for Fuel Cell Vehicles

Vehicle Gross Weight Rating in Pounds	Credit Amount
Vehicle ≤ 8,500	$8,000
8,500 < vehicle ≤ 14,000	$10,000
14,000 < vehicle ≤ 26,000	$20,000
26,000 < vehicle	$40,000

In the case of a fuel cell vehicle weighing less than 8,500 pounds and placed in service after December 31, 2009, the $8,000 amount in Table 2, above is reduced to $4,000.

Table 3, below, shows the proposed additional credits for passenger automobiles or light trucks.

Table 3.-Credit for Qualifying Fuel Cell Vehicles

Credit	If Fuel Economy of the Fuel Cell Vehicle Is:	
	At least	but less than
$1,000	150% of base fuel economy	175% of base fuel economy
$1,500	175% of base fuel economy	200% of base fuel economy
$2,000	200% of base fuel economy	225% of base fuel economy
$2,500	225% of base fuel economy	250% of base fuel economy
$3,000	250% of base fuel economy	275% of base fuel economy
$3,500	275% of base fuel economy	300% of base fuel economy
$4,000	300% of base fuel economy	

Hybrid motor vehicles

A qualifying hybrid vehicle is a motor vehicle that draws propulsion energy from onboard sources of stored energy which include both an internal combustion engine or heat engine using combustible fuel and a rechargeable energy storage system (e.g., batteries). A qualifying hybrid motor vehicle must be placed in service before January 1, 2010.

In the case of an automobile or light truck (vehicles weighing 8,500 pounds or less), the amount of credit for the purchase of a hybrid vehicle is the sum of two components: a fuel economy credit amount that varies with the rated fuel economy of the vehicle compared to a 2002 model year standard and a conservation credit based on the estimated lifetime fuel savings of a qualifying vehicle compared to a comparable 2002 model year vehicle. A qualifying hybrid automobile or light truck must have a maximum available power from the rechargeable energy storage system of at least five percent. In addition, the vehicle must meet or exceed certain EPA emissions standards. For a vehicle with a gross vehicle weight rating of 6,000 pounds or less the applicable emissions standards are the Bin 5 Tier II emissions standards. For a vehicle with a gross vehicle weight

Act Sec. 1341   ¶10,260

rating greater than 6,000 pounds and less than or equal to 8,500 pounds, the applicable emissions standards are the Bin 8 Tier II emissions standards.

Table 4, below, shows the fuel economy credit available to a hybrid passenger automobile or light truck whose fuel economy (on a gasoline gallon equivalent basis) exceeds that of a base fuel economy.

Table 4.-Fuel Economy Credit

Credit	If Fuel Economy of the Fuel Cell Vehicle Is:	
	At least	but less than
$400	125% of base fuel economy	150% of base fuel economy
$800	150% of base fuel economy	175% of base fuel economy
$1,200	175% of base fuel economy	200% of base fuel economy
$1,600	200% of base fuel economy	225% of base fuel economy
$2,000	225% of base fuel economy	250% of base fuel economy
$2,400	250% of base fuel economy	

In the case of a qualifying hybrid motor vehicle weighing more than 8,500 pounds, the amount of credit is determined by the estimated increase in fuel economy and the incremental cost of the hybrid vehicle compared to a comparable vehicle powered solely by a gasoline or diesel internal combustion engine and that is comparable in weight, size, and use of the vehicle. For a vehicle that achieves a fuel economy increase of at least 30 percent but less than 40 percent, the credit is equal to 20 percent of the incremental cost of the hybrid vehicle. For a vehicle that achieves a fuel economy increase of at least 40 percent but less than 50 percent, the credit is equal to 30 percent of the incremental cost of the hybrid vehicle. For a vehicle that achieves a fuel economy increase of 50 percent or more, the credit is equal to 40 percent of the incremental cost of the hybrid vehicle.

The credit is subject to certain maximum applicable incremental cost amounts. For a qualifying hybrid motor vehicle weighing more than 8,500 pounds but not more than 14,000 pounds, the maximum allowable incremental cost amount is $7,500. For a qualifying hybrid motor vehicle weighing more than 14,000 pounds but not more than 26,000 pounds, the maximum allowable incremental cost amount is $15,000. For a qualifying hybrid motor vehicle weighing more than 26,000 pounds, the maximum allowable incremental cost amount is $30,000.

A qualifying hybrid motor vehicle weighing more than 8,500 pounds but not more than 14,000 pounds must have a maximum available power from the rechargeable energy storage system of at least 10 percent. A qualifying hybrid vehicle weighing more than 14,000 pounds must have a maximum available power from the rechargeable energy storage system of at least 15 percent.

Alternative fuel vehicle

The credit for the purchase of a new alternative fuel vehicle would be 50 percent of the incremental cost of such vehicle, plus an additional 30 percent if the vehicle meets certain emissions standards, but not more than between $4,000 and $32,000 depending upon the weight of the vehicle. Table 5, below, shows the maximum permitted incremental cost for the purpose of calculating the credit for alternative fuel vehicles by vehicle weight class.

Table 5.-Maximum Allowable Incremental Cost for Calculation of Alternative Fuel Vehicle Credit

Vehicle Gross Weight Rating in Pounds	Maximum Allowable Incremental Cost
Vehicle ≤ 8,500	$5,000
8,500 < vehicle ≤ 14,000	$10,000
14,000 < vehicle ≤ 26,000	$25,000
26,000 < vehicle	$40,000

Alternative fuels comprise compressed natural gas, liquefied natural gas, liquefied petroleum gas, hydrogen, and any liquid fuel that is at least 85 percent methanol. Qualifying alternative fuel motor vehicles are vehicles that operate only on qualifying alternative fuels and are incapable of operating on gasoline or diesel (except in the extent gasoline or diesel fuel is part of a qualified mixed fuel, described below).

Certain mixed fuel vehicles, that is vehicles that use a combination of an alternative fuel and a petroleum-based fuel, are eligible for a reduced credit. If the vehicle operates on a mixed fuel that is at least 75 percent alternative fuel, the vehicle is eligible for 70 percent of the otherwise allowable alternative fuel vehicle credit. If the vehicle operates on a mixed fuel that is at least 90 percent alternative fuel, the vehicle is eligible for 90 percent of the otherwise allowable alternative fuel vehicle credit.

Base fuel economy

The base fuel economy is the 2002 model year city fuel economy for vehicles by inertia weight class by vehicle type. The "vehicle inertia weight class" is that defined in regulations prescribed by the Environmental Protection Agency for purposes of Title II of the Clean Air Act. Table 6, below, shows the 2002 model year city fuel economy for vehicles by type and by inertia weight class.

Table 6.-2002 Model Year City Fuel Economy

Vehicle Inertia Weight Class Pounds	Passenger Automobile (miles per gallon)	Light Truck (miles per gallon)
1,500	45.2	39.4
1,750	45.2	39.4
2,000	39.6	35.2
2,250	35.2	31.8
2,500	31.7	29.0
2,750	28.8	26.8
3,000	26.4	24.9
3,500	22.6	21.8
4,000	19.8	19.4
4,500	17.6	17.6
5,000	15.9	16.1
5,500	14.4	14.8
6,000	13.2	13.7
6,500	12.2	12.8
7,000	11.3	12.1
8,500	11.3	12.1

Joint Committee on Taxation (J.C.T. REP. NO. JCX-60-05)

⇛ *Caution: The Description and Technical Explanation of the Conference Agreement of H.R. 6, Title XIII, the "Energy Tax Incentives Act of 2005" (JCX-60-05), below, is included to assist the reader's understanding, but may not be cited as the official Conference Committee Report to H.R. 6—CCH.*

House Bill

The House bill provides a credit for each new qualified advanced lean-burn technology motor vehicle placed in service by the taxpayer during the taxable year. The amount of the credit for any vehicle is the sum of an amount for fuel efficiency and an amount for conservation. The amount for fuel efficiency is based on a comparison of the fuel efficiency of the vehicle compared to the Environmental Protection Agency's 2000 model year city fuel economy for a vehicle in the same inertia weight class. The amount for conservation is based on the qualifying vehicle's estimated lifetime fuel savings compared to the same 2000 model year standard.

Table 2, below, shows the credit amount for fuel efficiency of a qualified advanced lean-burn technology motor vehicle.

Table 2.—Fuel Efficiency Credit Amount for Qualified Advanced Lean-Burn Technology Motor Vehicles

Credit Amount	If Fuel Economy of the Vehicle Is:	
	at least	but less than
$500	125% of base fuel economy	150% of base fuel economy
$1,000	150% of base fuel economy	175% of base fuel economy
$1,500	175% of base fuel economy	200% of base fuel economy
$2,000	200% of base fuel economy	225% of base fuel economy
$2,500	225% of base fuel economy	250% of base fuel economy
$3,000	250% of base fuel economy	

The credit amount for conservation of a qualified advanced lean burn technology vehicle is computed as follows. The vehicle is assumed to be driven 120,000 miles over its life. The 120,000 miles of lifetime mileage is divided by the fuel economy rating of the vehicle. The 120,000 miles of lifetime mileage also is divided by the 2000 model year city economy for a vehicle in the same inertia weight class. The difference is the lifetime fuel savings. If the vehicle achieves a lifetime motor fuel savings between 1,500 and 2,500 gallons of fuel, the credit amount for the vehicle is $250. If the vehicle achieves a lifetime fuel savings of at least 2,500 gallons of motor fuel, the credit amount is $500.

The base fuel economy is the 2000 model year city fuel economy for vehicles by inertia weight class by vehicle type. The "vehicle inertia weight class" is that defined in regulations prescribed by the Environmental Protection Agency for purposes of Title II of the Clean Air Act. A qualifying advanced lean-burn technology motor vehicle means a motor vehicle the original use of which commences with the taxpayer, powered by an internal combustion engine that is designed to operate primarily using more air than is necessary for complete combustion of the fuel and incorporates direct injection, that uses only diesel fuel (as defined in section 4083(a)(3)), has sufficient fuel economy to qualify for the credit, and meets the Environmental Protection Agency's Tier II bin 8 emissions standards. In addition, in order to qualify for a credit, a vehicle must be in compliance with the applicable provisions of the Clean Air Act and the motor vehicle safety provisions.

In general, the credit is allowed to the vehicle owner, including the lessor of a vehicle subject to a lease. If the use of the vehicle is described in paragraph (3) or (4) of section 50(b) (relating to use by tax-exempts, governments, and foreign persons) and is not subject to a lease, the seller of the vehicle may claim the credit so long the seller clearly discloses to the user in a document the amount that is allowable as a credit. A vehicle must be used predominantly in the United States to qualify for the credit.

The provision permits the credit to offset both the regular tax and the alternative minimum tax. Credits in excess of this limitation may be carried forward for up to 20 years; credits may not be carried back to earlier years.

Conference Agreement

The conference agreement follows both the House bill and the Senate amendment with modifications.

Fuel cell vehicles

The conference agreement follows the Senate amendment with respect to fuel cell vehicles.

Alternate fuel vehicles

The conference agreement follows the Senate amendment with respect to alternate fuel vehicles.

Hybrid vehicles and advanced lean-burn technology vehicles

Qualifying hybrid vehicle

A qualifying hybrid vehicle is a motor vehicle that draws propulsion energy from onboard sources of stored energy which include both an internal combustion engine or heat engine using combustible fuel and a rechargeable energy storage system (e.g., batteries). A qualifying hybrid motor vehicle must be placed in service before January 1, 2011 (January 1, 2010 in the case of a hybrid motor vehicle weighing more than 8,500 pounds).

Hybrid vehicles that are automobiles and light trucks

In the case of an automobile or light truck (vehicles weighing 8,500 pounds or less), the amount of credit for the purchase of a hybrid vehicle is the sum of two components: a fuel economy credit amount that varies with the rated fuel economy of the vehicle compared to a 2002 model year standard and a conservation credit based on the estimated lifetime fuel savings of a qualifying vehicle compared to a comparable 2002 model year vehicle. A qualifying hybrid automobile or light truck must have a maximum available power from the rechargeable energy storage system of at least four percent. In addition, the vehicle must meet or exceed certain EPA emissions standards. For a vehicle with a gross vehicle weight rating of 6,000 pounds or less the applicable emissions standards are the Bin 5 Tier II emissions standards. For a vehicle with a gross vehicle weight rating greater than 6,000 pounds and less than or equal to 8,500 pounds, the applicable emissions standards are the Bin 8 Tier II emissions standards.

Table 8, below, shows the fuel economy credit available to a hybrid passenger automobile or light truck whose fuel economy (on a gasoline gallon equivalent basis) exceeds that of a base fuel economy.

Table 8.—Fuel Economy Credit

Credit	If Fuel Economy of the Hybrid Vehicle Is:	
	at least	but less than
$400	125% of base fuel economy	150% of base fuel economy
$800	150% of base fuel economy	175% of base fuel economy
$1,200	175% of base fuel economy	200% of base fuel economy
$1,600	200% of base fuel economy	225% of base fuel economy
$2,000	225% of base fuel economy	250% of base fuel economy
$2,400	250% of base fuel economy	

Table 9, below, shows the conservation credit.

Table 9.—Conservation Credit

Estimated Lifetime Fuel Savings	Conservation Amount
At least 1,200 but less than 1,800 . .	$250
At least 1,800 but less than 2,400 . .	$500
At least 2,400 but less than 3,000 . .	$750
At least 3,000	$1,000

Advanced lean-burn technology motor vehicles

The conference agreement a credit for the purchase of a new advanced lean burn technology motor vehicle. The amount of credit for the purchase of an advanced lean burn technology motor vehicle is the sum of two components: a fuel economy credit amount that varies with the rated fuel economy of the vehicle compared to a 2002 model year standard as described in Table 8, above and a conservation credit based on the estimated lifetime fuel savings of a qualifying vehicle compared to a comparable 2002 model year vehicle as described in Table 9 above.

A qualifying advanced lean burn technology motor vehicle that incorporates direct injection, achieves at least 125 percent of the 2002 model year city fuel economy, and 2004 and later model vehicles meets or exceeds certain Environmental Protection Agency emissions standards. For a vehicle with a gross vehicle weight rating of 6,000 pounds or less the applicable emissions standards are the Bin 5 Tier II emissions standards. For a vehicle with a gross vehicle weight rating greater than 6,000 pounds and less than or equal to 8,500 pounds, the applicable emissions standards are the Bin 8 Tier II emissions standards. A qualifying advanced lean burn technology motor vehicle must be placed in service before January 1, 2011.

Limitation on number of qualified hybrid and advanced lean-burn technology motor vehicles eligible for the credit

The conference agreement imposes a limitation on the number of qualified hybrid motor vehicles and advanced lean-burn technology motor vehicles sold by each manufacturer of such vehicles that are eligible for the credit. Taxpayers may claim the full amount of the allowable credit up to the end of the first calendar quarter after the quarter in which the manufacturer records its sale of the 60,000th hybrid and advanced lean-burn technology motor vehicle. Taxpayers may claim one half of the otherwise allowable credit during the two calendar quarters subsequent to the first quarter after the manufacturer has recorded its 60,000th such sale. In the third and fourth calendar quarters subsequent to the first quarter after the manufacturer has recorded its 60,000th such sale, the taxpayer may claim one quarter of the otherwise allowable credit.

Thus, summing the sales of qualifying hybrid motor vehicles of all weight classes and all sales of qualifying advanced lean-burn technology motor vehicles, if a manufacturer records the sale of its 60,000th in February of 2007, taxpayers purchasing such vehicles from the manufacturer may claim the full amount of the credit on their purchases of qualifying vehicles through June 30, 2007. For the period July 1, 2007, through December 31, 2007, taxpayers may claim one half of the otherwise allowable credit on purchases of qualifying vehicles of the manufacturer. For the period January 1, 2008, through June 30, 2008, taxpayers may claim one quarter of the otherwise allowable credit on the purchases of qualifying vehicles of the manufacturer. After June 30, 2008, no credit may be claimed for purchases of hybrid motor vehicles or advanced lean-burn technology motor vehicles sold by the manufacturer.

Hybrid vehicles that are medium and heavy trucks

In the case of a qualifying hybrid motor vehicle weighing more than 8,500 pounds, the conference agreement follows the Senate amendment.

Act Sec. 1341 ¶10,260

Other rules

The portion of the credit attributable to vehicles of a character subject to an allowance for depreciation is treated as a portion of the general business credit; the remainder of the credit is allowable to the extent of the excess of the regular tax (reduced by certain other credits) over the alternative minimum tax for the taxable year.

Termination of Code section 179A

The conference agreement provides that section 179A sunsets after December 31, 2005.

Effective Date

The provision applies to vehicles placed in service after December 31, 2005, in the case of qualified fuel cell motor vehicles, before January 1, 2015; in the case of qualified hybrid motor vehicles that are automobiles and light trucks and in the case of advanced lean-burn technology vehicles, before January 1, 2011; in the case of qualified hybrid motor vehicles that medium and heavy trucks, before January 1, 2010; and in the case of qualified alternative fuel motor vehicles, before January 1, 2011.

[Law at ¶5030, ¶5040, ¶5130, ¶5180, ¶5240 and ¶5440. CCH Explanation at ¶305, ¶310, ¶315, ¶320, ¶325 and ¶330.]

[¶10,270] Act Sec. 1342. Credit for installation of alternative fuel refueling property

Joint Committee on Taxation (J.C.T. REP. NO. JCX-44-05)

⟫→ *Caution: The Technical Explanation of the "Energy Policy Tax Incentives Act of 2005" (JCX-44-05), below, is included to assist the reader's understanding but may not be cited as the official Senate Committee Report to H.R. 6—CCH.*

[New Code Sec. 30C]

Present Law

Clean-fuel vehicle refueling property may be expensed and deducted when such property is placed in service (sec. 179A). Clean-fuel vehicle refueling property comprises property for the storage or dispensing of a clean-burning fuel, if the storage or dispensing is the point at which the fuel is delivered into the fuel tank of a motor vehicle. Clean-fuel vehicle refueling property also includes property for the recharging of electric vehicles, but only if the property is located at a point where the electric vehicle is recharged. Up to $100,000 of such property at each location owned by the taxpayer may be expensed with respect to that location. The deduction is unavailable for costs incurred after December 31, 2006.

For the purpose of sec. 179A clean fuels comprise natural gas, liquefied natural gas, liquefied petroleum gas, hydrogen, electricity, and any other fuel at least 85 percent of which is methanol, ethanol, or any other alcohol or ether.

Description of Proposal

The proposal permits taxpayers to claim a 50-percent credit for the cost of installing clean-fuel vehicle refueling property to be used in a trade or business of the taxpayer or installed at the principal residence of the taxpayer. In the case of retail clean-fuel vehicle refueling property the allowable credit may not exceed $30,000. In the case of residential clean-fuel vehicle refueling property the allowable credit may not exceed $1,000.

Under the proposal clean fuels are any fuel at least 85 percent of the volume of which consists of ethanol, natural gas, compressed natural gas, liquefied natural gas, liquefied petroleum gas, and hydrogen.

The taxpayer's basis in the property is reduced by the amount of the credit and the taxpayer may not claim deductions under section 179A with respect to property for which the credit is claimed. In the case of refueling property installed on property owned or used by a tax-exempt person, the taxpayer that installs the property may claim the credit. To be eligible for the credit, the property must be placed in service before January 1, 2010. The credit allowable for any taxable year cannot exceed the amount by which the taxpayer's regular tax (reduced by certain other credits) exceeds the taxpayer's tentative minimum tax. The taxpayer may carry forward unused credits for 20 years.

In the case of hydrogen fuel refueling property, to be eligible for the credit, the property must be placed in service before January 1, 2015.

Joint Committee on Taxation (J.C.T. Rep. No. JCX-60-05)

>>>→ *Caution: The Description and Technical Explanation of the Conference Agreement of H.R. 6, Title XIII, the "Energy Tax Incentives Act of 2005" (JCX-60-05), below, is included to assist the reader's understanding, but may not be cited as the official Conference Committee Report to H.R. 6—CCH.*

House Bill

No provision.

Conference Agreement

The conference agreement follows the Senate amendment with modifications. The conference agreement provides that the credit rate is 30 percent rather than 50 percent.

The portion of the credit attributable to property of a character subject to an allowance for depreciation is treated as a portion of the general business credit; the remainder of the credit is allowable to the extent of the excess of the regular tax (reduced by certain other credits) over the alternative minimum tax for the taxable year.

The conference agreement provides that the credit may not be claimed for property placed in service after December 31, 2007.

Effective Date

The provision is effective for property placed in service December 31, 2005 and before January 1, 2008.

[Law at ¶5035, ¶5040, ¶5130, ¶5240 and ¶5440. CCH Explanation at ¶730.]

[¶10,280] Act Sec. 1343. Diesel-water fuel emulsion

House Committee Report (H.R. Rep. No. 109-45)

>>>→ *Caution: Excerpts from H.R. Rep. No. 109-45, below, are included to assist the reader's understanding. H.R. Rep. No. 109-45 accompanies H.R. 1541, which was amended and reported favorably by the Committee on Ways and Means on April 18, 2005. H.R. 1541 contained the tax portions of the Energy Policy Bill of 2005, but was never voted on by the House as a standalone bill. Its provisions, however, were included in the larger energy bill (H.R. 6) that passed the House on April 21, 2005. The Committee did not issue a separate report on H.R. 6, but the provision described below is substantially similar to that contained in the Conference Report that accompanies H.R. 6.*

[Code Secs. 4081 and 6427]

Present Law

A 24.3-cents-per-gallon excise tax is imposed on diesel fuel to finance the Highway Trust Fund.[24] Gasoline and most special motor fuels are subject to tax at 18.3 cents per gallon for the Trust Fund.[25]

The tax rate for certain special motor fuels is determined, on an energy equivalent basis, as follows:[26]

Liquefied petroleum gas (propane)	13.6 cents per gallon
Liquefied natural gas	11.9 cents per gallon
Methanol derived from natural gas	9.15 cents per gallon
Compressed natural gas	48.54 cents per MCF

No special tax rate is provided for diesel fuel blended with water to form a diesel-water fuel emulsion.

Reasons for Change

Because diesel-water emulsion fuels have fewer British thermal units ("Btu") per gallon, larger quantities must be purchased to travel the same number of miles as regular diesel fuel. A Btu-based tax rate better correlates highway use and tax paid. The Committee further understands that the diesel-water emulsion fuel may reduce emissions of air pollutants relative to regular diesel fuel and believes that the Btu-based rate, by removing a tax disadvantage to use of the fuel, will be beneficial to the environment.

Explanation of Provision

A special tax rate of 19.7 cents per gallon is provided for diesel fuel blended with water into a diesel-water fuel emulsion to reflect the reduced Btu content per gallon resulting from the water. Emulsion fuels eligible for the special rate

---

[24] Sec. 4081(a)(2)(A)(iii).
[25] Secs. 4081(a)(2)(A)(i) and 4041(a)(2)(B)(i).
[26] See sec. 4041(a)(2)(B)(ii) and (iii), sec. 4041(a)(3) and sec. 4041(m)(1)(A).

must consist of not more than 83.1 percent diesel (and other minor chemical additives to enhance combustion) and at least 16.9 percent water. The emulsion addition must be registered by a United States manufacturer with the Environmental Protection Agency pursuant to section 211 of the Clean Air Act (as in effect on March 31, 2003). A refund of the difference between the regular rate (24.3 cents per gallon) and the incentive rate (19.7 cents per gallon) is available to the extent tax-paid diesel is used to produce a qualifying emulsion diesel fuel. Anyone who separates the diesel fuel from the diesel-water fuel emulsion on which a reduced rate of tax was imposed is treated as a refiner of the fuel and is liable for the difference between the amount of tax on the latest removal of the separated fuel and the amount of tax that was imposed upon the pre-mixture removal.

Effective Date

The provision is effective on January 1, 2006.

Joint Committee on Taxation (J.C.T. Rep. No. JCX-60-05)

⟫→ *Caution: The Description and Technical Explanation of the Conference Agreement of H.R. 6, Title XIII, the "Energy Tax Incentives Act of 2005" (JCX-60-05), below, is included to assist the reader's understanding, but may not be cited as the official Conference Committee Report to H.R. 6—CCH.*

Senate Amendment

No provision.

Conference Agreement

The conference agreement follows the House bill except the diesel-water emulsion fuels eligible for the special rate must consist of least 14 percent water. In addition, the person claiming entitlement to the special rate of tax must be registered with the Secretary. The conference agreement clarifies that claims for refund based on the incentive rate may be filed quarterly if such person can claim at least $750. If the person cannot claim at least $750 at the end of quarter, the amount can be carried over to the next quarter to determine if the person can claim at least $750. If the person cannot claim at least $750 at the end of the taxable year, the person must claim a credit on the person's income tax return.

[Law at ¶ 5290 and ¶ 5430. CCH Explanation at ¶ 720.]

[¶ 10,290] Act Secs. 1344 and 1346. Extend excise tax provisions and income tax credit for biodiesel and create similar incentives for renewable diesel

Joint Committee on Taxation (J.C.T. Rep. No. JCX-60-05)

⟫→ *Caution: The Description and Technical Explanation of the Conference Agreement of H.R. 6, Title XIII, the "Energy Tax Incentives Act of 2005" (JCX-60-05), below, is included to assist the reader's understanding, but may not be cited as the official Conference Committee Report to H.R. 6—CCH.*

[Code Secs. 40A, 6426 and 6427]

Present Law

Biodiesel income tax credit

Overview

The Code provides an income tax credit for biodiesel and qualified biodiesel mixtures, the biodiesel fuels credit.[81] The biodiesel fuels credit is the sum of the biodiesel mixture credit plus the biodiesel credit and is treated as a general business credit. The amount of the biodiesel fuels credit is includable in gross income. The biodiesel fuels credit is coordinated to take into account benefits from the biodiesel excise tax credit and payment provisions discussed below. The credit may not be carried back to a taxable year ending before or on December 31, 2004. The provision does not apply to fuel sold or used after December 31, 2006.

Biodiesel is monoalkyl esters of long chain fatty acids derived from plant or animal matter that meet (1) the registration requirements established by the Environmental Protection Agency under section 211 of the Clean Air Act and (2) the requirements of the American Society of Testing and Materials D6751. Agri-biodiesel is biodiesel derived solely from virgin oils including oils from corn, soybeans, sunflower seeds, cottonseeds, canola, crambe, rapeseeds, safflowers,

---

[81] Sec. 40A.

flaxseeds, rice bran, mustard seeds, or animal fats.

Biodiesel may be taken into account for purposes of the credit only if the taxpayer obtains a certification (in such form and manner as prescribed by the Secretary) from the producer or importer of the biodiesel which identifies the product produced and the percentage of the biodiesel and agri-biodiesel in the product.

Biodiesel mixture credit

The biodiesel mixture credit is 50 cents for each gallon of biodiesel used by the taxpayer in the production of a qualified biodiesel mixture. For agri-biodiesel, the credit is $1.00 per gallon. A qualified biodiesel mixture is a mixture of biodiesel and diesel fuel that is (1) sold by the taxpayer producing such mixture to any person for use as a fuel, or (2) is used as a fuel by the taxpayer producing such mixture. The sale or use must be in the trade or business of the taxpayer and is to be taken into account for the taxable year in which such sale or use occurs. No credit is allowed with respect to any casual off-farm production of a qualified biodiesel mixture.

Biodiesel credit

The biodiesel credit is 50 cents for each gallon of biodiesel which is not in a mixture with diesel fuel (100 percent biodiesel or B-100) and which during the taxable year is (1) used by the taxpayer as a fuel in a trade or business or (2) sold by the taxpayer at retail to a person and placed in the fuel tank of such person's vehicle. For agri-biodiesel, the credit is $1.00 per gallon.

Biodiesel mixture excise tax credit

The Code also provides an excise tax credit for biodiesel mixtures.[82] The credit is 50 cents for each gallon of biodiesel used by the taxpayer in producing a biodiesel mixture for sale or use in a trade or business of the taxpayer. In the case of agri-biodiesel, the credit is $1.00 per gallon. A biodiesel mixture is a mixture of biodiesel and diesel fuel that (1) is sold by the taxpayer producing such mixture to any person for use as a fuel, or (2) is used as a fuel by the taxpayer producing such mixture. No credit is allowed unless the taxpayer obtains a certification (in such form and manner as prescribed by the Secretary) from the producer of the biodiesel that identifies the product produced and the percentage of biodiesel and agri-biodiesel in the product.[83]

The credit is not available for any sale or use for any period after December 31, 2006. This excise tax credit is coordinated with the income tax credit for biodiesel such that credit for the same biodiesel cannot be claimed for both income and excise tax purposes.

Payments with respect to biodiesel fuel mixtures

If any person produces a biodiesel fuel mixture in such person's trade or business, the Secretary is to pay such person an amount equal to the biodiesel mixture credit.[84] To the extent the biodiesel fuel mixture credit exceeds the section 4081 liability of a person, the Secretary is to pay such person an amount equal to the biodiesel fuel mixture credit with respect to such mixture.[85] Thus, if the person has no section 4081 liability, the credit is refundable. The payment provision does not apply with respect to biodiesel fuel mixtures sold or used after December 31, 2006.

House Bill

No provision.

Senate Amendment

The Senate amendment extends the income tax credit, excise tax credit, and payment provisions through December 31, 2010.

Conference Agreement

The conference agreement extends the income tax credit, excise tax credit, and payment provisions through December 31, 2008. The conference agreement also creates a similar income tax credit, excise tax credit and payment system for renewable diesel; however, there is no credit for small producers of renewable diesel. Renewable diesel means diesel fuel derived from biomass (as defined in section 29(c)(3), thus excluding petroleum oil, natural gas, coal, or any product thereof) using a thermal depolymerization process.[86] Renewable diesel must meet the requirements of the American Society of Testing and Materials D975 or D396, and meet the registration requirements for fuels and fuel additives

---

[82] Sec. 6426(c).
[83] Sec. 6426(c)(4).
[84] Sec. 6427(e).
[85] Sec. 6427(e)(1) and 6327(e)(2). See also, Internal Revenue Service, *Notice 2005-4*, 2005-2 I.R.B. (December 15, 2004).
[86] Thermal depolymerization is a process for the reduction of complex organic materials (such as turkey offal) into light crude oil. The process uses pressure and heat to decompose long chain polymers of hydrogen, oxygen, and carbon into short-chain petroleum hydrocarbons with a maximum length of around 18 carbons.

established by the Environmental Protection Agency under section 211 of the Clean Air Act (42 USC 7545). The amount of the credit for renewable diesel is $1.00 per gallon. In addition, all producers of renewable diesel must be registered with the Secretary.

Effective Date

The extension of incentives is effective on the date of enactment. The renewable diesel provisions are effective for fuel sold or used after December 31, 2005.

[Law at ¶5045, ¶5050, ¶5425 and ¶5430. CCH Explanation at ¶705 and ¶715.]

[¶10,300] Act Sec. 1345. Small agri-biodiesel producer credit

Joint Committee on Taxation (J.C.T. REP. NO. JCX-46-05)

≫→ *Caution: The Technical Explanation of the "Energy Policy Tax Incentives Act of 2005" (JCX-46-05), below, is included to assist the reader's understanding but may not be cited as the official Senate Committee Report to H.R. 6— CCH.*

[Code Sec. 40A]

Present Law

Biodiesel income tax credit

The Code provides an income tax credit for biodiesel and qualified biodiesel mixtures, the biodiesel fuels credit. The biodiesel fuels credit is the sum of the biodiesel mixture credit plus the biodiesel credit and is treated as a general business credit. The amount of the biodiesel fuels credit is includible in gross income. The biodiesel fuels credit is coordinated to take into account benefits from the biodiesel excise tax credit and payment provisions created by the Act. The credit may not be carried back to a taxable year ending before or on December 31, 2004. The provision does not apply to fuel sold or used after December 31, 2006.

Biodiesel is monoalkyl esters of long chain fatty acids derived from plant or animal matter that meet (1) the registration requirements established by the EPA under section 211 of the Clean Air Act and (2) the requirements of the American Society of Testing and Materials D6751. Agri-biodiesel is biodiesel derived solely from virgin oils including oils from corn, soybeans, sunflower seeds, cottonseeds, canola, crambe, rapeseeds, safflowers, flaxseeds, rice bran, mustard seeds, or animal fats.

Biodiesel may be taken into account for purposes of the credit only if the taxpayer obtains a certification (in such form and manner as prescribed by the Secretary) from the producer or importer of the biodiesel which identifies the product produced and the percentage of the biodiesel and agri-biodiesel in the product.

The biodiesel income tax credit does not contain any incentives for small producers.

Small ethanol producer credit

Present law provides several tax benefits for ethanol and methanol produced from renewable sources that are used as a motor fuel or that are blended with other fuels (e.g., gasoline) for such a use. In the case of ethanol, a separate 10-cents-per-gallon credit for up to 15 million gallons per year for small producers, defined generally as persons whose production does not exceed 15 million gallons per year and whose production capacity does not exceed 30 million gallons per year. The alcohol fuels tax credits are includible in income. The alcohol fuels tax credit is scheduled to expire after December 31, 2010.

Description of Proposal

The proposal adds to the biodiesel fuels credit a small agri-biodiesel producer credit. The credit is a 10-cents-per-gallon credit for up to 15 million gallons of biodiesel produced by small producers, defined generally as persons whose production capacity does not exceed 60 million gallons per year.

Effective Date

The proposal is effective for taxable years ending after the date of enactment.

Joint Committee on Taxation (J.C.T. REP. NO. JCX-60-05)

⟫➤ *Caution: The Description and Technical Explanation of the Conference Agreement of H.R. 6, Title XIII, the "Energy Tax Incentives Act of 2005" (JCX-60-05), below, is included to assist the reader's understanding, but may not be cited as the official Conference Committee Report to H.R. 6—CCH.*

House Bill

No provision.

Conference Agreement

The conference agreement follows the Senate amendment except the credit sunsets after December 31, 2008.

[Law at ¶ 5050. CCH Explanation at ¶ 710.]

[¶ 10,310] Act Sec. 1347. Modifications to small ethanol producer credit

Joint Committee on Taxation (J.C.T. REP. NO. JCX-46-05)

⟫➤ *Caution: The Technical Explanation of the "Energy Policy Tax Incentives Act of 2005" (JCX-46-05), below, is included to assist the reader's understanding but may not be cited as the official Senate Committee Report to H.R. 6—CCH.*

[Code Sec. 40]

Present Law

Present law provides several tax benefits for ethanol and methanol that are used as a fuel or that are blended with other fuels (e.g., gasoline) for such a use. For example, the Code provides an income tax credit for alcohol and alcohol-blended fuels. In the case of ethanol, the Code provides an additional 10-cents-per-gallon credit for small producers, defined generally as persons whose production capacity does not exceed 30 million gallons per year.[2]

Description of Proposal

The proposal increases the limit on production capacity for small ethanol producers from 30 million gallons to 60 million gallons per year.

Effective Date

The proposal is effective for taxable years ending after the date of enactment.

Joint Committee on Taxation (J.C.T. REP. NO. JCX-60-05)

⟫➤ *Caution: The Description and Technical Explanation of the Conference Agreement of H.R. 6, Title XIII, the "Energy Tax Incentives Act of 2005" (JCX-60-05), below, is included to assist the reader's understanding, but may not be cited as the official Conference Committee Report to H.R. 6—CCH.*

House Bill

No provision.

Conference Agreement

The conference agreement follows the Senate amendment.

[Law at ¶ 5045. CCH Explanation at ¶ 735.]

---

[2] Secs. 40(b)(4) and (g)(1). The alcohol fuels tax credit (which is comprised of the small ethanol producer credit, the alcohol mixture credit, and the alcohol credit) is scheduled to expire after December 31, 2010 (sec. 40(e)(1)).

[¶10,320] Act Sec. 1351. Modify research credit for research relating to energy

Joint Committee on Taxation (J.C.T. Rep. No. JCX-46-05)

⮕ *Caution: The Technical Explanation of the "Energy Policy Tax Incentives Act of 2005" (JCX-46-05), below, is included to assist the reader's understanding but may not be cited as the official Senate Committee Report to H.R. 6— CCH.*

[Code Sec. 41]

Present Law

General rule

Section 41 provides for a research tax credit equal to 20 percent of the amount by which a taxpayer's qualified research expenses for a taxable year exceed its base amount for that year. The research tax credit is scheduled to expire and generally will not apply to amounts paid or incurred after December 31, 2005.

A 20-percent research tax credit also applies to the excess of (1) 100 percent of corporate cash expenses (including grants or contributions) paid for basic research conducted by universities (and certain nonprofit scientific research organizations) over (2) the sum of (a) the greater of two minimum basic research floors plus (b) an amount reflecting any decrease in nonresearch giving to universities by the corporation as compared to such giving during a fixed-base period, as adjusted for inflation. This separate credit computation is commonly referred to as the university basic research credit (see sec. 41(e)).

Alternative incremental research credit regime

Taxpayers are allowed to elect an alternative incremental research credit regime. If a taxpayer elects to be subject to this alternative regime, the taxpayer is assigned a three-tiered fixed-base percentage (that is lower than the fixed-base percentage otherwise applicable under present law) and the credit rate likewise is reduced. Under the alternative credit regime, a credit rate of 2.65 percent applies to the extent that a taxpayer's current-year research expenses exceed a base amount computed by using a fixed-base percentage of one percent (i.e., the base amount equals one percent of the taxpayer's average gross receipts for the four preceding years) but do not exceed a base amount computed by using a fixed-base percentage of 1.5 percent. A credit rate of 3.2 percent applies to the extent that a taxpayer's current-year research expenses exceed a base amount computed by using a fixed-base percentage of 1.5 percent but do not exceed a base amount computed by using a fixed-base percentage of two percent. A credit rate of 3.75 percent applies to the extent that a taxpayer's current-year research expenses exceed a base amount computed by using a fixed-base percentage of two percent. An election to be subject to this alternative incremental credit regime may be made for any taxable year beginning after June 30, 1996, and such an election applies to that taxable year and all subsequent years unless revoked with the consent of the Secretary of the Treasury.

Eligible expenses

Qualified research expenses eligible for the research tax credit consist of: (1) in-house expenses of the taxpayer for wages and supplies attributable to qualified research; (2) certain time-sharing costs for computer use in qualified research; and (3) 65 percent of amounts paid or incurred by the taxpayer to certain other persons for qualified research conducted on the taxpayer's behalf (so-called contract research expenses). In the case of amounts paid to a research consortium, 75 percent of amounts paid for qualified research is treated as qualified research expenses eligible for the research credit (rather than 65 percent under the general rule) if (1) such research consortium is a tax-exempt organization that is described in section 501(c)(3) (other than a private foundation) or section 501(c)(6) and is organized and operated primarily to conduct scientific research, and (2) such qualified research is conducted by the consortium on behalf of the taxpayer and one or more persons not related to the taxpayer.

To be eligible for the credit, the research must not only satisfy the requirements of present-law section 174 for the deduction for research expenses, but must be undertaken for the purpose of discovering information that is technological in nature, the application of which is intended to be useful in the development of a new or improved business component of the taxpayer, and substantially all of the activities of which must constitute elements of a process of experimentation for functional aspects, performance, reliability, or quality of a business component.

Description of Proposal

The proposal modifies the present-law research credit as it applies to qualified energy research. In particular, the proposal provides that the taxpayer may claim a credit equal to 20 percent of the taxpayer's expenditures on qualified energy research undertaken by an energy research consortium. The amount of credit claimed is determined only by regard to such expenditures by the taxpayer within the taxable year. Unlike the general rule for the research credit, the 20-percent credit for research by an energy research consortium applies to all such expenditures, not only those in excess of a base amount however determined. An energy research consortium is a qualified research consortium as under present law that also is organized and operated primarily to conduct energy research and development in the public interest and to which at least five unrelated persons paid, or incurred amounts, to such organization within the calendar year. In addition, to be a qualified energy research consortium, no single person shall pay or incur more than 50 percent of the total amounts received by the research consortium during the calendar year.

The proposal also provides that 100 percent of amounts paid or incurred by the taxpayer to eligible small businesses, universities, and the Federal government for qualified energy research would constitute qualified research expenses as contract research expenses, rather than 65 percent of qualified research expenditures allowed under present law. An eligible small business for this purpose is a business in which the taxpayer does not own a 50 percent or greater interest and the business has employed, on average, 500 or fewer employees in the two preceding calendar years.

Qualified energy research expenditures are expenditures that would otherwise qualify for the research credit under present law and relate to the production, supply, and conservation of energy, including otherwise qualifying research expenditures related to alternative energy sources or the use of alternative energy sources. For example, research relating to hydrogen fuel cell vehicles would qualify under this proposal, if the research expenditures otherwise satisfy the criteria of present-law section 41. Likewise, otherwise qualifying research undertaken to improve the energy-efficiency of lighting would qualify under this proposal.

Effective Date

The proposal is effective for amounts paid or incurred after the date of enactment in taxable years ending after such date.

Joint Committee on Taxation (J.C.T. REP. NO. JCX-60-05)

⟫→ *Caution: The Description and Technical Explanation of the Conference Agreement of H.R. 6, Title XIII, the "Energy Tax Incentives Act of 2005" (JCX-60-05), below, is included to assist the reader's understanding, but may not be cited as the official Conference Committee Report to H.R. 6—CCH.*

House Bill

No provision.

Conference Agreement

The conference agreement follows the Senate amendment.

[Law at ¶ 5055. CCH Explanation at ¶ 235.]

[¶ 10,330] Act Sec. 1352. National Academy of Sciences study

Joint Committee on Taxation (J.C.T. REP. NO. JCX-46-05)

⟫→ *Caution: The Technical Explanation of the "Energy Policy Tax Incentives Act of 2005" (JCX-46-05), below, is included to assist the reader's understanding but may not be cited as the official Senate Committee Report to H.R. 6—CCH.*

[Act Sec. 1352]

Present Law

Present law does not provide for a study of the health, environmental, security, and infrastructure external costs that may be associated with the use and production of energy.

Description of Proposal

The proposal requires the Secretary of Treasury to enter into an agreement, within 60 days, with the National Academy of Sciences to conduct a study to define and evaluate the health, environmental, security, and infrastructure external costs and benefits associated with energy activities that are not or may not be fully incorporated into the price of such activities, or into the Federal tax or fee or other applicable revenue measure related to such activities. The results of the study are to be submitted to Congress within two years of the agreement.

Effective Date

The proposal is effective on the date of enactment.

Joint Committee on Taxation (J.C.T. REP. NO. JCX-60-05)

⟫→ *Caution: The Description and Technical Explanation of the Conference Agreement of H.R. 6, Title XIII, the "Energy Tax Incentives Act of 2005" (JCX-60-05), below, is included to assist the reader's understanding, but may not be cited as the official Conference Committee Report to H.R. 6—CCH.*

House Bill

No provision.

Conference Agreement

The conference agreement follows the Senate amendment.

[Law at ¶ 7015. CCH Explanation at ¶ 1005.]

[¶ 10,340] Act Sec. 1353. Credit for equipment for processing or sorting materials gathered through recycling

Joint Committee on Taxation (J.C.T. REP. NO. JCX-60-05)

⟫→ *Caution: The Description and Technical Explanation of the Conference Agreement of H.R. 6, Title XIII, the "Energy Tax Incentives Act of 2005" (JCX-60-05), below, is included to assist the reader's understanding, but may not be cited as the official Conference Committee Report to H.R. 6—CCH.*

[Act Sec. 1353]

Present Law

There is no present law credit for equipment for processing or sorting materials gathered through recycling.

House Bill

No provision.

Senate Amendment

The provision provides a 15-percent business tax credit for the cost of qualified recycling equipment placed in service or leased by the taxpayer. Qualified recycling equipment is equipment, including connecting piping, (1) that is employed in sorting or processing residential and commercial qualified recyclable materials (any packaging or printed material which is glass, paper, plastic, steel, or aluminum generated by an individual or business) for the purpose of converting such materials for use in manufacturing tangible consumer products, including packaging, or (2) whose primary purpose is the shredding and processing of any electronic waste, including any cathode ray tube, flat panel screen, or similar video display device with a screen size greater than four inches measured diagonally, or a central processing unit.

Qualified recycling equipment does not include rolling stock or other equipment used to transport recyclable materials. Materials that are not packaging or printed material, such as tires or scrap metal from junked automobiles, are not qualified recyclable materials, and thus equipment used to process such materials are not qualified recycling equipment.

For the purposes of (1), qualified recycling equipment includes equipment that is utilized at commercial or public venues, including recycling collection centers, where the equipment is utilized to sort or process qualified recyclable materials for such purpose. For the purpose of (2), only the cost of each piece of equipment as exceeds $400,000 is eligible for the credit.

Conference Agreement

The conference agreement does not include the Senate amendment provision. The conference agreement directs the Secretary of the Treasury, in consultation with the Secretary of Energy, to conduct a study to determine and quantify the energy savings achieved through the recycling of glass, paper, plastic, steel, aluminum, and electronic devices, and to identify tax incentives that would encourage recycling of such material. The study is to be submitted to Congress within one year of the date of enactment.

Effective Date

The provision is effective on the date of enactment.

[Law at ¶ 7020. CCH Explanation at ¶ 1010.]

[¶10,350] Act Sec. 1361. Oil Spill Liability Trust Fund

Joint Committee on Taxation (J.C.T. Rep. No. JCX-46-05)

⟫→ *Caution: The Technical Explanation of the "Energy Policy Tax Incentives Act of 2005" (JCX-46-05), below, is included to assist the reader's understanding but may not be cited as the official Senate Committee Report to H.R. 6—CCH.*

[Code Sec. 4611]

Present Law

In general, a five-cent-per-barrel tax was imposed on crude oil received at a United States refinery and imported petroleum products received for consumption, use, or warehousing. The Fund's tax applied after December 31, 1989, and before January 1, 1995. The tax was effective only if the unobligated balance in the Fund was less than $1 billion.

Description of Proposal

The proposal reinstates the Oil Spill Liability Trust Fund tax. The tax applies on April 1, 2007, or if later, the last day of any calendar quarter for which the Secretary estimates that, as of the close of that quarter, the unobligated balance in the Oil Spill Liability Trust fund is less that $2 billion.

The tax will be suspended during a calendar quarter if the Secretary estimates that, as of the close of the preceding calendar quarter, the unobligated balance in the Oil Spill Liability Trust Fund exceeds $3 billion. The tax terminates after December 31, 2014.

Joint Committee on Taxation (J.C.T. Rep. No. JCX-60-05)

⟫→ *Caution: The Description and Technical Explanation of the Conference Agreement of H.R. 6, Title XIII, the "Energy Tax Incentives Act of 2005" (JCX-60-05), below, is included to assist the reader's understanding, but may not be cited as the official Conference Committee Report to H.R. 6—CCH.*

House Bill

No provision.

Senate Amendment

The Senate amendment reinstates the Oil Spill Liability Trust Fund tax. The tax applies on April 1, 2006, or if later, the last day of any calendar quarter for which the Secretary estimates that, as of the close of that quarter, the unobligated balance in the Oil Spill Liability Trust Fund is less than $2 billion.

* * *

Effective Date

The provision is effective on the date of enactment.

Conference Agreement

The conference agreement follows the Senate amendment with the following modification. The tax will be suspended during a calendar quarter if the Secretary estimates that, as of the close of the preceding calendar quarter, the unobligated balance in the Oil Spill Liability Trust Fund exceeds $2.7 billion.

[Law at ¶5365. CCH Explanation at ¶540.]

[¶10,360] Act Sec. 1362. Leaking Underground Storage Tank Trust Fund

Joint Committee on Taxation (J.C.T. Rep. No. JCX-46-05)

⇢ *Caution: The Technical Explanation of the "Energy Policy Tax Incentives Act of 2005" (JCX-46-05), below, is included to assist the reader's understanding but may not be cited as the official Senate Committee Report to H.R. 6—CCH.*

[Code Secs. 4041, 4081(d), 4082, 9508 and New Code Sec. 6430]

Present Law

The Code imposes an excise tax, generally at a rate of 0.1 cents per gallon, on gasoline, diesel, kerosene, and special motor fuels (other than liquefied petroleum gas and liquefied natural gas).[86] The taxes are deposited in the Leaking Underground Storage Tank ("LUST") Trust Fund. The tax expires on October 1, 2005.

Diesel fuel and kerosene that is to be used for a nontaxable purpose will not be taxed upon removal from the terminal if it is dyed to indicate its nontaxable purpose.

The Code requires the LUST Trust Fund to reimburse the General Fund for certain refund and credit claims related to the nontaxable use of fuel (only to the extent attributable to the LUST Trust fund financing rate).[87]

Description of Proposal

Under the proposal, the LUST Trust Fund tax is extended at the current rate through September 30, 2011. Further, dyed fuel is subject to the LUST tax and without refund. Under the proposal, the LUST Trust Fund is no longer required to reimburse the General Fund for claims and credits related to the nontaxable use of fuel.

Joint Committee on Taxation (J.C.T. Rep. No. JCX-60-05)

⇢ *Caution: The Description and Technical Explanation of the Conference Agreement of H.R. 6, Title XIII, the "Energy Tax Incentives Act of 2005" (JCX-60-05), below, is included to assist the reader's understanding, but may not be cited as the official Conference Committee Report to H.R. 6—CCH.*

Effective Date

The provision is generally effective for fuel entered, removed or sold after September 30, 2005. The extension of the trust fund tax is effective October 1, 2005.

House Bill

No provision.

Conference Agreement

The conference agreement follows the Senate amendment.

[Law at ¶5265, ¶5290, ¶5295, ¶5435 and ¶5495. CCH Explanation at ¶785 and ¶1035.]

---

[86] For qualified methanol and ethanol fuel the rate is 0.05 cents per gallon (sec. 4041(b)(2)(A)(ii). Qualified methanol or ethanol fuel is any liquid at least 85 percent of which consists of methanol, ethanol or other alcohol produced from coal (including peat) (sec. 4041(b)(2)(B)).

[87] Specifically, section 9508(c)(2) requires the LUST Trust Fund to reimburse the General Fund from time to time for claims paid pursuant to sections 6420 (relating to amounts paid in respect of gasoline used on farms), section 6421 (relating to amounts paid in respect of gasoline used for certain nonhighway purposes or by local transit systems), and section 6427 (relating to fuels not used for taxable purposes) and income credits allowed under section 34 for the purposes previously mentioned. No income tax credit is allowed for any amount payable under section 6421 or 6427 if a claim for such amount is timely filed and is payable under such section (sec. 34(b)).

[¶ 10,370] Act Sec. 1363. Modify recapture of section 197 amortization

Joint Committee on Taxation (J.C.T. REP. NO. JCX-60-05)

>>>→ *Caution: The Description and Technical Explanation of the Conference Agreement of H.R. 6, Title XIII, the "Energy Tax Incentives Act of 2005" (JCX-60-05), below, is included to assist the reader's understanding, but may not be cited as the official Conference Committee Report to H.R. 6—CCH.*

[Code Sec. 1245]

Present Law

Taxpayers are entitled to recover the cost of amortizable section 197 intangibles using the straight-line method of amortization over a uniform life of fifteen years.[189] With certain exceptions, amortizable section 197 intangibles generally are purchased intangibles held by a taxpayer in the conduct of a business.[190]

Gain on the sale of depreciable property must be recaptured as ordinary income to the extent of depreciation deductions previously claimed,[191] and the recapture amount is computed separately for each item of property. Section 197 intangibles, because they are treated as property of a character subject to the allowance for depreciation,[192] are subject to these recapture rules.

House Bill

No provision.

Senate Amendment

No provision.

Conference Agreement

Under the conference agreement, if multiple section 197 intangibles are sold (or otherwise disposed of) in a single transaction or series of transactions, the seller must calculate recapture as if all of the section 197 intangibles were a single asset. Thus, any gain on the sale (or other disposition) of the intangibles is recaptured as ordinary income to the extent of ordinary depreciation deductions previously claimed on any of the section 197 intangibles.

The following example illustrates present law and the conference agreement:

Example.—In year 1, a taxpayer acquires two section 197 intangible assets for a total of $45. Asset A is assigned a cost basis of $15 and asset B is assigned a cost basis of $30. The allocation is irrelevant for amortization purposes, as the taxpayer will be entitled to a total of $3 per year ($45 divided by 15 years).

In year 6, the basis of A is $10 and the basis of B is $20. Taxpayer sells the assets for an aggregate sale price of $45, resulting in gain of $15. The character of this gain depends on the recapture amount, which depends in turn on the relative sales prices of the individual assets. Taxpayer has claimed $5 of amortization, and therefore has $5 of recapture potential, with respect to A. Taxpayer has claimed $10 of amortization, and therefore has $10 of recapture potential, with respect to B.

Under present law, if the sale proceeds are allocated $15 to A and $30 to B, the gain on assets A and B will be $5 and $10, respectively. These amounts match the recapture potential for each asset, so the full amount of the gain will be recaptured as ordinary income. However, if the sale proceeds instead are allocated $25 to A and $20 to B, the full $15 gain will be recognized with respect to A, and only $5 (full recapture potential with respect to A) will be recaptured as ordinary income. The remaining $10 of gain attributable to A will be treated as capital gain. No gain (and thus no recapture) will be recognized with respect to Asset B, and only $5 of the $15 recapture potential is recognized.

Under the conference agreement, the taxpayer calculates recapture as if assets A and B were a single asset. For purposes of the calculation, the proceeds are $45 and the gain is $15. Because a total of $15 of amortization has been claimed with respect to assets A and B, the full $15 gain is recaptured as ordinary income.

Effective Date

The conference agreement is effective for dispositions of property after the date of enactment.

[Law at ¶ 5245. CCH Explanation at ¶ 245.]

---

[189] Sec. 197(a)
[190] Sec. 197(c)
[191] Sec. 1245.
[192] Sec. 197(f)(7).

[¶10,380] Act Sec. 1364. Clarification of tire excise tax

Joint Committee on Taxation (J.C.T. REP. NO. JCX-60-05)

⟫⟶ *Caution: The Description and Technical Explanation of the Conference Agreement of H.R. 6, Title XIII, the "Energy Tax Incentives Act of 2005" (JCX-60-05), below, is included to assist the reader's understanding, but may not be cited as the official Conference Committee Report to H.R. 6—CCH.*

[Code Sec. 4072(e)]

Present Law

The Code imposes an excise tax on highway tires with a rated load capacity exceeding 3,500 pounds, generally at a rate of 9.45 cents per 10 pounds of excess. Biasply tires and super single tires are taxed at a rate of 4.725 cents for each 10 pounds of rated load capacity exceeding 3,500 pounds. A super single tire is a single tire greater than 13 inches in cross section width designed to replace two tires in a dual fitment.

House Bill

No provision.

Senate Amendment

The Senate amendment subjects super single tires to a tax of 8 cents per 10 pounds of excess rated load capacity over 3,500 pounds. It redefines super single tire to be a single tire greater than 17.5 inches in cross section width designed to replace two tires in a dual fitment.

Conference Agreement

The conference agreement clarifies that the definition of super single tire does not include tires designed to serve as steering tires. It is understood that steering axles are not equipped with a dual fitment. Therefore, tires classified as steering tires are not "designed to replace two tires in a dual fitment." To the extent there is any perceived ambiguity in the present law definition, the conferees wish to clarify that steering tires are not included within the definition of super single tire eligible for the special rate of tax. Under the conference agreement, a "super single tire" is a single tire greater than 13 inches in cross section width designed to replace two tires in a dual fitment, but such term does not include any tire designed for steering.

With respect to the one-year period beginning on January 1, 2006, the IRS is required to report to the Congress on the amount of tax collected during such period for each class of taxable tire (e.g. biasply, super single, or other) and the number of tires in each such class on which tax is imposed during such period. The report must be submitted no later than July 1, 2007. The IRS is directed to revise the Form 720, Quarterly Federal Excise Tax Return, to collect the information necessary to prepare the report. The report is also to include total tire tax collections for an equivalent one-year period preceding the date of enactment of the American Jobs Creation Act of 2004.

Effective Date

The provision regarding the definition of a super single tire is effective as if included in section 869 of the American Jobs Creation Act of 2004. The study requirement is effective on the date of enactment.

[Law at ¶5285 and ¶7025. CCH Explanation at ¶345 and ¶1020.]

Committee Reports

Safe, Accountable, Flexible, Efficient Transportation Equity Act: A Legacy for Users

¶15,001 Introduction

The committee reports accompanying Title XI, the tax title, of the Safe, Accountable, Flexible, Efficient Transportation Equity Act: A Legacy for Users (H.R. 3) explain the intent of Congress regarding the revenue-related provisions of the Act. At the end of each committee reports section, references are provided to the corresponding CCH explanation and Internal Revenue Code provisions. Subscribers to the electronic version can link from these references to the corresponding material. *The pertinent sections of the Conference Report appear in Act Section order beginning at ¶15,010.*

¶15,005 Background

The Transportation Equity Act: A Legacy for Users (H.R. 3) was introduced in the House of Representatives on February 9, 2005. On March 10, 2005, the House passed H.R. 3 by a vote of 417 to 9. The Senate passed H.R. 3 with an amendment on May 17, 2005, by a vote of 89 to 11.

On March 1, 2005, the Highway Reauthorization Tax Act of 2005 was introduced in the House as H.R. 996. The House Committee on Ways and Means reported favorably on H.R. 996 on March 8, 2005 (H.R. REP. NO. 109-13).

On April 19, 2005, the Highway Reauthorization and Excise Tax Simplification Act of 2005 was introduced in the Senate as S. 1230. The Senate Finance Committee reported favorably on S. 1230 on June 14, 2005 (S. REP. NO. 109-82).

On May 26, 2005, the House disagreed to the Senate amendment to H.R. 3 and requested a conference. A conference report on H.R. 3 was filed on July 28, 2005 (H.R. CONF. REP. 109-203). The House agreed to the conference report on July 29, 2005, by a vote of 412 to 8. On that same day, the Senate agreed to the conference report by a vote of 91 to 4.

The following material includes the pertinent texts of the committee reports that explain the revenue-related changes made by Title XI, the tax title, of the Safe, Accountable, Flexible, and Efficient Transportation Equity Act: A Legacy for Users (H.R. 3). The sections include the text of the relevant House, Senate and Conference Committee Reports, as released by the Congressional committees. Headings have been added for convenience. Missions of text are indicated by asterisks (* * *). References are to the following reports:

• The Highway Reauthorization Tax Act of 2005 (H.R. 996), House Ways and Means Committee Report, as reported on March 8, 2005, is referred to as House Committee Report (H.R. REP. NO. 109-13).

• The Highway Reauthorization and Excise Tax Simplification Act of 2005 (S. 1230), Senate Finance Committee Report, as reported on June 14, 2005, is referred to as Senate Committee Report (S. REP. NO. 109-82).

• The Conference Committee Report on Title XI, the tax title, of the Safe, Accountable, Flexible, and Efficient Transportation Equity Act: A Legacy for Users (H.R. 3), as released on July 28, 2005, is referred to as Conference Committee Report (H.R. Conf. Rep. No. 109-203).

[¶15,010] Act Secs. 11101 and 11102. Extension of Highway Trust Fund and Aquatic Resources Trust Fund Expenditure Authority and related taxes

House Committee Report (H.R. REP. NO. 109-13)

[Code Secs. 4041, 4051, 4071, 4081, 4221, 4481, 4482, 4483, 6412, 9503 and 9504]

Present-Law Highway Trust Fund Excise Taxes

In general

Six separate excise taxes are imposed to finance the Federal Highway Trust Fund program. Three of these taxes are imposed on highway motor fuels. The remaining three are a retail sales tax on heavy highway vehicles, a manufacturers' excise tax on heavy vehicle tires, and an annual use tax on heavy vehicles. A substantial majority of the revenues produced by the Highway Trust Fund excise taxes are derived from the taxes on motor fuels. Except for 4.3 cents per gallon of the Highway Trust Fund fuels tax rates, and a portion of the tax on certain special motor fuels, all of these taxes are scheduled to expire after September 30, 2005. The 4.3-cents-per-gallon portion of the fuels tax rates is permanent.[1] The six taxes are summarized below.

Highway motor fuels taxes

The Highway Trust Fund motor fuels tax rates are as follows:[2]

Gasoline	18.3 cents per gallon
Diesel fuel and kerosene .	24.3 cents per gallon
Special motor fuels	18.3 cents per gallon generally[3]

---

[3] The statutory rate for certain special motor fuels is determined on an energy equivalent basis, as follows: Liquefied petroleum gas (propane): 13.6 cents per gallon (3.2 cents after September 30, 2005). Liquefied natural gas: 11.9 cents per gallon (2.8 cents after September 30, 2005). Methanol derived from natural gas: 9.15 cents per gallon (2.15 cents after September 30, 2005). Compressed natural gas: 48.54 cents per MCF. See secs. 4041(a)(2), 4041(a)(3) and 4041(m). The compressed natural gas tax rate is equivalent only to 4.3 cents per gallon of the rate imposed on gasoline and other special motor fuels rather than the full 18.3-cents-per-gallon rate. The tax rate for the other special motor fuels is equivalent to the full 18.3-cents-per-gallon gasoline and special motor fuels tax rate.

Non-fuel Highway Trust Fund excise taxes

In addition to the highway motor fuels excise tax revenues, the Highway Trust Fund receives revenues produced by three excise taxes imposed exclusively on heavy highway vehicles or tires. These taxes are:

1. A 12-percent excise tax imposed on the first retail sale of heavy highway vehicles, tractors, and trailers (generally, trucks having a gross vehicle weight in excess of 33,000 pounds and trailers having such a weight in excess of 26,000 pounds) (sec. 4051);

2. An excise tax imposed on highway tires with a rated load capacity exceeding 3,500 pounds, generally at a rate of 9.45 cents per 10 pounds of excess (sec. 4071(a)); and

3. An annual use tax imposed on highway vehicles having a taxable gross weight of 55,000 pounds or more (sec. 4481). (The maximum rate for this tax is $550 per year, imposed on vehicles having a taxable gross weight over 75,000 pounds.)

Present-Law Highway Trust Fund Expenditure Provisions

In general

Dedication of excise tax revenues to the Highway Trust Fund and expenditures from the Highway Trust Fund are governed by the Code (sec. 9503).[4] The Code authorizes expenditures (subject to appropriations) from the Fund through May 31, 2005, for the purposes provided in authorizing legislation, as in effect on the date of enactment of the Surface Transportation Extension Act of 2004, Part V.

Under present law, revenues from the highway excise taxes, as imposed through September 30, 2005, generally are dedicated to the Highway Trust Fund. Under section 9503(c)(2), the Highway Trust Fund reimburses the General Fund for

---

[1] This portion of the tax rates was enacted as a deficit reduction measure in 1993. Receipts from it were retained in the General Fund until 1997 legislation provided for their transfer to the Highway Trust Fund.

[2] Secs. 4081(a)(2)(A)(i), 4081(a)(2)(A)(iii), 4041(a)(2), 4041(a)(3), and 4041(m). Some of these fuels also are subject to an additional 0.1-cent-per-gallon excise tax to fund the Leaking Underground Storage Tank ("LUST") Trust Fund (secs. 4041(d) and 4081(a)(2)(B)).

[4] The Highway Trust Fund statutory provisions were placed in the Internal Revenue Code in 1982.

amounts paid in respect of gasoline used on farms, gasoline used for certain nonhighway purposes or by local transit systems, amounts relating to fuels not used for taxable purposes, and income tax credits for certain exempt uses of fuels.

Highway Trust Fund expenditure purposes

The Highway Trust Fund has a separate account for mass transit, the Mass Transit Account.[5] The Highway Trust Fund and the Mass Transit Account are funding sources for specific programs. Neither the Highway Trust Fund nor the Mass Transit Account receives interest on its unexpended balances.[6]

Highway Trust Fund expenditure purposes have been revised with each authorization Act enacted since establishment of the Highway Trust Fund in 1956. In general, expenditures authorized under those Acts (as the Acts were in effect on the date of enactment of the most recent such authorizing Act) are specified by the Code as Highway Trust Fund expenditure purposes.[7] The Code provides that authority to make expenditures from the Highway Trust Fund expires after May 31, 2005. Thus, no Highway Trust Fund expenditures may occur after May 31, 2005, without an amendment to the Code.

Interrelationship of the Highway Trust Fund and the Aquatic Resources Trust Fund

The Aquatic Resources Trust Fund is funded by a portion of the receipts from the excise taxes imposed on motorboat gasoline and special motor fuels and on gasoline used as a fuel in the nonbusiness use of small-engine outdoor power equipment. A portion of these taxes are transferred into the Highway Trust Fund and then retransferred into the Aquatic Resources Trust Fund. As a result, transfers to the Aquatic Resources Trust Fund are governed in part by Highway Trust Fund provisions (secs. 9503(c)(4) and 9503(c)(5)).

A total tax rate of 18.4 cents per gallon is imposed on gasoline and special motor fuels used in motorboats and on gasoline used as a fuel in the nonbusiness use of small-engine outdoor power equipment. Of this rate, 0.1 cent per gallon is dedicated to the Leaking Underground Storage Tank Trust Fund. Of the remaining 18.3 cents per gallon, 4.8 cents per gallon are retained in the General Fund. The balance of 13.5 cents per gallon is transferred to the Highway Trust Fund and then retransferred to the Aquatic Resources Trust Fund and the Land and Water Conservation Fund, as follows.

The Aquatic Resources Trust Fund is comprised of two accounts, the Boat Safety Account and the Sport Fish Restoration Account. Motorboat fuel taxes, not exceeding $70 million per year, are transferred to the Boat Safety Account. In addition, these transfers are subject to an overall annual limit equal to an amount that will not cause the Boat Safety Account to have an unobligated balance in excess of $70 million. To the extent there are excess motorboat fuel taxes, the next $1 million per year of motorboat fuel taxes is transferred from the Highway Trust Fund to the Land and Water Conservation Fund provided for in Title I of the Land and Water Conservation Fund Act of 1965. The balance of the motorboat fuel taxes in the Highway Trust Fund is transferred to the Sport Fish Restoration Account.

The Sport Fish Restoration Account also receives 13.5 cents per gallon of the small-engine fuel taxes from the Highway Trust Fund. This Account is also funded with receipts from an ad valorem manufacturers' excise tax on sport fishing equipment.

The retention in the General Fund of 4.8 cents per gallon of taxes on fuel used in motorboats and in the nonbusiness use of small-engine outdoor power equipment expires with respect to taxes imposed after September 30, 2005.

The expenditure authority for the Aquatic Resources Trust Fund expires after May 31, 2005.

H.R. 3: Transportation Equity Act: A Legacy for Users

On February 9, 2005, Representative Don Young introduced H.R. 3, the Transportation Equity Act: A Legacy for Users. Among other purposes, the bill reauthorizes the Federal highway, public transportation, highway safety and motor carrier safety programs for fiscal year 2004 through fiscal year 2009.

---

[5] Sec. 9503(e)(1).
[6] Sec. 9503(f)(2).
[7] The authorizing Acts that currently are referenced in the Highway Trust Fund provisions of the Code are: the Highway Revenue Act of 1956, Title I and II of the Surface Transportation Assistance Act of 1982, the Surface Transportation and Uniform Relocation Act of 1987, the Intermodal Surface Transportation Efficiency Act of 1991 and the Transportation Equity Act for the 21st Century, the Surface Transportation Extension Act of 2003, the Surface Transportation Extension Act of 2004; the Surface Transportation Extension Act of 2004, Part II; the Surface Transportation Extension Act of 2004 Part III; the Surface Transportation Extension Act of 2004, Part IV; and the Surface Transportation Extension Act of 2004, Part V.

Reasons for Change

The Committee believes that highway and transit spending sustains and creates jobs, providing valuable new opportunities in communities where the availability of jobs is declining. In addition, a long-term reauthorization provides stability for State transportation programs dependent on Federal funds. Thus, the Committee believes it is appropriate to reauthorize Highway Trust Fund expenditures through September 30, 2009 in coordination with new transportation legislation and to extend current Federal taxes payable to the Highway Trust Fund through September 30, 2011.

The Committee also believes that the full amount of excise taxes imposed on fuel used in motorboats and in the nonbusiness use of small-engine outdoor power equipment should not be retained in the General Fund and should instead be credited to the trust fund dedicated to the users who primarily bear such taxes. Fuel taxes imposed with respect to other uses are currently either dedicated to an appropriate fund or are being phased out. Therefore, the Committee believes that allowing the present-law General Fund retention of such taxes to expire as scheduled is consistent with the treatment of other fuel taxes.

Explanation Of Provision

The expenditure authority for the Highway Trust Fund and Aquatic Resources Trust Fund is extended through September 30, 2009. The Code provisions governing the purposes for which monies in the Highway Trust Fund may be spent are modified to include the reauthorization bill, H.R. 3, Transportation Equity Act: A Legacy for Users.

The provision also extends the motor fuel taxes and all three non-fuel excise taxes at their current rates through September 30, 2011.

The provision does not extend the retention in the General Fund of 4.8 cents per gallon of taxes on fuel used in motorboats and in the nonbusiness use of small-engine outdoor power equipment.

Effective Date

The provision is effective on the date of enactment.

Conference Committee Report (H.R. CONF. REP. NO. 109-203)

Present-Law Highway Trust Fund Excise Taxes

Exemptions

* * *

Present law includes numerous exemptions (including partial exemptions) for specified uses of taxable fuels or for specified fuels. Because the gasoline and diesel fuel taxes generally are imposed before the end use of the fuel is known, many exemptions are realized through refunds to end users of tax paid by a taxpayer earlier in the distribution chain. Exempt uses and fuels include:

• use in State and local government and nonprofit educational organization highway vehicles;

• use in buses engaged in transporting students and employees of schools;

• use in local mass transit buses having a seating capacity of at least 20 adults (not including the driver) when the buses operate under contract with (or are subsidized by) a State or local governmental unit to furnish the transportation; and

• use in intercity buses serving the general public along scheduled routes. (Such use is totally exempt from the gasoline excise tax and is exempt from 17 cents per gallon of the diesel fuel tax.)

In addition, fuels used in off-highway business use or on a farm for farming purposes generally are exempt from these motor fuels taxes.[5] The Highway Trust Fund does not receive excise taxes imposed on fuel used in off-highway activities. Rather, when tax is imposed on off-highway use fuel consumption, it is used to finance other Trust Funds (e.g., motorboat gasoline and special motor fuel taxes from non-business off-highway use dedicated to the Aquatic Resources Trust Fund) or is retained in the General Fund (e.g., tax on diesel fuel used in trains).

* * *

---

[5] Diesel fuel is the same fuel (#2 fuel oil) as that commonly used as home heating oil. Fuel oil used as heating oil is not subject to the Federal excise tax.

Present-Law Highway Trust Fund Expenditure Provisions

In general

* * *

Highway Trust Fund expenditure purposes

The Highway Trust Fund has a subaccount for Mass Transit. Both the Trust Fund and its sub-account are funding sources for specific programs. Neither the Highway Trust Fund nor its Mass Transit sub-account receive interest on unexpended balances. The Highway Fund's Mass Transit sub-account receives 2.86 cents per gallon of highway motor fuels excise taxes.

Highway Trust Fund expenditure purposes have been revised with each authorization Act enacted since establishment of the Highway Trust Fund in 1956. In general, expenditures authorized under those Acts (as the Acts were in effect on the date of enactment of the most recent such authorizing Act) are approved by the Code as Highway Trust Fund expenditure purposes.[7] Thus, no Highway Trust Fund monies may be spent for a purpose not approved by the tax-writing committees of Congress. The Code provides that authority to make expenditures from the Highway Trust Fund expires after July 27, 2005. Thus, no Highway Trust Fund expenditures may occur after July 27, 2005.

Anti-deficit provisions (the "Harry Byrd rule")

Highway projects can take multiple years to complete. As a result, the Highway Trust Fund carries positive unexpended balances, a large portion of which are reserved to cover existing obligations.[8] Highway Trust Fund spending is limited by anti-deficit provisions internal to the Highway Trust Fund, the so-called "Harry Byrd rule." Generally, the Harry Byrd rule prevents the further obligation of Federal highway funds if the current and expected balances of the Highway Trust Fund fall below a certain level. The rule requires the Treasury Department to determine, on a quarterly basis, the amount (if any) by which unfunded highway authorizations exceed projected net Highway Trust Fund tax receipts for the 24-month period beginning at the close of each fiscal year.[9] Similar rules apply to unfunded Mass Transit Account authorizations. If unfunded authorizations exceed projected 24-month receipts, apportionments to the States for specified programs funded by the relevant Trust Fund Account are to be reduced proportionately. Because of the Harry Byrd rule, taxes dedicated to the Highway Trust Fund typically are scheduled to expire at least 24 months after current authorizing Acts.

The Surface Transportation Extension Act of 2003, created a temporary rule (through February 29, 2004) for purposes of the anti-deficit provisions of the Highway Trust Fund. For purposes of determining 24 months of projected revenues for the anti-deficit provisions, the Secretary of the Treasury is instructed to treat each expiring provision relating to appropriations and transfers to the Highway Trust Fund to have been extended through the end of the 24-month period and to assume that the rate of tax during such 24-month period remains at the same rate in effect on the date of enactment of the provision. The temporary rule has been continuously extended since February 29, 2004. The last extension, enacted as part of the Surface Transportation Extension Act of 2005, Part IV, extended the rule through July 27, 2005.

Limitations on transfers to the Highway Trust Fund

The Code also contains a special enforcement provision to prevent expenditure of Highway Trust Fund monies for purposes not authorized in section 9503.[10] Should such unapproved expenditures occur, no further excise tax receipts will be transferred to the Highway Trust Fund. Rather, the taxes will continue to be imposed with receipts being retained in the General Fund. This enforcement provision provides specifically that it applies not only to unauthorized expenditures under the current Code provisions, but also to expenditures pursuant to future legislation that does not amend section 9503's expenditure authorization provisions or otherwise authorize the expenditure as part of a revenue Act.

* * *

---

[7] The authorizing Acts which currently are referenced in the Highway Trust Fund provisions of the Code are: the Highway Revenue Act of 1956; Titles I and II of the Surface Transportation Assistance Act of 1982; the Surface Transportation and Uniform Relocation Act of 1987; the Intermodal Surface Transportation Efficiency Act of 1991; and the Transportation Equity Act for the 21st Century; the Surface Transportation Extension Act of 2003; the Surface Transportation Extension Act of 2004; the Surface Transportation Extension Act of 2004 Part II; the Surface Transportation Extension Act of 2004, Part III; the Surface Transportation Extension Act of 2004, Part IV; the Surface Transportation Extension Act of 2004, Part V; the Surface Transportation Extension Act of 2005; the Surface Transportation Extension Act of 2005, Part II; the Surface Transportation Extension Act of 2005, Part III; and the Surface Transportation Extension Act of 2005, Part IV.

[8] Congressional Research Service, RL 32226, *Highway and Transit Program Reauthorization Legislation in the 2nd Session, 108th Congress* (December 15, 2004) at CRS-12.

[9] Sec. 9503(d).

[10] Sec. 9503(b)(6).

Effective Date

The House bill is effective on the date of enactment.

Conference Agreement

The conference agreement follows the House bill with the following modifications. The expenditure authority for the Highway Trust Fund expires after September 29, 2009, (after September 30, 2009, in the case of expenditures for administrative purposes, and expenditures from the Mass Transit Account).

The conference agreement changes the Harry Byrd rule from a 24-month to a 48-month receipt rule. Under the conference agreement, the Harry Byrd rule is not triggered unless unfunded highway authorizations exceed projected net Highway Trust Fund tax receipts for the 48-month period beginning at the close of each fiscal year. For purposes of the 48-month rule, taxes are assumed extended beyond their expiration date.

The conference agreement does not extend the General Fund retention of taxes on fuel used in motorboats and in the nonbusiness use of small-engine outdoor power equipment. The conference agreement addresses authorization of expenditures for fuel tax compliance elsewhere in the conference agreement and does not amend the Code for this purpose.

[Law at ¶5265, ¶5270, ¶5280, ¶5290, ¶5320, ¶5350, ¶5355, ¶5360, ¶5405, ¶5485, ¶5490 and ¶7050. CCH Explanation at ¶905 and ¶1025.]

[¶15,020] Act Sec. 11111. Modify gas guzzler tax

Senate Committee Report (S. REP. NO. 109-82)

[Code Sec. 4064]

Present Law

Under present law, the Code imposes a tax ("the gas guzzler tax") on automobiles that are manufactured primarily for use on public streets, roads, and highways and that are rated at 6,000 pounds unloaded gross vehicle weight or less.[12] The tax applies to limousines without regard to the weight requirement. The tax is imposed on the sale by the manufacturer of each automobile of a model type with a fuel economy of 22.5 miles per gallon or less. The tax range begins at $1,000 and increases to $7,700 for models with a fuel economy less than 12.5 miles per gallon.

Emergency vehicles and non-passenger automobiles are exempt from the tax. The tax also does not apply to non-passenger automobiles. The Secretary of Transportation determines which vehicles are "non-passenger" automobiles, thereby exempting these vehicles from the gas guzzler tax based on regulations in effect on the date of enactment of the gas guzzler tax.[13] Hence, vehicles defined in Title 49 C.F.R. sec. 523.5 (relating to light trucks) are exempt. These vehicles include those designed to transport property on an open bed (e.g., pick-up trucks) or provide greater cargo-carrying than passenger carrying volume including the expanded cargo-carrying space created through the removal of readily detachable seats (e.g., pick-up trucks, vans, and most minivans, sports utility vehicles and station wagons). Additional vehicles that meet the "non-passenger" requirements are those with at least four of the following characteristics: (1) an angle of approach of not less than 28 degrees; (2) a breakover angle of not less than 14 degrees; (3) a departure angle of not less than 20 degrees; (4) a running clearance of not less than 20 centimeters; and (5) front and rear axle clearances of not less than 18 centimeters each. These vehicles would include many sports utility vehicles.

Reasons for Change

The Committee observes that limousines are the only class of vehicles weighing in excess of 6,000 pounds subject to the gas guzzler tax. The Committee believes that, as equipment essential to a commercial enterprise, the present-law application of the gas guzzler tax to such limousines is inappropriate.

Explanation of Provision

The provision repeals the tax as it applies to limousines rated at greater than 6,000 pounds unloaded gross vehicle weight.

Effective Date

The provision is effective on October 1, 2005.

---

[12] Sec. 4064.

[13] Sec. 4064(b)(1)(B).

Conference Committee Report (H.R. Conf. Rep. No. 109-203)

Conference Agreement [Law at ¶ 5275. CCH Explanation at ¶ 335.]

The conference agreement follows the Senate amendment provision.

[¶ 15,030] Act Sec. 11112. Exclusion for tractors weighing 19,500 pounds or less from excise tax on heavy trucks and trailers

Conference Committee Report (H.R. Conf. Rep. No. 109-203)

[Code Sec. 4051]

Present Law

A 12-percent excise tax is imposed on the first retail sale of automobile truck chassis and bodies, truck trailer and semitrailer chassis and bodies, and tractors of the kind chiefly used for highway transportation in combination with a trailer or semitrailer.[14] The tax does not apply to automobile truck chassis and bodies suitable for use with a vehicle which has a gross vehicle weight of 33,000 pounds or less.[15] The tax also does not apply to truck trailer and semitrailer chassis and bodies suitable for use with a trailer or semitrailer which has a gross vehicle weight of 26,000 pounds or less.[16] In general, tractors are subject to tax regardless of their gross vehicle weight.

Temporary Treasury regulations provide that "tractor" means a highway vehicle which is primarily designed to tow a vehicle, such as a trailer or semitrailer, but which does not carry cargo on the same chassis as the engine. The regulations presume that a vehicle equipped with air brakes and/or towing package is primarily designed as a tractor.[17] The regulations further require an incomplete chassis cab to be treated as a tractor if it is equipped with any of the safety devices listed in the regulations, and require that it be treated as a truck if it is not equipped with any of the listed safety devices and the purchaser certifies in writing that the vehicle will not be equipped for use as a tractor.[18]

In *Freightliner of Grand Rapids, Inc. v. U.S.*, the district court held that certain vehicles primarily designed to tow large RV trailers but which had some cargo carrying capacity on their chassis are properly characterized as tractors.[19] The court also held that incomplete chassis cabs that do not include any of the listed safety devices are to be treated as tractors unless the purchaser certifies in writing that it will not equip the vehicles for use as tractors. Under the holding of this case, these types of vehicles are subject to tax regardless of their gross vehicle weight.

House Bill

No provision.

Senate Amendment

The Senate amendment excludes from tax tractors with a gross vehicle weight of 19,500 pounds or less.

Effective Date

The Senate amendment is effective for sales after September 30, 2005.

Conference Agreement

The conference agreement follows the Senate amendment except that it also requires that in order to be exempt the gross combined weight (as determined by the Secretary) of the tractor if combined with a towed vehicle (such as trailer or semi-trailer) would not exceed 33,000 pounds. No inference is intended from this provision regarding the proper classification of vehicles as tractors or trucks.

[Law at ¶ 5270. CCH Explanation at ¶ 340.]

---

[14] Sec. 4051(a)(1).
[15] Sec. 4051(a)(2).
[16] Sec. 4051(a)(3).
[17] Temp. Treas. Reg. sec. 145.4051-1(e)(1)(i).
[18] Temp. Treas. Reg. sec. 145.4051-1(e)(1)(ii).
[19] 351 F.Supp.2d 718 (W.D. Mich. 2004).

[¶15,040] Act Sec. 11113. Volumetric excise tax credit for alternative fuels

Conference Committee Report (H.R. CONF. REP. NO. 109-203)

[Code Secs. 4041, 4101, 6426 and 6427]

Present Law

Under section 4081 of the Code, an excise tax is imposed upon (1) the removal of any taxable fuel from a refinery or terminal, (2) the entry of any taxable fuel into the United States, or (3) the sale of any taxable fuel to any person who is not registered with the IRS to receive untaxed fuel, unless there was a prior taxable removal or entry.[25] The tax does not apply to any removal or entry of taxable fuel transferred in bulk by pipeline or vessel to a terminal or refinery if the person removing or entering the taxable fuel, the operator of such pipeline or vessel, and the operator of such terminal or refinery are registered with the Secretary.[26] Section 4081 also imposes an excise tax on taxable fuel removed or sold by the blender of the fuels.[27] However, the blender is entitled to a credit on any tax previous paid if that person establishes the amount of such tax.[28] A "taxable fuel" is gasoline, diesel fuel (including any liquid, other than gasoline, which is suitable for use as a fuel in a diesel-powered highway vehicle or train), and kerosene.[29]

Diesel fuel and kerosene generally are taxed at 24.3 cents per gallon excise (aviation-grade kerosene at 21.8 cents per gallon). Gasoline is taxed at 18.3 cents per gallon and aviation gasoline is taxed at 19.3 cents per gallon.

The Code imposes a backup retail tax for diesel fuel and kerosene not taxed under section 4081, and for special motor fuels.[30] Under section 4041, tax is imposed on special motor fuels (any liquid other than gas oil, fuel oil or any product taxable under section 4081) when there is a taxable sale by any person to an owner, lessee or other operator of a motor vehicle or motorboat, for use as fuel in the motor vehicle or motorboat or used by any person as a fuel in a motor vehicle or motorboat unless there was a prior taxable sale.[31]

Most special motor fuels are subject to tax at 18.3 cents per gallon, however, certain special motor fuels and compressed natural gas are determined on an energy equivalent basis, as follows:

Liquefied petroleum gas (propane)	13.6 cents per gallon
Liquefied natural gas	11.9 cents per gallon
Methanol derived from petroleum or natural gas	9.15 cents per gallon
Compressed natural gas	48.54 cents per MCF

Liquid hydrogen is a special motor fuel for purposes of the tax on special motor fuels and is subject to a tax of 18.3 cents per gallon.[32] Compressed hydrogen gas used or sold as a fuel is not subject to tax.

Prior to the American Jobs Creation Act of 2004, gasohol and gasoline to be blended into gasohol was taxed at a reduced rate based on the amount of ethanol contained in the mixture (e.g., 10 percent, 7.7 percent or 5.5 percent alcohol in the mixture). The Act eliminated reduced rates of excise tax for most alcohol-blended fuels. In place of the reduced rates, the Act amended the Code to create two new excise tax credits: the alcohol fuel mixture credit and the biodiesel mixture credit.[33] The sum of these credits may be taken against the tax imposed on taxable fuels (by section 4081). A person may also file a claim for payment equal to the amount of these credits for biodiesel or alcohol used to produce an eligible mixture.[34] The credits and payments are paid out of the General Fund. If the alcohol is ethanol with a proof of 190 or greater, the credit or payment amount is 51 cents per gallon. For agri-biodiesel, the credit or payment amount is $1.00 per gallon; for biodiesel other than agri-biodiesel, the credit or payment amount is 50 cents per gallon. Under the Code's coordination rules, a claim may be taken only once with respect to any particular gallon of alcohol or biodiesel.

No excise tax credit is available for the blending or sale of special motor fuels.

---

[25] Sec. 4081(a)(1).
[26] Sec. 4081(a)(1)(B).
[27] Sec. 4081(b)(1). Blended taxable fuel is a taxable fuel that is produced outside the bulk transfer/terminal system by mixing taxpayer fuel with respect to which tax has been imposed under section 4041(a)(1) or 4081(a) (other than taxable fuel for which a credit or payment has been allowed); and any other liquid on which tax has not been imposed under section 4081. Treas. Reg. sec. 48.4081-1(c)(i).
[28] Sec. 4081(b)(2).
[29] Sec. 4083(a).
[30] Sec. 4041.
[31] Sec. 4041(a)(2).
[32] An additional 0.1 cent per gallon is imposed by section 4041(d) for the Leaking Underground Storage Tank Trust Fund.
[33] Sec. 6426. The Act also created an income tax credit for biodiesel and biodiesel mixtures. Sec. 40A.
[34] Sec. 6427(e).

House Bill

No provision.

Senate Amendment

Under the Senate amendment, P Series fuels (as defined by the Secretary of Energy under 42 U.S.C. sec. 13211(2)) are taxed at 18.3 cents per gallon under section 4081. Compressed natural gas and hydrogen are taxed at 18.3 cents per energy equivalent of a gallon of gasoline, and liquefied natural gas, any liquid fuel (other than methanol or ethanol) derived from coal and liquid hydrocarbons derived from biomass are taxed at 24.3 cents per gallon under section 4081. Collectively, these fuels are referred to as "alternative fuels."

In addition, the Senate amendment creates two new excise tax credits, the alternative fuel credit, and the alternative fuel mixture credit. The credits are allowed against section 4081 liability. The alternative fuel credit is 50 cents per gallon of alternative fuel or gasoline gallon equivalents of nonliquid alternative fuel sold by the taxpayer for use as a motor fuel in a highway vehicle. The alternative fuel mixture credit is 50 cents per gallon of alternative fuel used in producing an alternative fuel mixture for sale or use in a trade or business of the taxpayer. The mixture must be sold by the taxpayer for use as a fuel in a highway vehicle or used by the taxpayer as a fuel in a highway vehicle. Liquid fuel derived from coal would only qualify for the credits if derived from the Fischer-Tropsch process. The credits generally expire after September 30, 2009. The proposal also allows persons to file a claim for payment equal to the amount of the alternative fuel credit and alternative fuel mixture credits. These payment provisions generally also expire after September 30, 2009. Both credits and payments are made out of the General Fund. Under coordination rules, a claim for payment or credit may only be taken once with respect to any particular gallon or gasoline-gallon equivalent of alternative fuel.

Conference Agreement

The conference agreement follows the Senate amendment with the following modifications.

Under the conference agreement, liquefied petroleum gas and P Series fuels (as defined by the Secretary of Energy under 42 U.S.C. sec. 13211(2)) are taxed at 18.3 cents per gallon under section 4041. Compressed natural gas is taxed at 18.3 cents per energy equivalent of a gallon of gasoline. Liquefied natural gas, any liquid fuel derived from coal (other than ethanol or methanol) and liquid hydrocarbons derived from biomass are taxed at 24.3 cents per gallon under section 4041. The conference agreement does not change the tax treatment of hydrogen, liquefied hydrogen remains subject to the tax imposed by section 4041.

In addition, the conference agreement creates two new excise tax credits, the alternative fuel credit, and the alternative fuel mixture credit. For this purpose, the term "alternative fuel" means liquefied petroleum gas, P Series fuels (as defined by the Secretary of Energy under 42 U.S.C. sec. 13211(2)), compressed or liquefied natural gas, liquefied hydrogen, liquid fuel derived from coal through the Fisher-Tropsch process, and liquid hydrocarbons derived from biomass. Such term does not include ethanol, methanol, or biodiesel.

The alternative fuel credit is allowed against section 4041 liability and the alternative fuel mixture credit is allowed against section 4081 liability. Neither credit is allowed unless the taxpayer is registered with the Secretary. The alternative fuel credit is 50 cents per gallon of alternative fuel or gasoline gallon equivalents[35] of nonliquid alternative fuel sold by the taxpayer for use as a motor fuel in a motor vehicle or motorboat, or so used by the taxpayer.

The alternative fuel mixture credit is 50 cents per gallon of alternative fuel used in producing an alternative fuel mixture for sale or use in a trade or business of the taxpayer. The mixture must be sold by the taxpayer producing such mixture to any person for use as a fuel or used by the taxpayer for use as a fuel.[36] The credits generally expire after September 30, 2009. The provision also allows persons to file a claim for payment equal to the amount of the alternative fuel credit and alternative fuel mixture credits. These payment provisions generally also expire after September 30, 2009. With respect to liquefied hydrogen, the credit and payment provisions expire after September 30, 2014. Both credits and payments are made out of the General Fund. Under coordination rules, a claim for

---

[35] "Gasoline gallon equivalent" means, with respect to any nonliquid alternative fuel, the amount of such fuel having a Btu content of 124,800 (higher heating value).

[36] For example, the taxpayer produces fish oil in its trade or business. The taxpayer uses this fish oil to make a blend of 50 percent fish oil and 50 percent diesel fuel to run in a generator that is part of the taxpayer's trade or business. This use of the fish oil-diesel blend made by the taxpayer qualifies as use of an alternative fuel mixture for purposes of the requirement that the fuel be used in the blender's trade or business.

payment or credit may only be taken once with respect to any particular gallon or gasoline-gallon equivalent of alternative fuel.

[Law at ¶ 5265, ¶ 5305, ¶ 5425 and ¶ 5430. CCH Explanation at ¶ 725.]

Effective Date

The provision is effective for any sale or use for any period after September 30, 2006.

[¶ 15,050] Act Sec. 11115. Eliminate Aquatic Resources Trust Fund and transform Sport Fish Restoration Account

Senate Committee Report (S. REP. NO. 109-82)

[Code Secs. 9503 and 9504]

Present Law

A total tax rate of 18.4 cents per gallon is imposed on gasoline and special motor fuels used in motorboats, and on gasoline used as a fuel in the nonbusiness use of small-engine outdoor power equipment.[14] Of this rate, 0.1 cent per gallon is dedicated to the Leaking Underground Storage Tank Trust Fund. Of the remaining 18.3 cents per gallon, tax collected in excess of 13.5 cents per gallon (i.e., 4.8 cents per gallon) is retained in the General Fund of the Treasury.[15] The balance is transferred to the Highway Trust Fund, and retransferred (except with respect to amounts transferred to the fund for land and water conservation, as described below) to the Aquatic Resources Trust Fund.[16] The taxes on gasoline and special motor fuels used in motorboats and the taxes on gasoline used as a fuel in the nonbusiness use of small-engine outdoor power equipment are collected under the same rules as apply to the Highway Trust Fund collections generally.

The Aquatic Resources Trust Fund is comprised of two accounts.[17] First, the Boat Safety Account is funded by a portion of the receipts from the excise tax imposed on motorboat gasoline and special motor fuels. Transfers to the Boat Safety Account are limited to amounts not exceeding $70 million per year. In addition, these transfers are subject to an overall annual limit equal to an amount that will not cause the Boat Safety Account to have an unobligated balance in excess of $70 million.[18]

Second, the Sport Fish Restoration Account receives the balance of the motorboat gasoline and special motor fuels receipts that are transferred to the Aquatic Resources Trust Fund.[19] The Sport Fish Restoration Account is also funded with receipts from an excise tax on sport fishing equipment sold by the manufacturer, producer or importer. The excise tax rate on sport fishing equipment is 10 percent of the sales price; the rate is reduced to 3 percent for electric outboard motors and fishing tackle boxes.[20] Examples of the items of sport fishing equipment subject to the 10-percent rate include fishing rods and poles, fishing reels, fly fishing lines and certain other fishing lines, fishing spears, spear guns, spear tips, items of terminal tackle, containers designed to hold fish, fishing vests, landing nets, and portable bait containers.[21] In addition, import duties on certain fishing tackle, yachts and pleasure craft are transferred into the Sport Fish Restoration Account.

The amounts of taxes on gasoline used as a fuel in the nonbusiness use of small-engine outdoor power equipment that are transferred to

---

[14] Sec. 4081(a)(2).

[15] The retention in the General Fund of the 4.8 cents per gallon of motorboat fuel taxes and taxes on gasoline used as a fuel in the nonbusiness use of small-engine outdoor power equipment expires after September 30, 2005.

[16] See Sec. 9503(b)(4), (c)(4) and (5). The transfer from the Highway Trust Fund to the Aquatic Resources Trust Fund of amounts of taxes on gasoline used a fuel in the nonbusiness use of small-engine outdoor power equipment expires after September 30, 2005. Between October 1, 2001 and September 30, 2003, the amount transferred to the Aquatic Resources Trust Fund was 13 cents per gallon. Prior to October 1, 2001, the amount transferred was 11.5 cents per gallon. Sec. 9503(b)(4)(D).

[17] Sec. 9504(a).

[18] Sec. 9503(c)(4)(A). Funding of the Boat Safety Account is scheduled to terminate after September 30, 2005.

[19] After funding of the Boat Safety Account, remaining motorboat fuel taxes, not exceeding $1,000,000 during any fiscal year, are transferred from the Highway Trust Fund into the land and water conservation fund provided in title I of the Land and Water Conservation Fund Act of 1965. Sec. 9503(c)(4)(B). After the transfer to the land and water conservation fund, motorboat fuel taxes remaining in the Highway Trust Fund are transferred to the Sport Fish Restoration Account. See 9503(c)(4)(C).

[20] Sec. 4161(a)(2) and (3).

[21] Items of "sport fishing equipment" are enumerated in section 4162(a).

the Highway Trust Fund and retransferred to the Aquatics Resources Trust Fund are directed to a separate sub-account of the Sport Fish Restoration Account, the Coastal Wetlands Sub-Account.

Expenditures from the Boat Safety Account are subject to annual appropriations. Amounts transferred, paid, or credited to the Sport Fish Restoration Account (including the Coastal Wetlands Sub-Account) are authorized to be appropriated for the uses authorized in the expenditure provisions.[22]

Reasons for Change

The Committee believes that the current Boat Safety Account is fully funded and that expenditures for boating safety relating to newly collected funds would be facilitated by treating these collections in the same manner as those currently required for the Sport Fish Restoration Account. The Committee further believes that combining the Boat Safety Account and Sport Fish Restoration Account will facilitate such uniform treatment in the future and better coordinate expenditures for sport fishing and boating safety.

Explanation of Provision

The proposal eliminates the Aquatics Resources Trust Fund and future transfers to the Boat Safety Account and transforms the Sport Fish Restoration Account into the Sport Fish Restoration and Boating Trust Fund. After funding of the land and water conservation fund as under present law, the balance of the taxes on motorboat fuels is transferred from the Highway Trust Fund into the Sport Fish Restoration and Boating Trust Fund. In addition, the transfers from the Highway Trust Fund to the Sport Fish Restoration and Boating Trust Fund of amounts of taxes on gasoline used as a fuel in the non-business use of small-engine outdoor power equipment are extended through September 30, 2011.

Existing amounts in the Boat Safety Account, plus interest accrued on interest-bearing obligations of such account, are made available as provided under expenditure provisions.[23] The expenditure provisions also authorize the appropriation of amounts in the Sport Fish Restoration and Boating Trust Fund, including for boating safety, for the uses authorized in the expenditure provisions.

Effective Date

The proposal is effective October 1, 2005.

Conference Committee Report (H.R. Conf. Rep. No. 109-203)

House Bill
No provision.

Conference Agreement
The conference agreement follows the Senate amendment.

[Law at ¶ 5485, ¶ 5490 and ¶ 7055. CCH Explanation at ¶ 1030.]

[¶ 15,060] Act Sec. 11116. Repeal of harbor maintenance tax on exports

Senate Committee Report (S. Rep. No. 109-82)

[Code Sec. 4461]

Present Law

The Code contains provisions imposing a 0.125-percent excise tax on the value of most commercial cargo loaded or unloaded at U.S. ports (other than ports included in the Inland Waterway Trust Fund system). The tax also applies to amounts paid for passenger transportation using these U.S. ports. Exemptions are provided for (1) cargo donated for overseas use, (2) cargo shipped between the U.S. mainland and Alaska (except for crude oil), Hawaii, and/or U.S. possessions and (3) cargo shipped between Alaska, Hawaii, and/or U.S. possessions.

---

[22] Act of August 9, 1950, 64 Stat. 430 (codified at 16 U.S.C. sec. 777 et seq.) ("An Act to provide that the United States shall aid the States in fish restoration and management projects, and for other purposes.")

[23] The expenditure provisions are codified at 16 U.S.C. sec. 777 et seq., as may be amended by the Sportfishing and Recreational Boating Safety Act of 2005.

Receipts from this tax are deposited in the Harbor Maintenance Trust Fund.

The U.S. Supreme Court has held that the harbor maintenance excise tax is unconstitutional as applied to exported cargo because it violates the "Export Clause" of the U.S. Constitution.[24] The tax remains in effect for imported cargo. Imposition of the tax on passenger transportation with respect to passengers on cruises that originate, stop, or terminate, at U.S. ports has been upheld.

Reasons for Change

The Committee believes the Internal Revenue Code should conform to the law of the land as interpreted by the Supreme Court and, thus, believes the harbor maintenance excise tax as applied to exported cargo should be repealed as deadwood.

Explanation of Provision

The provision conforms the Code to the Supreme Court decision and exempts exported commercial cargo from the harbor maintenance tax.

Effective Date

The provision is effective before, on, and after the date of enactment.

Conference Committee Report (H.R. CONF. REP. NO. 109-203)

House Bill
No provision.

Conference Agreement
The conference agreement follows the Senate amendment.

[Law at ¶ 5340 and ¶ 5345. CCH Explanation at ¶ 825.]

[¶ 15,065] Act Sec. 11117. Cap on excise tax on certain fishing equipment

Senate Committee Report (S. REP. NO. 109-82)

[Code Sec. 4161]

Present Law

In general, the Code imposes a 10-percent tax on the sale by the manufacturer, producer, or importer of specified sport fishing equipment.[25] A three percent rate, however, applies to the sale of electric outboard motors and fishing tackle boxes.[26] Sport fishing equipment subject to the 10-percent tax includes fishing rods and poles, fishing reels, fly fishing lines, and other fishing lines not over 130 pounds test, fishing spears, spear guns, and spear tips, and tackle items including leaders, artificial lures, artificial baits, artificial flies, fishing hooks, bobbers, sinkers, snaps, drayles, and swivels. In addition the following fishing supplies and accessories are subject to the 10-percent tax: fish stringers; creels; bags, baskets, and other containers designed to hold fish; portable bait containers; fishing vests; landing nets; gaff hooks; fishing hook disgorgers; dressing for fishing lines and artificial flies; fishing tip-ups and tilts; fishing rod belts, fishing rodholders; fishing harnesses; fish fighting chairs; and fishing outriggers and downriggers.

Revenues from the excise tax on sport fishing equipment are deposited in the Sport Fishing Account of the Aquatic Resources Trust Fund. Monies in the fund are spent, subject to an existing permanent appropriation, to support Federal-State sport fish enhancement and safety programs.

Reasons for Change

The Committee understands that as a tax on the manufacturer, the 10-percent ad valorem tax rate generally is imposed at the time a rod is sold to a wholesaler or retailer and thus the tax as a percentage of the ultimate retail price paid by the consumer is less than 10 percent. However, the Committee understands that most rods priced in excess of $100 are custom rods produced by businesses that are both the "manufacturer" and the retailer. In this circumstance the 10-percent tax rate would apply to the retail price. The Committee therefore believes that pre-

---

[24] *United States Shoe Corp. v. United States,* [98-1 USTC ¶ 70,091,] 523 U.S. 360, 118 S. Ct. 1290, 140 L. Ed. 2d 453 (1998).

[25] Sec. 4161(a)(1).

[26] Sec. 4161(a)(2) and (a)(3).

sent-law tax does not provide for neutral taxation of different segments of the fishing rod market. The Committee concludes that the tax on rods and poles the manufacturer's price of which exceeds $100 should be limited to $10.00.

Explanation of Provision

The provision provides that the tax applicable to a fishing rod or fishing pole is the lesser of 10 percent or $10.00.

Effective Date

The provision is effective for articles sold by the manufacturer, producer, or importer after September 30, 2005.

Conference Committee Report (H.R. CONF. REP. NO. 109-203)

[Code Sec. 4161]

House Bill

No provision.

Conference Agreement

The conference agreement follows the Senate amendment.

[Law at ¶ 5310. CCH Explanation at ¶ 845.]

[¶ 15,070] Act Sec. 11121. Clarification of excise tax exemptions for agricultural aerial applicators and exemption for fixed-wing aircraft engaged in forestry operations

Senate Committee Report (S. REP. NO. 109-82)

[Code Secs. 4261 and 6420]

Present Law

Excise taxes are imposed on aviation gasoline (19.4 cents per gallon) and jet fuel (21.9 cents per gallon).[27] All but 0.1 cent per gallon of the revenues from these taxes are dedicated to the Airport and Airway Trust Fund. The remaining 0.1 cent per gallon rate is imposed for the Leaking Underground Storage Tank Trust Fund.

Fuel used on a farm for farming purposes is a nontaxable use. Aerial applicators (crop dusters) are allowed to claim a refund instead of farm owners and operators in the case of aviation gasoline if the owners or operators give written consent to the aerial applicators.[28] This provision applies only to fuel consumed in the airplane while operating over the farm, i.e., fuel consumed traveling to and from the farm is not exempt.

Air passenger transportation is subject to an excise tax equal to 7.5 percent of the amount paid plus $3.20 per domestic flight segment.[29] The tax on transportation by air does not apply to air transportation by helicopter if the helicopter is used for (1) the exploration, or the development or removal of oil, gas, or hard minerals exploration, or (2) certain timber operations (planting, cultivating, cutting, transporting, or caring for trees, including logging operations).[30] The exemption applies only when the helicopters are not using the Federally funded airport and airway services. Helicopters and fixed-wing aircraft providing emergency medical services also are exempt from the air passenger tax regardless of the type of airport and airway services used.[31]

Reasons for Change

The Committee believes significant simplification and reduction of administrative burden will be achieved by eliminating the requirements that aerial applicators obtain written consent from the farm owner for exempt fuel use and by allowing exempt fuel use to extend to fuel consumed when flying between the farms where chemicals are applied and the airport where the airplane takes off and lands. In addition, the Committee notes that the purpose of the aviation excise taxes is to generate revenue for the Airport Improvement program, which builds new and retrofits and expands existing public airports. The Committee believes it is appropriate to extend the current exemption for helicopters engaged in timber operations to fixed wing air-

---

[27] Sec. 4081.
[28] Sec. 6420(c)(4).
[29] Sec. 4261(a) and (b).
[30] Sec. 4261(f)
[31] Sec. 4261(g).

craft when such aircraft are not using the Federally funded airport and airway services.

Explanation of Provision

With regard to the exemption for aerial applicators, written consent from the farm owner or operator is no longer needed for the aerial applicator to claim exemption for aviation gasoline. The exemption also is expanded to include fuels consumed when flying between the farms where chemicals are applied and the airport where the airplane takes off and lands. The present exemption for helicopters engaged in timber operations is expanded to include fixed-wing aircraft if such aircraft are not using the Federally funded airport and airway services.

Effective Date

The provision is effective for fuel use or air transportation after September 30, 2005.

Conference Committee Report (H.R. CONF. REP. NO. 109-203)

House Bill

No provision.

Conference Agreement

The conference agreement follows the Senate amendment.

[Law at ¶ 5330 and ¶ 5115. CCH Explanation at ¶ 820 and ¶ 822.]

[¶ 15,080] Act Sec. 11122. Modify the definition of rural airport

Senate Committee Report (S. REP. NO. 109-82)

[Code Sec. 4261]

Present Law

Air passenger transportation is subject to an excise tax equal to 7.5 percent of the amount paid plus $3.20 per domestic flight segment.[32] The $3.20 tax on flight segments does not apply to a domestic segment beginning or ending at a rural airport.

With respect to any calendar year, a rural airport is an airport that had fewer than 100,000 passengers departing by air during the second preceding calendar year for such airport and such airport either (1) is not located within 75 miles of a larger airport (one that had at least 100,000 passengers departing in the second preceding calendar year), or (2) was receiving essential air service subsidy payments as of August 5, 1997.

Reasons for Change

The Committee notes that the present-law definition of "rural airports" generally encompasses those airports that do not offer potential customers a viable alternative to a larger airport from which a ticket would subject the purchaser to the flight segment tax in addition to the ad valorem tax. The Committee observes that airports located on islands with no direct access by road from the mainland also would not offer potential customers a viable alternative to a larger airport, even if the island airport is within 75 miles of the larger airport.

Explanation of Provision

The provision expands the definition of qualified rural airport to include an airport that (1) is not connected by paved roads to another airport and (2) had fewer than 100,000 commercial passengers departing by air on flight segments of at least 100 miles during the second preceding calendar year.

Effective Date

The provision is effective on October 1, 2005.

Conference Committee Report (H.R. CONF. REP. NO. 109-203)

House Bill

No provision.

Conference Agreement

The conference agreement follows the Senate amendment.

[Law at ¶ 5325. CCH Explanation at ¶ 805.]

---

[32] Sec. 4261(a) and (b).

[¶ 15,090] Act Sec. 11123. Exempt from ticket taxes transportation provided by seaplanes

Senate Committee Report (S. Rep. No. 109-82)

[Code Sec. 4261]

Present Law

Air passenger transportation is subject to an excise tax equal to 7.5 percent of the amount paid plus $3.20 per domestic flight segment ("air passenger tax").[33] A 6.25-percent tax is imposed on amounts paid for transportation of property by air ("air cargo tax").[34] The air cargo tax applies only to amounts paid to persons engaged in the business of transporting property by air for hire. The air passenger tax and air cargo tax does not apply to amounts paid for the transportation if furnished on an aircraft having a maximum certificated takeoff weight of 6,000 pounds or less unless the aircraft is operated on an established line.[35]

Reasons for Change

The Committee observes that seaplanes do not make as full utilization of Federal Aviation Administration services as do planes that offer passenger service out of traditional airports. The Committee, therefore, believes it is appropriate to exempt such service from the air transportation excise taxes and instead impose only the fuels excise taxes.

Explanation of Provision

The provision provides that the air passenger tax and the air cargo tax do not apply to transportation by a seaplane with respect to any segment consisting of a takeoff from, and a landing on, water, but only if the places at which such takeoff and landing occur have not received and are not receiving financial assistance from the Airport and Airway Trust Fund.

Effective Date

The provision is effective for transportation after September 30, 2005.

Conference Committee Report (H.R. Conf. Rep. No. 109-203)

House Bill

No provision.

Conference Agreement

The conference agreement follows the Senate amendment but clarifies that for purposes of the fuel taxes, transportation by seaplane is treated as noncommercial aviation.

[Law at ¶ 5300 and ¶ 5330. CCH Explanation at ¶ 810.]

[¶ 15,100] Act Sec. 11124. Exempt certain sightseeing flights from taxes on air transportation

Senate Committee Report (S. Rep. No. 109-82)

[Code Sec. 4281]

Present Law

Under present law, taxable aviation transportation is subject to a 7.5-percent excise tax on the price of an airline ticket and a $3.20 segment tax. An exception to these taxes is provided for transportation by an aircraft having a maximum certificated takeoff weight of 6,000 pounds or less except when the aircraft is operated on an established line. Under the Treasury regulations to be "operated on an established line" means to be operated with "some degree of regularity between definite points. The term implies that the air carrier maintains control over the direction, routes, time, number of passengers carried, etc." Treasury regulations provide that transportation need not be between two definite points to be taxable: a payment for continuous transportation beginning and ending at the same point is subject to the tax.[36] The IRS position is that the words "between definite points" do not require two separate points for purposes of determining

---

[33] Sec. 4261(a) and (b).
[34] Sec. 4271.
[35] Sec. 4281.
[36] Treas. Reg. sec. 494261-1(c).

whether an aircraft is operated on an established line. At least one court has agreed.[37]

Reasons for Change

The Committee believes it is appropriate to exempt certain sightseeing flights from the taxes on air transportation. Examples of sightseeing flights include flights of short duration that overlook a glacier, volcano, the Grand Canyon, or other similar attraction and for which the air tour begins and ends at the same point. By short duration, the Committee intends that the tour occur within a calendar day, irrespective of intermittent stops to view the attraction. In addition, all passengers from the initial point of departure must return with the aircraft at the conclusion of the tour. The Committee believes that such flights are primarily for entertainment rather than for transportation from one place to another and so should be treated as noncommercial aviation.

Explanation of Provision

For purposes of the proposal exemption for small aircraft operated on nonestablished lines, an aircraft operated on a flight, the sole purpose of which is sightseeing, will not be considered as operated on an established line.

Effective Date

The provision is effective with respect to transportation beginning after September 30, 2005, but does not apply to any amount paid before such date for such transportation.

Conference Committee Report (H.R. CONF. REP. NO. 109-203)

House Bill   [Law at ¶ 5335. CCH Explanation at ¶ 815.]

No provision.

Conference Agreement

The conference agreement follows the Senate amendment.

[¶ 15,110] Act Sec. 11125. Repeal of special occupational taxes on producers and marketers of alcoholic beverages

Senate Committee Report (S. REP. NO. 109-82)

[Code Secs. 5081, 5091, 5111, 5112, 5113, 5117, 5121, 5122, 5123, 5125, 5131, 5132, 5141, 5147, 5148 and 5276]

Present Law

Under the law in effect prior to July 1, 2005, special occupational taxes are imposed on producers and others engaged in the marketing of distilled spirits, wine, and beer. These excise taxes are imposed as part of a broader Federal tax and regulatory structure governing the production and marketing of alcoholic beverages. The special occupational taxes are payable annually, on July 1 of each year. The tax rates in effect prior to July 1, 2005 are as follows:

Producers[38] Distilled spirits and wines (sec. 5081),[39] $1,000 per year, per premise;

Brewers (sec. 5091), 1,000 per year, per premise

Wholesale dealers (sec. 5111): Liquors, wines, or beer, $500 per year

Retail dealers (sec. 5121): Liquors, wines, or beer, $250 per year

Nonbeverage use of distilled spirits (sec. 5131): $500 per year

Industrial use of distilled spirits (sec. 5276) $250 per year

Section 246(a) of the American Jobs Creation Act of 2004[40] suspends the special occupational tax for the period beginning July 1, 2005 and ending June 30, 2008.[41]

---

[37] *Lake Mead Air Inc.* v. *United States*, 991 F. Supp. 1209 (D. Nev. 1997).

[38] A reduced rate of tax in the amount of $500.00 is imposed on small proprietors (as defined in the Code) (secs. 5081(b) and 5091(b)).

[39] Proprietors of plants producing distilled spirits exclusively for fuel use, with annual production not exceeding 10,000 proof gallons, are exempt. Secs. 5081(c), 5181(c)(4).

[40] Pub. L. No. 108-357.

[41] See sec. 5148.

Every person engaged in a trade or business on which a special occupational tax is imposed is required to register with the Secretary.⁴² In addition, every dealer in liquors, wine or beer is required to keep records of their transactions.⁴³ A dealer is any person who sells, or offers for sale, distilled spirits, wine, or beer.⁴⁴ A delegate of the Secretary of the Treasury is authorized to inspect the records of any dealer during business hours.⁴⁵ There are penalties for failing to comply with the recordkeeping requirements.⁴⁶ There are also registration and regulation requirements for the nonbeverage use of distilled spirits, and permit and recordkeeping requirements for the industrial use of distilled spirits.⁴⁷

The Code limits the persons from whom dealers may purchase their liquor stock intended for resale. A dealer may only purchase from:

1. a wholesale dealer in liquors who has paid the special occupational tax as such dealer to cover the place where such purchase is made; or

2. a wholesale dealer in liquors who is exempt, at the place where such purchase is made, from payment of such tax under any provision chapter 51 of the Code; or

3. a person who is not required to pay special occupational tax as a wholesale dealer in liquors.⁴⁸

Violation of this restriction in punishable by $1,000 fine, imprisonment of one year, or both.⁴⁹ A violation also makes the alcohol subject to seizure and forfeiture.⁵⁰

Reasons for Change

The special occupational tax is not a tax on alcoholic products but rather operates as a license fee on businesses. The Committee believes that this tax places an unfair burden on business owners. However, the Committee recognizes that the registration and recordkeeping requirements applicable to wholesalers and retailers engaged in such businesses are necessary enforcement tools to ensure the protection of the revenue arising from the excise taxes on these products. Thus, the Committee believes it appropriate to repeal the tax, while retaining present-law recordkeeping requirements.

Explanation of Provision

The provision repeals the special occupational taxes on producers and marketers of alcoholic beverages and on the nonbeverage or industrial use of distilled spirits. The registration, recordkeeping and inspection rules applicable to wholesale and retail dealers are retained.⁵¹ For purposes of the recordkeeping requirements for wholesale and retail liquor dealers, the provision provides a rebuttable presumption that a person who sells, or offers for sale, distilled spirits, wine, or beer, in quantities of 20 wine gallons or more to the same person at the same time is engaged in the business of a wholesale dealer in liquors or a wholesale dealer in beer. In addition, the provision retains the present-law rules that make it unlawful for any liquor dealer to purchase distilled spirits for resale from any person other than a wholesale liquor dealer subject to the recordkeeping requirements, or a proprietor of a distilled spirits plant subject to recordkeeping requirements.⁵² Existing general criminal penalties relating to records and reports apply to wholesalers and retailers who fail to comply with these requirements.

Effective Date

The provision is effective on July 1, 2008. The provision does not affect liability for taxes imposed with respect to periods before July 1, 2008.

---

⁴² Secs. 5141 and 7011. The registration is of such person's name or style, place of residence, trade or business, and the place where such trade or business is to be carried on.

⁴³ Secs. 5114 and 5124.

⁴⁴ Sec. 5112(a). Such definition includes producers and, in general, proprietors of warehouses.

⁴⁵ Sec. 5146.

⁴⁶ Sec. 5603.

⁴⁷ Secs. 5132 and 5275.

⁴⁸ Sec. 5117. For example, purchases from a proprietor of a distilled spirits plant at his principal business office would be covered under item (2) since such a proprietor is not subject to the special occupational tax on account of sales at his principal business office (sec. 5113(a)). Purchases from a liquor store operated by a State or by a political subdivision of a State would be covered under item (3) (sec. 5113(b)).

⁴⁹ Sec. 5687.

⁵⁰ Sec. 7302.

⁵¹ The provision also retains the present-law registration and regulation requirements for the nonbeverage use of distilled spirits, and the permit and recordkeeping requirements for the industrial use of distilled spirits.

⁵² Proprietors of distilled spirits plants remain subject to present law recordkeeping requirements under section 5207. Under present law, a limited retail dealer in liquors (such as a charitable organization selling liquor at a picnic) may lawfully purchase distilled spirits for resale from a retail dealer in distilled spirits. The provision retains this rule.

Conference Committee Report (H.R. Conf. Rep. No. 109-203)

House Bill

No provision.

Conference Agreement

The conference agreement follows the Senate amendment.

[Law at ¶ 5390, ¶ 5460, ¶ 5475 and ¶ 7060. CCH Explanation at ¶ 840.]

[¶ 15,120] Act Sec. 11126. Provide an income tax credit for cost of carrying tax-paid distilled spirits in wholesale inventories and in control State bailment warehouses

Senate Committee Report (S. Rep. No. 109-82)

[New Code Sec. 5011]

Present Law

As is true of most major Federal excise taxes, the excise tax on distilled spirits is imposed at a point in the chain of distribution before the product reaches the retail (consumer) level. The excise tax on distilled spirits produced in the United States is imposed when the distilled spirits are removed from the distilled spirits plant where they are produced. Distilled spirits that are bottled before importation into the United States are taxed on removal from the first U.S. custom bonded warehouse to which they are landed (including a warehouse located in a foreign trade zone). Distilled spirits imported in bulk containers from bottling in the United States may be transferred to a domestic distilled spirits plant without payment of tax; subsequently, these distilled spirits are taxed in the same way as domestically produced distilled spirits.

No tax credits are allowed under present law for business costs associated with having tax-paid products in inventory. Rather, excise tax that is included in the purchase price of a product is treated the same as the other components of the product cost, i.e., deductible as a cost of goods sold.

Reasons for Change

Under current law, wholesale importers of distilled spirits are not required to pay the Federal excise tax on imported spirits until after the product is removed from a bonded warehouse for sale to a retailer. In contrast, the tax on domestically produced spirits is included as part of the purchase price and passed on from the supplier to wholesaler. It is the Committee's understanding that in some instances, wholesalers can carry this tax-paid inventory for an average of 60 days before selling it to a retailer. The Committee believes it is appropriate to provide an income tax credit to approximate the interest charge—more commonly referred to as float—that results from carrying tax-paid distilled spirits in inventory.

Explanation of Provision

The provision creates a new income tax credit for eligible wholesalers, distillers, and importers, of distilled spirits. The credit is calculated by multiplying the number of cases of bottled distilled spirits by the average tax-financing cost per case for the most recent calendar year ending before the beginning of such taxable year. A case is 12 80-proof 750-milliliter bottles. The average tax-financing cost per case is the amount of interest that would accrue at corporate overpayment rates during an assumed 60-day holding period on an assumed tax rate of $25.68 per case of 12 80-proof 750-milliliter bottles.

The wholesaler credit only applies to domestically bottled distilled spirits[60] purchased directly from the bottler of such spirits. An eligible wholesaler is any person that holds a permit under the Federal Alcohol Administration Act as a wholesaler of distilled spirits that is not a State, or agency or political subdivision thereof.

For distillers and importers that are not eligible wholesalers, the credit is limited to bottled inventory in a warehouse owned and operated by, or on behalf of, a State when title to such inventory has not passed unconditionally. The

---

[60] Distilled spirits that are imported in bulk and then bottled domestically qualify as domestically bottled distilled spirits.

credit for distillers and importers applies to distilled spirits bottled both domestically and abroad.

The credit is in addition to present-law rules allowing tax included in inventory costs to be deducted as a cost of goods sold.

The credit is treated as part of the general business credits.

Effective Date

The provision is effective for taxable years beginning after September 30, 2005.

Conference Committee Report (H.R. CONF. REP. NO. 109-203)

House Bill

No provision.

Conference Agreement

The conference agreement follows the Senate amendment.

[Law at ¶ 5040 and ¶ 5370. CCH Explanation at ¶ 835.]

[¶ 15,130] Act Sec. 11127. Quarterly excise tax filing for small alcohol excise taxpayers

Senate Committee Report (S. REP. NO. 109-82)

[Code Sec. 5061]

Present Law

Excise taxes on distilled spirits, wines, and beers are collected on the basis of returns filed in accordance with rules prescribed by the Secretary of the Treasury.[61] Domestic producers of distilled spirits, beer, and wine are generally required to pay alcohol excise taxes within 14 days after the last day of the semi-monthly period during which the article is withdrawn under a deferred payment bond.[62] Treasury regulations also permit certain very small wine producers to file and pay on an annual basis.[63] In the case of distilled spirits, wines, and beer which are imported into the United States (other than in bulk containers), the importer is generally required to pay alcohol excise taxes within 14 days after the last day of the semi-monthly period during which the article is entered into the customs territory of the United States.[64] In the case of imported articles entered for warehousing, the taxes are generally due within 14 days after the last day of the semi-monthly period during which the article is removed from the first such warehouse.[65]

Special rules apply to accelerate payments made with respect to taxes allocable to the second half of the month of September.[66]

Reasons for Change

The Committee believes that the payment of alcohol excise taxes and filing of the related tax returns on a semi-monthly basis are a heavy burden for small businesses engaged in the production and importation of distilled spirits, wines and beers. The Committee wishes to lighten the paperwork load on these taxpayers by permitting filing and payment on a quarterly basis.

Explanation of Provision

Under the provision, domestic producers and importers of distilled spirits, wines, and beers with annual excise tax liability of $50,000 or less attributable to alcohol may file returns and pay taxes within 14 days after the end of the calendar quarter instead of on a semi-monthly basis. In order to qualify, the taxpayer's tax liability for such taxes during the immediately preceding year must have been $50,000 or less, and, as of the beginning of the current calendar year, the taxpayer must reasonably expect to pay less than $50,000 in such taxes for that year. The provision does not apply to a taxpayer for any portion of the calendar year following the first date on which the aggregate amount of tax due for that year exceeds the $50,000 threshold.

---

[61] Sec. 5061(a).

[62] Sec. 5061(d)(1).

[63] Annual filing and payment is permitted to a wine producer who has not given a deferred payment bond, and who either paid wine excise taxes in an amount less than $1,000 during the previous calendar year or is a proprietor of a new bonded wine premise and expects to pay less than $1,000 in wine excise taxes before the end of the calendar year. 27 CFR sec. 24.273(a).

[64] Sec. 5061(d)(2)(A).

[65] Sec. 5061(d)(2)(B).

[66] Sec. 5061(d)(4).

The special rules accelerating payments for taxes allocable to the second half of September do not apply to quarterly filers under the proposal.

Very small wine producers may still file and pay on an annual basis as under present law.

Conference Committee Report (H.R. CONF. REP. NO. 109-203)

Conference Agreement

The conference agreement follows the Senate amendment with the clarification that quarterly filing and payment applies only to withdrawals, removals, and entries (and articles brought into the United States from Puerto Rico) under deferred payment bonds. Transactions that are not made under deferred payment bonds do not qualify for quarterly filing and payment, but do count toward determining whether the $50,000 threshold has been reached.

[Law at ¶ 5375. CCH Explanation at ¶ 830.]

Effective Date

The provision is effective for quarterly periods beginning January 1, 2006.

[¶ 15,140] Act Sec. 11131. Custom gunsmiths

Senate Committee Report (S. REP. NO. 109-82)

[Code Sec. 4182]

Present Law

The Code imposes an excise tax upon the sale by the manufacturer, producer or importer of certain firearms and ammunition.[67] Pistols and revolvers are taxable at 10 percent. Firearms (other than pistols and revolvers), shells, and cartridges are taxable at 11 percent. The excise tax for firearms imposed on manufacturers, producers, and importers does not apply to machine guns and short barreled firearms. Sales to the Defense Department of firearms, pistols, revolvers, shells and cartridges also are exempt from the tax.

Reasons for Change

Many custom gunsmiths do not actually make new guns, rather they remodel or refurbish existing firearms. The provision establishes an exemption from the excise tax for manufacturers of fewer than 50 firearms per year. The Committee believes two objectives are accomplished under the provisions. First, this provision eliminates the imposition of the excise tax on custom gunmakers, and second, it eliminates an administrative burden placed on small businesses.

Explanation of Provision

The provision exempts from the firearms excise tax firearms, pistols, and revolvers manufactured, produced, or imported by a person who manufactures, produces, and imports less than 50 of such articles during the calendar year. Controlled groups are treated as a single person for determining the 50-article limit.

Effective Date

The provision is effective for articles sold by the manufacturer, producer, or importer after September 30, 2005. No inference is intended from the prospective effective date of this provision as to the proper treatment of pre-effective date sales.

Conference Committee Report (H.R. CONF. REP. NO. 109-203)

House Bill

No provision.

Conference Agreement

The conference agreement follows the Senate amendment.

[Law at ¶ 5315. CCH Explanation at ¶ 850.]

---

[67] Sec. 4181.

[¶ 15,150] Act Sec. 11141. Motor Fuel Tax Enforcement Advisory Commission

Senate Committee Report (S. REP. NO. 109-82)

[Act Sec. 11141]

Present Law

Present law does not require that there be an advisory commission on motor tax fuel enforcement.

Reasons for Change

The Committee believes that motor fuel tax administration can be improved through the cooperation and shared experiences of the various stakeholders in motor fuel tax enforcement. Therefore, the Committee believes it appropriate to create an advisory commission for motor fuel tax enforcement consisting of both Government and private sector members.

Explanation of Provision

The provision establishes a "Motor Fuel Tax Enforcement Advisory Commission" (the "Commission"). The purpose of the Commission is to (1) review motor fuel revenue collections, historical and current, (2) review the progress of investigations (3) develop and review legislative proposals with respect to motor fuel taxes, (4) monitor the progress of administrative regulation projects relating to fuel taxes, (5) review the results Federal and State agency cooperative efforts regarding motor fuel taxes, and (6) review the results of Federal interagency cooperative efforts regarding motor fuel taxes. The Commission also is to evaluate and make recommendations regarding (1) the effectiveness of existing Federal enforcement programs regarding motor fuel taxes, (2) enforcement personnel allocation, and (3) proposals for regulatory projects, legislation, and funding.

The Commission is to be composed of the following:

1. At least one representative from each of the following Federal entities: the Department of Homeland Security, the Department of Transportation—Office of Inspector General, the Federal Highway Administration, the Department of Defense, and the Department of Justice.

2. At least one representative from the Federation of State Tax Administrators,

3. At least one representative from any State Department of Transportation,

4. Two representatives from the highway construction industry,

5. Six representatives from industries relating to fuel distribution: refiners (2 representatives), distributors (1 representative), pipelines (1 representative), terminal operators (2 representatives),

6. One representative from the retail fuel industry, and

7. Two representatives each from the staff of the Senate Committee on Finance and the House Committee on Ways and Means.

Members of the Commission are to be appointed by the Senate Committee on Finance and the House Committee on Ways and Means. Representatives from the Department of Treasury and the IRS shall be available to consult with the Commission upon request. The Commission is to terminate after September 30, 2009.

Effective Date

The provision is effective on the date of enactment.

Conference Committee Report (H.R. CONF. REP. NO. 109-203)

House Bill

No provision.

Conference Agreement

The conference agreement follows the Senate amendment.

[Law at ¶ 7065. CCH Explanation at ¶ 780.]

¶ 15,150 Act Sec. 11141

[¶ 15,160] Act Sec. 11142. National Surface Transportation Infrastructure Financing Commission

Senate Committee Report (S. Rep. No. 109-82)

[Act Sec. 11142]

Present Law

Present law does not provide for any advisory commissions related Federal highway or mass transit funding.

Reasons for Change

The Committee observes that, as the fuel economy of the nation's vehicular fleet improves, receipts flowing to the Highway Trust Fund will not grow commensurately with highway use. At the same time, the Committee recognizes that the nation's need for transportation infrastructure improvements are great. The Committee believes now is the time to engage in a review of the nation's long-term transportation infrastructure needs and a thoughtful reassessment of how to finance those needs.

Explanation of Provision

The provision establishes a "National Surface Transportation Infrastructure Financing Commission" (the "Financing Commission"). The Financing Commission is to be composed of 15 members drawn from among individuals knowledgeable in the fields of public transportation finance or highway and transit programs, policy, and needs. Financing Commission members may include representatives of State and local governments or other public transportation agencies, representatives of the transportation construction industry, providers of transportation, persons knowledgeable in finance, and users of highway and transit systems. The 15 members will be appointed as follows:

1. The Secretary of Transportation, in consultation with the Secretary of the Treasury, will appoint seven members;

2. The chairman of the House Committee on Ways and Means will appoint two members;

3. The ranking minority member of the House Committee on Ways and Means will appoint two members;

4. The chairman of the Senate Committee on Finance will appoint two members; and

5. The ranking minority member of the Senate Committee on Finance will appoint two members.

The Financing Commission will make an investigation and study of revenues flowing into the Highway Trust Fund under present law, including the individual components of the flow of such revenues. The Financing Commission will consider whether the amount of such revenues is likely to increase, decline or remain unchanged absent changes in the law, particularly by taking into account the impact of possible changes in consumers' vehicle choice, fuel use or travel alternatives that could be expected to reduce or increase revenues in to the Highway Trust Fund. The Financing Commission will consider alternative approaches to generating revenues for the Highway Trust Fund, and the level of revenues that such alternatives would yield. The Financing Commission will consider highway and transit needs and whether additional revenues into the Highway Trust Fund, or other Federal revenues dedicated to highway and transit infrastructure, would be required in order to meet such needs. The Financing Commission's study should address the period between the present and through the year 2015.

Based on such investigation and study, the Financing Commission will develop a final report, with recommendations and the bases for those recommendations, indicating policies that the Congress may consider to achieve various levels of annual revenue for the Highway Trust Fund and to enable the Highway Trust Fund to receive revenues sufficient to meet highway and transit needs. The Financing Commission's recommendations will address: (1) what levels of revenue are required by the Highway Trust Fund in order for it to meet needs to maintain and improve the condition and performance of the nation's highway and transit systems; (2) what levels of revenue are required by the Highway Trust Fund in order to ensure that Federal levels of investment in highways and transit do not decline in real terms; and (3) the extent, if any, to which the Highway Trust Fund should be augmented by other mechanisms or funds as a Federal means of financing highway and transit infrastructure investments.

The Financing Commission will submit its report and recommendations within two years of the date of its first meeting to the Secretary of Transportation, the Secretary of the Treasury, the House Committee on Ways and Means, Senate

Committee on Finance, the House Committee on Transportation and Infrastructure, the Senate Committee on Environment and Public Works, and Senate Committee on Banking, Housing, and Urban Affairs. The Financing Commission will hold its first meeting within 90 days of the appointment of the eighth individual to the Financing Commission and the Financing Commission will terminate on the 180th day following the transmittal of its report and recommendations.

Effective Date

The provision is effective on the date of enactment.

Conference Committee Report (H.R. CONF. REP. NO. 109-203)

House Bill

No provision.

Conference Agreement

The conference agreement follows the Senate amendment with the following modification. The Commission also must consider a program that would exempt all or a portion of gasoline or other motor fuels used in a State from the Federal excise tax on such gasoline or other motor fuels if such State elects not to receive all or a portion of Federal transportation funding, including: (1) whether such State should be required to increase State gasoline or other motor fuels taxes by the amount of the decrease in the Federal excise tax on such gasoline or other motor fuels; (2) whether any Federal transportation funding should not be reduced or eliminated for States participating in such program; (3) whether there are any compliance problems related to enforcement of Federal transportation-related excise taxes; and (4) study such other matters closely related to the subjects described in the preceding subparagraphs as it may deem appropriate.

[Law at ¶ 7070. CCH Explanation at ¶ 920.]

[¶ 15,170] Act Sec. 11143. Tax-exempt financing of highway projects and rail-truck transfer facilities

Conference Committee Report (H.R. CONF. REP. NO. 109-203)

[Code Sec. 142]

Present law

Tax-exempt bonds

In general

Interest on bonds issued by State and local governments generally is excluded from gross income for Federal income tax purposes if the proceeds of the bonds are used to finance direct activities of these governmental units or if the bonds are repaid with revenues of the governmental units. Interest on State or local bonds to finance activities of private persons ("private activity bonds") is taxable unless a specific exception is contained in the Code (or in a non-Code provision of a revenue Act). The term "private person" generally includes the Federal government and all other individuals and entities other than States or local governments.

Qualified private activity bonds

Private activity bonds are eligible for tax-exemption if issued for certain purposes permitted by the Code ("qualified private activity bonds"). The definition of a qualified private activity bond includes an exempt facility bond, or qualified mortgage, veterans' mortgage, small issue, redevelopment, 501(c)(3), or student loan bond.[94] The definition of exempt facility bond includes bonds issued to finance certain transportation facilities (airports, ports, mass commuting, and high-speed intercity rail facilities); low-income residential rental property; privately owned and/or operated utility facilities (sewage, water, solid waste disposal, and local district heating and cooling facilities, certain private electric and gas facilities, and hydroelectric dam enhancements); public/private educational facilities; and, qualified green building/sustainable design projects.[95]

Issuance of most qualified private activity bonds is subject (in whole or in part) to annual State volume limitations.[96] Exceptions are provided for bonds for certain governmentally owned facilities (airports, ports, high-speed intercity rail, and solid waste disposal) and bonds which are subject to separate local, State, or na-

---

[94] Sec. 141(e).
[95] Sec. 142(a).
[96] Sec. 146.

tional volume limits (public/private educational facilities, enterprise zone facility bonds, and qualified green building/sustainable design projects).

House Bill

No provision.

Senate Amendment

The Senate amendment establishes new categories of exempt facility bonds: bonds issued to finance "qualified highway facilities" and bonds issued to finance "qualified surface freight transfer facilities" (collectively "qualified highway or surface freight transfer facilities"). Under the provision, a qualified highway facility is any surface transportation or international bridge or tunnel project (for which an international entity authorized under Federal or State law is responsible) which receives Federal assistance under title 23 of the United States Code (relating to Highways). A qualified surface freight transfer facility is a facility for the transfer of freight from truck to rail or rail to truck which receives Federal assistance under title 23 or title 49 of the United States Code (relating to Transportation).

Under the provision, bonds issued to finance qualified highway or surface freight transfer facilities are not subject to the State volume limitations. Rather, there is an annual limitation on the aggregate amount of bonds that may be issued to finance such facilities for each of the calendar years 2005 through 2015, as follows: $130 million for 2005; $750 million for each of the years 2006, 2007, 2008, and 2009; $1.87 billion for 2010; $2 billion for each of the years 2011, 2012, 2013, 2014, and 2015. The Secretary of Transportation may allocate the annual bond authority among qualified highway or surface freight transfer facilities in such manner as the Secretary of Transportation determines appropriate. The authority to issue qualified highway or surface freight transfer facility bonds terminates after December 31, 2015.

The Senate amendment requires the proceeds of qualified highway or surface freight transfer facility bonds to be spent on qualified projects within five years from the date of issuance of such bonds. Proceeds that remain unspent after five years must be used to redeem outstanding bonds. However, the provision authorizes the Secretary of the Treasury (or his delegate) to extend the five-year period if the issuer establishes that the need for the extension is appropriate and due to circumstances not within the control of the issuer.

Effective Date

The Senate amendment applies to bonds issued after the date of enactment.

Conference Agreement

The conference agreement follows the Senate amendment provision with modifications. The conference agreement eliminates the limitation on the aggregate amount of qualified highway or surface freight transfer facility bonds that may be issued in each of the calendar years 2005 through 2015. The Secretary of Transportation is authorized to allocate a total of $15 billion of issuance authority to qualified highway or surface freight transfer facilities in such manner as the Secretary determines appropriate. The conference agreement also clarifies that bonds are not treated as qualified highway or surface freight transfer facility bonds unless the aggregate amount of bonds issued with respect to qualified facilities does not exceed the amount of authority allocated to such facilities by the Secretary of Transportation. However, the aggregate limitation on bonds that may be issued does not apply to the "current refunding" of qualified highway or surface freight transfer facility bonds. Bonds are treated as a current refunding for this purpose if: (1) the average maturity date of the refunding bond is not later than the average maturity date of the refunded bonds; (2) the amount of the refunding bond does not exceed the outstanding amount of the refunded bond, and (3) the refunded bond is redeemed not later than 90 days after the date of the issuance of the refunding bond.

The conference agreement on this provision is not intended to expand the scope of any Federal requirement beyond its application under present law and does not broaden the application of any Federal requirement under present law in Title 49.

[Law at ¶ 5145 and ¶ 5150. CCH Explanation at ¶ 915.]

Act Sec. 11143   ¶ 15,170

[¶ 15,180] Act Sec. 11144. Treasury study of highway fuels used by trucks for non-transportation purposes

Conference Committee Report (H.R. Conf. Rep. No. 109-203)

[Act Sec. 11144]

Present Law

Present law does not provide for a study of the fuel use by trucks.

House Bill

No provision.

Senate Amendment

The Senate amendment directs the Secretary of the Treasury to study the use by trucks of highway motor fuel that is not used for the propulsion of the vehicle, both in the case of vehicles carrying equipment that is unrelated to the transportation function of the vehicle and in the case where non-transportation equipment is run by a separate motor. In addition, the Secretary is to estimate the amount of fuel consumed and pollutants emitted by trucks due to the long-term idling of diesel engines, and report on the cost of reducing long-term idling through various technologies. The Secretary is to propose options for implementing exemptions for classes of vehicles whose nonpropulsive fuel use exceeds 50 percent.

Effective Date

The Senate amendment is effective on the date of enactment.

Conference Agreement

The conference agreement follows the Senate amendment with modification that the Secretary is to propose options for implementing exemptions from tax for fuel used in non-transportation uses, but only if the Secretary determines such exemptions are administratively feasible, for the following: (1) mobile machinery whose nonpropulsive fuel use exceeds 50 percent and (2) any highway vehicle that consumes fuel for both transportation-and non-transportation-related equipment, using a single motor. With respect to item (2), it is intended that the Secretary take into consideration such factors as whether the fuel use for non-transportation equipment by the vehicle operator is significant both relative to transportation-related fuel consumption of the vehicle and relative to the vehicle operator's business. There may be significant non-transportation use of taxed fuel even if such use is small relative to the vehicle's transportation use, if the vehicle is used extensively. Also with respect to item (2), it is intended that the Secretary take into account variations in fuel use among the different types of vehicles, such as concrete mixers, refuse collection vehicles, tow trucks, mobile drills, and other vehicles that the Secretary identifies.

[Law at ¶ 7075. CCH Explanation at ¶ 1015.]

[¶ 15,190] Act Sec. 11145. Diesel fuel tax evasion report

Conference Committee Report (H.R. Conf. Rep. No. 109-203)

[Act Sec. 11145]

Present Law

An excise tax is imposed upon (1) the removal of any taxable fuel from a refinery or terminal, (2) the entry of any taxable fuel into the United States, or (3) the sale of any taxable fuel to any person who is not registered with the IRS to receive untaxed fuel, unless there was a prior taxable removal or entry.[107] The tax does not apply to any removal or entry of taxable fuel transferred in bulk by pipeline or vessel to a terminal or refinery if the person removing or entering the taxable fuel, the operator of such pipeline or vessel, and the operator of such terminal or refinery are registered with the Secretary.[108]

Diesel fuel and kerosene that is to be used for a nontaxable purpose will not be taxed upon removal from the terminal if it is dyed to indicate its nontaxable purpose.[109] In addition to requirement that fuel be dyed, the Secretary has the authority to prescribe marking requirements for diesel fuel and kerosene destined for a nontaxable use.[110] The Secretary has not prescribed any marking requirements.

---

[107] Sec. 4081(a)(1).
[108] Sec. 4081(a)(1)(B).
[109] Sec. 4082(a)(1) and (2).
[110] Sec. 4082(a)(3).

House Bill

No provision.

Senate Amendment

The Senate amendment requires the Commissioner of the IRS to report on the availability of new technologies that can be employed to enhance the collections of the excise tax on diesel fuel and the plans of the IRS to employ such technologies. The report is to be submitted within 360 days from the date of enactment to the Senate Committees on Finance and Environment and Public Works, and the House Committees on Ways and Means and Transportation and Infrastructure.

Conference Agreement

The conference agreement follows the Senate amendment except the conference agreement requires the report to contain certain additional information regarding the use of forensic or chemical molecular markers. Specifically, the conference agreement requires the report to cover the availability of forensic or chemical molecular markers, in addition to other technologies, to enhance collections of the excise tax on diesel fuel and the plans of the Internal Revenue Service to employ such technologies. The report must also cover the design of three tests: (1) the design of a test to place forensic or chemical molecular markers in any excluded liquid as that term is defined in Treasury regulations; (2) the design of a test, in consultation with the Department of Defense, to place forensic or chemical molecular markers in all nonstrategic bulk fuel deliveries of diesel fuel to the military, and (3) the design of a test to place forensic or chemical molecular markers in all diesel fuel bound for export utilizing the Gulf of Mexico.

Effective date

The provision is effective on the date of enactment.

[Law at ¶ 7080. CCH Explanation at ¶ 760.]

[¶ 15,200] Act Sec. 11146. Tax treatment of state ownership of railroad real estate investment trust

Conference Committee Report (H.R. CONF. REP. NO. 109-203)

[Code Secs. 103, 115, 336 and 337]

Present Law

A real estate investment trust ("REIT") is an electing entity that is engaged primarily in passive real estate activities (as specifically defined) and that, among other requirements, must have at least 100 shareholders. If a qualified entity elects REIT status, it can pay little or no corporate level tax, since a REIT is allowed a deduction for amounts distributed to its shareholders and is required to distribute at least 90 percent of its income to shareholders annually.

If an entity does not qualify to be treated as a REIT, it would generally be treated as a regular corporation subject to corporate level tax on its income under subchapter C and section 11 of the Code. Such a corporation can elect to be taxed as a partnership or disregarded entity under Treasury regulations. However, if it made such an election, the corporation would be treated as if it had liquidated and distributed its assets to shareholders, generally resulting in corporate-level tax on the excess of the fair market value over the basis of corporate assets.[97] A corporation that itself becomes a tax-exempt entity also must pay corporate tax on the excess of the fair market value over the basis of its assets.[98]

A State or local government is not subject to Federal income tax on income that accrues to the State or any political subdivision thereof and that is derived from any public utility or the exercise of any activity that is an essential governmental function.[99]

Interest on a State and local bond is excluded from gross income, with certain exceptions.[100] Special rules are also provided as requirements for tax exemption for State and local bonds.[101] State and local bonds can be classified by the type of entity using the proceeds as either governmental or private activity bonds. In general, bonds are governmental bonds if the proceeds of the bonds are used to finance direct activities of governmental entities or if the bonds are repaid with revenues of governmental enti-

---

[97] Sec. 336. An exception to this gain recognition applies to certain liquidations into a corporation that owns 80 percent of the liquidating entity and that is not itself tax-exempt. Sec. 337.

[98] Treas. Reg. sec. 1.337(d)-4(a)(2).

[99] Sec. 115.
[100] Sec. 103.
[101] Secs. 141-150.

ties. Private activity bonds are bonds with respect to which a State or local government serves as a conduit providing financing to private businesses or individuals. The exclusion from income for State and local bonds does not apply to private activity bonds unless the bonds are issued for certain purposes permitted by the Code. In addition, both governmental and private activity bonds must satisfy applicable rules provided for in the Code as a condition of tax exemption.[102]

House Bill

No provision.

Senate Amendment

Under the Senate amendment, the income of a qualified corporation that is derived from its railroad transportation and economic development activities, that constitute substantially all of its activities (as described below), is treated as accruing to the State for purposes of section 115, to the extent such activities are of a type which are an essential governmental function under section 115 of present law. For purposes of the provision, a qualified corporation is a corporation which is a REIT on the date of enactment and which is a non-operating Class III railroad that becomes 100 percent owned by a State after December 31, 2003 and before December 31, 2006. Moreover, substantially all activities of the corporation must consist of the ownership, leasing, and operation by such corporation of facilities, equipment, and other property used by the corporation or other persons for railroad transportation and for economic development for the benefit of the State and its citizens.

Under the Senate amendment, no gain or loss shall be recognized from the deemed conversion of such a REIT to such a qualified corporation and no change in the basis of the property of the entity shall occur.

Also, any obligation issued by a qualified corporation described above is treated as an obligation of a State for purposes of applying the tax exempt bond provisions if 95 percent of the net proceeds of such obligation are to be used to provide for the acquisition, construction, or improvement of railroad transportation infrastructure (including railroad terminal facilities). In addition, such an obligation shall not be treated as a private activity bond solely by reason of the ownership or use of such railroad transportation infrastructure by the corporation. All other present-law provisions relating to tax exempt bonds continue to apply to and govern bonds issued by the corporation. For example, the use by a private business of railroad property financed with the proceeds of bonds issued by a qualified corporation may cause such bonds to be taxable private activity bonds.

Effective date

The Senate amendment applies on and after the date a State becomes the owner of all the outstanding stock of a qualified corporation through action of such corporation's board of directors, provided that the State becomes the owner of all the voting stock of the corporation on or before December 31, 2003 and becomes the owner of all the outstanding stock of the corporation on or before December 31, 2006.

Conference Agreement

The conference agreement follows the Senate amendment.

[Law at ¶ 7085. CCH Explanation at ¶ 910.]

[¶ 15,210] Act Sec. 11147. Leaking Underground Storage Tank Trust Fund

Conference Committee Report (H.R. CONF. REP. NO. 109-203)

[Code Sec. 9508]

Present Law

Leaking Underground Storage Tank Trust Fund

The Code imposes an excise tax, generally at a rate of 0.1 cents per gallon, on gasoline, diesel, kerosene, and special motor fuels (other than liquefied petroleum gas and liquefied natural gas).[111] The taxes are deposited in the Leaking Underground Storage Tank ("LUST") Trust Fund. The tax expires on October 1, 2005.

Amounts in the LUST Trust Fund are available, subject to appropriation, only for purposes of making expenditures to carry out section 9003(h) of the Solid Waste Disposal Act as in

---

[102] Secs. 141-150.

[111] For qualified methanol and ethanol fuel the rate is 0.05 cents per gallon (sec. 4041(b)(2)(A)(ii)). Qualified methanol or ethanol fuel is any liquid at least 85 percent of which consists of methanol, ethanol or other alcohol produced from coal (including peat) (sec. 4041(b)(2)(B)).

effect on the date of enactment of the Superfund Amendments and Reauthorization Act of 1986.

Highway Trust Fund

The Highway Trust Fund provisions of the Code contain a special enforcement provision to prevent expenditure of Highway Trust Fund monies for purposes not authorized in section 9503 or a revenue Act.[112] If such unapproved expenditures occur, no further excise tax receipts will be transferred to the Highway Trust Fund. Rather, the taxes will continue to be imposed with receipts being retained in the General Fund. This enforcement provision provides specifically that it applies not only to unauthorized expenditures under the current Code provisions, but also to expenditures pursuant to future legislation that does not amend section 9503's expenditure authorization provisions or otherwise authorize the expenditure as part of a revenue Act.

House Bill

No provision.

Senate Amendment

No provision.

Conference Agreement

The conference agreement adds to the Code's LUST Trust Fund provisions a special enforcement provision similar to that applicable to the Highway Trust Fund to prevent expenditure of LUST Trust Fund monies for purposes not authorized by the Code or in a revenue Act.

Effective Date

The provision is effective on the date of enactment.

[Law at ¶ 5495. CCH Explanation at ¶ 1035.]

[¶ 15,220] Act Sec. 11151(a). Volumetric ethanol excise tax credit

House Committee Report (H.R. REP. NO. 109-13)

[Code Sec. 6427]

AJCA repealed the reduced tax rates for alcohol fuels and taxable fuels to be blended with alcohol. The technical correction makes a conforming amendment to eliminate the refund provision based on those reduced rates (secs. 6427(f) and 6427(o)).

Conference Committee Report (H.R. CONF. REP. NO. 109-203)

Senate Amendment

The Senate amendment is the same as the House bill.

Conference Agreement

The conference agreement follows the House bill and the Senate amendment.

[Law at ¶ 5430. CCH Explanation at ¶ 787.]

[¶ 15,230] Act Sec. 11151(b). Aviation fuel

Senate Committee Report (S. REP. NO. 109-82)

[Code Sec. 4081]

The provision includes two technical corrections to AJCA, described below. Such technical corrections take effect as if included in the section of AJCA to which the correction relates.

* * *

Section 853 of the AJCA moved the taxation of jet fuel (aviation-grade kerosene) from section 4091 to section 4081 of the Code and repealed section 4091. The termination date for the 21.8 cent per gallon rate for noncommercial aviation jet fuel was inadvertently omitted from the Act. The technical correction clarifies that after September 30, 2007, the rate for jet fuel used in noncommercial aviation will be 4.3 cents per gallon (sec. 4081(d)(2)).

An additional technical correction clarifies that users of aviation fuel in commercial aviation are required to be registered with the IRS in order for the 4.3-cents-per-gallon rate to apply (including for purposes of the self-assessment of tax by commercial aircraft operators) (sec. 4081(a)(2)(C)).

---

[112] Sec. 9503(b)(6).

Conference Committee Report (H.R. CONF. REP. NO. 109-203)

Senate Amendment

The Senate amendment generally follows the House bill with certain technical drafting changes to accommodate changes made by other provisions of the Senate amendment. The Senate amendment also corrects cross-references in section 6421(f)(2) to the definition of noncommercial aviation to reflect changes made by the AJCA change in the tax treatment of fuel used in aviation.

Conference Agreement

The conference agreement follows the Senate amendment.

[Law at ¶5290 and ¶5420. CCH Explanation at ¶790 and ¶795.]

[¶15,240] Act Sec. 11151(c). Coastal Wetlands sub-account

Senate Committee Report (S. REP. NO. 109-82)

[Code Sec. 9504]

The provision includes a technical correction to TEA 21, described below. The technical correction takes effect as if included in the section of TEA 21 to which it relates.

Section 9005(b)(3) of TEA 21 redesignated Code section 9504(b)(2)(B), referring to the purposes of the Coastal Wetlands Planning, Protection and Restoration Act, as 9504(b)(2)(C), but did not cross reference the limitation for such purposes of taxes on gasoline used in the non-business use of small-engine outdoor power equipment. The technical correction makes a conforming cross-reference amendment (sec. 9504(b)(2)).

Conference Committee Report (H.R. CONF. REP. NO. 109-203)

House Bill

No provision.

Conference Agreement

The conference agreement follows the Senate amendment.

[Law at ¶5490. CCH Explanation at ¶797.]

[¶15,250] Act Sec. 11151(d). Erroneous reference to highway reauthorization bill

Conference Committee Report (H.R. CONF. REP. NO. 109-203)

[Act Sec. 11151(d)]

The provision includes a technical correction to the Energy Tax Incentives Act ("ETIA") of 2005. The amendment made by the technical correction takes effect as if included in the section of the ETIA to which it relates.

House Bill

No provision.

Senate Amendment

No provision.

Conference Agreement

The conference agreement corrects an erroneous reference to the highway reauthorization bill in section 38 as added by the Energy Policy Act of 2005.

[Law at ¶7090.]

¶15,240   Act Sec. 11151(c)

[¶ 15,260] Act Sec. 11161. Treatment of kerosene for use in aviation

Conference Committee Report (H.R. Conf. Rep. No. 109-203)

[Code Secs. 4041, 4081, 4082, 6427, 9502 and 9503]

Present Law

In general, aviation-grade kerosene is taxed at a rate of 21.8 cents per gallon upon removal of such fuel from a refinery or terminal (or entry into the United States) and on the sale of such fuel to any unregistered person unless there was a prior taxable removal or entry of such fuel.[242] Aviation-grade kerosene may be removed at a reduced rate, either 4.3 or zero cents per gallon, if the aviation fuel is removed directly into the fuel tank of an aircraft for use in commercial aviation[243] or for a use that is exempt from the tax imposed by section 4041(c) (other than by reason of a prior imposition of tax),[244] or is removed or entered as part of an exempt bulk transfer.[245] These taxes are credited to the Airport and Airway Trust Fund.[246] If taxed aviation-grade kerosene is used for a nontaxable use, a claim for credit or refund may be made.[247] Such claims are paid from the Airport and Airway Trust Fund to the general fund of the Treasury.[248] All other removals and entries of kerosene used for surface transportation are taxed at the diesel tax rate of 24.3 cents per gallon,[249] and these taxes are credited to the Highway Trust Fund.[250] If aviation-grade kerosene is taxed upon removal or entry but fraudulently diverted for surface transportation, the taxes remain in the Airport and Airway Trust Fund, and the Highway Trust Fund is not credited for the taxes on such fuel.

A special rule of present law addresses whether a removal from a refueler truck, tanker, or tank wagon may be treated as a removal from a terminal for purposes of determining whether aviation-grade kerosene is removed directly into the wing of an aircraft for use in commercial aviation, and so eligible for the 4.3 cents per gallon rate.[251] For the special rule to apply, a qualifying truck, tanker, or tank wagon must be loaded with aviation-grade kerosene from a terminal: (1) that is located within a secured area of an airport, and (2) from which no vehicle licensed for highway use is loaded with aviation fuel, except in exigent circumstances identified by the Secretary in regulations. In order to qualify for the special rule, a refueler truck, tanker, or tank wagon must: (1) be loaded with fuel for delivery only into aircraft at the airport where the terminal is located; (2) have storage tanks, hose, and coupling equipment designed and used for the purposes of fueling aircraft; (3) not be registered for highway use; and (4) be operated by the terminal operator (who operates the terminal rack from which the fuel is unloaded) or by a person that makes a daily accounting to such terminal operator of each delivery of fuel from such truck, tanker, or tank wagon.

House Bill

No provision.

Senate Amendment

The Senate amendment imposes the kerosene tax rate of 24.3 cents per gallon upon the

---

[242] Sec. 4081(a)(2)(A)(iv). (An additional 0.1 cent is imposed on aviation-grade kerosene and credited to the Leaking Underground Storage Tank ("LUST") Trust Fund.) Sec. 4081(a)(2)(B). The LUST Trust Fund tax is set to expire after September 30, 2005. Sec. 4081(d)(3).

[243] Sec. 4081(a)(2)(C).

[244] Sec. 4082(e). Exempt uses include use in commercial aviation as supplies for vessels or aircraft, which includes use by certain foreign air carriers and for the international flights of domestic carriers, secs. 4082(e), 6427(l)(2), and 4221(d)(3).

[245] Sec. 4081(a)(1)(B).

[246] Sec. 9502(b)(1)(C).

[247] Sec. 6427(l)(1) and 6427(l)(4). Nontaxable uses include: (1) use other than as fuel in an aircraft (such as use in heating oil); (2) use on a farm for farming purposes; (3) use in a military aircraft owned by the United States or a foreign country; (4) use in a domestic air carrier engaged in foreign trade or trade between the United States and any of its possessions; (5) use in a foreign air carrier engaged in foreign trade or trade between the United States and any of its possessions (but only if the foreign carrier's country of registration provides similar privileges to United States carriers); (6) exclusive use of a State or local government; (7) sales for export, or shipment to a United States possession; (8) exclusive use by a nonprofit educational organization; (9) use by an aircraft museum exclusively for the procurement, care, or exhibition of aircraft of the type used for combat or transport in World War II, and (10) use as a fuel in a helicopter or a fixed-wing aircraft for purposes of providing transportation with respect to which certain requirements are met. Secs. 4041(f)(2), 4041(g), 4041(h), 4041(l), and 6427(l)(2)(B)(i).

[248] Sec. 9502(d)(2).

[249] Sec. 4081(a)(2)(iii).

[250] Sec. 9503(b)(1)(D).

[251] Sec. 4081(a)(3).

entry or removal of aviation-grade kerosene and on the sale of such fuel to any unregistered person unless there was a prior taxable removal or entry of the fuel. The present law reduced rates for removals of aviation-grade kerosene directly into the fuel tank of an aircraft apply,[252] except that in addition, under the proposal, if kerosene is removed directly into the fuel tank of an aircraft for use in aviation other than commercial aviation, the rate of tax is 21.8 cents per gallon.

The Senate amendment provides that amounts may be claimed as credits or refunds for kerosene that is taxed at the 24.3 cents per gallon rate and used for aviation purposes. If kerosene is used for noncommercial aviation, the amount is 2.5 cents; if kerosene is used for commercial aviation, the amount is 20 cents; if kerosene is used for a use that is exempt from tax (as determined under present law), the amount is 24.3 cents. Present law rules with respect to claims apply, except for claims with respect to kerosene used in noncommercial aviation, which may be claimed by the ultimate vendor. To be eligible to receive a payment, a vendor must be registered and must show either that the price of the fuel did not include the tax and the tax was not collected from the purchaser, the amount of tax was repaid to the ultimate purchaser, or the written consent of the purchaser to the making of the claim was filed with the Secretary.

Under the Senate amendment, all taxes collected at the 24.3 cents per gallon rate (under section 4081) initially are credited to the Highway Trust Fund. The Senate amendment requires the Secretary to transfer from time to time from the Highway Trust Fund into the Airport and Airway Trust Fund amounts equivalent to the taxes received under sections 4041 and 4081 with respect to fuels used in a nontaxable use to the extent such amounts exceed the amounts paid with respect to such use. Transfers are required to be made with respect to taxes received on or after October 1, 2005, and before October 1, 2011.

Effective Date

The Senate amendment is effective for fuels or liquids removed, entered, or sold after September 30, 2005.

Conference Agreement

The conference agreement follows the Senate amendment with the following modifications.

The conference agreement provides that the rate of tax on kerosene is 21.8 cents per gallon if the kerosene is removed from refueler trucks, tankers, and tank wagons that are loaded with fuel from a terminal that is located in an airport, without regard to whether the terminal is located in a secured area of the airport, as long as all the other requirements of the present law special rule related to such trucks, tankers, and wagons are met. The conference agreement clarifies that the rate of tax upon removal of kerosene is zero if the removal is from a refueler truck, tanker, or tank wagon that meets all of the requirements of present law, including the security requirement, the kerosene is delivered directly into the fuel tank of an aircraft, and the kerosene is exempt from the tax imposed by section 4041(c) (other than by prior imposition of tax).

The Senate amendment is clarified to provide that claims for payment for kerosene that is used for noncommercial aviation may be claimed by the ultimate vendor only.

The conference agreement clarifies the transfer mechanism for payments from the Highway Trust Fund to the Airport and Airway Trust Fund to provide that such transfers shall be made monthly in amounts equivalent to 21.8 cents per gallon for claims made with respect to kerosene used for noncommercial aviation purposes, 4.3 cents per gallon for claims made with respect to kerosene used for commercial aviation purposes, and the amounts attributable to taxes received with respect to amounts allowed as a credit under section 34 for kerosene used for aviation purposes. The conference agreement requires that transfers be made on the basis of estimates by the Secretary, with proper adjustments to be made subsequently to the extent prior estimates were in excess of or less than the amounts required to be transferred. The conference agreement clarifies that the Airport and Airway Trust Fund does not reimburse the General Fund for claims with respect to kerosene

---

[252] For example, for kerosene removed directly into the fuel tank of an aircraft for use in commercial aviation by a person registered for such use, the rate of tax is 4.3 cents per gallon. Kerosene removed directly into the fuel tank of an aircraft for an exempt use is not taxed. For purposes of these reduced rates, it is intended that the following airports be included on the Secretary's list of airports that include a secured area in which a terminal is located. The airports are listed by airport name, and the terminal with respect to the airport is identified by terminal control number: Los Angeles International Airport (T-95-CA-4812) and Federal Express Corporation Memphis Airport (T-62-TN-2220).

that is taxed at the 24.3 cents per gallon rate and used for aviation purposes, or with respect to credits allowed under section 34 to the extent the Highway Trust Fund is credited initially with the amount of tax with respect to which the credit is claimed.

[Law at ¶ 5265, ¶ 5290, ¶ 5295, ¶ 5430, ¶ 5480 and ¶ 5485. CCH Explanation at ¶ 740.]

[¶ 15,270] Act Sec. 11162. Repeal of ultimate vendor refund claims with respect to farming

Conference Committee Report (H.R. CONF. REP. NO. 109-203)

[Code Sec. 6427(l)]

Present Law

In general - ultimate purchaser refunds for nontaxable uses

In general, the Code provides that if diesel fuel or kerosene on which tax has been imposed is used by any person in a nontaxable use, the Secretary is to refund (without interest) to the ultimate purchaser the amount of tax imposed.[253] The refund is made to the ultimate purchaser of the taxed fuel by either income tax credit or refund payment.[254] Not more than one claim may be filed by any person with respect to fuel used during its taxable year. However, there are exceptions to this rule.

An ultimate purchaser may make a claim for a refund payment for any quarter of a taxable year for which the purchaser can claim at least $750.[255] If the purchaser cannot claim at least $750 at the end of quarter, the amount can be carried over to the next quarter to determine if the purchaser can claim at least $750. If the purchaser cannot claim at least $750 at the end of the taxable year, the purchaser must claim a credit on the person's income tax return.

As discussed below, these ultimate purchaser refund rules do not apply to diesel fuel or kerosene used on a farm. The Code precludes the ultimate purchaser from claiming a refund for such use. Instead, the refund claims are made by registered vendors as described below.

Special vendor rule for use on a farm for farming purposes

In the case of diesel fuel or kerosene used on a farm for farming purposes refund payments are paid to the ultimate, registered vendors ("registered ultimate vendor") of such fuels.

Thus a registered ultimate vendor that sells undyed diesel fuel or undyed kerosene to any of the following may make a claim for refund: (1) the owner, tenant, operator of a farm for use by that person on a farm for farming purposes; and (2) a person other than the owner, tenant, or operator of a farm for use by that person on a farm in connection with cultivating, raising or harvesting. The registered ultimate vendor is the only person who may make the claim with respect to diesel fuel or kerosene used on a farm for farming purposes. The purchaser of the fuel cannot make the claim for refund.

Registered ultimate vendors may make weekly claims if the claim is at least $200 ($100 or more in the case of kerosene).[256] If not paid within 45 days (20 days for an electronic claim), the Secretary is to pay interest on the claim.

House Bill

No provision.

Senate Amendment

The Senate amendment repeals ultimate vendor refund claims in the case of diesel fuel or kerosene used on a farm for farming purposes. Thus, refunds for taxed diesel fuel or kerosene used on a farm for farming purposes would be paid to the ultimate purchaser under the rules applicable to nontaxable uses of diesel fuel or kerosene.

Effective date

The Senate amendment is effective for sales after September 30, 2005.

Conference Agreement

The conference agreement follows the Senate amendment.

[Law at ¶ 5430. CCH Explanation at ¶ 750.]

---

[253] Sec. 6427(l)(1).
[254] Generally, refund payments are only made to governmental units and tax-exempt organizations. Sec. 6427(k). The quarterly payment claim rules for ultimate purchasers are an exception to this rule.
[255] Sec. 6427(i)(2).
[256] Sec. 6427(i)(4)(A).

[¶ 15,280] Act Sec. 11163. Refunds of excise taxes on exempt sales of taxable fuel by credit card

Conference Committee Report (H.R. CONF. REP. NO. 109-203)

[Code Sec. 4101, 6206, 6416, 6427 and 6675]

Present Law

Under the rules in effect prior to 2005, in the case of gasoline on which tax had been paid and sold to a State or local government, to a nonprofit educational organization, for supplies for vessels or aircraft, for export, or for the production of special fuels, the wholesale distributor that sold such gasoline was treated as the only person who paid the tax and thereby was the proper claimant for a credit or refund of the tax paid. A "wholesale distributor" included any person, other than an importer or producer, who sold gasoline to producers, retailers, or to users who purchased in bulk quantities and accepted delivery into bulk storage tanks. A wholesale distributor also included any person who made retail sales of gasoline at 10 or more retail motor fuel outlets.

Under a special administrative exception to these rules, a sale of gasoline charged on an oil company credit card issued to an exempt person described above is not considered a direct sale by the person actually selling the gasoline to the ultimate purchaser if the seller receives a reimbursement of the tax from the oil company (or indirectly through an intermediate vendor). Thus, the person that actually paid the tax, in most cases the oil company, is treated as the only person eligible to make the refund claim.[257]

The American Jobs Creation Act of 2004 ("AJCA")[258] modified the pre-existing statutory rules with respect to certain sales. Under AJCA, if a registered ultimate vendor purchases any gasoline on which tax has been paid and sells such gasoline to a State or local government or to a nonprofit educational organization, for its exclusive use, such ultimate vendor is treated as the only person who paid the tax and thereby is the proper claimant for a credit or refund of the tax paid.[259] However, AJCA did not change the special administrative oil company credit card rule described above.[260]

In addition, under AJCA, refund claims made by such an ultimate vendor may be filed for any period of at least one week for which $200 or more is payable. Any such claim must be filed on or before the last day of the first quarter following the earliest quarter included in the claim. The Secretary must pay interest on refunds unpaid after 45 days. If the refund claim was filed by electronic means, and the ultimate vendor has certified to the Secretary for the most recent quarter of the taxable year that all ultimate purchasers of the vendor are certified for highway exempt use as a State or local government or a nonprofit educational organization, refunds unpaid after 20 days must be paid with interest.[261]

In the case of diesel fuel or kerosene used in a nontaxable use, the ultimate purchaser is generally the only person entitled to claim a refund of excise tax.[262] However, in the case of diesel fuel or kerosene used on a farm for farming purposes or by a State or local government, aviation-grade kerosene, and certain nonaviation-grade kerosene, an ultimate vendor may claim the refund if the ultimate vendor is registered and bears the tax (or receives the written consent of the ultimate purchaser to claim the refund).[263]

House Bill

No provision.

Senate Amendment

The Senate amendment replaces the oil company credit card rule with a new set of rules applicable to certain credit card sales. The new rules apply to all taxable fuels. Under the Senate amendment, if a purchase of taxable fuel is made by means of a credit card issued to an ultimate purchaser that is either a State or local government or, in the case of gasoline, a nonprofit

---

[257] Notice 89-29, 1989-1 C.B. 669.
[258] Pub. L. No. 108-357.
[259] AJCA, sec. 865(a), effective January 1, 2005. See Code sec. 6416(a)(4)(A).
[260] In Notice 2005-4, 2005-2 I.R.B. 289, the Treasury Department confirmed that it would continue to apply the oil company credit card rule until March 1, 2005. On February 28, 2005, the Treasury Department issued Notice 2005-24,
2005-12 I.R.B. 1, modifying Notice 2005-4. Notice 2005-24 stated that the oil company credit card rule will remain in effect until it is modified by a statutory change or by future guidance.
[261] Sec. 6146(a)(4)(B).
[262] Sec. 6427(l)(1).
[263] See sec. 6427(l)(4)(B), (l)(5)(B), and (l)(5)(C), and sec. 6416(a)(1)(A), (B), and (D).

¶ 15,280   Act Sec. 11163

educational organization, for its exclusive use, a credit card issuer who is registered and who extends such credit to the ultimate purchaser with respect to such purchase shall be the only person entitled to apply for a credit or refund if the following two conditions are met: (1) such registered person has not collected the amount of the tax from the purchaser, or has obtained the written consent of the ultimate purchaser to the allowance of the credit or refund; and (2) such registered person has either repaid or agreed to repay the amount of the tax to the ultimate vendor, has obtained the written consent of the ultimate vendor to the allowance of the credit or refund, or has otherwise made arrangements that directly or indirectly provide the ultimate vendor with reimbursement of such tax. It is anticipated that such indirect arrangements may consist of the contractual undertaking of the relevant oil company to the credit card issuer that it will pay the amount of the tax to the ultimate vendor, and the corresponding contractual undertaking of the oil company to the ultimate vendor.

A credit card issuer entitled to claim a refund under the provision is responsible for collecting and supplying all the appropriate documentation currently required from ultimate vendors. The present-law refund amount and timing rules applicable to ultimate vendors, including the special rules for electronic claims, apply to refunds to credit card issuers under the provision.[264]

The Senate amendment also conforms present-law penalty provisions to the new rules.

The Senate amendment does not change the present-law rules applicable to non-credit card purchases.

Effective date

The Senate amendment is effective for sales after December 31, 2005.

Conference Agreement

The conference agreement follows the Senate amendment with the following modifications.

Under the conference agreement, if a credit card issuer is not registered, or if either condition (1) or (2) described above is not met (or if the ultimate purchaser is not exempt), then the credit card issuer is required to collect an amount equal to the tax from the ultimate purchaser and only an (exempt) ultimate purchaser may claim a credit or payment from the IRS.[265] The conferees intend that tax-paid fuel shall not be sold tax free to an exempt entity by means of a credit card unless the credit card issuer is registered. An unregistered credit card issuer that does not collect an amount equal to the tax from the exempt entity is liable for present-law penalties for failure to register.[266] The present-law regulatory authority of the Secretary to prescribe the form, manner, terms, conditions of registration, and conditions of use of registration extends to registration under this provision.[267] Such authority may include rules that preclude persons which are registered credit card issuers from issuing nonregistered credit cards.[268] The conferees also intend that the IRS will review the registration of a registered credit card issuer that has engaged in multiple or flagrant violations of the requirements of the provision.

[Law at ¶ 5305, ¶ 5395, ¶ 5410, ¶ 5430 and ¶ 5445. CCH Explanation at ¶ 745.]

[¶ 15,290] Act Sec. 11164. Reregistration in event of change in ownership

Conference Committee Report (H.R. Conf. Rep. No. 109-203)

[Code Secs. 4101, 6719, 7232 and 7272]

Present Law

Blenders, enterers, pipeline operators, position holders, refiners, terminal operators, and vessel operators are required to register with the Secretary with respect to fuels taxes imposed by

---

[264] See sec. 6416(a)(4)(B). Present law would continue to apply to the timing of ultimate purchaser claims. Under present law, claims by an ultimate purchaser are generally made on an annual basis. However, claims aggregating over $750 may be made quarterly. See secs. 6421(d) and 6427(i)(2).

[265] See sec. 6421(c).

[266] See secs. 6719, 7232, and 7272.

[267] Sec. 4101(a)(1).

[268] Because registration occurs at the "person" (legal entity) level, it is anticipated that a credit card issuer will use a separate (registered) entity for the issuance of credit cards entitled to the benefits of this provision.

sections 4041(a)(1) and 4081.[281] An assessable penalty for failure to register is $10,000 for each initial failure, plus $1,000 per day that the failure continues.[282] A non-assessable penalty for failure to register is $10,000.[283] A criminal penalty of $10,000, or imprisonment of not more than five years, or both, together with the costs of prosecution also applies to a failure to register and to certain false statements made in connection with a registration application.[284] Treasury regulations require that a registrant notify the Secretary of any change (such as a change in ownership) in the information a registrant submitted in connection with its application for registration within 10 days of the change.[285] The Secretary has the discretion to revoke the registration of a non-compliant registrant.

House Bill

No provision.

Senate Amendment

The Senate amendment requires that upon a change in ownership of a registrant, the registrant must reregister with the Secretary, as provided by the Secretary. A change in ownership means that after a transaction (or series of related transactions), more than 50 percent of the ownership interests in, or assets of, a registrant are held by persons other than persons (or persons related thereto) who held more than 50 percent of such interests or assets before the transaction (or series of related transactions). The provision does not apply to companies, the stock of which is regularly traded on an established securities market. There is an assessable penalty for failure to reregister of $10,000 for each initial failure, plus $1,000 per day that the failure continues, and a criminal penalty for failure to reregister of $10,000, or imprisonment of not more than five years, or both, together with the costs of prosecution. The Senate amendment applies to changes in ownership occurring prior to, on, or after the date of enactment.

Effective date

The Senate amendment is effective for actions or failures to act after the date of enactment.

Conference Agreement

The conference agreement follows the Senate amendment and in addition makes the penalties for failure to reregister identical to the present-law penalties for failure to register by also providing for a non-assessable penalty for failure to reregister of $10,000.

[Law at ¶5305, ¶5450, ¶5465 and ¶5470. CCH Explanation at ¶755.]

[¶15,300] Act Sec. 11165. Reconciliation of on-loaded cargo to entered cargo

Conference Committee Report (H.R. Conf. Rep. No. 109-203)

[Act Sec. 11165]

Present Law

The Trade Act of 2002 directed the Secretary to promulgate regulations pertaining to the electronic transmission to the Bureau of Customs and Border Patrol ("Customs") of information pertaining to cargo destined for importation into the United States or exportation from the United States, prior to such importation or exportation.[286] The Department of the Treasury issued final regulations on October 31, 2002. The regulations require the advance and accurate presentation of certain manifest information prior to lading at the foreign port and encourage the presentation of this information electronically. Customs must receive from the carrier the vessel's Cargo Declaration (Customs Form 1302) or the electronic equivalent within 24 hours before such cargo is laden aboard the vessel at the foreign port.[287]

Certain carriers of bulk cargo, however, are exempt from these filing requirements. Such bulk cargo includes that composed of free flowing articles such as oil, grain, coal, ore and the like, which can be pumped or run through a chute or handled by dumping.[288] Thus, taxable fuels are not required to file the Cargo Declaration within 24 hours before such cargo is laden aboard the vessel at the foreign port. Instead the

---

[281] Sec. 4101; Treas. Reg. secs. 48.4101-1(a) and 48.4101-1(c)(1).
[282] Sec. 6719.
[283] Sec. 7272(a).
[284] Sec. 7232.
[285] Treas. Reg. sec. 48.4101-1(h)(1)(v).
[286] Sec. 343(a) of Pub. L. No. 107-210 (2002).
[287] 19 CFR sec. 4.7(b)(2).
[288] 19 CFR sec. 4.7(b)(4)(i)(A).

Cargo Declaration must be filed within 24 hours prior arrival in the United States.

House Bill

No provision.

Senate Amendment

The Senate amendment provides that not later than one year after the date of enactment of this paragraph, the Secretary of Homeland Security, together with the Secretary of the Treasury, is to establish an electronic data interchange system through which Customs shall transmit to the Internal Revenue Service information pertaining to cargoes of taxable fuels (as defined in section 4083) that Customs has obtained electronically under its regulations adopted to carry out the Trade Act of 2002 requirement. For this purpose, not later than one year after the date of enactment, all filers of required cargo information for such taxable fuels, as defined, must provide such information to Customs through its approved electronic data interchange system.

Effective Date

The Senate amendment is effective upon date of enactment.

Conference Agreement

The conference agreement follows the Senate amendment.

[Law at ¶ 7095. CCH Explanation at ¶ 770.]

[¶ 15,310] Act Sec. 11166. Registration of operators of deep-draft vessels

Conference Committee Report (H.R. Conf. Rep. No. 109-203)

[Code Secs. 4041 and 4081]

Present Law

Blenders, enterers, pipeline operators, position holders, refiners, terminal operators, and vessel operators are required to register with the Secretary with respect to fuels taxes imposed by sections 4041(a)(1) and 4081.[289] Treasury regulations define a vessel operator as any person that operates a vessel within the bulk transfer/terminal system, excluding deep-draft ocean-going vessels.[290] Accordingly, operators of deep-draft ocean-going vessels are not required to register. A deep-draft ocean-going vessel is a vessel that is designed primarily for use on the high seas that has a draft of more than 12 feet.[291]

An assessable penalty for failure to register is $10,000 for each initial failure, plus $1,000 per day that the failure continues.[292] A non-assessable penalty for failure to register is $10,000.[293] A criminal penalty of $10,000, or imprisonment of not more than five years, or both, together with the costs of prosecution also applies to a failure to register and to certain false statements made in connection with a registration application.[294]

In general, gasoline, diesel fuel, and kerosene ("taxable fuel") are taxed upon removal from a refinery or a terminal.[295] Tax also is imposed on the entry into the United States of any taxable fuel for consumption, use, or warehousing. The tax does not apply to any removal or entry of a taxable fuel transferred in bulk (a "bulk transfer") by pipeline or vessel to a terminal or refinery if the person removing or entering the taxable fuel, the operator of such pipeline or vessel, and the operator of such terminal or refinery are registered with the Secretary as required by section 4101.[296] Transfer to an unregistered party subjects the transfer to tax.

House Bill

No provision.

Senate Amendment

The Senate amendment provides that the Secretary of the Treasury shall require the registration of every operator of a deep-draft ocean going vessel. Under the provision, if a deep-draft ocean-going vessel is used as part of a bulk transfer of taxable fuel, the transfer is subject to tax unless the operator of such vessel is registered.

---

[289] Sec. 4101; Treas. Reg. sec. 48.4101-1(a) and 48.4101-1(c)(1).

[290] Treas. Reg. sec. 48.4101-1(b)(8).

[291] Sec. 4042(c)(1).

[292] Sec. 6719.

[293] Sec. 7272(a).

[294] Sec. 7232.

[295] Sec. 4081(a)(1)(A).

[296] Sec. 4081(a)(1)(B). The sale of a taxable fuel to an unregistered person prior to a taxable removal or entry of the fuel is subject to tax. Sec. 4081(a)(1)(A).

Effective Date

The Senate amendment is effective on the date of enactment.

Conference Agreement

The conference agreement follows the Senate amendment except that an operator of a deep-draft ocean-going vessel is not required to register under the provision if such operator uses such vessel exclusively for purposes of the entry of the taxable fuel. For purposes of the bulk transfer exemption, a deep-draft ocean-going vessel operator is not required to be registered for the exemption to be available with respect to the entry of taxable fuel by such vessel.

[Law at ¶5290 and ¶7100. CCH Explanation at ¶775.]

[¶15,320] Act Sec. 11167. Impose assessable penalty on dealers of adulterated fuel

Conference Committee Report (H.R. Conf. Rep. No. 109-203)

[New Code Sec. 6720A]

Present Law

Diesel fuel, gasoline, and kerosene are taxable fuels. Diesel fuel is defined as (1) any liquid (other than gasoline) which is suitable for use as a fuel in a diesel-powered highway vehicle or a diesel powered train, (2) transmix, and (3) diesel fuel blend stocks identified by the Secretary.[323] As a defense to Federal and State excise tax liability, some taxpayers have contended that certain diesel fuel mixtures or additives do not meet the requirements of (1) above because they are not approved as additives or mixtures by the EPA. In addition, under present law, untaxed fuel additives, including certain contaminants, may displace taxed diesel fuel in a mixture.

The Code provides that any person who, in connection with a sale or lease (or offer for sale or lease) of an article, knowingly makes any false statement ascribing a particular part of the price of the article to a tax imposed by the United States, or intended to lead any person to believe that any part of the price consists of such a tax, is guilty of a misdemeanor.[324] Another Code provision provides that any person who has in his custody or possession any article on which taxes are imposed by law, for the purpose of selling the article in fraud of the internal revenue laws or with design to avoid payment of the taxes thereon, is liable for "a penalty of $500 or not less than double the amount of taxes fraudulently attempted to be evaded."[325]

House Bill

No provision.

Senate Amendment

The Senate amendment adds a new assessable penalty. Any person other than a retailer who knowingly transfers for resale, sells for resale, or holds out for resale for use in a diesel-powered highway vehicle (or train) any liquid that does not meet applicable EPA regulations (as defined in section 45H(c)(3)[326]) is subject to a penalty of $10,000 for each such transfer, sale or holding out for resale, in addition to the tax on such liquid, if any. Any retailer who knowingly holds out for sale (other than for resale) any such liquid, is subject to a $10,000 penalty for each such holding out for sale, in addition to the tax on such liquid, if any.

The penalty is dedicated to the Highway Trust Fund.

Effective Date

The Senate amendment is effective for any transfer, sale, or holding out for sale or resale occurring after the date of enactment.

Conference Agreement

The conference agreement follows the Senate amendment.

[Law at ¶5455 and ¶5485. CCH Explanation at ¶765.]

---

[323] Sec. 4083(a)(3)(A).

[324] Sec. 7211. Such a violation is punishable by a fine not to exceed $1,000, or by imprisonment for not more than one year, or both.

[325] Sec. 7268.

[326] Section 45H(c)(3) refers to "the Highway Diesel Fuel Sulfur Control Requirements of the Environmental Protection Agency."

¶ 20,001 Effective Dates

Energy Tax Incentives Act of 2005

This CCH-prepared table presents the general effective dates for major law provisions added, amended or repealed by the Energy Tax Incentives Act of 2005. Entries are listed in Code Section order.

Code Sec.	Act Sec.	Act Provision Subject	Effective Date
23(c)	1335(b)(1)	Credit For Residential Energy Efficient Property—Conforming Amendments	Property placed in service after December 31, 2005, in tax years ending after such date
25(e)(1)(C)	1335(b)(2)	Credit For Residential Energy Efficient Property—Conforming Amendments	Property placed in service after December 31, 2005, in tax years ending after such date
25C	1333(a)	Credit For Certain Nonbusiness Energy Property	Property placed in service after December 31, 2005
25D	1335(a)	Credit For Residential Energy Efficient Property	Property placed in service after December 31, 2005, in tax years ending after such date
29	1322(a)(1)	Modification of Credit For Producing Fuel From a Nonconventional Source—Treatment as Business Credit—Credit Moved to Subpart Relating to Business Related Credits	Credits determined under the Internal Revenue Code of 1986 for tax years ending after December 31, 2005
29(c)(2)(A)	1322(b)(1)(A)	Modification of Credit For Producing Fuel From a Nonconventional Source—Amendments Conforming to the Repeal of the Natural Gas Policy Act of 1978	August 8, 2005
29(e)-(h)	1322(b)(1)(B)	Modification of Credit For Producing Fuel From a Nonconventional Source—Amendments Conforming to the Repeal of the Natural Gas Policy Act of 1978	August 8, 2005

Code Sec.	Act Sec.	Act Provision Subject	Effective Date
29(g)(1)(A)-(B)	1322(b)(2)(A)-(B)	Modification of Credit For Producing Fuel From a Nonconventional Source—Amendments Conforming to the Repeal of the Natural Gas Policy Act of 1978—Conforming Amendments	August 8, 2005
29(h)	1321(a)	Extension of Credit For Producing Fuel From a Nonconventional Source for Facilities Producing Coke or Coke Gas	Fuel produced and sold after December 31, 2005, in tax years ending after such date
30(b)(3)(A)	1322(a)(3)(A)	Modification of Credit For Producing Fuel From a Nonconventional Source—Treatment as Business Credit—Conforming Amendments	Credits determined under the Internal Revenue Code of 1986 for tax years ending after December 31, 2005
30B	1341(a)	Alternative Motor Vehicle Credit	Property placed in service after December 31, 2005, in tax years ending after such date
30C	1342(a)	Credit For Installation of Alternative Fueling Stations	Property placed in service after December 31, 2005, in tax years ending after such date
38(b)(19)-(21)	1306(b)	Credit for Production From Advanced Nuclear Power Facilities—Credit Treated as Business Credit	Production in tax years beginning after August 8, 2005
38(b)(20)-(22)	1322(a)(2)	Modification of Credit For Producing Fuel From a Nonconventional Source—Treatment as Business Credit—Credit Treated as Business Credit	Credits determined under the Internal Revenue Code of 1986 for tax years ending after December 31, 2005
38(b)(21)-(23)	1332(b)	Credit For Construction of New Energy Efficient Homes—Credit Made Part of General Business Credit	Qualified new energy efficient homes acquired after December 31, 2005, in tax years ending after such date
38(b)(22)-(24)	1334(b)	Credit For Energy Efficient Appliances—Conforming Amendment	Appliances produced after December 31, 2005
38(b)(23)-(25)	1341(b)(1)	Alternative Motor Vehicle Credit—Conforming Amendments	Property placed in service after December 31, 2005, in tax years ending after such date

¶20,001

Code Sec.	Act Sec.	Act Provision Subject	Effective Date
38(b)(24)-(26)	1342(b)(1)	Credit For Installation of Alternative Fueling Stations—Conforming Amendments	Property placed in service after December 31, 2005, in tax years ending after such date
40(g)	1347(a)	Modification of Small Ethanol Producer Credit—Definition of Small Ethanol Producer	Tax years ending after August 8, 2005
40(g)(6)(A)(ii)	1347(b)	Modification of Small Ethanol Producer Credit—Written Notice of Election to Allocate Credit to Patrons	Tax years ending after August 8, 2005
40A	1346(b)(1)	Renewable Diesel—Clerical Amendments	August 8, 2005
40A(a)	1345(a)	Small Agri-Biodiesel Producer Credit	Tax years ending after August 8, 2005
40A(b)	1345(d)(2)	Small Agri-Biodiesel Producer Credit—Conforming Amendments	Tax years ending after August 8, 2005
40A(b)(4)	1345(d)(1)	Small Agri-Biodiesel Producer Credit—Conforming Amendments	Tax years ending after August 8, 2005
40A(b)(5)	1345(b)	Small Agri-Biodiesel Producer Credit—Small Agri-Biodiesel Producer Credit Defined	Tax years ending after August 8, 2005
40A(d)(3)(C)-(D)	1345(d)(3)	Small Agri-Biodiesel Producer Credit—Conforming Amendments	Tax years ending after August 8, 2005
40A(e)	1344(a)	Extension of Excise Tax Provisions and Income Tax Credit For Biodiesel	August 8, 2005
40A(e)-(f)	1345(c)	Small Agri-Biodiesel Producer Credit—Definitions and Special Rules	Tax years ending after August 8, 2005
40A(f)-(g)	1346(a)	Renewable Diesel	Fuel sold or used after December 31, 2005
41(a)(1)-(3)	1351(a)(1)	Expansion of Research Credit—Credit For Expenses Attributable to Certain Collaborative Energy Research Consortia	Amounts paid or incurred after August 8, 2005, in tax years ending after such date
41(b)(3)(C)	1351(a)(3)	Expansion of Research Credit—Credit For Expenses Attributable to Certain Collaborative Energy Research Consortia—Conforming Amendment	Amounts paid or incurred after August 8, 2005, in tax years ending after such date
41(b)(3)(D)	1351(b)	Expansion of Research Credit—Repeal of Limitation on Contract Research Expenses Paid to Small Businesses, Universities, and Federal Laboratories	Amounts paid or incurred after August 8, 2005, in tax years ending after such date

Code Sec.	Act Sec.	Act Provision Subject	Effective Date
41(f)(6)	1351(a)(2)	Expansion of Research Credit—Credit For Expenses Attributable to Certain Collaborative Energy Research Consortia—Energy Research Consortium Defined	Amounts paid or incurred after August 8, 2005, in tax years ending after such date
43(b)(2)	1322(a)(3)(B)	Modification of Credit For Producing Fuel From a Nonconventional Source—Treatment as Business Credit—Conforming Amendments	Credits determined under the Internal Revenue Code of 1986 for taxable years ending after December 31, 2005
45(b)(4)(A)	1301(c)(2)	Extension and Modification of Renewable Electricity Production Credit—Expansion of Qualified Resources to Certain Hydropower—Credit Rate	August 8, 2005
45(b)(4)(B)(i)	1301(b)(1)	Extension and Modification of Renewable Electricity Production Credit—Increase in Credit Period	August 8, 2005
45(b)(4)(B)(ii)	1301(f)(1)	Extension and Modification of Renewable Electricity Production Credit—Additional Technical Amendments	Electricity produced and sold after December 31, 2004 in tax years ending after such date
45(b)(4)(B)(iii)	1301(b)(2)	Extension and Modification of Renewable Electricity Production Credit—Increase in Credit Period	August 8, 2005
45(c)	1301(d)(4)	Extension and Modification of Renewable Electricity Production Credit—Indian Coal—Conforming Amendment	August 8, 2005
45(c)(1)(F)-(H)	1301(c)(1)	Extension and Modification of Renewable Electricity Production Credit—Expansion of Qualified Resources to Certain Hydropower	August 8, 2005
45(c)(3)(A)(ii)	1301(f)(2)	Extension and Modification of Renewable Electricity Production Credit—Additional Technical Amendments	Electricity produced and sold after October 22, 2004 in tax years ending after such date
45(c)(8)	1301(c)(3)	Extension and Modification of Renewable Electricity Production Credit—Expansion of Qualified Resources to Certain Hydropower—Definition of Resources	August 8, 2005
45(c)(9)	1301(d)(2)	Extension and Modification of Renewable Electricity Production Credit—Indian Coal—Resource	August 8, 2005

¶20,001

Effective Dates

Code Sec.	Act Sec.	Act Provision Subject	Effective Date
45(d)(1)-(3)	1301(a)(1)	Extension and Modification of Renewable Electricity Production Credit—2-Year Extension for Certain Facilities	August 8, 2005
45(d)(4)	1301(a)(2)	Extension and Modification of Renewable Electricity Production Credit—2-Year Extension for Certain Facilities	August 8, 2005
45(d)(5)-(7)	1301(a)(1)	Extension and Modification of Renewable Electricity Production Credit—2-Year Extension for Certain Facilities	August 8, 2005
45(d)(7)	1301(e)	Extension and Modification of Renewable Electricity Production Credit—Technical Amendment	Electricity produced and sold after October 22, 2004 in tax years ending after such date
45(d)(9)	1301(c)(4)	Extension and Modification of Renewable Electricity Production Credit—Expansion of Qualified Resources to Certain Hydropower—Facilities	August 8, 2005
45(d)(10)	1301(d)(3)	Extension and Modification of Renewable Electricity Production Credit—Indian Coal—Indian Coal Production Facility	August 8, 2005
45(e)(6)	1301(f)(3)	Extension and Modification of Renewable Electricity Production Credit—Additional Technical Amendments	Electricity produced and sold after October 22, 2004 in tax years ending after such date
45(e)(8)(C)	1301(f)(4)(B)	Extension and Modification of Renewable Electricity Production Credit—Additional Technical Amendments	Refined coal produced and sold after October 22, 2004
45(e)(9)	1301(f)(4)(A)	Extension and Modification of Renewable Electricity Production Credit—Additional Technical Amendments	Electricity produced and sold after October 22, 2004 in tax years ending after such date
45(e)(9)	1322(a)(3)(C)(i)-(ii)	Modification of Credit For Producing Fuel From a Nonconventional Source—Treatment as Business Credit—Conforming Amendments	Credits determined under the Internal Revenue Code of 1986 for tax years ending after December 31, 2005
45(e)(10)	1301(d)(1)	Extension and Modification of Renewable Electricity Production Credit—Indian Coal—Production Facilities	August 8, 2005
45(e)(11)	1302(a)	Application of Section 45 Credit to Agricultural Cooperatives	Tax years of cooperative organizations ending after August 8, 2005

¶20,001

Code Sec.	Act Sec.	Act Provision Subject	Effective Date
45I(b)(2)(C)(i)	1322(a)(3)(B)	Modification of Credit For Producing Fuel From a Nonconventional Source—Treatment as Business Credit—Conforming Amendments	Credits determined under the Internal Revenue Code of 1986 for tax years ending after December 31, 2005
45I(c)(2)(A)	1322(a)(3)(D)(i)	Modification of Credit For Producing Fuel From a Nonconventional Source—Treatment as Business Credit—Conforming Amendments	Credits determined under the Internal Revenue Code of 1986 for tax years ending after December 31, 2005
45I(d)(3)	1322(a)(3)(D)(ii)	Modification of Credit For Producing Fuel From a Nonconventional Source—Treatment as Business Credit—Conforming Amendments	Credits determined under the Internal Revenue Code of 1986 for tax years ending after December 31, 2005
45J	1306(a)	Credit for Production From Advanced Nuclear Power Facilities	Production in tax years beginning after August 8, 2005
45K	1322(a)(1)	Modification of Credit For Producing Fuel From a Nonconventional Source—Treatment as Business Credit—Credit Moved to Subpart Relating to Business Related Credits	Credits determined under the Internal Revenue Code of 1986 for tax years ending after December 31, 2005
45K(a)	1322(a)(3)(E)	Modification of Credit For Producing Fuel From a Nonconventional Source—Treatment as Business Credit—Conforming Amendments	Credits determined under the Internal Revenue Code of 1986 for tax years ending after December 31, 2005
45K(b)	1322(a)(3)(F)	Modification of Credit For Producing Fuel From a Nonconventional Source—Treatment as Business Credit—Conforming Amendments	Credits determined under the Internal Revenue Code of 1986 for tax years ending after December 31, 2005
45L	1332(a)	Credit For Construction of New Energy Efficient Homes	Qualified new energy efficient homes acquired after December 31, 2005, in tax years ending after such date
45M	1334(a)	Credit For Energy Efficient Appliances	Appliances produced after December 31, 2005

¶20,001

Effective Dates

Code Sec.	Act Sec.	Act Provision Subject	Effective Date
46(1)-(4)	1307(a)	Credit for Investment in Clean Coal Facilities	Periods after August 8, 2005 under rules similar to rules of section 48(m) of the Internal Revenue Code of 1986 as in effect on the day before date of enactment of the Revenue Reconciliation Act of 1990 [11-4-90]
48(a)(1)	1336(d)	Credit For Business Installation of Qualified Fuel Cells and Stationary Microturbine Power Plants—Conforming Amendment	Periods after December 31, 2005, in tax years ending after such date, under rules similar to rules of section 48(m) of the Internal Revenue Code of 1986 as in effect on the day before date of enactment of the Revenue Reconciliation Act of 1990 [11-4-90]
48(a)(2)(A)	1336(c)	Credit For Business Installation of Qualified Fuel Cells and Stationary Microturbine Power Plants—Energy Percentage	Periods after December 31, 2005, in tax years ending after such date, under rules similar to rules of section 48(m) of the Internal Revenue Code of 1986 as in effect on the day before date of enactment of the Revenue Reconciliation Act of 1990 [11-4-90]
48(a)(2)(A)	1337(a)	Business Solar Investment Tax Credit—Increase in Energy Percentage	Periods after December 31, 2005, in tax years ending after such date, under rules similar to rules of section 48(m) of the Internal Revenue Code of 1986 as in effect on the day before date of enactment of the Revenue Reconciliation Act of 1990 [11-4-90]

¶20,001

Energy and Highway Tax Acts of 2005

Code Sec.	Act Sec.	Act Provision Subject	Effective Date
48(a)(3)(A)(i)	1337(c)	Business Solar Investment Tax Credit—Limitation on Use of Solar Energy to Heat Swimming Pools	Periods after December 31, 2005, in tax years ending after such date, under rules similar to rules of section 48(m) of the Internal Revenue Code of 1986 as in effect on the day before date of enactment of the Revenue Reconciliation Act of 1990 [11-4-90]
48(a)(3)(A)(i)-(iii)	1336(a)	Credit For Business Installation of Qualified Fuel Cells and Stationary Microturbine Power Plants	Periods after December 31, 2005, in tax years ending after such date, under rules similar to rules of section 48(m) of the Internal Revenue Code of 1986 as in effect on the day before date of enactment of the Revenue Reconciliation Act of 1990 [11-4-90]
48(a)(3)(A)(i)-(iii)	1337(b)	Business Solar Investment Tax Credit—Hybrid Solar Lighting Systems	Periods after December 31, 2005, in tax years ending after such date, under rules similar to rules of section 48(m) of the Internal Revenue Code of 1986 as in effect on the day before date of enactment of the Revenue Reconciliation Act of 1990 [11-4-90]
48(c)	1336(b)	Credit For Business Installation of Qualified Fuel Cells and Stationary Microturbine Power Plants—Qualified Fuel Cell Property; Qualified Microturbine Property	Periods after December 31, 2005, in tax years ending after such date, under rules similar to rules of section 48(m) of the Internal Revenue Code of 1986 as in effect on the day before date of enactment of the Revenue Reconciliation Act of 1990 [11-4-90]

¶20,001

Code Sec.	Act Sec.	Act Provision Subject	Effective Date
48A	1307(b)	Credit for Investment in Clean Coal Facilities—Amount of Credits	Periods after August 8, 2005 under rules similar to rules of section 48(m) of the Internal Revenue Code of 1986 as in effect on the day before date of enactment of the Revenue Reconciliation Act of 1990 [11-4-90]
48B	1307(b)	Credit for Investment in Clean Coal Facilities—Amount of Credits	Periods after August 8, 2005 under rules similar to rules of section 48(m) of the Internal Revenue Code of 1986 as in effect on the day before date of enactment of the Revenue Reconciliation Act of 1990 [11-4-90]
49(a)(1)(C)(ii)-(iv)	1307(c)(1)	Credit for Investment in Clean Coal Facilities—Conforming Amendments	Periods after August 8, 2005 under rules similar to rules of section 48(m) of the Internal Revenue Code of 1986 as in effect on the day before date of enactment of the Revenue Reconciliation Act of 1990 [11-4-90]
53(d)(1)(B)(iii)	1322(a)(3)(G)	Modification of Credit For Producing Fuel From a Nonconventional Source—Treatment as Business Credit—Conforming Amendments	Credits determined under the Internal Revenue Code of 1986 for tax years ending after December 31, 2005
54	1303(a)	Clean Renewable Energy Bonds	Bonds issued after December 31, 2005
55(c)(1)	1302(b)	Application of Section 45 Credit to Agricultural Cooperatives—Conforming Amendment	Tax years of cooperative organizations ending after August 8, 2005
55(c)(2)	1341(b)(3)	Alternative Motor Vehicle Credit—Conforming Amendments	Property placed in service after December 31, 2005, in tax years ending after such date

¶20,001

Code Sec.	Act Sec.	Act Provision Subject	Effective Date
55(c)(2)	1342(b)(3)	Credit For Installation of Alternative Fueling Stations—Conforming Amendments	Property placed in service after December 31, 2005, in tax years ending after such date
55(c)(3)	1322(a)(3)(H)	Modification of Credit For Producing Fuel From a Nonconventional Source—Treatment as Business Credit—Conforming Amendments	Credits determined under the Internal Revenue Code of 1986 for tax years ending after December 31, 2005
56(a)(1)(B)	1326(d)	Natural Gas Gathering Lines Treated as 7-Year Property—Alternative Minimum Tax Exception	Property placed in service after April 11, 2005, generally
141(c)(2)(A)-(C)	1327(b)	Arbitrage Rules Not to Apply to Prepayments For Natural Gas—Private Loan Financing Test Not to Apply to Prepayments For Natural Gas	Obligations issued after August 8, 2005
141(d)(7)	1327(c)	Arbitrage Rules Not to Apply to Prepayments For Natural Gas—Exception For Qualified Electric and Natural Gas Supply Contracts	Obligations issued after August 8, 2005
148(b)(4)	1327(a)	Arbitrage Rules Not to Apply to Prepayments For Natural Gas	Obligations issued after August 8, 2005
167(h)-(i)	1329(a)	Amortization of Geological and Geophysical Expenditures	Amounts paid or incurred in tax years beginning after August 8, 2005
168(e)(3)(B)(vi)(I)	1301(f)(5)	Extension and Modification of Renewable Electricity Production Credit—Additional Technical Amendments	Property placed in service after October 22, 2004
168(e)(3)(C)(iii)-(v)	1326(a)	Natural Gas Gathering Lines Treated as 7-Year Property	Property placed in service after April 11, 2005, generally
168(e)(3)(E)(v)-(vii)	1308(a)	Electric Transmission Property Treated as 15-Year Property	Property placed in service after April 11, 2005, generally
168(e)(3)(E)(vi)-(viii)	1325(a)	Natural Gas Distribution Lines Treated as 15-Year Property	Property placed in service after April 11, 2005, generally
168(g)(3)(B)	1308(b)	Electric Transmission Property Treated as 15-Year Property—Alternate System	Property placed in service after April 11, 2005, generally
168(g)(3)(B)	1325(b)	Natural Gas Distribution Lines Treated as 15-Year Property—Alternative System	Property placed in service after April 11, 2005, generally

¶20,001

Effective Dates

Code Sec.	Act Sec.	Act Provision Subject	Effective Date
168(g)(3)(B)	1326(c)	Natural Gas Gathering Lines Treated as 7-Year Property—Alternative System	Property placed in service after April 11, 2005, generally
168(i)(17)	1326(b)	Natural Gas Gathering Lines Treated as 7-Year Property—Natural Gas Gathering Line	Property placed in service after April 11, 2005, generally
169(d)	1309(c)	Expansion of Amortization for Certain Atmospheric Pollution Control Facilities in Connection With Plants First Placed in Service After 1975—Conforming Amendment	Facilities placed in service after April 11, 2005
169(d)(3)	1309(d)	Expansion of Amortization for Certain Atmospheric Pollution Control Facilities in Connection With Plants First Placed in Service After 1975—Technical Amendment	Facilities placed in service after April 11, 2005
169(d)(4)(B)	1309(b)	Expansion of Amortization for Certain Atmospheric Pollution Control Facilities in Connection With Plants First Placed in Service After 1975—Treatment as New Identifiable Treatment Facility	Facilities placed in service after April 11, 2005
169(d)(5)	1309(a)	Expansion of Amortization for Certain Atmospheric Pollution Control Facilities in Connection With Plants First Placed in Service After 1975—Eligibility of Post-1975 Pollution Control Facilities	Facilities placed in service after April 11, 2005
172(b)(1)(I)	1311	5-Year Net Operating Loss Carryover For Certain Losses	August 8, 2005
179A(f)	1348(a)	Sunset of Deduction For Clean-Fuel Vehicles and Certain Refueling Property	August 8, 2005
179B(e)	1324(a)	Pass Through to Owners of Deduction For Capital Costs Incurred By Small Refiner Cooperatives in Complying With Environmental Protection Agency Sulfur Regulations	Expenses paid or incurred after December 31, 2002 in tax years ending after such date
179C	1323(a)	Temporary Expensing For Equipment Used in Refining of Liquid Fuels	Properties placed in service after August 8, 2005
179D	1331(a)	Energy Efficient Commercial Buildings Deduction	Property placed in service after December 31, 2005

¶20,001

Code Sec.	Act Sec.	Act Provision Subject	Effective Date
196(c)(11)-(13)	1332(d)	Credit For Construction of New Energy Efficient Homes—Deduction For Certain Unused Business Credits	Qualified new energy efficient homes acquired after December 31, 2005, in tax years ending after such date
263(a)(1)(H)-(J)	1323(b)(2)	Temporary Expensing For Equipment Used in Refining of Liquid Fuels—Conforming Amendments	Properties placed in service after August 8, 2005
263(a)(1)(I)-(K)	1331(b)(4)	Energy Efficient Commercial Buildings Deduction—Conforming Amendments	Property placed in service after December 31, 2005
263A(c)(3)	1329(b)	Amortization of Geological and Geophysical Expenditures—Conforming Amendment	Amounts paid or incurred in tax years beginning after August 8, 2005
312(k)(3)(B)	1323(b)(3)	Temporary Expensing For Equipment Used in Refining of Liquid Fuels—Conforming Amendments	Properties placed in service after August 8, 2005
312(k)(3)(B)	1331(b)(5)	Energy Efficient Commercial Buildings Deduction—Conforming Amendments	Property placed in service after December 31, 2005
451(i)(3)	1305(a)	Dispositions of Transmission Property to Implement FERC Restructuring Policy	Transactions occurring after August 8, 2005
451(i)(4)(B)(ii)	1305(b)	Dispositions of Transmission Property to Implement FERC Restructuring Policy—Technical Amendment	Transactions occurring after October 22, 2004, in tax years ending after such date
468A(b)	1310(a)	Modifications to Special Rules For Nuclear Decommissioning Costs—Repeal of Limitation on Deposits Into Fund Based on Cost of Service; Contributions After Funding Period	Tax years beginning after December 31, 2005
468A(d)(1)	1310(c)	Modifications to Special Rules For Nuclear Decommissioning Costs—New Ruling Amount Required Upon License Renewal	Tax years beginning after December 31, 2005
468A(d)(2)(A)	1310(b)(2)	Modifications to Special Rules For Nuclear Decommissioning Costs—Treatment of Certain Decommissioning Costs—New Ruling Amount to Take Into Account Total Costs	Tax years beginning after December 31, 2005
468A(e)(2)	1310(e)(1)-(3)	Modifications to Special Rules For Nuclear Decommissioning Costs—Technical Amendments	Tax years beginning after December 31, 2005

¶20,001

Code Sec.	Act Sec.	Act Provision Subject	Effective Date
468A(e)(3)	1310(d)	Modifications to Special Rules For Nuclear Decommissioning Costs—Conforming Amendment	Tax years beginning after December 31, 2005
468A(f)-(h)	1310(b)(1)	Modifications to Special Rules For Nuclear Decommissioning Costs—Treatment of Certain Decommissioning Costs	Tax years beginning after December 31, 2005
501(c)(12)(C)	1304(a)	Treatment of Income of Certain Electric Cooperatives—Elimination of Sunset on Treatment of Income From Open Access and Nuclear Decommissioning Transactions	August 8, 2005
501(c)(12)(H)(x)	1304(b)	Treatment of Income of Certain Electric Cooperatives—Elimination of Sunset on Treatment of Income From Load Loss Transactions	August 8, 2005
613A(c)(6)(C)	1322(a)(3)(B)	Modification of Credit For Producing Fuel From a Nonconventional Source—Treatment as Business Credit—Conforming Amendments	Credits determined under the Internal Revenue Code of 1986 for tax years ending after December 31, 2005
613A(d)(4)	1328(a)	Determination of Small Refiner Exception to Oil Depletion Deduction	Tax years ending after August 8, 2005
772(a)(9)-(11)	1322(a)(3)(I)	Modification of Credit For Producing Fuel From a Nonconventional Source—Treatment as Business Credit—Conforming Amendments	Credits determined under the Internal Revenue Code of 1986 for tax years ending after December 31, 2005
772(d)(5)	1322(a)(3)(J)	Modification of Credit For Producing Fuel From a Nonconventional Source—Treatment as Business Credit—Conforming Amendments	Credits determined under the Internal Revenue Code of 1986 for tax years ending after December 31, 2005
1016(a)(30)-(32)	1331(b)(1)	Energy Efficient Commercial Buildings Deduction—Conforming Amendments	Property placed in service after December 31, 2005
1016(a)(31)-(33)	1332(c)	Credit For Construction of New Energy Efficient Homes—Basis Adjustment	Qualified new energy efficient homes acquired after December 31, 2005, in tax years ending after such date
1016(a)(32)-(34)	1333(b)(1)	Credit For Certain Nonbusiness Energy Property—Conforming Amendments	Property placed in service after December 31, 2005

Code Sec.	Act Sec.	Act Provision Subject	Effective Date
1016(a)(33)-(35)	1335(b)(4)	Credit For Residential Energy Efficient Property—Conforming Amendments	Property placed in service after December 31, 2005, in tax years ending after such date
1016(a)(34)-(36)	1341(b)(2)	Alternative Motor Vehicle Credit—Conforming Amendments	Property placed in service after December 31, 2005, in tax years ending after such date
1016(a)(35)-(37)	1342(b)(2)	Credit For Installation of Alternative Fueling Stations—Conforming Amendments	Property placed in service after December 31, 2005, in tax years ending after such date
1245(a)(2)(C)	1323(b)(1)	Temporary Expensing For Equipment Used in Refining of Liquid Fuels—Conforming Amendments	Properties placed in service after August 8, 2005
1245(a)(2)(C)	1331(b)(2)	Energy Efficient Commercial Buildings Deduction—Conforming Amendments	Property placed in service after December 31, 2005
1245(a)(3)(C)	1323(b)(1)	Temporary Expensing For Equipment Used in Refining of Liquid Fuels—Conforming Amendments	Properties placed in service after August 8, 2005
1245(a)(3)(C)	1331(b)(2)	Energy Efficient Commercial Buildings Deduction—Conforming Amendments	Property placed in service after December 31, 2005
1245(b)(9)	1363(a)	Modification of Recapture Rules for Amortizable Section 197 Intangibles	Dispositions of property after August 8, 2005
1250(b)(3)	1331(b)(3)	Energy Efficient Commercial Buildings Deduction—Conforming Amendments	Property placed in service after December 31, 2005
1397E(c)(2)	1303(c)(2)	Clean Renewable Energy Bonds—Conforming Amendments	Bonds issued after December 31, 2005
1397E(h)	1303(c)(3)	Clean Renewable Energy Bonds—Conforming Amendments	Bonds issued after December 31, 2005
1400C(d)	1335(b)(3)	Credit For Residential Energy Efficient Property-Conforming Amendments	Property placed in service after December 31, 2005, in tax years ending after such date
4041(a)(1)(B)	1362(b)(2)(A)	Extension of Leaking Underground Storage Tank Trust Fund Financing Rate—No Exemptions From Tax Except For Exports—Amendments Relating to Section 4041	Fuel entered, removed, or sold after September 30, 2005

Effective Dates

Code Sec.	Act Sec.	Act Provision Subject	Effective Date
4041(a)(2)(A)	1362(b)(2)(A)	Extension of Leaking Underground Storage Tank Trust Fund Financing Rate—No Exemptions From Tax Except For Exports—Amendments Relating to Section 4041	Fuel entered, removed, or sold after September 30, 2005
4041(b)(1)(A)	1362(b)(2)(B)	Extension of Leaking Underground Storage Tank Trust Fund Financing Rate—No Exemptions From Tax Except For Exports—Amendments Relating to Section 4041	Fuel entered, removed, or sold after September 30, 2005
4041(c)(2)	1362(b)(2)(A)	Extension of Leaking Underground Storage Tank Trust Fund Financing Rate—No Exemptions From Tax Except For Exports—Amendments Relating to Section 4041	Fuel entered, removed, or sold after September 30, 2005
4041(d)(5)	1362(b)(2)(C)	Extension of Leaking Underground Storage Tank Trust Fund Financing Rate—No Exemptions From Tax Except For Exports—Amendments Relating to Section 4041	Fuel entered, removed, or sold after September 30, 2005
4072(e)	1364(a)	Clarification of Tire Excise Tax	Sales in calendar years beginning more than 30 days after October 22, 2004
4081(a)(2)(D)	1343(a)	Reduced Motor Fuel Excise Tax on Certain Mixtures of Diesel Fuel	January 1, 2006
4081(c)	1343(b)(2)	Reduced Motor Fuel Excise Tax on Certain Mixtures of Diesel Fuel—Special Rules For Diesel-Water Fuel Emulsions—Later Separation of Fuel	January 1, 2006
4081(d)(3)	1362(a)	Extension of Leaking Underground Storage Tank Trust Fund Financing Rate	October 1, 2005
4082(a)	1362(b)(1)	Extension of Leaking Underground Storage Tank Trust Fund Financing Rate—No Exemptions From Tax Except For Exports	Fuel entered, removed, or sold after September 30, 2005
4611(f)	1361	Oil Spill Liability Trust Fund Financing Rate	August 8, 2005
6049(d)(8)	1303(b)	Clean Renewable Energy Bonds—Reporting	Bonds issued after December 31, 2005
6401(b)(1)	1303(c)(4)	Clean Renewable Energy Bonds—Conforming Amendments	Bonds issued after December 31, 2005
6426(c)(6)	1344(a)	Extension of Excise Tax Provisions and Income Tax Credit For Biodiesel	August 8, 2005
6427(e)(4)(B)	1344(a)	Extension of Excise Tax Provisions and Income Tax Credit For Biodiesel	August 8, 2005

¶20,001

Code Sec.	Act Sec.	Act Provision Subject	Effective Date
6427(i)(1)-(2)	1343(b)(3)	Reduced Motor Fuel Excise Tax on Certain Mixtures of Diesel Fuel—Special Rules For Diesel-Water Fuel Emulsions—Credit Claims	January 1, 2006
6427(m)-(q)	1343(b)(1)	Reduced Motor Fuel Excise Tax on Certain Mixtures of Diesel Fuel—Special Rules For Diesel-Water Fuel Emulsions—Refunds For Tax-Paid Purchases	January 1, 2006
6430	1362(b)(3)(A)	Extension of Leaking Underground Storage Tank Trust Fund Financing Rate—No Exemptions From Tax Except For Exports—No Refund	Fuel entered, removed, or sold after September 30, 2005
6501(m)	1341(b)(4)	Alternative Motor Vehicle Credit—Conforming Amendments	Property placed in service after December 31, 2005, in tax years ending after such date
6501(m)	1342(b)(4)	Credit For Installation of Alternative Fueling Stations—Conforming Amendments	Property placed in service after December 31, 2005, in tax years ending after such date
9508(c)	1362(c)	Extension of Leaking Underground Storage Tank Trust Fund Financing Rate—Certain Refunds and Credits Not Charged to LUST Trust Fund	October 1, 2005
. . .	1301(f)(6)	Extension and Modification of Renewable Electricity Production Credit—Additional Technical Amendments	Electricity produced and sold after October 22, 2004 in tax years ending after such date

¶20,001

¶20,005 Effective Dates

SAFE Transportation Equity Act of 2005

This CCH-prepared table presents the general effective dates for major law provisions added, amended or repealed by the SAFE Transportation Equity Act of 2005. Entries are listed in Code Section order.

Code Sec.	Act Sec.	Act Provision Subject	Effective Date
38(b)(18)-(20)	11126(b)	Income Tax Credit for Distilled Spirits Wholesalers and for Distilled Spirits in Control State Bailment Warehouses for costs of Carrying Federal Excise Taxes on Bottled Distilled Spirits—Credit Treated as Part of General Business Credit	Tax years beginning after September 30, 2005
142(a)(13)-(15)	11143(a)	Tax-Exempt Financing of Highway Projects and Rail-Truck Transfer Facilities—Treatment as Exempt Facility Bond	Bonds issued after August 10, 2005
142(m)	11143(b)	Tax-Exempt Financing of Highway Projects and Rail-Truck Transfer Facilities—Qualified Highway or Surface Freight Transfer Facilities	Bonds issued after August 10, 2005
146(g)(3)	11143(c)	Tax-Exempt Financing of Highway Projects and Rail-Truck Transfer Facilities—Exemption From General State Volume Caps	Bonds issued after August 10, 2005
4041(a)(1)(B)	11161(b)(3)(A)	Treatment of Kerosene for Use in Aviation—Reduced Rates for Use of Certain Liquids—Conforming Amendments	Fuels or liquids removed, entered, or sold after September 30, 2005
4041(a)(1)(C)(iii)(I)	11101(a)(1)(A)	Extension of Highway-Related Taxes and Trust Funds—Extension of taxes	August 10, 2005
4041(a)(2)	11113(a)(3)	Volumetric Excise Tax Credit For Alternative Fuels—Imposition of Tax—New Reference	Any sale or use for any period after September 30, 2006
4041(a)(2)(B)	11101(a)(1)(B)	Extension of Highway-Related Taxes and Trust Funds—Extension of taxes	August 10, 2005
4041(a)(2)(B)	11113(a)(1)	Volumetric Excise Tax Credit For Alternative Fuels—Imposition of Tax	Any sale or use for any period after September 30, 2006
4041(a)(2)(B)(ii)	11151(e)(2)	Highway-Related Technical Corrections—Clerical Amendments	Fuel entered, removed, or sold after September 30, 2005

Code Sec.	Act Sec.	Act Provision Subject	Effective Date
4041(a)(3)(A)	11113(a)(2)(A)	Volumetric Excise Tax Credit For Alternative Fuels—Imposition of Tax—Treatment of Compressed Natural Gas	Any sale or use for any period after September 30, 2006
4041(a)(3)(C)	11113(a)(2)(B)	Volumetric Excise Tax Credit For Alternative Fuels—Imposition of Tax—Treatment of Compressed Natural Gas	Any sale or use for any period after September 30, 2006
4041(c)	11161(b)(1)	Treatment of Kerosene for Use in Aviation—Reduced Rates for Use of Certain Liquids	Fuels or liquids removed, entered, or sold after September 30, 2005
4041(m)(1)	11101(a)(1)(C)	Extension of Highway-Related Taxes and Trust Funds—Extension of taxes	August 10, 2005
4051(a)(4)-(5)	11112(a)	Exclusion For Tractors Weighing 19,500 Pounds or Less From Federal Excise Tax on Heavy Trucks and Trailers	Sales after September 30, 2005
4051(c)	11101(a)(1)(D)	Extension of Highway-Related Taxes and Trust Funds—Extension of taxes	August 10, 2005
4064(b)(1)(A)	11111(a)	Modification of Gas Guzzler Tax—Uniform Application of Tax	October 1, 2005
4071(d)	11101(a)(1)(E)	Extension of Highway-Related Taxes and Trust Funds—Extension of taxes	August 10, 2005
4081(a)(1)(B)	11166(b)(1)	Treatment of Deep-Draft Vessels—Exemption for Domestic Bulk Transfers by Deep-Draft Vessels	August 10, 2005
4081(a)(2)(A)(ii)-(iv)	11161(a)(1)	Treatment of Kerosene for Use in Aviation—All Kerosene Taxed at Highest Rate	Fuels or liquids removed, entered, or sold after September 30, 2005
4081(a)(2)(C)	11151(b)(1)	Highway-Related Technical Corrections—Amendments Related to Section 853 of the American Jobs Creation Act of 2004	Aviation-grade kerosene removed, entered, or sold after December 31, 2004
4081(a)(2)(C)	11161(a)(2)	Treatment of Kerosene for Use in Aviation—All Kerosene Taxed at Highest Rate—Exception For Use in Aviation	Fuels or liquids removed, entered, or sold after September 30, 2005
4081(a)(3)(A)	11161(a)(4)(A)	Treatment of Kerosene for Use in Aviation—All Kerosene Taxed at Highest Rate—Conforming Amendments	Fuels or liquids removed, entered, or sold after September 30, 2005
4081(a)(3)(A)(i)	11161(a)(3)(A)	Treatment of Kerosene for Use in Aviation—All Kerosene Taxed at Highest Rate—Applicable Rate in Case of Certain Refueler Trucks, Tankers, and Tank Wagons	Fuels or liquids removed, entered, or sold after September 30, 2005

¶20,005

Code Sec.	Act Sec.	Act Provision Subject	Effective Date
4081(a)(3)(D)	11161(a)(3)(B)	Treatment of Kerosene for Use in Aviation—All Kerosene Taxed at Highest Rate—Applicable Rate in Case of Certain Refueler Trucks, Tankers, and Tank Wagons	Fuels or liquids removed, entered, or sold after September 30, 2005
4081(a)(4)	11161(a)(4)(B)-(C)	Treatment of Kerosene for Use in Aviation—All Kerosene Taxed at Highest Rate—Conforming Amendments	Fuels or liquids removed, entered, or sold after September 30, 2005
4081(d)(1)	11101(a)(1)(F)	Extension of Highway-Related Taxes and Trust Funds—Extension of taxes	August 10, 2005
4081(d)(2)	11151(b)(2)	Highway-Related Technical Corrections—Amendments Related to Section 853 of the American Jobs Creation Act of 2004	Aviation-grade kerosene removed, entered, or sold after December 31, 2004
4081(d)(2)	11161(a)(4)(D)	Treatment of Kerosene for Use in Aviation—All Kerosene Taxed at Highest Rate—Conforming Amendments	Fuels or liquids removed, entered, or sold after September 30, 2005
4082(b)	11161(a)(4)(A)	Treatment of Kerosene for Use in Aviation—All Kerosene Taxed at Highest Rate—Conforming Amendments	Fuels or liquids removed, entered, or sold after September 30, 2005
4082(d)(2)(B)	11161(b)(3)(C)	Treatment of Kerosene for Use in Aviation—Reduced Rates for Use of Certain Liquids—Conforming Amendments	Fuels or liquids removed, entered, or sold after September 30, 2005
4082(e)	11161(a)(4)(E)	Treatment of Kerosene for Use in Aviation—All Kerosene Taxed at Highest Rate—Conforming Amendments	Fuels or liquids removed, entered, or sold after September 30, 2005
4083(b)	11123(b)	Exemption From Taxes on Transportation Provided by Seaplanes—Rate of Fuel Tax for Sea Planes Subject to Exemption	Transportation beginning after September 30, 2005
4101(a)(1)	11113(c)	Volumetric Excise Tax Credit For Alternative Fuels—Additional Registration Requirements	Any sale or use for any period after September 30, 2006
4101(a)(4)	11163(a)	Refunds of Excise Tax on Exempt Sales of Fuel by Credit Card—Registration of Person Extending Credit on Certain Exempt Sales of Fuel	Sales after December 31, 2005
4101(a)(4)	11164(a)	Reregistration in Event of Change in Ownership	Actions, or failures to act, after August 10, 2005
4161(a)(1)	11117(a)	Cap on Excise Tax on Certain Fishing Equipment	Articles sold by manufacturer, producer, or importer after September 30, 2005

¶20,005

Code Sec.	Act Sec.	Act Provision Subject	Effective Date
4161(a)(2)	11117(b)	Cap on Excise Tax on Certain Fishing Equipment-Conforming Amendments	Articles sold by manufacturer, producer, or importer after September 30, 2005
4182(c)-(d)	11131(a)	Custom Gunsmiths—Small Manufacturers Exempt From Firearms Excise Tax	Articles sold by manufacturer, producer, or importer after September 30, 2005, generally
4221(a)	11101(b)(1)	Extension of Highway-Related Taxes and Trust Funds—Extension of Certain Exemptions—Certain Tax-Free Sales	August 10, 2005
4261(e)(1)(B)(i)	11122(a)(1)	Modification of Rural Airport Definition	October 1, 2005
4261(e)(1)(B)(ii)(I)-(III)	11122(a)(2)	Modification of Rural Airport Definition	October 1, 2005
4261(f)	11121(c)	Clarification of Excise Tax Exemptions for Agricultural Aerial Applicators and Exemption for Fixed-Wing Aircraft Engaged in Forestry Operations—Exemption From Tax on Air Transportation of Persons for Forestry Purposes Extended to Fixed-Wing Aircraft	Fuel use or air transportation after September 30, 2005
4261(i)-(j)	11123(a)	Exemption From Taxes on Transportation Provided by Seaplanes	Transportation beginning after September 30, 2005
4281	11124(a)	Certain Sightseeing Flights Exempt From Taxes on Air Transportation	Transportation beginning after September 30, 2005, but not on any amount paid before such date for such transportation
4461(c)(1)(A)-(C)	11116(b)(1)	Repeal of Harbor Maintenance Tax on Exports-Conforming Amendments	Before, on, and after the August 10, 2005
4461(c)(2)	11116(b)(2)	Repeal of Harbor Maintenance Tax on Exports—Conforming Amendments	Before, on, and after the August 10, 2005
4462(d)	11116(a)	Repeal of Harbor Maintenance Tax on Exports	Before, on, and after the August 10, 2005
4481(f)	11101(a)(2)(A)	Extension of Highway-Related Taxes and Trust Funds—Extension of Taxes—Extension of Tax, Etc., on Use of Certain Heavy Vehicles	August 10, 2005
4482(c)(4)	11101(a)(2)(B)	Extension of Highway-Related Taxes and Trust Funds—Extension of Taxes—Extension of Tax, Etc., on Use of Certain Heavy Vehicles	August 10, 2005

Code Sec.	Act Sec.	Act Provision Subject	Effective Date
4482(d)	11101(a)(2)(C)	Extension of Highway-Related Taxes and Trust Funds—Extension of Taxes—Extension of Tax, Etc., on Use of Certain Heavy Vehicles	August 10, 2005
4483(h)	11101(b)(2)	Extension of Highway-Related Taxes and Trust Funds—Extension of Certain Exemptions—Termination of Exemptions For Highway Use Tax	August 10, 2005
5002(b)	11125(b)(13)	Repeal of Special Occupational Taxes on Producers and Marketers of Alcoholic Beverages—Conforming Amendments	July 1, 2008, but does not apply to taxes imposed for periods before such date
5010(c)(2)(A)	11125(b)(14)	Repeal of Special Occupational Taxes on Producers and Marketers of Alcoholic Beverages—Conforming Amendments	July 1, 2008, but does not apply to taxes imposed for periods before such date
5011	11126(a)	Income Tax Credit for Distilled Spirits Wholesalers and for Distilled Spirits in Control State Bailment Warehouses for costs of Carrying Federal Excise Taxes on Bottled Distilled Spirits	Tax years beginning after September 30, 2005
5052(d)	11125(b)(15)	Repeal of Special Occupational Taxes on Producers and Marketers of Alcoholic Beverages—Conforming Amendments	July 1, 2008, but does not apply to taxes imposed for periods before such date
5061(d)(4)-(6)	11127(a)	Quarterly Excise Tax Filing for Small Alcohol Excise Taxpayers	Quarterly periods beginning on and after January 1, 2006
5061(d)(6)	11127(b)	Quarterly Excise Tax Filing For Small Alcohol Excise Taxpayers—Conforming Amendment	Quarterly periods beginning on and after January 1, 2006
5081	11125(a)(1)(A)	Repeal of Special Occupational Taxes on Producers and Marketers of Alcoholic Beverages—Repeal of Occupational Taxes	July 1, 2008, but does not apply to taxes imposed for periods before such date
5091	11125(a)(1)(B)	Repeal of Special Occupational Taxes on Producers and Marketers of Alcoholic Beverages—Repeal of Occupational Taxes	July 1, 2008, but does not apply to taxes imposed for periods before such date
5092	11125(a)(1)(B)	Repeal of Special Occupational Taxes on Producers and Marketers of Alcoholic Beverages—Repeal of Occupational Taxes	July 1, 2008, but does not apply to taxes imposed for periods before such date

¶20,005

Code Sec.	Act Sec.	Act Provision Subject	Effective Date
5093	11125(a)(1)(B)	Repeal of Special Occupational Taxes on Producers and Marketers of Alcoholic Beverages—Repeal of Occupational Taxes	July 1, 2008, but does not apply to taxes imposed for periods before such date
5111	11125(a)(1)(C)	Repeal of Special Occupational Taxes on Producers and Marketers of Alcoholic Beverages—Repeal of Occupational Taxes	July 1, 2008, but does not apply to taxes imposed for periods before such date
5111	11125(b)(3)(A)	Repeal of Special Occupational Taxes on Producers and Marketers of Alcoholic Beverages—Conforming Amendments	July 1, 2008, but does not apply to taxes imposed for periods before such date
5111	11125(b)(3)(C)(i)	Repeal of Special Occupational Taxes on Producers and Marketers of Alcoholic Beverages—Conforming Amendments	July 1, 2008, but does not apply to taxes imposed for periods before such date
5111(a)	11125(b)(3)(C)(ii)	Repeal of Special Occupational Taxes on Producers and Marketers of Alcoholic Beverages—Conforming Amendments	July 1, 2008, but does not apply to taxes imposed for periods before such date
5111(b)	11125(b)(3)(C)(iii)	Repeal of Special Occupational Taxes on Producers and Marketers of Alcoholic Beverages—Conforming Amendments	July 1, 2008, but does not apply to taxes imposed for periods before such date
5112	11125(a)(1)(C)	Repeal of Special Occupational Taxes on Producers and Marketers of Alcoholic Beverages—Repeal of Occupational Taxes	July 1, 2008, but does not apply to taxes imposed for periods before such date
5112	11125(b)(3)(A)	Repeal of Special Occupational Taxes on Producers and Marketers of Alcoholic Beverages—Conforming Amendments	July 1, 2008, but does not apply to taxes imposed for periods before such date
5113	11125(a)(1)(C)	Repeal of Special Occupational Taxes on Producers and Marketers of Alcoholic Beverages—Repeal of Occupational Taxes	July 1, 2008, but does not apply to taxes imposed for periods before such date
5113	11125(b)(3)(A)	Repeal of Special Occupational Taxes on Producers and Marketers of Alcoholic Beverages—Conforming Amendments	July 1, 2008, but does not apply to taxes imposed for periods before such date
5114	11125(b)(3)(A)	Repeal of Special Occupational Taxes on Producers and Marketers of Alcoholic Beverages—Conforming Amendments	July 1, 2008, but does not apply to taxes imposed for periods before such date

Effective Dates

Code Sec.	Act Sec.	Act Provision Subject	Effective Date
5114(c)-(d)	11125(b)(5)(B)	Repeal of Special Occupational Taxes on Producers and Marketers of Alcoholic Beverages—Conforming Amendments	July 1, 2008, but does not apply to taxes imposed for periods before such date
5116	11125(b)(11)	Repeal of Special Occupational Taxes on Producers and Marketers of Alcoholic Beverages—Conforming Amendments	July 1, 2008, but does not apply to taxes imposed for periods before such date
5117	11125(a)(1)(C)	Repeal of Special Occupational Taxes on Producers and Marketers of Alcoholic Beverages—Repeal of Occupational Taxes	July 1, 2008, but does not apply to taxes imposed for periods before such date
5121	11125(a)(1)(D)	Repeal of Special Occupational Taxes on Producers and Marketers of Alcoholic Beverages—Repeal of Occupational Taxes	July 1, 2008, but does not apply to taxes imposed for periods before such date
5121(d)(3)	11125(b)(5)(C)	Repeal of Special Occupational Taxes on Producers and Marketers of Alcoholic Beverages—Conforming Amendments	July 1, 2008, but does not apply to taxes imposed for periods before such date
5122	11125(a)(1)(D)	Repeal of Special Occupational Taxes on Producers and Marketers of Alcoholic Beverages—Repeal of Occupational Taxes	July 1, 2008, but does not apply to taxes imposed for periods before such date
5123	11125(a)(1)(D)	Repeal of Special Occupational Taxes on Producers and Marketers of Alcoholic Beverages—Repeal of Occupational Taxes	July 1, 2008, but does not apply to taxes imposed for periods before such date
5123	11125(b)(7)	Repeal of Special Occupational Taxes on Producers and Marketers of Alcoholic Beverages—Conforming Amendments	July 1, 2008, but does not apply to taxes imposed for periods before such date
5124	11125(b)(8)	Repeal of Special Occupational Taxes on Producers and Marketers of Alcoholic Beverages—Conforming Amendments	July 1, 2008, but does not apply to taxes imposed for periods before such date
5124(c)-(d)	11125(b)(6)(B)	Repeal of Special Occupational Taxes on Producers and Marketers of Alcoholic Beverages—Conforming Amendments	July 1, 2008, but does not apply to taxes imposed for periods before such date
5125	11125(a)(1)(D)	Repeal of Special Occupational Taxes on Producers and Marketers of Alcoholic Beverages—Repeal of Occupational Taxes	July 1, 2008, but does not apply to taxes imposed for periods before such date

Code Sec.	Act Sec.	Act Provision Subject	Effective Date
5131	11125(a)(2)	Repeal of Special Occupational Taxes on Producers and Marketers of Alcoholic Beverages—Repeal of Occupational Taxes—Nonbeverage Domestic Drawback	July 1, 2008, but does not apply to taxes imposed for periods before such date
5131	11125(b)(3)(A)	Repeal of Special Occupational Taxes on Producers and Marketers of Alcoholic Beverages—Conforming Amendments	July 1, 2008, but does not apply to taxes imposed for periods before such date
5131(a)	11125(b)(11)	Repeal of Special Occupational Taxes on Producers and Marketers of Alcoholic Beverages—Conforming Amendments	July 1, 2008, but does not apply to taxes imposed for periods before such date
5132	11125(b)(3)(A)	Repeal of Special Occupational Taxes on Producers and Marketers of Alcoholic Beverages—Conforming Amendments	July 1, 2008, but does not apply to taxes imposed for periods before such date
5132	11125(b)(12)	Repeal of Special Occupational Taxes on Producers and Marketers of Alcoholic Beverages—Conforming Amendments	July 1, 2008, but does not apply to taxes imposed for periods before such date
5133	11125(b)(3)(A)	Repeal of Special Occupational Taxes on Producers and Marketers of Alcoholic Beverages—Conforming Amendments	July 1, 2008, but does not apply to taxes imposed for periods before such date
5134	11125(b)(3)(A)	Repeal of Special Occupational Taxes on Producers and Marketers of Alcoholic Beverages—Conforming Amendments	July 1, 2008, but does not apply to taxes imposed for periods before such date
5141	11125(a)(1)(E)	Repeal of Special Occupational Taxes on Producers and Marketers of Alcoholic Beverages—Repeal of Occupational Taxes	July 1, 2008, but does not apply to taxes imposed for periods before such date
5142	11125(b)(20)(A)	Repeal of Special Occupational Taxes on Producers and Marketers of Alcoholic Beverages—Conforming Amendments	July 1, 2008, but does not apply to taxes imposed for periods before such date
5143	11125(b)(20)(A)	Repeal of Special Occupational Taxes on Producers and Marketers of Alcoholic Beverages—Conforming Amendments	July 1, 2008, but does not apply to taxes imposed for periods before such date
5145	11125(b)(20)(A)	Repeal of Special Occupational Taxes on Producers and Marketers of Alcoholic Beverages—Conforming Amendments	July 1, 2008, but does not apply to taxes imposed for periods before such date

Effective Dates 535

Code Sec.	Act Sec.	Act Provision Subject	Effective Date
5146	11125(b)(7)	Repeal of Special Occupational Taxes on Producers and Marketers of Alcoholic Beverages—Conforming Amendments	July 1, 2008, but does not apply to taxes imposed for periods before such date
5147	11125(a)(1)(E)	Repeal of Special Occupational Taxes on Producers and Marketers of Alcoholic Beverages—Repeal of Occupational Taxes	July 1, 2008, but does not apply to taxes imposed for periods before such date
5148	11125(a)(1)(E)	Repeal of Special Occupational Taxes on Producers and Marketers of Alcoholic Beverages—Repeal of Occupational Taxes	July 1, 2008, but does not apply to taxes imposed for periods before such date
5149	11125(a)(1)(E)	Repeal of Special Occupational Taxes on Producers and Marketers of Alcoholic Beverages—Repeal of Occupational Taxes	July 1, 2008, but does not apply to taxes imposed for periods before such date
5182	11125(b)(16)	Repeal of Special Occupational Taxes on Producers and Marketers of Alcoholic Beverages—Conforming Amendments	July 1, 2008, but does not apply to taxes imposed for periods before such date
5276	11125(a)(3)	Repeal of Special Occupational Taxes on Producers and Marketers of Alcoholic Beverages—Repeal of Occupational Taxes—Industrial Use of Distilled Spirits	July 1, 2008, but does not apply to taxes imposed for periods before such date
5402(b)	11125(b)(17)	Repeal of Special Occupational Taxes on Producers and Marketers of Alcoholic Beverages—Conforming Amendments	July 1, 2008, but does not apply to taxes imposed for periods before such date
5671	11125(b)(18)	Repeal of Special Occupational Taxes on Producers and Marketers of Alcoholic Beverages—Conforming Amendments	July 1, 2008, but does not apply to taxes imposed for periods before such date
5691	11125(b)(19)(A)	Repeal of Special Occupational Taxes on Producers and Marketers of Alcoholic Beverages—Conforming Amendments	July 1, 2008, but does not apply to taxes imposed for periods before such date
5731(c)-(d)	11125(b)(20)(E)	Repeal of Special Occupational Taxes on Producers and Marketers of Alcoholic Beverages—Conforming Amendments	July 1, 2008, but does not apply to taxes imposed for periods before such date
5732	11125(b)(20)(A)	Repeal of Special Occupational Taxes on Producers and Marketers of Alcoholic Beverages—Conforming Amendments	July 1, 2008, but does not apply to taxes imposed for periods before such date

Code Sec.	Act Sec.	Act Provision Subject	Effective Date
5732	11125(b)(20)(B)	Repeal of Special Occupational Taxes on Producers and Marketers of Alcoholic Beverages—Conforming Amendments	July 1, 2008, but does not apply to taxes imposed for periods before such date
5733	11125(b)(20)(A)	Repeal of Special Occupational Taxes on Producers and Marketers of Alcoholic Beverages—Conforming Amendments	July 1, 2008, but does not apply to taxes imposed for periods before such date
5733(c)(2)	11125(b)(20)(C)	Repeal of Special Occupational Taxes on Producers and Marketers of Alcoholic Beverages—Conforming Amendments	July 1, 2008, but does not apply to taxes imposed for periods before such date
5734	11125(b)(20)(A)	Repeal of Special Occupational Taxes on Producers and Marketers of Alcoholic Beverages—Conforming Amendments	July 1, 2008, but does not apply to taxes imposed for periods before such date
6071(c)	11125(b)(21)	Repeal of Special Occupational Taxes on Producers and Marketers of Alcoholic Beverages—Conforming Amendments	July 1, 2008, but does not apply to taxes imposed for periods before such date
6206	11163(d)(1)	Refunds of Excise Tax on Exempt Sales of Fuel by Credit Card—Conforming Penalty Amendments	Sales after December 31, 2005
6412(a)(1)	11101(a)(3)	Extension of Highway-Related Taxes and Trust Funds—Extension of Taxes—Floor Stocks Refunds	August 10, 2005
6416(a)(4)	11163(b)(1)	Refunds of Excise Tax on Exempt Sales of Fuel by Credit Card—Refunds of Tax on Gasoline	Sales after December 31, 2005
6416(b)(2)	11163(b)(2)	Refunds of Excise Tax on Exempt Sales of Fuel by Credit Card—Refunds of Tax on Gasoline—Conforming Amendment	Sales after December 31, 2005
6420(c)(4)	11121(b)	Clarification of Excise Tax Exemptions for Agricultural Aerial Applicators and Exemption for Fixed-Wing Aircraft Engaged in Forestry Operations—Exemption Includes Fuel Used Between Airfield and Farm	Fuel use or air transportation after September 30, 2005
6420(c)(4)(B)	11121(a)	Clarification of Excise Tax Exemptions for Agricultural Aerial Applicators and Exemption for Fixed-Wing Aircraft Engaged in Forestry Operations—No Waiver by Farm Owner, Tenant, or Operator Necessary	Fuel use or air transportation after September 30, 2005

¶20,005

Effective Dates

Code Sec.	Act Sec.	Act Provision Subject	Effective Date
6421(f)(2)	11151(b)(3)	Highway-Related Technical Corrections—Amendments Related to Section 853 of the American Jobs Creation Act of 2004	Aviation-grade kerosene removed, entered, or sold after December 31, 2004
6426	11113(b)(3)(A)	Volumetric Excise Tax Credit For Alternative Fuels—Alternative Fuel and Alternative Fuel Mixture Credit—Conforming Amendments	Any sale or use for any period after September 30, 2006
6426(a)	11113(b)(1)	Volumetric Excise Tax Credit For Alternative Fuels—Credit for Alternative Fuel and Alternative Fuel Mixtures	Any sale or use for any period after September 30, 2006
6426(d)(2)(F)	11151(e)(2)	Highway-Related Technical Corrections—Clerical Amendments	Credits determined under the Internal Revenue Code of 1986 for tax years ending after December 31, 2005
6426(d)-(g)	11113(b)(2)	Volumetric Excise Tax Credit For Alternative Fuels—Alternative Fuel and Alternative Fuel Mixture Credit	Any sale or use for any period after September 30, 2006
6427(e)	11113(b)(3)(C)	Volumetric Excise Tax Credit For Alternative Fuels—Alternative Fuel and Alternative Fuel Mixture Credit—Conforming Amendments	Any sale or use for any period after September 30, 2006
6427(f)	11151(a)(1)	Highway-Related Technical Corrections—Amendments Related to Section 301 of the American Jobs Creation Act of 2004	Fuel sold or used after December 31, 2004.
6427(i)(4)(A)	11161(b)(3)(D)	Treatment of Kerosene for Use in Aviation—Reduced Rates for Use of Certain Liquids—Conforming Amendments	Fuels or liquids removed, entered, or sold after September 30, 2005
6427(l)	11161(b)(3)(B)	Treatment of Kerosene for Use in Aviation—Reduced Rates for Use of Certain Liquids—Conforming Amendments	Fuels or liquids removed, entered, or sold after September 30, 2005
6427(l)(2)	11161(b)(2)(A)	Treatment of Kerosene for Use in Aviation—Reduced Rates for Use of Certain Liquids—Partial Refund of Full Rate	Fuels or liquids removed, entered, or sold after September 30, 2005
6427(l)(4)	11161(b)(3)(E)	Treatment of Kerosene for Use in Aviation—Reduced Rates for Use of Certain Liquids—Conforming Amendments	Fuels or liquids removed, entered, or sold after September 30, 2005

Code Sec.	Act Sec.	Act Provision Subject	Effective Date
6427(l)(5)-(6)	11161(b)(2)(B)	Treatment of Kerosene for Use in Aviation—Reduced Rates for Use of Certain Liquids—Partial Refund of Full Rate—Refunds for Noncommercial Aviation	Fuels or liquids removed, entered, or sold after September 30, 2005
6427(l)(6)	11162(b)	Repeal of Ultimate Vendor Refund Claims With Respect to Farming—Conforming Amendment	Sales after September 30, 2005
6427(l)(6)(A)	11162(a)	Repeal of Ultimate Vendor Refund Claims With Respect to Farming	Sales after September 30, 2005
6427(l)(6)(B)	11161(b)(3)(F)	Treatment of Kerosene for Use in Aviation—Reduced Rates for Use of Certain Liquids—Conforming Amendments	Fuels or liquids removed, entered, or sold after September 30, 2005
6427(l)(6)(C)-(D)	11163(c)	Refunds of Excise Tax on Exempt Sales of Fuel by Credit Card—Diesel Fuel or Kerosene	Sales after December 31, 2005
6427(o)-(p)	11151(a)(2)	Highway-Related Technical Corrections—Amendments Related to Section 301 of the American Jobs Creation Act of 2004	Fuel sold or used after December 31, 2004.
6675(a)	11163(d)(2)	Refunds of Excise Tax on Exempt Sales of Fuel by Credit Card—Conforming Penalty Amendments	Sales after December 31, 2005
6675(b)(1)	11163(d)(3)	Refunds of Excise Tax on Exempt Sales of Fuel by Credit Card—Conforming Penalty Amendments	Sales after December 31, 2005
6719	11164(b)(1)	Reregistration in Event of Change in Ownership—Conforming Amendments—Civil Penalty	Actions, or failures to act, after August 10, 2005
6720A	11167(a)	Penalty With Respect to Certain Adulterated Fuels	Any transfer, sale, or holding out for sale or resale occurring after August 10, 2005
7012(4)-(6)	11125(b)(9)	Repeal of Special Occupational Taxes on Producers and Marketers of Alcoholic Beverages—Conforming Amendments	July 1, 2008, but does not apply to taxes imposed for periods before such date
7232	11164(b)(2)	Reregistration in Event of Change in Ownership—Conforming Amendments—Criminal Penalty	Actions, or failures to act, after August 10, 2005
7272	11164(b)(3)	Reregistration in Event of Change in Ownership—Conforming Amendments—Additional Civil Penalty	Actions, or failures to act, after August 10, 2005

¶20,005

Code Sec.	Act Sec.	Act Provision Subject	Effective Date
7652(g)(1)	11125(b)(22)	Repeal of Special Occupational Taxes on Producers and Marketers of Alcoholic Beverages—Conforming Amendments	July 1, 2008, but does not apply to taxes imposed for periods before such date
7652(g)(1)	11125(b)(22)(A)	Repeal of Special Occupational Taxes on Producers and Marketers of Alcoholic Beverages—Conforming Amendments	July 1, 2008, but does not apply to taxes imposed for periods before such date
7652(g)(1)	11125(b)(22)(B)	Repeal of Special Occupational Taxes on Producers and Marketers of Alcoholic Beverages—Conforming Amendments	July 1, 2008, but does not apply to taxes imposed for periods before such date
9502(a)	11161(c)(2)(A)	Treatment of Kerosene for Use in Aviation—Transfers From Highway Trust Fund of Taxes on Fuels Used in Aviation to Airport and Airway Trust Fund—Conforming Amendments	Fuels or liquids removed, entered, or sold after September 30, 2005
9502(b)(1)(A)	11161(c)(2)(B)(i)	Treatment of Kerosene for Use in Aviation—Transfers From Highway Trust Fund of Taxes on Fuels Used in Aviation to Airport and Airway Trust Fund—Conforming Amendments	Fuels or liquids removed, entered, or sold after September 30, 2005
9502(b)(1)(C)	11161(c)(2)(B)(ii)	Treatment of Kerosene for Use in Aviation—Transfers From Highway Trust Fund of Taxes on Fuels Used in Aviation to Airport and Airway Trust Fund—Conforming Amendments	Fuels or liquids removed, entered, or sold after September 30, 2005
9502(d)(2)-(3)	11161(d)	Treatment of Kerosene for Use in Aviation—Certain Refunds Not Transferred From Airport and Airway Trust Fund	Fuels or liquids removed, entered, or sold after September 30, 2005
9503(b)	11161(c)(2)(C)	Treatment of Kerosene for Use in Aviation—Transfers From Highway Trust Fund of Taxes on Fuels Used in Aviation to Airport and Airway Trust Fund—Conforming Amendments	Fuels or liquids removed, entered, or sold after September 30, 2005
9503(b)(1)-(2)	11101(c)(1)	Extension of Highway-Related Taxes and Trust Funds—Extension of Transfers of Certain Taxes	August 10, 2005
9503(b)(5)	11167(b)	Penalty With Respect to Certain Adulterated Fuels—Dedication of Revenue	Any transfer, sale, or holding out for sale or resale occurring after August 10, 2005
9503(b)(6)(B)	11101(d)(1)(C)	Extension of Highway-Related Taxes and Trust Funds—Extension and Expansion of Expenditures From Trust Funds—Highway Trust Fund—Exception to Limitation on Transfers	August 10, 2005

Code Sec.	Act Sec.	Act Provision Subject	Effective Date
9503(c)(1)	11101(d)(1)(A)	Extension of Highway-Related Taxes and Trust Funds—Extension and Expansion of Expenditures From Trust Funds—Highway Trust Fund—Highway Account	August 10, 2005
9503(c)(2)-(3)	11101(c)(1)	Extension of Highway-Related Taxes and Trust Funds—Extension of Transfers of Certain Taxes	August 10, 2005
9503(c)(4)(A)-(E)	11115(a)(1)	Elimination of Aquatic Resources Trust Fund and Transformation of Sport Fish Restoration Account—Simplification of Funding for Boat Safety Account	October 1, 2005
9503(c)(5)(A)	11101(c)(2)(A)	Extension of Highway-Related Taxes and Trust Funds—Extension of Transfers of Certain Taxes—Motorboat and Small-Engine Fuel Tax Transfers	August 10, 2005
9503(c)(5)(A)	11115(a)(2)	Elimination of Aquatic Resources Trust Fund and Transformation of Sport Fish Restoration Account—Simplification of Funding for Boat Safety Account—Conforming Amendment	October 1, 2005
9503(c)(7)	11161(c)(1)	Treatment of Kerosene for Use in Aviation—Transfers From Highway Trust Fund of Taxes on Fuels Used in Aviation to Airport and Airway Trust Fund	Fuels or liquids removed, entered, or sold after September 30, 2005
9503(d)(1)(B)	11102(a)(1)	Modification of Adjustments of Apportionments	August 10, 2005
9503(d)(3)	11102(a)(2)	Modification of Adjustments of Apportionments	August 10, 2005
9503(d)(6)-(7)	11102(b)	Modification of Adjustments of Apportionments—Measurement of Net Highway Receipts	August 10, 2005
9503(e)(3)	11101(d)(1)(B)	Extension of Highway-Related Taxes and Trust Funds—Extension and Expansion of Expenditures From Trust Funds—Highway Trust Fund—Mass Transit Account	August 10, 2005
9504	11115(b)(2)(D)	Elimination of Aquatic Resources Trust Fund and Transformation of Sport Fish Restoration Account—Merging Accounts—Conforming Amendments	October 1, 2005

Effective Dates

Code Sec.	Act Sec.	Act Provision Subject	Effective Date
9504(a)	11115(b)(1)	Elimination of Aquatic Resources Trust Fund and Transformation of Sport Fish Restoration Account—Merging Accounts	October 1, 2005
9504(b)	11115(b)(2)(A)	Elimination of Aquatic Resources Trust Fund and Transformation of Sport Fish Restoration Account—Merging Accounts—Conforming Amendments	October 1, 2005
9504(b)(2)	11101(d)(2)(A)	Extension of Highway-Related Taxes and Trust Funds—Extension and Expansion of Expenditures From Trust Funds—Aquatic Resources Trust Fund—Sport Fish Restoration Account	August 10, 2005
9504(b)(2)	11151(c)	Highway-Related Technical Corrections—Amendment Related to Section 9005 of the Transportation Equity Act for the 21st Century	June 9, 1998
9504(b)(2)(A)	11151(e)(1)	Highway-Related Technical Corrections—Clerical Amendments	August 10, 2005
9504(c)	11115(c)	Elimination of Aquatic Resources Trust Fund and Transformation of Sport Fish Restoration Account—Phaseout of Boat Safety Account	October 1, 2005
9504(d)	11115(b)(2)(B)	Elimination of Aquatic Resources Trust Fund and Transformation of Sport Fish Restoration Account—Merging Accounts—Conforming Amendments	October 1, 2005
9504(d)(2)	11101(d)(2)(B)	Extension of Highway-Related Taxes and Trust Funds—Extension and Expansion of Expenditures From Trust Funds—Aquatic Resources Trust Fund—Exception to Limitation on Transfers	August 10, 2005
9504(e)	11115(b)(2)(C)	Elimination of Aquatic Resources Trust Fund and Transformation of Sport Fish Restoration Account—Merging Accounts—Conforming Amendments	October 1, 2005
9508(e)	11147(a)	Limitation on Transfers to the Leaking Underground Storage Tank Trust Fund	August 10, 2005

¶20,005

Code Sec.	Act Sec.	Act Provision Subject	Effective Date
. . .	11101(c)(2)(B)	Extension of Highway-Related Taxes and Trust Funds—Extension of Transfers of Certain Taxes—Motorboat and Small-Engine Fuel Tax Transfers—Conforming Amendments to Land and Water Conservation Fund	August 10, 2005
. . .	11141	Motor Fuel Tax Enforcement Advisory Commission	August 10, 2005
. . .	11142	National Surface Transportation Infrastructure Financing Commission	August 10, 2005
. . .	11144	Treasury Study of Highway Fuels Used by Trucks For Non-Transportation Purposes	August 10, 2005
. . .	11145	Diesel Fuel Tax Evasion Report	August 10, 2005
. . .	11146	Tax Treatment of State Ownership of Railroad Real Estate Investment Trust	August 10, 2005
. . .	11151(d)(1)	Highway-Related Technical Corrections—Amendment Related to Section 1306 of the Energy Policy Act of 2005	Production in tax years beginning after August 8, 2005
. . .	11151(d)(2)	Highway-Related Technical Corrections—Amendment Related to Section 1306 of the Energy Policy Act of 2005	August 10, 2005
. . .	11166(a)	Treatment of Deep-Draft Vessels	August 10, 2005
. . .	11165(a)	Reconciliation of On-Loaded Cargo to Entered Cargo	August 10, 2005

¶25,001 Code Section to Explanation Table

Code Sec.	Explanation
23(c)	¶210
25C	¶205
25D	¶210
25(e)(1)(C)	¶210
29	¶615
29(c)(2)(A)	¶615
29(e)-(h)	¶615
29(h)	¶610
30(b)(3)(A)	¶615
30B	¶305, ¶310, ¶315, ¶320, ¶325
30C	¶730
38(b)	¶220, ¶305, ¶310, ¶315, ¶320, ¶325, ¶615, ¶730
38(b)(19)-(21)	¶440
38(b)(20)	¶835
38(b)(22)	¶225, ¶615
38(b)(23)	¶220, ¶225
38(b)(24)	¶225
40(g)	¶735
40(g)(6)	¶735
40A	¶715
40A(a)-(b)	¶710
40A(d)(3)(C)-(D)	¶710
40A(e)	¶710
40A(f)	¶710, ¶715
40A(g)	¶705, ¶715
41(a)	¶235
41(b)(3)	¶235
41(b)(3)(C)	¶235
41(f)	¶235
43(b)(2)	¶615
45(b)(4)(A)-(B)	¶415
45(c)	¶405
45(c)(1)(H)	¶405
45(c)(3)(A)(ii)	¶405
45(c)(8)-(9)	¶405
45(d)	¶410
45(d)(9)	¶415
45(e)(6)	¶415
45(e)(8)(C)	¶410
45(e)(9)	¶410, ¶615
45(e)(10)	¶415
45(e)(11)	¶420
45I(b)(2)(C)(i)	¶615
45I(c)(2)(A)	¶615
45I(d)(3)	¶615
45J	¶440
45K	¶615
45K(a)-(b)	¶615
45K(c)(2)(A)(e)-(g)	¶615
45K(h)	¶610
45L	¶220
45M	¶225
46(3)-(4)	¶605
48(a)(1)	¶240
48(a)(2)(A)	¶230, ¶240
48(a)(3)(A)	¶230, ¶240
48(a)(3)(A)(i)	¶230
48(c)	¶240
48A	¶605
48B	¶605
49(a)(1)(C)	¶605
53(d)(1)(B)(iii)	¶615
54	¶455
55(c)(1)	¶420
55(c)(2)	¶305, ¶310, ¶315, ¶320, ¶325, ¶730
55(c)(3)	¶615
56(a)(1)	¶520
141(c)(2)	¶530
141(d)(7)	¶530
142(a)(15)	¶915
142(m)	¶915
146(g)(3)	¶915
148(b)(4)	¶530
167(h)-(i)	¶525
168(e)(3)(B)(ii)(I)	¶415
168(e)(3)(C)(iv)-(v)	¶520
168(e)(3)(E)(vii)	¶425
168(e)(3)(E)(viii)	¶515
168(g)(3)(B)	¶425, ¶515, ¶520
168(i)(17)	¶520
169(d)	¶620
169(d)(3)	¶620
169(d)(4)(B)	¶620
169(d)(5)	¶620
172(b)(1)(I)	¶430
179A(f)	¶330

Code Sec.	Explanation
179B(e)	¶535
179C	¶505
179D	¶215
196(c)	¶220
196(c)(13)	¶220
263(a)(1)	¶505
263(a)(1)(K)	¶215
263A(c)(3)	¶525
312(k)(3)(B)	¶215, ¶505
451(i)(3)	¶435
451(i)(4)(B)(ii)	¶435
468A(b)	¶445
468A(d)(1)	¶445
468A(d)(2)(A)	¶445
468A(e)(2)-(3)	¶445
468A(f)-(h)	¶445
501(c)(12)(C)	¶450
501(c)(12)(H)	¶450
613A(c)(6)(C)	¶615
613A(d)(4)	¶510
772(a)	¶615
772(d)(5)	¶615
1016(a)	¶205, ¶220, ¶305, ¶315, ¶320, ¶325, ¶730
1016(a)(32)	¶215
1016(a)(33)	¶220
1016(a)(34)	¶205
1016(a)(35)	¶210
1245(a)	¶215, ¶505
1245(b)(9)	¶245
1250(b)(3)	¶215
1397E(c)(2)	¶455
1397E(h)	¶455
1400C(d)	¶210
4041(a)	¶905
4041(a)(1)	¶725
4041(a)(1)(B)	¶740, ¶785
4041(a)(2)	¶725
4041(a)(2)(A)	¶785
4041(a)(3)	¶725
4041(b)(1)(A)	¶785
4041(c)	¶740
4041(c)(2)	¶785
4041(d)(5)	¶785
4041(m)(1)	¶905
4051(a)	¶340
4051(c)	¶905
4064(b)(1)(A)	¶335
4071(d)	¶905
4072(e)	¶345

Code Sec.	Explanation
4081(a)	¶740
4081(a)(1)(B)	¶775
4081(a)(2)(C)	¶790
4081(a)(2)(D)	¶720
4081(c)	¶720
4081(d)(1)	¶905
4081(d)(2)	¶795
4081(d)(2)(B)	¶740
4081(d)(3)	¶785
4082(a)	¶785
4082(b)	¶740
4082(d)(2)(B)	¶740
4082(d)-(e)	¶740
4083(b)	¶810
4101(a)	¶755
4101(a)(4)	¶745
4161(a)(1)-(2)	¶845
4182(c)-(d)	¶850
4221(a)	¶905
4261(e)(1)(B)	¶805
4261(f)	¶820
4261(i)-(j)	¶810
4281	¶815
4461(c)(1)-(2)	¶825
4462(d)	¶825
4481(f)	¶905
4482	¶905
4483(h)	¶905
4611(f)	¶540
5011	¶835
5061(d)(4)-(6)	¶830
6049(d)(8)	¶455
6071(c)	¶840
6206	¶745
6401(b)(1)	¶455
6412(a)(1)	¶905
6416(a)(4)	¶745
6416(b)(2)	¶745
6420(c)(4)	¶820
6420(c)(4)(B)	¶820
6421(f)(2)	¶790
6426	¶725
6426(c)(6)	¶705
6427(e)	¶725
6427(e)(3)(B)	¶705
6427(f)	¶787
6427(i)	¶720
6427(i)(4)(A)	¶740
6427(l)	¶740
6427(l)(6)	¶745, ¶750
6427(l)(6)(A)	¶750
6427(m)	¶720

Code Sec.	Explanation
6427(m)-(q)	¶720
6427(o)-(p)	¶787
6430	¶785
6501(m)	¶305, ¶310, ¶315, ¶320, ¶325, ¶730
6675	¶745
6719	¶755
6720A	¶765
7012	¶840
7232	¶755
7272	¶755
7652(g)	¶840
9502(a)	¶740
9502(b)(1)	¶740
9502(d)(2)-(3)	¶740
9503(b)	¶765, ¶905
9503(b)(3)	¶740

Code Sec.	Explanation
9503(b)(6)(B)	¶905
9503(c)	¶905
9503(c)(1)	¶905
9503(c)(4)	¶1030
9503(c)(7)	¶740
9503(d)(1)(B)	¶1025
9503(d)(3)	¶1025
9503(d)(6)-(7)	¶1025
9503(e)(3)	¶905
9504(a)-(b)	¶1030
9504(b)(2)	¶797, ¶905
9504(c)	¶1030
9504(d)-(e)	¶1030
9504(d)(2)	¶905
9508(c)	¶1035
9508(e)	¶1035

¶25,001

¶25,005 Code Sections Added, Amended or Repealed

The list below notes all the Code Sections or subsections of the Internal Revenue Code that were added, amended or repealed by the Energy Tax Incentives Act of 2005 and the SAFE Transportation Equity Act of 2005. The first column indicates the Code Section added, amended or repealed, and the second column indicates the Act Section.

Energy Tax Incentives Act of 2005

Code Sec.	Act Sec.	Code Sec.	Act Sec.
25(e)(1)(C)	1335(b)(2)	45(c)(3)(A)(ii)	1301(f)(2)
25C	1333(a)	45(c)(8)	1301(c)(3)
25D	1335(a)	45(c)(9)	1301(d)(2)
29	1322(a)(1)	45(d)(1)-(3)	1301(a)(1)
29(c)(2)(A)	1322(b)(1)(A)	45(d)(4)	1301(a)(2)
29(e)-(h)	1322(b)(1)(B)	45(d)(5)-(7)	1301(a)(1)
29(g)(1)(A)-(B)	1322(b)(2)(A)-(B)	45(d)(7)	1301(e)
29(h)	1321(a)	45(d)(9)	1301(c)(4)
30(b)(3)(A)	1322(a)(3)(A)	45(d)(10)	1301(d)(3)
30B	1341(a)	45(e)(6)	1301(f)(3)
30C	1342(a)	45(e)(8)(C)	1301(f)(4)(B)
38(b)(19)-(21)	1306(b)	45(e)(9)	1301(f)(4)(A)
38(b)(20)-(22)	1322(a)(2)	45(e)(9)	1322(a)(3)(C)(i)-(ii)
38(b)(21)-(23)	1332(b)	45(e)(10)	1301(d)(1)
38(b)(22)-(24)	1334(b)	45(e)(11)	1302(a)
38(b)(23)-(25)	1341(b)(1)	45I(b)(2)(C)(i)	1322(a)(3)(B)
38(b)(24)-(26)	1342(b)(1)	45I(c)(2)(A)	1322(a)(3)(D)(i)
40(g)	1347(a)	45I(d)(3)	1322(a)(3)(D)(ii)
40(g)(6)(A)(ii)	1347(b)	45J	1306(a)
40A	1346(b)(1)	45K	1322(a)(1)
40A(a)	1345(a)	45K(a)	1322(a)(3)(E)
40A(b)	1345(d)(2)	45K(b)(6)	1322(a)(3)(F)
40A(b)(4)	1345(d)(1)	45L	1332(a)
40A(b)(5)	1345(b)	45M	1334(a)
40A(d)(3)(C)-(D)	1345(d)(3)	46(1)-(4)	1307(a)
40A(e)	1344(a)	48(a)(1)	1336(d)
40A(e)-(f)	1345(c)	48(a)(2)(A)	1336(c)
40A(f)-(g)	1346(a)	48(a)(2)(A)	1337(a)
41(a)(1)-(3)	1351(a)(1)	48(a)(3)(A)(i)	1337(c)
41(b)(3)(C)	1351(a)(3)	48(a)(3)(A)(i)-(iii)	1336(a)
41(b)(3)(D)	1351(b)	48(a)(3)(A)(i)-(iii)	1337(b)
41(f)(6)	1351(a)(2)	48(c)	1336(b)
43(b)(2)	1322(a)(3)(B)	48A	1307(b)
45(b)(4)(A)	1301(c)(2)	48B	1307(b)
45(b)(4)(B)(i)	1301(b)(1)	49(a)(1)(C)(ii)-(iv)	1307(c)(1)
45(b)(4)(B)(ii)	1301(f)(1)	53(d)(1)(B)(iii)	1322(a)(3)(G)
45(b)(4)(B)(iii)	1301(b)(2)	54	1303(a)
45(c)	1301(d)(4)	55(c)(1)	1302(b)
45(c)(1)(F)-(H)	1301(c)(1)	55(c)(2)[(3)]	1341(b)(3)

Code Sec.	Act Sec.	Code Sec.	Act Sec.
55(c)(2)[(3)]	1342(b)(3)	613A(c)(6)(C)	1322(a)(3)(B)
55(c)(3)	1322(a)(3)(H)	613A(d)(4)	1328(a)
56(a)(1)(B)	1326(d)	772(a)(9)-(11)	1322(a)(3)(I)
141(c)(2)(A)-(C)	1327(b)	772(d)(5)	1322(a)(3)(J)
141(d)(7)	1327(c)	1016(a)(30)-(32)	1331(b)(1)
148(b)(4)	1327(a)	1016(a)(31)-(33)	1332(c)
167(h)-(i)	1329(a)	1016(a)(32)-(34)	1333(b)(1)
168(e)(3)(B)(vi)(I)	1301(f)(5)	1016(a)(33)-(35)	1335(b)(4)
168(e)(3)(C)(iii)-(v)	1326(a)	1016(a)(34)-(36)	1341(b)(2)
168(e)(3)(E)(v)-(vii)	1308(a)	1016(a)(35)-(37)	1342(b)(2)
168(e)(3)(E)(vi)-(viii)	1325(a)	1245(a)(2)(C)	1323(b)(1)
168(g)(3)(B)	1308(b)	1245(a)(2)(C)	1331(b)(2)
168(g)(3)(B)	1325(b)	1245(a)(3)(C)	1323(b)(1)
168(g)(3)(B)	1326(c)	1245(a)(3)(C)	1331(b)(2)
168(i)(17)	1326(b)	1245(b)(9)	1363(a)
169(d)	1309(c)	1250(b)(3)	1331(b)(3)
169(d)(3)	1309(d)	1397E(c)(2)	1303(c)(2)
169(d)(4)(B)	1309(b)	1397E(h)	1303(c)(3)
169(d)(5)	1309(a)	1400C(d)	1335(b)(3)
172(b)(1)(I)	1311	4041(a)(1)(B)	1362(b)(2)(A)
179A(f)	1348	4041(a)(2)(A)	1362(b)(2)(A)
179B(e)	1324(a)	4041(b)(1)(A)	1362(b)(2)(B)
179C	1323(a)	4041(c)(2)	1362(b)(2)(A)
179D	1331(a)	4041(d)(5)	1362(b)(2)(C)
196(c)(11)-(13)	1332(d)	4072(e)	1364(a)
263(a)(1)(H)-(J)	1323(b)(2)	4081(a)(2)(D)	1343(a)
263(a)(1)(I)-(K)	1331(b)(4)	4081(c)	1343(b)(2)
263A(c)(3)	1329(b)	4081(d)(3)	1362(a)
312(k)(3)(B)	1323(b)(3)	4082(a)	1362(b)(1)
312(k)(3)(B)	1331(b)(5)	4611(f)	1361
451(i)(3)	1305(a)	6049(d)(8)	1303(b)
451(i)(4)(B)(ii)	1305(b)	6401(b)(1)	1303(c)(4)
468A(b)	1310(a)	6426(c)(6)	1344(a)
468A(d)(1)	1310(c)	6427(e)(4)[(3)](B)	1344(a)
468A(d)(2)(A)	1310(b)(2)	6427(i)(1)-(2)	1343(b)(3)
468A(e)(2)(A)-(D)	1310(e)(1)-(3)	6427(m)-(q)	1343(b)(1)
468A(e)(3)	1310(d)	6430	1362(b)(3)(A)
468A(f)-(h)	1310(b)(1)	6501(m)	1341(b)(4)
501(c)(12)(C)	1304(a)	6501(m)	1342(b)(4)
501(c)(12)(H)(x)	1304(b)	9508(c)	1362(c)

SAFE Transportation Equity Act of 2005

Code Sec.	Act Sec.	Code Sec.	Act Sec.
38(b)(18)-(20)	11126(b)	4041(a)(2)(B)(ii)	11151(e)(2)
142(a)(13)-(15)	11143(a)	4041(a)(3)(A)	11113(a)(2)(A)
142(m)	11143(b)	4041(a)(3)(C)	11113(a)(2)(B)
146(g)(3)	11143(c)	4041(a)(2)	11113(a)(3)
4041(a)(1)(B)	11161(b)(3)(A)	4041(c)	11161(b)(1)(A)-(D)
4041(a)(1)(C)(iii)(I)	11101(a)(1)(A)	4041(m)(1)	11101(a)(1)(C)
4041(a)(2)(B)	11101(a)(1)(B)	4051(a)(4)-(5)	11112(a)
4041(a)(2)(B)(i)-(iii)	11113(a)(1)(A)-(D)	4051(c)	11101(a)(1)(D)

¶25,005

Code Sections Added, Amended or Repealed

Code Sec.	Act Sec.	Code Sec.	Act Sec.
4064(b)(1)(A)	11111(a)	5114	11125(b)(3)(A)
4071(d)	11101(a)(1)(E)	5114	11125(b)(5)(B)(i)
4081(a)(1)(B)	11166(b)(1)	5114(c)-(d)	11125(b)(5)(B)(ii)
4081(a)(2)(A)(ii)-(iv)	11161(a)(1)	5116	11125(b)(11)
4081(a)(2)(C)	11151(b)(1)	5117	11125(a)(1)(C)
4081(a)(2)(C)	11161(a)(2)	5121	11125(a)(1)(D)
4081(a)(3)	11161(a)(3)(A)-(B)	5121(d)(3)	11125(b)(5)(C)
4081(a)(3)(A)	11161(a)(4)(A)	5122	11125(a)(1)(D)
4081(a)(4)	11161(a)(4)(B)	5123	11125(a)(1)(D)
4081(a)(4)	11161(a)(4)(C)	5123	11125(b)(7)
4081(d)(1)	11101(a)(1)(F)	5124	11125(b)(6)(A)
4081(d)(2)	11151(b)(2)	5124	11125(b)(6)(B)(i)-(iii)
4081(d)(2)	11161(a)(4)(D)	5124	11125(b)(8)
4082(b)	11161(a)(4)(A)	5125	11125(a)(1)(D)
4082(d)(2)(B)	11161(b)(3)(C)	5131	11125(a)(2)
4082(e)	11161(a)(4)(E)(i)-(iv)	5131	11125(b)(3)(A)
4083(b)	11123(b)	5131	11125(b)(11)
4101(a)(1)	11113(c)	5132	11125(b)(3)(A)
4101(a)(4)	11163(a)	5132	11125(b)(12)
4101(a)(4)[5]	11164(a)	5133	11125(b)(3)(A)
4161(a)(1)	11117(a)	5134	11125(b)(3)(A)
4161(a)(2)	11117(b)	5141	11125(a)(1)(E)
4182(c)-(d)	11131(a)	5142	11125(b)(20)(A)
4221(a)	11101(b)(1)	5143	11125(b)(20)(A)
4261(e)(1)(B)(i)-(ii)	11122(a)(1)-(2)	5145	11125(b)(20)(A)
4261(f)	11121(c)	5146	11125(b)(7)
4261(i)-(j)	11123(a)	5147	11125(a)(1)(E)
4281	11124(a)	5148	11125(a)(1)(E)
4461(c)(1)(A)-(C)	11116(b)(1)	5149	11125(a)(1)(E)
4461(c)(2)	11116(b)(2)	5182	11125(b)(16)
4462(d)	11116(a)	5276	11125(a)(3)
4481(f)	11101(a)(2)(A)	5402(b)	11125(b)(17)
4482(c)(4)	11101(a)(2)(B)	5432[5121]	11125(b)(5)(B)(i)
4482(d)	11101(a)(2)(C)	5671	11125(b)(18)
4483(h)	11101(b)(2)	5691	11125(b)(19)(A)
5002(b)	11125(b)(13)(A)-(C)	5731(c)-(d)	11125(b)(20)(E)
5010(c)(2)(A)	11125(b)(14)	5732	11125(b)(20)(A)
5011	11126(a)	5732	11125(b)(20)(B)
5052(d)	11125(b)(15)	5733	11125(b)(20)(A)
5061(d)(4)-(6)	11127(a)	5733(c)(2)	11125(b)(20)(C)
5061(d)(6)	11127(b)	5734	11125(b)(20)(A)
5081	11125(a)(1)(A)	6071(c)	11125(b)(21)
5091	11125(a)(1)(B)	6206	11163(d)(1)(A)-(D)
5092	11125(a)(1)(B)	6412(a)(1)	11101(a)(3)(A)-(B)
5093	11125(a)(1)(B)	6416(a)(4)	11163(b)(1)(A)-(E)
5111	11125(a)(1)(C)	6416(b)(2)	11163(b)(2)
5111	11125(b)(3)(A)	6420(c)(4)	11121(b)
5111	11125(b)(3)(C)(i)-(iii)	6420(c)(4)(B)	11121(a)
5112	11125(a)(1)(C)	6421(f)(2)(A)-(B)	11151(b)(3)(A)-(B)
5112	11125(b)(3)(A)	6426	11113(b)(3)(A)
5113	11125(a)(1)(C)	6426(a)	11113(b)(1)
5113	11125(b)(3)(A)	6426(d)(2)(F)	11151(e)(2)

¶25,005

Code Sec.	Act Sec.	Code Sec.	Act Sec.
6426(d)-(g)	11113(b)(2)	9503(b)(3)	11161(c)(2)(C)
6427(e)(1)-(5)	11113(b)(3)(C)(i)-(ix)	9503(b)(5)	11167(b)
6427(f)	11151(a)(1)	9503(b)(6)(B)	11101(d)(1)(C)
6427(i)(4)(A)	11161(b)(3)(D)(i)-(ii)	9503(c)(1)	11101(d)(1)(A)
6427(l)	11161(b)(3)(B)	9503(c)(2)-(3)	11101(c)(1)(A)-(B)
6427(l)(2)	11161(b)(2)(A)	9503(c)(4)	11115(a)(1)(A)-(C)
6427(l)(4)	11161(b)(3)(E)(i)-(iv)	9503(c)(5)(A)	11101(c)(2)(A)
6427(l)(5)-(6)	11161(b)(2)(B)	9503(c)(5)(A)	11115(a)(2)
6427(l)(6)	11162(b)	9503(c)(7)	11161(c)(1)
6427(l)(6)(A)	11162(a)	9503(d)(1)(B)	11102(a)(1)
6427(l)(6)(B)	11161(b)(3)(F)	9503(d)(3)	11102(a)(2)
6427(l)(6)(C)-(D)	11163(c)(1)-(2)	9503(d)(6)-(7)	11102(b)
6427(o)-(p)	11151(a)(2)	9503(e)(3)	11101(d)(1)(B)
6675(a)	11163(d)(2)	9504	11115(b)(2)(D)
6675(b)(1)	11163(d)(3)	9504(a)	11115(b)(1)
6719	11164(b)(1)(A)-(C)	9504(b)	11115(b)(2)(A)(i)-(iii)
6720A	11167(a)	9504(b)(2)	11101(d)(2)(A)
7012(4)-(6)	11125(b)(9)	9504(b)(2)	11151(c)
7232	11164(b)(2)(A)-(C)	9504(b)(2)(A)	11151(e)(1)
7272	11164(b)(3)(A)-(B)	9504(c)	11115(c)
7652(g)(1)	11125(b)(22)(A)-(B)	9504(d)	11115(b)(2)(B)(i)-(iii)
9502(a)	11161(c)(2)(A)	9504(d)(2)	11101(d)(2)(B)
9502(b)(1)	11161(c)(2)(B)(i)-(ii)	9504(e)	11115(b)(2)(C)
9502(d)(2)	11161(d)(1)	9508(e)	11147(a)
9502(d)(3)	11161(d)(2)		
9503(b)(1)-(2)	11101(c)(1)(A)-(B)		

¶25,005

¶25,010 Table of Amendments to Other Acts

Energy Tax Incentives Act of 2005

Amended Act Sec.	H.R. 6 Sec.	Par. (¶)

American Jobs Creation Act of 2004

Amended Act Sec.	H.R. 6 Sec.	Par. (¶)
710(g)(4)	1301(f)(6)	7005

SAFE Transportation Equity Act of 2005

Amended Act Sec.	H.R. 3 Sec.	Par. (¶)	Amended Act Sec.	H.R. 3 Sec.	Par. (¶)
			\- Energy Tax Incentives Act of 2005		
Land and Water Conservation Fund Act of 1965			1306(b)	11151(d)(1)	7090
201(b)	11101(c)(2)(B)	7050	**Trade Act of 2002**		
Homeland Security Act of 2002			343(a)	11165(a)	7095
1511(e)	11115(b)(2)(F)	7055			

¶25,010

¶25,015 Table of Act Sections Not Amending Internal Revenue Code Sections

Energy Tax Incentives Act of 2005

	Paragraph
Sec. 1300. Short title; amendment of 1986 Code	¶7003
Sec. 1303. Clean renewable energy bonds	¶7010
Sec. 1352. National Academy of Sciences study and report	¶7015
Sec. 1353. Recycling study	¶7020
Sec. 1364. Clarification of tire excise tax	¶7025

SAFE Transportation Equity Act of 2005

	Paragraph
Sec. 11100. Amendment of 1986 Code	¶7045
Sec. 11125. Repeal of special occupational taxes on producers and marketers of alcoholic beverages	¶7060
Sec. 11141. Motor fuel tax enforcement advisory commission	¶7065
Sec. 11142. National surface transportation infrastructure financing commission	¶7070
Sec. 11144. Treasury study of highway fuels used by trucks for non-transportation purposes	¶7075
Sec. 11145. Diesel fuel tax evasion report	¶7080
Sec. 11146. Tax treatment of state ownership of railroad real estate investment trust	¶7085
Sec. 11166. Treatment of deep-draft vessels	¶7100

¶ 25,020 Act Sections Amending Code Sections

Energy Tax Incentives Act of 2005

Act Sec.	Code Sec.	Act Sec.	Code Sec.
1301(a)(1)	45(d)(1)-(3)	1310(c)	468A(d)(1)
1301(a)(1)	45(d)(5)-(7)	1310(d)	468A(e)(3)
1301(a)(2)	45(d)(4)	1310(e)(1)-(3)	468A(e)(2)(A)-(D)
1301(b)(1)	45(b)(4)(B)(i)	1311	172(b)(1)(I)
1301(b)(2)	45(b)(4)(B)(iii)	1321(a)	29(h)
1301(c)(1)	45(c)(1)(F)-(H)	1322(a)(1)	29
1301(c)(2)	45(b)(4)(A)	1322(a)(1)	45K
1301(c)(3)	45(c)(8)	1322(a)(2)	38(b)(20)-(22)
1301(c)(4)	45(d)(9)	1322(a)(3)(A)	30(b)(3)(A)
1301(d)(1)	45(e)(10)	1322(a)(3)(B)	43(b)(2)
1301(d)(2)	45(c)(9)	1322(a)(3)(B)	45I(b)(2)(C)(i)
1301(d)(3)	45(d)(10)	1322(a)(3)(B)	613A(c)(6)(C)
1301(d)(4)	45(c)	1322(a)(3)(C)(i)-(ii)	45(e)(9)
1301(e)	45(d)(7)	1322(a)(3)(D)(i)	45I(c)(2)(A)
1301(f)(1)	45(b)(4)(B)(ii)	1322(a)(3)(D)(ii)	45I(d)(3)
1301(f)(2)	45(c)(3)(A)(ii)	1322(a)(3)(E)	45K(a)
1301(f)(3)	45(e)(6)	1322(a)(3)(F)	45K(b)(6)
1301(f)(4)(A)	45(e)(9)	1322(a)(3)(G)	53(d)(1)(B)(iii)
1301(f)(4)(B)	45(e)(8)(C)	1322(a)(3)(H)	55(c)(3)
1301(f)(5)	168(e)(3)(B)(vi)(I)	1322(a)(3)(I)	772(a)(9)-(11)
1302(a)	45(e)(11)	1322(a)(3)(J)	772(d)(5)
1302(b)	55(c)(1)	1322(b)(1)(A)	29(c)(2)(A)
1303(a)	54	1322(b)(1)(B)	29(e)-(h)
1303(b)	6049(d)(8)	1322(b)(2)(A)-(B)	29(g)(1)(A)-(B)
1303(c)(2)	1397E(c)(2)	1323(a)	179C
1303(c)(3)	1397E(h)	1323(b)(1)	1245(a)(2)(C)
1303(c)(4)	6401(b)(1)	1323(b)(1)	1245(a)(3)(C)
1304(a)	501(c)(12)(C)	1323(b)(2)	263(a)(1)(H)-(J)
1304(b)	501(c)(12)(H)(x)	1323(b)(3)	312(k)(3)(B)
1305(a)	451(i)(3)	1324(a)	179B(e)
1305(b)	451(i)(4)(B)(ii)	1325(a)	168(e)(3)(E)(vi)-(viii)
1306(a)	45J	1325(b)	168(g)(3)(B)
1306(b)	38(b)(19)-(21)	1326(a)	168(e)(3)(C)(iii)-(v)
1307(a)	46(1)-(4)	1326(b)	168(i)(17)
1307(b)	48A	1326(c)	168(g)(3)(B)
1307(b)	48B	1326(d)	56(a)(1)(B)
1307(c)(1)	49(a)(1)(C)(ii)-(iv)	1327(a)	148(b)(4)
1308(a)	168(e)(3)(E)(v)-(vii)	1327(b)	141(c)(2)(A)-(C)
1308(b)	168(g)(3)(B)	1327(c)	141(d)(7)
1309(a)	169(d)(5)	1328(a)	613A(d)(4)
1309(b)	169(d)(4)(B)	1329(a)	167(h)-(i)
1309(c)	169(d)	1329(b)	263A(c)(3)
1309(d)	169(d)(3)	1331(a)	179D
1310(a)	468A(b)	1331(b)(1)	1016(a)(30)-(32)
1310(b)(1)	468A(f)-(h)	1331(b)(2)	1245(a)(2)(C)
1310(b)(2)	468A(d)(2)(A)	1331(b)(2)	1245(a)(3)(C)

Energy and Highway Tax Acts of 2005

Act Sec.	Code Sec.	Act Sec.	Code Sec.
1331(b)(3)	1250(b)(3)	1343(b)(1)	6427(m)-(q)
1331(b)(4)	263(a)(1)(I)-(K)	1343(b)(2)	4081(c)
1331(b)(5)	312(k)(3)(B)	1343(b)(3)	6427(i)(1)-(2)
1332(a)	45L	1344(a)	40A(e)
1332(b)	38(b)(21)-(23)	1344(a)	6426(c)(6)
1332(c)	1016(a)(31)-(33)	1344(a)	6427(e)(4)[(3)](B)
1332(d)	196(c)(11)-(13)	1345(a)	40A(a)
1333(a)	25C	1345(b)	40A(b)(5)
1333(b)(1)	1016(a)(32)-(34)	1345(c)	40A(e)-(f)
1334(a)	45M	1345(d)(1)	40A(b)(4)
1334(b)	38(b)(22)-(24)	1345(d)(2)	40A(b)
1335(a)	25D	1345(d)(3)	40A(d)(3)(C)-(D)
1335(b)(1)	23(c)	1346(a)	40A(f)-(g)
1335(b)(2)	25(e)(1)(C)	1346(b)(1)	40A
1335(b)(3)	1400C(d)	1347(a)	40(g)
1335(b)(4)	1016(a)(33)-(35)	1347(b)	40(g)(6)(A)(ii)
1336(a)	48(a)(3)(A)(i)-(iii)	1348	179A(f)
1336(b)	48(c)	1351(a)(1)	41(a)(1)-(3)
1336(c)	48(a)(2)(A)	1351(a)(2)	41(f)(6)
1336(d)	48(a)(1)	1351(a)(3)	41(b)(3)(C)
1337(a)	48(a)(2)(A)	1351(b)	41(b)(3)(D)
1337(b)	48(a)(3)(A)(i)-(iii)	1361	4611(f)
1337(c)	48(a)(3)(A)(i)	1362(a)	4081(d)(3)
1341(a)	30B	1362(b)(1)	4082(a)
1341(b)(1)	38(b)(23)-(25)	1362(b)(2)(A)	4041(a)(1)(B)
1341(b)(2)	1016(a)(34)-(36)	1362(b)(2)(A)	4041(a)(2)(A)
1341(b)(3)	55(c)(2)[(3)]	1362(b)(2)(A)	4041(c)(2)
1341(b)(4)	6501(m)	1362(b)(2)(B)	4041(b)(1)(A)
1342(a)	30C	1362(b)(2)(C)	4041(d)(5)
1342(b)(1)	38(b)(24)-(26)	1362(b)(3)(A)	6430
1342(b)(2)	1016(a)(35)-(37)	1362(c)	9508(c)
1342(b)(3)	55(c)(2)[(3)]	1363(a)	1245(b)(9)
1342(b)(4)	6501(m)	1364(a)	4072(e)
1343(a)	4081(a)(2)(D)		

SAFE Transportation Equity Act of 2005

Act Sec.	Code Sec.	Act Sec.	Code Sec.
11101(a)(1)(A)	4041(a)(1)(C)(iii)(I)	11101(c)(2)(A)	9503(c)(5)(A)
11101(a)(1)(B)	4041(a)(2)(B)	11101(d)(1)(A)	9503(c)(1)
11101(a)(1)(C)	4041(m)(1)	11101(d)(1)(B)	9503(e)(3)
11101(a)(1)(D)	4051(c)	11101(d)(1)(C)	9503(b)(6)(B)
11101(a)(1)(E)	4071(d)	11101(d)(2)(A)	9504(b)(2)
11101(a)(1)(F)	4081(d)(1)	11101(d)(2)(B)	9504(d)(2)
11101(a)(2)(A)	4481(f)	11102(a)(1)	9503(d)(1)(B)
11101(a)(2)(B)	4482(c)(4)	11102(a)(2)	9503(d)(3)
11101(a)(2)(C)	4482(d)	11102(b)	9503(d)(6)-(7)
11101(a)(3)(A)-(B)	6412(a)(1)	11111(a)	4064(b)(1)(A)
11101(b)(1)	4221(a)	11112(a)	4051(a)(4)-(5)
11101(b)(2)	4483(h)	11113(a)(1)(A)-(D)	4041(a)(2)(B)(i)-(iii)
11101(c)(1)(A)-(B)	9503(b)(1)-(2)	11113(a)(2)(A)	4041(a)(3)(A)
11101(c)(1)(A)-(B)	9503(c)(2)-(3)	11113(a)(2)(B)	4041(a)(3)(C)

¶25,020

Act Sections Amending Code Sections

Act Sec.	Code Sec.	Act Sec.	Code Sec.
11113(a)(3)	4041(a)(2)	11125(b)(3)(C)(i)-(iii)	5111
11113(b)(1)	6426(a)	11125(b)(5)(B)(i)	5114
11113(b)(2)	6426(d)-(g)	11125(b)(5)(B)(i)	5432[5121]
11113(b)(3)(A)	6426	11125(b)(5)(B)(ii)	5114(c)-(d)
11113(b)(3)(C)(i)-(ix)	6427(e)(1)-(5)	11125(b)(5)(C)	5121(d)(3)
11113(c)	4101(a)(1)	11125(b)(6)(A)	5124
11115(a)(1)(A)-(C)	9503(c)(4)	11125(b)(6)(B)(i)-(iii)	5124
11115(a)(2)	9503(c)(5)(A)	11125(b)(7)	5123
11115(b)(1)	9504(a)	11125(b)(7)	5146
11115(b)(2)(A)(i)-(iii)	9504(b)	11125(b)(8)	5124
11115(b)(2)(B)(i)-(iii)	9504(d)	11125(b)(9)	7012(4)-(6)
11115(b)(2)(C)	9504(e)	11125(b)(11)	5116
11115(b)(2)(D)	9504	11125(b)(11)	5131
11115(c)	9504(c)	11125(b)(12)	5132
11116(a)	4462(d)	11125(b)(13)(A)-(C)	5002(b)
11116(b)(1)	4461(c)(1)(A)-(C)	11125(b)(14)	5010(c)(2)(A)
11116(b)(2)	4461(c)(2)	11125(b)(15)	5052(d)
11117(a)	4161(a)(1)	11125(b)(16)	5182
11117(b)	4161(a)(2)	11125(b)(17)	5402(b)
11121(a)	6420(c)(4)(B)	11125(b)(18)	5671
11121(b)	6420(c)(4)	11125(b)(19)(A)	5691
11121(c)	4261(f)	11125(b)(20)(A)	5142
11122(a)(1)-(2)	4261(e)(1)(B)(i)-(ii)	11125(b)(20)(A)	5143
11123(a)	4261(i)-(j)	11125(b)(20)(A)	5145
11123(b)	4083(b)	11125(b)(20)(A)	5732
11124(a)	4281	11125(b)(20)(A)	5733
11125(a)(1)(A)	5081	11125(b)(20)(A)	5734
11125(a)(1)(B)	5091	11125(b)(20)(B)	5732
11125(a)(1)(B)	5092	11125(b)(20)(C)	5733(c)(2)
11125(a)(1)(B)	5093	11125(b)(20)(E)	5731(c)-(d)
11125(a)(1)(C)	5111	11125(b)(21)	6071(c)
11125(a)(1)(C)	5112	11125(b)(22)(A)-(B)	7652(g)(1)
11125(a)(1)(C)	5113	11126(a)	5011
11125(a)(1)(C)	5117	11126(b)	38(b)(18)-(20)
11125(a)(1)(D)	5121	11127(a)	5061(d)(4)-(6)
11125(a)(1)(D)	5122	11127(b)	5061(d)(6)
11125(a)(1)(D)	5123	11131(a)	4182(c)-(d)
11125(a)(1)(D)	5125	11143(a)	142(a)(13)-(15)
11125(a)(1)(E)	5141	11143(b)	142(m)
11125(a)(1)(E)	5147	11143(c)	146(g)(3)
11125(a)(1)(E)	5148	11147(a)	9508(e)
11125(a)(1)(E)	5149	11151(a)(1)	6427(f)
11125(a)(2)	5131	11151(a)(2)	6427(o)-(p)
11125(a)(3)	5276	11151(b)(1)	4081(a)(2)(C)
11125(b)(3)(A)	5111	11151(b)(2)	4081(d)(2)
11125(b)(3)(A)	5112	11151(b)(3)A)-(B)	6421(f)(2)(A)-(B)
11125(b)(3)(A)	5113	11151(c)	9504(b)(2)
11125(b)(3)(A)	5114	11151(e)(1)	9504(b)(2)(A)
11125(b)(3)(A)	5131	11151(e)(2)	6426(d)(2)(F)
11125(b)(3)(A)	5132	11151(e)(2)	4041(a)(2)(B)(ii)
11125(b)(3)(A)	5133	11161(a)(1)	4081(a)(2)(A)(ii)-(iv)
11125(b)(3)(A)	5134	11161(a)(2)	4081(a)(2)(C)

¶25,020

Act Sec.	Code Sec.	Act Sec.	Code Sec.
11161(a)(3)(A)-(B)	4081(a)(3)	11161(d)(1)	9502(d)(2)
11161(a)(4)(A)	4081(a)(3)(A)	11161(d)(2)	9502(d)(3)
11161(a)(4)(A)	4082(b)	11162(a)	6427(l)(6)(A)
11161(a)(4)(B)	4081(a)(4)	11162(b)	6427(l)(6)
11161(a)(4)(C)	4081(a)(4)	11163(a)	4101(a)(4)
11161(a)(4)(D)	4081(d)(2)	11163(b)(1)(A)-(E)	6416(a)(4)
11161(a)(4)(E)(i)-(iv)	4082(e)	11163(b)(2)	6416(b)(2)
11161(b)(1)(A)-(D)	4041(c)	11163(c)(1)-(2)	6427(l)(6)(C)-(D)
11161(b)(2)(A)	6427(l)(2)	11163(d)(1)(A)-(D)	6206
11161(b)(2)(B)	6427(l)(5)-(6)	11163(d)(2)	6675(a)
11161(b)(3)(A)	4041(a)(1)(B)	11163(d)(3)	6675(b)(1)
11161(b)(3)(B)	6427(l)	11164(a)	4101(a)(4)[5]
11161(b)(3)(C)	4082(d)(2)(B)	11164(b)(1)(A)-(C)	6719
11161(b)(3)(D)(i)-(ii)	6427(i)(4)(A)	11164(b)(2)(A)-(C)	7232
11161(b)(3)(E)(i)-(iv)	6427(l)(4)	11164(b)(3)(A)-(B)	7272
11161(b)(3)(F)	6427(l)(6)(B)	11166(b)(1)	4081(a)(1)(B)
11161(c)(1)	9503(c)(7)	11167(a)	6720A
11161(c)(2)(A)	9502(a)	11167(b)	9503(b)(5)
11161(c)(2)(B)(i)-(ii)	9502(b)(1)		
11161(c)(2)(C)	9503(b)(3)		

¶27,001 Provisions Dropped in Conference

Energy Tax Incentives Act of 2005

The following proposed law changes were originally included in the House or Senate amendment versions of the Energy Tax Incentives Act of 2005, H.R. 6, but were dropped by the conferees. References to the House Bill are to the Enhanced Energy Infrastructure and Technology Tax Act of 2005, H.R. 1541. H.R. 1541, which was never voted on, contained the tax portions of the larger Energy Policy Act of 2005, which was passed by the House on April 21, 2005. References to the Senate Bill are to the Energy Policy Tax Incentives Act of 2005, H.R. 6, as passed by the Senate on June 28, 2005.

Energy Infrastructure Tax Incentives
- Tax credit bonds, Clean Energy Coal Bonds ("CIECos") (Senate Bill Sec. 1509).
- Investment tax credit for qualified investments in clean coke/cogeneration facilities property (Senate Bill Sec. 1511).
- Modification of enhanced oil recovery credit (Senate Bill Sec. 1514).

Miscellaneous Energy Tax Incentives
- Amortization of delay rental payments incurred in connection with the development of oil or gas in the United States (House Bill Sec. 1314).
- Repeal of the phase out of the credit for electric vehicles (Senate Bill Sec. 1532).
- Volumetric excise tax for alternative fuels (Senate Bill Sec. 1534). [Note: This provision was included in the Highway Act, see ¶725.]
- Deduction for business energy property (Senate Bill Sec. 1523).
- Energy credit for the purchase of combined heat and power system property (Senate Bill Sec. 1525).
- Offset of regular and alternative minimum tax by nonbusiness energy credits (House Bill Sec. 1321).
- Allowance of certain business energy credits against alternative minimum tax (House Bill Sec. 1322 and Senate Bill Sec. 1548(c)).

Additional Energy Tax Incentives
- Shortened recovery period for underground natural gas storage facilities and cushion gas (Senate Bill Sec. 1541).
- Investment tax credit for pollution control equipment (Senate Bill Sec. 1547).
- Credit for the replacement of an EPA non-compliant wood stove (Senate Bill Sec. 1549).
- Exemption for bulk beds from excise tax on retail sale of heavy trucks and trailers (Senate Bill Sec. 1550).
- Exclusion for certain fuel costs of rural carpoolers (Senate Bill Sec. 1552).
- Allowance of three-year applicable recovery period for depreciation of qualified energy management devices (Senate Bill Sec. 1553).
- Exception from volume cap for certain cooling facilities (Senate Bill Sec. 1554).

Revenue Raising Provisions
- Treatment of kerosene for use in aviation (Senate Bill Sec. 1561). [Note: This provision was included in the Highway Act, see ¶740.]
- Repeal of ultimate vendor refund claims with respect to farming (Senate Bill Sec. 1562). [Note: This provision was included in the Highway Act, ¶750.]
- Refund of excise tax on exempt sales of taxable fuel by credit card (Senate Bill Sec. 1563). [Note: This provision was included in the Highway Act, see ¶745.]
- Recertification of exempt status (Senate Bill Sec. 1564).
- Reregistration in event of change of ownership (Senate Bill Sec. 1565). [Note: This provision was included in the Highway Act, see ¶755.]
- Registration of operators of deep-draft vessels (Senate Bill Sec. 1566). [Note: This provision was included in the Highway Act, see ¶775.]
- Reconciliation of on-loaded cargo to entered cargo (Senate Bill Sec. 1567). [Note: This provision was included in the Highway Act, see ¶770.]
- Partial repeal of exemption for gasoline blend stocks and modification of definition of kerosene (Senate Bill Sec. 1568).
- Nonapplication of export exemption to delivery of fuel to motor vehicles removed from the United States (Senate Bill Sec. 1569).
- Assessable penalty for dealers of adulterated fuel (Senate Bill Sec. 1570). [Note: This provision was included in the Highway Act, see ¶765.]

SAFE Transportation Equity Act of 2005

The following proposed law changes were originally included in the House or Senate amendment versions of the SAFE Transportation Equity Act of 2005, H.R. 3, but were dropped by the conferees. References to the House Bill are to the Transportation Equity Act: A Legacy for Users, H.R. 3, as passed by the House on March 10, 2005. References to the Senate Bill are to the Highway Reauthorization and Excise Tax Simplification Act of 2005, as passed by the Senate on May 17, 2005.

Excise Tax Reform and Simplification
- Exemption for bulk beds from excise tax on retail sale of heavy trucks and trailers (Senate Bill Sec. 5203).
- Modification of limit on rate of rum excise tax cover over to Puerto Rico and the Virgin Islands (Senate Bill Sec. 5232).

Miscellaneous Provisions
- Expansion of Highway Trust Fund authority to include funding for studies of supplemental or alternative financing for Highway Trust Fund (Senate Bill Sec. 5303).
- Study of transportation in the Delta region (Senate Bill Sec. 5304).
- Establishment of Build America Corporation (Senate Bill Sec. 5305).
- Increase of dollar limits for qualified transportation fringe benefits (Senate Bill Sec. 5306).
- Credit for installation of alternative refueling property (Senate Bill Secs. 5310 and 2011). [Note: This provision was included in the Energy Act, see ¶730.]

- Modification of recapture rules for amortizable Code Sec. 197 intangibles (Senate Bill Sec. 5311). [Note: This provision was included in the Energy Act, see ¶ 245.]
- Treatment of contingent payment convertible debt instruments (Senate Bill Sec. 5501).
- Frivolous tax submissions (Senate Bill Sec. 5502).
- Increase of certain criminal penalties (Senate Bill Sec. 5503).
- Increase of penalties, fines and interest on underpayments related to certain offshore financial arrangements (Senate Bill Sec. 5504).
- Modification of coordination rules for controlled foreign corporations and passive foreign investment company regimes (Senate Bill Sec. 5505).
- Declaration by chief executive officer on federal annual corporate income tax return (Senate Bill Sec. 5506).
- Treasury regulatory authority to address certain foreign tax credit transactions (Senate Bill Sec. 5507).
- Reformation of whistleblower rules (Senate Bill Sec. 5508).
- Modification of rules for determining nondeductible fines and penalties (Senate Bill Sec. 5509).
- Freeze of interest suspension rules for listed transactions (Senate Bill Sec. 5510).
- Repeal of loss deferral exception for qualified transportation property (Senate Bill Sec. 5511).
- Imposition of mark-to-market rules on expatriates (Senate Bill Sec. 5512).
- Disallowance of deduction for punitive damages (Senate Bill Sec. 5513).
- Application of earnings stripping rules to corporate partners (Senate Bill Sec. 5514).
- Prohibition of deferral of certain stock option and restricted stock gains (Senate Bill Sec. 5515).
- Limitation on employer deduction of certain entertainment expenses (Senate Bill Sec. 5516).
- Increase in penalty for bad checks and money orders (Senate Bill Sec. 5517).
- Elimination of double deduction of mining and exploration and development costs under the minimum tax (Senate Bill Sec. 5518).
- Clarification of economic substance doctrine (Senate Bill Sec. 5521).
- Penalty for understatements attributable to transactions lacking economic substance (Senate Bill Sec. 5522).
- Extension of disallowance of interest deduction to interest attributable to noneconomic substance transactions (Senate Bill Sec. 5523).
- Waiver of user fee for installment agreements using automated withdrawals (Senate Bill Sec. 5531).
- Termination of installment agreements (Senate Bill Sec. 5532).

- Repeal of requirement that Office of Chief Counsel review certain offers-in-compromise (Senate Bill Sec. 5533).
- Partial payment requirements with submissions of offers-in-compromise (Senate Bill Sec. 5534).
- Establishment of joint task force to review offers-in-compromise determinations (Senate Bill Sec. 5535).
- Suspension of transfers from Highway Trust Fund for certain repayments and credits (Senate Bill Sec. 5601).
- Dedication of gas guzzler tax to Highway Trust Fund (Senate Bill Sec. 5602).
- Recertification of exempt status (Senate Bill Sec. 5614).
- Partial repeal of exemption for gasoline blend stocks and modification of definition of kerosene (Senate Bill Sec. 5618).
- Nonapplication of export exemption to delivery of fuel to motor vehicles removed from the United States (Senate Bill Sec. 5619).

Topical Index

References are to paragraph (¶) numbers

A

Air passenger transportation tax
. rural airports
. . defined . . . 805
. . ticket segment tax . . . 805
. seaplanes
. . ticket segment tax . . . 810
. sightseeing flights
. . established lines . . . 815
. . non-established lines . . . 815

Airport and Airway Trust Fund
. aviation-grade kerosene
. . excise taxes . . . 740

Alcohol fuels
. excise taxes
. . rate reductions delayed . . . 905
. . refund claims repealed . . . 787
. small ethanol producer credit
. . cooperative's election to pass through to patrons . . . 735
. . eligible small producer expanded . . . 735

Alcoholic beverages
. distilled spirits
. . tax credit for wholesalers . . . 835
. producers and marketers
. . occupational tax repealed . . . 840
. small importers and producers
. . quarterly payment of tax . . . 830

Alternative fuels
. excise tax
. . credits . . . 725
. . diesel-water emulsion . . . 720
. . payments in lieu of credits . . . 725
. . rates . . . 725
. fueling station credit . . . 730

Alternative motor vehicles credit
. advanced lean burn technology vehicles . . . 305; 315
. alternative fuel motor vehicles . . . 305; 325
. clean-fuel vehicles
. . deduction termination date . . . 330
. qualified fuel cell motor vehicles . . . 305; 310
. qualified hybrid motor vehicles . . . 305; 320

Amortization
. atmospheric pollution control facilities
. . deduction expanded . . . 620
. Code Sec. 197
. . recapture modified . . . 245
. oil and gas geological and geophysical expenses . . . 525

Appliances
. energy efficient appliances
. . manufacturing credit . . . 225

Aquatic Resources Trust Fund
. fund eliminated . . . 1030

Arbitrage profits
. natural gas supply contracts
. . safe harbor rules for government bonds . . . 530

Automobiles—see Vehicles

Aviation fuel
. aviation-grade kerosene
. . excise tax . . . 795
. . excise tax termination date . . . 795
. crop dusters
. . excise tax waiver . . . 820
. fixed-wing aircraft
. . forestry operations . . . 822
. registered commercial user
. . reduced tax rate . . . 790

B

Biodiesel fuels
. agri-biodiesel
. . small agri-biodiesel producer credit . . . 710
. excise and income tax credits . . . 705

Bonds
. clean renewable energy bonds . . . 455
. government arbitrage
. . safe harbor rules for natural gas contracts . . . 530
. highway or surface freight transfer facilities
. . exempt facility bonds . . . 915
. state-owned railroad real estate investment trust bonds . . . 910

Business credits
. advanced nuclear power facility credit . . . 440
. alternative fueling station credit . . . 730
. energy credit
. . qualified fuel cells property . . . 240
. energy efficient appliance credit . . . 225
. energy efficient residential construction credit . . . 220
. . stationery microturbine power plant . . . 240
. investment tax credit
. . qualifying advanced coal project credit . . . 605
. . qualifying gasification project credit . . . 605
. . solar energy property credit increased . . . 230
. renewable diesel fuels credit . . . 715
. research credit
. . energy research credit expanded . . . 235

C

Carryback and carryforward
. net operating losses
. . public utilities . . . 430
. nonconventional fuel source credit . . . 615

Coal
. clean coal facilities credits
. . qualifying advanced coal project credit . . . 605
. . qualifying gasification project credit . . . 605
. coke or coke gas
. . nonconventional fuel source credit . . . 610
. Indian coal
. . renewable electricity production credit . . . 405; 410; 415

564   Topical Index

References are to paragraph (¶) numbers

Commercial cargo vessels
. exports
. . harbor maintenance tax repealed . . . 825
Cooperatives
. electrical
. . asset exchange or conversion . . . 450
. . income exclusion for rural cooperatives . . . 450
. . load loss transactions . . . 450
. . nuclear decommissioning transaction . . . 450
. farmers
. . renewable electricity production credit . . . 420
. refinery property expensing
. . election to pass through to patrons . . . 505
. small business refiners
. . election to pass through EPA compliance deduction to patrons . . . 535
. small ethanol producer credit
. . election to pass through to patrons . . . 735
Credits against tax
. advanced nuclear power facilities . . . 440
. alcohol fuels
. . small ethanol producer credit . . . 735
. alternative fueling stations . . . 730
. alternative motor vehicles
. . advanced lean burn vehicles . . . 305; 315
. . alternative fuel vehicles . . . 305; 325
. . qualified fuel cell vehicles . . . 305; 310
. . qualified hybrid vehicles . . . 305; 320
. biodiesel fuels
. . credit extended . . . 705
. . small agri-biodiesel producer credit . . . 710
. clean coal facilities
. . qualifying advanced coal project credit . . . 605
. . qualifying gasification project credit . . . 605
. clean renewable energy bonds . . . 455
. distilled spirits
. . wholesaler inventory . . . 835
. energy efficient appliance manufacturing . . . 225
. energy efficient home construction
. . comparable dwelling unit . . . 220
. . contractor's credits . . . 220
. investment tax credit
. . clean coal facilities credits . . . 605
. . solar energy property credit . . . 230
. nonconventional source fuels
. . coke or coke gas . . . 610
. . oil, gas, synthetic fuels . . . 615
. qualified fuel cell property
. . telecommunications companies . . . 240
. renewable diesel fuels . . . 715
. renewable electricity production
. . agricultural cooperative's election to pass through credit to patrons . . . 420
. . computation of credit . . . 415
. . credit period . . . 415
. . placed-in-service dates expanded . . . 410
. . qualified energy resources expanded . . . 405
. . qualified facilities expanded . . . 410
. . research
. . energy research credit expanded . . . 235
. residential alternative energy expenditures
. . qualified fuel cell property . . . 210
. . solar equipment . . . 210
. . residential energy property . . . 205
. solar property investments
. . percentage increased . . . 230

Credits against tax—continued
. state tax credits
. . energy conservation and production income tax credits . . . 195
. stationary microturbine power plant
. . telecommunications companies . . . 240

D

Deductions
. energy efficient commercial building property . . . 215
. EPA sulfur regulations compliance costs
. . small refiner cooperatives . . . 535
. qualified clean-fuel vehicle
. . repealed . . . 330
. refinery property
. . temporary election to expense . . . 505
Department of Energy
. recycling study . . . 1010
Depletion
. independent producers
. . refinery limitation increased . . . 510
Depreciation—see also Modified Accelerated Cost Recovery System (MACRS)
. Code Sec. 197 recapture modified . . . 245
Diesel fuels
. excise taxes
. . rate reductions delayed . . . 905
. fuel tax evasion
. . IRS report . . . 760
. renewable diesel
. . excise tax credit . . . 715
. . income tax credit . . . 715
. ultimate vendor refund
. . exempt sales by credit card . . . 745
. . farming . . . 750
Distilled spirits
. income tax credit
. . wholesaler inventory . . . 835

E

Electric transmission property
. depreciation
. . 15-year recovery period . . . 425
. public utilities
. . net operating loss five-year carryback amount limited . . . 430
. sales or dispositions
. . Federal Energy Regulatory Commission (FERC) . . . 435
. . independent transmission company . . . 435
. . qualified gains . . . 435
Electricity production—see also Renewable electricity production credit
. clean coal facilities
. . credits for investment . . . 605
. external costs
. . National Academy of Sciences study . . . 1005
. tax-exempt producers
. . clean renewable energy bonds . . . 455

COM

Topical Index 565

References are to paragraph (¶) numbers

Environmental Protection Agency (EPA)
. gas and diesel sulfur regulations
. . capital costs deduction . . . 535

Ethanol
. small producer credit
. . cooperative's election to pass through to patrons . . . 735
. . eligible small producer expanded . . . 735

Excise taxes
. aviation-grade kerosene
. . Airport and Airway Trust Fund . . . 740
. . Highway Trust Fund . . . 740
. biodiesel fuel credits
. . extended through 2008 . . . 705
. commercial cargo
. . harbor maintenance tax on exports . . . 825
. crop dusters waiver . . . 820
. custom firearms . . . 850
. diesel-water fuel emulsion
. . reduced tax rate . . . 720
. distilled spirits
. . income tax credits for wholesaler inventory . . . 835
. fishing equipment . . . 845
. fixed-wing aircraft
. . forestry operations . . . 822
. fuel taxes
. . alcohol fuels . . . 905
. . alternative fuels credits . . . 725
. . aviation . . . 740; 790; 795; 820; 822
. . diesel fuel . . . 905
. . floor stock refunds . . . 905
. . gasoline tax . . . 905
. . refunds on exempt sales . . . 745
. . renewable diesel mixtures excise tax credit . . . 715
. . special motor fuels . . . 905
. . transfer to Highway Trust Fund . . . 905
. gas guzzler tax
. . repealed for limousines . . . 335
. highway-related taxes
. . highway tractors retail sales exemption . . . 340
. . National Surface Transportation Infrastructure Financing Commission established . . . 920
. . six-year extension . . . 905
. Highway Trust Fund
. . anti-deficit provisions modified . . . 1025
. . aviation-grade kerosene . . . 740
. . deposits extended . . . 905
. Leaking Underground Storage Tanks (LUST)
. . fuel excise taxes . . . 785
. . trust fund transfers limited . . . 1035
. liquor taxes
. . occupational tax repealed . . . 840
. . quarterly payments by small importers and producers . . . 830
. Motor Fuel Tax Enforcement Advisory Committee . . . 780
. oil spills
. . tax on domestic and imported oil . . . 540
. sightseeing flights
. . exemption for small engine aircraft . . . 815
. special fuels
. . registration of deep-draft ocean-going vessels . . . 775
. Sport Fish Restoration Account
. . small engine fuels appropriation . . . 797
. . Sport Fish Restoration and Boating Trust Fund . . . 1030

Excise taxes—continued
. tires
. . floor stock refunds . . . 905
. . steering tires . . . 345
. . super single tires . . . 345
. . tax extended . . . 905
. . Treasury collection study . . . 1020
. trucks and trailers
. . heavy trucks and trailers . . . 340; 905

F

Farming
. cooperatives
. . renewable electricity production credit . . . 420
. cropdusters
. . aerial fuel excise tax waiver . . . 820
. diesel fuel
. . ultimate vendor refund . . . 750

Firearms
. small manufacturers
. . excise tax . . . 850

Fishing equipment
. excise taxes . . . 845

Fuel cell property
. purchase for residential use
. . residential alternative energy credit . . . 210

Fuels—see also Special fuels
. adulterated fuels
. . penalties . . . 765
. alcohol fuels
. . excise tax rate reductions delayed . . . 905
. . small ethanol producer credit . . . 735
. alternative fuels
. . excise tax credits . . . 725
. . excise tax rates . . . 725
. . fueling station credit . . . 730
. . payments in lieu of credits . . . 725
. aviation-grade kerosene
. . crop dusters . . . 820
. . registered commercial user . . . 790
. . tax termination date . . . 795
. biodiesel
. . fuels mixture credit . . . 705
. . income tax credit . . . 705
. . small agri-biodiesel producer credit . . . 710
. cargo taxable fuels
. . electronic data interchange system . . . 770
. coke or coke gas
. . production credit . . . 610
. diesel
. . agricultural use refund . . . 750
. . excise tax rate reductions delayed . . . 905
. . exempt sales refund . . . 745
. . Highway Diesel Fuel Sulfur Control Requirements . . . 765
. . IRS fuel tax evasion report . . . 760
. . renewable diesel . . . 715
. diesel additives and EPA standards
. . penalties . . . 765
. fixed-wing aircraft
. . forestry operations . . . 822
. gasohol refund claims repealed . . . 787
. gasoline
. . excise tax rate reductions delayed . . . 905

FUE

566 Topical Index

References are to paragraph (¶) numbers

Fuels—see also Special fuels—continued
. gasoline—continued
.. excise tax refund . . . 745
. import and export cargo information
.. electronic data interchange system . . . 770
. kerosene
.. commercial aviation . . . 740
.. excise tax rate reductions delayed . . . 905
. Leaking Underground Storage Tanks (LUST)
.. credits and refunds . . . 785
.. trust fund transfers limited . . . 1035
. Motor Fuel Tax Enforcement Advisory Commission . . . 780
. oil, gas, synthetic fuels
.. production credit . . . 615
. small engine fuels tax
.. coastal wetlands use . . . 797
. special motor fuels
.. excise tax rate reductions delayed . . . 905
. technical corrections
.. aviation-grade kerosene . . . 790
.. commercial aviation fuel . . . 790
.. gasohol refund claims . . . 787
. Treasury highway fuels study
.. non-transportation use by trucks . . . 1015

G

Gasoline
. excise taxes
.. rate reductions delayed . . . 905
.. refund on exempt sales by credit cards . . . 745
General business credit—see Business credits
Gunsmiths
. custom firearms
.. excise tax . . . 850

H

Harbor Maintenance Tax
. exemption for cargo exports . . . 825
Highways
. bond financing
.. exempt facility bonds . . . 915
. Highway Trust Fund
.. anti-deficit provisions modified . . . 1025
.. apportionment adjustments modified . . . 1025
.. excise tax transfers . . . 740; 905
.. mass transit account . . . 905
.. Motor Fuel Tax Enforcement Advisory Commission . . . 780
. National Surface Transportation Infrastructure Financing Commission . . . 920
. Treasury highway fuels study
.. non-transportation use by trucks . . . 1015
Hydropower
. renewable electricity production credit . . . 405; 410; 415

I

Intangibles
. Code Sec. 197
.. recapture modification . . . 245

IRS hearings, reports and records
. diesel fuel
.. tax evasion report . . . 760

K

Kerosene
. aviation-grade fuel
.. excise tax . . . 740
. excise tax rate reductions delayed . . . 905

L

Leaking Underground Storage Tanks (LUST)
. fuel credits and refunds . . . 785
. fuels and excise taxes
.. refunds and credits . . . 785
. trust fund transfers limited . . . 1035

M

Manufacturing
. appliances
.. energy efficient appliance credit . . . 225
Modified Accelerated Cost Recovery System (MACRS)
. electric transmission property
.. 15-year recovery period . . . 425
. natural gas distribution lines
.. 15-year recovery period . . . 515
. natural gas gathering lines
.. 7-year recovery period . . . 520
Motor vehicles—see Vehicles

N

National Surface Transportation Infrastructure Financing Commission . . . 920
Natural gas
. arbitrage bond rules
.. safe harbor . . . 530
. distribution lines
.. 15-year depreciation recovery period . . . 515
. gathering lines
.. 7-year depreciation recovery period . . . 520
. state and local governments
.. pre-paid supply contracts . . . 530
Net operating losses
. carrybacks and carryovers
.. public utilities . . . 430
Nonconventional fuel source credit
. coke or coke gas facilities . . . 610
. modification of credit
.. carryback and carryforward . . . 615
. oil, gas, synthetic fuels . . . 615
Nuclear power
. advanced facilities credit . . . 440
. decommissioning funds
.. contributions after close of funding period . . . 445
.. costs of service requirement repealed . . . 445
. treatment of rural electric cooperative income . . . 450

GAS

Topical Index

References are to paragraph (¶) numbers

O

Ocean-going vessels
- deep-draft vessel
- . . bulk fuel transfer system registration . . . 775

Oil and gas
- depletion
- . . refinery limitation on independent producers increased . . . 510
- geological and geophysical expenses
- . . amortization . . . 525
- government bond arbitrage
- . . natural gas supply safe harbor . . . 530
- natural gas distribution lines
- . . 15-year depreciation recovery period . . . 515
- natural gas gathering lines
- . . 7-year depreciation recovery period . . . 520
- Oil Spill Liability Trust Fund . . . 540
- oil spill tax
- . . domestic and imported oil . . . 540
- . . imported petroleum products . . . 540
- refinery property
- . . temporary election to expense . . . 505

P

Petroleum products
- spill tax
- . . domestic products . . . 540
- . . imported products . . . 540

Pollution control facilities
- atmospheric pollution control facilities
- . . amortization deduction expanded . . . 620
- public utilities
- . . net operating loss five-year carryback amount limited . . . 430

Public utilities
- net operating losses
- . . five-year carryback . . . 430

R

Railroads
- National Surface Transportation Infrastructure Financing Commission . . . 920
- rail-truck transfer facilities
- . . exempt facility bonds . . . 915
- railroad real estate investment trust
- . . state ownership . . . 910

Real estate investment trusts (REITs)
- railroad REITs
- . . state ownership . . . 910

Recycling
- energy savings study . . . 1010

Renewable electricity production credit
- computation . . . 415
- credit period extension
- . . geothermal . . . 415
- . . hydropower . . . 415
- . . Indian coal . . . 415
- . . irrigation . . . 415
- . . landfill gas . . . 415
- . . open-loop biomass . . . 415

Renewable electricity production credit—continued
- credit period extension—continued
- . . solar . . . 415
- . . trash combustion . . . 415
- placed-in-service dates
- . . closed-loop biomass . . . 410
- . . geothermal . . . 410
- . . irrigation . . . 410
- . . landfill gas . . . 410
- . . open-loop biomass . . . 410
- . . trash combustion . . . 410
- . . wind . . . 410
- qualified energy resources added
- . . hydropower . . . 405; 410; 415
- . . Indian coal . . . 405; 410; 415

Research credit
- energy research
- . . contract research expenses . . . 235
- . . energy research consortium payments . . . 235

Residential property
- alternative energy expenditures credit . . . 210
- energy efficient home construction credit . . . 220
- residential energy property credit . . . 205

S

Safe harbor rules
- government bond arbitrage
- . . prepaid natural gas contracts . . . 530

Small engine aircraft
- sightseeing flights
- . . transportation excise taxes . . . 815

Solar energy property
- investment tax credit
- . . percentage increased . . . 230
- . . purchase for residential use
- . . residential alternative energy credit . . . 210
- renewable electricity production
- . . credit period increased . . . 415

Special fuels
- bulk transfers
- . . ocean-going vessels . . . 775
- changes in fuel operation ownership
- . . reregistration required . . . 755
- transport vessels
- . . deep-draft ocean-going vessel registration . . . 775

Sport Fish Restoration Account
- renamed Sport Fish Restoration and Boating Trust Fund . . . 1030

Sport Fish Restoration and Boating Trust Fund
- funding
- . . gas-powered outdoor equipment . . . 1030
- . . motorboat fuel taxes . . . 1030

Sporting goods
- fishing equipment
- . . excise tax limit . . . 845

State and local bonds—see Bonds

State tax energy incentives
- energy conservation and production income tax credits . . . 195

References are to paragraph (¶) numbers

T

Taxpayers affected
. coal and coke
. . effect on coal and coke producers . . . 149
. cooperatives
. . effect on energy cooperatives . . . 147
. electricity
. . effect on electric utilities . . . 145
. . effect on electricity producers . . . 139
. . effect on electricity transmission . . . 143
. energy
. . effect on energy cooperatives . . . 147
. . effect on energy research . . . 176
. . overview of effect on energy . . . 129
. farmers
. . effect on farmers . . . 182
. fuels
. . effect on alcohol fuels producers . . . 163
. . effect on diesel and biodiesel producers . . . 153
. . effect on ethanol producers . . . 159
. . effect on fuel blenders, pipeline operators, inventory position holders, and terminal and vessel operators . . . 171
. . effect on fuel importers . . . 173
. . effect on gasoline producers . . . 151
. . effect on kerosene producers . . . 155
. . effect on liquefied petroleum gas producers . . . 157
. . effect on liquid hydrocarbons from biomass . . . 169
. . effect on motor boat and small engine fuel producers . . . 165
. . effect on P series fuels producers . . . 167
. . effect on refiners . . . 175
. . effect on special motor fuels producers . . . 161
. general business
. . effect on appliance manufacturers . . . 127
. . effect on business expenditures for energy savings and research . . . 119
. . effect on business purchasers of environmentally friendly vehicles . . . 121
. . effect on commercial building owners . . . 125
. . effect on home builders . . . 123
. . overall effect on business . . . 117
. government trust funds
. . effect on government trust funds . . . 191
. individuals
. . effect on homeowners . . . 109
. . effect on patrons of cooperatives . . . 113
. . effect on purchasers of environmentally friendly vehicles . . . 107
. . effect on sport fishermen . . . 115
. . effect on tax-exempt bond investors . . . 111
. . overall effect on individuals . . . 105
. natural gas
. . effect on natural gas distributors . . . 137
. effect on natural gas producers . . . 133
. effect on natural gas utilities . . . 135
. lear power
. .t on nuclear power industry . . . 141
. . n oil producers . . . 131

Taxpayers affected—continued
. oil—continued
. . effect on oil tanker operators . . . 185
. other affected businesses
. . alcoholic beverage producers . . . 179
. . credit card issuers . . . 183
. . custom gunsmiths . . . 184
. . exporters . . . 181
. . oil tanker operators . . . 185
. . operators of deep draft vessels . . . 186
. . overall effects . . . 177
. . recycling industry . . . 187
. state implications of energy legislation . . . 195
. transportation
. . effect on aviation . . . 180
. . effect on trucking and limousine companies . . . 178
Telecommunications companies
. qualified fuel cell property credit . . . 240
. stationary microturbine property credit . . . 240
Tires
. excise taxes
. . extension . . . 905
. . floor stock refunds . . . 905
. . steering tires . . . 345
. . super single tires . . . 345
. . Treasury collection study . . . 1020
Treasury
. studies
. . National Academy of Sciences external energy costs study . . . 1005
. . non-transportation use of highway fuels by trucks . . . 1015
. . recycling . . . 1010
. . tire tax collection . . . 1020
Trucks and trailers
. heavy trucks and trailers
. . excise tax extended . . . 905
. . retail sales exemption . . . 340
. highway use
. . excise tax extended . . . 905
. rail-truck transfer facilities
. . exempt facility bonds . . . 915
. Treasury highway fuels study
. . non-transportation use . . . 1015

V

Vehicles—see also **Trucks and trailers**
. alternative motor vehicles credit
. . advanced lean burn technology vehicles . . . 305; 315
. . alternative fuel motor vehicles . . . 305; 325
. . qualified fuel cell motor vehicles . . . 305; 310
. . qualified hybrid motor vehicles . . . 305; 320
. gas guzzler tax
. . repealed for limousines . . . 335
. qualified clean-fuel vehicles
. . deduction repealed . . . 330